P9-DMB-222

Exam Ref 70-740 Installation, Storage and Compute with Windows Server 2016

Craig Zacker

Exam Ref 70-740 Installation, Storage, and Compute with Windows Server 2016

Published with the authorization of Microsoft Corporation by:
Pearson Education, Inc.

Copyright © 2017 by Craig Zacker

All rights reserved. Printed in the United States of America. This publication is protected by copyright, and permission must be obtained from the publisher prior to any prohibited reproduction, storage in a retrieval system, or transmission in any form or by any means, electronic, mechanical, photocopying, recording, or likewise. For information regarding permissions, request forms, and the appropriate contacts within the Pearson Education Global Rights & Permissions Department, please visit www.pearsoned.com/permissions/. No patent liability is assumed with respect to the use of the information contained herein. Although every precaution has been taken in the preparation of this book, the publisher and author assume no responsibility for errors or omissions. Nor is any liability assumed for damages resulting from the use of the information contained herein.

ISBN-13: 978-0-7356-9882-6
ISBN-10: 0-7356-9882-1

Library of Congress Control Number: 2016962646

1 17

Trademarks

Microsoft and the trademarks listed at https://www.microsoft.com on the "Trademarks" webpage are trademarks of the Microsoft group of companies. All other marks are property of their respective owners.

Warning and Disclaimer

Every effort has been made to make this book as complete and as accurate as possible, but no warranty or fitness is implied. The information provided is on an "as is" basis. The authors, the publisher, and Microsoft Corporation shall have neither liability nor responsibility to any person or entity with respect to any loss or damages arising from the information contained in this book or programs accompanying it.

Special Sales

For information about buying this title in bulk quantities, or for special sales opportunities (which may include electronic versions; custom cover designs; and content particular to your business, training goals, marketing focus, or branding interests), please contact our corporate sales department at corpsales@pearsoned.com or (800) 382-3419.

For government sales inquiries, please contact governmentsales@pearsoned.com.

For questions about sales outside the U.S., please contact intlcs@pearson.com.

Editor-in-Chief	Greg Wiegand
Acquisitions Editor	Trina MacDonald
Development Editor	Rick Kughen
Managing Editor	Sandra Schroeder
Senior Project Editor	Tracey Croom
Editorial Production	Backstop Media
Copy Editor	Christina Rudloff
Indexer	Julie Grady
Proofreader	Christina Rudloff
Technical Editor	Ajay Kakkar
Cover Designer	Twist Creative, Seattle

Contents at a glance

	Introduction	*xv*
	Preparing for the exam	*xix*
CHAPTER 1	**Install Windows Servers in host and compute environments**	**1**
CHAPTER 2	**Implement storage solutions**	**81**
CHAPTER 3	**Implement Hyper-V**	**165**
CHAPTER 4	**Implement Windows containers**	**259**
CHAPTER 5	**Implement high availability**	**297**
CHAPTER 6	**Maintain and monitor server environments**	**387**
	Index	*445*

Contents

Introduction **xv**

Organization of this book xvi

Microsoft certifications xvi

Free ebooks from Microsoft Press xvi

Microsoft Virtual Academy xvi

Quick access to online references xvii

Errata, updates, & book support xvii

We want to hear from you xvii

Stay in touch xvii

Preparing for the exam *xix*

Chapter 1 Install Windows Servers in host and compute environments **1**

Skill 1.1: Install, upgrade, and migrate servers and workloads 1

Determine Windows Server 2016 installation requirements 2

Determine appropriate Windows Server 2016 editions per workloads 4

Install Windows Server 2016 6

Install Windows Server 2016 features and roles 11

Install and configure Windows Server Core 17

Manage Windows Server Core installations using Windows PowerShell, command line, and remote management capabilities 21

What do you think of this book? We want to hear from you!

Microsoft is interested in hearing your feedback so we can continually improve our books and learning resources for you. To participate in a brief online survey, please visit:

https://aka.ms/tellpress

Implement Windows PowerShell Desired State Configuration (DSC) to install and maintain integrity of installed environments 26

Perform upgrades and migrations of servers and core workloads from Windows Server 2008 and Windows Server 2012 to Windows Server 2016 27

Determine the appropriate activation model for server installation 35

Skill 1.2: Install and configure Nano Server 42

Determine appropriate usage scenarios and requirements for Nano Server 43

Install Nano Server 44

Implement Roles and Features on Nano Server 48

Manage and configure Nano Server 50

Managing Nano Server remotely using PowerShell 55

Skill 1.3: Create, manage, and maintain images for deployment 58

Plan for Windows Server virtualization 58

Plan for Linux and FreeBSD deployments 61

Assess virtualization workloads using the Microsoft Assessment and Planning (MAP) Toolkit 61

Determine considerations for deploying workloads into virtualized environments 69

Update images with patches, hotfixes, and drivers 70

Install Roles and Features in offline images 75

Manage and maintain Windows Server Core, Nano Server images, and VHDs using Windows PowerShell 76

Chapter summary 79

Thought experiment. 80

Thought experiment answer. 80

Chapter 2 Implement storage solutions 81

Skill 2.1: Configure disks and volumes. 81

Configure sector sizes appropriate for various workloads 82

Configure GUID partition table (GPT) disks 84

Create VHD and VHDX files using Server Manager or Windows PowerShell 88

Mount Virtual Hard Disks (VHDs) 91

Determine when to use NTFS and ReFS File Systems 93
Configure NFS and SMB shares using Server Manager 95
Configure SMB share and session settings using Windows PowerShell 106
Configure SMB server and SMB client configuration settings using Windows PowerShell 108
Configure file and folder permissions 112
Skill 2.2: Implement server storage 123
Configure storage pools 123
Implement simple, mirror, and parity storage layout options for disks or enclosures 125
Configure tiered storage 131
Configure iSCSI target and initiator 133
Configure iSNS 140
Configure Datacenter Bridging (DCB) 142
Configure Multipath I/O (MPIO) 145
Determine usage scenarios for Storage Replica 148
Implement Storage Replica for server-to-server, cluster-to-cluster, and stretch cluster scenarios 151
Skill 2.3: Implement data deduplication 155
Implement and configure deduplication 155
Determine appropriate usage scenarios for deduplication 158
Monitor deduplication 160
Implement a backup and restore solution with deduplication 162
Chapter summary 162
Thought experiment. 164
Thought experiment answer. 164

Chapter 3 Implement Hyper-V 165

Skill 3.1: Install and configure Hyper-V. 165
Determine hardware and compatibility requirements for installing Hyper-V 166
Install Hyper-V 170
Install management tools 172

Upgrade from existing versions of Hyper-V 173
Delegate virtual machine management 174
Perform remote management of Hyper-V hosts 174
Configure virtual machines using Windows PowerShell Direct 180
Implement nested virtualization 181

Skill 3.2: Configure virtual machine (VM) settings 182
Creating a virtual machine 182
Add or remove memory in running a VM 185
Configure dynamic memory 186
Configure Non-Uniform Memory Access (NUMA) support 189
Configure smart paging 192
Configure resource metering 193
Manage Integration Services 195
Create and configure Generation 1 and 2 VMs and determine appropriate usage scenarios 197
Implement enhanced session mode 199
Create Linux and FreeBSD VMs 201
Install and configure Linux Integration Services (LIS) 204
Install and configure FreeBSD Integration Services (BIS) 205
Implement Secure Boot for Windows and Linux environments 205
Move and convert VMs from previous versions of Hyper-V to Windows Server 2016 Hyper-V 208
Export and import VMs 209
Implement Discrete Device Assignment (DDA) 212

Skill 3.3: Configure Hyper-V storage 213
Create VHDs and VHDX files using Hyper-V Manager 214
Create shared VHDX files 220
Configure differencing disks 222
Modify virtual hard disks 223
Configure pass-through disks 225
Resize a virtual hard disk 226
Manage checkpoints 228
Implement production checkpoints 230

Implement a virtual fibre channel adapter 231
Configure Storage Quality of Service (QoS) 233
Skill 3.4: Configure Hyper-V networking 235
Add and remove virtual network interface cards (vNICs) 236
Configure Hyper-V virtual switches 238
Optimize network performance 243
Configure MAC addresses 244
Configure network isolation 246
Configure synthetic and legacy virtual network adapters 247
Configure NIC teaming in VMs 249
Configure virtual machine queue (VMQ) 251
Enable Remote Direct Memory Access (RDMA) on network adapters bound to a Hyper-V virtual switch using Switch Embedded Teaming (SET) 253
Configure bandwidth management 254
Chapter summary 256
Thought experiment. 258
Thought experiment answer. 258

Chapter 4 Implement Windows containers 259

Skill 4.1: Deploy Windows containers 259
Determine installation requirements and appropriate scenarios for Windows containers 260
Install and configure Windows Server Container Host in physical or virtualized environments 261
Install and configure Windows Server container host to Windows Server Core or Nano Server in a physical or virtualized environment 264
Install Docker on Windows Server and Nano Server 266
Configure Docker Daemon start-up options 269
Configure Windows PowerShell for use with containers 270
Install a base operating system 271
Tag an image 272
Uninstall an operating system image 273

Create Windows Server containers 274
Create Hyper-V containers 275
Skill 4.2: Manage Windows containers 277
Manage Windows or Linux containers using the Docker daemon 277
Manage Windows or Linux containers using Windows PowerShell 279
Manage container networking 281
Manage container data volumes 286
Manage resource control 287
Create new container images using Dockerfile 289
Manage container images using DockerHub Repository for public and private scenarios 291
Manage container images using Microsoft Azure 293
Chapter summary 293
Thought experiment. 295
Thought experiment answer. 295

Chapter 5 Implement high availability 297

Skill 5.1: Implement high availability and disaster recovery options in Hyper-V 297
Implement Hyper-V Replica 298
Implement live migration 303
Implement shared nothing live migration 307
Configure CredSSP or Kerberos authentication protocol for Live Migration 308
Implement storage migration 309
Skill 5.2: Implement failover clustering 311
Implement workgroup, single, and multi domain clusters 314
Configure quorum 317
Configure cluster networking 321
Restore single node or cluster configuration 324
Configure cluster storage 326
Implement cluster-aware updating 328
Implement cluster operating system rolling upgrade 332

Configure and optimize clustered shared volumes (CSVs) 333
Configure clusters without network names 337
Implement Scale-Out File Server (SoFS) 337
Determine different scenarios for the use of SoFS vs. clustered file server 341
Determine usage scenarios for implementing guest clustering 341
Implement a clustered Storage Spaces solution using shared SAS storage enclosures 342
Implement Storage Replica 345
Implement cloud witness 345
Implement VM resiliency 348
Implement shared VHDX as a storage solution for guest clusters 349

Skill 5.3: Implement Storage Spaces Direct 352
Determine scenario requirements for implementing Storage Spaces Direct 352
Enable Storage Spaces direct using Windows PowerShell 354
Implement a disaggregated Storage Spaces Direct scenario in a cluster 355
Implement a hyper-converged Storage Spaces Direct scenario in a cluster 357

Skill 5.4: Manage failover clustering 359
Configure role-specific settings, including continuously available shares 359
Configure VM monitoring 361
Configure failover and preference settings 364
Implement stretch and site-aware failover clusters 365
Enable and configure node fairness 367

Skill 5.5: Manage VM movement in clustered nodes 369
Perform a live migration 369
Perform a quick migration 370
Perform a storage migration 371
Import, export, and copy VMs 372
Configure VM network health protection 373
Configure drain on shutdown 374

Skill 5.6: Implement Network Load Balancing (NLB) 375
Configure NLB prerequisites 375
Install NLB nodes 377
Configure affinity 381
Configure port rules 382
Configure cluster operation mode 384
Upgrade an NLB cluster 384
Chapter summary 385
Thought experiment 386
Thought experiment answer 386

Chapter 6 Maintain and monitor server environments 387

Skill 6.1: Maintain server installations 387
Implement Windows Server Update Services (WSUS) solutions 388
Configure WSUS groups 398
Manage patch management in mixed environments 401
Implement an antimalware solution with Windows Defender 405
Integrate Windows Defender with WSUS and Windows Update 409
Perform backup and restore operations using Windows Server Backup 411
Determine backup strategies for different Windows Server roles and workloads, including Hyper-V Host, Hyper-V Guests, Active Directory, File Servers, and Web Servers using Windows Server 2016 native tools and solutions 421
Skill 6.2: Monitor server installations 425
Monitor workloads using Performance Monitor 425
Configure data collector sets 431
Determine appropriate CPU, memory, disk, and networking counters for storage and compute workloads 433
Configure alerts 438
Monitor workloads using Resource Monitor 440

Chapter summary 442
Thought experiment. 443
Thought experiment answer. 443

Index *445*

What do you think of this book? We want to hear from you!

Microsoft is interested in hearing your feedback so we can continually improve our books and learning resources for you. To participate in a brief online survey, please visit:

https://aka.ms/tellpress

Introduction

Many Windows Server books take the approach of teaching you every detail about the product. Such books end up being huge and tough to read. Not to mention that remembering everything you read is incredibly challenging. That's why those books aren't the best choice for preparing for a certification exam such as the Microsoft Exam 70-740, "Installation, Storage, and Compute with Windows Server 2016." For this book, we focus on your review of the Windows Server skills that you need to maximize your chances of passing the exam. Our goal is to cover all of the skills measured on the exam, while bringing a real-world focus to the information. This book shouldn't be your only resource for exam preparation, but it can be your primary resource. We recommend combining the information in this book with some hands-on work in a lab environment (or as part of your job in a real-world environment).

The 70-740 exam is geared toward IT professionals who have a minimum of 3 years of experience working with Windows Server. That doesn't mean you can't take and pass the exam with less experience, but it probably means that it will be harder. Of course, everyone is different. It is possible to get the knowledge and skills required to pass the 70-740 exam in fewer than 3 years. But whether you are a senior-level Windows Server administrator or just a couple of years into your Windows Server journey, we think you'll find the information in this book valuable as your primary exam prep resource.

This book covers every major topic area found on the exam, but it does not cover every exam question. Only the Microsoft exam team has access to the exam questions, and Microsoft regularly adds new questions to the exam, making it impossible to cover specific questions. You should consider this book a supplement to your relevant real-world experience and other study materials. If you encounter a topic in this book that you do not feel completely comfortable with, use the "Need more review?" links you'll find in the text to find more information and take the time to research and study the topic. Great information is available on MSDN, TechNet, and in blogs and forums.

Organization of this book

This book is organized by the "Skills measured" list published for the exam. The "Skills measured" list is available for each exam on the Microsoft Learning website: *https://aka.ms/examlist*. Each chapter in this book corresponds to a major topic area in the list, and the technical tasks in each topic area determine a chapter's organization. If an exam covers six major topic areas, for example, the book will contain six chapters.

Microsoft certifications

Microsoft certifications distinguish you by proving your command of a broad set of skills and experience with current Microsoft products and technologies. The exams and corresponding certifications are developed to validate your mastery of critical competencies as you design and develop, or implement and support, solutions with Microsoft products and technologies both on-premises and in the cloud. Certification brings a variety of benefits to the individual and to employers and organizations.

MORE INFO **ALL MICROSOFT CERTIFICATIONS**

For information about Microsoft certifications, including a full list of available certifications, go to *https://www.microsoft.com/learning*.

Free ebooks from Microsoft Press

From technical overviews to in-depth information on special topics, the free ebooks from Microsoft Press cover a wide range of topics. These ebooks are available in PDF, EPUB, and Mobi for Kindle formats, ready for you to download at:

https://aka.ms/mspressfree

Check back often to see what is new!

Microsoft Virtual Academy

Build your knowledge of Microsoft technologies with free expert-led online training from Microsoft Virtual Academy (MVA). MVA offers a comprehensive library of videos, live events, and more to help you learn the latest technologies and prepare for certification exams. You'll find what you need here:

https://www.microsoftvirtualacademy.com

Quick access to online references

Throughout this book are addresses to webpages that the author has recommended you visit for more information. Some of these addresses (also known as URLs) can be painstaking to type into a web browser, so we've compiled all of them into a single list that readers of the print edition can refer to while they read.

Download the list at *https://aka.ms/examref740/downloads.*

The URLs are organized by chapter and heading. Every time you come across a URL in the book, find the hyperlink in the list to go directly to the webpage.

Errata, updates, & book support

We've made every effort to ensure the accuracy of this book and its companion content. You can access updates to this book—in the form of a list of submitted errata and their related corrections—at:

https://aka.ms/examref740/errata

If you discover an error that is not already listed, please submit it to us at the same page.

If you need additional support, email Microsoft Press Book Support at *mspinput@microsoft.com.*

Please note that product support for Microsoft software and hardware is not offered through the previous addresses. For help with Microsoft software or hardware, go to *http://support.microsoft.com.*

We want to hear from you

At Microsoft Press, your satisfaction is our top priority, and your feedback our most valuable asset. Please tell us what you think of this book at:

https://aka.ms/tellpress

We know you're busy, so we've kept it short with just a few questions. Your answers go directly to the editors at Microsoft Press. (No personal information will be requested.) Thanks in advance for your input!

Stay in touch

Let's keep the conversation going! We're on Twitter: *http://twitter.com/MicrosoftPress.*

Important: How to use this book to study for the exam

Certification exams validate your on-the-job experience and product knowledge. To gauge your readiness to take an exam, use this Exam Ref to help you check your understanding of the skills tested by the exam. Determine the topics you know well and the areas in which you need more experience. To help you refresh your skills in specific areas, we have also provided "Need more review?" pointers, which direct you to more in-depth information outside the book.

The Exam Ref is not a substitute for hands-on experience. This book is not designed to teach you new skills.

We recommend that you round out your exam preparation by using a combination of available study materials and courses. Learn more about available classroom training at *https://www.microsoft.com/learning*. Microsoft Official Practice Tests are available for many exams at *https://aka.ms/practicetests*. You can also find free online courses and live events from Microsoft Virtual Academy at *https://www.microsoftvirtualacademy.com*.

This book is organized by the "Skills measured" list published for the exam. The "Skills measured" list for each exam is available on the Microsoft Learning website: *https://aka.ms/examlist*.

Note that this Exam Ref is based on this publicly available information and the author's experience. To safeguard the integrity of the exam, authors do not have access to the exam questions.

CHAPTER 1

Install Windows Servers in host and compute environments

Windows Server 2016 provides administrators with a variety of ways to deploy servers. You can install the operating system on a physical computer, as always, but you can also create a virtual deployment, using Hyper-V virtual machines and also the new Nano Server installation option.

IMPORTANT

Have you read page xix?

It contains valuable information regarding the skills you need to pass the exam.

Skills in this chapter:

- Install, upgrade, and migrate servers and workloads
- Install and configure Nano Server
- Create, manage, and maintain images for deployment

Skill 1.1: Install, upgrade, and migrate servers and workloads

There is more to installing Windows Server 2016 than running a setup wizard. Deploying servers, however you choose to do it, requires careful planning before you touch any hardware. This planning includes selecting the proper operating system edition and the best installation option for your organization's needs. If you have existing servers running prior Windows Server versions, you must decide how to upgrade or migrate them to Windows Server 2016.

This section covers how to:

- Determine Windows Server 2016 installation requirements
- Determine appropriate Windows Server 2016 editions per workloads
- Install Windows Server 2016
- Install Windows Server 2016 features and roles
- Install and configure Windows Server Core
- Manage Windows Server Core installations using Windows PowerShell, command line, and remote management capabilities
- Implement Windows PowerShell Desired State Configuration (DSC) to install and maintain integrity of installed environments
- Perform upgrades and migrations of servers and core workloads from Windows Server 2008 and Windows Server 2012 to Windows Server 2016
- Determine the appropriate activation model for server installation, such as Automatic Virtual Machine Activation (AVMA), Key Management Service (KMS), and Active Directory-based Activation

Determine Windows Server 2016 installation requirements

Planning a Windows Server 2016 installation requires several important decisions that affect not only the initial deployment of the server, but also its ongoing maintenance. While the Windows installation process is relatively simple, there are options to be considered both before you purchase the server hardware and the operating system, and after the initial installation is complete.

Some of the questions you must consider when planning a server deployment are as follows:

- **Which Windows Server 2016 edition should you install?** Microsoft provides Windows Server 2016 in several editions, which vary in the features they include, the resources they support, and the cost of the license. The details of the editions are described later in this chapter.
- **Which installation option should you use?** Most of the Windows Server 2016 editions include two installation options: Desktop Experience and Server Core. Desktop Experience includes all of the Windows features and a full graphical user interface (GUI). Server Core has a minimal user interface and a significantly reduced resource footprint, so it can utilize less memory and disk space than a Desktop Experience installation. There is also a third installation option, Nano Server, which requires an even smaller resource footprint, but this option does not appear in the initial installation wizard; you deploy Nano Server later, using Windows PowerShell.
- **Which roles and features does the server need?** The type and number of roles and features you plan to install can greatly affect the hardware resources the server will need, as well as the edition you purchase. For example, complex roles such as

Active Directory Certificate Services and Failover Clustering typically require additional resources and are not available in all editions. Third-party applications also affect resource utilization.

- **What virtualization strategy should you use?** The increased emphasis on virtualization in enterprise networking has profoundly altered the server deployment process. The ease with which administrators can migrate virtual machines from one host server to another has led then to consider not only what roles the physical server runs, but what roles could be needed on any virtual servers it is hosting. It is also important to consider what resources could be required if a server has to host additional virtual machines during a disaster situation.

By answering these questions, you can begin to determine what resources a server will need. Microsoft publishes minimum hardware requirements for a Windows Server 2016 installation, but it is difficult to predict just what resources a server will need to run efficiently, once you have installed all of the roles, features, and applications it requires to function.

Minimum hardware requirements

If your computer does not meet the following minimum hardware specifications, Windows Server 2016 will not install correctly (or possibly not install at all):

- Processor: 1.4-GHz 64-bit
- RAM: 512 MB ECC for Server Core, 2 GB ECC for Server with Desktop Experience
- Disk space: 32 GB minimum on a SATA or comparable drive
- Network adapter: Ethernet, with gigabit throughout
- Monitor: Super VGA (1024 x 768) or higher resolution
- Keyboard and mouse (or other compatible pointing device)
- Internet access

32 GB of available disk space should be considered the absolute minimum. A minimal Server Core installation with only the Web Server (IIS) role added should install successfully in 32 GB, but using the Desktop Experience installation option and installing additional roles will require more storage.

Windows Server 2016 does not support the use of the ATA, PATA, IDE, or EIDE interfaces for boot, page, or data drives. The system partition also needs additional space if you install the system over a network or if the computer has more than 16 GB of RAM. The additional disk space is required for paging, hibernation, and dump files.

NOTE **INSTALLING A MINIMUM HARDWARE CONFIGURATION**

A Windows Server 2016 installation on a virtual machine with the minimum single processor core and 512 MB of RAM fails. However, you can allocate more memory for the installation and then reduce it 512 MB afterwards, and the operating system runs.

Maximum hardware and virtualization limits

Virtualization has complicated the issue of the maximum hardware configurations supported by Windows Server 2016. It's no longer a simple matter of how many processors, how much memory, and largest possible disk size. While processor maximums were at one time measured in the number of sockets, now they refer to numbers of cores and logical processors. There are now also different maximums for physical and virtual machines in some resources.

The maximum hardware configurations for Windows Server 2016 are as follows:

- **Processors** A server host supports up to 512 logical processors (LPs) if Hyper-V is installed.
- **Memory** Up to 24 terabytes per host server and up to 12 terabytes per virtual machine.
- **VHDX size** Up to 64 terabytes.
- **Virtual machines** Up to 1,024 per host server.
- **Virtual machine processors** Up to 240 per virtual machine.

NOTE **UNDERSTANDING LPS**

Intel processors have a feature called hyperthreading, which enables a single core to process two threads simultaneously when Hyper-V is running. Thus, an Intel processor is considered to have two LPs per core when Hyper-V is running and one LP per core when it is not. In an AMD processor with multiple cores, each core is equivalent to one LP.

Determine appropriate Windows Server 2016 editions per workloads

Windows Server 2016 is available in multiple editions, with varying prices and features. To select an edition for your server deployment, you should consider the following questions:

- What roles and features will you need to run on the server?
- How will you obtain licenses for the servers?
- Will you be running Windows Server 2016 on virtual or physical machines?

The current trend in server deployment is to use relatively small servers that perform a single task, rather than large servers that perform many tasks. In cloud deployments, whether public, private, or hybrid, it is common to see virtual machines performing one role, such as a web server or a DNS server. It is for this reason that Microsoft introduced the Server Core installation option in Windows Server 2008 and Nano Server in Windows Server 2016, so that virtual machines could function with a smaller resource footprint.

Before you choose an installation option, however, you must select the appropriate Windows Server 2016 edition for the server workload you intend to implement. The Windows Server 2016 editions are as follows:

- **Windows Server 2016 Datacenter** The Datacenter edition is intended for large and powerful servers in a highly virtualized environment. The license allows for an unlimited number of operating system environments (OSEs) or Hyper-V containers. The Datacenter edition also includes additional features not available in the other editions, such as Storage Spaces Direct, Storage Replica, shielded virtual machines, and a new networking stack with additional virtualization options.

- **Windows Server 2016 Standard** The Standard edition license allows for two OSEs and includes the same core set of features as the Datacenter edition. However, it lacks the new storage and networking features listed in the Datacenter description.

Data Center
STANDARD
essential -
- S. core

- **Windows Server 2016 Essentials** The Essentials edition includes nearly all the features in the Standard and Datacenter editions; it does not include the Server Core installation option. The Essentials edition is also limited to one OSE (physical or virtual) and a maximum of 25 users and 50 devices. Unlike the Standard and Datacenter editions, Essential includes a configuration wizard that installs and configures Active Directory Domain Services and other essential components needed for a single-server network.
- **Windows Server 2016 MultiPoint Premium Server** Available only through academic licensing, the Multipoint edition enables multiple users to access a single server installation.

- ACADEMIC

- **Windows Storage Server 2016 Server** Available only through original equipment manufacturer (OEM) channels, the Storage Server edition is bundled as part of a dedicated storage hardware solution.

- OEM

- **Windows Hyper-V Server 2016** Available at no cost, the Hyper-V Server edition is a hypervisor-only download, without a graphical interface, that hosts virtual machines as its only function.

> ***NOTE*** **UNDERSTANDING OSES**
>
> **Microsoft now uses the term operating system environment (OSE) to refer to the Windows instances running on a computer. An OSE can be physical or virtual. For example, a server running one virtual machine in Hyper-V would be using two OSEs because the physical server installation counts for one. The Standard edition license therefore enables you to run one virtual machine in Hyper-V.**

In Windows Server 2012, the Datacenter and Standard editions were functionally identical. The only difference was in the number of Hyper-V virtual machines the license authorized you to create. In Windows Server 2016, the Datacenter edition includes several new features that could affect your decision to choose that edition over Standard. The features in the Datacenter edition that are not included in the Standard edition are as follows:

- **Storage Spaces Direct** Enables administrators to use relatively inexpensive drive arrays to create high-availability storage solutions. Instead of using an expensive array or controller with built-in storage management intelligence, the intelligence is incorporated into the operating system, enabling the use of inexpensive JBOD (just a bunch of disks) arrays.

- SOFTWARE
RAID

- **Storage Replica** Provides storage-agnostic, synchronous or asynchronous volume replication between local or remote servers, using the Server Message Blocks Version 3 protocol.
- **Shielded virtual machines** Provides VMs with protection from compromised administrators that have access to the Hyper-V host computer by encrypting the VM state and its virtual disks.
- **Network controller** Provides a central automation point for network infrastructure configuration, monitoring, and troubleshooting.

For most organizations, the selection of an edition will be based on cost. The Essentials edition is inexpensive and easy to deploy, but it is limited in its features. For a small organization, it can be ideal, however.

For medium to large-sized organizations, the typical choice is between the Standard and Datacenter editions. If the new Datacenter features are not important to you, the decision will likely be based on your virtualization strategy. If the plan is for a server to run a relatively small number of virtual machines, it could be more economical to purchase multiple Standard edition licenses than one Datacenter license. At the current prices, you can purchase up to seven Standard licenses (with two OSEs each) for less than the cost of a single Datacenter license.

Another issue to consider is your organization's potential for growth. If you intend to run 10 virtual machines now, it could be better to spend a few hundred dollars more for a Datacenter license, which provides unlimited OSEs for future expansion, rather than five Standard licenses.

EXAM TIP

The 70-740 exam can include licensing questions in which you must determine which Windows edition and how many licenses are needed to support a specific number of virtual machines on a Hyper-V server, while minimizing the licensing cost.

Clean = Bare metal

Install Windows Server 2016

The process of installing Windows Server 2016 can be relatively simple, when you are performing a clean installation on a single, new computer. It can also be extremely complex, when you are automating a mass deployment or migrating existing servers to the new operating system.

Performing a clean installation

A clean installation—also called a bare-metal installation—is when you are installing an operating system on a computer that does not already have one. To do this, you must have the operating system files on a bootable installation medium. Windows Server 2016 is still available on a bootable DVD, but most administrators download the installation package as a disk image file with an ISO extension.

- To install an ISO on a physical computer, you have to burn it to a removable disk, such as a flash drive or a DVD. You can do this on any other computer running Windows Server 2016 or Windows 10 by selecting the ISO in File Manager, and then selecting the Disk Image Tools\Manage menu, and clicking the Burn button.

- To install Windows Server 2016 on a virtual machine in Hyper-V, you can use the ISO file directly. When you create a VM, you can specify the ISO as you configure the virtual DVD drive. When you start the VM, the ISO appears and functions as a bootable disk on the system.

Once you have a bootable disk, you can perform a clean installation of Windows Server 2016 on a physical machine using the following procedure.

1. Turn on the computer and insert the Windows Server 2016 installation flash drive or disk.
2. Press any key to boot from the installation medium (if necessary). A progress indicator screen appears as Windows loads files.

> ***NOTE*** **MODIFYING BIOS SETTINGS**
>
> **The device that a PC uses to boot is specified in its system (or BIOS) settings. In some cases, you could have to modify these settings to enable the computer to boot from the installation medium you are using. If you are not familiar with the operation of a particular computer, watch the screen carefully as the system starts and look for an instruction specifying what key to press to access the system settings.**

3. The computer loads the graphical user interface and the Windows Setup page appears, as shown in Figure 1-1.

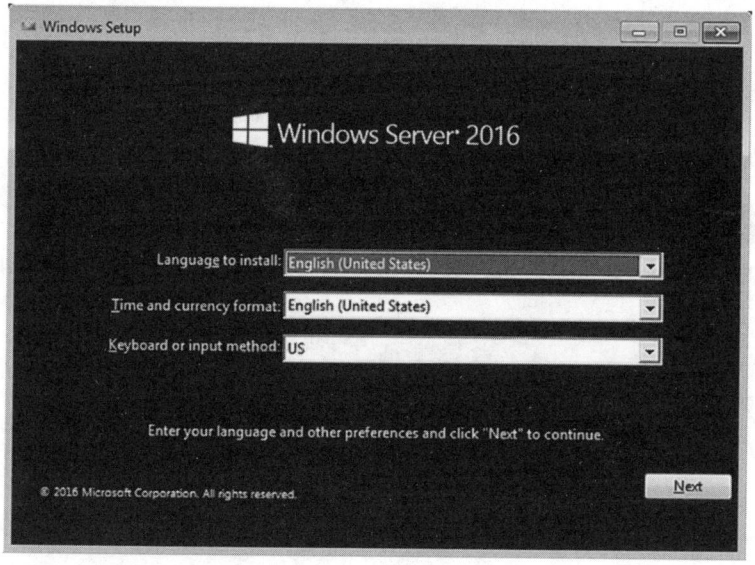

FIGURE 1-1 The Windows Setup page

4. Using the drop-down lists provided, select the appropriate Language To Install, Time And Currency Format, and Keyboard Or Input Method, and then click Next. Another Windows Setup page appears.

5. Click Install Now. The Windows Setup Wizard appears, displaying the Select The Operating System You Want To Install page.
6. Select the operating system edition and installation option you want to install and click Next. The Applicable Notices And License Terms page appears.
7. Select the I Accept The License Terms check box and click Next. The Which Type Of Installation Do You Want page appears, as shown in Figure 1-2.

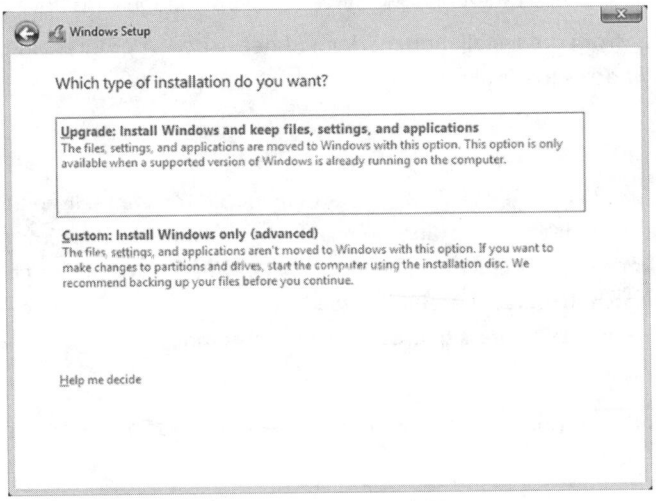

FIGURE 1-2 The Which Type Of Installation Do You Want page

8. Because you are performing a clean installation and not an upgrade, click the Custom: Install Windows Only (Advanced) option. The Where Do You Want To Install Windows page appears, as shown in Figure 1-3.

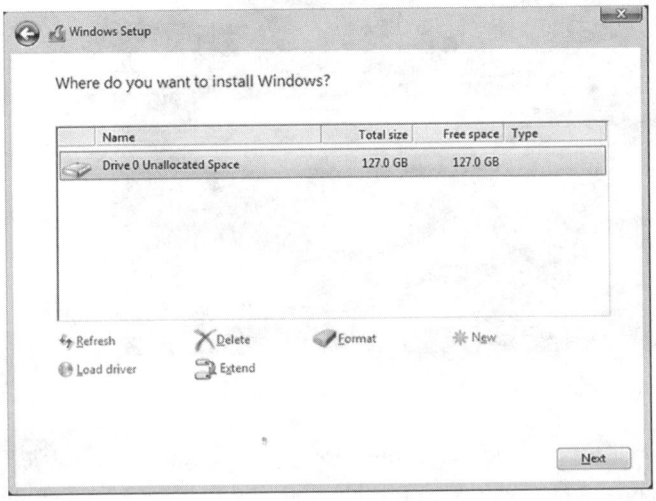

FIGURE 1-3 The Where Do You Want To Install Windows page

9. From the list provided, select the partition on which you want to install Windows Server 2016, or select an area of unallocated disk space where the Setup program can create a new partition. Then click Next. The Installing Windows page appears.
10. After several minutes, during which the Setup program installs Windows Server 2016, the computer restarts and the Customize Settings page appears, as shown in Figure 1-4.

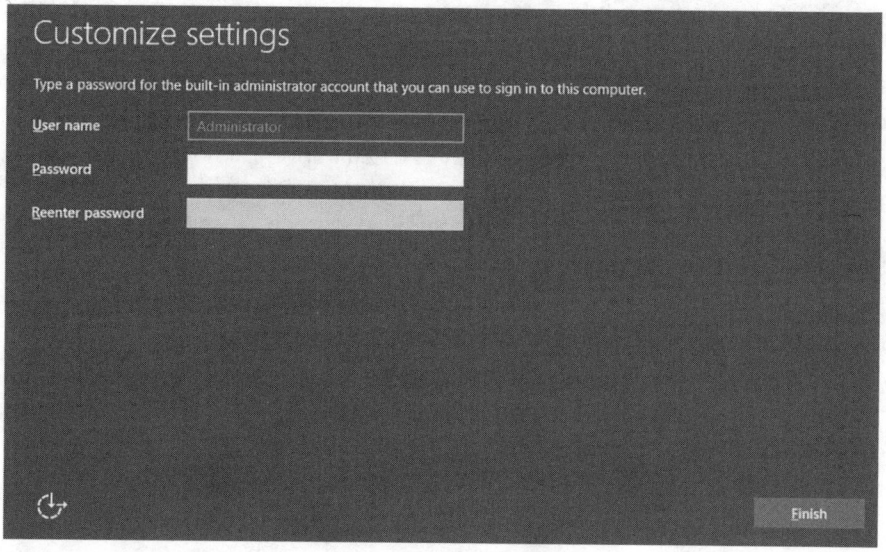

FIGURE 1-4 The Customize Settings page

11. In the Password and Reenter Password text boxes, type the password to be associated with the system's local Administrator account and press Enter. The system finalizes the installation and the Windows lock screen appears.

Working with partitions

In some cases, as you install Windows Server 2016, you could find it necessary to work with your disks and partitions. For this reason, the Setup program includes controls on the Where Do You Want To Install Windows page that enable you to create, manage, and delete the partitions on your disks.

The buttons on the page have the following functions:

- **Refresh** Displays partitions that are available as the result of a newly loaded driver.
- **Load driver** Enables you to add disk drivers from an external medium, such as a CD-ROM, DVD, or USB drive.
- **Delete** Removes an existing partition from a disk, permanently erasing all its data. You might want to delete partitions to consolidate unallocated disk space, enabling you to create a new, larger partition.

- **Extend** Enables you to make an existing partition larger, as long as unallocated space is available immediately following the selected partition on the disk.
- **Format** Enables you to format an existing partition on a disk, thereby erasing all its data. You do not need to format any new partitions you create for the install, but you might want to format an existing partition to eliminate unwanted files before installing Windows Server ~~2012 R2~~ 2016 on it.
- **New** Creates a new partition of a user-specified size in the selected area of unallocated space.

Sometimes, during an installation, you might see no partitions listed at all on the Where Do You Want To Install Windows page. This page lists the partitions on all the computer's disk drives that the Setup program can detect with its default drivers. If no partitions appear, it is because the computer's disk controller requires a device driver that is not included in the Windows default driver set. Some high-end controllers, such as those for disk arrays, require their own drivers, which you can install during the Setup process.

Check the disk controller manufacturer's website for a driver supporting Windows Server 2016, or another recent version of Windows Server, and use the following procedure to install it.

1. On the Where Do You Want To Install Windows page, click the Load Driver button. A Load Driver message box appears, as shown in Figure 1-5.

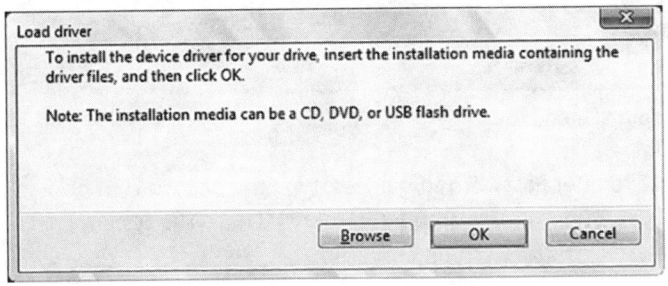

FIGURE 1-5 The Load Driver message box

2. Insert the storage medium containing the driver into the computer. You can supply drivers on a CD, DVD, USB flash drive, or floppy disk.
3. Click OK if the driver is in the root directory of the storage medium, or Browse if you need to locate the driver in the directory structure of the disk. A list of the drivers found on the disk appears on the Select The Driver To Install page.
4. Select one of the drivers in the list, and click Next.
5. When the driver loads, the partitions and unallocated space on the associated disks appear in the list on the Where Do You Want To Install Windows page.
6. Select the partition or area of unallocated space where you want to install Windows Server 2016, and then continue with the rest of the installation procedure, as covered earlier in this chapter.

Performing a mass deployment

When you have a large number of servers to install, you can conceivably mount a disk and perform a manual installation on each one, but that can become impractical. For a mass operating system deployment, you can use a server-based technology, such as Windows Deployment Services (WDS), to deploy image files automatically.

WDS is a role included with Windows Server 2016, which you can use to provide disk images to clients on the network. For this to work, however, the client must have some way to contact the WDS server and initiate the process. WDS enables you to create boot images, which you can burn to removable disks, but this still requires you to travel to each computer and run through the installation process.

A better way of deploying the WDS boot image is to use the *Preboot Execution Environment (PXE)* feature included with most network interface adapters. PXE is built into the adapter's firmware and enables a computer with no operating system to discover a Dynamic Host Configuration Protocol (DHCP) server on the network and request a configuration from it. The DHCP server supplies the client with the IP address of a WDS server, which the client then uses to connect to the server and download a boot image. The client system can then boot from that image and run a WDS client program that initiates the operating system installation.

Installing and configuring an automated software deployment service, such as WDS or System Center Configuration Manager, can be a complex task in itself. It is up to the administrators to decide whether the number of servers they have to deploy is worth the time and expense.

Install Windows Server 2016 features and roles

Windows Server 2016 includes predefined combinations of services, called *roles*, which are designed to configure the server to perform specific tasks. The operating system also includes other, smaller components called *features*. Windows Server 2016 can run as many roles as it has the hardware resources to support, but the current trend is toward more specialized servers that run only one or two roles.

To add roles and features in Windows Server 2016, you can use a graphical wizard in the Server Manager console, or you can install them from the Windows PowerShell command line, as described in the following sections.

Using Server Manager to install roles

To install roles and services on a computer running Windows Server 2016 with Server Manager, use the following procedure:

1. In Server Manager, open the Manage menu and select Add Roles And Features. The Add Roles And Features Wizard launches.
2. Bypass the Before You Begin page to proceed to the Select Installation Type page, as shown in Figure 1-6.

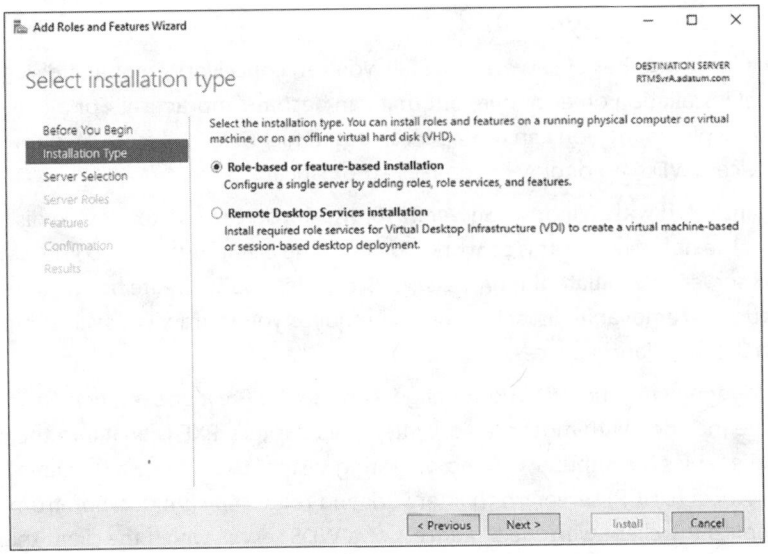

FIGURE 1-6 The Select Installation Type page in the Add Roles And Features Wizard

3. Click Next to accept the default Role-Based or Feature-Based Installation option selected. The Select Destination Server page appears, as shown in Figure 1-7.

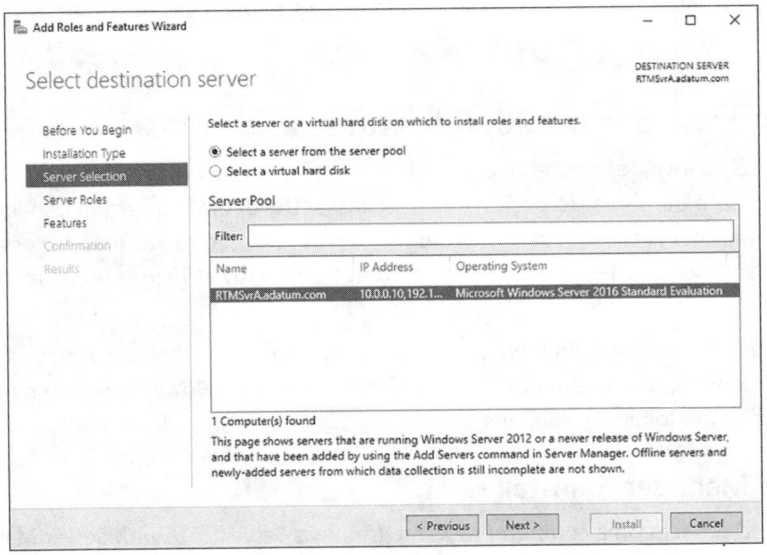

FIGURE 1-7 The Select Destination Server page in the Add Roles And Features Wizard

4. Click Next to accept the default server settings. The Select Server Roles page opens, as shown in Figure 1-8.

NOTE **CONFIGURING MULTIPLE SERVERS**

When you first run Server Manager, only the local server appears on the Select Destination Server page. However, you can add other servers to Server Manager, enabling you to manage them remotely. When you do this, you can use the Add Roles And Features Wizard to install components to any server you have added, though you cannot use it to install components to multiple servers at once. You can, however, do this by using the Install-WindowsFeature cmdlet in Windows PowerShell.

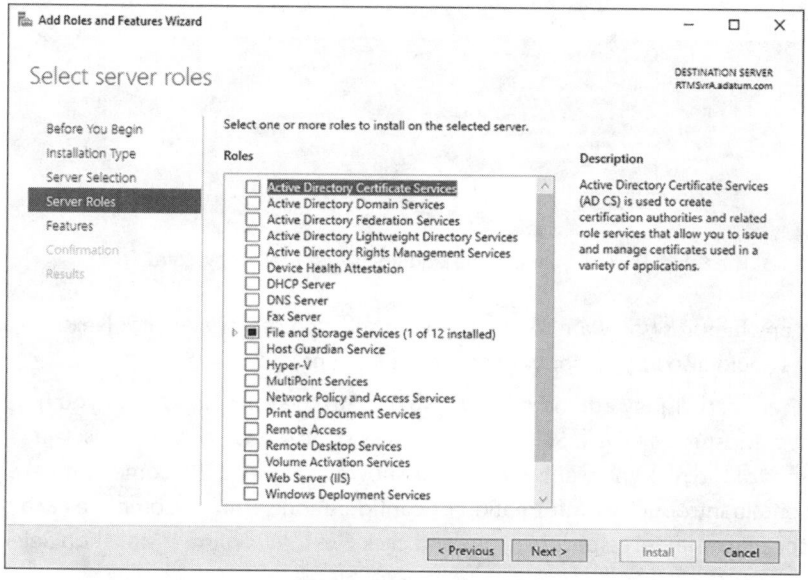

FIGURE 1-8 The Select Server Roles page in the Add Roles And Features Wizard

5. Select the role or roles you want to install on the selected server. If the roles you select have other roles or features as dependencies, an Add Features That Are Required dialog box appears.
6. Click Add Features to accept the dependencies, and then click Next to open the Select Features page, as shown in Figure 1-9.

Roles are predefined services, programs and config settings that allow a computer to full fill a specific Req. ie File in print Services

Feature - a smaller add on package. ie LPR Service

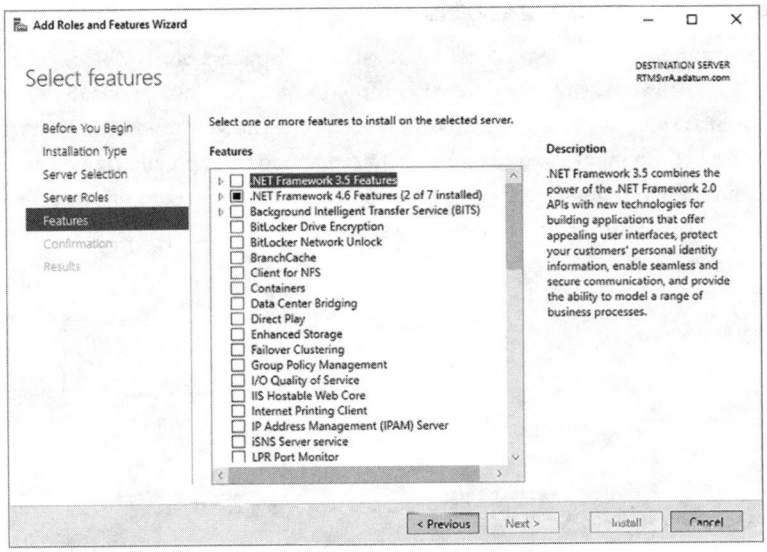

FIGURE 1-9 The Select Features page in the Add Roles And Features Wizard

7. Select any features you want to install on the selected server and click Next. Dependencies could also appear for your feature selections.
8. The wizard can display additional pages specific to the roles or features you have selected. Most roles have a Select Role Services page, on which you can select which elements of the role you want to install, as shown in Figure 1-10. Some also have pages that contain introductory information or configuration settings. Complete each of the role-specific or feature-specific pages and click Next. A Confirm Installation Selections page appears.

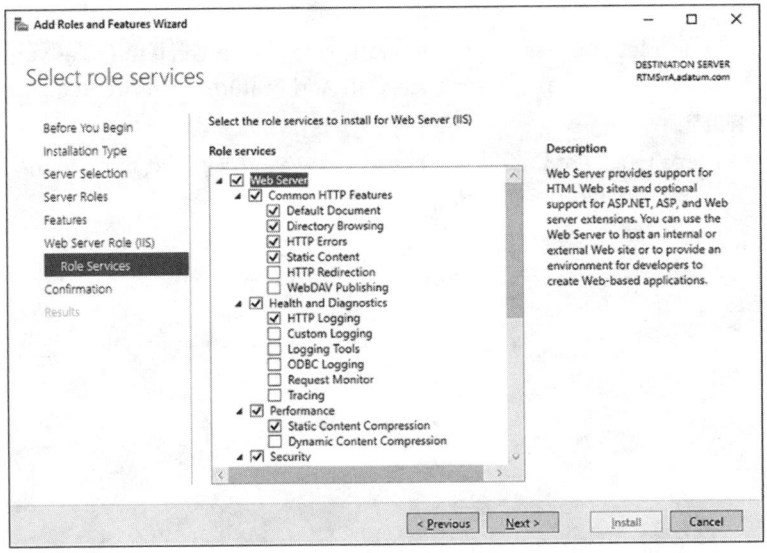

FIGURE 1-10 A Select Role Services page in the Add Roles And Features Wizard

9. On the Confirm Installation Selections page, you can perform the following optional tasks:
   - **Restart The Destination Server Automatically If Required** Selecting this check box causes the server to restart automatically when the installation is completed, if the selected roles and features require it.
   - **Export Configuration Settings** Creates an XML script containing the procedures performed by the wizard. You can use the script to install the same configuration on another server by using Windows PowerShell.
   - **Specify An Alternate Source Path** Specifies the location of an image file containing the software needed to install the selected roles and features. In a default Windows Server 2016 installation, this is not necessary, but if you have previously deleted the source files from the system using Features on Demand, you will need an image file to install roles and features.
10. Click Install to open the Installation Progress page. Depending on the roles and features you have selected, the wizard might display hyperlinks to the tools or wizards needed to perform required post installation tasks. When the installation is complete, click Close to complete the wizard.

Confirm - Restart, Export, Specify alternate -

Using Windows PowerShell to install roles

For administrators who prefer working from the command line, or for those working on systems using the Server Core installation option, it is also possible to install roles and features using the Install-WindowsFeature cmdlet in Windows PowerShell. The basic syntax of the cmdlet is as follows:

```
install-windowsfeature -name featurename [-includeallsubfeature]
[-includemanagementtools]
```

To install a role or feature, you must use a PowerShell session with administrative privileges. Then, you must determine the correct name to use for the role or feature you want to install. To do this, you can list all of the available roles and features available in Windows by running the Get-WindowsFeature cmdlet, the first part of which is shown in Figure 1-11.

INSTALL-WINDOWSFEATURE } are a server thing only.
GET-WINDOWSFEATURE

```
Windows PowerShell
Copyright (C) 2016 Microsoft Corporation. All rights reserved.

PS C:\Users\Administrator> get-windowsfeature

Display Name                                            Name                       Install State
------------                                            ----                       -------------
[ ] Active Directory Certificate Services               AD-Certificate                 Available
    [ ] Certification Authority                         ADCS-Cert-Authority            Available
    [ ] Certificate Enrollment Policy Web Service       ADCS-Enroll-Web-Pol            Available
    [ ] Certificate Enrollment Web Service              ADCS-Enroll-Web-Svc            Available
    [ ] Certification Authority Web Enrollment          ADCS-Web-Enrollment            Available
    [ ] Network Device Enrollment Service               ADCS-Device-Enrollment         Available
    [ ] Online Responder                                ADCS-Online-Cert               Available
[ ] Active Directory Domain Services                    AD-Domain-Services             Available
[ ] Active Directory Federation Services                ADFS-Federation                Available
[ ] Active Directory Lightweight Directory Services     ADLDS                          Available
[ ] Active Directory Rights Management Services         ADRMS                          Available
    [ ] Active Directory Rights Management Server       ADRMS-Server                   Available
    [ ] Identity Federation Support                     ADRMS-Identity                 Available
[ ] Device Health Attestation                           DeviceHealthAttestat...        Available
[ ] DHCP Server                                         DHCP                           Available
[ ] DNS Server                                          DNS                            Available
[ ] Fax Server                                          Fax                            Available
[X] File and Storage Services                           FileAndStorage-Services        Installed
    [ ] File and iSCSI Services                         File-Services                  Available
        [ ] File Server                                 FS-FileServer                  Available
        [ ] BranchCache for Network Files               FS-BranchCache                 Available
        [ ] Data Deduplication                          FS-Data-Deduplication          Available
        [ ] DFS Namespaces                              FS-DFS-Namespace               Available
        [ ] DFS Replication                             FS-DFS-Replication             Available
        [ ] File Server Resource Manager                FS-Resource-Manager            Available
        [ ] File Server VSS Agent Service               FS-VSS-Agent                   Available
        [ ] iSCSI Target Server                         FS-iSCSITarget-Server          Available
        [ ] iSCSI Target Storage Provider (VDS and V... iSCSITarget-VSS-VDS            Available
        [ ] Server for NFS                              FS-NFS-Service                 Available
        [ ] Work Folders                                FS-SyncShareService            Available
    [X] Storage Services                                Storage-Services               Installed
[ ] Host Guardian Service                               HostGuardianServiceRole        Available
[ ] Hyper-V                                             Hyper-V                        Available
[ ] MultiPoint Services                                 MultiPointServerRole           Available
[ ] Network Policy and Access Services                  NPAS                           Available
```

FIGURE 1-11 Output from the Get-WindowsFeature cmdlet

NOTE **POWERSHELL TERMINOLOGY**

Windows PowerShell, in its command language, does not distinguish between roles and features, as Server Manager does. All of the components are referred to as features and are installed using the Install-WindowsFeature cmdlet. There are no cmdlets that use the term role.

The resulting list displays all of the roles first, and then all of the features. The Name column specifies the exact string you should use in the Name parameter of your Install-WindowsFeature command line.

The check boxes specify which components are currently installed on the system. The list is indented to show which components are subordinate role services or subfeatures, so that you can install specific elements of a role, just as you can in Server Manager. You can also add the IncludeAllSubFeature parameter to install all of the subordinate components for a role.

Unlike Server Manager, which automatically includes the management tools associated with a role when you install it, the Install-WindowsFeature cmdlet does not. If you want to install the Microsoft Management Console snap-in or other tools used to manage a role or feature, you must add the IncludeManagementTools parameter on the command line.

Install and configure Windows Server Core

For many network administrators, running a graphical user interface (GUI) on a server that will spend its life in a data center or server closet seems like a waste of resources. In many cases, administrators rarely have to touch servers after their initial installation and configuration, except to check logs, which can be done remotely. Server Core is an installation option in Windows Server 2016 that eliminates most of the GUI, leaving a default screen with only a command line interface, as shown in Figure 1-12.

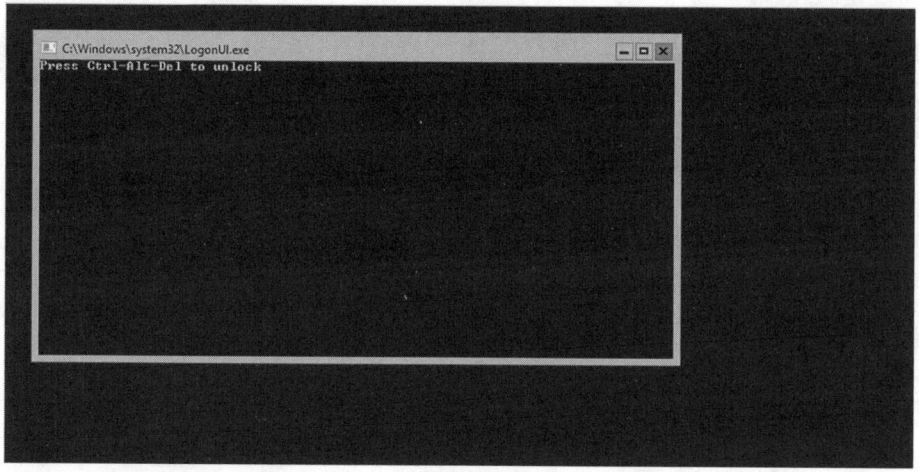

FIGURE 1-12 The default Server Core screen in Windows Server 2016

Installing Server Core

When you install Windows Server 2016, the Select The Operating System You Want To Install page of the Windows Setup Wizard appears, with the Server Core option selected by default, as shown in Figure 1-13. Unlike Windows Server 2012 R2, the term Server Core does not appear on the page; the full GUI option is identified by the term Desktop Experience. (In Windows Server 2012 R2, the options are called Server With A GUI and Server Core Installation.) With the exception of this page, the operating system installation is the same as for the Desktop Experience option, described earlier in this chapter.

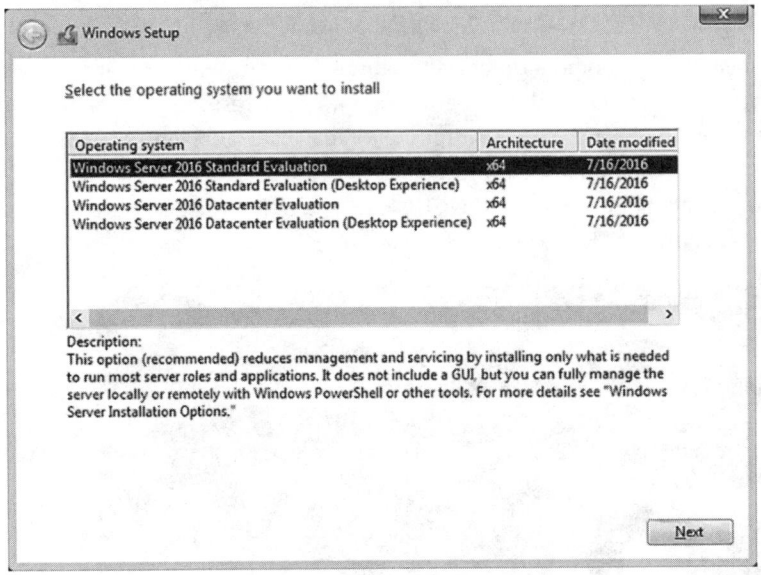

FIGURE 1-13 The Select The Operating System You Want To Install page of the Windows Setup Wizard

EXAM TIP

In Windows Server 2016, you can no longer add or remove the GUI elements after the operating system installation. In addition, there is no Minimal Server Interface option, as in Windows Server 2012 R2. This means that, at installation time, you must choose between a full graphical interface, similar to that of Windows 10, and a command line only. In Windows Server 2012 R2, it was possible to install and configure the server using the full GUI option, and then remove GUI features once the server was up and running. This is no longer possible. Administrators familiar with this practice should be aware of the change when taking Exam 70-740.

When you select the Windows Server Core installation option, you get a stripped-down version of the operating system. There is no Taskbar, no Explorer shell, no Server Manager, no Microsoft Management Console, and virtually no other graphical applications.

However, the advantages of running servers using the Server Core option are several, including the following:

- **Hardware resource conservation** Server Core eliminates some of the most memory- and processor-intensive elements of the Windows Server 2016 operating system, thus devoting more of the system resources to running applications and essential services.
- **Reduced disk space** Server Core requires less disk space for the installed operating system elements, as well as less storage space devoted to memory swapping, which maximizes the utilization of the server's storage resources.

- **Fewer updates** The graphical elements of Windows Server 2016 are among the most frequently updated features, so running Server Core reduces the number of updates that administrators must apply. Fewer updates also means fewer server restarts and less downtime.
- **Reduced attack surface** The less software there is running on the computer, the fewer entrances there are available for attackers to exploit. Server Core reduces the potential openings presented by the operating system, increasing its overall security.

Configuring Server Core

To work interactively with a computer installed using the Server Core option, you can use the CMD command line interface, or you can use Windows PowerShell. It is also possible to connect to the server remotely, using graphical tools such as Server Manager and MMC snap-ins.

Immediately after the installation, however, you might be forced to perform some basic post-installation tasks interactively, such as configuring the network adapter, renaming the computer, and joining the server to a domain. To complete these tasks on a computer running Server Core using Windows PowerShell, you must first type **powershell** in the CMD window to invoke a PowerShell session.

If your network does not have a DHCP server to automatically configure the computer's network adapter, you can do it manually with the New-NetIpAddress cmdlet. First, you must discover the interface index of the adapter by using the Get-NetAdapter cmdlet, which produces the output shown in Figure 1-14.

```
PS C:\Users\Administrator> get-netadapter

Name                      InterfaceDescription                    ifIndex Status       MacAddress             LinkSpeed
----                      --------------------                    ------- ------       ----------             ---------
Ethernet 2                Microsoft Hyper-V Network Adapter #2          6 Up           00-15-5D-02-01-32        10 Gbps
Ethernet                  Microsoft Hyper-V Network Adapter             4 Up           00-15-5D-02-01-30        10 Gbps

PS C:\Users\Administrator>
```

FIGURE 1-14 Output of the Get-NetAdapter cmdlet

With this information, you can select the interface of the adapter you want to configure and use a command like the following to configure it:

```
new-netipaddress -interfaceindex 6 -ipaddress 192.168.0.200 -prefixlength 24
-defaultgateway 192.168.0.1
```

The functions of the command line parameters are as follows:

- **interfaceindex** Identifies the adapter in the computer to be configured, using index numbers displayed by the Get-NetAdapter cmdlet.
- **ipaddress** Specifies the IP address to be assigned to the adapter.
- **prefixlength** Specifies the subnet mask value to be associated with the IP address. The numeral specifies the number of network bits in the IP address. For example, a prefixlength value of 24 is the equivalent of a subnet mask value of 255.255.255.0.

- **defaultgateway** Specifies the IP address of a local router that the computer should use to access other networks.

The resulting output is shown in Figure 1-15.

```
PS C:\Users\Administrator> new-netipaddress -interfaceindex 4 -ipaddress 10.0.0.200 -prefixlength 24 -defaultgateway 10.
0.0.1


IPAddress         : 10.0.0.200
InterfaceIndex    : 4
InterfaceAlias    : Ethernet
AddressFamily     : IPv4
Type              : Unicast
PrefixLength      : 24
PrefixOrigin      : Manual
SuffixOrigin      : Manual
AddressState      : Tentative
ValidLifetime     : Infinite ([TimeSpan]::MaxValue)
PreferredLifetime : Infinite ([TimeSpan]::MaxValue)
SkipAsSource      : False
PolicyStore       : ActiveStore

IPAddress         : 10.0.0.200
InterfaceIndex    : 4
InterfaceAlias    : Ethernet
AddressFamily     : IPv4
Type              : Unicast
PrefixLength      : 24
PrefixOrigin      : Manual
SuffixOrigin      : Manual
AddressState      : Invalid
ValidLifetime     : Infinite ([TimeSpan]::MaxValue)
PreferredLifetime : Infinite ([TimeSpan]::MaxValue)
SkipAsSource      : False
PolicyStore       : PersistentStore
```

FIGURE 1-15 Output of the New-NetIpAddress cmdlet

To configure the DNS server addresses for the adapter, you use the Set-DnsClient-ServerAddress cmdlet, as in the following example:

```
Set-dnsclientserveraddress -interfaceindex 6 -serveraddresses
("192.168.0.1","192.168.0.2")
```

To rename the computer and join it to a domain, you can use the Add-Computer cmdlet, as in the following example:

```
add-computer -domainname adatum.com -newname ServerB -credential adatum\administrator
```

The functions of the command line parameters are as follows:

- **domainname** Specifies the name of the domain that you want the computer to join
- **newname** Specifies a computer name that you want to assign to the computer
- **credential** Specifies the domain and account names for a domain user with domain join privileges

Manage Windows Server Core installations using Windows PowerShell, command line, and remote management capabilities

Although most of the standard graphical utilities are not available on a computer installed using the Server Core option, there are still many ways to manage the server, both locally and remotely. In the previous section, you learned how to configure the network adapter and join a domain using Windows PowerShell cmdlets. There are thousands of other PowerShell cmdlets available on a Server Core computer, which can perform virtually any tasks that the graphical tools can, except display results in a fancy, colorful window. PowerShell also provides a powerful scripting capability that you can use to automate complex tasks.

To display a long list of the PowerShell cmdlets available, run the Get-Command cmdlet. To learn how to use any one of the cmdlets, run the Get-help cmdlet with the name of the cmdlet about which you want to learn.

In addition to Windows PowerShell, Server Core also includes the standard CMD command shell, which you can use to run any of the command line programs included with Windows Server 2016.

For example, as an alternative to the Add-Computer PowerShell cmdlet, you can use the Netdom.exe tool from the command prompt to rename a computer and join it to a domain. To rename a computer, you use the following command:

```
netdom renamecomputer %computername% /newname: newcomputername
```

To restart the computer after changing its name, you use the Shutdown.exe tool, as follows:

```
shutdown /r
```

To join a computer to a domain using Netdom.exe, use the following command:

```
netdom join %computername% /domain: domainname /userd: username /passwordd:*
```

In this command, the asterisk (*) in the `/password` parameter causes the program to prompt you for the password to the user account you specified.

Using remote PowerShell

For Server Core computers that are locked in server closets or data centers, or that are at remote locations, you can access their PowerShell prompts remotely. In Windows Server 2016, the Windows Remote Management (WinRM) service is enabled by default, so you can create a remote PowerShell session using the New-PsSession cmdlet, as in the following example:

```
new-pssession -computername rtmsvrd
```

In this example, Rtmsvrd is the remote Server Core computer you want to manage. Running this command creates a connection to remote computer and assigns it an ID number as shown in Figure 1-16.

```
PS C:\Users\administrator.ADATUM> new-pssession -computername rtmsvrd

 Id Name            ComputerName    ComputerType    State         ConfigurationName     Availability
 -- ----            ------------    ------------    -----         -----------------     ------------
  3 Session3         rtmsvrd         RemoteMachine   Opened        Microsoft.PowerShell     Available


PS C:\Users\administrator.ADATUM> _
```

FIGURE 1-16 Output of the New-PsSession cmdlet

Once you have created the session, you can connect to it using the Enter-PsSession cmdlet, specifying the ID number of the session you just created, as shown in Figure 1-17. Notice that the command prompt changes to indicate the name of the computer you are working on.

```
PS C:\Users\administrator.ADATUM> new-pssession -computername rtmsvrd

 Id Name            ComputerName    ComputerType    State         ConfigurationName     Availability
 -- ----            ------------    ------------    -----         -----------------     ------------
  3 Session3         rtmsvrd         RemoteMachine   Opened        Microsoft.PowerShell     Available


PS C:\Users\administrator.ADATUM> enter-pssession 3
[rtmsvrd]: PS C:\Users\Administrator.ADATUM\Documents>
```

FIGURE 1-17 Output of the Enter-PsSession cmdlet

While you are connected to the session, the commands you type are running on the remote computer, configuring the remote computer's settings, and utilizing the remote computer's resources.

To leave the session and return to the local PowerShell prompt, you run the Exit-PsSession cmdlet, or just type exit. When you do this, the session remains in force, however, and you can return to it by running the Enter-PsSession cmdlet again. To terminate the session, run the Disconnect-PsSession cmdlet.

Using Server Manager remotely

For administrators who are not comfortable working at the CMD or PowerShell command line, it is possible to use graphical management tools on another system to manage a computer running Server Core. The Server Manager console included with the Windows Server 2016 Desktop Experience installation option enables you to add multiple servers to its interface, add and remove roles and features on any server, and monitor the installed roles.

To add servers in Server Manager, use the following procedure.

1. Open Server Manager and, in the left pane, click All Servers. The Servers pane appears, as shown in Figure 1-18.

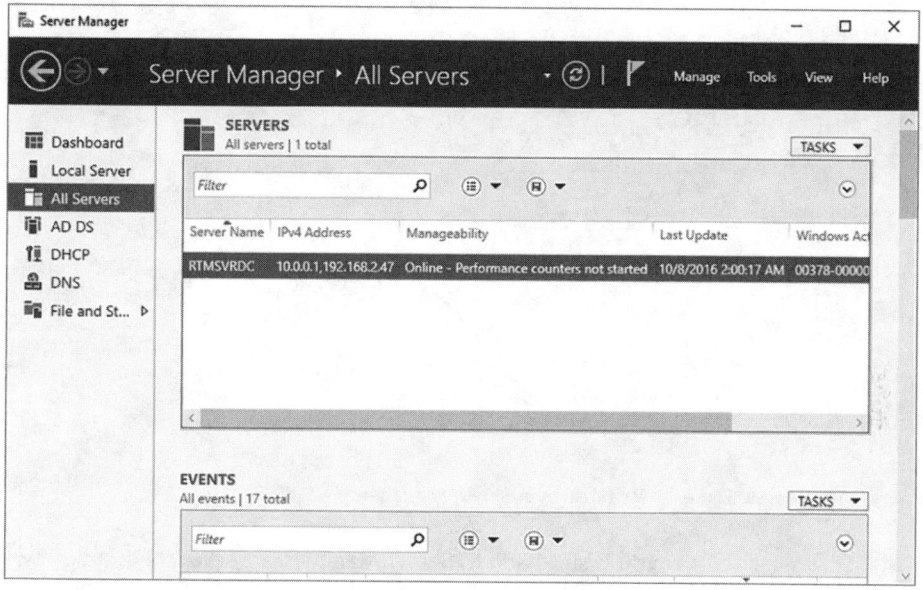

FIGURE 1-18 The Servers pane in Server Manager

2. From the Manage menu, select Add Servers. The Add Servers dialog box appears.
3. Select one of the following tabs to search for servers:
   - **Active Directory** Enables you to search for servers running specific Windows versions in specific Active Directory locations
   - **DNS** Enables you to search the Domain Name System (DNS) for servers
   - **Import** Enables you to supply a text file specifying server names

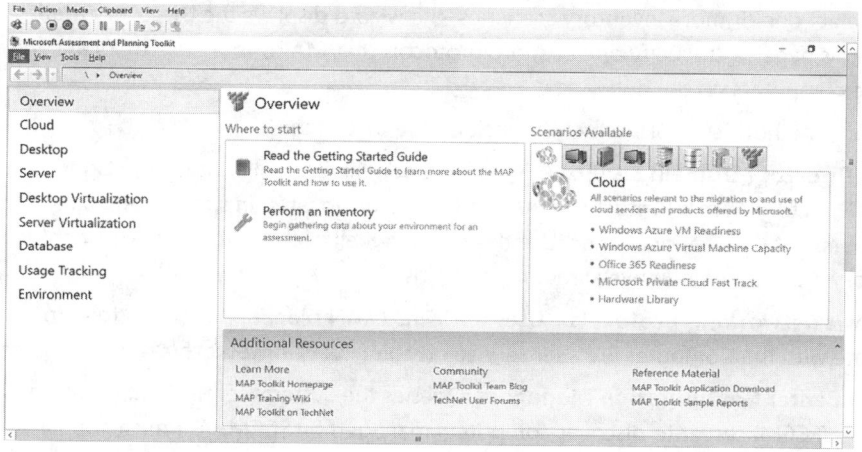

FIGURE 1-42 The Microsoft Assessment and Planning Toolkit console

Once you have configured MAP with a database, you can select one of several methods for collecting inventory information from the computers on the network. Clicking Perform An Inventory on the console's Overview page launches the Inventory And Assessment Wizard. This wizard is the starting point for all inventory scenarios. The Inventory Scenarios page, shown in Figure 1-43, lists the basic types of information discoverable by MAP and specifies the collector technologies that the program uses to probe the network. A *collector technology* specifies the means and the protocol by which MAP communicates with the other computers on the network.

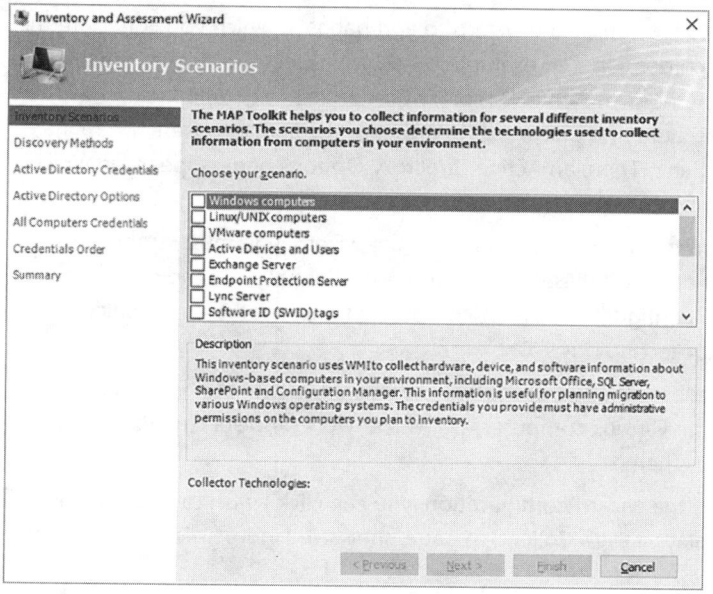

FIGURE 1-43 The Inventory Scenarios page

After you select one or more inventory scenarios, the wizard displays the Discovery Methods page. On this page, you specify one or more protocols that MAP should use to locate and connect to the computers on the network.

The discovery methods supported by MAP include the following:

- **Active Directory Domain Services** Queries a domain controller using the Lightweight Directory Access Protocol (LDAP) for computers located in specific domains, containers, or organizational units. Use this method if all of the computers you want to inventory are located in Active Directory domains.
- **Windows networking protocols** Uses the Win32 LAN Manager interface to communicate with the Computer Browser service on computers in workgroups or domains.
- **System Center Configuration Manager** Queries the System Center Configuration Manager (SCCM) server to discover computers managed by SCCM. You must supply credentials for an account with access to the Configuration Manager WMI provider on the server.
- **Scan an IP address range** Queries up to 100,000 devices using IP addresses within a specified range. This enables the wizard to connect to computers without credentials and regardless of their operating systems.
- **Manually enter computer names** Enables you to inventory a small number of computers by entering their computer names, NetBIOS names, or fully-qualified domain names (FQDNs).
- **Import computer names from a file** Enables you to specify the name of a text file containing up to 120,000 computer names, NetBIOS names, FQDNs, or IPv4 addresses.

Making selections on this page causes the wizard to add pages in which you configure the discovery method or supply credentials. For example, when you select the Active Directory Domain Services discovery method, an Active Directory Credentials page appears, on which you must supply a domain account and password for a user in the Domain Users group in each domain you intend to query. Then, an Active Directory Options page appears, in which you can select specific domains, containers, and organizational units.

Depending on which inventory scenario you select in the wizard, you must supply appropriate credentials that MAP needs to access the computers on the network and their software. In some cases, you must also configure the target computers to accept the communication protocol used by the collector technology.

On the All Computers Credentials page of the wizard, you can create multiple account entries, providing access to the various computers on the network, and specifying the order in which the MAP Toolkit uses them.

Once you have completed the wizard configuration, you can click Finish to start the inventory process. The wizard displays a Data Collection page, shown in Figure 1-44, which tracks the progress of the inventory.

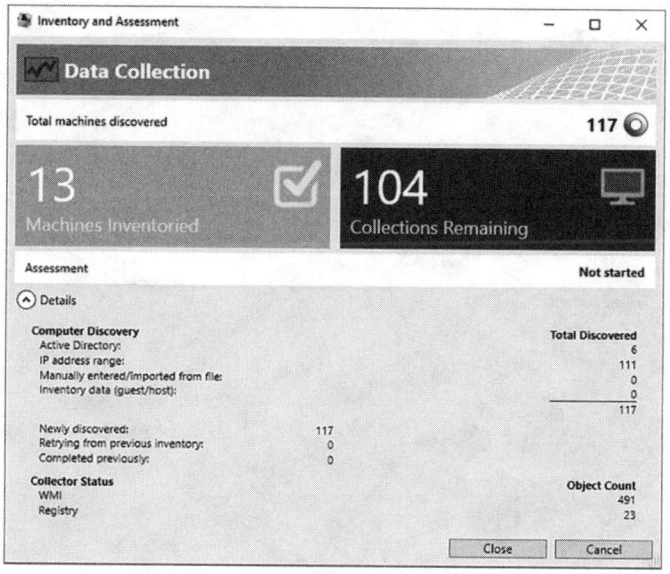

FIGURE 1-44 The Data Collection page

Once you have performed a hardware inventory, you can view the Server Virtualization page (shown in Figure 1-45), which guides you through the rest of the data collection procedure.

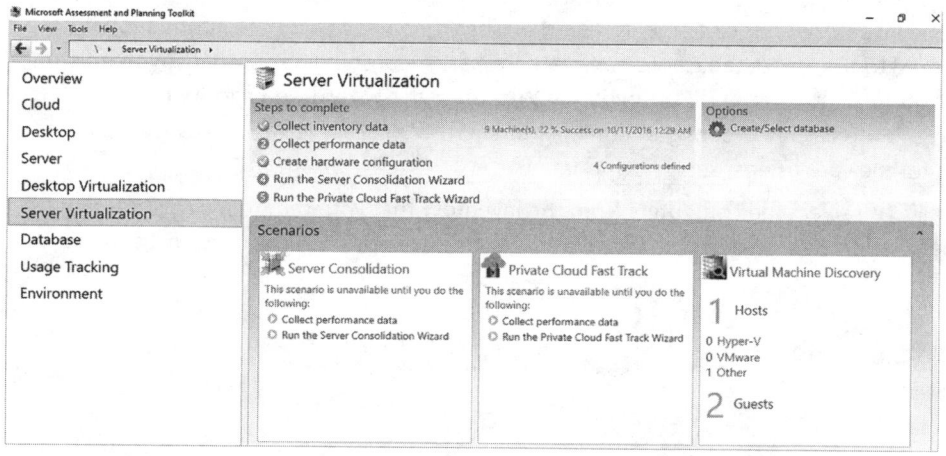

FIGURE 1-45 The Inventory Scenarios page

Clicking Collect Performance Data launches the Performance Metrics Wizard. This wizard collects performance data from the computers on the network over a period of time, which you specify on the Collection Configuration page.

You select the computers from which you want to collect data and supply credentials, as you did earlier. Once the wizard begins, it samples performance counter data from each computer every five minutes, as shown in Figure 1-46, until the specified time expires.

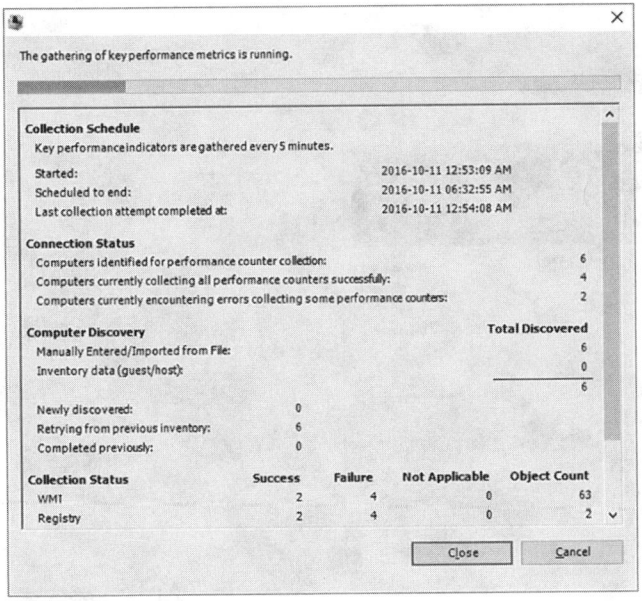

FIGURE 1-46 The Performance Metrics Wizard

Evaluating results

Once the Inventory And Assessment Wizard finishes running, it saves the information it has discovered to the SQL database. To complete the server consolidation scenario, you must run the Server Virtualization And Consolidation Wizard. In this wizard, you specify the operating system and the hardware configuration of your Hyper-V host server, as well as a utilization ceiling for the various host server components.

Finally, you select the computers from the inventory that you want to include in the assessment. After the assessment is completed, the results appear on the console, as shown in Figure 1-47.

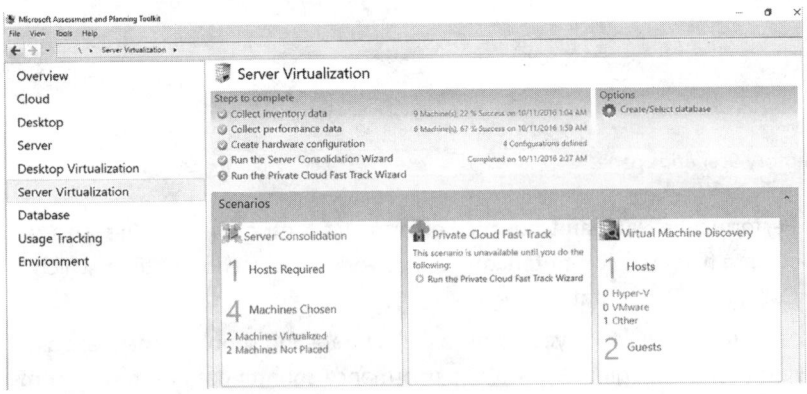

FIGURE 1-47 The completed Server Virtualization page

The MAP Toolkit also creates reports as Excel workbooks, which in this scenario provides details about the recommended server consolidation strategy, as shown in Figure 1-48.

	A	B	C	D	E
1	**Pre-Consolidation Utilization Report**				
2	This report provides details of the current utilization of machines in your network based on performance details collected earlier. The values indicate the utilization before each machine is virtualized for consolidation. All values are for the 95th percentile, except for disk space, for which the maximum utilization is shown. See the HowItWorks worksheet for more details.				
3					
4	Machine Name	Operating System	CPU Utilization (%)	Memory Utilization (MB)	Disk I/O Utilization (IOPS)
5	POM-6VW8E-RTM-1.USA.CONTOSO.COM	Microsoft Windows 8 Enterprise	0.26	221.97	4.3
6	pom-6v3s-05.MAP2012.COM	Microsoft(R) Windows(R) Server 2003 Standard x64 Edition	0.08	366.71	1.05
7	POM-3SQL12BM-01.USA.CONTOSO.COM	Microsoft® Windows Server® 2008 Datacenter	0.27	1387.42	0.74
8	POM-6EX-07MBS-1.CONTOSO.COM	Microsoft Windows Server 2008 R2 Enterprise	1.9	1312.76	1.53
9	pom-3v3w-sp1-01.WA.USA.CONTOSO.COM	Microsoft(R) Windows(R) Server 2003, Web Edition	0.13	269.18	0.66
10	POM-6V3S-SP1-01.WA.USA.CONTOSO.COM	Microsoft(R) Windows(R) Server 2003 Standard x64 Edition	0.18	207.14	0.68
11	POM-3SP03NSPS-1.CONTOSO.COM	Microsoft(R) Windows(R) Server 2003, Enterprise Edition	1.52	889.73	3.11
12	POM-6VVB-02.WA.USA.CONTOSO.COM	Microsoft® Windows Vista™ Business	0.39	343.07	1.29
13	POM-3VVE-03.CONTOSO.COM	Microsoft® Windows Vista™ Enterprise	0.63	603.39	1.35

FIGURE 1-48 The Server Consolidation report

Determine considerations for deploying workloads into virtualized environments

Many of the workloads used on today's networks can easily be converted from physical to virtual servers, but not all of them can be, and even more important, not all of them should be. To determine which existing servers are the best candidates for virtualization, consider first the following resource utilization factors:

- **Memory** Applications that have large memory requirements might not be good candidates for virtualization, because they might consume an inordinate amount of the host server's memory resources. For example, an application that uses 32 GB of memory would not be cost effective on a VM running on a host server with 48 GB total.
- **Processor** Much like the memory requirement, an application that consistently uses a large amount of the physical server's CPU capacity might not be efficient on a virtual machine because it could leave too few of the host server's processor capacity for other VMs.
- **Network** Network throughput is a critical factor in a virtualization project because you must consider the combined requirements of all the virtual machines running on the server. You must consider the combined network throughput requirements of all the virtual machines running on the host server to make sure that they do not overwhelm the capacity of the physical network adapters. This is often the reason why administrators cannot deploy dozens of VMs on a single host server.
- **Storage** Physical servers with a high storage throughput might not work well in a virtualized environment because they could slow down the input/output (I/O) performance of the other VMs.

Enhancing the hardware configuration of the host server can mitigate all of these factors. For example, you could purchase a physical computer with 512 GB of memory instead of 48 GB, or several multicore processors, or a high performance storage array, or multiple network connections, but you also must consider whether these additional expenses are worth it. The higher the hardware costs go, the less likely that the ROI will pay for the project. It might be more economical just to leave certain resource-intensive applications on their physical servers.

Update images with patches, hotfixes, and drivers

Windows includes a command line tool called *Deployment Image Servicing and Management (DISM.exe)* that enables you to modify virtual hard disk (VHD) and Windows Imaging files while they are offline. With that same tool, you can also perform the following maintenance tasks:

- Add and remove device drivers
- Add and remove language packs
- Add and remove packaged updates
- Add and remove files and folders
- Enable or disable operating system features
- Execute answer files
- Add or remove app packages

Administrators can use this capability in several ways. If you capture images from reference computers so that you can use them to deploy new computers, those images will eventually become outdated. At first, you can apply operating system and application updates to your deployed workstations as they are released. However, eventually, deploying new workstations become increasingly difficult because of all the updates and changes you must apply to each one. When this happens, it is time to consider updating your image files, and this is when an alternative to recapturing new images is welcome.

The 10.0 version of DISM.exe included in Windows Server 2016 can service images of the following operating systems:

- Windows 10
- Windows 8.1
- Windows 8
- Windows 7
- Windows Server 2016
- Windows Server 2012 R2
- Windows Server 2012
- Windows Server 2008 R2
- Windows Server 2008 SP2
- Windows Preinstallation Environment (Windows PE) 5.0

- Windows PE 4.0
- Windows 3.0

While DISM was originally designed to service WIM images, like the ones on the Windows installation disks, many (but not all) of its functions also work with virtual hard disk (VHD and VHDX) images. For example, you can use DISM.exe to mount VHD or VHDX images and add or remove drivers and packages, as well as enable and disable Windows features. In addition to working with image files in their offline state, you can also use DISM to perform certain functions on the computer's currently running operating system.

Mounting an image

The standard procedure for modifying image files offline is to mount an image to a folder, make changes to the expanded files, and then commit the changes back to the image file. To modify an image file using DISM.exe, you must first mount it to a folder. This process creates copies of all the files in the image in their expanded form. You can then work with the copies, making any changes you need.

To mount an image, open a command prompt with administrative privileges and use the following syntax:

```
dism /mount-image /imagefile:filename /index:# /name:imagename /mountdir:pathname
```

The functions of the parameters are as follows:

- **/mount-image** Specifies that the command should mount an image to a folder
- **/imagefile:filename** Specifies the name and location of the image file you want to mount
- **/index:#** Specifies the number of the image within the WIM file that you want to mount
- **/name:imagename** Specifies the name of the image within the WIM file that you want to mount
- **/mountdir:pathname** Specifies a location on the local disk where you want to mount the image

A typical mount command would appear as follows:

```
Dism /mount-image /imagefile:c:\images\install.wim /index:4 /mountdir:c:\mount
```

This command takes the fourth image in the Install.wim file, found in the C:\Images folder, and mounts it in the C:\Mount folder. The result of the command is as shown in Figure 1-49.

FIGURE 1-49 Mounting an image using DISM.exe

NOTE MOUNTING READ/WRITE IMAGES

If you mount an image directly from a read-only source, such as a Windows installation DVD, the DISM.exe program mounts the image in read-only mode. You can't make any changes to the image, even though it is mounted to a folder on a read/write hard disk. To modify the image from a Windows disk, you must first copy the Install.wim file from the DVD to a hard disk.

WIM files can contain multiple images, but you can only mount one of the images in the file at a time. This is the reason for the /index and /name options on the command line. To determine the index number or name value for a specific image in a file containing more than one, you can use the following command:

```
dism /get-imageinfo /imagefile:x:\filename
```

Once the image is mounted, you can proceed to work with it, as shown in the following sections.

Adding drivers to an image file

For a workstation with a storage host adapter or other hardware device that Windows Server 2016 does not support natively, an administrator might find it easier to add a device driver for the adapter to an existing image file rather than capture a new one. This would be especially true if there are several workstation configurations with different drivers involved.

To add a driver to an image file that you have already mounted, use a DISM command with the following syntax:

```
dism /image:foldername /add-driver /driver:drivername [/recurse]
```

- **/image:foldername** Specifies the location of the mounted image that you want to modify.
- **/add-driver** Indicates that you want to add a driver to the image specified by the /image parameter.
- **/driver:drivername** Specifies the location of the driver to be added to the image, either as a path to the driver file (with an .inf extension) or to the folder where the driver is located.
- **/recurse** When you specify a folder without a file name in the /driver option, causes the program to search for drivers in the subdirectories of the folder specified in the /driver parameter.

NOTE THE /IMAGE PARAMETER

Once you have mounted an image using DISM.exe, nearly all of the commands you use to work with the image begin with the /image parameter, with which you specify the mount location, so that DISM knows what image it should access. For some commands, you can substitute the /online option for the /image option, to service the currently running operating system. The commands that you can perform with the /online option depend on the Windows version that is currently running.

An example of the command is shown in Figure 1-50.

```
C:\Windows\system32>dism /image:c:\mount /add-driver /driver:c:\drivers /recurse

Deployment Image Servicing and Management tool
Version: 10.0.14393.0

Image Version: 10.0.14393.0

Searching for driver packages to install...
Found 2 driver package(s) to install.
Installing 1 of 2 - oem0.inf: The driver package was successfully installed.
Installing 2 of 2 - oem0.inf: The driver package was successfully installed.
The operation completed successfully.

C:\Windows\system32>
```

FIGURE 1-50 Adding a driver with DISM.exe

NOTE INSTALLING DRIVERS

DISM.exe can only manage drivers that include a Windows Information file (with an .inf extension). If you have drivers packaged as executable (.exe) files or Microsoft Windows Installer (.msi) packages, you cannot add them to an image using the /add-driver parameter. You can however, use Windows System Image Manager (SIM) to create an answer file that installs these drivers and then apply the answer file to the image using DISM with the /Apply-Unattend parameter.

During the driver addition process, DISM renames the driver files with consecutively numbered file names, such as oem1.inf and oem2.inf. From that point on, you must use the new file names when referring to the drivers on the command line. To display information about the drivers in an image, use the following command:

```
dism /image:c:\mount /get-drivers
```

You can also use the /Get-DriverInfo option to display detailed information about a specific driver, as in the following example:

```
dism /image:c:\mount /get-driverinfo /driver:c:\drivers\driver.inf
```

Once you know this information, you can remove a driver from an image by substituting the /Remove-Driver option instead of /Add-Driver. An example would appear as follows:

```
dism /image:c:\mount /remove-driver /driver:oem1.inf
```

Adding updates to an image file

In roughly the same way that you can add drivers to a mounted image, you can also add operating system updates, such as hotfixes and language packs, which have been packaged as cabinet (CAB) or Windows Update Stand-Alone Installer (MSU) files.

To add an update to a mounted image, you use a command like the following:

```
dism /image:c:\mount /add-package /packagepath:c:\updates\package.msu [/ignorecheck]
```

- **/image:c:\mount** Specifies the location of the image that you want to modify.
- **/add-package** Indicates that you want to add a package to the image specified by the /image parameter.
- **/packagepath:c:\updates\package.msu** Specifies the location of the package to be added to the image. This option can point to a single CAB or MSU file, a folder that contains a single expanded CAB or a single MSU file, or a folder containing multiple CAB or MSU files. If the option points to a folder containing a CAB or MSU file, the program recursively checks any subdirectories for additional packages.
- **/ignorecheck** By default, DISM checks each package file to determine if it applies to the operating system specified by the /image option. This option suppresses this check and applies the package regardless of the operating system version.

DISM.exe can only add packages that take the form of cabinet (.cab) or Windows Update Stand-alone Installer (.msu) files.

> ***NOTE*** **FINDING CABS AND MSUS**
>
> **Although it might seem as though most of the updates that you can download from the Microsoft Download center do not qualify for addition to mounted images, because they are executable (.exe) or sector-based image (.iso) files, these packages often do contain appropriate .cab or .msu files inside the archive. You can expand an executable archive or mount an .iso file to access the files inside.**

You can specify multiple /packagepath options in a single DISM command, to install multiple packages. The program installs the packages in the order in which they appear on the command line.

To remove a package from an image file, you can use the /remove-package option, with the /packagepath option specifying the package you want to remove. You can also use the /get-packages option, to display information about all of the packages in an image, or the /get-packageinfo option, to display information about a specific package.

Committing and unmounting images

When you have made all of your modifications to the mounted image, you must commit the changes you made to the mounted copy back to the original Windows Imaging file and unmount the image, using a command like the following:

```
dism /unmount-image /mountdir:c:\mount /commit
```

The result of the command is shown in Figure 1-51. The /commit parameter causes DISM to save the changes you made. To abandon the changes and unmount the image without saving, use the /discard parameter instead of /commit.

```
C:\Windows\system32>dism /unmount-image /mountdir:c:\mount2 /commit

Deployment Image Servicing and Management tool
Version: 10.0.14393.0

Saving image
[==========================100.0%==========================]
Unmounting image
[==========================100.0%==========================]
```

FIGURE 1-51 Unmounting an image with DISM.exe

Install Roles and Features in offline images

DISM also enables you to enable and disable Windows features in a mounted image. To do this, you must first determine the exact name of the feature using DISM with the /get-features option, as in the following example:

```
dism /image:c:\mount /get-features
```

The result of this command is a long list of Windows features, the beginning of which is shown in Figure 1-52.

```
C:\Windows\system32>dism /image:c:\mount2 /get-features

Deployment Image Servicing and Management tool
Version: 10.0.14393.0

Image Version: 10.0.14393.0

Features listing for package : Microsoft-Windows-Foundation-Package~31bf3856ad364e35~amd64~~10.0.14393.0

Feature Name : NetFx4ServerFeatures
State : Enabled

Feature Name : NetFx4
State : Enabled

Feature Name : NetFx4Extended-ASPNET45
State : Disabled

Feature Name : MicrosoftWindowsPowerShellRoot
State : Enabled

Feature Name : MicrosoftWindowsPowerShell
State : Enabled

Feature Name : iSCSITargetServer-PowerShell
State : Disabled

Feature Name : PKIClient-PSH-Cmdlets
State : Disabled
```

FIGURE 1-52 Displaying Windows features with DISM.exe

Once you have found the feature you want to add, you must create a DISM command using the /enable-feature option and the exact feature name, as shown in the /get-features list, which you insert into the /featurename option.

The syntax for the DISM /enable-feature command is as follows:

```
dism /image:folder /enable-feature /featurename:feature [/packagename:package] [/
source:path] [/all]
```

- **/image:folder** Specifies the location of the image that you want to modify.
- **/enable-feature** Indicates that you want to enable a Windows feature in the image specified by the /image parameter.
- **/featurename:feature** Specifies the name of the feature you want to enable, using the name specified by the /get-features option.
- **[/packagename:package]** Specifies the name of the feature's parent package. This option is not needed when enabling a Windows Foundation feature.
- **[/source:path]** Specifies the path to the files needed to re-enable a feature that has previously been removed. This can be the /Windows folder in a mounted image or a Windows side-by-side (SxS) folder.
- **[/all]** Causes the program to enable all of the parent features for the specified feature.

An example of an /enable-feature command is shown in Figure 1-53.

```
C:\Windows\system32>dism /image:c:\mount2 /enable-feature /featurename:iis-webserverrole

Deployment Image Servicing and Management tool
Version: 10.0.14393.0

Image Version: 10.0.14393.0

Enabling feature(s)
[==========================100.0%==========================]
The operation completed successfully.

C:\Windows\system32>
```

FIGURE 1-53 Enabling a feature using DISM.exe

You can include multiple /featurename options in a single DISM command, as long as the features you specify all have the same common parent. For example, you can enable several IIS features at once, but you cannot enable an IIS and a Hyper-V feature in the same command.

The /disable-feature command functions in the same way as /enable-feature and uses the same basic syntax.

Manage and maintain Windows Server Core, Nano Server images, and VHDs using Windows PowerShell

As noted earlier in this chapter, the Windows Server 2016 Server Core installation option relies heavily on Windows PowerShell for system management and maintenance. On a Server Core system, Windows PowerShell and the CMD command prompt are your only choices for interactive management on the local console.

The Nano Server installation option relies on PowerShell for the creation of the image files that you use to deploy Nano Servers. You can also use the Edit-NanoServerImage cmdlet to modify those image files by configuring their network adapter settings and adding role and feature packages.

Windows includes a DISM module for Windows PowerShell that enables you to perform most of the same modifications on VHD image files as the DISM.exe command line executable.

Many of the Windows PowerShell cmdlets in the DISM module correspond directly to their command line equivalents and use exactly the same options and syntax. Some are slightly different, however. Table 1-2 lists the DISM.exe command line options and their equivalent Windows PowerShell cmdlets.

TABLE 1-2 Windows PowerShell equivalents for basic DISM.exe command line options

Dism.exe command	DISM cmdlet
Dism.exe /Append-Image	Add-WindowsImage
Dism.exe /Apply-Image	Expand-WindowsImage
Dism.exe /Capture-Image	New-WindowsImage
Dism.exe /Commit-Image	Save-WindowsImage
Dism.exe /Export-Image	Export-WindowsImage
Dism.exe /Get-ImageInfo	Get-WindowsImage
Dism.exe /Get-MountedImageInfo	Get-WindowsImage -Mounted
Dism.exe /List-Image	Get-WindowsImageContent
Dism.exe /Mount-Image	Mount-WindowsImage
Dism.exe /Remove-Image	Remove-WindowsImage
Dism.exe /Remount-Image	Mount-WindowsImage -Remount
Dism.exe /Unmount-Image	Dismount-WindowsImage
Dism.exe /Image:foldername /Add-Driver	Add-WindowsDriver
Dism.exe /Image:foldername /Add-Package	Add-WindowsPackage
Dism.exe /Image:foldername /Add-ProvisionedAppxPackage	Add-AppxProvisionedPackage
Dism.exe /Image:foldername /Apply-Unattend	Apply-WindowsUnattend
Dism.exe /Image:foldername /Disable-Feature	Disable-W.indowsOptionalFeature
Dism.exe /Image:foldername /Enable-Feature	Enable-WindowsOptionalFeature
Dism.exe /Image:foldername /Export-Driver	Export-WindowsDriver

Dism.exe /Image:foldername /Get-Driverinfo	Get-WindowsDriver -Driver
Dism.exe /Image:foldername /Get-Drivers	Get-WindowsDriver
Dism.exe /Image:foldername /Get-Featureinfo	Get-WindowsOptionalFeature -FeatureName
Dism.exe /Image:foldername /Get-Features	Get-WindowsOptionalFeature
Dism.exe /Image:foldername /Get-Packageinfo	Get-WindowsPackage -PackagePath | -PackageName
Dism.exe /Image:foldername /Get-Packages	Get-WindowsPackage
Dism.exe /Image:foldername /Get-ProvisionedAppxPackages	Get-AppxProvisionedPackage
Dism.exe /Image:foldername /Remove-Driver	Remove-WindowsDriver
Dism.exe /Image:foldername /Remove-Package	Remove-WindowsPackage
Dism.exe /Image:foldername /Remove-ProvisionedAppxPackage	Remove-AppxProvisionedPackage
Dism.exe /Image:foldername /Set-ProvisionedAppxDataFile	Set-AppXProvisionedDataFile

Quick check

Which of the following are the correct activation thresholds for the Key Management System (KMS)?

1. **5 workstations**
2. **5 servers**
3. **25 workstations**
4. **25 servers**

Quick check answer

KMS requires a minimum of 25 workstation systems (#3) or 5 server systems as clients. This is called the activation threshold.

Chapter summary

- Windows Server 2016 is available in multiple editions that vary in features, capabilities, market, and price.
- Installing Windows Server 2016 on a single computer is usually simple, but mass deployments can be extremely complex.
- Windows Server 2016 includes a collection of roles and features, which you can install using Server Manager or Windows PowerShell.
- Server Core is an installation option that provides a reduced resource footprint, which you manage remotely or from the command line.
- An upgrade is when you install Windows Server 2016 on a computer running an earlier version of Windows. A migration is when you transfer the roles, settings, and data from an existing server to a new one.
- After installation, the Windows Server 2016 operating system must be activated, and there are several ways to do that, including the Key Management Service (KMS) and Active Directory-Based Activation.
- Nano Server is a Windows Server 2016 installation option that provides a stripped-down, headless server.
- To install Nano Server, you create a VHD image file using PowerShell and deploy it as Hyper-V virtual machine.
- Nano Server includes a limited selection of roles and features, which are not interchangeable with those used by the other Windows Server installation options.
- To manage Nano Server, you use remote installation tools from another computer.
- Virtualizing Windows servers requires a careful planning process that takes business factors into account, as well as technical factors.
- Windows Server 2016 Hyper-V provides support for FreeBSD and many Linux operating system distributions. The integration services that provide support for many of Hyper-V's features are integrated into the kernels of the latest FreeBSD and Linux versions.
- The MAP Toolkit includes a series of wizards that collect information about the configuration and performance of the computers on your network. Using that information, the toolkit can create a server consolidation report that specifies which of your servers should be migrated to virtual machines.
- When developing a virtualization plan, you should consider not only when [articular workloads should be migrated to virtual machines, but if they should be migrated.
- To update image files by adding patches, hotfixes, and features, you can use the DISM.exe command line tool.

Thought experiment

In this thought experiment, demonstrate your skills and knowledge of the topics covered in this chapter. You can find answer to this thought experiment in the next section.

Alice is responsible for deploying four new computers, which run Windows Server 2016. The computers function as Hyper-V servers and run as a cluster. To ensure that all of the computers are installed and configured identically, Alice has copied the Install.wim file from a Windows Server 2016 installation image to her working computer. Her intention is to mount the image using DISM.exe, add all of the drivers the computers need, and enable the Hyper-V role.

Alice mounts the image she needs to a local directory called c:\winsvr using the DISM /mount-image command. Then she adds the required drivers using the /add-drivers command. Both of these procedures complete flawlessly. Next, she attempts to enable the Hyper-V role using the following command:

```
dism /image:c:\winsvr /enable-feature /featurename:Hyper-V
```

This time, the command fails. What must Alice do to successfully enable the Hyper-V role using DISM? After she determines how to install Hyper-V successfully, what must Alice do before she can deploy the image to the computers?

Thought experiment answer

This section contains the solution to the thought experiment.

Alice must use the DISM /get-features command to list the available features in the image. When she does so, she discovers that the correct name for the role is Microsoft-Hyper-V. She must use this name in the /featurename option. After she installs Hyper-V, Alice must commit her changes to the image file an unmount it, using the following command:

```
dism /unmount-image /mountdir:c:\winsvr /commit
```

CHAPTER 2

Implement storage solutions

Enhancing the storage infrastructure in Windows Server has been a clear priority for the operating system developers for some years. Windows Server 2016 maintains many of the venerable storage mechanisms and management tools from previous versions, deprecates others, but also builds on these foundations with new capabilities that enable administrators to build larger and more reliable storage systems.

Skills in this chapter:

- Configure disks and volumes
- Implement server storage
- Implement data deduplication

Skill 2.1: Configure disks and volumes

Many of the fundamental storage technologies in Windows Server 2016 are unchanged from the previous version. However, it is still common for certification exams to test your knowledge of these technologies because they involve some of the most common tasks performed by server administrators.

This section covers how to:

- Configure sector sizes appropriate for various workloads
- Configure GUID partition table (GPT) disks
- Create VHD and VHDX files using Server Manager or Windows PowerShell
- Mount virtual hard disks
- Determine when to use NTFS and ReFS file systems
- Configure NFS and SMB shares using Server Manager
- Configure SMB share and session settings using Windows PowerShell
- Configure SMB server and SMB client configuration settings using Windows PowerShell
- Configure file and folder permissions

Configure sector sizes appropriate for various workloads

In its correct usage, a disk sector is a subdivision of a track. Each platter of a hard disk drive is split into circular tracks, and each track is split into sectors, as shown in Figure 2-1. Hard disks traditionally use 512-byte sectors, although new Advanced Format disks use 4,096-byte sectors. The sector size is created during the manufacture of the drive; it cannot be changed.

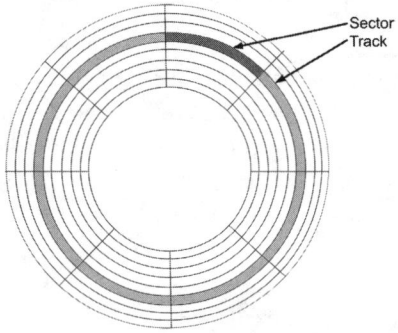

FIGURE 2-1 On a hard disk platter, a sector is a segment of a track

You can, however, change the *allocation unit* size of a disk volume, which is often incorrectly called a sector. Allocation unit is the Windows term, but it is also commonly called a block or a cluster. An allocation unit is the smallest amount of disk space that the computer can allocate when storing a file. For example, storing a 10-kilobyte file on a disk with an allocation unit size of 4 kilobytes requires three allocation units, or 12 kilobytes. Allocation units cannot be split among files, so this means that 2 kilobytes of storage space is wasted in what is called *slack space*.

You select the allocation unit size of a volume when you format it, as shown in Figure 2-2. Selecting an allocation unit size for a workload is a tradeoff between slack space and drive efficiency. You typically select an allocation unit size based on the average size of the files that you intend to store on the volume. If you select a larger allocation unit size, any small files that you store on the volume incurs a larger amount of space wasted.

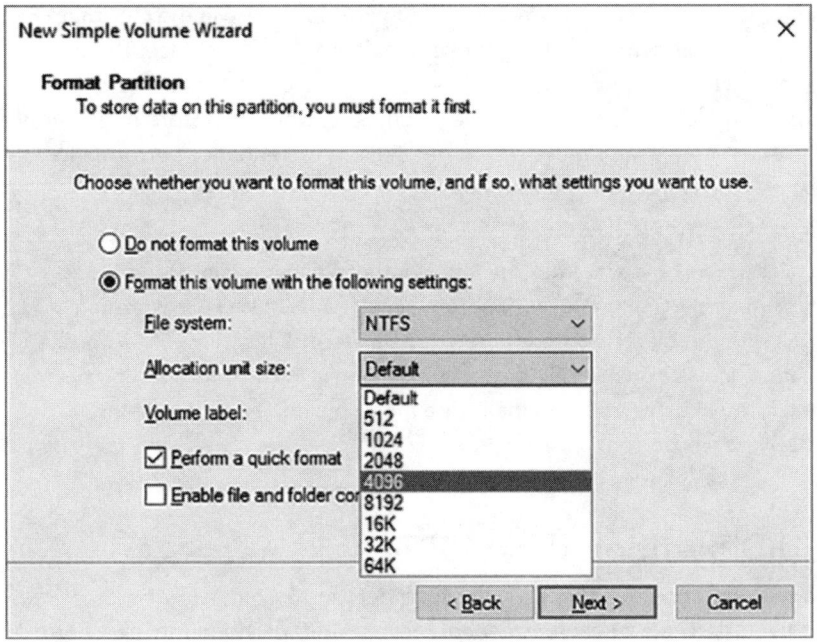

FIGURE 2-2 The Format Partition page of the New Simple Volume Wizard

For example, storing the 10 KB file mentioned earlier on a volume with a 4 KB allocation unit size wastes 2 KB. If the volume has a 64 KB allocation unit size, only one allocation unit is needed, but 54 KB of storage space would be wasted. Multiply that by thousands of files and you end up wasting a substantial part of the volume.

On the other hand, if you are storing a 1-megabyte file on a volume with a 4 KB allocation unit size, 250 allocation units are required. If the volume uses a 64 KB allocation unit size, the file only requires 16 allocation units. To access the file, the drive must seek and read each allocation unit individually. Seeking and reading 250 allocation units is inherently less efficient than seeking and reading 16 allocation units, so the drive performs better.

Also, the issue is complicated by the degree of fragmentation on the volume. The more a volume is written and rewritten, the more likely it is that the allocation units for a file are not adjacent to each other, and the drive has to pick up its heads and place them at a new location to read each allocation unit.

Hard disks have grown so large that the difference between allocation unit sizes does not matter all that much. For a typical volume, the average amount of slack space per file is half of the allocation unit size. For example, on a volume with a 4 KB allocation unit size, the slack space averages 2 KB per file. On a volume with a 64 KB allocation unit size, the slack space averages 32 KB per file. If you store 10,000 files on each volume, the wasted space is 20 MB on the 4 KB volume, and 312 MB on the 64 KB volume. On a disk that is 2 TB or larger, the loss of 300 MB is not such a big deal, especially when you achieve better efficiency in the bargain.

This does not mean, however, that by formatting all of your drives to use the maximum 64 KB allocation unit size, you realize a dramatic improvement in drive performance. The default allocation unit size for an NTFS volume under 16 TB is 4,096 bytes, or 4 KB, and this is usually appropriate for a system drive. However, if you have volumes on which you store mostly large files, such as databases or videos, raising the allocation unit size can enhance performance.

NOTE **HYPER-V ALLOCATION UNIT SIZES**

In Hyper-V, VHD files use 512-byte internal disk input/output (I/O) operations, and VHDX files use 4,096 byte internal I/O operations. Therefore, the default 4,096 NTFS allocation unit size aligns well with the characteristics of the VHDX virtual disk file. However, if you use a 64 KB allocation unit size on a VHDX, the system must read each 64 KB allocation unit, cache it, modify 4,096 bytes of it, and then write the whole thing back to the VHDX file, which negatively affects performance.

Configure GUID partition table (GPT) disks

Hard disk drives have a partition table that provides the operating system with the locations of the partitions on the disk. The original *master boot record (MBR)* partition table was introduced in 1983. It is still supported by Windows, and it is still used on many computers. The MBR partition table has shortcomings, however, which is why the *GUID partition table (GPT)* was created in the late 1990s.

When you add a new hard disk to a computer running Windows Server 2016, your first step after installing the hardware is to initialize the disk. When you launch the Disk Management snap-in, the tool detects the new disk and presents the Initialize Disk dialog box, as shown in Figure 2-3.

FIGURE 2-3 The Initialize Disk dialog box in the Disk Management snap-in

This dialog box provides the following options:

- **Master Boot Record (MBR)** The MBR partition style has been around since PC DOS 2.0, before Windows, and provides the most compatibility. It is still a common partition style for x86-based and x64-based computers.
- **GUID Partition Table (GPT)** GPT has existed since the late 1990s, but no x86 versions of Windows prior to Windows Server 2008 and Windows Vista support it. Today, most operating systems support GPT, including Windows Server 2016.

MBR shortcomings

Selecting the MBR option creates a boot sector at the beginning of the disk that points to the locations of the partitions and provides a boot loader for the operating system. Because this vital information is stored in only one place on the disk, if that boot sector is corrupted or overwritten, the disk is not recognized by the operating system. This partition style was the industry standard for many years and is still supported by nearly all operating systems.

The MBR disk partitioning style supports volumes up to 2 TB in size, and up to four primary partitions. The size limitation is due to the 32-bit maximum size of the partition entries in the MBR boot sector. At the time the MBR style was designed, the idea of a 2 TB hard drive was pure fantasy, but today they are commonplace, making this limitation a major shortcoming.

The four-partition limit is also a disadvantage for some. Beginning with PC DOS 3.3 in 1987, if you wanted more than four partitions on an MBR drive, you had to create three primary partitions and make the fourth an extended partition. You could then create multiple logical drives on the extended partition, as shown in Vol4, Vol5, and Vol6 in Figure 2-4. This is a workaround that exists in the MBR partition style to this day.

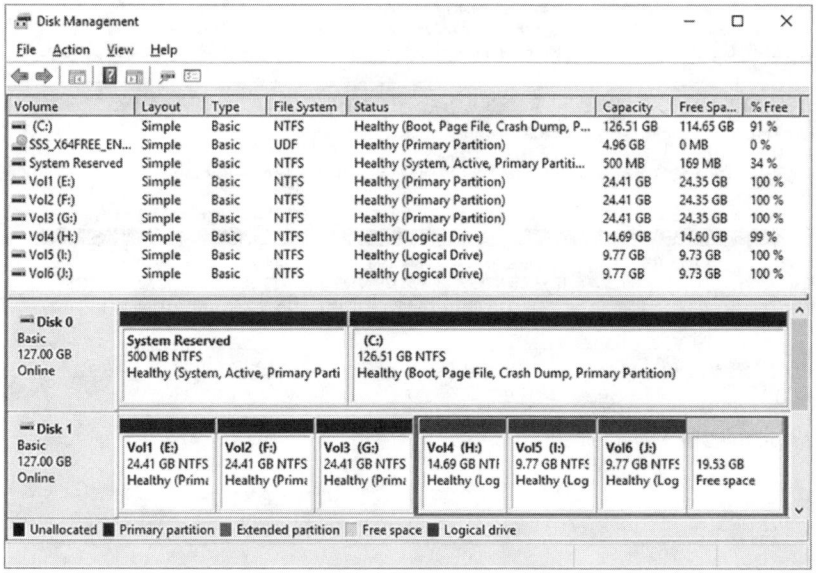

FIGURE 2-4 An MBR disk in the Disk Management snap-in

GPT advantages

The GUID partition table style is so named because each of the partitions on the disk has a globally-unique identifier (GUID). GPT is part of the *Unified Extensible Firmware Interface (UEFI)* developed by Intel in the late 1990s to replace the venerable Basic Input/Output System (BIOS) firmware standard.

GPT varies from MBR in that the partitioning information is stored in multiple places spread throughout the disk, along with cyclical redundancy check (CRC) information that makes it possible to detect corruption in the partition table and recover the data from another location. This makes the GPT partitioning style more robust than MBR.

Most importantly, GPT disks are not limited to 2 TB, as are MBR disks. The GPT disk partitioning style supports volumes up to 18 exabytes (1 exabyte = 1 billion gigabytes, or 260 bytes).

GPT is also not subject to the four-partition limit of MBR. The GPT specification permits an unlimited number of partitions, but the Windows GPT implementation limits the number of partitions to 128 per disk. Therefore, it is possible to create a GPT disk with six partitions, as shown in Figure 2-5.

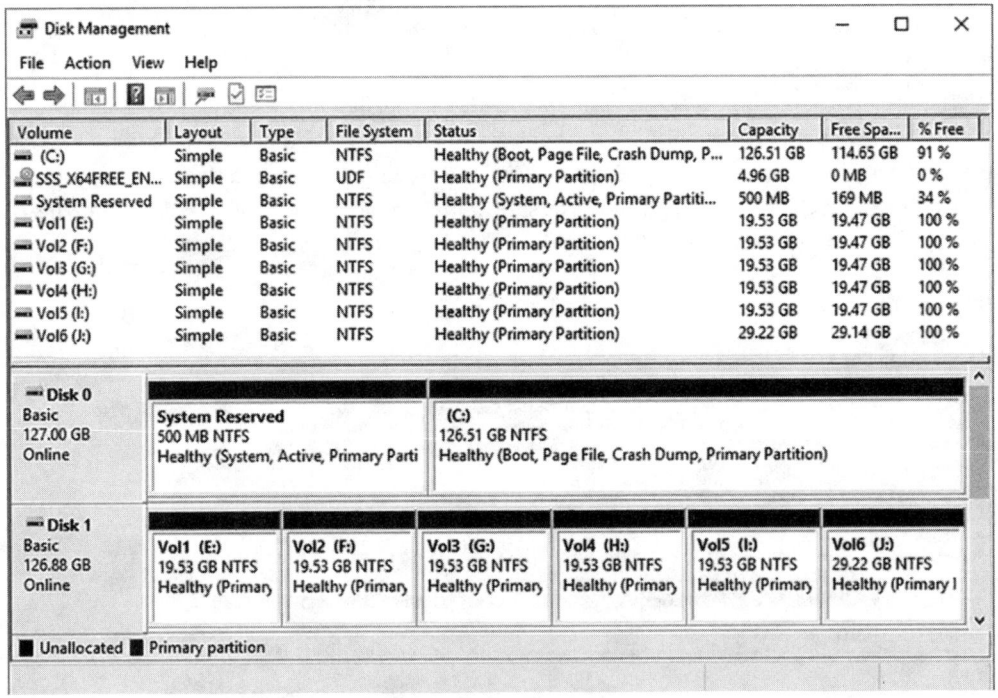

FIGURE 2-5 A GPT disk in the Disk Management snap-in

Selecting a partition style

Unless the computer's architecture provides support for an Extensible Firmware Interface (EFI)-based boot partition, it is not possible to boot from a GPT disk. If this is the case, the system drive must be an MBR disk, and you can use GPT only on separate non-bootable disks used for data storage.

Before Windows Server 2008 and Windows Vista, all x86-based Windows computers could use only the MBR partition style. Computers based on the x64 platform could use either the MBR or GPT partition style, if the GPT disk was not the boot disk.

Now that hard disk drives larger than 2 TB are readily available, the selection of a partition style is more critical than ever. When you initialize a physical disk using the traditional Disk Management snap-in, MBR is the default partition style, as it always has been. You can also use the snap-in to convert a disk between MBR and GPT partition styles, although you can do so only on disks that do not have partitions or volumes created on them.

When you use Server Manager to initialize a disk in Windows Server 2016, it uses the GPT partition style, whether the disk is physical or virtual. Server Manager has no controls supporting MBR, although it does display the partition style in the Disks tile.

Table 2-1 compares some of the characteristics of the MBR and GPT partition styles.

TABLE 2-1 MBR and GPT Partition Style Comparison

Master Boot Record (MBR)	GUID partition table (GPT)
Supports up to four primary partitions or three primary partitions and one extended partition, with unlimited logical drives on the extended partition	Supports up to 128 primary partitions
Supports volumes up to 2 terabytes	Supports volumes up to 18 exabytes
Hidden (unpartitioned) sectors store data critical to platform operation	Partitions store data critical to platform operation
Replication and cyclical redundancy checks (CRCs) are not features of the MBR partition table	Replication and CRC protection of the partition table provide increased reliability

Booting from GPT disks

The main compatibility issue with the partition styles is the ability to boot from a GPT disk. Windows can only boot from a GPT disk if the computer has UEFI firmware and if it is running a 64-bit version of Windows. Servers must be running at least Windows Server 2008, and workstations must be running at least Windows Vista.

Nearly all of the servers on the market today have UEFI firmware, and Windows Server 2016 is available only in a 64-bit version. If you are running older hardware, you must confirm that the computer is UEFI-compatible before you can boot from a GPT disk.

If you cannot boot from a GPT disk, you can still use MBR for your partition style on the boot disk and GPT for the other hard disks in the computer. GPT is essential if your other disks are larger than 2 TB in size.

In Windows Server 2016 Hyper-V, Generation 1 virtual machines emulate the BIOS boot firmware and must boot from a virtual MBR disk. You can create additional virtual GPT disks, just as in a physical computer. When you create a Generation 2 VM, however, the firmware is UEFI and the boot disk uses the GPT partition style. You can create additional virtual disks using either the GPT or MBR partition style, although there is no compelling reason to use MBR.

Create VHD and VHDX files using Server Manager or Windows PowerShell

Hyper-V relies on the Virtual Hard Disk (VHD) format to store virtual disk data in files that can easily be transferred from one computer to another. You can create new VHD files on a computer running Hyper-V by using the New Virtual Hard Disk Wizard, but it is also possible to create and use VHDs on computers that are not running the Hyper-V role.

Windows Server 2016 supports two types of virtual hard disk images, differentiated by their file name extensions, as follows:

- **VHD** VHD images are limited to maximum size of 2 TB and are compatible with servers running Windows Server 2008 or later, or workstations running Windows 7 or later.
- **VHDX** VHDX image files can be as large as 64 TB, and they also support 4 KB logical sector sizes, to provide compatibility with new 4 KB native drives. VHDX files are not backward compatible and can be read only by servers running Windows Server 2012, or later or workstations running Windows 8 or later.

Creating VHD or VHDX files using Disk Management

The Disk Management snap-in in Windows Server 2016 enables you to create VHD and VHDX files, and mount them on the computer. As soon as a VHD or VHDX file is mounted, you can treat it just like a physical disk and use it to store data. Dismounting a VHD or VHDX packages the stored data in the file, so you can copy or move it as needed.

To create a VHD in Disk Management, use the following procedure.

1. Log on to Windows Server 2016, using an account with Administrator privileges. The Server Manager window appears.
2. Click Tools, and Computer Management.
3. In the Computer Management console, click Disk Management. The Disk Management snap-in appears.

NOTE **LAUNCHING DISK MANAGEMENT**

You can also launch the Disk Management snap-in by right-clicking the Start button, and selecting Disk Management from the context menu that appears, or by executing the Diskmgmt.msc file.

4. From the Action menu, select Create VHD. The Create And Attach Virtual Hard Disk dialog box appears, as shown in Figure 2-6.

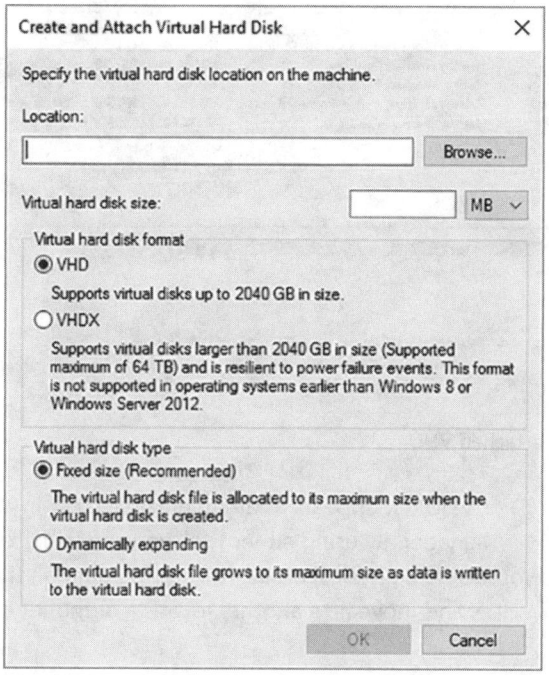

FIGURE 2-6 The Create And Attach Virtual Hard Disk dialog box

5. In the Location text box, specify the path and name for the file you want to create.
6. In the Virtual Hard Disk Size text box, specify the maximum size of the disk you want to create.
7. In the Virtual Hard Disk Format box, select the VHD or VHDX option.
8. Select one of the following Virtual Hard Disk Type options:
   - **Fixed Size** Allocates all disk space for the entire size of the VHD or VHDX file at once
   - **Dynamically Expanding** Allocates disk space to the VHD or VHDX file as you add data to the virtual hard disk
9. Click OK. The system creates the VHD or VHDX file and attaches it, so that it appears as a new disk in the snap-in, as shown in Figure 2-7.

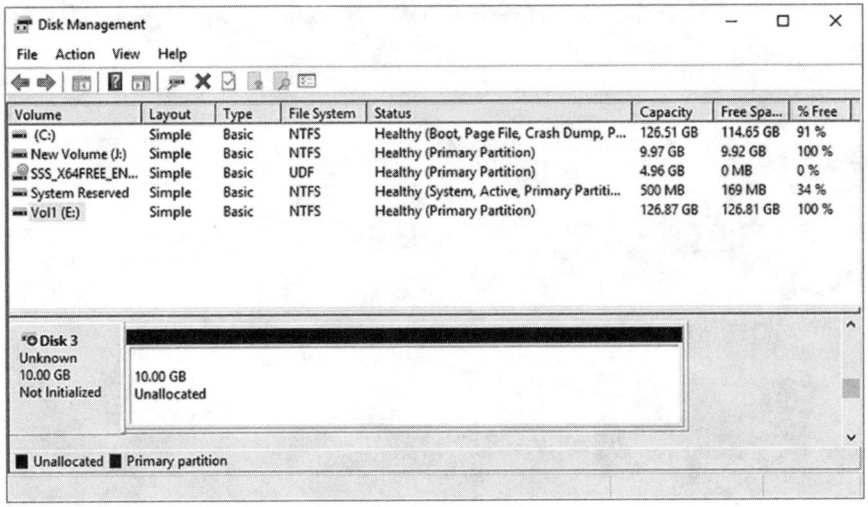

FIGURE 2-7 A newly created and attached VHD

After you create and attach the VHD or VHDX, it appears as an uninitialized disk in the Disk Management snap-in and in Server Manager. By using either tool, you can initialize the disk and create volumes on it, just as you would a physical disk. After storing data on the volumes, you can detach the VHD or VHDX and move it to another location or mount it on a Hyper-V virtual machine.

Creating VHD or VHDX files using Windows PowerShell

To create a VHD or VHDX in Windows PowerShell, you use the New-VHD cmdlet, which is included in the Hyper-V module. This module is installed as part of the Hyper-V Management Tools feature. If you do not have Hyper-V installed on your system, you can add just the PowerShell tools with the following command:

```
install-windowsfeature -name hyper-v-powershell
```

This module includes cmdlets that enable you to list, create, mount, merge, and resize VHDs. To create a new VHD, you can use the New-VHD cmdlet as in the following example:

```
new-vhd -path c:\data\disk1.vhdx -sizebytes 10gb
```

This simple command creates a 10 gigabyte VHDX disk called Disk1 in the c:\data folder. To configure other VHD features, you can use any of the following parameters:

- **Path** Specifies the location where the VHD is to be created and its filename. The filename extension you use specifies whether to create a VHD or a VHDX file.
- **SizeBytes** Specifies the size if the VHD to be created, or in the case of a dynamic disk, the maximum size. You can specify sizes using the following abbreviations: MB, GB, TB.

- **Fixed** Allocates all of the storage space specified in the SizeBytes parameter immediately on creating the VHD.
- **Dynamic** Creates a small-sized VHD and enables it to expand as needed to the maximum size specified in the SizeBytes parameter.
- **Differencing** Creates a differencing disk for the parent specified in the ParentPath parameter.
- **ParentPath** Specifies the location and filename of the parent disk for which a differencing disk is to be created.
- **SourceDisk** Specifies the location and filename of a physical disk to be copied to the new VHD upon creation.

To create a VHD and prepare it for use with one command, you can combine New-VHD with other cmdlets using the pipe character, as in the following example:

```
new-vhd -path c:\data\disk1.vhdx -sizebytes 256gb -dynamic | mount-vhd -passthru |
initialize-disk -passthru | new-partition -driveletter x -usemaximumsize | format-volume
-filesystem ntfs -filesystemlabel data1 -confirm:$false -force
```

This command creates a new 256 gigabyte dynamic VHDX file in the c:\data folder, mounts the disk, initializes the disk, creates a partition using drive letter X, and finally formats the partition using the NTFS file system. On completion of this command, the new VHD is ready to receive data.

Mount Virtual Hard Disks (VHDs)

One of the advantages of VHD and VHDX files is that you can easily move them to any system. In addition, you can mount a VHD or VHDX file on a physical or virtual machine and access it through the file system, using a standard drive letter. Mounting an image file provides you with full read/write capabilities, enabling you to access single files or entire folders as needed.

To mount a VHD or VHDX file, you can use the Disk Management snap-in, or Windows PowerShell cmdlets.

Mounting a VHD or VHDX with Disk Management

You can mount or dismount an existing VHD or VHDX file using the Disk Management snap-in, which uses the terms Attach and Detach instead. To mount a file, use the following procedure.

1. Log on to Windows Server 2016, using an account with Administrator privileges. The Server Manager window appears.
2. Click Tools, and Computer Management.
3. In the Computer Management console, click Disk Management. The Disk Management snap-in appears.

4. From the Action menu, click Attach VHD. The Attach Virtual Hard Disk dialog box appears, as shown in Figure 2-8.

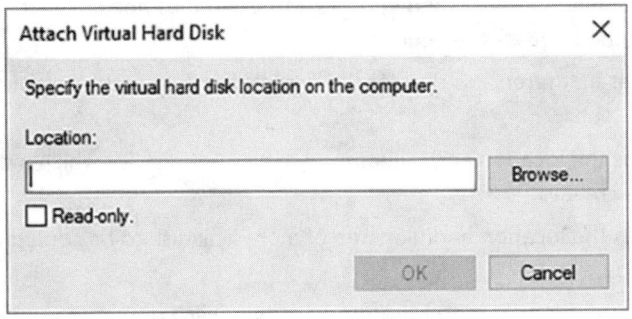

FIGURE 2-8 The Attach Virtual Hard Disk dialog box

5. In the Location text box, type or browse to the location and filename of the VHD or VHDX file to be mounted and click OK. The mounted disk appears in the Disk Management console.

If the virtual disk has already been initialized, partitioned, and formatted, its volumes appear using their assigned drive letters, and are ready for use. If the disk is still in its raw state, you must initialize it, create a volume, and format it using the file system of your choice before you can use it to store data.

When you are finished using the disk, you can select it and choose Detach VHD from the Action menu. Any changes you have made to the disk or its contents are saved back to the original VHD or VHDX file.

Mounting a VHD or VHDX with Windows PowerShell

There are two PowerShell cmdlets you can use to mount an existing VHD or VHDX files. Their syntaxes are similar, but not identical. The Mount-DiskImage cmdlet is part of the Storage module, and is found on all computers running Windows Server 2016. The Mount-VHD cmdlet is part of the Hyper-V module, and is only available on systems that have the Hyper-V management tools installed.

To mount a VHD or VHDX file with the Mount-DiskImage cmdlet, use the following syntax:

```
mount-diskimage -imagepath filename
```

To dismount a mounted image, you can use the Dismount-DiskImage cmdlet with the same imagepath parameter.

To mount a VHD or VHDX file with the Mount-VHD cmdlet, use the following syntax:

```
mount-vhd -path filename
```

To dismount a mounted image, you can use the Dismount-VHD cmdlet with the same path parameter.

Examples of the command lines for the two cmdlets are as follows:

```
mount-diskimage -imagepath c:\temp\diskimage.vhdx

mount-vhd -path c:\temp\diskimage.vhdx
```

Determine when to use NTFS and ReFS File Systems

To organize and store data or programs on a hard drive, you must install a file system, the underlying disk drive structure that enables you to store information on your computer. You install file systems by formatting a volume on the hard disk, as shown in Figure 2-9. In Windows Server 2016, five file system options are available, but only NTFS and ReFS are suitable for use on a modern server.

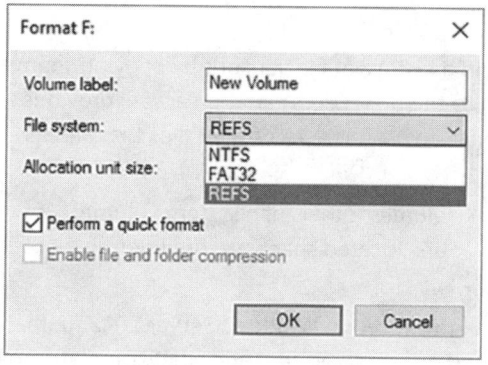

FIGURE 2-9 Formatting a volume using ReFS

NTFS has been the default file system for the Windows Server operating systems since the Windows NT 3.1 release in 1993. The primary advantage of NTFS over the FAT file systems it replaces is the ability to authorize user access to files and folders using permissions stored in discretionary access control lists (DACLs).

NTFS also supports long file names and larger files and volumes than FAT. The maximum size for an NTFS volume using the default 4KB allocation unit size is 16 TB; with the maximum 64 KB allocation units, the maximum volume size is 256 TB.

NOTE **FAT FILE SYSTEMS**

Because the FAT (File Allocation Table) file systems lack the security that NTFS provides, any user who gains access to your computer can read any file without restriction. FAT file systems also have disk size limitations. FAT32 cannot handle a partition greater than 32 GB, or a file greater than 4 GB. FAT cannot handle a hard disk greater than 4 GB, or a file greater than 2 GB. Because of these limitations, the only viable reason for using FAT16 or FAT32 is the need to dual boot the computer with a non-Windows operating system or a previous version of Windows that does not support NTFS, which is not a likely configuration for a server.

In addition to these capabilities, NTFS also includes the following additional features:

- **File compression** NTFS supports transparent, on-the-fly compression, but only for volumes using the 4 KB allocation unit size. The rate of compression is based on the type of file, with those containing repetitive bit patterns compressing more than those that don't. Volume size, number of files, and write frequency can all affect the efficiency of the compression system, which can be significantly processor-intensive.
- **Encrypting File System (EFS)** NTFS can provide on-the-fly encryption of selected files and folders using the public key belonging to a specific user. The file system then decrypts the files on demand with the user's public key. EFS and NTFS compression are mutually exclusive; files can be compressed or encrypted, but not both.
- **Quotas** Administrators can impose a quota governing the amount of storage space allowed to a specific user and specify the thresholds at which the user should receive a warning and be denied access.
- **Volume Shadow Copy** NTFS can maintain a history of file versions by copying them to an alternate location as they are written to the disk. Users can then access previous versions as needed, and backup applications can use them to protect files that are currently in use.
- **Resizing** Users can shrink or expand NTFS volumes (other than system volumes), if there is sufficient free space in the volume or unallocated space on the disk to support the requested action.

ReFS (Resilient File System) is a new file system introduced in Windows Server 2012 R2 that offers practically unlimited file and volume sizes and an increased resiliency that eliminates the need for error-checking tools, such as Chkdsk.exe. The maximum ReFS volume size is 280 bytes, or 1 yobibyte. The maximum file size is 16 exabytes (or one million terabytes), which is far larger than any storage technology available today can provide. But then again, who expected to be talking about terabyte drives a few years ago?

ReFS uses checksums to protect the metadata on a volume and, optionally, the data itself. Periodic checks occur in the background, while the volume is in use. When corruption is detected, the system repairs it immediately, without the need to take the drive offline.

The error detection and repair capabilities of ReFS make it particularly useful in Storage Spaces pools. In a storage pool that uses a mirror or parity space, a corrupted file detected on a ReFS volume can be repaired automatically using the duplicate mirror or parity data. On Hyper-V virtual disks, ReFS implements checkpointing and backups as file system metadata operations, increasing their speed and efficiency.

ReFS uses the same system of permissions as NTFS, and is completely compatible with existing ACLs. However, ReFS does not include support for NTFS features such as file compression, Encrypted File System (EFS), and disk quotas. ReFS disks also cannot be read by any operating systems older than Windows Server 2012 R2 and Windows 8.

Improvements in ReFS in Windows Server 2016, and particularly its improvements in Hyper-V use, have led Microsoft to state that it is now the preferred data volume for the operating system. System drives and volumes requiring compression, encryption, and other NTFS-only features should continue to use that file system, but all others can benefit from the resiliency that ReFS provides.

Configure NFS and SMB shares using Server Manager

Sharing server folders enables network users to access them. After you initialize, partition, and format your disks on a file server, you must create shares for users to be able to access those disks over the network.

Before you begin to create shares, you should devise a sharing strategy that consists of answers to questions like the following:

- Which disk folders are you sharing?
- What names are you assigning to the shares?
- What share permissions are you granting to your users?
- What Offline Files settings are you using for the shares?

If you are the designated Creator Owner of a folder, you can share it in Windows Server 2016 by right-clicking the folder in any File Explorer window, selecting Share With, and then Specific People from the context menu, and following the instructions in the File Sharing dialog box, as shown in Figure 2-10.

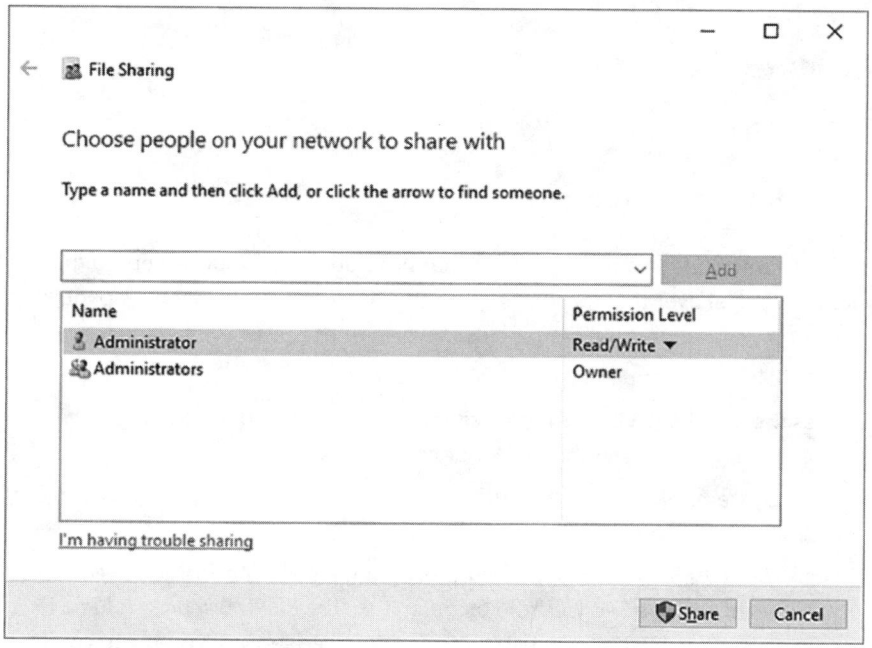

FIGURE 2-10 The File Sharing dialog box

This method of creating shares provides a simplified interface that contains only limited control over elements such as share permissions. You can specify only that the share users receive Read or Read/Write permissions to the share.

If you are not the Creator Owner of the folder, you can access the Sharing tab of the folder's Properties sheet instead. Clicking the Share button on this tab launches the same File Sharing dialog box, but clicking the Advanced Sharing button and selecting the Share This Folder check box displays the dialog box shown in Figure 2-11. Clicking the Permissions button in the Advanced Sharing dialog box provides you with greater control over share permissions through the standard Windows security interface.

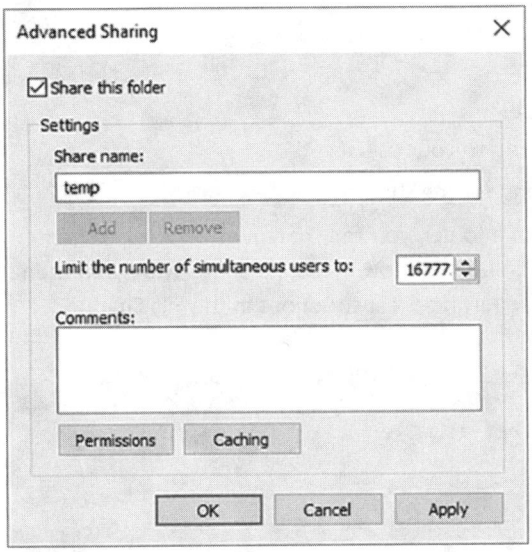

FIGURE 2-11 The Advanced Sharing dialog box

However, to take control of the shares on all of your disks and all of your servers so that you can exercise full control over their properties, use the File And Storage Services page in Server Manager.

Windows Server 2016 supports two types of folder shares:

- **Server Message Blocks (SMB)** An application layer protocol that has long been the standard for file and printer sharing on Windows networks.
- **Network File System (NFS)** A standardized file system protocol typically used by UNIX and Linux distributions.

When you install Windows Server 2016, the setup program installs the Storage Services role service in the File and Storage Services role by default. To create SMB shared folders in Server Manager, however, you must first install the File Server role service. When you create your first folder share using File Explorer, the system automatically installs the File Server role service.

To create NFS shares, you must install the Server for NFS role service. To install either of these role services, you can use the Add Roles And Features Wizard in Server Manager, or the Install-WindowsFeature cmdlet in Windows PowerShell, as in the following commands:

```
install-windowsfeature -name fs-fileserver

install-windowsfeature -name fs-nfs-service
```

Creating an SMB share

To create an SMB share using Server Manager, use the following procedure.

1. Log on to Windows Server 2016, using an account with Administrator privileges. The Server Manager window appears.
2. Click the File and Storage Services icon and, in the submenu that appears, click Shares. The Shares page appears, as shown in Figure 2-12.

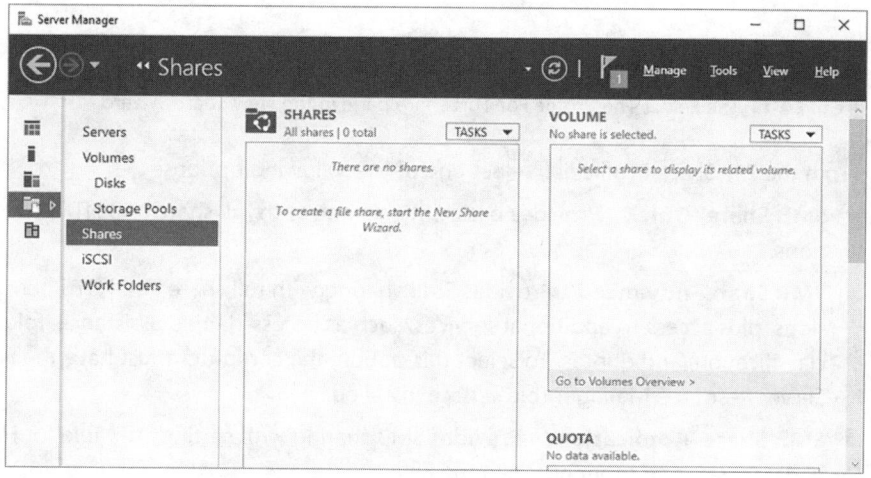

FIGURE 2-12 The Shares page in Server Manager

3. From the Tasks menu in the Shares tile, select New Share. The New Share Wizard appears, displaying the Select The Profile For This Share page, as shown in Figure 2-13.

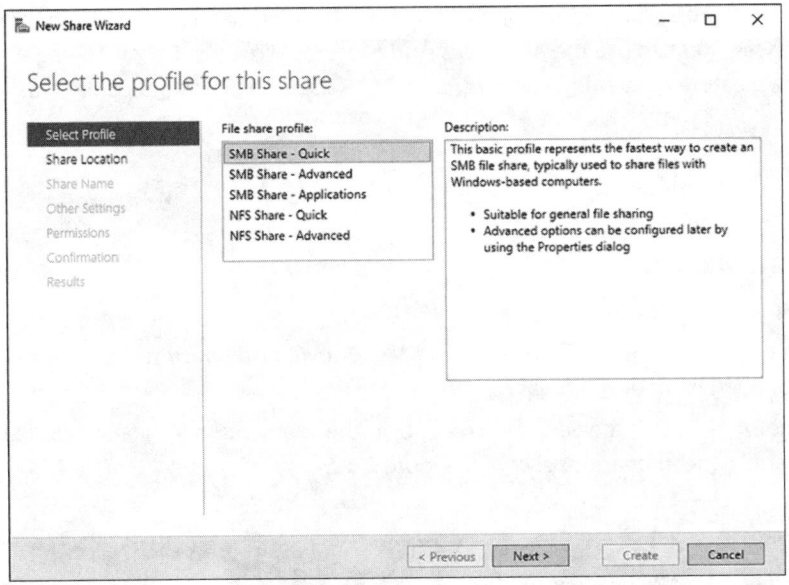

FIGURE 2-13 The Select The Profile For This Share page in the New Share Wizard

4. From the File Share Profile list, select one of the following options:
   - **SMB Share–Quick** Provides basic SMB sharing with full share and NTFS permissions.
   - **SMB Share–Advanced** Provides SMB sharing with full share and NTFS permissions, plus access to additional services, such as access-denied assistance, folder classification, and quotas. To select this option, the computer must have the File Server Resource Manager role service installed.
   - **SMB Share–Applications** Provides SMB sharing with settings suitable for Hyper-V, databases, and other applications.
5. Click Next. The Select The Server And Path For This Share page appears, as shown in Figure 2-14.

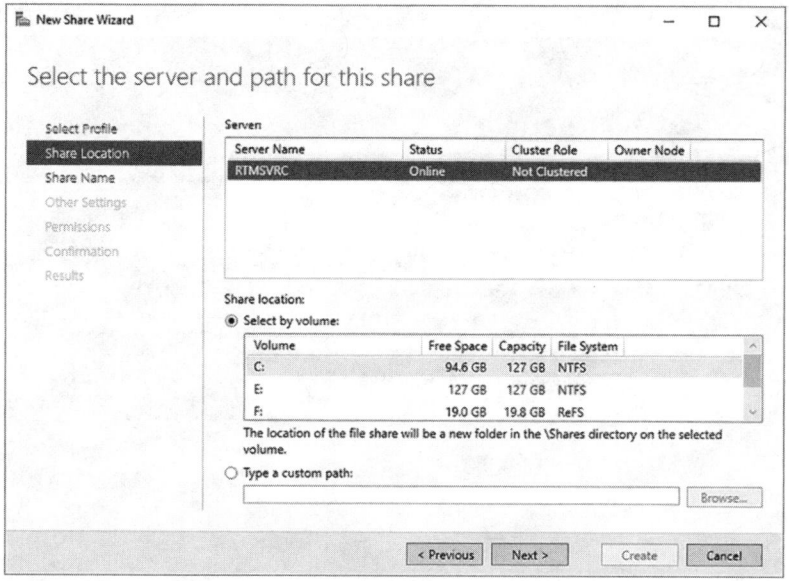

FIGURE 2-14 The Select The Server And Path For This Share page of the New Share Wizard

6. Select the server on which you want to create the share, and then either select a volume on the server or specify a path to the folder you want to share. Then click Next. The Specify Share Name page appears.
7. In the Share Name text box, specify the name you want to assign to the share and click Next. The Configure Share Settings Page appears.
8. Select any, or all of the following options:
   - **Enable Access-Based Enumeration** Applies filters to shared folders based on the individual user's permissions to the files and subfolders in the share. Users who cannot access a shared resource cannot see that resource on the network. This feature prevents users from searching through files and folders they cannot access.
   - **Allow Caching Of Share** Enables client systems to maintain local copies of files they access from server shares. When a client selects the Always Available Offline option for a server-based file, folder, or share, the client system copies the selected data to the local drive and updates it regularly, so that the client user can always access it, even if the server is offline.
   - **Enable BranchCache On The File Share** Enables client computers at remote locations running BranchCache to cache files accessed from this share, so that other computers at the remote location can access them.
   - **Encrypt Data Access** Causes the server to encrypt the files in the share before transmitting them to the remote client.
9. Click Next. The Specify Permissions To Control Access page appears, as shown in Figure 2-15.

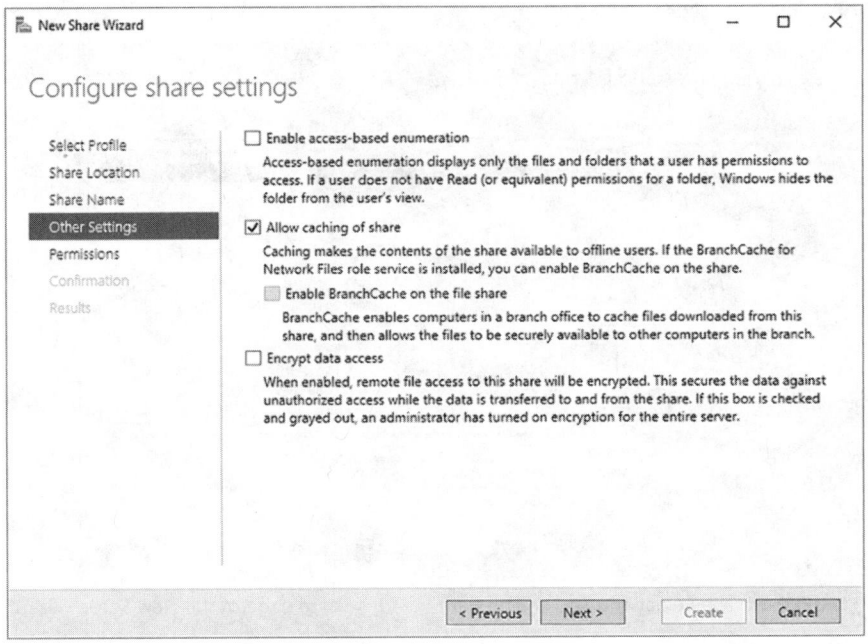

FIGURE 2-15 The Specify Permissions To Control Access page of the New Share Wizard

10. Modify the default share and NTFS permissions as needed, and click Next. The Confirm Selections page appears.
11. Click Create. The View Results page appears as the wizard creates the share.
12. Click Close. The new share appears in the Shares tile of the Shares page in Server Manager.

You can use the tile to manage a share by right-clicking it and opening its Properties sheet, or by clicking Stop Sharing. The Properties sheet for a share in Server Manager (see Figure 2-16) provides access to the same controls found on the Specify Permissions *To Control Access and Configure Share Settings pages in the New Share Wizard.*

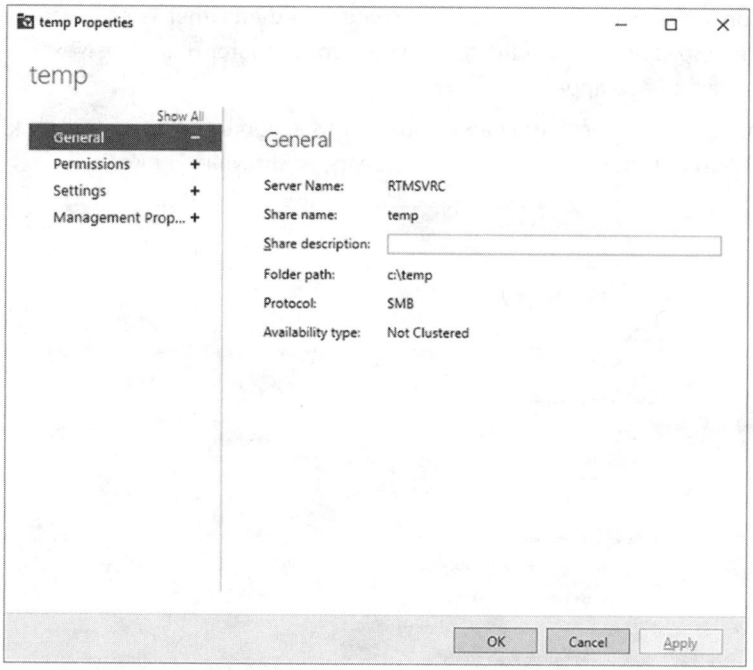

FIGURE 2-16 A share's Properties sheet in Server Manager

Creating an NFS share

To create an NFS share using Server Manager, use the following procedure.

1. Log on to Windows Server 2016, using an account with Administrator privileges. The Server Manager window appears.
2. Click the File And Storage Services icon and, in the submenu that appears, Click Shares. The Shares page appears.
3. From the Tasks menu in the Shares tile, select New Share. The New Share Wizard appears, displaying the Select The Profile For This Share page.
4. From the File Share Profile list, select one of the following options:
   - **NFS Share–Quick** Provides basic NFS sharing with authentication and permissions.
   - **NFS Share–Advanced** Provides NFS sharing with full share and NTFS permissions, plus access to additional services, such as access-denied assistance, folder classification, and quotas. To select this option, the computer must have the File Server Resource Manager role service installed.
5. Click Next. The Select The Server And Path For This Share page appears.

6. Select the server on which you want to create the share, and then either select a volume on the server or specify a path to the folder you want to share. Then click Next. The Specify Share Name page appears.
7. In the Share Name text box, specify the name you want to assign to the share and click Next. The Specify Authentication Methods page appears, as shown in Figure 2-17.

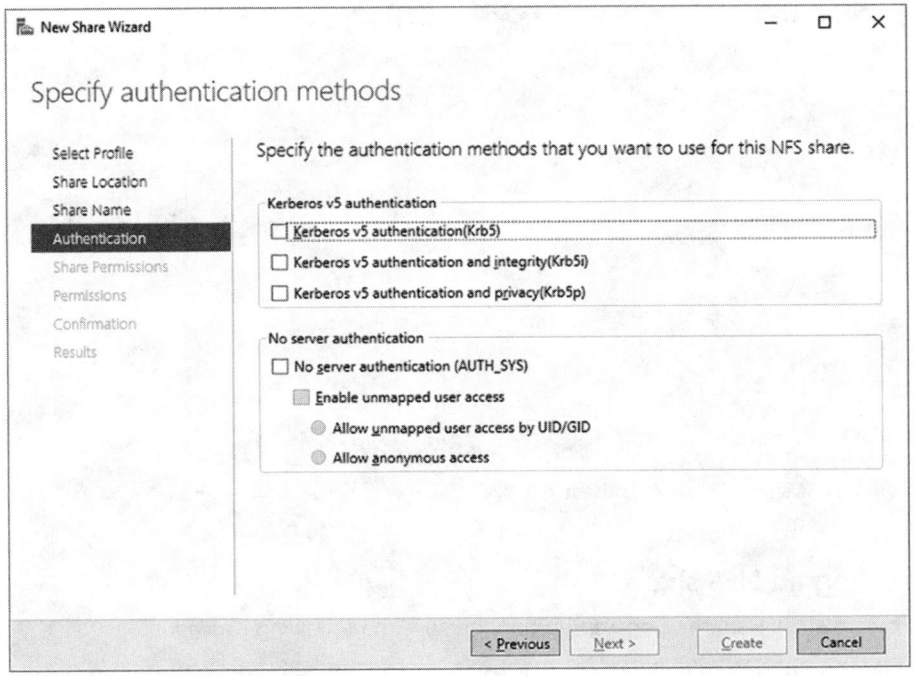

FIGURE 2-17 The Specify Authentication Methods page of the New Share Wizard

8. Select the check boxes for the authentication methods you want to use for share access, if any.
9. Click Next. The Specify The Share Permissions page appears.
10. Click Add. The Add Permissions dialog box appears, as shown in Figure 2-18.

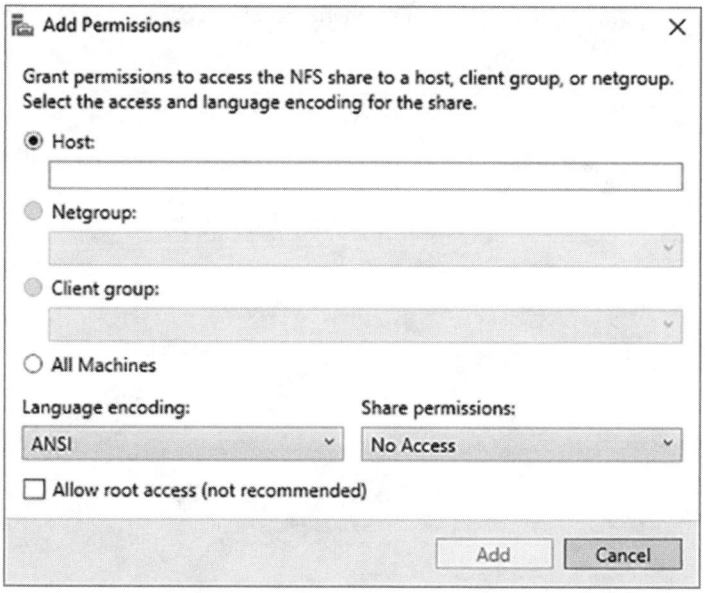

FIGURE 2-18 The Add Permissions dialog box

11. Specify the name of a host to be granted permission to the share or select the All Machines option. In the Share Permissions drop-down list, specify whether the selected host(s) should receive Read/Write, No Access, or Read Only access.
12. Click Add. The host is added to the wizard page. Repeat steps 10 to 12 to add more hosts, if necessary.
13. Click Next. The Specify Permissions To Control Access page appears.
14. Modify the default NTFS permissions as needed and click Next. The Confirm Selections page appears.
15. Click Create. The View Results page appears as the wizard creates the share.
16. Click Close. The new share appears in the Shares tile of the Shares page in Server Manager.

Creating advanced shares

When you select the SMB Share-Advanced or NFS Share-Advanced profile, two additional pages appear in the New Share Wizard. The first is a Specify Folder Management Properties page, as shown in Figure 2-19, on which you can select Folder Usage property values for the share. These values identify the type of data stored in the shared folder. You can use them to configure classification rules in the File Server Resource Manager (FSRM) that perform actions on files based on their classification properties. You can also specify the email addresses of the folder's owner or administrator, which are notified when a user is denied access to the share.

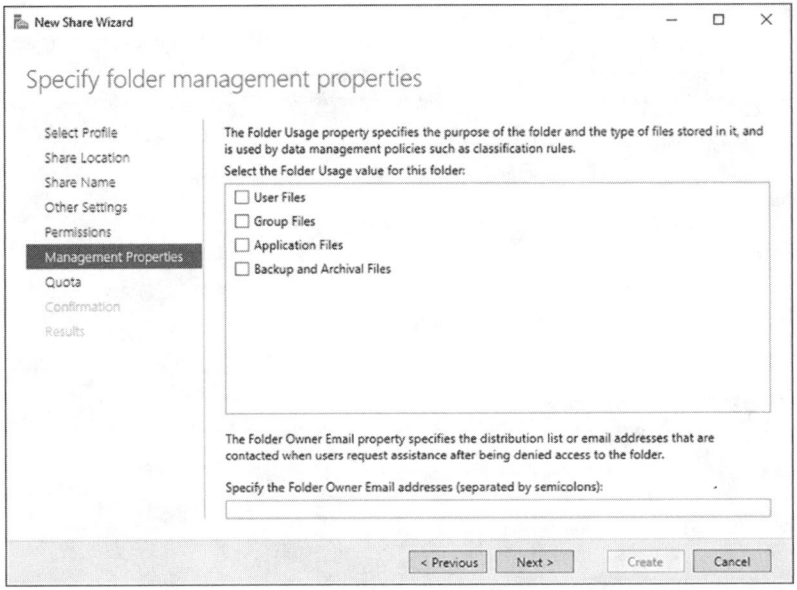

FIGURE 2-19 The Specify Folder Management Properties page of the New Share Wizard

The second added page is the Apply A Quota To A Folder Or Volume page, on which you can select a quota to be applied to the share from the list of predefined quota templates. For more granular control of quotas, you must use FSRM.

Configuring share permissions

On Windows systems, shared folders have their own permission system, which is completely independent from the NTFS and other permission systems. For network users to access a share on a file server, an administrator must grant them the appropriate share permissions. By default, the Everyone special identity receives the Allow Read share permission to any new shares you create using File Explorer. In shares you create using Server Manager, the Everyone special identity receives the Allow Full Control share permission.

It is important to understand that network users can possess the share permissions required to access a folder, but still be denied access to it because they lack the necessary NTFS permissions. The opposite is also true; users with the correct NTFS permissions cannot access a share over the network if they lack the required share permissions. You should also understand that share permissions only control access to a share over the network, while NTFS permissions control access both over the network and on the local machine.

When you create an SMB share using Server Manager, you can use the Specify Permissions To Control Access page to configure both NTFS and share permissions for the shared folder. Clicking Customize Permissions opens the Advanced Security Settings dialog box for the shared folder. The Permissions tab that is selected by default displays the NTFS permissions. To configure the share permissions for the folder, select the Share tab, as shown in Figure 2-20.

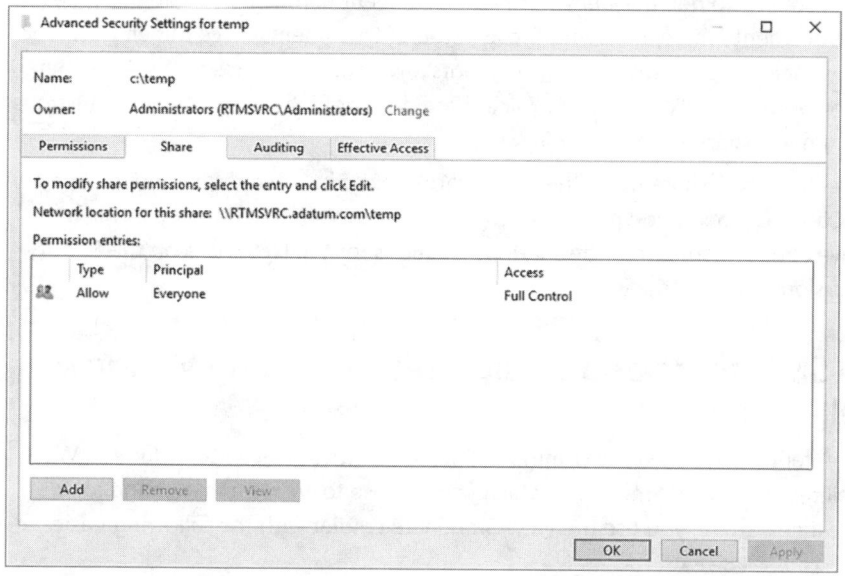

FIGURE 2-20 The Share tab on the Advanced Security Settings dialog box

Clicking the Add button opens a Permission Entry dialog box for the folder, on which you select a principal—a user or group to receive the permissions—and the permissions you want the principal to receive.

The Windows share permission system is relatively simple and has only three permissions. The permissions and the abilities they grant to users are listed in Table 2-2.

TABLE 2-2 Share permissions and their functions

Share permission	Allows or denies security principals the ability to:
Full Control	■ Change file permissions ■ Take ownership of files ■ Perform all tasks allowed by the Change permission
Change	■ Create folders ■ Add files to folders ■ Change data in files ■ Append data to files ■ Change file attributes ■ Delete folders and files ■ Perform all actions permitted by the Read permission
Read	■ Display folder names, filenames, file data and attributes ■ Execute program files ■ Access other folders within the shared folder

When assigning share permissions, you must also be aware that they do not combine like NTFS permissions. If you grant a user named Alice the Allow Read and Allow Change permissions to the shared C:\Documents\Alice folder and later deny her all three permissions to the shared C:\Documents folder, the Deny permissions prevent her from accessing any files through the C:\Documents share, including those in the C:\Documents\Alice folder. However, she can still access her files through the C:\Documents\Alice share because of the Allow permissions. In other words, the C:\Documents\Alice share does not inherit the Deny permissions from the C:\Documents share.

When you create an NFS share using the New Share Wizard in Server Manager, the Specify Permissions To Control Access page provides access only to the NTFS permissions. This is because you have already configured the share permissions for the NFS share on the Specify The Share Permissions page on the wizard.

Configure SMB share and session settings using Windows PowerShell

For those who prefer to work from the command line, Windows Server 2016 includes a Windows PowerShell module called SmbShare, which you can use to create and manage folder shares. To create a new share, you use the New-SmbShare cmdlet with the following basic syntax:

```
new-smbshare -name sharename -path pathname [-fullaccess groupname] [-readaccess
groupname] [-changeaccess groupname] [-noaccess groupname]
```

For example, to create a new share called Data from the C:\Docs folder with the Allow Full Control permission granted to the Everyone special identity, use the following command:

```
new-smbshare -name data -path c:\docs -fullaccess everyone
```

In addition to the access parameters listed here, there are other parameters you can include on the command line, to implement features available in the New Share Wizard, including the following:

- **ConcurrentUserLimit #** Specifies the maximum number of users that can connect to the share simultaneously. A value of 0 allows unlimited users.
- **CachingMode value** Specifies the type of offline file caching permitted to share clients, using the following values:
  - **None** Disables offline file caching at the client
  - **Manual** Enables users to select files for offline caching
  - **Programs** Automatically caches programs and documents offline
  - **Documents** Automatically caches documents offline
  - **BranchCache** Enables BranchCache caching on the remote client
- **EncryptData True|False** Causes the server to encrypt the files in the share before transmitting them to the remote client

- **FolderEnumerationMode AccessBased|Unrestricted** Implements or disables access-based enumeration. The default setting is Unrestricted.
- **Temporary** Causes the share to persist only to the next computer restart

Managing sessions

Once you have created a share, by any means, you can monitor and manage its use using PowerShell cmdlets. For example, running the Get-SmbSession cmdlet displays all the current client sessions that are connected to the server's shares, as shown in Figure 2-21.

```
PS C:\Users\Administrator> get-smbsession

SessionId    ClientComputerName ClientUserName       NumOpens
---------    ------------------ --------------       --------
154618822713 10.0.0.10          ADATUM\Administrator 1
154618822717 10.0.0.11          ADATUM\Administrator 1


PS C:\Users\Administrator> _
```

FIGURE 2-21 Output of the Get-SmbSession cmdlet

With the information in this listing, you can terminate a specific session using the Close-SmbSession cmdlet, as in the following example, which uses the Session ID to specify the session to close.

```
close-smbsession -sessionid 154618822713
```

By default, the cmdlet displays a warning, prompting you to confirm that you want to terminate the session, as shown in Figure 2-22. Adding the Force parameter to the command line eliminates the prompt. There is no warning displayed on the client computer, and closing the session can cause any work in progress by the client to be lost.

```
PS C:\Users\Administrator> get-smbsession

SessionId    ClientComputerName ClientUserName       NumOpens
---------    ------------------ --------------       --------
154618822713 10.0.0.10          ADATUM\Administrator 1
154618822717 10.0.0.11          ADATUM\Administrator 1


PS C:\Users\Administrator> close-smbsession -sessionid 154618822713

Confirm
Are you sure you want to perform this action?
Performing operation 'Close-Session' on Target '154618822713'.
[Y] Yes  [A] Yes to All  [N] No  [L] No to All  [S] Suspend  [?] Help (default is "Y"): y
PS C:\Users\Administrator> _
```

FIGURE 2-22 Output of the Close-SmbSession cmdlet

You can also close sessions based on the other information in the Get-SmbSession output, as shown in the following examples.

```
close-smbsession -clientcomputername 10.0.0.11

close-smbsession -clientusername adatum\Administrator
```

In addition to listing sessions, you can also use the Get-SmbOpenFile cmdlet to display the files that clients are currently accessing, as shown in Figure 2-23.

```
PS C:\Users\Administrator> get-smbopenfile

FileId       SessionId    Path                ShareRelativePath ClientComputerName ClientUserName
------       ---------    ----                ----------------- ------------------ --------------
154618822929 154618822721 c:\temp\                                10.0.0.10          ADATUM\Administrator
154618822953 154618822717 c:\temp\                                10.0.0.11          ADATUM\Administrator
154618822961 154618822717 c:\temp\disk2.vhdx disk2.vhdx           10.0.0.11          ADATUM\Administrator


PS C:\Users\Administrator>
```

FIGURE 2-23 Output of the Get-SmbOpenFile cmdlet

To forcefully close an open file, you can use the Close-SmbOpenFile cmdlet, as in the following example:

```
close-smbopenfile -fileid 154618822961
```

Removing a share

To terminate a share completely, along with all its sessions, you can use the Remove-SmbShare cmdlet, specifying the name of the share on the command line, as in the following example:

```
remove-smbshare -name data
```

Configure SMB server and SMB client configuration settings using Windows PowerShell

You can configure the attributes of a share as you create it, whether you use Server Manager or PowerShell to do so, but you can also modify a share's configuration settings at any time after its creation using other cmdlets in the SmbShare PowerShell module.

Setting share permissions

You can modify the share permissions for a specific share, using the following cmdlets:

- **Get-SmbShareAccess** Displays the access control list for a named share, as shown in Figure 2-24.

fault tolerance, because you are paying for two or three times the price for the storage space you need.

- **Parity** The computer stripes the data across three or more physical disks in the pool along with parity information, which the system can use to recreate the data if a physical disk fails. Performance is slightly reduced, because the server is writing additional parity data, but this option is less expensive than mirroring.

When you select the Mirror option, a Configure The Resiliency Settings page is added to the wizard, as shown in Figure 2-36. The Two-Way Mirror option requires two physical disks and provides protection against a single disk failure. The Three-Way Mirror option requires five physical disks and provides protection against the failure of two disk.

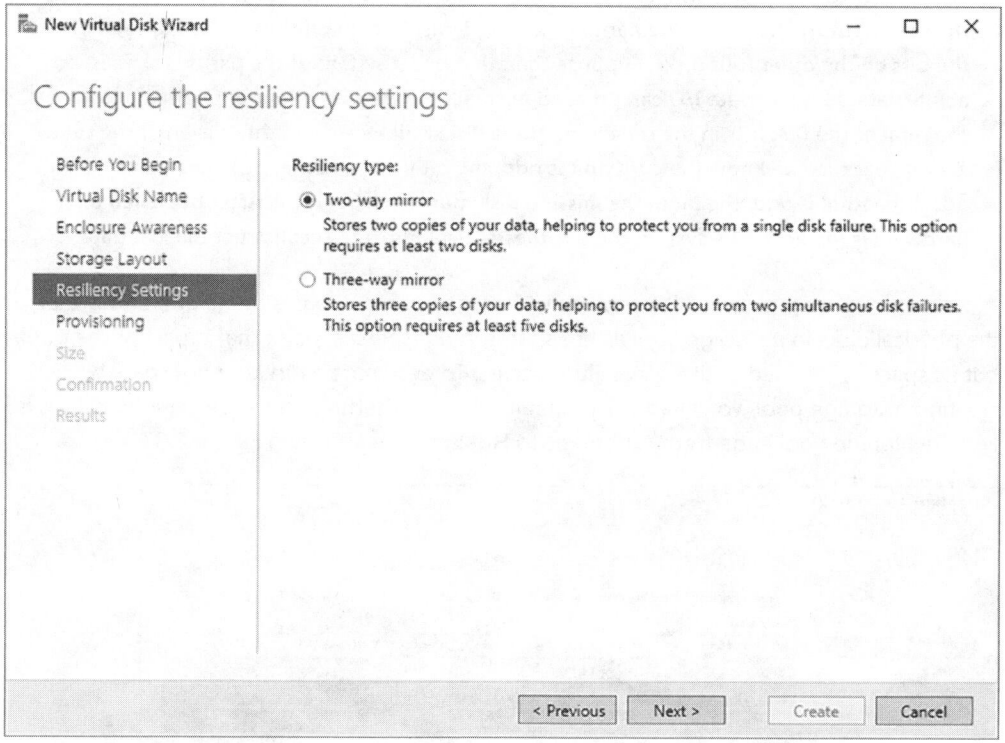

FIGURE 2-36 The Configure The Resiliency Settings page, in which you select between two-way and three-way mirroring

Choosing the Parity option on the Select The Storage Layout page requires no additional configuration. However, if your storage pool does not contain enough physical disks to support the layout, the wizard displays an error and forces you to select another option.

NOTE UNDERSTANDING PARITY

Parity is a mathematical algorithm that some disk storage technologies use to provide data redundancy in their disk write operations. To calculate the parity information for a drive array, the system takes the values for the same data bit on each drive in the array and adds them together, to determine whether the total is odd or even. The system then uses the resulting total to calculate a value for a parity bit corresponding to those data bits. The system then repeats the process for every bit location on the drives. If one drive is lost due to a hardware failure, the system can restore each lost data bit by calculating its value using the remaining data bits and the parity bit.

For example, in an array with five disks, suppose the first four disks have the values 1, 1, 0, and 1 for their first bit. The total of the four bits is 3, an odd number, so the system sets the first bit of the fifth disk, the parity disk, to 0, indicating an odd result for the total of the bits on the other four disks. Suppose then that one disk fails. If the parity disk fails, no actual data is lost, so data I/O can proceed normally. If one of the four data disks is lost, the total of the first bits in the remaining three disks will be either odd or even. If the total is even, because we know the parity bit is odd, the bit in the missing disk must have been a 1. If the total is odd, the bit in the missing disk must have been a 0. After the failed disk hardware is replaced, the system can use these calculations to reconstruct the lost data.

Another way to provide fault tolerance in Storage Spaces is to designate one or more of the physical disks in a storage pool as hot spares. A *hot spare* is a disk that is part of the pool, but its space is not used until a disk failure occurs. To designate a disk as a hot spare while creating a storage pool, you change its default Allocation setting on the Select Physical Disks For The Storage Pool page from Automatic to Hot Spare, as shown in Figure 2-37.

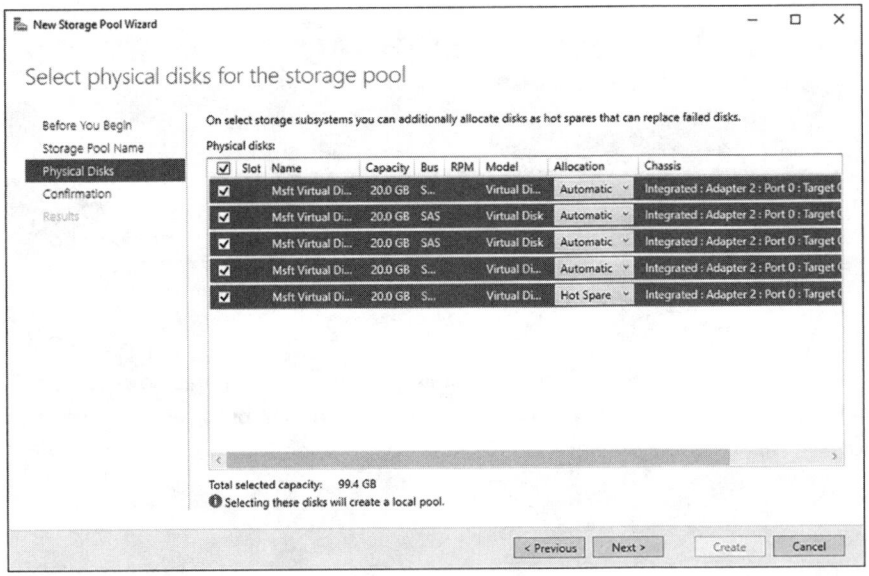

FIGURE 2-37 The Select Physical Disks For The Storage Pool page, with a hot spare

When a physical hard drive reports a write error to the operating system (usually after silently recovering from several failures), it marks the disk as failed and activates a hot spare, if one exists. In the case of a read error, the system will try to recover from the failure, if possible, by writing the missing data back to the disk using a mirror or parity copy. If this fails, the write error procedure begins.

Expand storage pools

One of the advantages of Storage Spaces is that you can expand a storage pool at any time by adding physical disks. The disks can be new ones that you've installed in the server or its storage array, or you can repurpose existing disks by deleting any volumes on them. When you add a physical disk to an existing storage pool, the new space is simply added to it. If you have created a pool that is larger than the physical disk space available in the computer, the space on the added disk does to make up the difference.

To expand an existing storage pool, use the following procedure.

1. In Server Manager, on the Storage Pools page, select an existing pool in the Storage Pools tile.
2. Right-click the existing pool and, from the context menu, select Add Physical Disk. The Add Physical Disk dialog box appears, as shown in Figure 2-38.

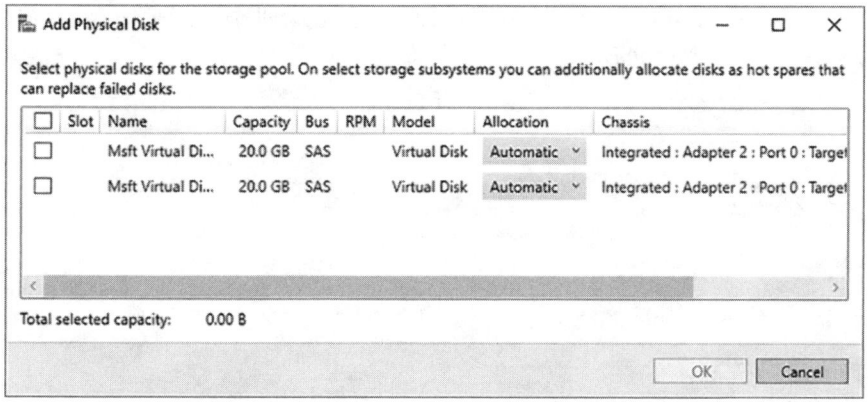

FIGURE 2-38 The Add Physical Disk dialog box

3. Select the disk(s) that you want to add to the pool and click OK. The storage space from the new disks is added to the storage pool.

Configure tiered storage

Tiered storage, in Windows Server 2016, is a Storage Spaces feature that enables administrators to use their higher-performance storage devices for their most commonly used files. To use tiered storage in Windows Server 2016, you create a storage pool that contains both solid state drives (SSDs) and standard hard disk drives (HDDs). SSDs are faster than HDDs, but they are also more expensive. You then create a virtual disk that includes space from both drive types. Once users begin storing data on the virtual disk, the system transparently copies the most frequently-used files from the HDDs to the SSDs, thus providing improved access times for those files.

When you create a virtual disk in Server Manager, using the New Virtual Disk Wizard, the Specify The Virtual Disk Name page includes a Create Storage Tiers On This Virtual Disk check box. The check box is only enabled when the storage pool contains both SSD and HDD physical disks. You also must have enough physical disks of each type to support the layout you intend to use when you create the virtual disk. For example, to create a tiered virtual disk with a two-way mirror layout, you must have a minimum of two SSDs and two HDDs available.

NOTE **RECOGNIZING MEDIA TYPES**

Windows recognizes the types of storage devices installed in, or connected to, the computer and assigns them media types—SSD and HDD—so that Storage Spaces can determine which devices to use for each tier. In situations where the system fails to identify the drives correctly (such as when you create VHDs on the physical disks for use in Hyper-V virtual machines), you can manually set the media type using the Set-PhysicalDisk cmdlet in Windows PowerShell, with the MediaType parameter.

Selecting the check box modifies the Specify The Size Of The Virtual Disk page of the wizard, as shown in Figure 2-39. Instead of specifying an overall size for the virtual disk, you specify separate sizes for the Faster Tier and the Standard Tier.

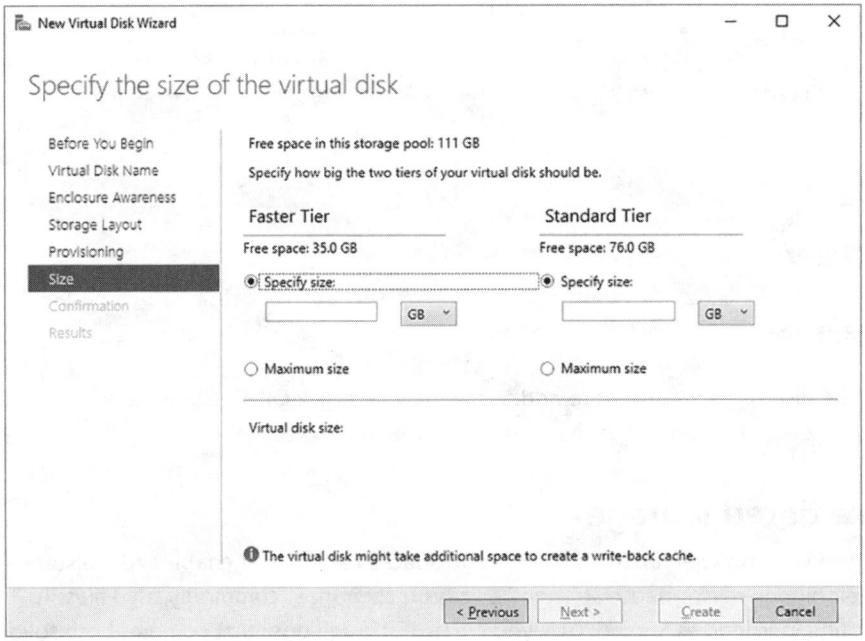

FIGURE 2-39 Tiered storage controls in the New Virtual Disk Wizard

Once the virtual disk is in use, administrators can use Set-FileStorageTier cmdlet to pin specific files to one tier or the other, so that they are always accessed from the specified disk type.

Configure iSCSI target and initiator

A *storage area network (SAN)* is a technology that enterprises use to deploy storage resources and make this storage available to other connected devices. At its most basic level, a SAN is simply a network dedicated solely to high-speed connections between servers and storage devices. Instead of installing disk drives into servers or using directly-connected drive enclosures, a SAN consists of one or more drive arrays equipped with network interface adapters, which connect to servers using standard twisted pair or fiber optic network cables.

The earliest SANs used a serial networking technology called Fibre Channel. Fibre Channel networks provide excellent SAN performance, but the expense and special skills required to install and maintain them have made them a rarity in all but the largest enterprise installations. *Internet Small Computer System Interface* (*iSCSI*, pronounced *eye-scuzzy*) is an alternative storage area networking technology that enables servers and storage devices to exchange SCSI traffic using a standard IP network instead of a dedicated Fibre Channel network. This makes iSCSI a far more economical and practical solution, placing SAN technology within reach of small and medium-sized installations.

Because iSCSI uses a standard IP network for its lower layer functionality, you can use the same cables, network adapters, switches, and routers for a SAN as you would for a LAN or wide area network (WAN), without any modifications. You simply connect your servers and storage devices to an existing Ethernet network or build a new one using low-cost, widely available components.

Because of its relatively low cost and its simplicity, iSCSI has come to dominate the SAN industry. The addition of widespread support for iSCSI in the Windows Server 2016 and other operating systems has led to the introduction of many iSCSI storage device products at a wide range of price points. Whereas a SAN at one time required a huge investment in money and time, the technology is now available to modest organizations.

Initiators and targets

iSCSI communication is based on two elements: initiators and targets. An *iSCSI initiator*, so-called because it initiates the SCSI communication process, is a hardware or software device running on a computer that accesses the storage devices on the SAN. On an iSCSI network, the initiator takes the place of the host adapter that traditional SCSI implementations used to connect storage devices to a computer. The initiator receives I/O requests from the operating system and sends them, in the form of SCSI commands, to specific storage devices on the SAN.

Hardware-based initiators typically take the form of a host bus adapter (HBA), an expansion card that includes the functionality of a SCSI host adapter and a Gigabit Ethernet network adapter in one device. Hardware-based initiators offload some of the SCSI processing from the computer's main processor.

Initiators can also be software-based, such as the iSCSI Initiator module included in Windows Server 2016. When using a software initiator, the computer connects to the storage devices using a standard Ethernet network adapter.

The other half of the iSCSI equation is the *iSCSI target*, which is integrated into a storage device, such as a drive array or computer. The target receives SCSI commands from the initiator and passes them to a storage device, which is represented by a *logical unit number (LUN)*. A LUN is essentially an address that SCSI devices use to identify a specific storage resource. A single LUN can represent an entire hard disk, part of a disk, or a part of a drive array. Therefore, a single computer or drive array can have many LUNs, represented by multiple targets.

Drive arrays supporting iSCSI have targets implemented in their firmware, automatically making the various volumes in the array available to iSCSI initiators on the network. It is also possible for iSCSI targets to be implemented in software, in the form of a service or daemon that makes all or part of a hard disk in a computer available to initiators.

Windows Server 2016 includes an iSCSI target, in the form of the iSCSI Target Server role service, part of the File and Storage Services role. Using the iSCSI initiator and target capabilities in Windows Server 2016, you can designate a drive on one server as a target, and then access it using the initiator on another computer. On a more practical level, you can also purchase a drive array with an integrated iSCSI target, connect it to your network, and let Windows computers all over the network access it with their initiators.

Creating an iSCSI target

To create an iSCSI target in Windows Server 2016, you must first install the iSCSI Target Server role service, using the Add Roles And Features Wizard in Server Manager, as shown in Figure 2-40, or by running the following command in a Windows PowerShell window with administrative privileges:

```
install-windowsfeature -name fs-iscsitarget-server -installmanagementtools
```

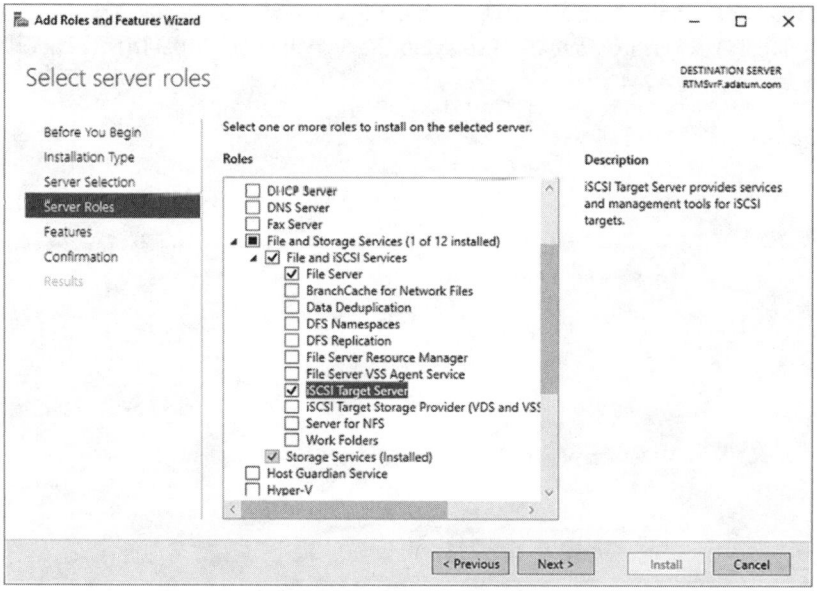

FIGURE 2-40 Installing the iSCSI Target Server role service

Once you have installed the role service, you can proceed to demonstrate the use of iSCSI by creating an iSCSI virtual disk and an iSCSI target, using space on one of the computer's disks, as described in the following procedure.

1. In Server Manager, click the File and Storage Services icon and, in the submenu that appears, click iSCSI. The iSCSI page appears, as shown in Figure 2-41.

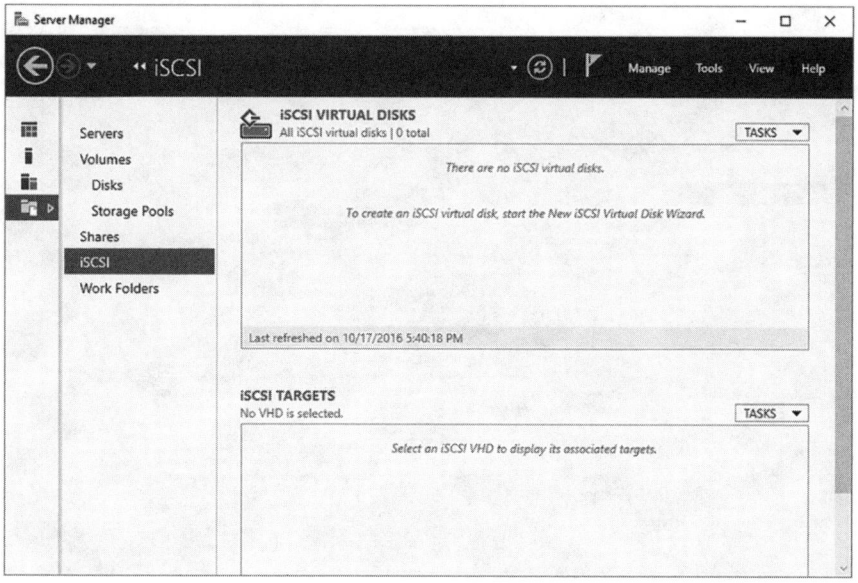

FIGURE 2-41 The iSCSI page in Server Manager

2. From the Tasks menu in the iSCSI Virtual Disks tile, select New iSCSI Virtual Disk. The New iSCSI Virtual Disk Wizard appears, displaying the Select iSCSI Virtual Disk Location page, as shown in Figure 2-42.

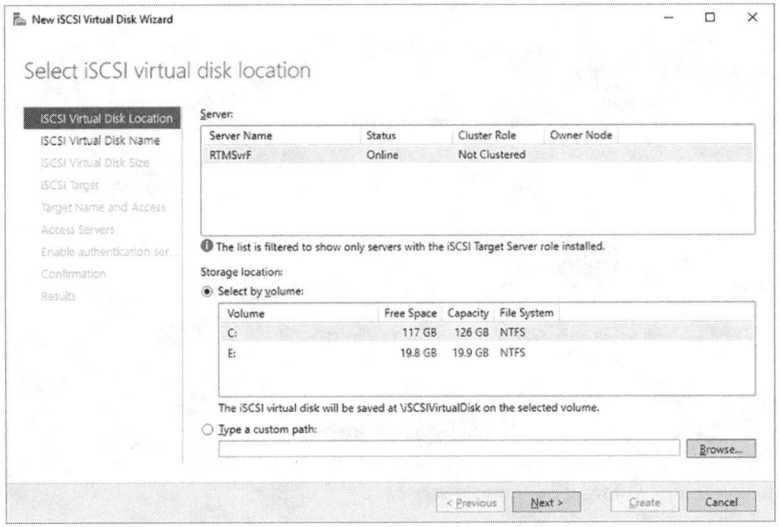

FIGURE 2-42 The Select iSCSI Virtual Disk Location page

3. Select the volume on which you want to create an iSCSI virtual disk and click Next. The Specify iSCSI Virtual Disk Name page appears.
4. Type a name for the iSCSI virtual disk and click Next. The Specify iSCSI Virtual Disk Size page appears, as shown in Figure 2-43.

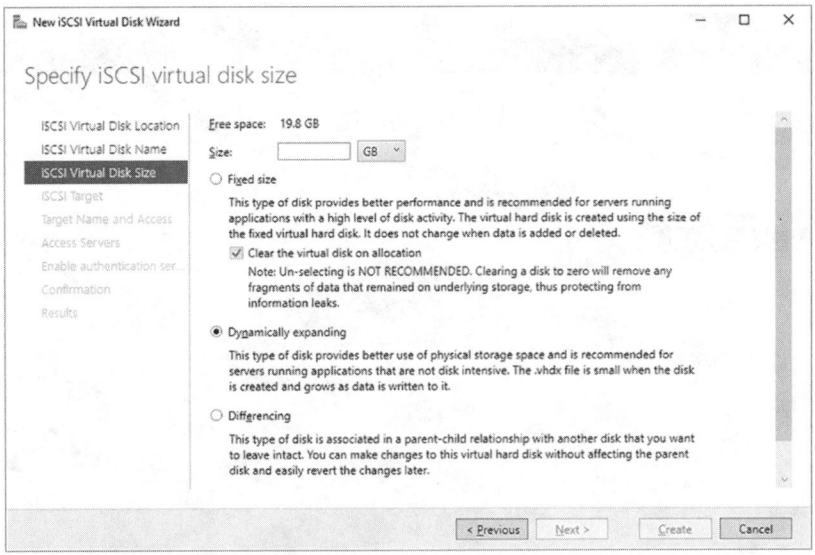

FIGURE 2-43 The Select iSCSI Virtual Disk Size page

5. Specify a size for the iSCSI virtual disk and choose from the Fixed Size, Dynamically Expanding, or Differencing options. The wizard will create a VHDX file, so these options have the same functions as a virtual disk you create in Hyper-V. Click Next. The Assign iSCSI Target page appears.
6. Leave the New iSCSI Target option selected and click Next. The Specify Target Name appears.
7. Type a name for the iSCSI target and click Next. The Specify Access Servers page appears, on which you will identify the iSCSI initiators that will access the new virtual disk.
8. Click Add. The Select A Method To Identify The Initiator dialog box appears, as shown in Figure 2-44.

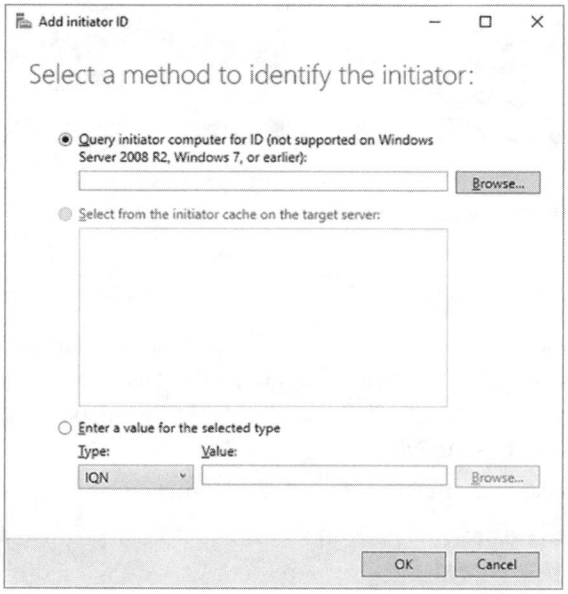

FIGURE 2-44 The Select A Method To Identify the Initiator dialog box

9. Select the Enter A Value For The Selected Type option. Then, select IP Address in the Type drop-down list and type the IP address of the server that will function as the iSCSI initiator and click OK. The initiator computer is added to the wizard.
10. Click Next. The Enable Authentication page appears.
11. Click Next to bypass the optional authentication settings. The Confirm Selections page appears.
12. Click Create. The wizard creates the new iSCSI virtual disk and an iSCSI target.
13. Click Close. The disk and target appear in the tiles on the iSCSI page, as shown in Figure 2-45.

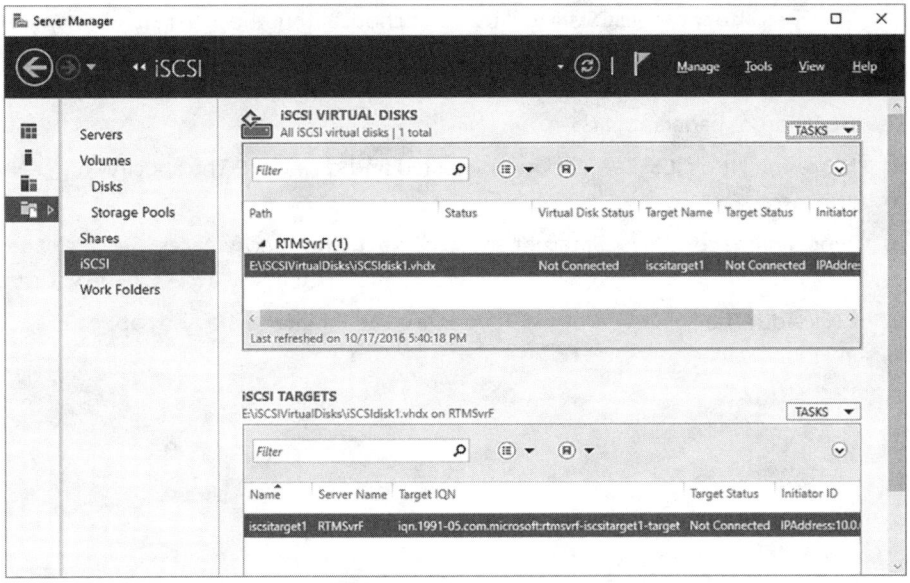

FIGURE 2-45 The iSCSI page in Server Manager

Using iSCSI initiator

When an iSCSI target is available—one you have created on a server or one built into a hardware device—you can connect to it and access its storage using the iSCSI initiator in Windows Server 2016. Unlike the iSCSI Target Server, the iSCSI initiator is installed by default in Windows Server 2016; there is nothing you need to install.

To connect to a target using the iSCSi initiator, use the following procedure.

1. Log on to the computer you have designated as an access server when creating a target in the New iSCSI Virtual Disk Wizard.
2. In Server Manager, click Tools, and iSCSI Initiator. The iSCSI Initiator Properties sheet appears, as shown in Figure 2-46.

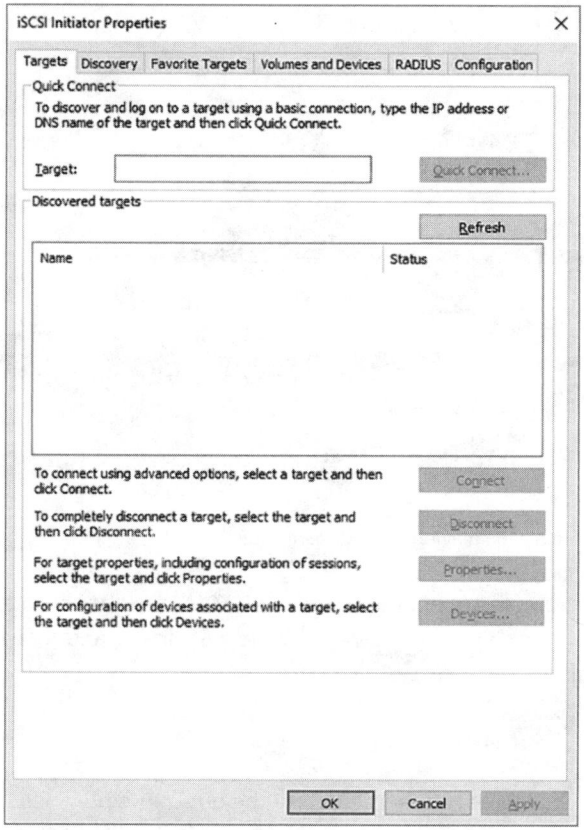

FIGURE 2-46 The iSCSI Initiator Properties sheet

3. On the Targets tab, in the Target text box, type the IP address of the computer where you created the iSCSI target and click Quick Connect. The target appears in the Discovered Targets box.
4. Click OK.

Once the initiator is connected to the target, you can open the Disk Management console and see that the iSCSI virtual disk you created on the target computer is now listed, as shown in Figure 2-47.

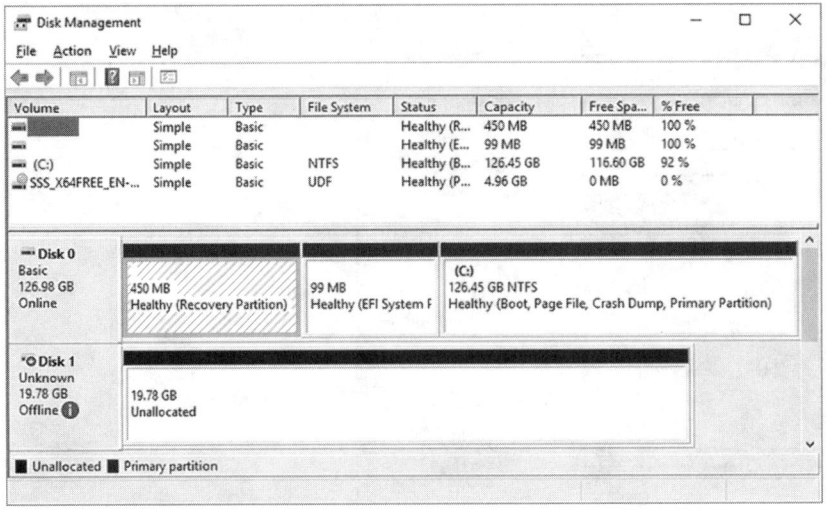

FIGURE 2-47 The Disk Management console, displaying an iSCSi target disk

Because the virtual disk was just created, it appears in the Disk Management console as Offline and Uninitialized. To use the disk, you must bring it online, initialize it, and then create a volume on it, just as if it was a disk in the local system.

Configure iSNS

In a simple demonstration of the iSCSI target and initiator, like the one in the previous section, you can easily determine the IP addresses of the computers involved and use them to establish the iSCSI connection over the network. In an enterprise environment, however, where you might have many iSCSI targets and many initiators accessing them, using IP addresses is not practical.

After the iSCSI targets and initiators are in place, the main problem remaining in iSCSI communications is how the two locate each other. The *Internet Storage Name Service (iSNS)* makes this possible by registering the presence of initiators and targets on a network and responding to queries from iSNS clients. Windows Server 2016 includes an iSNS implementation as a feature, which can provide the identification service for an entire network.

iSNS consists of four components, as follows:

- **iSNS server** Receives and processes registration requests and queries from clients on the network, using the iSNS database as an information store.
- **iSNS database** Information store on an iSNS server that contains data supplied by client registrations. The server retrieves the data to respond to client queries.
- **iSNS clients** Component in iSCSI initiators and targets that registers information about itself with an iSNS server and sends queries to the server for information about other clients.

- **iSNS Protocol (iSNSP)** Protocol used for all registration and query traffic between iSNS servers and clients.

To create an iSNS server on Windows Server 2016, you must install the iSNS feature, using the Add Roles And Features Wizard or the following PowerShell command:

```
install-WindowsFeature -name isns
```

Once the iSNS server is installed, it automatically registers the iSCSI targets available on the network, but you must register your iSCSI initiators with it manually, using the following procedure.

1. In Server Manager, click Tools, iSCSI Initiator. The iSCSI Initiator Properties dialog box appears.
2. Click the Discovery tab, as shown in Figure 2-48.

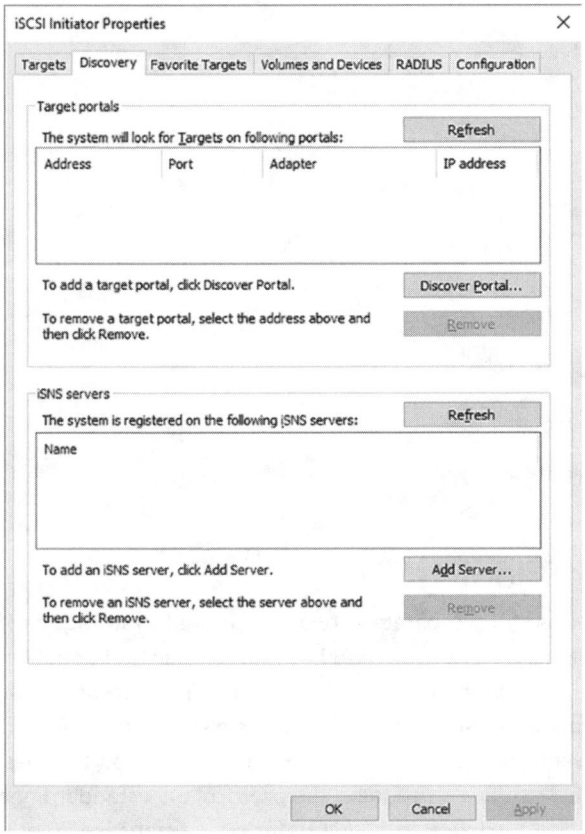

FIGURE 2-48 The Discovery tab in the iSCSI Initiator Properties dialog box

3. In the iSNS Servers box, click Add Server. The Add iSNS Server dialog box appears.

4. Type the IP address or DNS name of the server on which you installed the iSNS Server feature, and click OK.
5. Click OK to close the iSCSI Initiator Properties dialog box.

Once you have added the iSNS server to your iSCSI initiators, they are registered in the iSNS database. When you select Tools, iSNS Server in Server Manager, the iSNS Server Properties sheet appears, as shown in Figure 2-49, listing the iSCSI initiators you have registered.

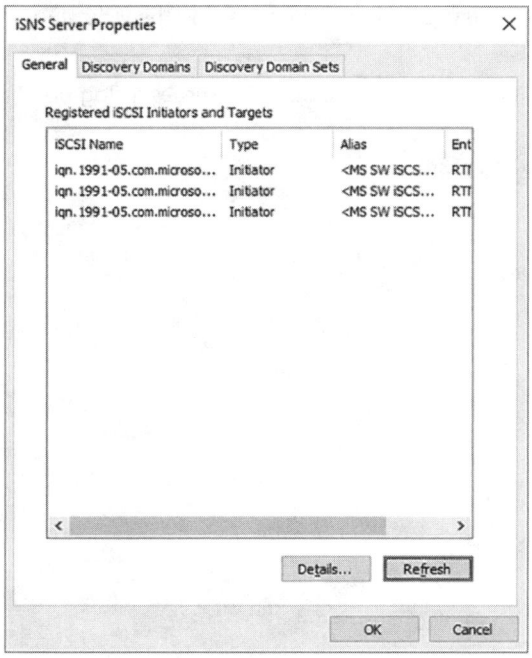

FIGURE 2-49 The iSNS Server Properties sheet

Configure Datacenter Bridging (DCB)

The original concept of the SAN called for a separate network dedicated to storage traffic. Servers already connected to the local area network (LAN) would have an additional network adapter to connect to the SAN, to provide them with access to standalone storage devices. One of the most important innovations of iSCSI is its ability to use a standard Ethernet network for its communications between initiators and targets. Fibre Channel now also has a Fiber Channel over Ethernet (FCoE) standard for running the protocol on a standard network. This raises a question, however. If it is possible to run SAN traffic over a standard Ethernet network, why not just use the network that is already in place and run both SAN and LAN traffic together?

The reasons why this is not a good idea have to do with the way that Ethernet controls access to the network medium. Ethernet is a "lossy" protocol, meaning that packet collisions are an expected occurrence. The more traffic there is on the network, the greater the number of collisions. The TCP/IP traffic running on a LAN has error detection and correction mechanisms in place to deal with the lost packets that result from the collisions. SAN protocols are more finicky about lost packets and are generally in need of an uninterrupted flow of traffic to function efficiently.

The result is that SAN and LAN traffics do not function well together unless there is a mechanism in place to ensure that each gets the bandwidth it needs at all times. This is where datacenter bridging comes into the picture. *Datacenter bridging (DCB)* is a series of standards, published by the Institute of Electrical and Electronics Engineers (IEEE), that define mechanisms for flow control and bandwidth management on a network with multiple traffic types. Windows Server 2016 includes a DCB implementation that enables administrators to allocate a specific amount of bandwidth to the different types of traffic on the network. The result is what is known as a *converged network*. By allocating a percentage of the network bandwidth to iSCSI traffic, for example, the SAN will continue to function properly, even when the LAN is in heavy use.

Windows Server 2016 includes Datacenter Bridging as a feature that you can install in the usual manner, using the Add Roles And Features Wizard in Server Manager or the Install-WindowsFeature cmdlet in PowerShell. However, implementing DCB on your network requires specialized hardware as well as software.

For a server to use DCB, it must have a converged network adapter (CNA) that supports the DCB standards. A CNA is a combination device that includes standard Ethernet networking capabilities, plus a SAN host bus adapter supporting iSCSI, FCoE, or a combination of SAN types. Your storage devices must also support DCB, as must the switches linking your devices together.

The DCB implementation in Windows Server 2016 includes a PowerShell module called DcbQos, which includes cmdlets that enable you to configure the CNA in the server, as described in the following sections.

Set the DCBX Willing bit

DCBX Willing is a single bit function defined in the DCB standards that controls the source of the CNA configuration settings. DCBX is a mechanism by which DCB devices on the network can propagate their configuration settings to other devices. By default, the DCBX Willing bit in a CNA is set to True, enabling your storage devices or switches to alter its settings. Changing the bit to False enables the CNA to receive only local configuration settings, the ones you create with the DcbQos cmdlets in PowerShell.

To set the DCBX Willing bit to false, you use the Set-NetQoSbcdxSetting cmdlet, as in the following example:

```
set-netqosdcbxsetting -willing 0
```

Once the CNA is under your control, you can configure it to function per your specifications.

Create traffic classes

Traffic classes are how you separate the types of traffic on your converged network. By default, there is a single traffic class that gets 100 percent of the network bandwidth and all eight priority ratings. You can create up to seven additional traffic classes, for a total of eight, although you should confirm that all of the other DCB devices on your network can recognize that many.

To create a new traffic class, you use the New-NetQosTrafficClass cmdlet, as in the following example:

```
new-netqostrafficclass -name "smb class" -priority 2 -bandwidthpercentage 60 -algorithm
ets
```

In this example, you are creating a new traffic class for SMB traffic, using 60 percent of the network bandwidth, with a priority of 2. The Algorithm parameter specifies which of two transmission selection algorithms, EBS or Strict, defined in the DCB standard the traffic class should use.

Create QoS policies

A quality of service (QoS) policy specifies the type of traffic to which a class is dedicated. To create a QoS policy, you use the New-NetQosPolicy cmdlet, as in the following example:

```
new-netqospolicy -name "smb policy" -smb -priorityvalue8021action 2
```

In this example, the Smb parameter filters the traffic based on Traffic Control Protocol (TCP) and User Datagram Protocol (UDP) port 445, which is the well-known port reserved for SMB traffic. The cmdlet accepts the following filter parameters:

- **SMB** Filters traffic matching TCP or UDP port 445
- **iSCSI** Filters traffic matching TCP or UDP port 3260
- **NFS** Filters traffic matching TCP or UDP port 2049
- **LiveMigration** Filters traffic matching TCP port 6600
- **NetDirect portnumber** Filters traffic matching the specified port number
- **Default** Matches all traffic not otherwise classified

In addition to these predefined filters, you can also identify a traffic type in other ways, using the parameters like the following:

- **AppPathNameMatchCondition** Filters traffic generated by an executable file
- **IpDstMatchCondition** Filters traffic based on a specific destination port number
- **IpDstPrefixMatchCondition** Filters traffic based on a specific destination IPv4 or IPv6 address

Enabling Priority-based Flow Control (PFC)

Priority-based Flow Control (PFC), as defined by one of the DCB standards, is a method of regulating network traffic, to provide lossless data transmissions. Typically, you would enable PFC for storage traffic that cannot tolerate packet loss.

To enable PFC for a specific traffic priority, you use the Enable-NetQosFlowControl cmdlet, as in the following example:

```
enable-netqosflowcontrol -priority 3
```

Configure Multipath I/O (MPIO)

Multipath I/O is a Windows Server 2016 feature that enables a server connected to iSCSI, Fibre Channel, or Serial Attached SCSI (SAS) SAN devices to revert to an alternate path through the network when a connection fails.

To implement Multipath I/O, you must have the following components:

- **Multipath I/O feature** Windows Server 2016 includes a Multipath I/O feature, which you install using the Add Roles And Features Wizard in Server Manager or the Install-WindowsFeature cmdlet in PowerShell.
- **Device Specific Module (DSM)** Every network adapter or host bus adapter in the server that connects to the SAN must have a DSM. The Multipath I/O implementation in Windows Server 2016 includes a DSM that is compatible with many devices, but some might require a hardware-specific DSM supplied by the manufacturer.
- **Redundant network components** The server, the network, and the storage device must have redundant components providing separate paths through the network. This means that the server must have at least two network adapters or host bus adapters connected to different network segments and different switches, so that a failure of any component still leaves an available path to the destination. MPIO can support up to 32 redundant paths.

Once you have installed the Multipath I/O feature, you can access the MPIO Properties sheet by selecting Tools | MPIO in Server Manager. By default, the MPIO Devices tab appears, as shown in Figure 2-50.

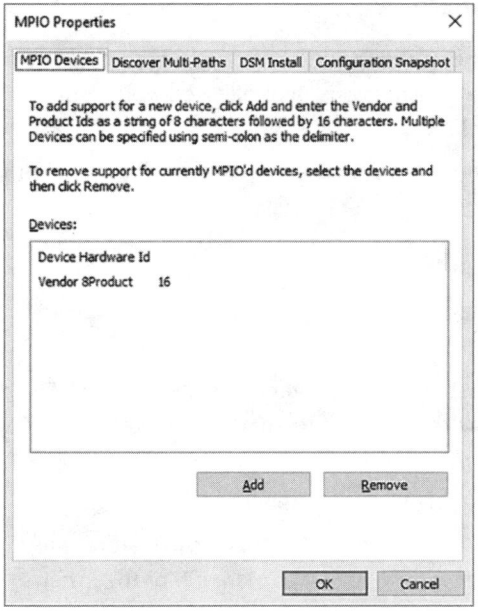

FIGURE 2-50 The MPIO Devices tab on the MPIO Properties sheet

Only the Microsoft DSM appears in the Devices box initially. To add DSMs supplied by the manufacturer of your hardware, select the DSM Install tab, as shown in Figure 2-51, browse to the location of the INF file supplied with the DSM, and click Install. This method only applies to DSMs that are not supplied with their own installation software.

FIGURE 2-51 The DSM Install tab on the MPIO Properties sheet

The Discover Multi-Paths tab, shown in Figure 2-52, displays devices for which MPIO has detected multiple paths through the network. By default, iSCSI devices do not appear on this tab, but you can enable them by selecting the Add Support For iSCSI Devices check box.

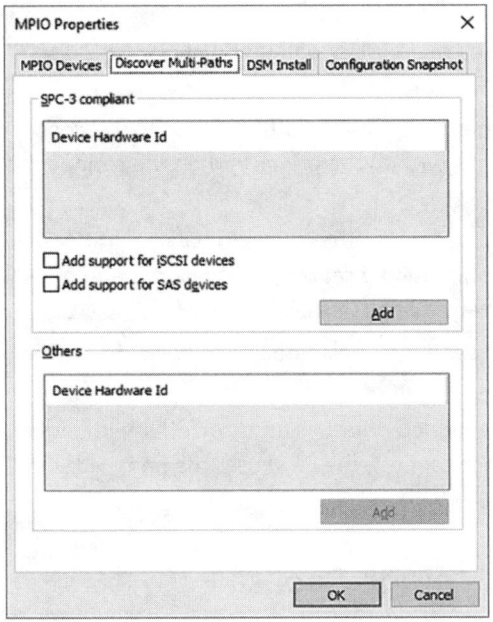

FIGURE 2-52 The Discover Multi-Paths tab on the MPIO Properties sheet

NOTE **IDENTIFYING DEVICES**

Devices in the MPIO Properties sheet are identified by their hardware IDs, which consist of an eight-character vendor ID (VID) plus a 16-character product ID (PID). The combination is sometimes called a VID/PID.

Detecting devices

Windows Server 2016 relies on Plug and Play (PnP) to detect and identify the storage devices to which the server is connected. Without Multipath I/O, a server with two network interfaces connected to a single storage device would be seen by PnP as two storage devices.

With MPIO installed, each time PnP detects a new storage device, the MPIO driver scans the available DSMs to find the one that corresponds to the device. Once the DSM claims the device, the MPIO driver verifies that the device is active and ready for data. When PnP detects the same device again through a different network interface, the MPIO driver and the DSM identify it as such and create a multipath group that is addressed using a single identifier.

DSM policies

In addition to failover, Multipath I/O can also support load balancing, in which storage requests use different paths to the SAN device to minimize network traffic congestion. The Microsoft DSM supports the following policies:

- **Failover** The server designates one path as the primary path and only switches to a secondary path when the primary fails.
- **Failback** The server designates one path as the primary path, switches to a secondary path when the primary fails, and switches back to the primary when the connection is restored.
- **Round Robin** The DSM uses each of the available paths in turn to balance traffic among them. Variations include a round robin using a set of primary paths, with one or more paths reserved as a standby in the event that all of the primaries fail.
- **Dynamic Least Queue Depth** For each storage request, the DSM selects the path with the fewest outstanding requests.
- **Weighted Path** The available paths are assigned priorities using weights, with higher numbers indicating a lower priority. For each request, the DSM uses the path with the lowest weight.

Determine usage scenarios for Storage Replica

Storage Replica (SR) is a Windows Server 2016 feature that enables administrators to replicate volumes, synchronously or asynchronously, for disaster preparedness and disaster recovery purposes. The storage devices to be replicated can be located in the same computer, the same datacenter, or in distant cities.

Storage Replica supports two types of replication: synchronous and asynchronous.

- **Synchronous replication** Data is written to two destinations at the same time before the acknowledgment of the I/O request to the originating application. In SR, this occurs when the replicated volumes share a fast connection, and data can be mirrored between volumes immediately. This type of replication ensures that there will be no data loss if a failure occurs and the system must fail over to a volume replica.
- **Asynchronous replication** Data is written to a single destination and acknowledged immediately. Then, it is replicated to a second destination, with acknowledgment sent to the replication partner, but not to the original application that generated the write request. In SR, this occurs when the volumes are connected using a relatively slow technology, usually over longer distances, such as a WAN link. The data write is acknowledged quickly, and the data is mirrored between the volumes, but there is no guarantee that the data will be identical at any given time, in the event of a failure.

Storage Replica is designed to function in three primary scenarios, as follows:

- **Server-to-server** Provides synchronous or asynchronous replication between local or shared storage volumes on two standalone servers, as shown in Figure 2-53. The servers can be using Storage Spaces with local disks, SAN storage, or shared SAS. Failover of one server to the replica is manual.

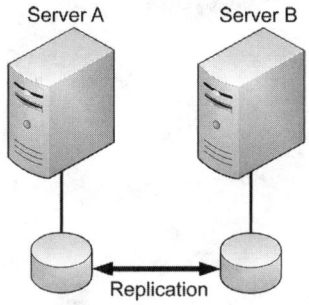

FIGURE 2-53 Storage Replica server-to-server configuration

- **Cluster-to-cluster** Provides synchronous or asynchronous replication between two clusters, as shown in Figure 2-54. The clusters can be using Storage Spaces with SAN storage or shared SAS, or Storage Spaces Direct. Failover of one cluster to the replica is manual.

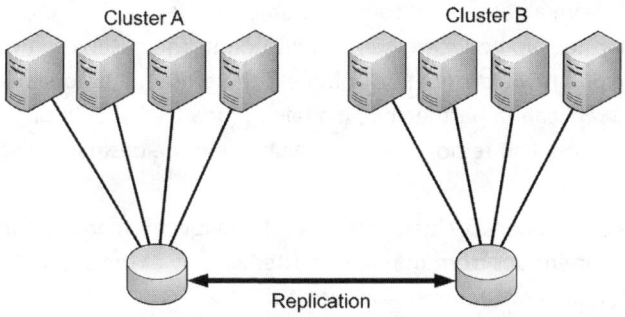

FIGURE 2-54 Storage Replica cluster-to-cluster configuration

- **Stretch cluster** Provides synchronous or asynchronous replication between the storage devices in an asymmetric cluster. In a stretch cluster, the cluster nodes are divided between two sites, each with its own storage, as shown in Figure 2-55. The cluster sites can be using Storage Spaces with SAN storage or shared SAS, or Storage Spaces Direct. The stretch cluster configuration is the only one supported by Storage Replica that includes an automated failover capability.

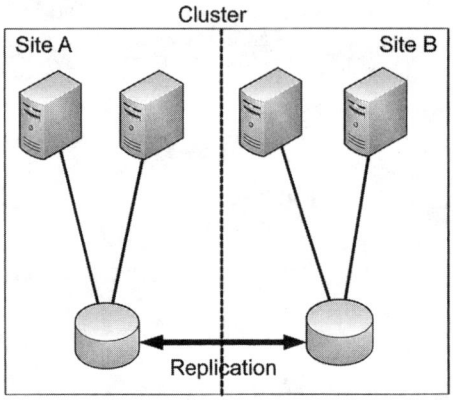

FIGURE 2-55 Storage Replica stretch cluster configuration

While there are many applications for data replication, SR is designed to provide failover capabilities if an equipment failure or other disaster occurs. By replicating your data to another room, another building, or another city, you can easily shift your workload to another location after, or even before, a catastrophic event occurs. In the event of an imminent disaster, such as an approaching hurricane, an organization with its data replicated to a server or node or cluster in another city is prepared to revert to the replica at a few minutes' notice.

SR replication is one-way, from a designated source volume to a destination volume. When you create the replication partnership between them, SR dismounts the destination volume and its drive letter or mount point. The destination volume is therefore not accessible to users while it is involved in a replication partnership. If a failure (or a test) should occur, and you need to access the replication, you remove the partnership and the destination volume becomes available again.

Thus, in a server-to-server or cluster-to-cluster scenario, the failover is manual, but in a stretch cluster, because there are nodes from the same cluster already at the alternate location, along with the replicated data, the failover is automatic.

The replication performed by Storage Replica is designed to improve on Windows tools that administrators might have used in the past, such as Distributed File System (DFS) Replication, which is file-based and exclusively asynchronous. SR uses SMB version 3 for its communication, which provides features such as multichannel link aggregation, data encryption, and digital signatures. The replication is also block-based, not file-based, as in DFS Replication. Because of this, there are no issues of data missing in the replica due to open files that could not be accessed by the replication process.

Even when running asynchronously, RA replication operates continuously; it is not based on checkpoints, which can result is more lost data, depending on the time since the last checkpoint when a failure occurs. The potential for data loss during asynchronous operation is typically based only on the latency of the connection between the replication volumes.

Implement Storage Replica for server-to-server, cluster-to-cluster, and stretch cluster scenarios

Implementing Storage Replica on your network requires careful planning and a lot of prerequisites. Creating the replication partnership is simply a matter of running one PowerShell cmdlet (New-SRPartnership), but this happens at the end of the procedure.

Storage Replica is a Windows feature that is available only in the Datacenter edition of Windows Server 2016. You install the feature through the Add Roles and Features Wizard in Server Manager or by running the following PowerShell command:

```
install-windowsfeature -name storage-replica, fs-fileserver -includemanagementtools
-restart
```

NOTE **INSTALLING FILE SERVER WITH SR**

The File Server role service (FS-FileServer) is not required for the operation of Storage Replica itself. It is included because it is required to run the Test-SRTopology cmdlet.

The next step is to prepare the storage infrastructure for replication. The individual tasks for this part of the procedure vary depending on whether you are using the server-to-server, cluster-to-cluster, or stretch cluster scenario. After you configure the server or cluster storage infrastructure, all three scenarios proceed with testing the replication topology and creating the SR partnership between servers.

Preparing the storage infrastructure

To use SR, the servers that will function as the replication partners, whether standalone or in a cluster, must be running Windows Server 2016 Datacenter edition. Two gigabytes of memory in each server is the bare minimum; at least four gigabytes is recommended. In addition, the infrastructure should be configured as follows:

- Each server, cluster, or cluster site must have its own storage infrastructure. A server-to-server implementation is the only one that can use internal disks, but all the scenarios can use virtually any kind of external disk technology, including iSCSI, a Fibre Channel SAN, or SAS. In each case, however, a mixture of SSD and HDD drives is recommended.
- To provision the storage, you use Storage Spaces to create at least two virtual disks, one for logs and one for data, with the SSD drives being used for the log volume. All the physical disks used for the logs in both replication partners must use the same sector size, as must all the physical disks used for data. All the disks must use the GPT partition style. None of the replicated storage can be located on the system disk containing the operating system. The data volumes on the two replication partners must be the same size; the log volumes must also be the same size, at least 9 GB. The data volumes can use tiered storage, and mirrored or parity disks.

- The network connecting the replication partners should have sufficient speed and bandwidth to support your workload, with a ~5ms round-trip latency, to support synchronous replication. There is no recommended latency for asynchronous operation.
- All servers must be joined to an Active Directory Domain Services (AD DS) domain, although the domain controllers do not necessarily have to be running Windows Server 2016.
- Firewall rules for the replication partners must allow the following traffic in both directions: Internet Control Message Protocol, SMB (ports 445, and 5445 for SMB Direct), and Web Services Management (WS-MAN, port 5985).

Testing the SR topology

Among the PowerShell cmdlets included with the SR feature is one called Test-SRTopology, which runs a variety of prerequisite and performance tests on the two servers that become replication partners and their network connection, and creates an HTML report containing the results.

The cmdlet takes parameters specifying the names of the servers that become the source and destination replication partners, the volumes to be replicated, the length of the test, and the location for the resulting report, as shown in the following example:

```
test-srtopology -sourcecomputername servera -sourcevolumename f: -sourcelogvolumename e:
-destinationcomputername serverb -destinationvolumename f: -destinationlogvolumename e:
-durationinminutes 30 -resultpath c:temp
```

The cmdlet initially checks whether the servers and the storage subsystems meet the requirements for SR, as shown in Figure 2-56.

Requirements Tests

The following tests were attempted. Hover over each test below to get more details.

	Test
ⓘ	**Volume Availability Test:** Volume **F:** exists on **RTMSvrH**
ⓘ	**Volume Availability Test:** Volume **E:** exists on **RTMSvrH**
ⓘ	**Volume Availability Test:** Volume **F:** exists on **RTMSvrI**
ⓘ	**Volume Availability Test:** Volume **E:** exists on **RTMSvrI**
ⓘ	**Partition Style Test:** Partition **F:** on **RTMSvrH** is a GPT-style partition
ⓘ	**Partition Style Test:** Partition **E:** on **RTMSvrH** is a GPT-style partition
ⓘ	**Partition Style Test:** Partition **F:** on **RTMSvrI** is a GPT-style partition
ⓘ	**Partition Style Test:** Partition **E:** on **RTMSvrI** is a GPT-style partition
ⓘ	**Volume Size Test:** Volume **F:** on **RTMSvrH** and **F:** on **RTMSvrI** are identical in size
ⓘ	**File System Test:** File system on volume **E:** on **RTMSvrH** is **NTFS**
ⓘ	**File System Test:** File system on volume **E:** on **RTMSvrI** is **NTFS**
ⓘ	**Disk Sector Size Test:** Sector size of the volume **F:** on **RTMSvrH** and **F:** on **RTMSvrI** is identical
ⓘ	**Log Disk Sector Size Test:** Sector size of the volume **E:** on **RTMSvrH** and **E:** on **RTMSvrI** is identical
ⓘ	**Log Volume Free Disk Space Test:** The log volume **E:** in **RTMSvrH** has enough free space to hold the recommended log volume size of **8**GB
ⓘ	**Log Volume Free Disk Space Test:** The log volume **E:** in **RTMSvrI** has enough free space to hold the recommended log volume size of **8**GB
ⓘ	**Remote Server Management Test:** Target server **RTMSvrI** can be managed remotely using WMI
ⓘ	**SMB Connectivity Test:** Firewalls are configured to allow SMB protocol traffic to and from **RTMSvrI**

FIGURE 2-56 Storage Replica requirements test results

Then, the cmdlet runs performance tests for a time interval that you specify in the command line. The ideal way to run this test is while the source server is running under its usual workload. The test proceeds to measure the synchronization performance between the source and the destination, to determine if the throughout is sufficient for synchronous replication, and presents the results in a chart, as shown in Figure 2-57.

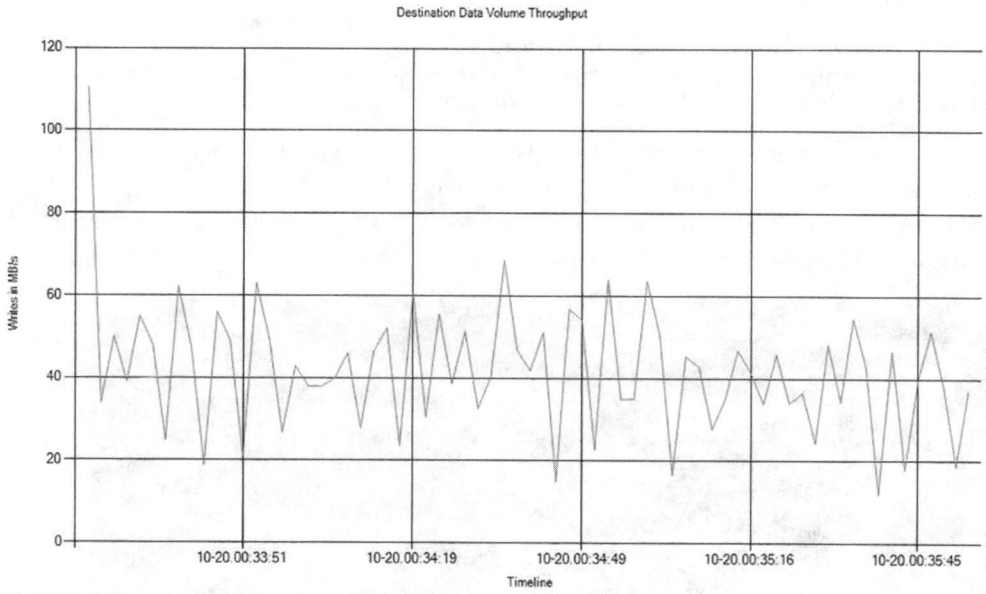

FIGURE 2-57 Storage Replica throughput test results

Configuring clustering

After configuring the replication partners, you can proceed to implement the clustering solution, for the cluster-to-cluster or stretch cluster scenarios. For the cluster-to-cluster scenario, you create two separate failover clusters, in the normal manner. Then, you configure each cluster to have full access to the other, using the Grant-SRAccess cmdlet, as in the following examples:

```
grant-sraccess -computername servera -cluster clustera

grant-sraccess -computername serverb -cluster clusterb
```

For a stretch cluster scenario, you create the cluster and make the replication source disk a cluster shared volume (CSV), using the Add-ClusterSharedVolume cmdlet. You can also do that and create the replication partnership using the graphical Failover Cluster Manager console.

Creating the SR partnership

Assuming that your servers and storage infrastructure have passed the Test-SRTopology checks, and your cluster(s) are in place, you can proceed to establish the actual replication partnership between the source and the destination servers. You do this by running the New-SRPartnership cmdlet, with many of the same parameters as Test-SRTopology, as in the following example:

```
new-srpartnership -sourcecomputername servera -sourcergname group1 -sourcevolumename
f: -sourcelogvolumename e: -destinationcomputername serverb -destinationrgname group2
-destinationvolumename f: -destinationlogvolumename e:
```

Once you create the partnership, the initial synchronization begins, which can take some time, depending on the size of the volumes. To monitor the replication progress, you can use the Get-WinEvent cmdlet to check the Windows event logs for the following codes: 5015, 5002, 5004, 1237, 5001, and 2200, as shown in Figure 2-58.

```
PS E:\> get-winevent -providername microsoft-windows-storagereplica -max 40


   ProviderName: Microsoft-Windows-StorageReplica

TimeCreated                     Id LevelDisplayName Message
-----------                     -- --------------- -------
10/20/2016 1:43:10 PM         5015 Information      Successfully established a connection to a partner replica....
10/20/2016 1:43:05 PM         5002 Information      Source entered ready state....
10/20/2016 1:43:04 PM         5004 Information      Source entered wait-for-quorum state....
10/20/2016 1:43:04 PM         1237 Information      Block copy is in progress....
10/20/2016 1:43:04 PM         1201 Information      Source completed preparing for replication....
10/20/2016 1:43:04 PM         5001 Information      Entered preparation state....
10/20/2016 1:43:04 PM         2231 Information      Replication group is online....
10/20/2016 1:43:04 PM         2200 Information      Start replication for replica....
10/20/2016 1:43:04 PM         9004 Warning          Resetting the recovery bitmap....
10/20/2016 1:43:04 PM         9007 Information      The disk is not thinly-provisioned....
10/20/2016 12:08:48 AM       10330 Information      A GPT partition was detected and prepared for replication operat...
10/20/2016 12:08:48 AM       10330 Information      A GPT partition was detected and prepared for replication operat...
10/20/2016 12:08:47 AM       10002 Information      Filter driver started successfully.
10/19/2016 11:01:54 PM       10330 Information      A GPT partition was detected and prepared for replication operat...
10/19/2016 11:00:16 PM       10330 Information      A GPT partition was detected and prepared for replication operat...


PS E:\> _
```

FIGURE 2-58 Storage Replica event log entries

You can also display the status of the partnership using the Get-SRGroup cmdlet, as shown in Figure 2-59.

```
PS E:\> get-srgroup


AllowVolumeResize  : False
AsyncRPO           :
ComputerName       : RTMSVRH
Description        :
Id                 : 36049202-434a-4e62-98e2-72246549e56c
IsAutoFailover     :
IsCluster          : False
IsEncrypted        : False
IsInPartnership    : True
IsPrimary          : True
IsSuspended        : False
IsWriteConsistency : False
LastInSyncTime     :
LogSizeInBytes     : 8589934592
LogVolume          : e:\
Name               : sr1
NumOfReplicas      : 1
Partitions         : {5c98190e-5064-4a1e-b6f9-e8bfd2f224fd}
Replicas           : {MSFT_WvrReplica (PartitionId = "5c98190e-5064-4a1e-b6f9-e8bfd2f224fd")}
ReplicationMode    : Synchronous
ReplicationStatus  : InitialBlockCopy
PSComputerName     :


PS E:\>
```

FIGURE 2-59 Storage Replica event log entries

Once the synchronization partnership is in place, you can trigger a failover by using the Set-SRPartnership cmdlet to reverse the source and destination roles, as in the following example. This makes the destination volumes available for use again.

```
set-srpartnership -newsourcecomputername serverb -sourcergname group2
-destinationcomputername servera -destinationrgname group1
```

Skill 2.3: Implement data deduplication

Data deduplication is a role service in Windows Server 2016 that conserves storage space on an NTFS volume by locating redundant data and storing one only copy of that data instead of multiple copies. This is the basic operating principle for many data compression products, but Data Duplication improves on many other technologies by operating at the volume level, and not the file level.

This section covers how to:

- Implement and configure deduplication
- Determine appropriate usage scenarios for deduplication
- Monitor deduplication
- Implement a backup and restore solution with deduplication

Implement and configure deduplication

To use Data Deduplication on your volumes, you must first install the Data Deduplication role service, which is part of the File and Storage Services Role. You can do this using the Add Roles And Features Wizard, or by using the Install-WindowsFeature cmdlet in PowerShell, as follows:

```
install-windowsfeature -name fs-data-deduplication
```

Once Data Deduplication is installed, you manage it in Server Manager or by using PowerShell cmdlets.

Configuring deduplication using server manager

To use data deduplication, you must enable it on specific volumes. To do this in Server Manager, use the following procedure.

1. In Server Manager, click File And Storage Services, Volumes. The Volumes page appears.
2. Right-click one of the volumes in the Volumes tile and, in the context menu, select Configure Data Deduplication. The Deduplication Settings dialog box for the selected volume appears, as shown in Figure 2-60.

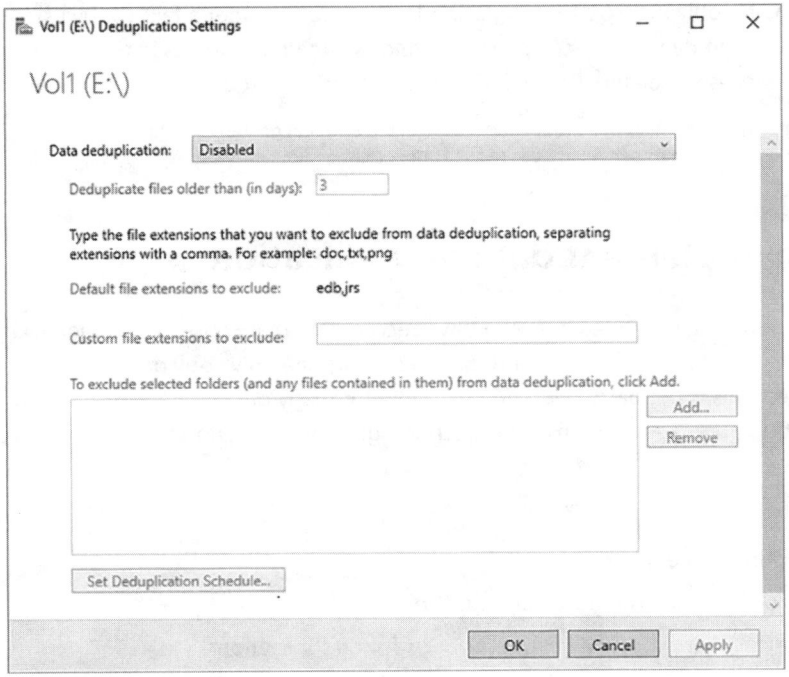

FIGURE 2-60 The Deduplication Settings dialog box

3. In the Data Deduplication drop-down list, select one of the following options:
   - **Disabled** Prevents any duplication from occurring
   - **General Purpose File Server** Intended for use with typical file server functions, such as shared folders, Work Folders, and Folder Redirection. Deduplication occurs in the background, and in-use files are ignored.
   - **Virtual Desktop Infrastructure (VDI) Server** Intended for use with Hyper-V. Deduplication occurs in the background, and in-use and partial files are optimized.
   - **Virtualized Backup Server** Intended for use with backup applications, such as Microsoft DPM. Deduplication is a priority process, and in-use files are optimized.
4. In the Deduplicate Files Older Than box, specify in days how old files must be before they are deduplicated.
5. The Default File Extensions To Exclude list specifies file types that will not be deduplicated, based on the option you chose in the Data Deduplication drop-down list. To exclude additional file types, specify their file name extensions in the Custom File Extensions To Exclude text box.
6. Click Add to open a Select Folder dialog box, in which you specify any folders that you want to be excluded from the deduplication process.
7. Click Set Duplication Schedule. The Deduplication Schedule dialog box for the selected volume appears, as shown in Figure 2-61.

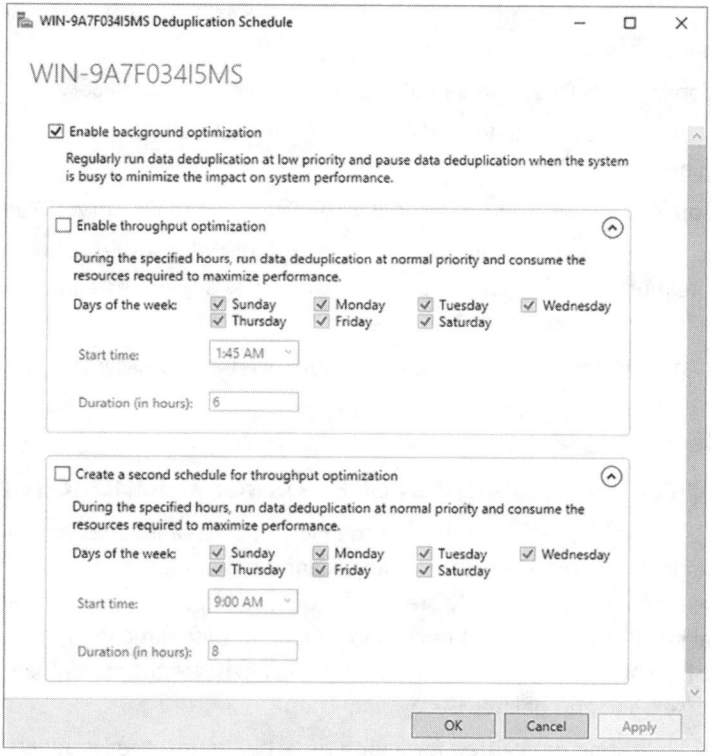

FIGURE 2-61 The Deduplication Schedule dialog box

8. By default, deduplication occurs in the background, as a low-priority process, when the system is not busy. To create a schedule for running the deduplication with normal priority and maximum performance, select the Enable Throughput Optimization check box.
9. Select the days of the week, the time of day, and the duration of the deduplication process.
10. Optionally, create another scheduled deduplication process by selecting the Create A Second Schedule For Throughput Optimization check box and configuring the days, time, and duration. Then click OK.
11. Click OK to close the Deduplication Settings dialog box.

Configuring deduplication using PowerShell

To enable deduplication for a volume using PowerShell, you run the Enable-DedupVolume cmdlet, as in the following example:

```
enable-dedupvolume -volume "e:" -usagetype default
```

The functions of the parameters are as follows:

- **UsageType** Specifies the type of workload for which the selected volume is used. The possible values are as follows:
  - **Default** Corresponds to the General Purpose File Server option in Server Manager
  - **Hyper-V** Corresponds to the Virtual Desktop Infrastructure (VDI) Server option in Server Manager
  - **Backup** Corresponds to the Virtualized Backup Server option in Server Manage
- **Volume** Specifies the volume on which to enable deduplication, using the format "X:" You can separate multiple volumes with commas, or specify a GUID instead of a drive letter, as in the following example:

```
enable-dedupvolume -volume "\\?\volume{26a21bda-a627-11d7-9931-806e6f6e6963}" -usagetype
backup
```

Determine appropriate usage scenarios for deduplication

Data deduplication optimizes a volume by selecting the files that are candidates for optimization, breaking them up into variable-sized chunks, and scanning them for their uniqueness. A chunk that is unique is copied to a separate area of the disk, called the *chunk store*, and replaced in its original locations by a special tag called a *reparse point*, directing it to the chunk's new location. If a chunk is identical to one that already exists in the store, the system replaces it with a reparse point and deletes the original chunk.

This principle of deduplication has existed for a long time, but many other products use it on individual files. Data deduplication in Windows Server 2016 works on the entire volume, not on one file at a time. Therefore, instead of having a copy of the same unique chunk in every file, there is only one copy for the entire volume. In the case of the Single Instance Store (SIS) technology in earlier versions of Windows Server, which data deduplication replaces, a volume maintains a single copy of an entire file, instead of multiple duplicates. Chunks, being typically smaller than files, have a much greater chance of being duplicated on a volume, thus generating a greater compression rate.

When an application or a user requests read access to an optimized file, the system uses the reparse points to redirect the request to the appropriate locations in the chunk store. The requestor is completely unaware that the file has been deduplicated.

If the application or user modifies the file, the system writes it back to the volume in its standard, unoptimized form. The file remains unoptimized until the next deduplication job occurs. This accumulation of unoptimized files due to the volume's workload is called *churn*. The post-processing nature of the system prevents any delay or interference with the volume writes.

Data deduplication also performs other jobs besides optimizations. *Garbage collection* is the term for a job that searches the chunk store for chunks that no longer have reparse points associated with them, typically due to modified or deleted files. *Integrity scrubbing* is a job that searches for damage or corruption in the chunk store, replacing the missing data with mirror or parity data. Finally, *unoptimization* is a job that restores all of the optimized files on a volume to their original states, disabling Data Deduplication for that volume in the process.

Optimization rates

The amount of storage space freed up by the application of data deduplication to a volume is dependent on multiple factors, including the formats of the files and the nature of the workload that generated the data. In traditional, file-based compression products, a software binary file might compress at 80 percent, and a bitmap image at 80 percent. If you were to apply the data deduplication process to a single file, the results are likely to be similar.

However, when you apply the deduplication process to an entire volume, you are comparing chunks to a much larger pool. While you might find 10 identical copies of a specific chunk in a single file, comparing that same chunk to an entire volume might yield thousands or millions of copies. Therefore, the space savings resulting from the disk deduplication process tend to be far higher than those from file-based compression.

Take, as an example, a volume that contains many Hyper-V VHD image files, all of which contain Windows 10 guest operating system installations used by a software development team. Since the contents of the VHD files will all be very similar, there will be a great many identical chunks. Microsoft estimates the storage space savings for a volume containing image files like these to be 80 to 95 percent. Thus, a nearly full volume containing 1 TB of data can be reduced to 100 GB or less, leaving 900 GB of newly created free space.

This is a best case example. A volume on a file server containing a typical mixture of user files might optimize at 50 to 60 percent.

Evaluating workloads

Before implementing data deduplication on your volumes, you should consider whether the workloads that generate your data are good candidates for optimization. The factors that can affect this decision include the nature of the work load that generates the data and the nature of the data itself.

The optimization process imposes a burden on a server's processor and memory resources that can have a significant effect on server performance. Because data deduplication uses a post-processing model, there is no effect on performance as the data write occurs. However, you should consider whether your workflow allows for a period when the optimization can occur without compromising production. A workflow that is idle at night is a good candidate for deduplication, in this respect, but one that operates around the clock might not be.

The next consideration is the data itself. The usage scenarios that are predefined in data deduplication are ones in which the data involved is particularly susceptible to redundancy. They are therefore good candidates for optimization. For example, on general purpose file servers, users often tend to store multiple copies of the same files. In the same way, software developers typically store multiple builds that differ only slightly. However, if a volume contains a large amount of encrypted files, the encryption will hide the redundancy, preventing data deduplication from being effective.

Data deduplication includes a Data Deduplication Savings Evaluation Tool (Ddpeval.exe) that you can use to test a volume to see how much storage savings can result from optimization. Ddpeval is a command line tool that you run, by specifying a drive letter to evaluate. The results specify how much saving you can expect in the selected data set, as shown in Figure 2-62.

```
PS F:\> ddpeval e: /v
Data Deduplication Savings Evaluation Tool
Copyright (c) 2013 Microsoft Corporation.  All Rights Reserved.

Evaluated Target OS: Windows 10.0
Evaluated folder: e:
Evaluated folder size: 14.85 GB
Files in evaluated folder: 3358

Processed files: 957
Processed files size: 14.84 GB
Optimized files size: 4.15 GB
Space savings: 10.69 GB
Space savings percent: 72

Optimized files size (no compression): 4.28 GB
Space savings (no compression): 10.56 GB
Space savings percent (no compression): 71

Files excluded by policy: 2401
     Small files (<32KB): 2401
Files excluded by error: 0
PS F:\> _
```

FIGURE 2-62 Output of the Ddpeval program

Other types of data might not be good candidates for optimization because of the way in which they store and access data. Data deduplication tries to organize the chunk store along file boundaries. A file read request will, in many cases, require access to successive chunks in the store, which enhances performance. Database files, however, tend to have read patterns that are more random, and the way that data deduplication stores a chunked database might require a read process to access chunks scattered all over the disk, decreasing efficiency. Before implementing data deduplication on a production server, you should perform a test deployment, to determine whether the realized savings can offset any performance degradation that might occur.

Monitor deduplication

Once you have installed data deduplication and enabled it on volumes, the Volumes tile in Server Manager is modified to include Deduplication Rate and Deduplication Savings columns, as shown in Figure 2-63. The Deduplication Rate specifies the percentage of the files' original disk space that has been cleared, and the Deduplication Saving specifies the amount of disk space cleared, in gigabytes.

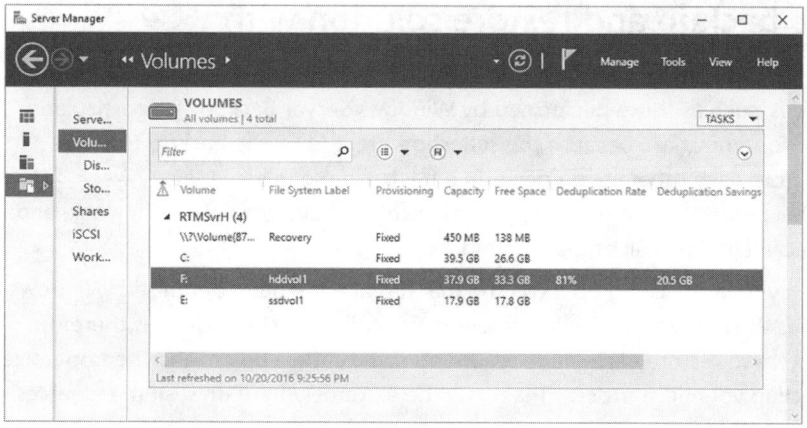

FIGURE 2-63 The Volumes tile in Server Manager

You can also monitor the deduplication process using PowerShell with the Get-DedupStatus cmdlet. When you run the cmdlet by itself, it displays only a few statistics. To see the entire display, as shown in Figure 2-64, pipe the output to the Format-List cmdlet, as follows:

```
get-dedupostatus | format-list
```

```
PS C:\Users\administrator.ADATUM> get-dedupstatus |fl

Volume                          : F:
VolumeId                        : \\?\Volume{5c98190e-5064-4a1e-b6f9-e8bfd2f224fd}\
Capacity                        : 37.87 GB
FreeSpace                       : 33.25 GB
UsedSpace                       : 4.62 GB
UnoptimizedSize                 : 25.08 GB
SavedSpace                      : 20.46 GB
SavingsRate                     : 81 %
OptimizedFilesCount             : 1550
OptimizedFilesSize              : 24.71 GB
OptimizedFilesSavingsRate       : 82 %
InPolicyFilesCount              : 1550
InPolicyFilesSize               : 24.71 GB
LastOptimizationTime            : 10/20/2016 9:13:27 PM
LastOptimizationResult          : 0x00000000
LastOptimizationResultMessage   : The operation completed successfully.
LastGarbageCollectionTime       :
LastGarbageCollectionResult     :
LastGarbageCollectionResultMessage :
LastScrubbingTime               :
LastScrubbingResult             :
LastScrubbingResultMessage      :

PS C:\Users\administrator.ADATUM>
```

FIGURE 2-64 Output of the Get-DedupStatus cmdlet

A LastOptimizationResult value of zero indicates that the operation was successful. If, after the initial deduplication, jobs start to show as being unsuccessful, it is typically because the deduplication process did not have enough time to keep up with the changes generated by the workload (called the *churn*). You might have to increase the duration of the deduplication jobs, or the priority allotted to them, to resolve the problem.

To monitor the history of a server's deduplication jobs, you can review the Windows event logs. Data deduplication events are located in the Applications and Services Logs\Windows\Deduplication\Operational container.

Implement a backup and restore solution with deduplication

Backups to disk drives, such as those performed by Windows Server Backup, are particularly good candidates for optimization, because the snapshots created by the backup software tend to differ little from each other. If you perform a full backup of a server every week, for example, only a small percentage of the server data is likely to have changed each week, and data deduplication can eliminate all of that redundancy.

In addition, when you are backing up a volume that has already been optimized, Windows Server Backup copies the data to the backup target in its optimized state. There is therefore no need for the system to restore each file to its unoptimized state, copy it, and then optimize the copy on the backup volume, a process that could be extremely hard on system resources.

The Virtualized Backup Server usage option is designed specifically to work with backup software solutions like Microsoft System Center Data Protection Manager (DPM), in which the backup software runs on a Hyper-V virtual machine and stores its backups in VHD or VHDX files on a volume with data deduplication enabled.

Because a backup job can generate a relatively large amount of new data, the optimization settings for the backup scenario differ from those of the other presets, in that they enable the optimization process to run with a high priority on the server. Administrators must monitor the optimization jobs on a regular basis, to ensure that they are keeping up with this higher rate of churn than is typically found on a general-purpose file server.

Chapter summary

- The GUID Partition Table (GPT) is an alternative to the Master Boot Record partition style. GPT supports larger disks than MBR, allows for the creation of more partitions, and provides better recovery from disk errors that corrupt the partition table.
- Windows supports a virtual hard disk (VHD) format that you can use on Hyper-V guests or other purposes. You can create image files using VHD or the newer VHDX format with the Disk Management snap-in or the Get-VHD cmdlet in Windows PowerShell.
- VHD and VHDX image files can be mounted on a physical or virtual computer, so that they function just like physical disks.
- Windows Server 2016 includes support for the NTFS file system, as well as the newer ReFS file system, which supports larger volumes, but lacks some of the NTFS capabilities.
- Windows can share folders using SMB, the original standard for Windows drive sharing, and NFS, which the standard used on many UNIX and Linux distributions.

- Windows PowerShell includes a collection of cmdlets that you can use to manage folder shares and their permissions.
- NTFS has a system of permissions that you can use to authorize specific degrees of user access to files and folders.
- Storage Spaces enables administrators to create storage pools out of physical disks. They can then create virtual disks from the pooled storage, irrespective of the boundaries between physical disks.
- Virtual disks in storage pools can be configured to use mirroring, in which data is stored in duplicate, and parity, in which data bits are stored with parity information for data recovery purposes.
- Tiered storage is a feature of virtual that uses faster SSD drives in a storage pool to store the most frequently used files.
- iSCSI is a storage area networking protocol that enables Windows servers (called initiators) to connect to storage devices (called targets) using standard Ethernet hardware.
- iSNS is essentially a registry for iSCSI components that enables initiators to locate the targets available on the network.
- Datacenter Bridging (DCB) is a mechanism for separating LAN and SAN traffic on a converged network. DCB works by creating classes of network traffic that are assigned a specific percentage of the available bandwidth.
- Multipath I/O is a fault tolerance mechanism that enables a server to access a networked storage device through redundant paths, in the event of a component failure.
- Storage Replica is a feature in the Datacenter edition that enables administrators to create replication partnerships between servers, between clusters, or within a stretch cluster.
- Data Deduplication is a Windows Server 2016 feature that conserves storage space by splitting files into chunks and storing only one copy each redundant chunk. By operating on entire volumes instead of individual files, the savings rate for many data types can range from 50% to over 90%.
- Data Deduplication has three predefined usage scenarios that contain settings to maximize storage savings and server performance.
- Once enabled, you can use PowerShell cmdlets and Windows Event logs to monitor the ongoing progress of Data Deduplication jobs.
- Data Deduplication is particularly suitable for backup targets because of the redundant nature of the data stored there.

Thought experiment

In this thought experiment, demonstrate your skills and knowledge of the topics covered in this chapter. You can find answer to this thought experiment in the next section.

You are working the help desk for Contoso Corp., a government contractor, and a user named Ralph calls to request access to the files for Alamo, a new classified project. The Alamo project files are stored in a shared folder on a Windows Server 2016 workgroup file server, which is locked in a secured underground data storage facility. After verifying that Ralph has the appropriate security clearance for the project, you create a new group on the file server called ALAMO_USERS and add Ralph's user account to that group. Then, you add the ALAMO_USER group to the access control list for the Alamo folder on the file server, and assign the group the following NTFS permissions:

- Allow Modify
- Allow Read & Execute
- Allow List Folder Contents
- Allow Read
- Allow Write

Sometime later, Ralph calls you to tell you that he is able to access the Alamo folder and read the files stored there, but he has been unable to save changes back to the server. What is the most likely cause of the problem?

Thought experiment answer

This section contains the solution to the thought experiment.

Ralph probably does not have sufficient share permissions for read/write access to the Alamo files. By default, when you share a folder on a workgroup server using File Explorer, the Everyone special identity receives only the Read share permission. After you grant the ALAMO_USER group the Allow Full Control share permission, Ralph should be able to save his changes to the Alamo files.

CHAPTER 3

Implement Hyper-V

Hyper-V is the hypervisor and hardware virtualization platform incorporated into Windows Server 2016 as a role. Using Hyper-V, you can create virtual machines (VMs) that consist of virtualized equivalents of computer hardware, storage resources, and network components, such as network interface adapters and switches. VMs function like physical computers, but administrators can easily save them, move them, and reconfigure them to accommodate their needs.

Skills in this chapter:

- Install and configure Hyper-V
- Configure virtual machine (VM) settings
- Configure Hyper-V storage
- Configure Hyper-V networking

Skill 3.1: Install and configure Hyper-V

Hyper-V is a Windows Server 2016 role that makes it possible to create virtual machines on which you can install an operating system and use as though it is a separate computer. A server running Windows Server 2016 that has the Hyper-V role installed is known as a host. The virtual machines that you create in Hyper-V are known as guests.

This section covers how to:

- Determine hardware and compatibility requirements for installing Hyper-V
- Install Hyper-V
- Install management tools
- Upgrade from existing versions of Hyper-V
- Delegate virtual machine management
- Perform remote management of Hyper-V hosts
- Configure virtual machines using Windows PowerShell Direct
- Implement nested virtualization

Determine hardware and compatibility requirements for installing Hyper-V

Windows Server 2016 includes the *Hyper-V* role, which enables you to create virtual machines, each of which runs in its own isolated environment. *Virtual machines (VMs)* are self-contained units that you can easily move from one Hyper-V host server to another, greatly simplifying the process of deploying network applications and services.

Server virtualization in Windows Server 2016 is based on a module called a *hypervisor.* Sometimes called a *virtual machine monitor (VMM),* the hypervisor is responsible for abstracting the computer's physical hardware and creating a virtualized hardware environment for each virtual machine. Each VM has its own (virtual) hardware configuration and can run a separate copy of an operating system, called a *guest.* Therefore, with sufficient physical hardware and the correct licensing, a single computer running Windows Server 2016 with the Hyper-V role installed can support dozens, or even hundreds, of VMs, which you can manage as though they are standalone computers.

Virtualization architectures

In early virtualization products, including Microsoft Virtual Server, the virtualization software adds the hypervisor component. The hypervisor essentially runs as an application on the host operating system, as shown in Figure 3-1, and enables you to create as many virtual machines as the computer has hardware to support.

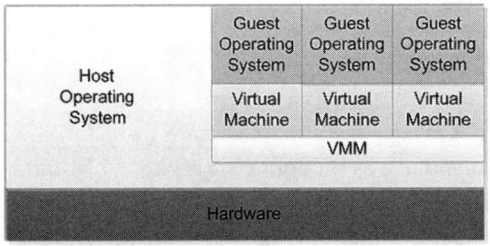

FIGURE 3-1 Type II virtualization

This arrangement, in which the hypervisor runs on top of a host operating system, is called a *Type II virtualization.* The host operating system shares access to the computer's processor with the hypervisor, with each taking the clock cycles it needs and passing control of the processor back to the other.

Type II virtualization can provide adequate virtual machine performance, particularly in classroom and laboratory environments, but it does not provide performance equivalent to separate physical computers. Therefore, it is not recommended for high-traffic servers in production environments.

The Hyper-V virtualization built into Windows Server 2016 uses a different type of architecture. Hyper-V uses *Type I virtualization*, in which the hypervisor is an abstraction layer that interacts directly with the computer's physical hardware—that is, without an intervening host operating system.

The hypervisor creates individual environments called *partitions*, each of which has its own operating system installed and accesses the computer's hardware via the hypervisor. Unlike Type II virtualization, no host operating system shares processor time with the hypervisor. Instead, the hypervisor designates the first partition it creates as the parent partition and all subsequent partitions as child partitions, as shown in Figure 3-2.

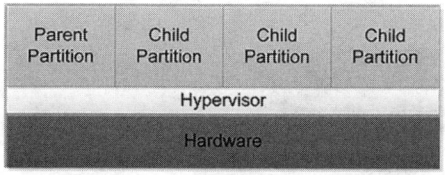

FIGURE 3-2 Type 1 virtualization

The parent partition accesses the system hardware through the hypervisor, just as the child partitions do. The only difference is that the parent runs the virtualization stack, which creates and manages the child partitions. The parent partition is also responsible for the subsystems that directly affect the performance of the computer's physical hardware, such as Plug and Play, power management, and error handling. These subsystems run in the operating systems on the child partitions as well, but they address only virtual hardware, whereas the parent, or root, partition handles the real thing.

Hyper-V hardware limitations

The Windows Server 2016 version of Hyper-V contains improvements in the scalability of the system over previous versions. A Windows Server 2016 Hyper-V host system can have up to 512 logical processors, supporting up to 2,048 virtual CPUs and up to 24 terabytes (TB) of physical memory.

One server can host as many as 1,024 active virtual machines, and each Generation 2 virtual machine can have up to 240 virtual CPUs and up to 12 TB of memory. Generation 1 VMs can have up to 64 virtual CPUs and up to 1 TB of memory.

Hyper-V can also support clusters with up to 64 nodes and 8,000 virtual machines.

NOTE **HYPER-V SERVER**

Microsoft also provides a dedicated Hyper-V Server product, which is a subset of Windows Server 2016. Hyper-V Server 2016 includes the Hyper-V role, which it installs by default during the operating system installation. Except for some limited File and Storage Services and Remote Desktop capabilities, the operating system includes no other roles.

The Hyper-V Server product is also limited to the Server Core interface, although it also includes Sconfig. a simple, script-based configuration interface, as shown in Figure 3-3. You can also manage Hyper-V Server remotely, using Server Manager and Hyper-V Manager, just as you would with any other Server Core installation.

```
Microsoft (R) Windows Script Host Version 5.812
Copyright (C) Microsoft Corporation. All rights reserved.

Inspecting system...


===========================================================================
                         Server Configuration
===========================================================================

1) Domain/Workgroup:                    Workgroup:  WORKGROUP
2) Computer Name:                       WIN-LLHUG0OK15A
3) Add Local Administrator
4) Configure Remote Management          Enabled

5) Windows Update Settings:             DownloadOnly
6) Download and Install Updates
7) Remote Desktop:                      Disabled

8) Network Settings
9) Date and Time
10) Telemetry settings                  Enhanced

11) Log Off User
12) Restart Server
13) Shut Down Server
14) Exit to Command Line


Enter number to select an option:
```

FIGURE 3-3 The Server Core interface in Hyper-V Server

Hyper-V Server is a free product, available for download from the Microsoft website. However, Hyper-V Server does not include any licenses for virtual instances. You must obtain and license all the operating systems you install on the virtual machines you create.

Microsoft recommends that you do not install other roles with Hyper-V. Any other roles that you need the physical computer to perform are better off implemented within one of the virtual machines you create with Hyper-V. You also might want to consider installing Hyper-V on a computer using the Server Core installation option to minimize the overhead expended on the partition. As with other roles, installing Hyper-V on Server Core excludes the management tools, which you must install separately as a feature.

The Hyper-V role has general hardware requirements that exceed those of the Windows Server 2016 operating system itself. Before you can install the Hyper-V role on a server running Windows Server 2016, you must have the following hardware:

- A 64-bit processor that includes hardware-assisted virtualization and second-level address translation (SLAT). This type of virtualization is available in processors that include a virtualization option, such as Intel Virtualization Technology (Intel VT) or AMD Virtualization (AMD-V) technology.
- Hardware-enforced Data Execution Prevention (DEP), which Intel describes as eXecuted Disable (XD) and AMD describes as No eXecute (NS). CPUs use this technology to segregate areas of memory for either storage of processor instructions or for storage of data. Specifically, you must enable Intel XD bit (execute disable bit) or AMD NX bit (no execute bit).
- VM Monitor Mode extensions, found on Intel processors as VT-c.
- A system BIOS or UEFI that supports the virtualization hardware and on which the virtualization feature has been enabled.
- A minimum of 4 gigabytes (GB) of memory. In addition to running the Hyper-V host operating system, the computer must have sufficient physical memory for all of the guest operating systems running on the virtual machines.

NOTE **HYPER-V MANAGEMENT TOOLS**

Virtualization hardware and BIOS/UEFI support is necessary to install the Hyper-V role itself, but it is not necessary to install the Hyper-V management tools. You can manage a Hyper-V server from any remote Windows computer by installing the Hyper-V Management Tools feature.

To determine if a computer has the hardware necessary to install the Hyper-V role, you can open a Windows PowerShell session and run the Systeminfo.exe program, to produce a display like the one shown in Figure 3-4. At the bottom of the listing, the Hyper-V Requirements item lists the computer's hypervisor capabilities.

```
PS C:\Users\Administrator> systeminfo.exe

Host Name:                 CZ10
OS Name:                   Microsoft Windows Server 2016 Datacenter Evaluation
OS Version:                10.0.14393 N/A Build 14393
OS Manufacturer:           Microsoft Corporation
OS Configuration:          Standalone Server
OS Build Type:             Multiprocessor Free
Registered Owner:          N/A
Registered Organization:   N/A
Product ID:                00377-10000-00000-AA360
Original Install Date:     10/17/2016, 10:24:18 PM
System Boot Time:          10/22/2016, 3:55:40 PM
System Manufacturer:       LENOVO
System Model:              Lenovo ThinkServer TS130
System Type:               x64-based PC
Processor(s):              1 Processor(s) Installed.
                           [01]: Intel64 Family 6 Model 58 Stepping 9 GenuineIntel ~1600 Mhz
BIOS Version:              LENOVO FAKT22BUS, 5/29/2013
Windows Directory:         C:\WINDOWS
System Directory:          C:\WINDOWS\system32
Boot Device:               \Device\HarddiskVolume2
System Locale:             en-us;English (United States)
Input Locale:              en-us;English (United States)
Time Zone:                 (UTC-05:00) Eastern Time (US & Canada)
Total Physical Memory:     3,902 MB
Available Physical Memory: 2,923 MB
Virtual Memory: Max Size:  4,606 MB
Virtual Memory: Available: 3,660 MB
Virtual Memory: In Use:    946 MB
Page File Location(s):     C:\pagefile.sys
Domain:                    WORKGROUP
Logon Server:              \\CZ10
Hotfix(s):                 3 Hotfix(s) Installed.
                           [01]: KB3192137
                           [02]: KB3199209
                           [03]: KB3194798
Network Card(s):           1 NIC(s) Installed.
                           [01]: Intel(R) 82579LM Gigabit Network Connection
                                 Connection Name: Ethernet
                                 DHCP Enabled:    Yes
                                 DHCP Server:     192.168.2.2
                                 IP address(es)
                                 [01]: 192.168.2.36
                                 [02]: fe80::d459:e49d:1350:3c5b
Hyper-V Requirements:      VM Monitor Mode Extensions: Yes
                           Virtualization Enabled In Firmware: Yes
                           Second Level Address Translation: Yes
                           Data Execution Prevention Available: Yes
PS C:\Users\Administrator>
```

FIGURE 3-4 Output of the Systeminfo.exe program

Install Hyper-V

As soon as you have the appropriate hardware and the required licenses, you can add the Hyper-V role to Windows Server 2016 using the Add Roles And Features Wizard in Server Manager or the Install-WindowsFeature cmdlet in Windows PowerShell.

Installing Hyper-V using Server Manager

To install the Hyper-V role with Server Manager, use the following procedure.

1. Log on to the server running Windows Server 2016 using an account with administrative privileges.
2. In the Server Manager console, select Manage, Add Roles And Features. The Add Roles And Features Wizard appears, displaying the Before You Begin page.

3. Click Next. The Select Installation Type page appears.
4. Leave the Role-Based Or Feature-Based Installation option selected and click Next. The Select Destination Server page appears.
5. Select the server on which you want to install Hyper-V and click Next. The Select Server Roles page appears.
6. Select the Hyper-V role check box. The Add Features That Are Required For Hyper-V dialog box appears.
7. Click Add Features to accept the dependencies, and then click Next. The Select Features Page appears.
8. Click Next. The Hyper-V page appears.
9. Click Next. The Create Virtual Switches page appears.
10. Select the check box for a network adapter and click Next. The Virtual Machine Migration page appears.
11. Click Next. The Default Stores page appears.
12. Optionally, specify alternatives to the default locations for virtual hard disk and virtual machine configuration files, and click Next. The Confirm Installation Selection page appears.
13. Click Install. The Installation Progress page appears as the wizard installs the role.
14. Click Close to close the wizard.
15. Restart the server.

Installing the role modifies the Windows Server 2016 startup procedure, so that the newly installed hypervisor can address the system hardware directly and then load the operating system as the primary partition on top of that.

Installing Hyper-V using Windows PowerShell

You can also install the Hyper-V role with the Install-WindowsFeature cmdlet, using the following command:

```
install-windowsfeature -name hyper-v -includemanagementtools -restart
```

As always, the Install-WindowsFeature cmdlet does not install the management tools associated with a role by default. You must include the IncludeManagementTools parameter to install Hyper-V Manager and the Hyper-V PowerShell module along with the role.

EXAM TIP

When working with Windows Server 2016 installed as a guest operating system on a Hyper-V host server running an earlier version of Windows Server, such as in a lab or training environment, you cannot install the Hyper-V role using the Add Roles And Features Wizard or the Install WindowsFeature cmdlet. In both cases, the installation terminates with an error message. This is because the virtual machine does not have hardware virtualization capability, and both tools perform prerequisite checks before allowing the installation of the role. However, the Deployment Image Servicing and Management tool (DISM.exe) does not perform these checks, and can install the Hyper-V role on a running system, even if it is a virtual machine. To install Hyper-V using DISM.exe, run the following command from an elevated command prompt:

```
dism /online /enable-feature /featurename:microsoft-hyper-v
```

A Hyper-V installation on a guest operating system is suitable only for training and practice, such as preparing for the 70-740 exam. You can create and configure VMs, but you can't start them, because the requisite hardware is not present. If the Hyper-V host server is running Windows Server 2016 and has the correct hardware, however, Hyper-V nesting is possible.

Install management tools

Adding the Hyper-V role installs the hypervisor software, and, in the case of a Server Manager installation, the management tools as well. The primary tool for creating and managing virtual machines and their components on Hyper-V servers is the Hyper-V Manager console. Hyper-V Manager provides you with a list of all the virtual machines on Windows Server 2016 systems and enables you to configure both the server environments and those of the individual VMs. Windows PowerShell also includes a Hyper-V module containing cmdlets that enable you to exercise complete control over VMs using that interface.

Both the Hyper-V Manager and the PowerShell cmdlets can manage remote Hyper-V servers. To do this, you can install the management tools by themselves, without installing the Hyper-V role. There are no prerequisites for installing or using the tools, so no special hardware is required.

To install the Hyper-V management tools with Server Manager, use the following procedure.

1. Log on to the server running Windows Server 2016 using an account with administrative privileges.
2. In Server Manager, launch the Add Roles And Features Wizard.
3. Leave the default settings selected on the Select Installation Type page and the Select Destination Server page.
4. Click Next to bypass the Select Server Roles page.

5. On the Select Features Page, browse to Remote Server Administration Tools\Role Administration Tools and select the Hyper-V Administration Tools check box. You can also choose to install only the Hyper-V GUI Management Tools or the Hyper-V Module for Windows PowerShell instead, by selecting the appropriate check box. Then click Next.
6. Click Install. The Installation Progress page appears as the wizard installs the features.
7. Click Close to close the wizard.

To install the management tools with Windows PowerShell, you use the Install-WindowsFeature cmdlet, as follows:

```
install-windowsfeature -name rsat-hyper-v-tools
```

To install just the Hyper-V Manager or just the Hyper-V PowerShell module, you use one of the following commands:

```
install-windowsfeature -name hyper-v-tools

install-windowsfeature -name hyper-v-powershell
```

Upgrade from existing versions of Hyper-V

When you upgrade a server to Windows Server 2016, Hyper-V is an important factor in the planning and execution process. Windows Server 2016 Hyper-V has many new features, and it is worthwhile to take advantage of them, but you must care for your existing virtual machines before you can upgrade the host operating system.

The first step in upgrading a host server to Windows Server 2016 is to get the virtual machines off the host, for their own protection. You can do this in two ways:

- **Export** Saves the VM files, including the virtual disks, to a folder that you specify. Later, you can import the VMs back into the host, after the upgrade is complete. Exporting and importing VMs can be a lengthy process, because you must work with each VM individually. The VMs are also offline while they are stored as exported files. You can import them into another server temporarily and run them there, but this doubles the length of the process.
- **Hyper-V Replica** Creates a copy of a running VM as an offline replica on another host server, including virtual disks. Because the source VM remains online as the replication occurs, downtime is minimal, and production can continue. After the upgrade is complete, you can replicate the copy back to the original host.
- **Share Nothing Live Migration** Moves a running VM with no shared storage to another host server in the same or a trusted domain, with virtually no downtime.

The solution you choose should depend primarily on whether your VMs are production servers that need to be running during the upgrade process. Once the guest VMs are safely located in another location, you can proceed to upgrade the host server, or migrate its roles to a clean Windows Server 2016 installation on another computer (which is the recommended method).

Delegate virtual machine management

To install the Hyper-V role, you must be logged on using an account with local Administrator or Domain Admin privileges, but once the role is installed, it might not be practical to grant this type of access to every person who works with virtual machines on the Hyper-V host.

To address this issue, installing the Hyper-V role in Windows Server 2016 creates a local Hyper-V Administrators group that you can use to grant users and groups permission to create, manage, and connect to virtual machines. Members of this group have no other access to the host operating system, so you can grant this privilege to non-administrators without endangering the rest of the operating system.

NOTE **AUTHORIZING HYPER-V ADMINISTRATORS**

In previous versions of Windows Server, there was a tool called Authorization Manager (Azman.msc) that enabled administrators to grant specific privileges to users. For example, you could authorize a user to start and stop virtual machines, but not alter any of their settings. This tool was deprecated in the Windows Server 2012 R2 release, although it still exists in Windows Server 2016. The current approved method for assigning granular Hyper-V administration tasks is to use System Center Virtual Machine Manager (VMM), a separate product that must be purchased.

Perform remote management of Hyper-V hosts

Once the Hyper-V role is installed, you can manage it locally using the Hyper-V Manager console or the cmdlets provided in the Hyper-V PowerShell module. This is frequently not practical, such as when the Hyper-V host server is in a distant data center or server closet. As with many other Windows services, you can manage Hyper-V remotely in a variety of ways.

Remote management using Hyper-V Manager

Like most snap-ins for Microsoft Management Console (MMC), Hyper-V Manager can connect to a remote server and perform the same functions there that it does on the local system. You can install Hyper-V Manager on any computer running Windows Server 2016, whether it has the Hyper-V role installed or not. Using Hyper-V Manager, you can connect to any computer running the Hyper-V role, whether it has Hyper-V Management Tools installed or not.

To run Hyper-V Manager on Windows 10, you must download and install the Remote Server Administration Tools package for Windows 10. The Windows Server 2016 and Windows 10 versions of Hyper-V Manager can connect to Hyper-V running on any Windows version since Windows Server 2012 and Windows 8. The opposite is not necessarily true, however. Earlier versions of Hyper-V Manager are limited in their ability to manage a Windows Server 2016 host server.

LIS package, as the vast majority of Hyper-V features are already integrated into the operating system.

The downloadable versions of the LIS package are assigned version numbers, which the integrated versions are not. If you decide to use the downloaded LIS, you should always obtain the latest version, after ensuring that Microsoft supports it for the version of the guest operating system you are running. Microsoft provides the LIS package in two forms, as a gzipped tar file that you can download to the guest operating system and install, or as a disk image in the ISO format, which you can load into a virtual DVD drive.

Install and configure FreeBSD Integration Services (BIS)

Since version 10, FreeBSD has included full support for FreeBSD Integration Services (BIS) in its operating system releases. There is no need to install additional software unless you are running FreeBSD version 9 or earlier. For versions 8.x and 9.x, there are ports available at: *https://svnweb.freebsd.org/ports/head/emulators/hyperv-is*, which can provide BIS functionality.

Implement Secure Boot for Windows and Linux environments

Secure Boot is a mechanism built into the Unified Extensible Firmware Interface (UEFI) that is designed to ensure that every component loaded during a computer's boot sequence has been digitally signed, and is therefore trusted by the computer's manufacturer. In Hyper-V, Generation 2 VMs support Secure Boot as part of their UEFI implementation.

In a traditional system boot, the computer performs a power-on self-test (POST), after which it initializes the BIOS, detects the system hardware, and loads the firmware into memory. After that, the system runs the bootloader. Because the firmware and the bootloader are not verified, it is possible for them to contain some form of malware, such as a rootkit or bootkit. These are not detectible by ordinary anti-virus software, and can therefore infect the system while remaining invisible to the operating system.

Secure Boot replaces the traditional BIOS firmware with UEFI firmware, which is responsible for verifying that the firmware, the bootloader, and other components originate from trusted sources. UEFI uses trusted certificates for the operating system and a platform key supplied by the computer vendor to ensure that no unauthorized software is being loaded during the boot process.

Windows and Secure Boot

When you create a Generation 2 virtual machine in Hyper-V, the computer manufacturer is Microsoft, and the UEFI firmware includes certificates for the Windows bootloaders. This means that Windows boots on the VM, because there is a chain of trusted certificates going back to the root. If you attempt to boot the VM into a non-Windows operating system, the system silently proceeds to the next item in the boot order. If you find that a VM is constantly trying to boot from the network or from a DVD, no matter what boot order you specify, the problem is likely to be that the Secure Boot failed, and the system is bypassing the hard disk boot.

Secure Boot in enabled by default on Generation 2 VMs. To disable it, you open the Security page in the VM Settings dialog box, and clear the Enable Secure Boot check box, as shown in Figure 3-28.

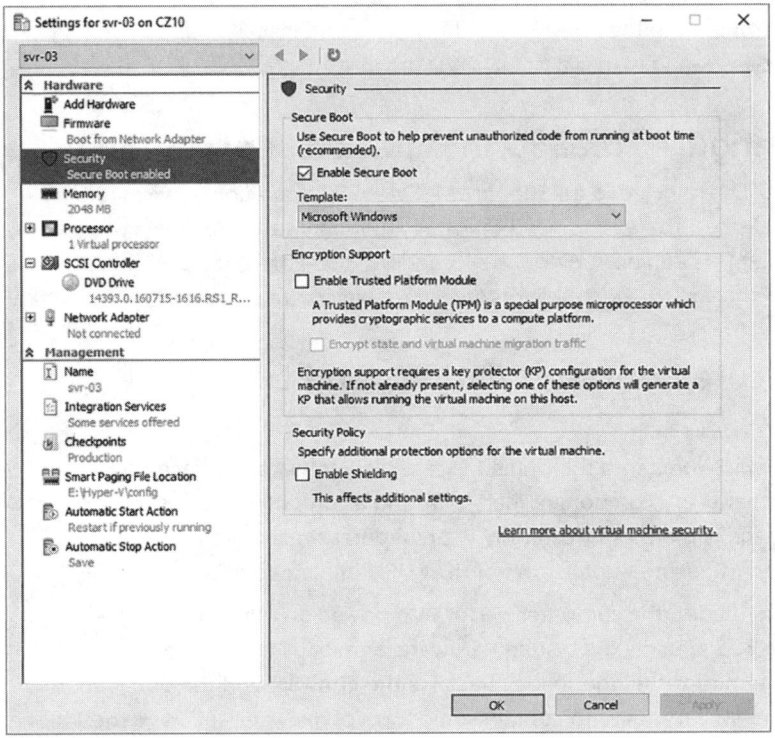

FIGURE 3-28 The Security page of a VM Settings dialog box

You can also disable Secure Boot using the Set-VMFirmware cmdlet in Windows PowerShell, as in the following example:

```
set-vmfirmware -vmname server1 -enablesecureboot off
```

Linux and Secure Boot

When you install a Linux distribution in a Generation 2 VM, the problem described earlier happens when Secure Boot is enabled. UEFI has no certificates for non-Windows operating systems by default, so it cannot run the Linux bootloader and the system keeps trying to boot from the network, as shown in Figure 3-29.

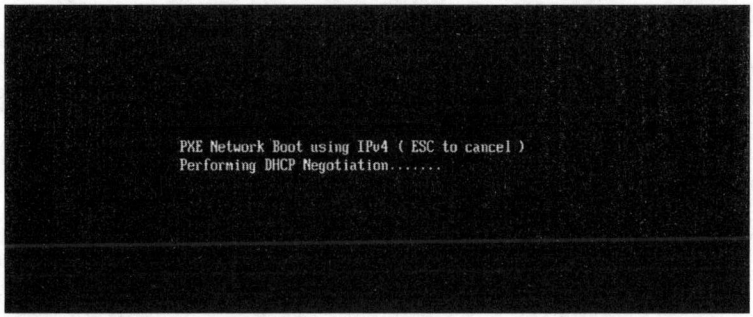

FIGURE 3-29 Secure Boot failure

One of the ways in which certain Linux distributions are supported by Microsoft is the inclusion of certificates for their bootloaders in Windows Server 2016 Hyper-V. To access those certificates and enable the VM to boot into Linux, you must change the Secure Boot template on the Security page in the Settings dialog box. By default, the Microsoft Windows template is selected. The certificates for the Linux operating systems are in the Microsoft UEFI Certificate Authority template, as shown in Figure 3-30.

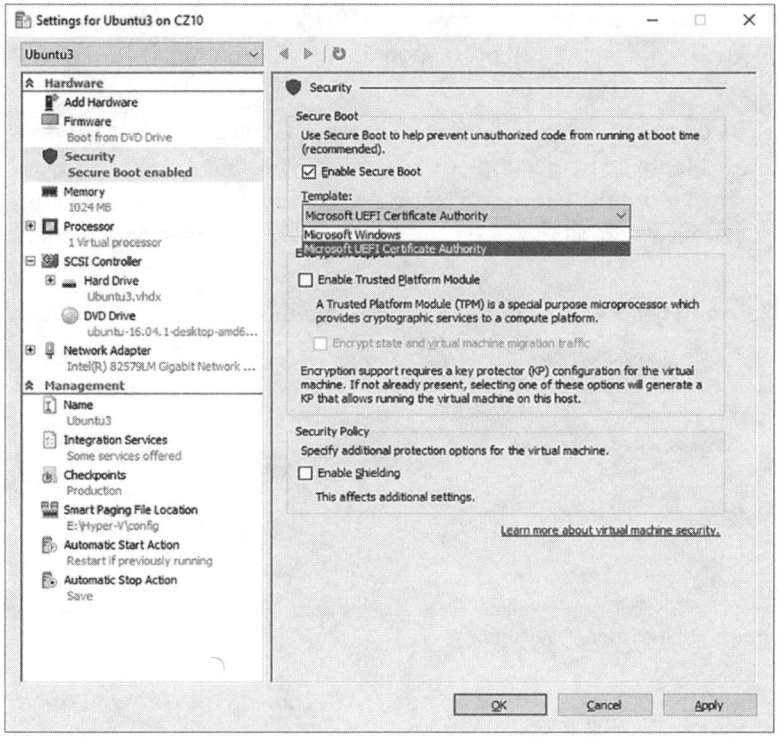

FIGURE 3-30 Secure Boot templates on the Security page of a VM Settings dialog box

To change the template setting using the Set-VMFirmware cmdlet, use a command like the following:

```
set-vmfirmware -vmname server1 -secureboottemplate microsoftueficertificate authority
```

Move and convert VMs from previous versions of Hyper-V to Windows Server 2016 Hyper-V

Each version of Hyper-V creates virtual machines of a specific version. The version indicates the features that are available on that VM. The VMs created in Windows Server 2016 are version 8.0. If you have upgraded a Hyper-V server to Windows Server 2016 from a previous version, you should also consider upgrading your virtual machines as well.

In previous versions of Windows, upgrading the operating system caused the VMs to be upgraded as well. In Windows Server 2016 (and Windows 10), this is not the case, because these versions of Hyper-V enable you to move VMs to servers running different versions of Windows.

For example, if you have virtual machines you created in Windows Server 2012 R2 Hyper-V, you can import them into a Windows Server 2016 Hyper-V, and they run perfectly well. However, if you want to take advantage of the latest Hyper-V features, such as adding a network adapter or memory to a running VM, you must upgrade the VM from version 5.0 (the Windows Server 2012 R2 version) to version 8.0.

Unfortunately, once you upgrade the VM, you can no longer run it on a Windows Server 2012 R2 server. Therefore, VMs are no longer upgrade automatically with the operating system. If you might ever have to move the VM back to the old server, you should not upgrade it. If you intend to run it exclusively on Windows Server 2016 Hyper-V, go ahead and upgrade it.

Each VM Summary tab in Hyper-V Manager displays its Configuration Version, as shown in Figure 3-31.

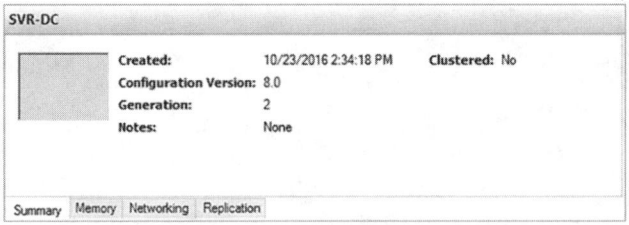

FIGURE 3-31 Summary tab of a VM in Hyper-V Manager

You can also display the versions of all the VMs on a server by running the Get-VM PowerShell cmdlet with the asterisk (*) wildcard character, as shown in Figure 3-32.

```
PS C:\WINDOWS\system32> get-vm

Name      State CPUUsage(%) MemoryAssigned(M) Uptime   Status             Version
----      ----- ----------- ----------------- ------   ------             -------
SVR-01    Off   0           0                 00:00:00 Operating normally 8.0
freebsd1  Off   0           0                 00:00:00 Operating normally 8.0
temptest1 Off   0           0                 00:00:00 Operating normally 5.0
CentOS1   Off   0           0                 00:00:00 Operating normally 8.0
svr-02    Off   0           0                 00:00:00 Operating normally 8.0
Ubuntu3   Off   0           0                 00:00:00 Operating normally 8.0
wsvr-01   Off   0           0                 00:00:00 Operating normally 8.0
svr-03    Off   0           0                 00:00:00 Operating normally 8.0
Ununtu2   Off   0           0                 00:00:00 Operating normally 8.0
SVR-DC    Off   0           0                 00:00:00 Operating normally 8.0

PS C:\WINDOWS\system32> _
```

FIGURE 3-32 Output of the Get-VM cmdlet

To move a VM to another server, you can export it in the old one and import it into the new one. To list the VM versions supported on a server, run the Get-VMHostSupportedVersion cmdlet, as shown in Figure 3-33.

```
PS C:\WINDOWS\system32> get-vmhostsupportedversion

Name                                                    Version IsDefault
----                                                    ------- ---------
Microsoft Windows 8.1/Server 2012 R2                    5.0     False
Microsoft Windows 10 1507/Server 2016 Technical Preview 3 6.2     False
Microsoft Windows 10 1511/Server 2016 Technical Preview 4 7.0     False
Microsoft Windows Server 2016 Technical Preview 5       7.1     False
Microsoft Windows 10 Anniversary Update/Server 2016     8.0     True
Prerelease                                              254.0   False
Experimental                                            255.0   False

PS C:\WINDOWS\system32> _
```

FIGURE 3-33 Output of the Get-VMHostSupportedVersion cmdlet

Then, to upgrade the VM to the version used by the new server, select Upgrade Configuration in the Actions pane, and confirm your action. The version in the Summary tab changes and the new server's features are now available in the VM.

You can also upgrade the VM by using the Update-VMVersion PowerShell cmdlet, as in the following example:

```
update-vmversion -vm server1
```

You can also specify multiple VM names on this command line, to upgrade multiple VMs using a single command.

Export and import VMs

The export and import functions in Hyper-V are a means of moving a virtual machine to a different server or creating a copy of a VM on the same server. When you export a VM, you specify the name of a folder where the system creates a copy of all the files of the VM, including its configuration files, virtual hard disks, and even checkpoints. You can then import the VM into the same or another server.

To export a VM, you select Export in the Actions pane, to display the Export Virtual Machine dialog box, as shown in Figure 3-34. Once you specify a location and click Export, the system begins to copy the files to a subfolder named for the VM. You can export a VM while it is running or stopped.

FIGURE 3-34 The Export Virtual Machine dialog box

To export a VM with Windows PowerShell, you use the Export-VM cmdlet, as in the following example:

```
export-vm -name server1 -path c\export
```

The only indication in Hyper-V Manager that the export is ongoing is that the Actions pane has a Cancel Exporting item in it. Once the export is completed, this item is replaced by the Export item again. At this point, you can copy the export folder to another server, or import it to the same server to make a copy of the VM.

Importing VMs using Hyper-V Manager

To import an exported VM into a Hyper-V server using Hyper-V Manager, use the following procedure:

1. In Hyper-V Manager, in the Actions pane, select Import Virtual Machine. The Import Virtual Machine Wizard appears.
2. On the Locate Folder page, type or browse to the folder containing the exported files.
3. On the Select Virtual Machine page, select the VM to import.
4. On the Choose Import Type page, shown in Figure 3-35, select one of the following options:
   - **Register The Virtual Machine In Place** Leaves the exported files where they are and registers the VM in the Hyper-V server, using the same ID as the VM from which they were exported. If the VM was exported from the same server, you cannot run both at the same time.
   - **Restore The Virtual Machine** Copies the exported files, either to the default locations on the server or to different locations that you specify, and registers the VM in the Hyper-V server, using the same ID as the VM from which they were exported. If the VM was exported from the same server, you cannot run both at the same time. Once the import is complete, you can delete the exported files or import them again.
   - **Copy The Virtual Machine** Copies the exported files, either to the default locations on the server or to different locations that you specify, and registers the VM in the Hyper-V server with a new ID. This enables you to create a copy of an existing VM on the same server and run it together with the original.

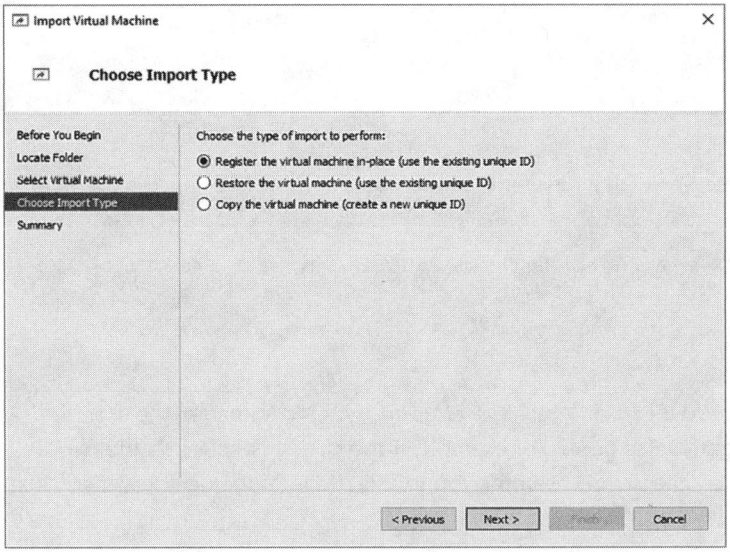

FIGURE 3-35 The Choose Import Type page of the Import Virtual Machine Wizard

5. If you choose either the Restore or Copy option, a Choose Folders For Virtual Machine Files page appears, on which you can specify different locations for the configuration, checkpoint, and Smart Paging files.
6. If you choose either the Restore or Copy option, a Choose Folders To Store Virtual Hard Disks page appears, on which you can specify an alternate location for the VHD files of the virtual machine. If you are importing a VM from the same server, you must specify a different folder, because VHD files with the same names already exist.
7. Click Finish to begin the import process.

Importing VMs using Windows PowerShell

To import a VM with Windows PowerShell, you use the Import-VM cmdlet. To import a VM using the Register option, in which the exported files are not copied, you use a command like the following. Note that, for this cmdlet, you must type the entire path to the VM configuration file:

```
import-vm -path c:\export\server1\virtualmachines\2b197d10-4dbe-4ea9-a54e-cc0bb0f12d09.
vcmx
```

To import a VM using the Restore option, you add the Copy parameter, which causes the cmdlet to copy the exported files to the new server's default folders, as follows.

```
import-vm -path c:\export\server1\virtualmachines\2b197d10-4dbe-4ea9-a54e-cc0bb0f12d09.
vcmx -copy
```

To specify different locations for the copied files, you can add the following parameters to the command line:

- VirtualMachinePath
- VhdDestinationPath
- SnapshotFilePath
- SmartPagingFilePath

To create a new copy of a VM with a different ID, you add the GenerateNewId parameter, as in the following:

```
import-vm -path c:\export\server1\virtualmachines\2b197d10-4dbe-4ea9-a54e-cc0bb0f12d09.
vcmx -copy -generatenewid
```

Handling conflicts

When you are importing a VM into a different server using Hyper-V Manager, the wizard prompts you if any incompatibilities occur. For example, if the virtual switches on the two servers have different names, the wizard prompts you to select one of the new server's virtual switches.

If an incompatibility occurs during a VM import using the Import-VM cmdlet, an error occurs and the command is not completed. You must then use the Compare-VM cmdlet with the same parameters to generate a report that specifies the incompatibility. Depending on the nature of the problem, you then use other cmdlets to rectify the situation. For the virtual switch incompatibility described here, you would use the Disconnect-VMNetwork Adapter cmdlet to remove the switch assignment before reattempting the import.

Implement Discrete Device Assignment (DDA)

Hyper-V has long had the ability to create pass-through disks, in which you assign a physical disk in the Hyper-V host to a guest virtual machine. The VM accesses the disk directly, without using a VHD. *Discrete Device Assignment (DDA)* is a similar concept, except that it enables you to pass any PCI Express device through to a VM.

You can, for example, pass a graphics processing unit (GPU) through to a VM with DDA, providing the VM with graphics performance that was previously impossible. You can also pass a wireless network adapter through to a VM, providing the virtual machine with WiFi capability.

DDA is implemented strictly through PowerShell, presumably to keep all but advanced administrators from playing with it. Any sort of pass-through arrangement between the host server and a guest operating sytem is an inherent security risk. An attack to the guest can use that pass-through conduit to get to the host, possibly bringing down the entire server with an error on the PCI Express bus.

From a high-level perspective, the steps involved in passing through a device using DDA are as follows:

1. Identify the device to be passed.
2. Disable the device on the host.

3. Dismount the device on the host.
4. Attach the device to the virtual machine.

If you think this makes the process look easy, think again. Here are the cmdlets you use to implement each of these steps:

1. The Get-PnpDevice -PresentOnly command generates a long list of the devices that Plug and Play has installed on the computer and displays information about them. By selecting one device and formatting the output of the cmdlet, you can determine the Instance ID of the device, a long string that you need for the next step. The instance ID can also be found in Device Manager on the Details tab, under the name Device Instance Path.
2. The Disable-PnpDevice -InstanceID command disables the device by removing the installed drivers on the host.
3. The Dismount-VmHostAssignableDevice -LocationPath command removes the device from the control of the host. To obtain a value for the LocationPath parameter, you use the Get-PnpDeviceProperty cmdlet, for which you must supply KeyName and InstanceID values. The location path is also available in Device Manager.
4. The Add-VMAssignableDevice -VM -LocationPath cmdlet attaches the device to a specific virtual machine.

Before this last command completes successfully, you must configure the following settings in the virtual machine Settings dialog box:

- The Automatic Stop Action setting must be set to Turn Off The Virtual Machine.
- The VM can use dynamic memory, but the RAM and Minimum RAM settings must be equal.

Finally, and perhaps most important, there are many low-level requirements that the host server BIOS/UEFI and the proposed device must meet. Some of these requirements are visible in software and some are not. The Dismount-VmHostAssignableDevice cmdlet supports a Force parameter that enables it to ignore the Access Control Services (ACS) checks that prevent PCI Express traffic from going to the wrong places. This parameter should only be used with extreme caution.

Skill 3.3: Configure Hyper-V storage

This section covers the various features and mechanisms that Windows Server 2016 uses to enhance the storage subsystem for its virtual machines.

This section covers how to:

- Create VHDs and VHDX files using Hyper-V Manager
- Create shared VHDX files
- Configure differencing disks
- Modify virtual hard disks
- Configure pass-through disks
- Resize a virtual hard disk
- Manage checkpoints
- Implement production checkpoints
- Implement a virtual Fibre Channel adapter
- Configure storage Quality of Service (QoS)

Create VHDs and VHDX files using Hyper-V Manager

When you create a new Generation 1 virtual machine in Hyper-V Manager, the New Virtual Machine Wizard creates a virtual storage subsystem that consists of two IDE (Integrated Drive Electronics) controllers and one SCSI (Small Computer Systems Interface) controller, as shown in Figure 3-36.

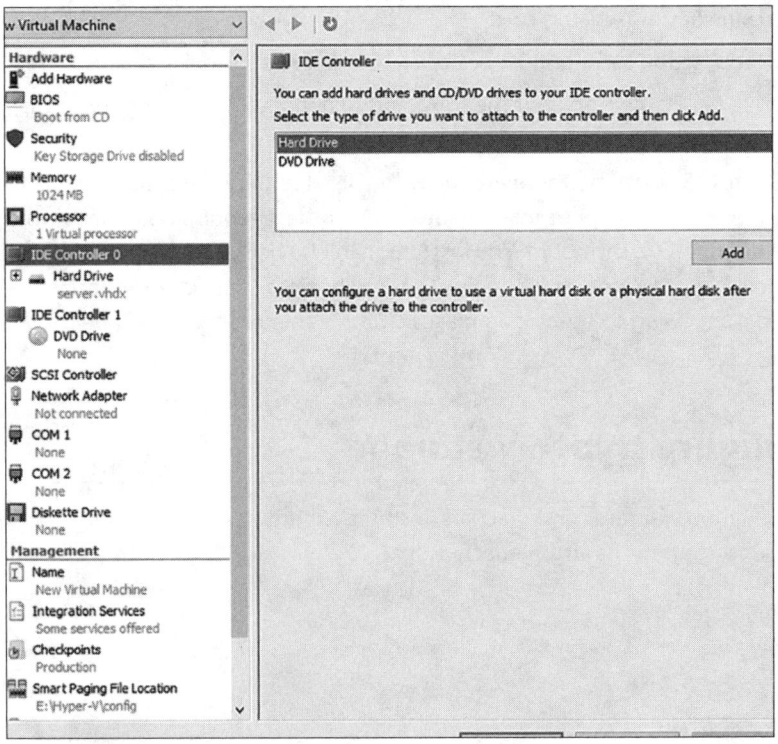

FIGURE 3-36 The default VM drive controller configuration

The IDE controllers host the virtual machine system drive and its DVD drive. As with their physical equivalents, each IDE controller can host two devices, so you can create two additional virtual drives and add them to the system. The SCSI controller is unpopulated; you can create additional disks and add them to that controller to provide the VM with more storage.

In a Generation 2 VM, there is no IDE controller, so the system and DVD drives are both connected to the default SCSI controller. In a VM of either generation, you can also create additional SCSI controllers and add drives to them. By creating multiple drives and controllers, Hyper-V makes it possible to construct virtual storage subsystems that emulate almost any physical storage solution you might devise.

Understanding virtual disk formats

Windows Server 2016 Hyper-V supports the original VHD disk image file and the new VHDX format. The original VHD format is limited to a maximum size of 2 terabytes (TB) and is compatible with all versions of Hyper-V. Windows Server 2012 R2 introduced an updated version of the format, which uses a VHDX filename extension. VHDX image files can be as large as 64 TB, and they also support 4 KB logical sector sizes, to provide compatibility with 4 KB native physical drives. VHDX files can also use larger block sizes (up to 256 MB), which enable you to fine tune the performance level of a virtual storage subsystem to accommodate specific applications and data file types.

However, VHDX files are not backwards compatible and can be read only by the Hyper-V servers in Windows Server 2012 R2 or later and Windows 8.1 or later. If migrating your virtual machines from Windows Server 2016 to an older Hyper-V version is a possibility, you should continue to use the VHD file format.

Creating a Virtual Disk with a VM

Windows Server 2016 Hyper-V provides several ways to create virtual disk files. You can create them as part of a new virtual machine, or create them later and add them to a VM. The graphical interface in Hyper-V Manager provides access to most of the VHD parameters, but the Windows PowerShell cmdlets included in Windows Server 2016 provide the most granular control over the disk image format.

When you create a new VM in Hyper-V Manager, the New Virtual Machine Wizard includes a Connect Virtual Hard Disk page, as shown in Figure 3-37, with which you can add a single disk to your new VM. The options for this disk are limited and consist of the following:

- **Create A Virtual Hard Disk** Enables you to specify the name, location, and size for a new virtual hard disk, but this option can only create a dynamically expanding disk using the VHDX format.
- **Use An Existing Virtual Hard Disk** Enables you to specify the location of an existing VHD or VHDX disk, which the VM uses as its system disk.
- **Attach A Virtual Hard Disk Later** Prevents the wizard from adding any virtual hard disks to the VM configuration. You must manually add a disk later, before you can start the virtual machine.

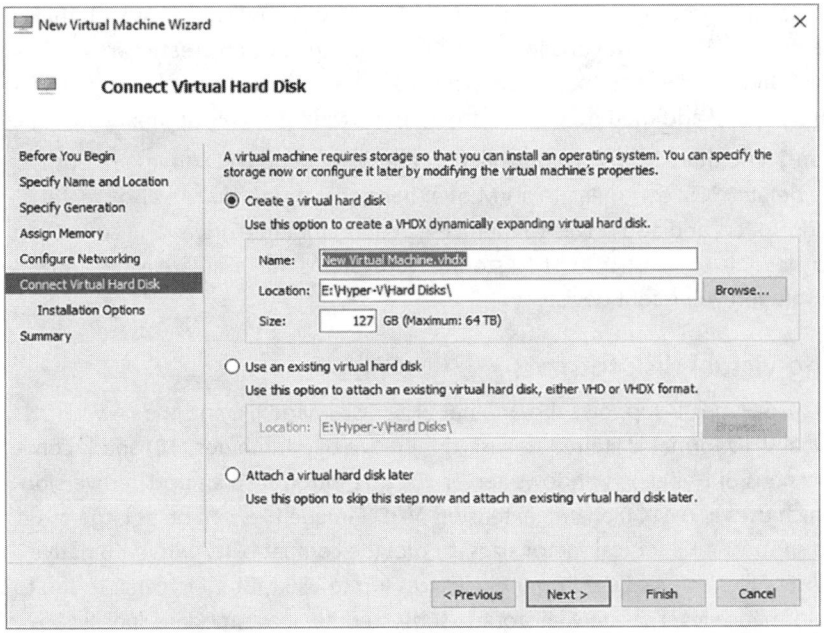

FIGURE 3-37 The Connect Virtual Hard Disk page of the New Virtual Machine Wizard

The object of this wizard page is to create the disk on which you install the guest operating system of the virtual machine, or select an existing disk on which an operating system is already installed. The disk the wizard creates is always a dynamically expanding one, connected to IDE Controller 0 on a Generation 1 VM or the SCSI Controller on a Generation 2 VM. To create a disk using any settings other than the defaults, you must select Attach A Virtual Hard Disk Later, create a new VHD or VHDX using the New Virtual Hard Disk Wizard, and then add the disk to the virtual machine.

NOTE **DOWNLOADING VHDS**

It is a common practice for Microsoft to release evaluation copies of its products as preinstalled VHD files, as an alternative to the traditional installable disk images. After downloading one of these files, you can create a VM on a Hyper-V server and select the Use An Existing Virtual Hard Disk option to mount the VHD as its system drive.

Creating a new virtual disk in Hyper-V Manager

You can create a virtual hard disk file at any time, without adding it to a virtual machine, by using the New Virtual Hard Disk Wizard in Hyper-V Manager.

To create a new virtual disk, use the following procedure.

1. Log on to the server running Windows Server 2016 using an account with administrative privileges.

2. Launch Hyper-V Manager and, in the left pane, select a Hyper-V server.
3. From the Action menu, select New | Hard Disk. The New Virtual Hard Disk Wizard appears.
4. On the Choose Disk Format page, shown in Figure 3-38, select one of the following disk format options:
   - **VHD** Creates an image no larger than 2 TB, using the highly compatible VHD format
   - **VHDX** Creates an image up to 64 TB in size, using the new VHDX format
   - **VHD Set** Creates an image for disk sharing among guest operating systems that supports features like online disk resizing and host-based backups

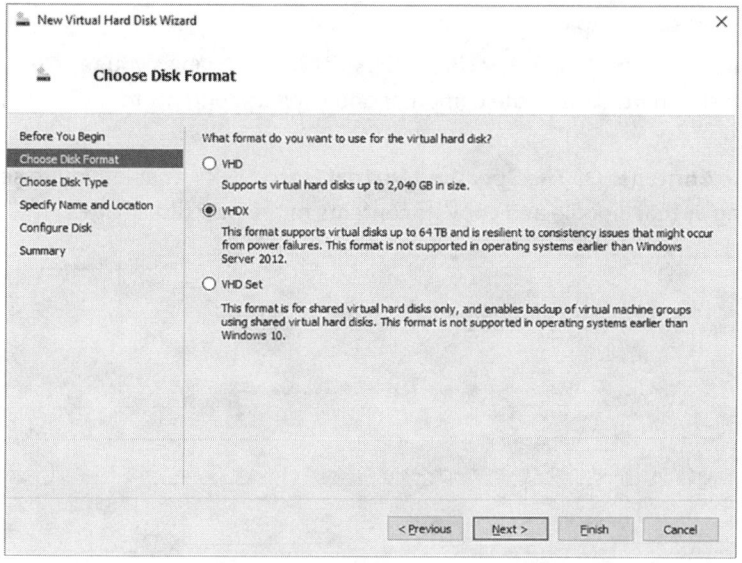

FIGURE 3-38 The Choose Disk Format page of the New Virtual Hard Disk Wizard

5. On the Choose Disk Type page, select one of the following disk type options:
   - **Fixed Size** The image file is a specified size, in which all the disk space required to create the image is allocated during its creation. Fixed disk images can be considered wasteful in terms of storage, because they can contain large amounts of empty space, but they are also efficient from a performance standpoint, because there is no overhead due to dynamic expansion and less fragmentation of the file.
   - **Dynamically Expanding** The image file has a specified maximum size, which starts out small and expands as needed to accommodate the data the system writes to it. Dynamically expanding disks are initially conservative of disk space, but their

continual growth can cause them to be highly fragmented, negatively affecting performance.

- **Differencing** The image file, called a child, is associated with a specific parent image. The system writes all changes made to the data on the parent image file to the child image, to facilitate a rollback later.

6. On the Specify Name And Location page, specify a filename for the disk image in the Name text box and, if desired, specify a location for the file other than the server default.
7. On the Configure Disk page, shown in Figure 3-39, select and configure one of the following options:
   - **Create A New Blank Virtual Hard Disk** Specifies the size (or the maximum size) of the disk image file to create.
   - **Copy The Contents Of The Specified Physical Disk** Enables you to select one of the physical hard disks in the computer and copy its contents to the new disk image.
   - **Copy The Contents Of The Specified Virtual Hard Disk** Enables you to select an existing virtual disk file and copy its contents to the new disk image.

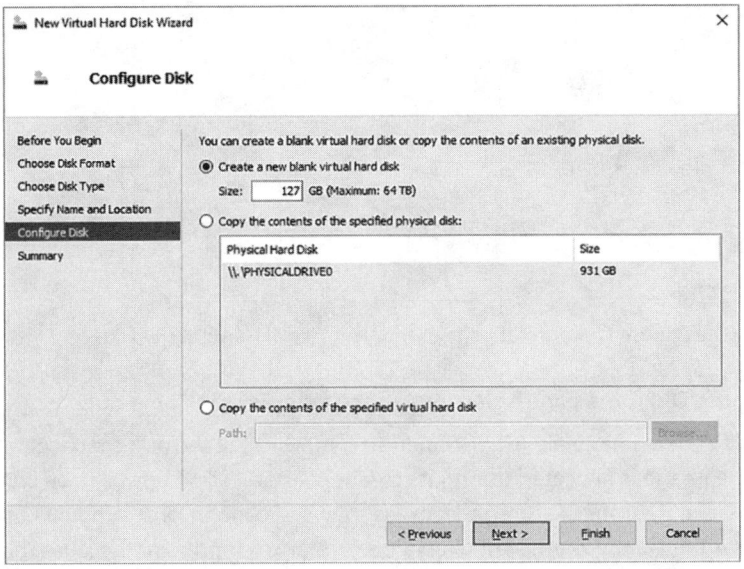

FIGURE 3-39 The Configure Disk page of the New Virtual Hard Disk Wizard

8. On the Completing The New Virtual Hard Disk Wizard page, click Finish.

The wizard creates the new image disk and saves it to the specified location.

Creating a new virtual disk in Windows PowerShell

You can create new virtual hard disk files using Windows PowerShell, with more control than is available through the graphical interface. To create a new disk image, you use the New-VHD cmdlet with the following basic syntax:

```
new-vhd -path c:\filename.vhd|c:\filename.vhdx -fixed|-dynamic|-differencing -sizebytes
size [-blocksizebytes blocksize] [-logicalsectorsizebytes 512|4096]
```

When you use the cmdlet to create a virtual disk, the extension you specify for the filename determines the format (VHD or VHDX), and you can specify the block size and the logical sector size for the image, which you cannot do in the GUI. For example, the following command creates a 500 GB fixed VHDX image file with a logical sector size of 4 KB:

```
new-vhd -path c:\diskfile.vhdx -fixed -sizebytes 500gb -logicalsectorsizebytes 4096
```

Adding virtual disks to virtual machines

Creating virtual disk image files as a separate process enables you to exercise more control over their capabilities. After creating the VHD or VHDX files, you can add them to a virtual machine.

To add a hard disk drive to a physical computer, you must connect it to a controller, and the same is true with a virtual machine in Hyper-V. When you open the Settings dialog box for a Generation 1 virtual machine in its default configuration, you see three controllers, labeled IDE Controller 0, IDE Controller 1, and SCSI Controller. Each of the IDE controllers can support two devices, and the default virtual machine configuration uses one channel on IDE Controller 0 for the system hard disk and one channel on IDE Controller 1 for the system's DVD drive.

If you did not create a virtual disk as part of the new Virtual Machine Wizard (that is, if you chose the Attach A Virtual Hard Disk Later option), you must add a hard disk image to IDE Controller 0 to use as a system drive. A Generation 1 virtual machine cannot boot from the SCSI controller.

To add an existing virtual system drive to a virtual machine, use the following procedure.

1. In Hyper-V Manager, select a virtual machine and open its Settings dialog box.
2. Select IDE Controller 0 and, on the IDE Controller page, select Hard Drive, and click Add.
3. On the Hard Drive page, shown in Figure 3-40, in the Controller and Location drop-down lists, select the IDE controller and the channel you want to use for the hard disk.

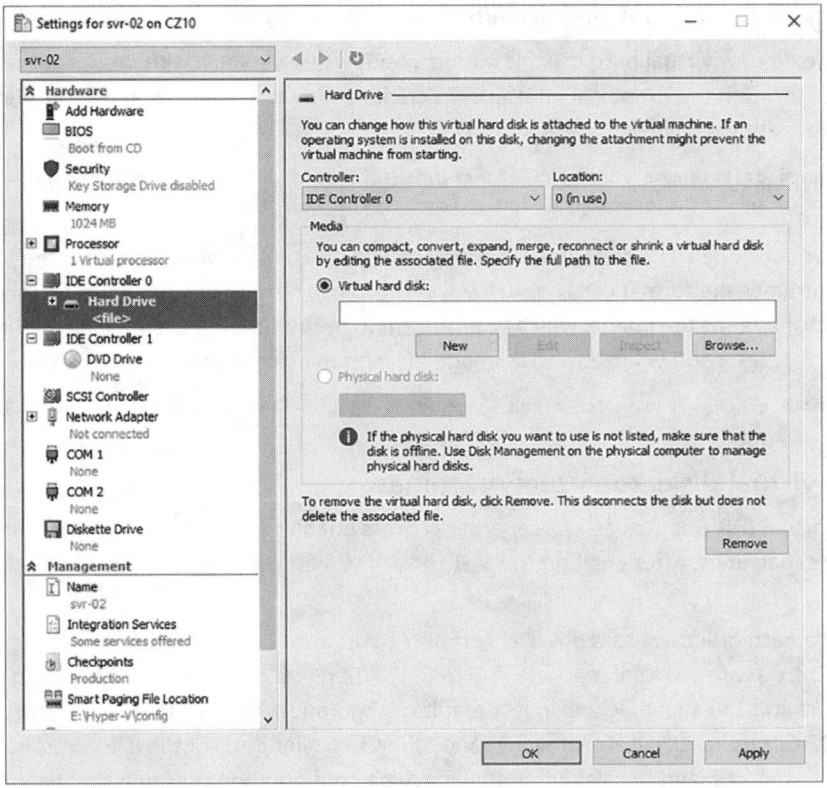

FIGURE 3-40 The Hard Drive page in a Generation 1 VM Settings dialog box

4. With the Virtual Hard Disk option selected, click Browse, and select the disk image file you want to add.
5. Click OK to close the Settings dialog box.

Although you cannot use a SCSI drive as the system disk in a Generation 1 virtual machine, you can add virtual data disks to the SCSI controller, and you must do so on a Generation 2 VM. The procedure is all but identical to that of a Generation 1 VM.

Unlike the IDE Controllers, which support only two devices each, a SCSI connector in Hyper-V can support up to 64 drives. You can also add multiple SCSI controllers to a virtual machine, providing almost unlimited scalability for your virtual storage subsystem.

Create shared VHDX files

Windows Server 2016 Hyper-V can create shared virtual disk files, for use in Hyper-V guest failover clusters. A failover cluster is a group of computers, physical or virtual, that all run the same application. If one of the computers should fail, the others are there to take up the slack. For a failover cluster to function, the computers must access the same data, which means the store hardware—again, physical or virtual—must be shared.

For example, you can create a failover cluster with multiple computers running Microsoft SQL Server. Each computer, called a node, runs its own copy of the application, but all of the nodes must be able to access the same copy of the database. By storing the database on a shared virtual disk, you can configure each of the computers in the cluster to access it, as shown in Figure 3-41.

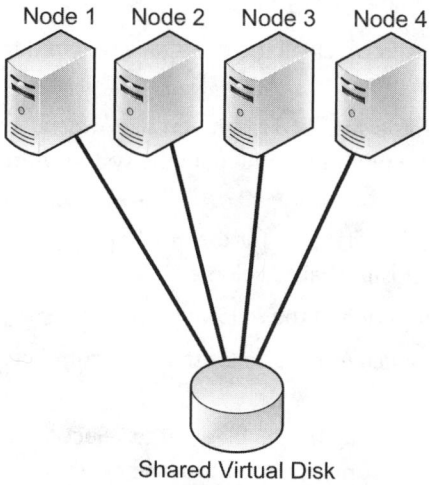

FIGURE 3-41 Failover cluster with a shared virtual disk

Before the release of Windows Server 2012 R2, the only way to create shared storage for clustered virtual machines was to use physical storage hardware. Windows Server 2012 R2 introduced a virtual solution by making it possible to create shared VHDX files. That capability still exists in Windows Server 2016, so that your existing storage configurations remain functional after an upgrade. There is now also a second option, called a *VHD set*.

Shared VHDX files have some shortcomings. You cannot resize them or migrate them, nor can you back up or replicate them from the host server. You can do all these things with VHD sets. Their only drawback is that only Windows Server 2016 can access them.

To create a shared VHDX file or VHD set with Hyper-V Manager, use the following procedure.

1. In Hyper-V Manager, open the Settings dialog box for the VM in which you want to create the shared disk.
2. Select the SCSI Controller and, on the SCSI Controller page, select Shared Drive, and click Add.
3. On the Shared Drive page, click New to launch the New Virtual Hard Disk Wizard.
4. On the Choose Disk Format page, select one of the following options:
   - **VHDX** Creates a single VHDX file that is accessible by multiple virtual machines running Windows Server 2016 or Windows Server 2012 R2.

- **VHD Set** Creates a 260 MB VHDS file and an AVHDX backing storage file, which will contain the actual stored data. The VHDS file contains metadata used to coordinate the disk activities of the cluster nodes. The AVHDX file is just a standard VHDX file, which has been placed under the control of the hypervisor. VHD sets are only accessible by Windows Server 2016.

5. On the Choose Disk Type page, select one of the following options. Both VHDX files and VHD Sets can use either option:
   - **Fixed size** The image file is a specified size, in which all the disk space required to create the image is allocated during its creation.
   - **Dynamically expanding** The image file has a specified maximum size, which starts out small and expands as needed to accommodate the data the system writes to it.
6. On the Specify Name And Location page, specify a filename for the disk image in the Name text box and a location for the file on a cluster shared volume (CSV).
7. On the Configure Disk page, select and configure one of the following options:
   - **Create A New Blank Virtual Hard Disk** Specifies the size (or the maximum size) of the disk image file to create.
   - **Copy The Contents Of The Specified Physical Disk** Enables you to select one of the physical hard disks in the computer and copy its contents to the new disk image.
   - **Copy The Contents Of The Specified Virtual Hard Disk** Enables you to select an existing virtual disk file and copy its contents to the new disk image.
8. On the Completing the New Virtual Hard Disk Wizard page, click Finish. The wizard creates the new image disk and saves it to the specified location.
9. Click OK to close the Settings dialog box.

To create a VHD set in Windows PowerShell, you use the New-VHD cmdlet, just as you would to create any virtual disk file, except that you use VHDS for the extension of the file you are creating, as in the following example:

```
new-vhd -path c:\diskfile.vhds -dynamic -sizebytes 1tb
```

Configure differencing disks

A differencing disk enables you to preserve an existing virtual disk image file in its original state, while mounting it in an operating system and even modifying its contents. For example, when building a laboratory system, you can create a baseline by installing a clean copy of an operating system on a new virtual disk and configuring the environment to your needs. Then, you can create a new child differencing disk, using your baseline image as the parent. All subsequent changes you make to the system are written to the differencing disk, while the parent remains untouched. You can experiment freely on the system, knowing that you can revert to your baseline configuration by creating a new differencing disk.

You can create multiple differencing disks that point to the same parent image, enabling you to populate a lab network with as many virtual machines as you need, without having to repeatedly install the operating system and while saving on disk space. This can be particularly useful for software development efforts that require testing of subsequent product builds.

You can also create multiple generations of differencing disks, by creating a child of a child. In this case, all of the disks descending from the parent are essential to the disk's functionality.

When you create a differencing disk by using the New Virtual Hard Disk Wizard, selecting the Differencing option on the Choose Disk Type page causes the wizard's Configure Disk page to change, as shown in Figure 3-42. In the Location text box, you must specify the name of the file to use as the parent image.

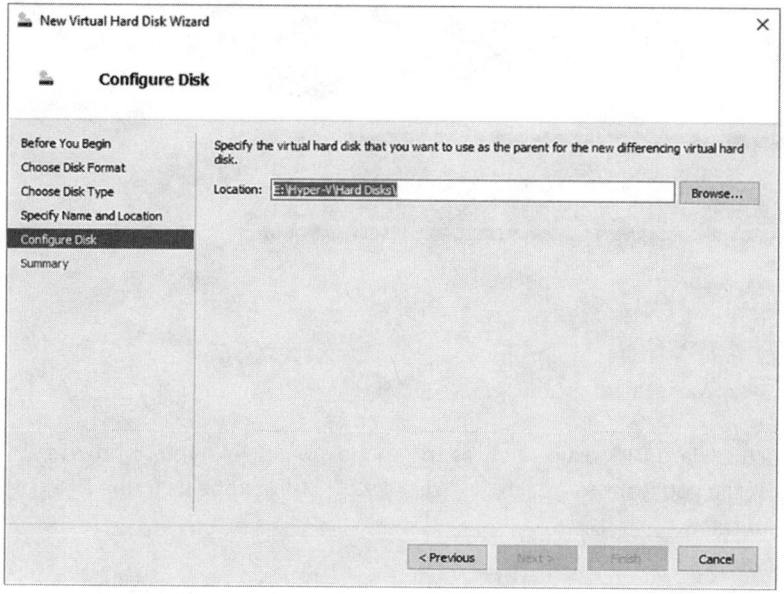

FIGURE 3-42 The Configure Disk page for the Differencing option in the New Virtual Hard Disk Wizard

To create a differencing disk using Windows PowerShell, you must run the New-VHD cmdlet with the Differencing parameter and the ParentPath parameter, specifying the location of the parent disk, as in the following example:

```
new-vhd -path c:\disks\diffdisk.vhdx -sizebytes 1tb -differencing -parentpath c:\disks\
parentdisk.vhdx
```

Modify virtual hard disks

Windows Server 2016 provides several ways for you to manage and manipulate virtual hard disk images without adding them to a virtual machine. For example, you can use the Disk Management snap-in or Windows PowerShell to mount a virtual disk in a computer's file system and access its contents, just as if it was a physical disk.

Mounting a VHD

To mount a virtual hard disk file using the Disk Management snap-in, use the following procedure.

1. From the Tools menu in the Server Manager console, select Computer Management.
2. In the left pane of the Computer Management console, select Disk Management.
3. In the Disk Management snap-in, as shown in Figure 3-43, from the Action menu, select Attach VHD.

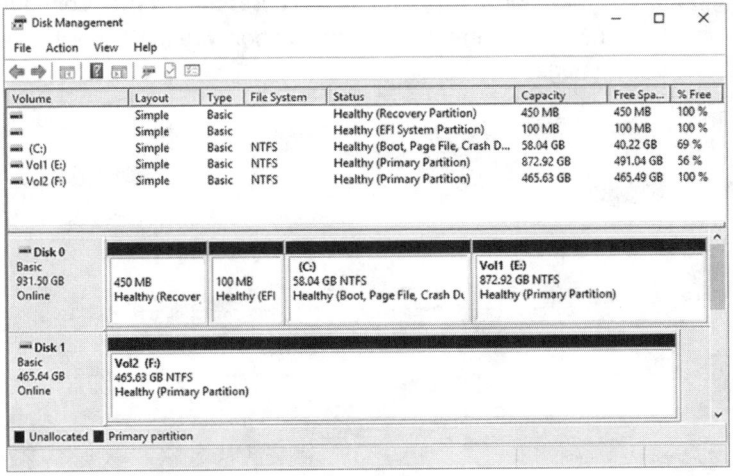

FIGURE 3-43 The Disk Management snap-in

4. In the Attach Virtual Hard Disk dialog box, as shown in Figure 3-44, type or browse to the image disk file you want to attach, and click OK. The disk appears in the Disk Management interface.

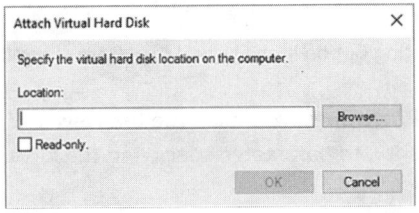

FIGURE 3-44 The Attach Virtual Hard Disk dialog box

5. Close the Computer Management console.

At this point, the contents of the virtual disk are mounted using a drive letter, and you can work with the contents using any standard tools, just as you would the files on a physical hard disk drive. To dismount the disk, saving any changes you have made back to the virtual disk file, you select Detach VHD from the Action menu, and specify the location of the original image file.

You can also mount and dismount a VHD or VHDX file by using the Mount-VHD and Dismount-VHD PowerShell cmdlets, as in the following examples:

```
mount-vhd -path c:\disks\server1.vhdx

dismount-vhd -path c:\disks\server1.vhdx
```

Installing roles and features offline

To install Windows roles and features on a running virtual machine, you can use the Install-WindowsFeature PowerShell cmdlet. However, you can also use this cmdlet to install roles and features to the VHD or VHDX image of a system disk while it is offline.

To install a Windows role or feature to an offline virtual disk, you add the Vhd parameter to the Install-WindowsFeature command, as in the following example:

```
install-windowsfeature -vhd c:\disks\server1.vhdx -name web-server
-includemanagementtools
```

Configure pass-through disks

The default Hyper-V behavior when creating a VM is to create a virtual hard disk. You also learned how to create VHD or VHDX files, to provide VMs with additional storage. However, it is also possible for VMs to access physical disks in the host server directly.

A *pass-through disk* is a type of virtual disk that points not to a file stored on a physical disk, but to a physical disk drive itself, installed on the host server. When you add a hard drive to any of the controllers in a virtual machine, you can select a physical hard disk, as opposed to a virtual one.

To add a physical hard disk to a virtual machine, however, the VM must have exclusive access to it. That is, you must first take the disk offline in the host operating system, by using the Disk Management snap-in, as shown in Figure 3-45, or the Set-Disk PowerShell cmdlet.

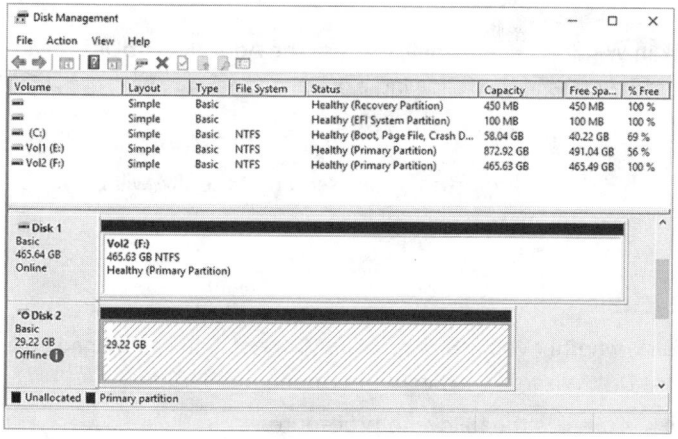

FIGURE 3-45 An offline disk in the Disk Management snap-in

To use the Set-Disk cmdlet to take a disk offline, you must first discover the number of the disk you want to modify by running the Get-Disk cmdlet. You then run Set-Disk using a command like the following:

```
set-disk -number 2 -isoffline $true
```

Once the disk is offline, the Physical Hard Disk option is enabled on the Hard Drive page of the Settings dialog box, as shown in Figure 3-46, and the disk is available for selection in the drop-down list.

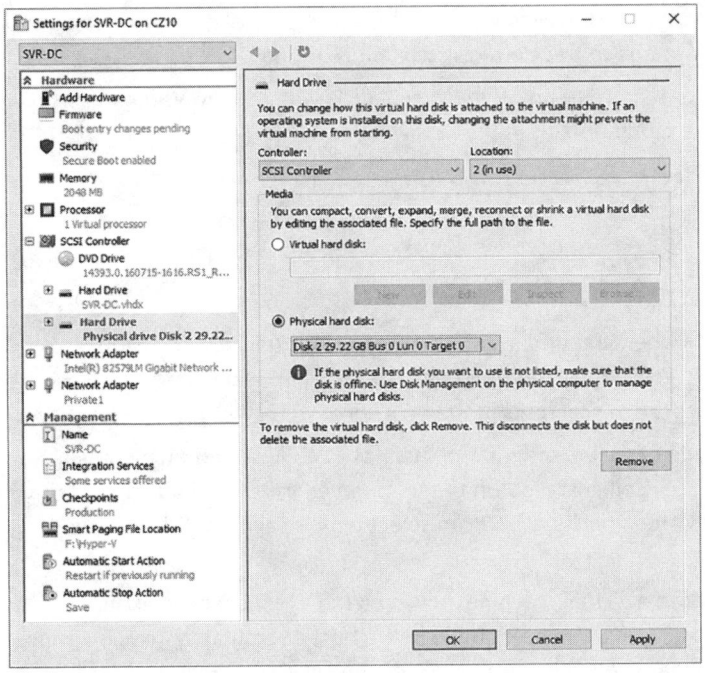

FIGURE 3-46 The Physical Hard Disk option in the Hard Drive page of a Settings dialog box

To create a pass-through disk in Windows PowerShell, you use the Add-VMHardDiskDrive cmdlet with the DiskNumber parameter, as in the following example:

```
add-vmharddiskdrive -vmname server1 -controllertype scsi -disknumber 2
```

When you create a pass-through disk, it is import to understand that the VM will be accessing the actual physical disk; it does not make a copy of it.

Resize a virtual hard disk

After you create a virtual hard disk, whether you attach it to a VM or not, you can manage its size by using the Edit Virtual Hard Disk Wizard in Hyper-V Manager.

To edit an existing VHD or VHDX file, use the following procedure.

1. In Hyper-V Manager, in the Actions pane, select Edit Disk to launch the Edit Virtual Hard Disk Wizard.
2. On the Locate Disk page, type or browse to the name of the VHD or VHDX file you want to open.
3. On the Choose Action page, shown in Figure 3-47, select one of the following functions. The functions that appear depend on the type of disk you have selected.
   - **Compact** Reduces the size of a dynamically expanding or differencing disk by deleting empty space, while leaving the disk's capacity unchanged.
   - **Convert** Creates a copy of the disk image file, enabling you to change the format (VHD or VHDX) or the type (fixed size or dynamically expanding) in the process.
   - **Expand** Increases the capacity of the disk by adding empty storage space to the image file.
   - **Shrink** Reduces the capacity of the disk by deleting empty storage space from the file. The Shrink option only appears when there is unpartitioned space available at the end of the virtual disk.
   - **Merge** Combines the data on a differencing disk with that on its parent disk, to form a single composite image file. The Merge option only appears when you select a differencing disk.

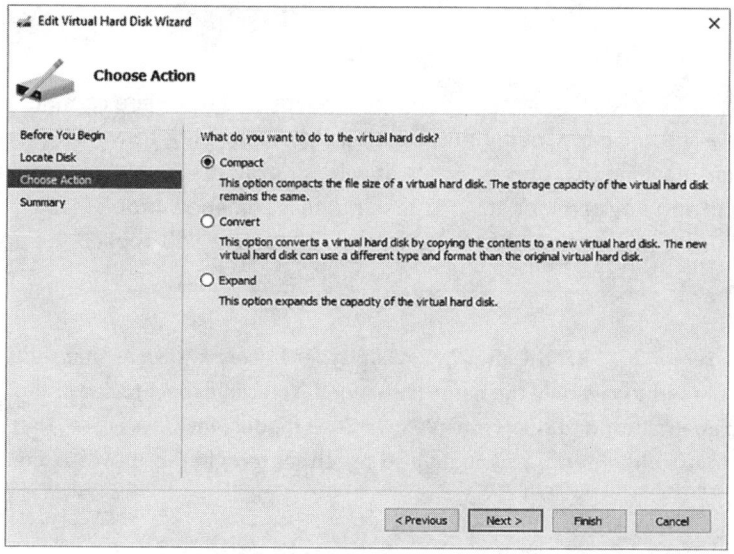

FIGURE 3-47 The Choose Action page in the Edit Virtual Hard Disk Wizard

4. Complete any new pages presented by the wizard based on your selection and click Finish.

You can also execute the functions of the Edit Virtual Hard Disk Wizard using Windows PowerShell cmdlets. To compact a virtual hard disk file (mounted as a read-only disk), you use the Optimize-VHD cmdlet, as in the following example:

```
optimize-vhd -path c:\disks\server1.vhdx -mode full
```

To convert a virtual hard disk file, you use the Convert-VHD cmdlet, as in the following examples that converts a fixed VHD file to a dynamic VHDX:

```
convert-vhd -path c:\disks\server1.vhd -destinationpath c:\disks\server1.vhdx -vhdtype
dynamic
```

To expand or shrink a virtual disk, you use the Resize-VHD cmdlet with the SizeBytes parameter, as in the following example. The same command can expand or shrink a disk, depending on its original size. To shrink a disk to is smallest possible size, you can add the ToMinimumSize parameter.

```
resize-vhd -path c:\disks\server1.vhdx -sizebytes 500gb
```

To merge a differencing disk into its parent disk, you use the Merge-VHD cmdlet, as in the following command. If there are multiple generations of child disks involved, merging the youngest child disk into the parent merges all of the intervening child disks as well.

```
merge-vhd -path c:\disks\child.vhdx -destionationpath c:\disks\parent.vhdx
```

Manage checkpoints

In Hyper-V, a *checkpoint* is a captured image of the state, data, and hardware configuration of a virtual machine at a specific moment in time. Creating checkpoints is a convenient way for you to revert a virtual machine to a previous state at will. For example, if you create a checkpoint just before applying a system update, and the update is somehow problematic, you can apply the checkpoint and return the VM to the state it was in before you applied the update.

EXAM TIP

Prior to Windows Server 2012 R2, the checkpoints in Hyper-V were known as snapshots. They function in the same way; only the name is changed. You can expect to see either term used in documentation, and the Hyper-V PowerShell module includes aliases that make it possible to use either term. You might also see either term in the 70-740 exam.

Creating a checkpoint

Creating a checkpoint is as simple as selecting a running virtual machine in Hyper-V Manager and selecting Checkpoint from the Actions pane or running the Checkpoint-VM PowerShell cmdlet with the name of the VM. The system creates a checkpoint file, with an AVHD or AVHDX extension, in the same folder as the virtual hard disk file, and adds the checkpoint to Hyper-V Manager display, as shown in Figure 3-48.

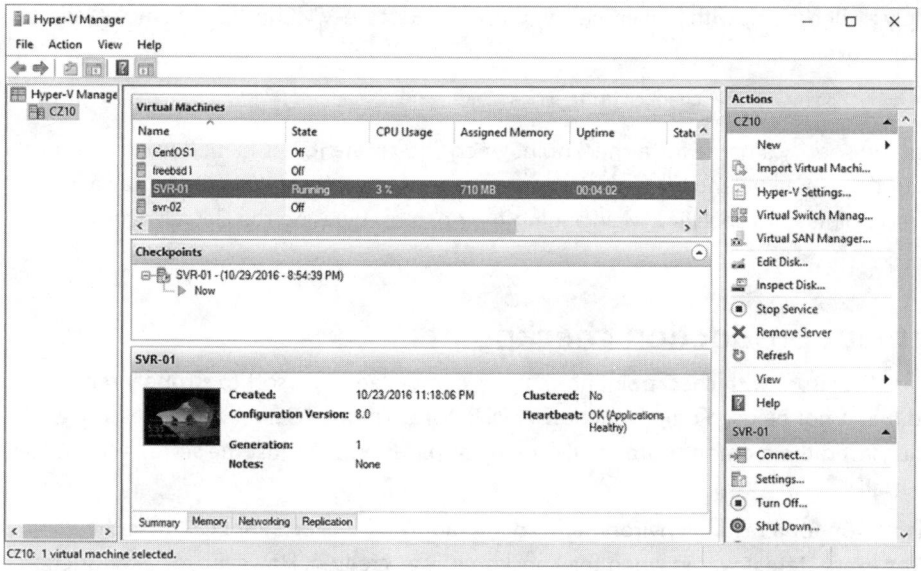

FIGURE 3-48 A checkpoint in Hyper-V Manager

Checkpointing is a useful tool for development and testing environments in Hyper-V, but they are not recommended for use in production environments, nor are they to be considered a replacement for backup software. Apart from consuming disk space, the presence of checkpoints can reduce the overall performance of a virtual machine's storage subsystem.

Applying a checkpoint

To apply a previously created checkpoint, returning the virtual machine to its previous state, you right-click the checkpoint in Hyper-V Manager and select Apply from the Actions menu to open the Apply Checkpoint dialog box, as shown in Figure 3-49.

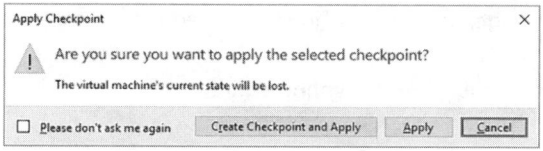

FIGURE 3-49 The Apply Checkpoint dialog box

In this dialog box, you can choose from the following options:

- **Apply** Applies the selected checkpoint, overwriting the current state of the VM.
- **Create Checkpoint And Apply** Creates a new checkpoint of the VM, to preserve its current state, and then applies the selected checkpoint.

To apply a checkpoint with PowerShell, you use the Restore-VMCheckpoint cmdlet, as in the following example.

```
restore-vmcheckpoint -name checkpoint1 -vmname server1
```

Unless you specify a name for a checkpoint when you create it, it is named using a combination of the VM name and the timestamp from the creation time. You can display a list of all the checkpoints for a specific VM, including their names, by using the Get-VMCheckpoint cmdlet.

Implement production checkpoints

There is another issue with checkpointing that has compelled Microsoft to strongly recommend that it not be used on production VMs. Before Windows Server 2016, creating a checkpoint saved the memory state of all running applications, not just the state of the virtual machine itself.

This is a boon for a testing environment, so that applying a checkpoint can take the VM back to the exact state it was in when the checkpoint was created. However, for a production VM to which clients are connected, such as a database or mail server, or one that replicates data to other systems, such as domain controller, restoring a previous memory state can interrupt ongoing processes.

For this reason, Windows Server 2016 Hyper-V includes *production checkpoints*, which use the Volume Shadow Copy Service in Windows, or File System Freeze in Linux, to create a snapshot of the data from a VM, without saving its memory state. The use of production checkpoints is now the default on all Windows Server 2016 VMs. The previous type of checkpoint, still available in Windows Server 2016, is now known as a *standard checkpoint*

To administrators, production checkpoints behave exactly like standard checkpoints. You can create them and apply them using the same tools and techniques.

To modify the default checkpointing settings for a VM, you can open its Settings dialog box in Hyper-V Manager to the Checkpoints page, as shown in Figure 3-50, and select the Standard Checkpoints option. You can also use the controls on this page to specify the location for the checkpoint files from the VM, and disable checkpointing entirely.

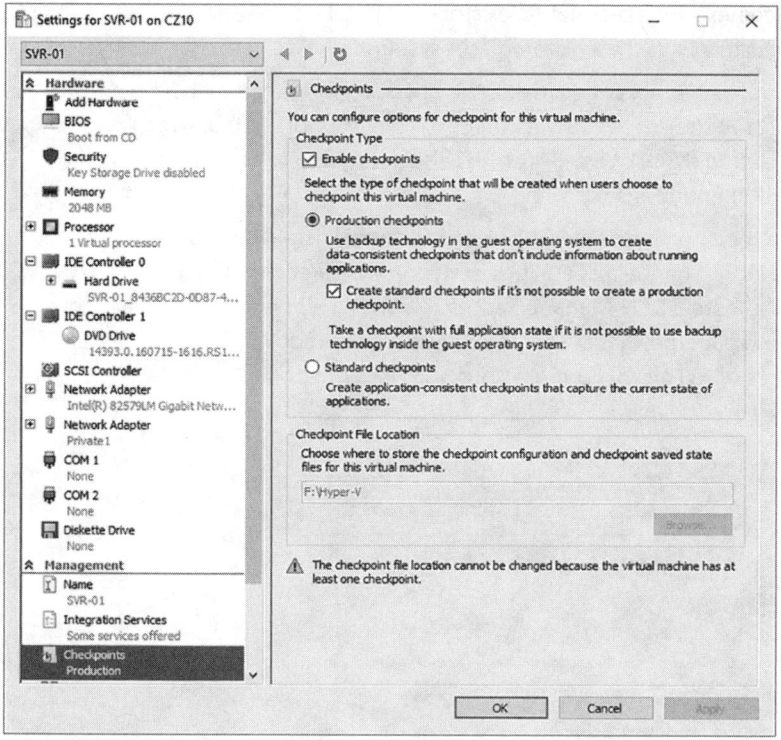

FIGURE 3-50 The Checkpoints page in a VM Settings dialog box

To modify the checkpointing defaults in PowerShell, you use the Set-VM cmdlet, as in the following example:

```
set-vm -name server1 -checkpointtype standard
```

In addition to Standard, the CheckpointType parameter supports the Production value, to return the setting to its default; and the Disabled value, to disable all checkpointing for the VM. You can also use the SnapshotFileLocation parameter to specify where the system should create its checkpoint files.

Implement a virtual fibre channel adapter

In the past, the specialized networking technologies used to build Fibre Channel storage area networks (SANs) made it difficult to use them with virtualized servers. However, since the Windows Server 2012 implementation, Hyper-V has supported the creation of virtual Fibre Channel adapters.

A Hyper-V Fibre Channel adapter is essentially a pass-through device that enables a virtual machine to access a physical Fibre Channel adapter installed in the computer, and through that, the external storage resources connected to the SAN. With this capability, applications running on virtual machines can access data files stored on SAN devices, and you can use VMs to create server clusters with shared storage subsystems.

To support virtual Fibre Channel connectivity, the physical Fibre Channel host bus adapter(s) in the host server must have drivers that explicitly support virtual Fibre Channel and N_Port ID Virtualization (NPIV). Your SAN must also be able to address its connected resources using logical unit numbers (LUNs).

Assuming you have the appropriate hardware and software installed on the host commuter, you implement the Fibre Channel capabilities in Hyper-V by first creating a virtual SAN. You do this by using the Virtual SAN Manager, accessible from Hyper-V Manager, as shown in Figure 3-51. When you create the virtual SAN, the World Wide Node Names (WWNNs) and World Wide Port Names (WWPNs) of your host bus adapter appear.

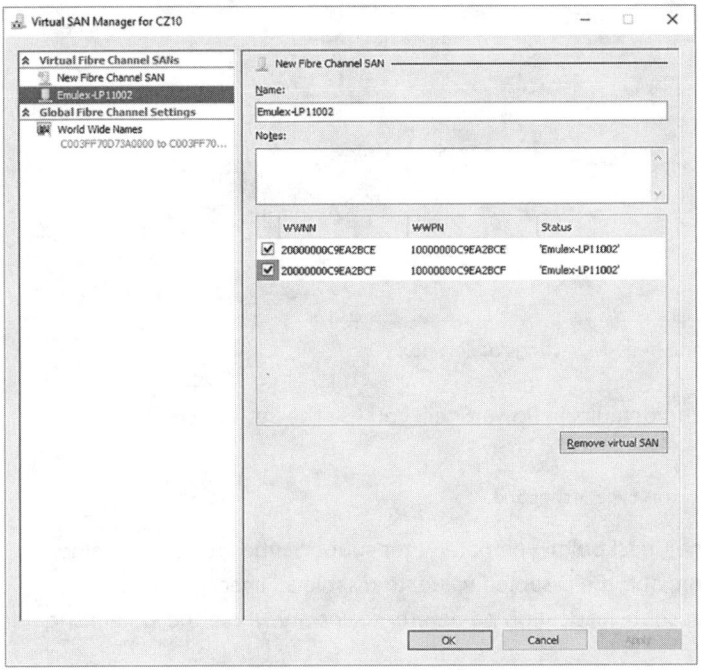

FIGURE 3-51 WWNNs and WWPNs in a virtual SAN

The next step is to add a Fibre Channel Adapter to your virtual machine from the Add Hardware page in the Settings dialog box. Then, the virtual SAN you created previously is available in the Fibre Channel Adapter page, as shown in Figure 3-52. Hyper-V virtualizes the SAN and makes the WWNNs and WWPNs available to the virtual machine.

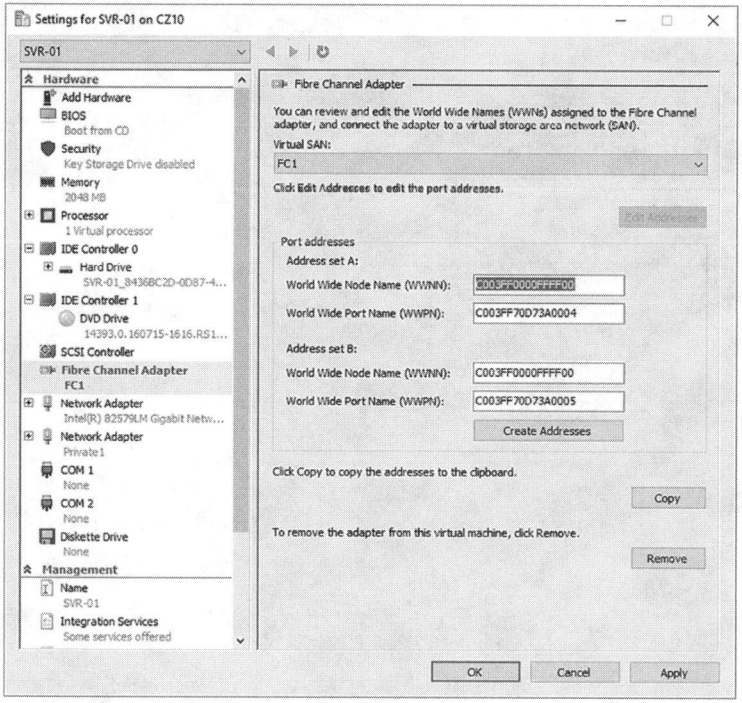

FIGURE 3-52 A Fibre Channel adapter in a VM

Configure Storage Quality of Service (QoS)

When you create virtual machines on a single Hyper-V host, it is common for there to be multiple virtual disks stored on a single physical disk. With VMs running simultaneously and accessing their virtual disks from the same physical disk, it is possible for one virtual disk to monopolize the physical disk's input/output (I/O) capacity, causing the other virtual disks to slow down. To help prevent this, Windows Server 2016 enables you to control the Quality of Service (QoS) for a given virtual hard disk.

QoS management in Hyper-V takes the form of controls that enables you to specify the minimum and maximum input/output operations per second (IOPS) for a disk. To configure storage QoS, you open the Settings dialog box for a VM, expand a hard drive component, select Quality Of Service, and, on the Quality Of Service page, select the Enable Quality Of Service Management check box, as shown in Figure 3-53.

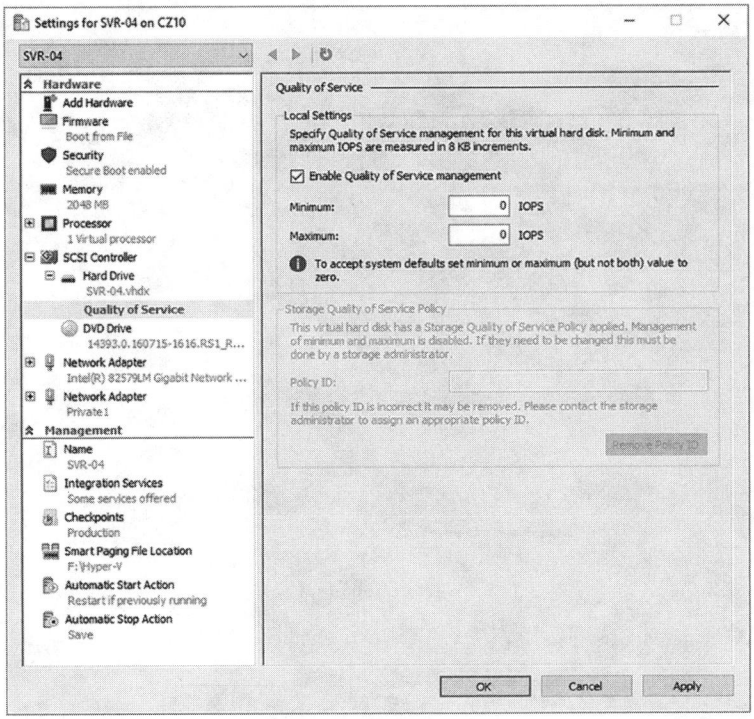

FIGURE 3-53 Quality of Service controls in the Settings dialog box in Hyper-V Manager

After selecting the Enable Quality Of Service Management check box, you can specify minimum and maximum IOPS values for the disk, to throttle its throughout in 8 KB increments. To configure these settings with Windows PowerShell, you use the Set-VMHardDiskDrive cmdlet, as in the following example. The ControllerType and ControllerNumber parameters specify which drive to configure, and the MinimumIOPS and MaximumIOPS parameters specify the QoS settings.

```
set-vmharddiskdrive -vmname server1 -controllertype scsi -controllernumber 0
-minimumiops 10 -maximumiops 500
```

Determining the optimum QoS settings for a specific drive likely takes some monitoring and adjustment. After enabling resource metering on the VM, you can use the Measure-VM cmdlet to display its current disk usage, as shown in the following examples. The output of the Measure-VM cmdlet is shown in Figure 3-54. After checking the IOPS under workload of the VM, you can zero in on appropriate QoS settings.

```
enable-vmresourcemetering -vmname server1

measure-vm -vmname server1 | fl
```

```
PS C:\WINDOWS\system32> measure-vm svr-04 |fl


VMId                                : 10426a2d-2ea2-4855-ac67-39cf1f10cb42
VMName                              : SVR-04
CimSession                          : CimSession: .
ComputerName                        : CZ10
MeteringDuration                    :
AverageProcessorUsage               : 50
AverageMemoryUsage                  : 732
MaximumMemoryUsage                  : 2048
MinimumMemoryUsage                  : 548
TotalDiskAllocation                 : 40960
AggregatedAverageNormalizedIOPS     : 514
AggregatedAverageLatency            : 5675
AggregatedDiskDataRead              : 572
AggregatedDiskDataWritten           : 207
AggregatedNormalizedIOCount         : 106573
NetworkMeteredTrafficReport         : {Microsoft.HyperV.PowerShell.VMNetworkAdapterPortAclMeteringReport,
                                      Microsoft.HyperV.PowerShell.VMNetworkAdapterPortAclMeteringReport,
                                      Microsoft.HyperV.PowerShell.VMNetworkAdapterPortAclMeteringReport,
                                      Microsoft.HyperV.PowerShell.VMNetworkAdapterPortAclMeteringReport...}
HardDiskMetrics                     : {Microsoft.HyperV.PowerShell.VHDMetrics}
AvgCPU                              : 50
AvgRAM                              : 732
MinRAM                              : 548
MaxRAM                              : 2048
TotalDisk                           : 40960


PS C:\WINDOWS\system32> _
```

FIGURE 3-54 Output of the Measure-VM cmdlet

Skill 3.4: Configure Hyper-V networking

Hyper-V includes networking capabilities that enable administrators to create a virtualized equivalent of nearly any physical network configuration.

This section covers how to:

- Add and remove virtual network interface cards (VNICs)
- Configure Hyper-V virtual switches
- Optimize network performance
- Configure MAC addresses
- Configure network isolation
- Configure synthetic and legacy virtual network adapters
- Configure NIC teaming in VMs
- Configure virtual machine queue (VMQ)
- Enable Remote Direct Memory Access (RDMA) on network adapters bound to a Hyper-V virtual switch using Switch Embedded Teaming (SET)
- Configure Bandwidth Management

Add and remove virtual network interface cards (vNICs)

As in a physical computer, a virtual machine can have multiple network interface adapters in it, providing connections to different networks or for carrying different types of traffic. When you create a new virtual machine, the default configuration includes one virtual network adapter. The New Virtual Machine Wizard includes a Configure Networking page, as shown in Figure 3-55, on which you can select one of the virtual switches on the host server.

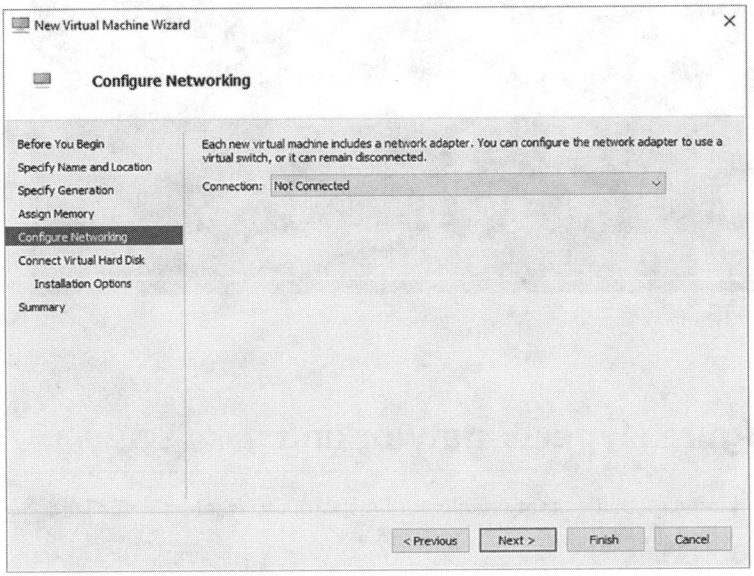

FIGURE 3-55 The Configure Networking page in the New Virtual Machine Wizard

If you create only the default external virtual switch when installing Hyper-V, connecting a virtual machine to the switch joins the system to the physical network. To create additional network adapters in your virtual machines, use the following procedure.

1. Launch Hyper-V Manager, select a virtual machine, and open its Settings dialog box.
2. In the Add Hardware list, select Network Adapter, and click Add.

> ***NOTE*** **ADDING NETWORK ADAPTERS**
>
> **On a Generation 2 VM, you can add and configure a network adapter while the system is running. For Generation 1 VMs the system must be shut down.**

3. On the new Network Adapter page, shown in Figure 3-56, in the Virtual Switch drop-down list, select the switch to which you want to connect the network adapter.

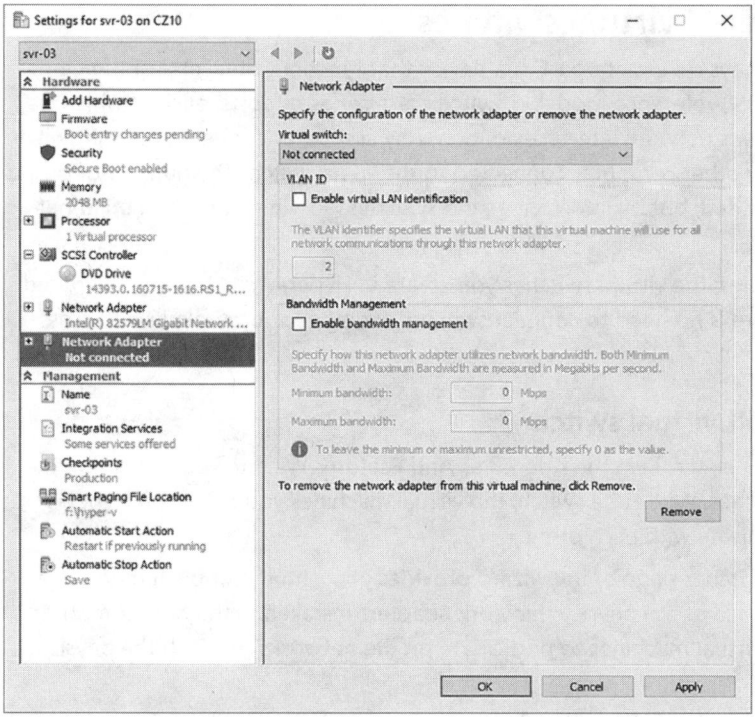

FIGURE 3-56 The Network Adapter page in the Settings dialog box

4. If your host computer is connected to a physical switching infrastructure that uses VLANs to create separate subnets, you can select the Enable Virtual LAN Identification check box and enter a VLAN identifier to associate the network adapter with a specific VLAN on your physical network.
5. Click OK to create the new network adapter and close the Settings dialog box.

You can create up to eight network adapters in a Windows Server 2016 Hyper-V virtual machine. To create a network adapter with PowerShell, you use the Add-VMNetworkAdapter cmdlet, as in the following example:

```
add-vmnetworkadapter -vmname server1 -switchname private1
```

To remove a network adapter in Hyper-V Manager, you select the adapter in the Settings dialog box and click the Remove button. The adapter appears crossed out, until you click the OK or Apply button. To remove a network adapter with PowerShell, you use the Remove-VMNetworkAdapter cmdlet, as in the following example:

```
remove-vmnetworkadapter -vmname server1 -vmnetworkadapter nic1
```

Configure Hyper-V virtual switches

A *virtual switch*, like its physical counterpart, is a device that functions at layer 2 of the Open Systems Interconnect (OSI) reference model. A switch has a series of ports, each of which is connected to a computer's network interface adapter. Any computer connected to the switch can transmit data to any other computer connected to the same switch. The number of ports in a physical switch is limited, but by interconnecting switches, administrators can build networks of nearly any size.

Unlike physical switches, the virtual switches you create in Hyper-V can have an unlimited number of ports, so there is no need to connect switches together or use uplinks and crossover circuits.

Creating the default virtual switch

When you install the Hyper-V role in the Add Roles And Features Wizard, you can create the server's first virtual switches. Without a switch, the virtual machines you create on Hyper-V are not able to communicate with each other.

The Create Virtual Switches page of the wizard provides you with the opportunity to create a virtual switch for each of the physical network adapters installed in the host computer. These switches enable virtual machines to participate on the networks to which the physical adapters are connected.

When you create a virtual switch in this manner, the networking configuration in the host operating system changes. The new virtual switch appears in the Network Connections window. If you examine its properties, notice that the switch is bound to the operating system's TCP/IP client, as shown in Figure 3-57.

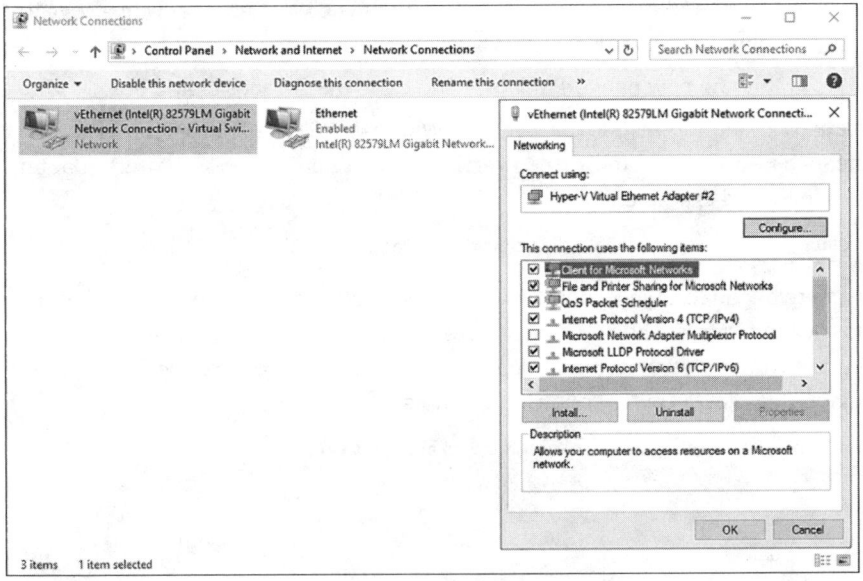

FIGURE 3-57 A virtual switch and its properties, displayed in the host operating system

Meanwhile, Hyper-V also changes the properties of original network connection representing the physical network interface adapter in the computer. The physical network adapter is now bound only to the virtual switch, as shown in Figure 3-58.

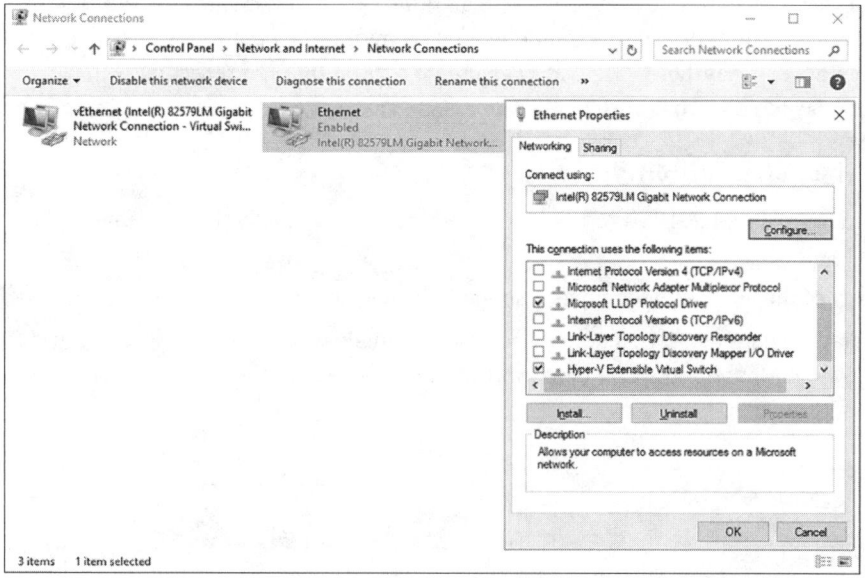

FIGURE 3-58 A network interface adapter in the host operating system, bound to a virtual switch

The result is that the computer's physical network configuration, in which its network adapter is connected to an external physical switch, is overlaid by the virtual network configuration created by Hyper-V. In this virtual configuration, the virtual switch is connected to the physical switch and the network adapter in the host operating system is connected to the virtual switch. The internal virtual network and the external physical network are joined into a single local area network (LAN), just as if you connected two physical switches together.

After Hyper-V creates the virtual switch and makes the configuration changes, any new virtual machines that you connect to the virtual switch become part of this conjoined network, as do any physical computers connected to the physical network through an external switch.

This type of virtual switch is, in Hyper-V terminology, an *external network switch*, because it provides connections external to the Hyper-V environment. This is typically the preferred arrangement for a production network in which Hyper-V virtual machines provide and consume services for the entire network.

For example, a virtual machine connected to this switch automatically obtains an IP address from a DHCP server on the physical network, if one exists. You can also configure a VM as a DHCP server and let it provide addresses to all the system on the network, virtual or physical.

This arrangement also enables your virtual machines to access the Internet by using the router and DNS servers on the external network. The virtual machines can then download operating system updates from servers on the Internet, just as external machines often do.

This type of virtual switch is not appropriate in all situations. If you create a laboratory network for product testing or a classroom network, you might not want it to be connected to the external network. For these cases, you can create a different type of virtual switch, by using the Virtual Switch Manager in Hyper-V Manager.

Creating a new virtual switch

Hyper-V in Windows Server 2016 supports three types of switches that you can create in the Virtual Switch Manager.

To create any of the virtual switch types, use the following procedure.

1. In Hyper-V Manager, in the Actions pane, select Virtual Switch Manager to open the Virtual Switch Manager dialog box, as shown in Figure 3-59.

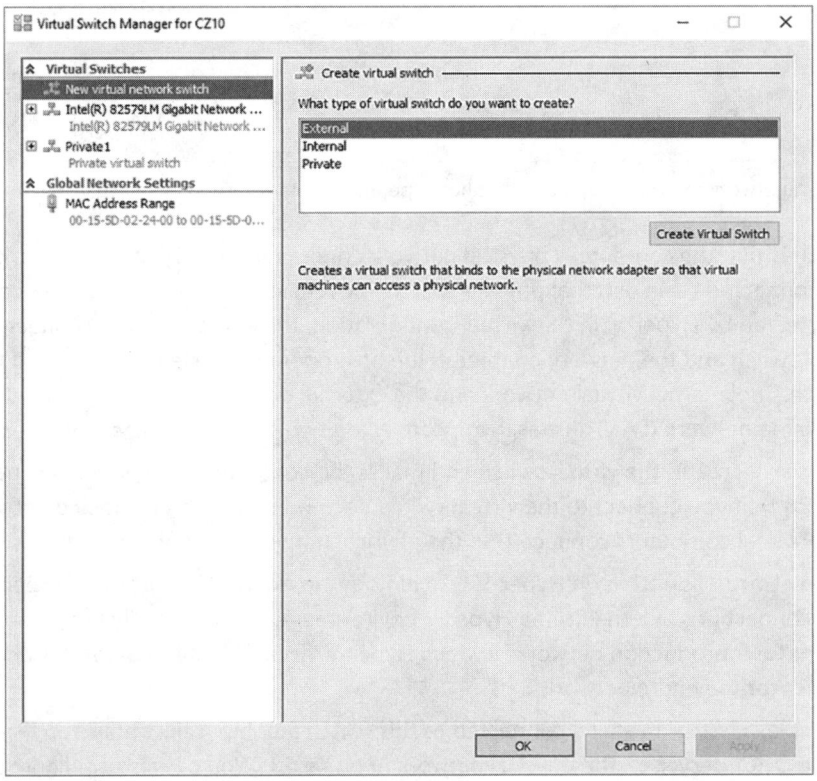

FIGURE 3-59 The Virtual Switch Manager dialog box in Hyper-V Manager

2. In the Create Virtual Switch box, select one of the following switch types, and click Create Virtual Switch.

- **External** The virtual switch is bound to networking protocol stack in the host operating system and connected to a physical network interface adapter in the Hyper-V server. Virtual machines running on the server can access the network to which the physical adapter is connected.
- **Internal** An internal network switch is bound to a separate instance of the networking protocol stack in the host operating system, independent from the physical network interface adapter and its connected network. Virtual machines running on the server can access the virtual network implemented by the virtual switch, and the host operating system can access the physical network through the physical network interface adapter, but the virtual machines cannot access the physical network through the physical adapter.
- **Private** A private network switch exists only in the Hyper-V server and is accessible only to the virtual machines running on the server. The host operating system can still access the physical network through the physical network interface adapter, but it cannot access the virtual network created by the virtual switch.

3. On the Virtual Switch Properties page, as shown in Figure 3-60, type a name for the new switch.

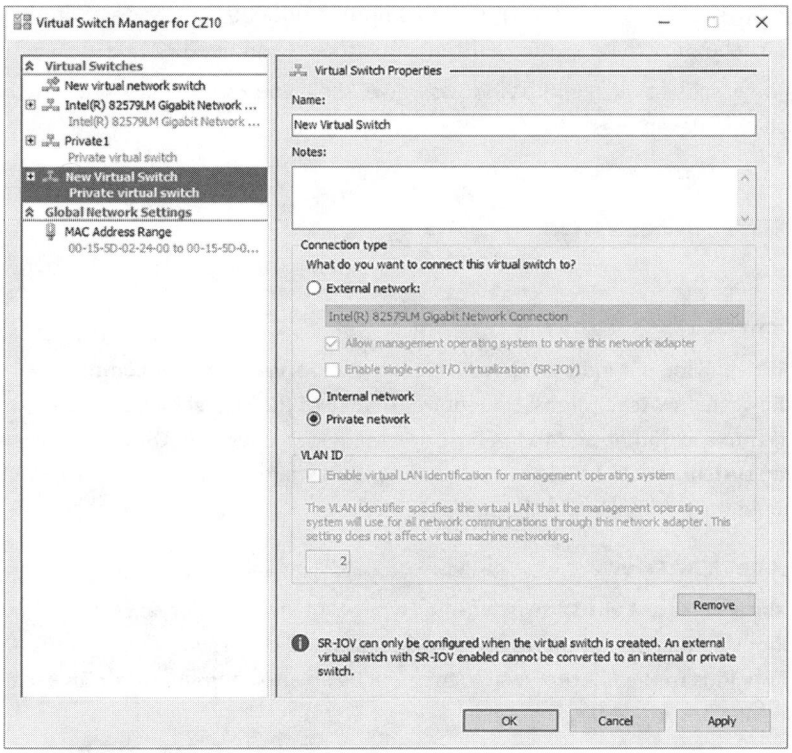

FIGURE 3-60 The Virtual Switch Properties page, with the External Network option selected

4. For an External Network switch, select the physical network adapter to which the virtual switch will be bound, and configure the following options, if desired:
   - **Allow Management Operating System To Share This Network Adapter** Selected by default when you create an external virtual switch, clearing this check box excludes the host operating system from the physical network, while allowing access to the virtual machines.
   - **Enable Single Root I/O Virtualization (SR-IOV)** Enables you to create an external virtual switch that is associated with a physical network adapter capable of supporting SR-IOV. This option is only available when creating a new virtual switch; you cannot modify an existing switch to use this option.
   - **Enable Virtual LAN Identification For Management Operating System** If your host computer is connected to a physical switching infrastructure that uses virtual LANs (VLANs) to create separate subnets, you can select the check box and enter a VLAN identifier to associate the virtual switch with a specific VLAN on your physical network.
5. Click OK. The new virtual switch is created.

You can proceed to create additional virtual switches as needed. You can create only one switch for each physical network adapter in the computer, but you can create multiple internal or private switches, to create as many virtual networks as you need.

To create a new virtual switch with Windows PowerShell, you use the New-VMSwitch cmdlet, as in the following examples:

```
new-vmswitch -name lan1 -netadaptername "ethernet 2"

new-vmswitch -name private1 -switchtype private
```

Quick check

Harold is deploying a Windows Server 2016 Hyper-V server, and he is confused about the virtual switch options. He requires that all of the virtual machines be networked to each other, and to the host operating system as well. Only the host operating system should be connected to the external network and the Internet. How should Harold implement this in Hyper-V?

Quick check answer

Harold should create a virtual switch using Hyper-V Manager in Server Manager. When choosing the type of the virtual switch, he should choose Internal. By connecting the VMs to the Internal switch, they will be able to communicate with each other and the host operating system.

Optimize network performance

Some physical network interface adapters have features that are designed to improve performance by offloading certain functions from the system processor to components built into the adapter itself. Hyper-V includes support for some of these features, if the hardware in the physical network adapter supports them properly.

When you expand a network adapter in the Settings dialog box of a VM, you gain access to the Hardware Acceleration page, as shown in Figure 3-61. On this page, you can configure the following hardware acceleration settings:

- **Enable Virtual Machine Queue** Virtual machine queue (VMQ) is a technique that stores incoming packets intended for virtual machines in separate queues on the physical network adapter and delivers them directly to the VMs, bypassing the processing normally performed by the virtual switch on the host server.
- **Enable IPsec Task Offloading** This setting uses the processing capabilities of the network adapter to perform some of the cryptographic functions required by IPsec. You can also specify the maximum number of security associations you want the adapter to be able to calculate.
- **Single-Root I/O Virtualization** This setting enables the virtual adapter to use the SR-IOV capabilities of the physical adapter. SR-IOV enables virtual machines to share the hardware resources of a PCI Express device, such as a network adapter.

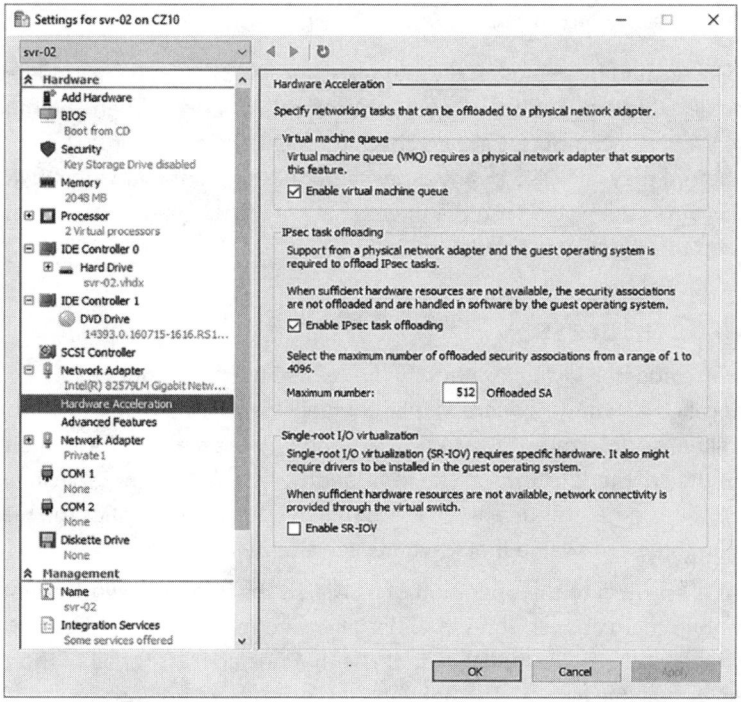

FIGURE 3-61 A network adapter's Hardware Acceleration page in the Settings dialog box

Create multiple switches

If your Hyper-V server has multiple physical network adapters, you should create a virtual switch for each one and split the VMs with network-intensive workloads among them, to achieve best performance.

Create a private network

When you have multiple VMs on a Hyper-V server that frequently communicate with each other, create a private virtual network in Virtual Switch Manager and configure the VMs to use it wherever possible. Network communication is more efficient on a private network than it is on the external network, in which other computers are sharing the same medium.

To create a private network, use the following procedure.

1. Create a private virtual network in Virtual Switch Manager.
2. Add a network adapter to each of your VMs, and assign it to the private switch.
3. Configure the adapter for each VM with a static IP address.
4. Modify the HOSTS file on each VM by adding the names and IP addresses of the other VMs on the Hyper-V server, as in the following example:

```
192.168.10.11   vm-01.contoso.com
192.168.10.12   vm-02.contoso.com
192.168.10.13   vm-03.contoso.com
192.168.10.14   vm-04.contoso.com
192.168.10.15   vm-05.contoso.com
```

HOSTS is a text file, located by default in the \Windows\system32\drivers\etc folder, that contains nothing but IP addresses and their equivalent computer names. When communicating on the network, Windows computers always check the HOSTS file as their first name resolution mechanism, before they use DNS or any other solution. Adding the private network addresses to this file causes the VMs to use the private network first, when communicating with the other VMs on the Hyper-V server.

Configure MAC addresses

Every network interface adapter, virtual or physical, has a Media Access Control (MAC) address (sometimes called a *hardware address*) that uniquely identifies the device on the network. On physical network adapters, the MAC is assigned by the manufacturer and permanently entered in the adapter's firmware. The MAC address is a six-byte hexadecimal value consisting of a three-bytes organizationally unique identifier (OUI) that specifies the manufacturer, and a unique three-byte value that identifies the adapter itself.

The MAC address is essential to the operation of a LAN, so the virtual network adapters on a Hyper-V server require them as well. The server has at least one real MAC address, provided in its physical network adapter, but Hyper-V cannot use that one address for all of the virtual adapters connecting virtual machines to the network.

To provide MAC addresses for the virtual adapters, Hyper-V creates a pool of addresses and assigns them from this pool to virtual network adapters as you create them. To view or modify the MAC address pool for the Hyper-V server, you open the Virtual Switch Manager and select MAC Address Range under Global Network Settings, as shown in Figure 3-62.

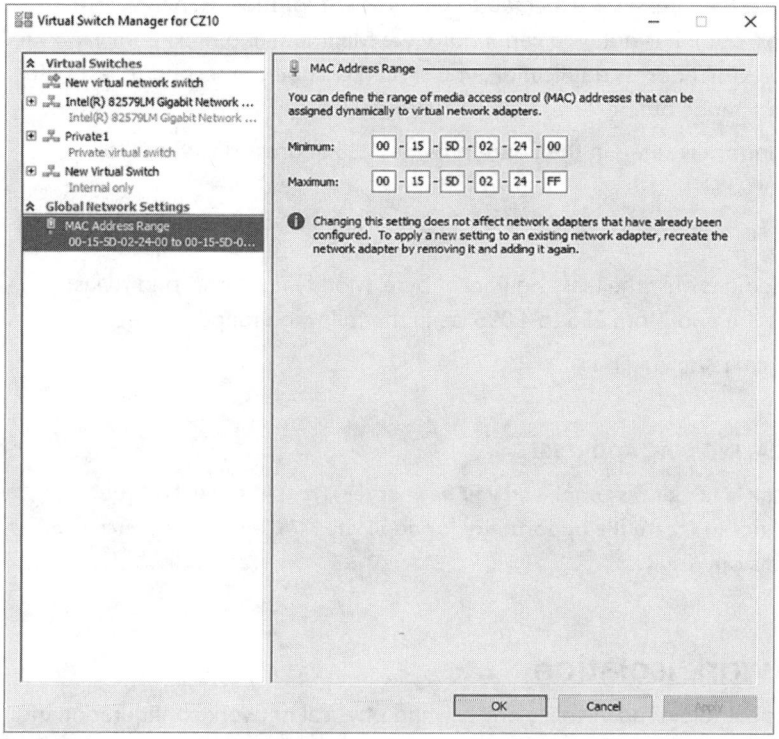

FIGURE 3-62 The MAC Address Range page in Virtual Switch Manager

NOTE **ASSIGNING MAC ADDRESSES**

Virtual network adapters in Hyper-V receive dynamically assigned MAC addresses by default, but you can choose to configure individual adapters in your virtual machines with static MAC addresses. You do this on the adapter's Advanced Features page in the Settings dialog box.

The Hyper-V MAC address range uses values constructed as follows:

- **Bytes 1 to 3** Consists of the value 00-15-5D, which is an OUI registered by Microsoft
- **Bytes 4 and 5** Consists of the last two bytes of the IP address assigned to the server's physical network adapter, converted to hexadecimal notation
- **Byte 6** Consists of a range of values from 00 to FF, which provides 256 possible addresses

The Hyper-V server assigns the MAC addresses to the network adapters in virtual machines as you create the adapters. The adapters retain their MAC addresses permanently, or until the adapter is removed from the virtual machine. The server reclaims any unused addresses and reuses them.

The default pool of 256 addresses is expected to be sufficient for most Hyper-V virtual machine configurations, but if it is not, you can modify the Minimum and Maximum values to enlarge the pool. To prevent address duplication, you should change the second to last byte only, by making it into a range of addresses like the last byte.

For example, the range illustrated in the figure provides 256 addresses with the following values:

```
00-15-1D-02-24-00 to 00-15-1D-02-24-FF
```

This value range modifies only the least significant byte. Modifying the second to last bytes as well increases the pool from 256 to 4,096, as in the following range:

```
00-15-1D-02-20-00 to 00-15-1D-02-2F-FF
```

CAUTION **DUPLICATING MAC ADDRESSES**

When you modify the MAC address pool, and you have other Hyper-V servers on your network, be careful not to create the opportunity for duplicate MAC addresses to occur, or networking problems can result.

Configure network isolation

Hyper-V makes it possible to extend virtually any existing physical network configuration into its virtual space, or create a completely separated and isolated network within the Hyper-V environment.

The basic default configuration of a Hyper-V virtual machine connects its network adapter to an external virtual switch, thus attaching the guest operating system on the virtual machine to the outside network. The VM can then take advantage of services running on the outside network and send traffic through routers to other networks, including the Internet.

This type of arrangement can enable you to consolidate many physical servers into virtual machines on a single Hyper-V server, by providing them all with access to the entire network. There is no distinction here between the physical network and the virtual one in the Hyper-V space.

Extending a production network into virtual space

A Hyper-V server can have multiple physical network adapters installed in it, which might be connected to different networks to separate traffic, or to the same network to increase available bandwidth. You might also have adapters dedicated to SAN connections, for shared storage and server clustering.

Microsoft recommends using at least two physical network adapters in a Hyper-V server, with one adapter servicing the host operating system and the other connected to the VMs. When you have more than two physical adapters in the server, you can create separate external virtual network switches for the physical adapters, and connect each one to a separate VM.

Creating an isolated network

For testing, development, and evaluation purposes, or for classroom situations, you might want to create an isolated network environment. By creating internal or private virtual switches, you can create a network that exists only within the Hyper-V space, with or without the host operating system included.

An isolated network such as this suffers from the weaknesses of its strengths. If you want to install the guest operating systems using Windows Deployment Services or configure the virtual machines using DHCP, you must install and configure these services on the private network. The guest operating systems also do not have access to the Internet, which prevents them from downloading operating system updates. Again, you must deploy appropriate substitutes on the private network.

To provide your systems with software updates, you can install two network adapters on each of your virtual machines and connect one to a private switch and one to an external switch. This procedure enables the virtual machines to access the Internet and the private network.

Another method for creating an isolated network is to use virtual LANs (VLANs). This is particularly helpful if you have virtual machines on different Hyper-V servers that you want to add to the isolated network. By connecting the network adapters to an external switch and configuring them with the same VLAN identifier, you can create a network within a network that isolates the VLAN from other computers. You can, for example, deploy a DHCP server on your VLAN without it interfering with other DHCP servers in your production environment.

Configure synthetic and legacy virtual network adapters

When you select the Network Adapter option in the Add Hardware page of the Settings dialog box, you create what is known in Hyper-V terminology as a *synthetic network adapter.* Generation 1 virtual machines support two types of network and storage adapters: synthetic and legacy (sometimes called emulated).

A synthetic adapter is a virtual device that does not correspond to a real-world product. Synthetic devices in a virtual machine communicate with the host operating system using a high-speed conduit called the VMBus.

Hyper-V virtual switches exist in the host server operating system and are part of a component called the network Virtualization Service Provider (VSP). The synthetic network adapter in the VM is a Virtualization Service Client (VSC). The VSP and the VSC are both connected to the VMBus, which provides communication between the two, as shown in Figure 3-63. The VSP, in the host operating system, provides the VSC, in the guest operating system, with access to the physical hardware in the host computer, that is, the physical network interface adaptor.

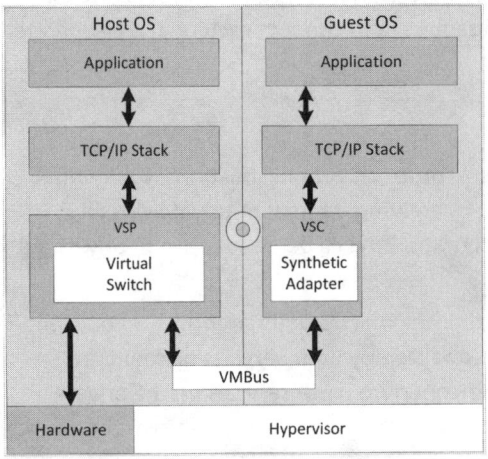

FIGURE 3-63 Synthetic network adapters communicate using the VMBus

Because they have access to the hardware through the VMBus, synthetic adapters provide a much higher level of performance than the alternative—a legacy adapter. Synthetic adapters are implemented as part of the Integration Services package that runs on supported guest operating systems. The one main drawback of synthetic network adapters is that they are not operational until Integration Services is loaded with the operating system on the virtual machine.

A *legacy network adapter* (sometimes called an emulated adapter) is a standard network adapter driver that communicates with the host operating system by making calls directly to the hypervisor, as shown in Figure 3-64. This communication method is substantially slower than the VMBus used by the synthetic network adapters, and is therefore less desirable.

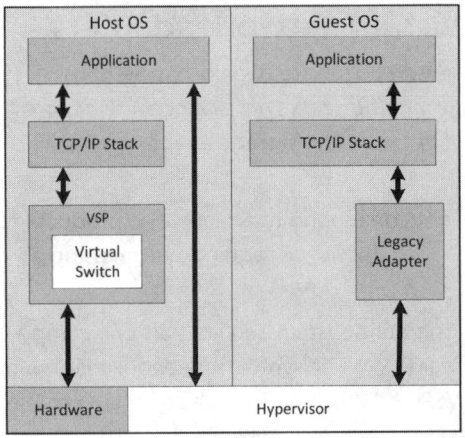

FIGURE 3-64 Legacy network adapter communicating with the host through the hypervisor

The primary advantage of the legacy adapter is that you can use it to boot a Generation 1 VM from the network, using the Preboot Execution Environment (PXE). PXE is a mechanism that software deployment tools, such as Windows Deployment Services (WDS) and System Center Configuration Manager (SCCM), use to install operating systems to new computers over the network. The synthetic network adapter in Generation 1 VMs does not support PXE.

To install a legacy adapter, you use the same procedure described earlier, except that you select Legacy Network Adapter in the Add Hardware list. Unlike synthetic adapters, legacy adapters load their drivers before the operating system, so you can boot the virtual machine using PXE and deploy an operating system over the network. Performance suffers with the legacy adapter, however, so you might consider using a synthetic adapter instead, after the operating system is installed.

This is one of the only scenarios in which an legacy adapter is preferable to a synthetic adapter. The other is when you install an operating system on your virtual machines that does not have an Integration Services package available for it.

In Generation 2 VMs, the distinction between synthetic and legacy adapters disappears. There is no more legacy adapter, and the synthetic adapter is capable of performing a PXE boot.

Configure NIC teaming in VMs

NIC teaming is a Windows feature that enables administrators to join multiple network adapters into a single entity, for performance enhancement or fault tolerance purposes. Hyper-V virtual machines can also take advantage of NIC teaming, but they are limited to teams of only two, as opposed to the host operating system, which can have teams of up to 32 NICs.

To use NIC teaming in Hyper-V, you must complete three basic tasks, as follows:

1. Create the NIC team in the Windows Server 2016 host operating system.
2. In Hyper-V Manager, create an external virtual switch using the NIC team.
3. Configure the network adapter in a virtual machine to connect to the virtual switch representing the NIC team.

Creating the NIC team

NIC teams must consist of physical network interface adapters, so before you can use a NIC team in a virtual machine, you must create it in the host operating system. After installing two physical network adapters in the computer, you can create a NIC team with Server Manager, as shown in Figure 3-65, using the following settings:

- **Teaming Mode** Switch Independent
- **Load Balancing Mode** Hyper-V Port
- **Standby Adapter** None (All Adapters Active)

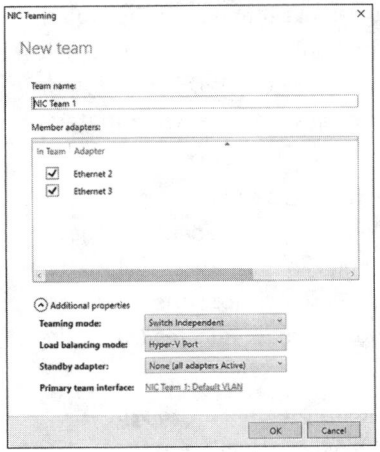

FIGURE 3-65 The NIC Teaming dialog box

Creating the team installs the Microsoft Network Adapter Multiplexor Driver, which appears as one of the components of the network connection representing the team.

Creating the team virtual switch

Once you have created the NIC team, you can open Virtual Switch Manager and create a new virtual switch by selecting the External option and choosing Microsoft Network Adapter Multiplexor Driver from the drop-down list, as shown in Figure 3-66.

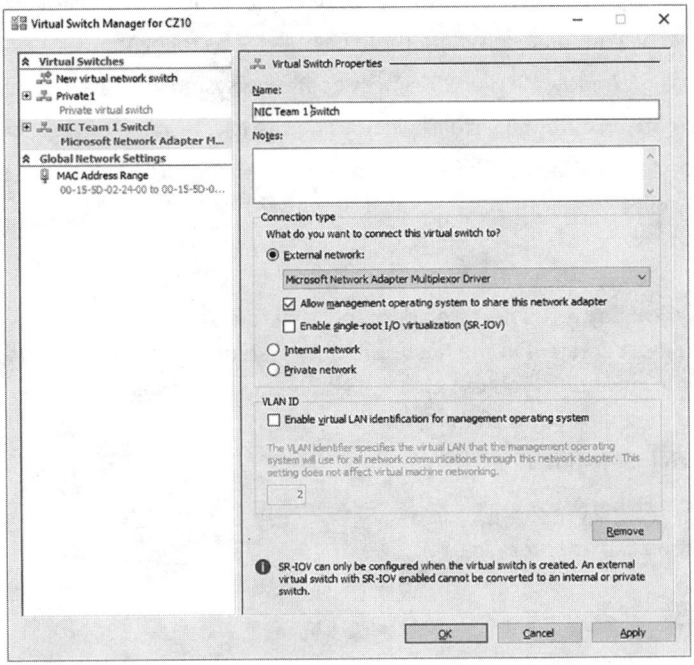

FIGURE 3-66 The Virtual Switch Properties settings for a NIC team switch

Configuring a NIC team virtual network adapter

To configure a virtual machine to use a NIC team, you must use the Settings dialog box to add a virtual network adapter or modify the properties of an existing one, configuring it to use the NIC team switch you created in the previous section, as shown in Figure 3-67.

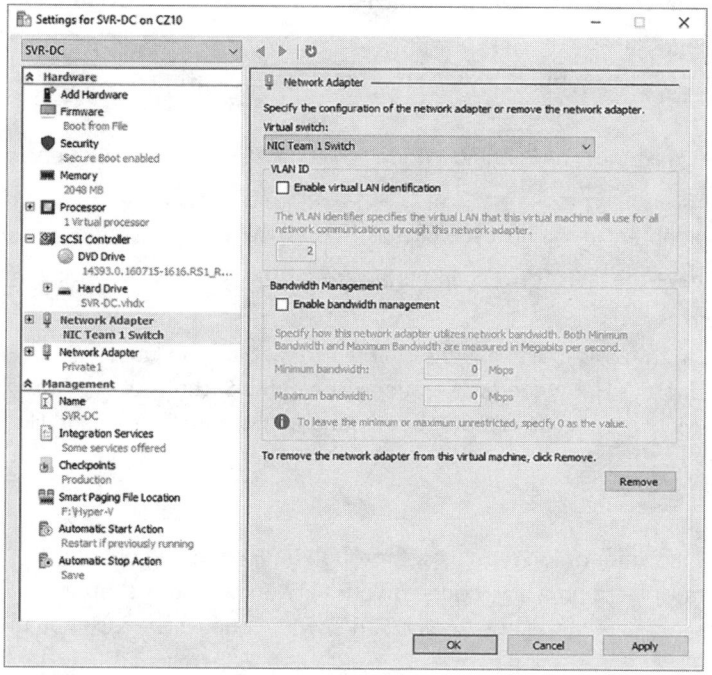

FIGURE 3-67 The Network Adapter settings for a NIC team adapter

Finally, you must open the Advanced Features page for the network adapter and select the Enable This Network Adapter To Be Part Of A Team In The Guest Operating System check box. At this point, the NIC team is operational for the virtual machine. You can unplug one of the network cables, and the system maintains its connection to the network.

Configure virtual machine queue (VMQ)

Virtual machine queue (VMQ) is a network performance enhancement feature that Windows Server 2016 enables automatically when it detects physical network adapters that run at 10 gigabits per second (Gbps) or faster. The VMQ process for incoming network traffic is as follows:

1. A network adapter that supports VMQ performs its own internal packet filtering based on the destination address. The packets for each destination are added to a separate queue.
2. The adapter sends the queued data for each destination to the host operating system.
3. The host operating system forwards each queue to a different logical processor, so that it can handle the traffic for multiple destinations simultaneously.

4. The host operating system sends the packets for each queue to the virtual switch.
5. The virtual switch routes the packets in each queue out through the appropriate port to the destination VM.

Because the filtering takes place in the physical network adapter, there is less processing needed in the virtual switch. Any traffic that does not match the filters is sent to a default queue, which the switch must then process.

For the Hyper-V implementation to support VMQ, it must meet the following requirements:

- Both the host and the guest must be running Windows Server 2016 or Windows Server 2012 R2.
- The physical network adapters in the host server must support VMQ.
- The host server must have the latest drivers and firmware for the physical network adapters installed.
- The network adapters in the VMs must have the Enable Virtual Machine Queue check box selected on the adapter's Hardware Acceleration page in the Settings dialog box. You can also enable VMQ on a specific adapter by running a PowerShell command like the following:

```
enable-netadaptervmq -name nic1
```

Modifying the default VMQ configuration requires a thorough understanding of your hardware's capabilities. You must learn how many queues your network adapters support, how many logical processors there are in the host server, and how the queues are assigned to the processors.

To discover whether your physical network adapters support VMQ, run the Get-NetAdapterVmq cmdlet in a PowerShell window with Administrator privileges. A blank response indicates that your adapters do not support VMQ. If they do, the cmdlet displays the identifying information for the physical adapters it detects in the computer, as well as the following information:

- **Enabled** Indicates whether the adapter is currently using VMQ
- **BaseVmqProcessor** Identifies the first logical processor that VMQ uses to assign queues from the network adapter
- **MaxProcessors** Specifies the maximum number of logical processors that VMQ uses to assign queues from the network adapter
- **NumberOfReceiveQueues** Specifies the number of queues supported by the network adapter

Next, you can use the Get-NetAdapterVmqQueue cmdlet to see which queues are assigned to which logical processors. The information displayed by this cmdlet is as follows:

- **QueueID** Specifies the number of the queue being assigned.

- **MacAddress** Specifies the MAC address to which the queue is assigned. A blank value for this property indicates the default queue used to process all unfiltered traffic.
- **VlanID** Specifies the VLAN to which the queue is assigned, if VLANs are in use.
- **Processor** Specifies the number of the processor to which the queue is assigned.
- **VmFriendlyName** Specifies the name of the virtual machine that is the destination for the queue's traffic. The presence of the host server name in this property indicates the default queue.

To modify the default VMQ settings, you use the Set-NetAdapterVmq PowerShell cmdlet. The parameters that are most commonly modified by administrators are as follows:

- **BaseProcessorNumber** Specifies the number of the lowest logical processor that the system should use when assigning queues. The recommended practice is to leave the first one or two processors for use by the host operating system.
- **MaxProcessorNumber** Specifies the number of the highest logical processor that the system should use when assigning queues.
- **MaxProcessors** Specifies how many of the logical processors in the host server should be used to service queues

For example, the following command sets the network adapter called NIC1 to reserve logical processors 0 and 1 for the host server, and begin assigned queues at processor 2.

```
Set-netadaptervmq -name nic1 -baseprocessornumber 2
```

Enable Remote Direct Memory Access (RDMA) on network adapters bound to a Hyper-V virtual switch using Switch Embedded Teaming (SET)

NIC teaming is a function of Windows Server 2016, which you can use with or without Hyper-V. *Switch Embedded Teaming (SET)* is a Hyper-V-only variation on the concept of NIC teaming that is implemented wholly within a Hyper-V virtual switch.

Remote Direct Memory Access (RDMA) is a high-speed network transmission method that can send large amounts of data with low latency and without processor intervention. RDMA-capable network adapters transfer data directly to and from application memory, without having to buffer it. Networking technologies such as SMB Direct rely on RDMA to achieve their high-performance levels.

Windows Server 2016 can, for the first time, combine these two technologies to provide Hyper-V with a high-performance networking solution using multiple physical network adapters.

To create a Hyper-V virtual switch that uses SET with RDMA adapters, the requirements are as follows:

- The host server can have up to eight physical network adapters.

- All physical network adapters that have passed the Windows Hardware Qualification and Logo (WHQL) test are supported.
- All the physical network adapters must be identical, with the same model, the same firmware, and the same drivers.
- Physical network adapters capable of running at various speeds must all be configured to run at the same speed.
- The physical adapters do not have to be connected to the same physical switch.
- The use of Data Center Bridging (DCB) is strongly recommended, to separate the RDMA from standard networking traffic.

To create a virtual switch with SET enabled, you must run the New-VMSwitch PowerShell cmdlet with the EnableEmbeddedTeaming parameter. There is no graphical equivalent in Virtual Switch Manager. An example of the command is as follows:

```
new-vmswitch -name setswitch -netadaptername "nic1","nic2" -enableembeddedteaming $true
```

After creating the switch, you can add new virtual network adapters to your VMs, using commands like the following:

```
add-vmnetworkadapter -vmname server1 -switchname setswitch -name set1
```

Once you have done this, you can enable RDMA on the adapters in the SET team. The Get-NetAdapterRdma cmdlet displays the current RDMA status of the adapters, plus the names assigned to them. To enable RDMA, you run the Enable-NetAdapterRdma cmdlet with the name listed in the Get-NetAdapterRdma output, as shown in Figure 3-68.

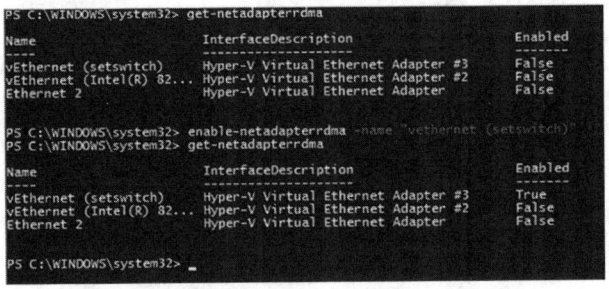

FIGURE 3-68 Enabling RDMA for SET team adapters

Configure bandwidth management

To prevent any one virtual network adapter from monopolizing the bandwidth available in a virtual switch, you can configure the minimum and maximum amount of bandwidth it is permitted to use. When you open the Settings dialog box for a virtual machine and select a network adapter, there is an Enable Bandwidth Management check box the activates the settings shown in Figure 3-69.

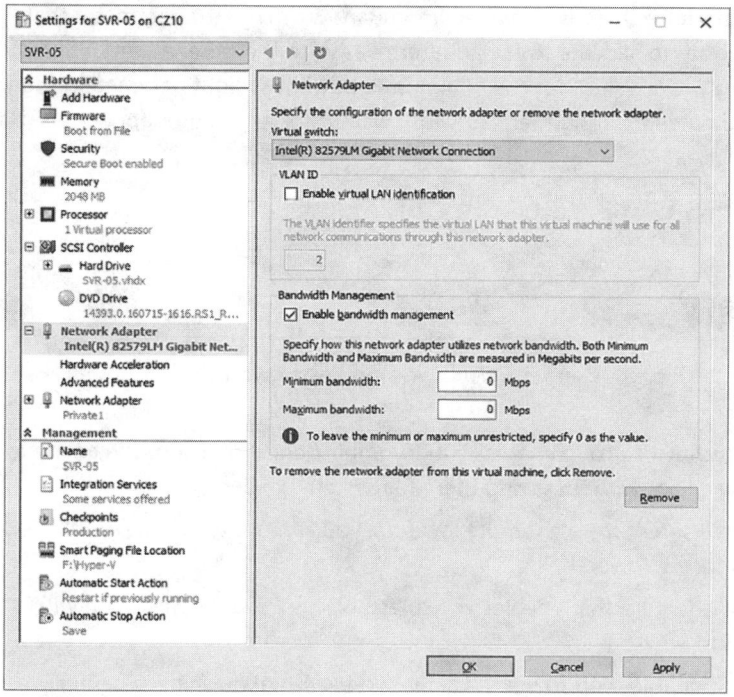

FIGURE 3-69 The Bandwidth Management settings for a virtual network adapter

The Minimum Bandwidth and Maximum Bandwidth settings in Hyper-V Manager are absolute, meaning that they measure the bandwidth in megabits per second (Mbps). Therefore, the settings you use depend on the speed of the physical network adapter in the host server, the number of VMs contending for the available bandwidth of the virtual switch, and the importance of the workloads on the VMs.

The Minimum Bandwidth setting ensures that a specific adapter does not get overwhelmed by the other VMs contending for the same bandwidth. Even if another VM malfunctions and floods the network, this setting should ensure that the adapter is not denied access. The Maximum Bandwidth setting can prevent a malfunctioning or noisy adapter from taking all the bandwidth, shutting the other VMs out.

Make sure that the Maximum Bandwidth settings for all VMs connected to the virtual switch do not exceed the actual bandwidth provided by the physical network adapter. If, for example, the host server has a 1 Gbps physical adapter, and the Maximum Bandwidth settings for the VMs using it add up to more than 1 Gbps, there is contention for the network, and the host server itself might end up being denied access.

You can also configure these settings using the Set-VMNetworkAdapter cmdlet in Windows PowerShell, which also has an additional capability. The parameters corresponding the settings in Hyper-V Manager are MaximumBandwidth and MinimumBandwidthAbsolute.

The latter is so named because there is also a MinimumBandwidthWeight parameter that specifies how much bandwidth to allocate to the adapter relative to the other adapters connected to the same virtual switch. Values for the MinimumBandwidthWeight parameter range from 1 to 100. A typical command setting the bandwidth weight for an adapter appears as follows:

```
set-vmnetworkadapter -vmname server1 -name nic1 -minimumbandwidthweight 75
```

Chapter summary

- To install the Hyper-V role, your server must have a processor with virtualization capabilities.
- The Hyper-V Administrators group enables you to grant users and groups the ability to work with virtual machines without giving them full system privileges.
- To manage a Hyper-V server from a remote location, you can use the Hyper-V Manager console or Windows PowerShell.
- PowerShell Direct is a feature that enables you to establish a PowerShell session with a guest OS from its host server.
- Nested virtualization enables you to install Hyper-V on a virtual machine, essentially creating a host out of a guest.
- In Windows Server 2016, you can modify the amount of memory allotted to a virtual machine while it is running.
- Dynamic Memory is a Hyper-V function that automatically assigns memory to and reclaims it from a virtual machine as it is needed.
- NUMA is a system architecture that pairs processors with local memory for optimum performance. Hyper-V includes a virtualized NUMA architecture that mirrors the one in the physical computer by default, but which you can modify to suit the needs of your VMs.
- Smart Paging is a feature used with Dynamic Memory that enables Hyper-V to restart VMs when the system is short of physical memory by paging to disk during the boot process.
- Integration Services is a suite of programs that runs on the guest operating system and facilitates communication with the host operating system. Hyper-V enables administrators to control which Integration Services components are running for each VM.
- Enhanced Session Mode enables administrators to remotely access virtual machines while taking advantage of local hardware, such as printers and USB devices.
- Hyper-V supports VMs running FreeBSD and various Linux distributions as guest operating systems.

NOTE **ADDING A DATA VOLUME**

To add a data volume to an existing container, your only option is to use Docker Commit to save any changes you've made to the existing container to a new image, and then use Docker Run to create a new container from the new image, including the -v switch to add the data volume.

Manage resource control

As noted earlier, the Docker Run command supports many parameters and switches, some of which have already been demonstrated in this chapter. For example, you have seen how the it switches create an interactive container that runs a specific shell or other command. To create a container that runs in the background—in what is called detached mode—you use the -d switch, as in the following example:

```
docker run -d -p 80:80 microsoft/iis
```

To interact with a detached container, you can use network connections or file system shared. You can also connect to the container using the Docker Attach command.

Working with container names

By default, when you create a container using the Docker Run command, the Dockerd engine assigns three identifiers to the container, as shown in Figure 4-20:

- **Long UUID** A 32-byte hexadecimal string, represented by 64 digits, as in the following example: 0e38bdac48ca0120eff6491a7b9d1908e65180213b-2c1707b924991ae8d1504f
- **Short UUID** The first six bytes of the long UUID, represented as 12 digits, as in the following example: 0e38bdac48ca.
- **Name** A randomly chosen name consisting of two words separated by an underscore character, as in the following example: drunk_jones

```
PS C:\WINDOWS\system32> docker ps --no-trunc
CONTAINER ID                                                       IMAGE                        COMMAND            CREATED
    STATUS              PORTS                   NAMES
0e38bdac48ca0120eff6491a7b9d1908e65180213b2c1707b924991ae8d1504f   microsoft/windowsservercore   "powershell"       3 days ago
    Up 32 minutes                               drunk_jones
PS C:\WINDOWS\system32> _
```

FIGURE 4-20 Output of the Docker ps --no-trunc command

You can use any of the three identifiers when referencing the container on the command line. You can also assign your own name to the container when you create it by adding the name parameter to the Docker Run command line, as in the following example:

```
docker run -it microsoft/windowsservercore powershell --name core1
```

Constraining memory

The Docker Run command supports parameters that enable you to specify how much memory a container is permitted to use. By default, container processes can use as much host memory and swap memory as they need. If you are running multiple containers on the same host or a memory intensive application on the host itself, you might to impose limits on the memory certain containers can use.

The memory parameters you can use in a Docker Run command are as follows:

- **-m (or --memory)** Specifies the amount of memory the container can use. Values consist of an integer and the unit identifier b, k, m, or g (for bytes, kilobytes, megabytes, or gigabytes, respectively).
- **-memory-swap** Specifies the total amount of memory plus virtual memory that the container can use. Values consist of an integer and the unit identifier b, k, m, or g.
- **-memory-reservation** Specifies a soft memory limit that the host retains for the container, even when there is contention for system memory. For example, you might use the -m switch to set a hard limit of 1 GB, and a memory reservation value of 750 MB. When other containers or processes require additional memory, the host might reclaim up to 250 MB of the container's memory, but will leave at least 750 MB intact. Values consist of an integer smaller than that of the m or --memory-swap value and the unit identifier b, k, m, or g.
- **-kernel-memory** Specifies the amount of the memory limit set using the -m switch that can be used for kernel memory. Values consist of an integer and the unit identifier b, k, m, or g.
- **-oom-kill-disable** Prevents the kernel from killing container processes when an out of memory error occurs. Never use this option without the -m switch, to create a memory limit for the container. Otherwise, the kernel could start to kill processes on the host when an OOM error occurs.

Constraining CPU cycles

You can also specify parameters that limit the CPU cycles allocated to a container. By default, all the containers on a host share the available CPU cycles equally. Using these parameters, you can assign priorities to the containers, which take effect when cpu contention occurs.

The Docker Run parameters that you can use to control container access to CPUs are as follows:

- **-c (or --cpu-shares)** Specifies a value from 0 to 1024 that specifies the weight of the container in contention for the CPU cycles. The actual amount of processor cycles that a container receives depends on the number of containers running on the host and their respective weights.
- **-cpuset-cpus** Specifies which CPUs in a multiprocessor host system that the container can use. Values consist of integers representing the CPUs in the host computer, separated by commas.

- **-cpuset-mems** Specifies which nodes on a NUMA host that the container can use. Values consist of integers representing the CPUs in the host computer, separated by commas.

Create new container images using Dockerfile

If you have made changes to a container since you first created it with the Docker Run command, you can save those changes by creating a new container image using Docker Commit. However, the recommended method for creating container images is to build them from scratch using a script called a dockerfile.

A *dockerfile* is a plain text file, with the name dockerfile, which contains the commands needed to build your new image. Once you have created the dockerfile, you use the Docker Build command to execute it and create the new file. The dockerfile is just a mechanism that automates the process of executing the steps you used to modify your container manually. When you run the Docker Build command with the dockerfile, the Dockerd engine runs each command in the script by creating a container, making the modifications you specify, and executing a Docker Commit command to save the changes as a new image.

A dockerfile consists of instructions, such as FROM or RUN, and a statement for each instruction. The accepted format is to capitalize the instruction. You can insert remarks into the script by preceding them with the pound (#) character.

An example of a simple dockerfile is as follows:

```
#install DHCP server
FROM microsoft/windowsservercore
RUN powershell -command install-windowsfeature dhcp -includemanagementtools
RUN powershell -configurationname microsoft.powershell -command add-dhcpserverv4scope
-state active -activatepolicies $true  -name scopetest -startrange 10.0.0.100 -endrange
10.0.0.200 -subnetmask 255.255.255.0
RUN md boot
COPY ./bootfile.wim c:/boot/
CMD powershell
```

In this example:

- The FROM instruction specifies the base image from which the new image is created. In this case, the new image starts with the microsoft/windowsservercore image.
- The first RUN command opens a PowerShell session and uses the Install-WindowsFeature cmdlet to install the DHCP role.
- The second RUN command uses the Add-DhcpServerv4Scope cmdlet to create a new scope on the DHCP server.
- The third RUN command creates a new directory called boot.
- The COPY command copies a file called bootfile.wim from the current folder on the container host to the c:\boot folder on the container.
- The CMD command opens a PowerShell session when the image is run.

Once you have created the dockerfile script, you use the Docker Build command to create the new image, as in the following example:

```
docker build -t dhcp .
```

This command reads the dockerfile from the current directory and creates an image called dhcp. As the Dockerd engine builds the image, it displays the results of each command and the IDs of the interim containers it creates, as shown in Figure 4-21. Once you have created the image, you can then create a container from it using the Docker Run command in the usual manner.

```
PS C:\temp> docker build --no-cache --force-rm -t dhcp4 .
Sending build context to Docker daemon 8.192 kB
Step 1/6 : FROM microsoft/windowsservercore
 ---> 93a9c37b36d0
Step 2/6 : RUN powershell install-windowsfeature dhcp -includemanagementtools
 ---> Running in 71a7f8f39e4f

Success Restart Needed Exit Code      Feature Result
------- -------------- ---------      --------------
True    No             Success        {DHCP Server}


 ---> 92a23f1b115c
Removing intermediate container 71a7f8f39e4f
Step 3/6 : RUN powershell -configurationname microsoft.powershell -command Add-dhcpserverv4scope -state active -activatepolicies $true -name scopetest -startrange 172.25.112.10 -end
nge 172.25.112.20 -subnetmask 255.255.240.0
 ---> Running in 41b6925364f7
 ---> bef09e926948
Removing intermediate container 41b6925364f7
Step 4/6 : RUN md boots
 ---> Running in 2d6d8cb82ee7
 ---> 0da73c9a2291
Removing intermediate container 2d6d8cb82ee7
Step 5/6 : COPY ./bootfile.wim c:/boots/
 ---> 365faa0f2ee0
Removing intermediate container 53498275c410
Step 6/6 : CMD powershell
 ---> Running in 4f23c9326a9d
 ---> bce3bfd56322
Removing intermediate container 4f23c9326a9d
Successfully built bce3bfd56322
PS C:\temp>
```

FIGURE 4-21 Output of the Docker Build command

This is a simple example of a dockerfile, but they can be much longer and more complex.

✔ Quick check

Which of the following Docker commands can you use to create new container image files?

1. **Docker Run**
2. **Docker Commit**
3. **Docker Build**
4. **Docker Images**

Quick check answer

Answers 2 and 3 are correct. Docker Commit is the command used to create a new image from an existing container. Docker Build is the command used to create a new container image using the instructions in a dockerfile.

Manage container images using DockerHub Repository for public and private scenarios

DockerHub is a public repository that you can use to store and distribute your container images. When you download container images using the Docker Pull command, they come from DockerHub by default, unless you specify another repository in the command. However, you can upload images as well, using the Docker Push command.

Uploading images to DockerHub enables you to share them with your colleagues, and even with yourself, so you don't have to transfer files manually to deploy a container image on another host.

Before you can upload images to the Docker Hub, you must register at the site at *http://hub.docker.com*. Once you have done this, your user name becomes the name of your repository on the service. For example, the microsoft/windowsservercore image you pulled earlier is an image called windowsservercore in the Microsoft repository. If your user name on DockerHub is hholt, your images will all begin with that repository name, followed by the image name, as in the following example:

```
hholt/nano1
```

Once you have an account, you must login to the DockerHub service from the command line before you can push images. You do this with the following command:

```
docker login
```

Docker prompts you for your user name and password, and then provides upload access to your repository.

Searching for images

You can search for images on the DockerHub by using the web site, as shown in Figure 4-22. This interface provides the latest information about the image, as well as comments from other users in the Docker community.

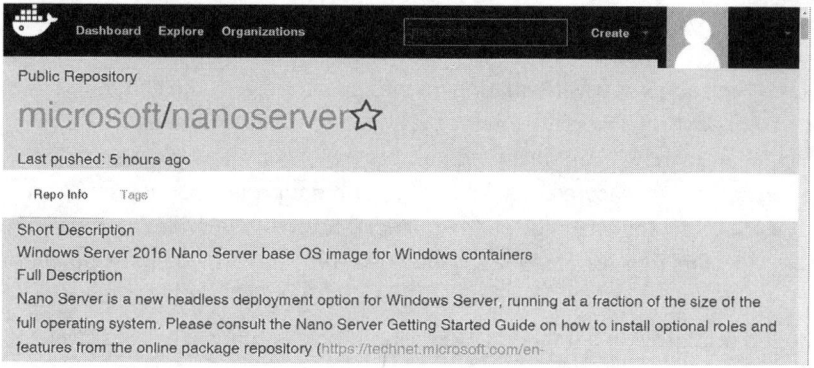

FIGURE 4-22 Screen capture of a DockerHub web search

You can also search the DockerHub from the command line, using the Docker Search command, as in the following example:

```
docker search microsoft --no-trunc
```

Adding the no-trunc parameter prevents the command from truncating the image descriptions, as shown in Figure 4-23.

```
PS C:\temp> docker search microsoft --no-trunc
NAME                                      DESCRIPTION                                                                     STARS     OFFICIAL   AUTOMATED
microsoft/aspnet                          ASP.NET is an open source server-side Web application framework                 498                  [OK]
microsoft/dotnet                          Official images for .NET Core for Linux and Windows Server 2016 Nano Server     331                  [OK]
mono                                      Mono is an open source implementation of Microsoft's .NET Framework             196       [OK]
microsoft/windowsservercore               Windows Server 2016 Server Core base OS image for Windows containers            71
microsoft/nanoserver                      Windows Server 2016 Nano Server base OS image for Windows containers            68
microsoft/azure-cli                       Docker image for Microsoft Azure Command Line Interface                         66                   [OK]
microsoft/iis                             Internet Information Services (IIS) installed in a Windows Server Core based container  50
microsoft/mssql-server-2014-express-windows  Microsoft SQL Server 2014 Express installed in Windows Server Core based containers.  42
microsoft/mssql-server-2016-express-windows  Microsoft SQL Server 2016 Express installed in Windows Server Core based containers.  29
microsoft/aspnetcore                      Official images for running compiled ASP.NET Core applications.                 29                   [OK]
microsoft/dotnet-framework                The official Docker images for .NET Framework on Windows Server 2016 Server Core.  11
microsoft/powershell                      Official PowerShell Core releases from https://github.com/PowerShell/PowerShell/releases  9  [OK]
microsoft/oms                             Monitor your containers using the Operations Management Suite (OMS). For minimal OS like CoreOS.  7  [OK]
microsoft/aspnetcore-build                Official images for building ASP.NET Core applications.                         7                    [OK]
microsoft/applicationinsights             Application Insights for Docker helps you monitor your containerized applications.  4  [OK]
microsoft/vsts-agent                      Official images for the Visual Studio Team Services (VSTS) agent.               4
microsoft/dotnet35                        The .NET Framework 3.5 image has moved to microsoft/dotnet-framework:3.5        4
microsoft/dotnet-nightly                  Preview bits of the .NET Core CLI                                               2                    [OK]
microsoft/powershell-nightly              Nightly builds of PowerShell Core for CI                                        2                    [OK]
cvugrinec/microsoft-prep70533                                                                                             0
microsoft/aspnetcore-build-nightly        Images to build preview versions of ASP.NET Core applications.                  0                    [OK]
berlius/microsoft-malmo                   Microsoft-malmo - artificial intelligence - training agent on MINECRAFT         0
microsoft/dotnet-samples                  .NET Core Docker Samples                                                        0                    [OK]
microsoft/cntk                            CNTK                                                                            0                    [OK]
dreher/microsoft                          Microsoft Test Repo                                                             0
PS C:\temp>
```

FIGURE 4-23 Output of the Docker Search command

Pushing images

To upload your own images to the repository, you use the Docker Push command, as in the following example:

```
docker push hholt/nano1
```

By default, the Docker Push command uploads the specified image to your public repository on the DockerHub, as shown in Figure 4-24. Anyone can access images pushed in this way.

```
PS C:\temp> docker push craigz3/nano1
The push refers to a repository [docker.io/craigz3/nano1]
0bc9597871ad: Pushed
2c195a33d84d: Skipped foreign layer
342d4e407550: Skipped foreign layer
0.9: digest: sha256:1518e997672c384bad70aeb897de64689fef78fcb420e9fda86b933e25f1cd6b size: 1155
PS C:\temp>
```

FIGURE 4-24 Output of the Docker Push command

Because Docker is open source software, sharing images and code with the community is a large part of the company's philosophy. However, it is also possible to create private repositories, which you can share with an unlimited number of collaborators you select. This enables you to use DockerHub for secure application development projects or any situation in which you do not want to deploy an image to the public. DockerHub provides a single private repository as part of its free service, but for additional repositories, you must purchase a subscription.

In addition to storing and providing images, DockerHub provides other services as well, such as automated builds. By uploading a dockerfile and any other necessary files to a repository, you can configure DockerHub to automatically execute builds for you, to your exact specifications. The code files are available to your collaborators, and new builds can occur whenever the code changes.

Manage container images using Microsoft Azure

In addition to creating containers locally, you can also use them on Microsoft Azure. By creating a Windows Server 2016 virtual machine on Azure, you can create and manage containers just as you would on a local server. Azure also provides the Azure Container Service (ACS), which enables you to create, configure, and manage a cluster of virtual machines, configured to run container-based applications using various open source technologies.

Microsoft Azure is a subscription-based cloud service that enables you to deploy virtual machines and applications and integrate them into your existing enterprise. By paying a monthly fee, you can create a Windows Server 2016 virtual machine, as shown in Figure 4-25. Once you have created the virtual machine, you can install the Containers feature and the Docker engine. Containers and images that you create on an Azure virtual machine are completely compatible with the Docker implementations on your local computers.

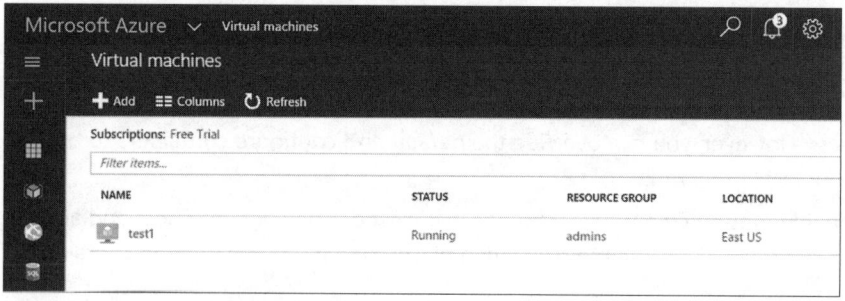

FIGURE 4-25 Microsoft Azure Resource Center

Chapter summary

- Containers are based on images. You create a container by running an image, and you create an image by saving the contents of a container.
- Windows Server 2016 includes the Containers feature, which provides the support environment for the Docker platform.
- Both the Server Core and Nano Server installation options support the creation of Windows Server and Hyper-V containers. In Nano Server, you can run the Docker.exe client on a remote system.
- Docker is an open source container solution that consists of two files: Dockerd.exe, which is the engine that runs as a service on Windows, and Docker.exe, which is the command line client that controls the Dockerd engine.

- Using a text file called daemon.json, you can configure start-up options for the Dockerd engine.
- The Docker client is one way to control the Docker engine, but it is not the only way. You can also use the Docker module for Windows PowerShell to perform the same tasks.
- To download images from the Docker Hub, you use the Docker Pull command.
- Tags are version indicators that developers can use to track the builds or versions of a container image. To assign tag values, you use the Docker Tag command.
- To uninstall a container image, you use the Docker RMI command.
- To create a Windows Server container, you use the Docker Run command, specifying the name of a container image.
- The procedure for creating a Hyper-V container using Docker differs from a Windows Server container only in the inclusion of the --isolation parameter.
- The Docker.exe client enables you to control containers by starting, stopping, saving, and removing them.
- The Docker module for Windows PowerShell provides an alternative to the Docker.exe client that can perform most, if not all, of the same functions.
- By default, Docker uses network address translation to provide containers with network access. However, you can override the default and configure containers to be part of your larger network.
- Docker enables you to create data volumes that exist on the container host and add them to a container. Data volumes remain in place, even if you remove the container itself.
- Using parameters on the Docker Run command line, you can limit the amount of memory and CPU resources a container is permitted to use.
- A dockerfile is a script that contains instructions for building a new container image. You use the Docker Build command to execute the script and create the image.
- Docker Hub is a free repository, based in the cloud, on which you can upload your
- Microsoft Azure enables you to create virtual machines that you can use as container hosts.

Thought experiment

In this thought experiment, demonstrate your skills and knowledge of the topics covered in this chapter. You can find answer to this thought experiment in the next section.

Ralph wants to create a virtual machine called Core1 that functions as a container host for both Windows Server and Hyper-V containers. To create the container host, he plans to perform the following tasks:

- Create a virtual machine.
- Configure the virtual machine with 4 GB of memory, two virtual processors, and MAC address spoofing enabled.
- Install Windows Server 2016 on the virtual machine.
- Install the Containers feature.
- Install the Hyper-V role.
- Install the dockermsftprovider module.
- Install the Docker package.
- Pull the Server Core image from DockerHub.
- Create containers using the Docker Run command.

What step has Ralph forgotten, that prevents him from creating the containers he needs? What task must he perform to complete his plan, and when should he complete it?

Thought experiment answer

This section contains the solution to the thought experiment.

Ralph has forgotten to expose the virtualization extensions of the physical computer's processor to the VM, so that it can run the Hyper-V role. To do this, he must run the following command in a PowerShell session after creating the virtual machine and before he starts it:

```
set-vmprocessor -vmname server1 -exposevirtualizationextensions $true
```

CHAPTER 5

Implement high availability

Keeping applications running at all times is a major priority for many system administrators, and Windows Server 2016 includes features that enable you to create redundant server solutions that can anticipate nearly any type of disaster. Failover clusters enable you to create servers that share data, which ensures that an application runs in spite of multiple failures. Network Load Balancing clusters enable you to provide an application with both fault tolerance and scalability.

Skills in this chapter:

- Implement high availability and disaster recovery options in Hyper-V
- Implement failover clustering
- Implement Storage Spaces Direct
- Manage failover clustering
- Manage VM movement in clustered nodes
- Implement Network Load Balancing (NLB)

Skill 5.1: Implement high availability and disaster recovery options in Hyper-V

Hyper-V enables administrators to consolidate multiple physical servers into a single Hyper-V server. One of the advantages of virtualizing servers in this way is that you can easily move virtual machines (VMs) from one Hyper-V host to another. Whether it is for fault tolerance reasons or load balancing, Hyper-V provides several technologies for replicating and migrating VMs.

This section covers how to:

- Implement Hyper-V Replica
- Implement Live Migration
- Implement Shared Nothing Live Migration
- Configure CredSSP or Kerberos authentication protocol for Live Migration
- Implement Storage Migration

Implement Hyper-V Replica

Hyper-V Replica is a feature of the Hyper-V role that enables you to create a replica of the virtual machines on a Hyper-V server to another server, locally or at a remote site. The replication is asynchronous, and the failover process to the replica is not automatic. However, Hyper-V Replica is easy to set up and does not require advanced networking features, such as shared storage or a failover cluster. It is a simple way to create a replica of a Hyper-V server that you can start up whenever the primary server is unavailable.

Hyper-V replica is based on checkpoints, so after the initial replication is completed, only the changes made to the primary server are checkpointed and replicated. This minimizes the amount of data transmitted over the network and enables the replica server to load the virtual machine be accessing its checkpoints.

Hyper-V Replica has a lot of options. It does not require a failover cluster, but it works on one. It does not require certificates for encrypted transmissions, but it can use them. This enables administrators to create as simple or as complex a configuration as they need.

Planning the replication environment

In its simplest form, a Hyper-V Replica implementation uses two servers in the following configuration:

- Hyper-V installed on both servers
- Servers are located behind the same firewall
- Servers are not part of a cluster
- Servers are joined to the same Active Directory Domain Services (AD DS) domain or to domains with mutual trust relationships
- Servers use Kerberos-authenticated, unencrypted communication

Any exceptions to these policies require additional setup procedures, such as the following:

- If the servers are located at different sites, you must configure the intervening firewalls to allow the replication traffic to pass.
- If the replication traffic is to be encrypted, you must obtain a security certificate from an appropriate certification authority (or use a self-signed certificate).
- If the servers are part of a failover cluster, you must configure the Hyper-V Replica Broker role and make note the client access point name.
- If you want to use a third server to create an additional replica, you must configure Hyper-V Replica to use Extended Replication.

Configuring the Hyper-V Servers

To configure replication in one direction, you must configure Hyper-V Replica on the destination server, also called the replica server. However, to use Hyper-V Replica as a failover solution, the recommended practice is to configure both servers as replica servers. This way, after a failover incident in which you activate a replica server, you can replicate any changes made in the interim back to the original server once it is back online.

To configure a Hyper-V server as a replica server with Hyper-V Manager, use the following procedure:

1. Open Hyper-V Manager, select the server, and, in the Actions pane, click Hyper-V Settings to display the Hyper-V Settings dialog box.
2. On the Replication Configuration page, select the Enable This Computer As A Replica Server checkbox, as shown in Figure 5-1.

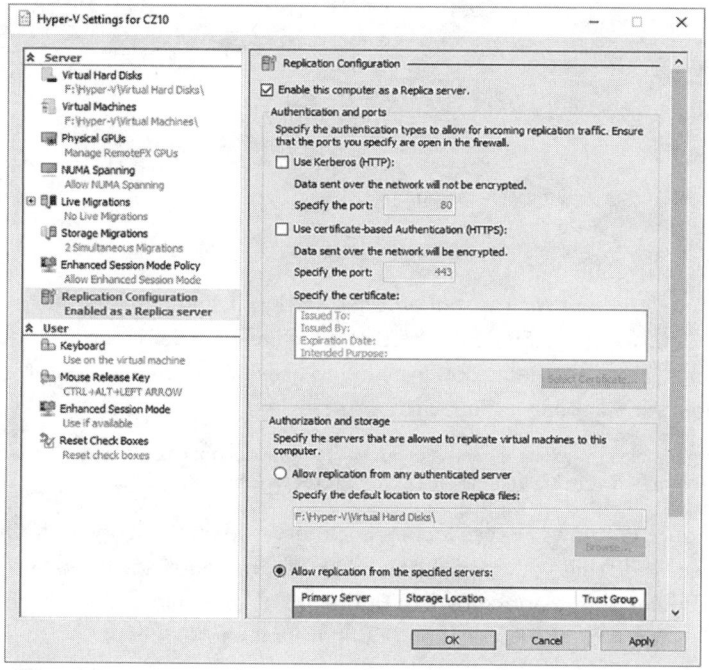

FIGURE 5-1 The Replication Configuration page of the Hyper-V Settings dialog box

3. In the Authentication and Ports box, select one of the following options:
   - **Use Kerberos (HTTP)** Replica traffic will not be encrypted, and the servers must be joined to the same domain (or trusted domains).
   - **Use Certificate-Based Authentication (HTTPS)** Click Select Certificate to specify the certificate to use for replica traffic encryption.
4. In the Authorization and Storage box, select one of the following options:

- **Allow Replication From Any Authenticated Server** Enables replication from any server, and saves replicas to the location you specify.
- **Allowed Replication From The Specified Servers** Click Add to open the Add Authorization Entry dialog box, shown in Figure 5-2, in which you specify a server name, a location for the replicas from that server, and a trust group to which it belongs.

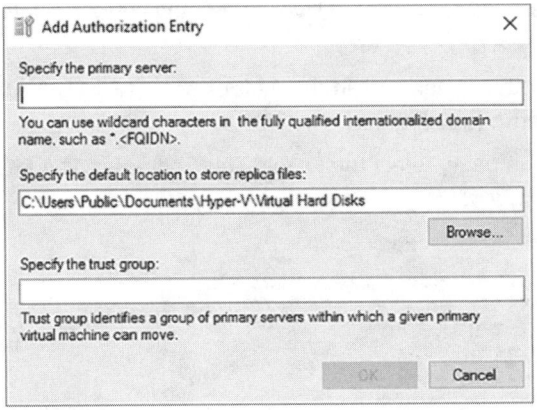

FIGURE 5-2 The Add Authorization Entry dialog box

5. Click OK.

You can also configure a server's replica configuration settings using the Set-VmReplicationServer cmdlet for Windows PowerShell. This cmdlet is included in the Hyper-V module, so you must have the Hyper-V management tools installed to use it. The command for a simple Hyper-V Replica configuration appears as follows:

```
set-vmreplicationserver -replicationenabled $true -allowedauthenticationtype kerberos
-replicationallowedfromanyserver $true -defaultstoragelocation d:\replicas
```

You must also configure Windows Firewall on a replica server to allow incoming traffic from the primary server. To do this, you open the Windows Firewall with Advanced Security console and, on the Inbound Rules page, shown in Figure 5-3, enable one of the following rules, based on your selections on the Replication Configuration page:

- If you selected the Use Kerberos (HTTP) option, enable the Hyper-V Replica HTTP Listener (TCP-In) rule.
- If you selected the Use certificate-based authentication (HTTPS) option, enable the Hyper-V Replica HTTPS Listener (TCP-In) rule.

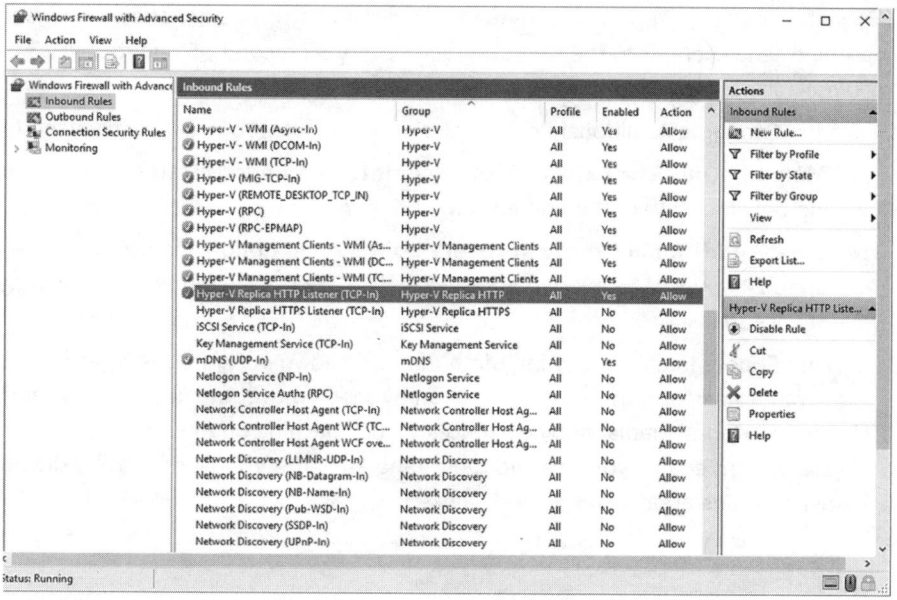

FIGURE 5-3 The Windows Firewall with Advanced Security console

To configure the firewall rule using PowerShell, you use the Enable-NetFirewallRule cmdlet, as in the following examples:

```
enable-netfirewallrule -displayname "hyper-v replica http listener (tcp-in)"

enable-netfirewallrule -displayname "hyper-v replica https listener (tcp-in)"
```

As mentioned earlier, this configuration process is only required on the replica server, but you might want to consider configuring the primary server in the same way, in anticipation of a recovery from a failover situation.

Configuring the virtual machines

Once the replica server is configured, you can proceed to configure the virtual machines on the primary server that you intend to replicate. To do this, use the following procedure.

1. In Hyper-V Manager, right-click a virtual machine and in the context menu, select Enable Replication to launch the Enable Replication Wizard.
2. On the Specify Replica Server page, type the name of the replica server you have configured, or click Browse to open a Select Computer dialog box.
3. On the Specify Connection Parameters page, in the Authentication Type box, specify whether to use Kerberos or certificate-based authentication, using the same setting you chose on the replica server. You can also specify whether to compress the replication data.
4. On the Choose Replication VHDs page, clear the checkboxes for any VHDs on the virtual machine that you do not want to replicate.

5. On the Configure Replication Frequency page, specify how often the primary server should send changes to the replica server—every 30 seconds, 5 minutes, or 15 minutes.
6. On the Configure Additional Recovery Points page, select one of the following options:
   - **Maintain Only The Latest Recovery Point** This option creates a replica containing only the state of the primary VM at the time of the last replication event.
   - **Create Additional Hourly Recovery Points** This option enables you to replicate up to 24 hours of recovery points and up to 12 hours of Volume Shadow Copy Service snapshots.
7. On the Choose Initial Replication Method page, shown in Figure 5-4, specify whether you want to perform the initial replication by sending over the network, by hand carrying it on external media, or by creating a virtual machine on the replica server yourself. These options enable you to avoid replicating an entire VM over relatively slow or expensive wide area network (WAN) links.

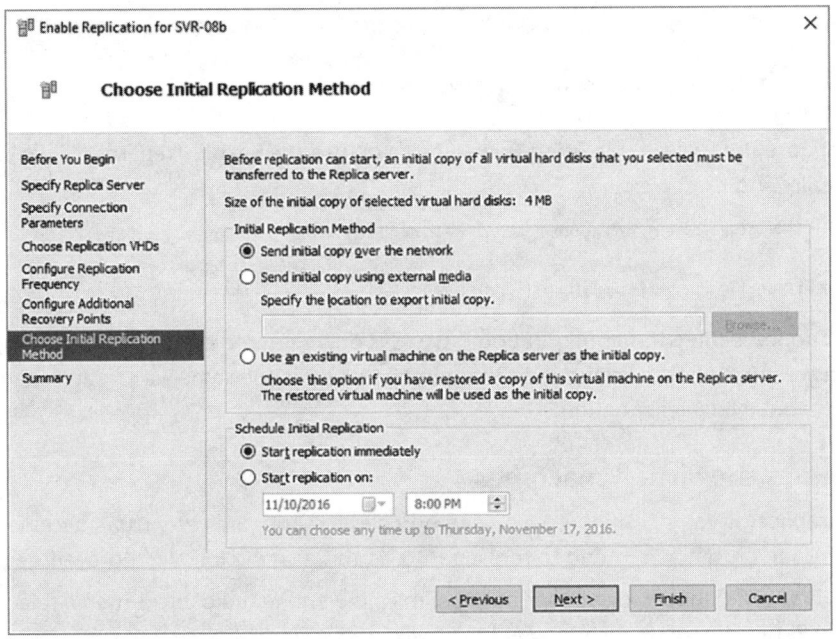

FIGURE 5-4 The Choose Initial Replication Method page of the Enable Replication Wizard

8. In the Schedule Initial Replication box, specify when the replication process should begin—immediately or at a time you specify.
9. Click Finish.

Once the replication process begins, a Replication context menu appears when you right-click the VM, enabling you to initiate a planned failover, pause or remove the replication process, and display a Replication Heath dialog box, as shown in Figure 5-5.

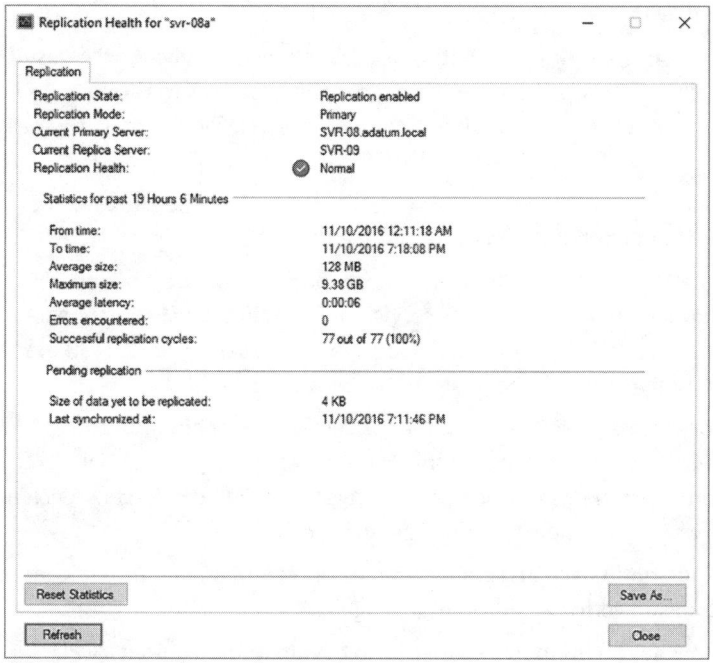

FIGURE 5-5 The Replication Health dialog box

Implement live migration

One of the main advantages of server virtualization, if not the main advantage, is the ability to consolidate multiple physical servers into one Hyper-V server running multiple virtual machines. Because the VMs all run on the same virtualized hardware platform, it is easy to move them around to different Hyper-V hosts, for load balancing or fault tolerance purposes. *Live Migration* is a Hyper-V feature that makes it possible to move a virtual machine from one Hyper-V host to another while it is running, with almost no interruption of service.

Live Migration is not an alternative to Hyper-V Replica; it does not move the virtual machine's data files. Live Migration is designed for environments in which virtual machines already have access to shared data storage; what is migrated is the system state and the live memory contents. If, for example, you have a Hyper-V failover cluster that runs a web server, with the cluster nodes all accessing the same storage array containing the web site files, Live Migration can move a VM from Hyper-V host to another without interrupting the client transactions in progress.

Originally conceived for use on failover clusters with physical shared storage subsystems, Live Migration in Windows Server 2016 can now work with non-clustered systems, systems in different domains, or no domains at all, and systems using nearly any type of shared storage, physical or virtual.

A typical Live Migration of a virtual machine takes place as follows:

1. The source server establishes a connection with the destination server, which creates an unpopulated virtual machine and confirms that it has the resources to recreate the source VM, such as sufficient memory and access to the shared storage containing the VM files.
2. The destination allocates memory and other resources to the new VM, essentially recreating the virtual hardware configuration of the source VM.
3. The source server begins transmitting the VM's memory pages to the destination VM. The source VM is still functioning at this point, servicing clients in the usual manner. As the memory transfer proceeds, however, Hyper-V on the source server starts marking any pages in its memory that have changed since the transfer began.
4. After the initial memory transfer is completed, the process begins again, with the source server transferring any memory pages that have changed since the initial transfer began. This process repeats through several iterations, until the servers reach a critical point at which point their memory states are identical.
5. At this point, processing and I/O are suspended on the source VM and control of the storage resources is transferred to the destination VM.
6. The destination VM now has an up to date "working set" of memory contents, CPU state, and storage resources, and can take over the VM's functionality.
7. With the destination VM up and running, Hyper-V notifies the network switch of the change, causing it to register the MAC addresses of the destination VM and associate them with its IP address, so that network traffic is diverted to the new virtual machine.

Despite all this activity, a live migration is typically completed in less time than the VM's TCP time-to-live interval. The changeover is therefore invisible, both to the clients and to the software running on the virtual machine. There are many factors that can affect the speed of a live migration, including the amount of memory to be transferred, the available bandwidth on the network, and the workload on the source and destination servers. However, any perceptible delay that occurs is usually caused by the time needed for the network to propagate the change in destination.

Live migration in a cluster

When you use the Failover Clustering feature in Windows Server 2016 to create a Hyper-V cluster, you use the Failover Cluster Manager console to initiate the New Virtual Machine Wizard. The wizard itself is the same as the one you can access through the Hyper-V Manager, but after the VM is created, Failover Cluster Manager launches the High Availability Wizard, which configures the VM to support Live Migration. In the PowerShell equivalent, you use the standard cmdlets to create the VM, and then run the Add-ClusterVirtualMachineRole cmdlet to make the virtual machine highly available.

Live migration without a cluster

It is possible, in Windows Server 2016, to perform live migrations between Hyper-V servers that are not clustered, although they must be members of the same domain (or trusted domains). Before you can do this, however, you must configure the Live Migration settings, in both the source and the destination server.

To do this using the Hyper-V Manager, open the Hyper-V Settings dialog box, select the Live Migration page, and select the Enable Incoming And Outgoing Live Migrations checkbox, as shown in Figure 5-6.

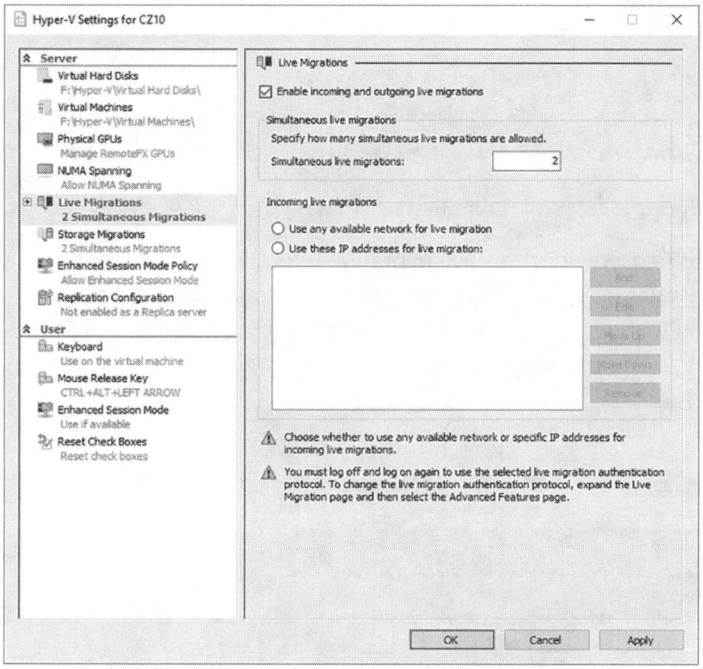

FIGURE 5-6 The Live Migrations page in the Hyper-V Settings dialog box

Then, configure the following settings on that page and the Live Migrations/Advanced Features page:

- **Simultaneous Live Migrations** Enables you to specify how many live migrations the server can perform at the same time, based on the bandwidth and traffic levels of your network and the workload on the server. The default setting is 2.
- **Incoming Live Migrations** If the server is connected to more than one network, this setting enables you to specify which network the server should use for live migration traffic and the order in which multiple networks should be used. Whenever possible, the best practice is to separate live migration traffic from standard local area network traffic (LAN).

- **Authentication Protocol** Enables you to specify whether to use CredSSP or Kerberos for authentication between the servers. Kerberos requires additional configuration of constrained delegation in Active Directory.
- **Performance Options** Enables you to specify whether to use the TCP/IP or Server Message Block (SMB) protocols for the live migration data transfers. If you have a network dedicated to storage traffic, or a network that uses datacenter bridging to separate LAN and storage traffic, SMB is probably a better choice. On a standard LAN connection, use TCP/IP.

To configure these settings using PowerShell, you use commands like the following:

```
enable-vmmmigration

set-vmmigrationnetwork 192.168.4.0

set-vmhost -virtualmachinemigrationauthenticatiuontype kerberos

set-vmhost -virtualmachinemigrationperformanceoption smbtransport
```

Once the servers are configured, you initiate a live migration using the Move Wizard, which you access by selecting a VM in Hyper-V Manager, choosing Move from the Actions pane. On the wizard's Choose Move Type page, shown in Figure 5-7, the Move The Virtual Machine option enables you to perform a live migration.

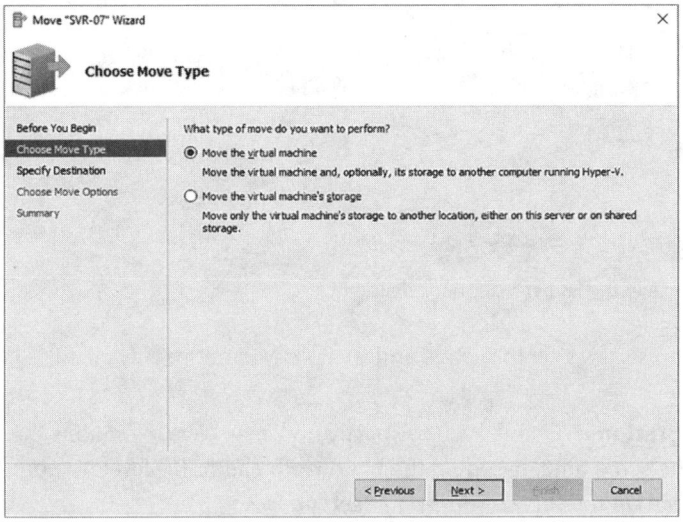

FIGURE 5-7 The Choose Move Type page in the Move Wizard

When you select Move The Virtual Machine, the Choose Move Options page, shown in Figure 5-8, provides the following options:

- **Move The Virtual Machine's Data To A Single location** Causes the wizard to move the virtual machine and its storage to the default location on the destination server

- **Move The Virtual Machine's Data By Selecting Where To Move The Items** Causes the wizard to move the virtual machine and its storage to a location you specify on the destination server.
- **Move Only The Virtual Machine** Causes the wizard to move the virtual machine to the destination server without its storage. This option provided the non-clustered equivalent of a live migration.

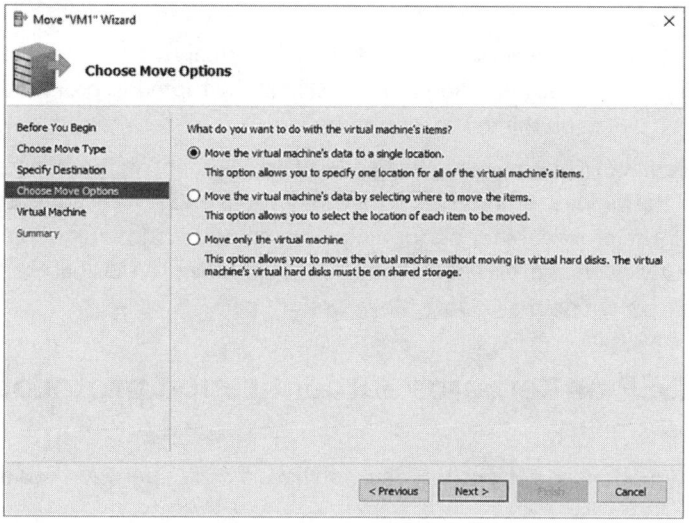

FIGURE 5-8 The Choose Move Options page in the Move Wizard

To perform a live migration with PowerShell, you use the Move-VM cmdlet, as in the following example:

```
Move-vm -vm server1 -destinationhost hyper2
```

Implement shared nothing live migration

Live Migration was originally a tool with highly restrictive requirements. Your servers had to be part of a cluster and the virtual machines had to have access to shared storage.Windows Server 2016 makes it possible to migrate virtual machines between Hyper-V hosts with neither of those requirements, using a feature known as Shared Nothing Live Migration.

Shared Nothing Live Migration is essentially a combination of a live migration and a storage migration. On the surface, the procedure is essentially the same as the one described for a live migration, except that the source server copies the VM's storage to the destination, in addition to its memory and system state. Obviously, the migration process takes much longer than that of a standard live migration, depending on the amount of storage involved and the network bandwidth available, but as with a live migration, the source VM continues to remain active until the data transfer is complete.

A shared nothing live migration has the following prerequisites:

- The source and destination VMs must be members of the same AD DS domain (or trusted domains).
- The source and domain servers must be using the same processor family (Intel or AMD).
- The source and destination servers must be connected by an Ethernet network running at a minimum of 1 gigabit per second (Gbps).
- The source and destination servers should have identical virtual switches that use the same name. If they do not, the migration process will be interrupted to prompt the operator to select a switch on the destination server.

As with a non-clustered live migration, you must enable Live Migration in the Hyper-V Settings dialog box, and the various settings on the Live Migrations and Advanced Features pages apply here as well. The procedure for performing a shared nothing live migration is the same also, using the Move Wizard, except that you select the Move The Virtual Machine's Data To A Single Location option on the Choose Move Options page.

Configure CredSSP or Kerberos authentication protocol for Live Migration

When you enable Live Migration on a Hyper-V server, you have a choice between two authentication protocols:

- **Credential Security Support Provider (CredSSP)** CredSSP is an authentication protocol that enables a client to delegate a user's credentials for authentication on a remote server. In Hyper-V, CredSSP is the default authentication protocol for Live Migration. The protocol requires no special configuration, but it does require a user to sign in to the source server before performing a live migration.
- **Kerberos** The default authentication protocol for Active Directory, Kerberos does not require you to sign on, as CredSSP does, but you do have to configure it to use constrained delegation before you can perform live migrations.

Constrained delegation is an element of the Kerberos protocol that enables a server to act on behalf of a user, but only for specific services. To configure constrained delegation, you must be logged on as a domain administrator and use the following procedure.

1. Open the Active Directory Users And Computers console.
2. Browse to the Computers container and locate the computer object for the Live Migration source server.
3. Open the Properties sheet for the source server's computer object and select the Delegation tab, as shown in Figure 5-9.

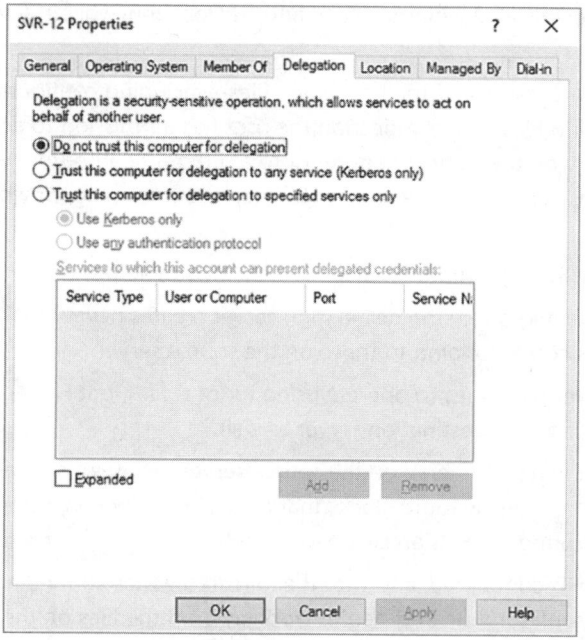

FIGURE 5-9 The Delegation tab of a computer object's Properties sheet

4. Select the Trust This Computer For Delegation To The Specified Services Only option, and leave the Use Kerberos Only option selected.
5. Click Add and, in the Add Services dialog box, click Users or Computers.
6. In the Select Users or Computers dialog box, type the name of the destination server and click OK.
7. In the Available Services box, select one or both of the following services, as needed, and click OK.
   - **cifs** Enables the computer user to move virtual machine storage, with or without the virtual machine itself.
   - **Microsoft Virtual System Migration Service** Enables the computer to move virtual machines.
8. Click OK to close the Properties sheet.
9. Repeat the procedure for the Live Migration destination computer, specifying the name of the source computer in the Select Users Or Computers dialog box.

Implement storage migration

Live Migration is designed to move a virtual machine from one Hyper-V host server to another, without touching the files, which are presumed to be accessible on shared storage. Storage Migration (sometimes referred to, somewhat inaccurately, as Storage Live Migration) is the exact opposite; it moves the virtual machine's files to another location, while the VM itself remains in place.

You can use Storage Migration to move a virtual machine's files—including configuration files, checkpoints, and Smart Paging files—to any location the user has permission to access, including another disk or directory on the same computer or to a different computer. As with Live Migration, storage migrations can occur while the virtual machine is running, or while it's stopped.

Compared to a Live Migration, Storage Migration uses a relatively simple process:

1. When you initiate a storage migration, the destination server creates new virtual hard disk files of sizes and types corresponding to those on the source server.
2. The VM on the source server continues to operate using its local files, but Hyper-V begins mirroring disk writes to the destination server as well.
3. While continuing to mirror writes, Hyper-V on the source server initiates a single-pass copy of the source disks to the destination. Blocks that have already been written to the destination by the mirroring process are skipped.
4. When the single-pass copy is completed, and with the mirrored writes continuing, Hyper-V updates the VM configuration and begins working from the files on the destination server.
5. Once the VM is running successfully from the migrated files, Hyper-V deletes the source files.

If the source VM is turned off, there is no need for any special procedure. Hyper-V simply copies the files from the source to the destination, reconfigures the VM to use the destination files, and then deletes the source files.

There are hardly any special requirements for performing a storage migration, except that you cannot migrate VMs that use pass-through disks for their storage. The files must be stored on virtual hard disk (either VHD or VHDX) files.

To perform a storage migration, use the same Move Wizard as for non-clustered live migrations and shared nothing live migrations. On the wizard's Choose Move Type page, you select the Move The Virtual Machine's Storage option. The Choose Options For Moving Storage page appears, as shown in Figure 5-10, with the following options:

- **Move All Of The Virtual Machine's Data To A Single Location** Enables you to specify one destination for all of the source VM's files.
- **Move All Of The Virtual Machine's Data To Different Locations** Adds multiple screen to the wizard, on which you can select the file types to migrate and specify a destination for each type.
- **Move Only The Virtual Machine's Virtual Hard Disks** Enables you to select which VHD/VHDX files to migrate and specify a destination for each one.

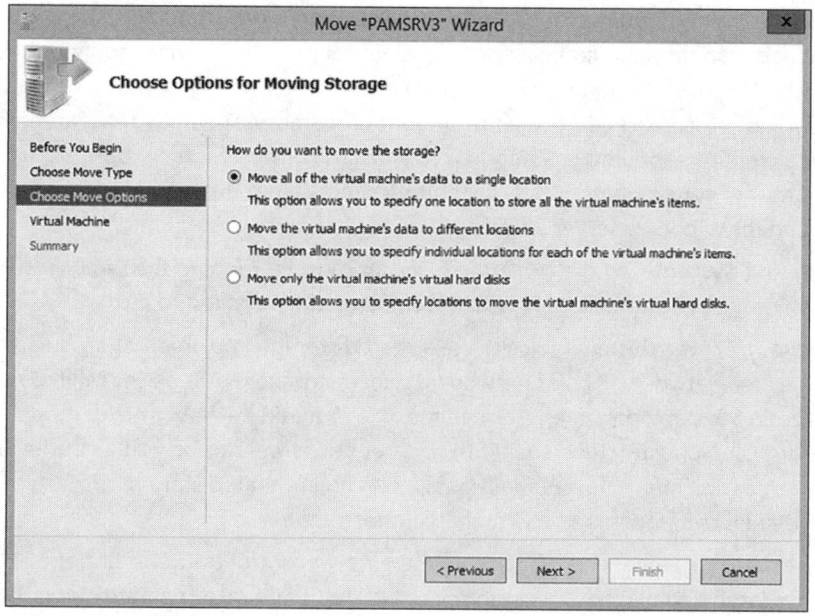

FIGURE 5-10 The Choose Options For Moving Storage page in the Move Wizard

Skill 5.2: Implement failover clustering

A *failover cluster* is a group of two or more computers—physical or virtual, and running the same application—that functions as a single entity to provide a highly available, scalable, and fault tolerant service to clients on the network. Clustered applications typically provide essential user services, such as database and email server applications, or infrastructure services, such as Hyper-V and file servers. With multiple computers—called *nodes*— running the same application, the services are always available, even when a node fails. When demand for the service increases, administrators can easily add more nodes to the cluster, increasing its overall capacity.

In Windows Server 2016, the Failover Clustering feature provides the tools needed to create a cluster of as many as 64 computers, supporting up to 8,000 virtual machines, with a maximum of 1,024 VMs per node. The feature includes a graphical management tool, the Failover Cluster Manager console, plus a Windows PowerShell module with a comprehensive collection of cmdlets.

Although it's possible to create a simple two-node cluster in a lab environment, even on a single Hyper-V server, failover clusters typically have sophisticated hardware and software requirements, especially when they provide vital services to many clients in a production environment. Hardware and software requirements include the following:

- **Servers** The computers that function as cluster nodes are intended to be interchangeable, so they should be as close to identical in their hardware configurations as possible. The ideal situation is one in which every cluster node has the same number and type of processors and the same amount of memory. The network adapters in all of the computers should be configured identically. For Microsoft support, all hardware and software components in the cluster nodes must meet the qualifications for the Certified for Windows Server 2016 logo.
- **Operating System** All the servers in a cluster must be running the same version and edition of the operating system, with the same updates applied to it.
- **Storage** Failover clusters typically use a shared storage implementation, such as a storage area network (SAN) or network attached storage (NAS), so that all the nodes can access the same data files. At one time, this required an elaborate, dedicated storage hardware infrastructure, even if the cluster nodes were to be virtual, but technologies such as iSCSI have now made it possible to create shared storage subsystems using off-the-shelf components and virtual disk infrastructures.
- **Networking** Failover clusters exchange their own control traffic among the nodes, and in a large deployment, it is recommended that there be a separate network dedicated to cluster traffic. In addition, the shared storage infrastructure should typically have its own dedicated network as well. Thus, a failover cluster implementation can have three or more network interfaces per node, supporting these various kinds of traffic, as well as the additional switches, cabling, and other components necessary to support the additional networks. For mission critical applications, it can also be necessary to compound the network implementations with redundant adapters, switches, and cabling, to avoid single points of failure. For smaller deployments, such as in a lab environment, it is also possible to use Quality of Service technologies, such as Datacenter Bridging, to reserve bandwidth on a single network for these various types of traffic.
- **Applications** In addition to the hardware requirements for the cluster itself, you must also consider the requirements for the application that will be running on the cluster nodes. For example, the nodes in a Hyper-V cluster must meet the virtualization hardware requirements specified for the Hyper-V role.

Because the hardware configuration is such an integral part of building a cluster, the Failover Cluster Manager includes a Validate Cluster Wizard that performs a series of tests on the servers you select, to determine if they are eligible for membership in a cluster. You can also use the Test-Cluster PowerShell cmdlet to initiate these tests. The validation process generates a detailed report, like the one shown in Figure 5-11.

Microsoft

Failover Cluster Validation Report

Node:	SVR-10.adatum.local	Validated
Node:	SVR-11.adatum.local	Validated
Started	11/12/2016 5:06:49 PM	
Completed	11/12/2016 6:07:34 PM	

The Validate a Configuration Wizard must be run after any change is made to the configuration of the cluster or hardware. For more information, see http://go.microsoft.com/fwlink/p/?LinkId=280145.

Results by Category

Name	Result Summary	Description
Cluster Configuration		Success
Hyper-V Configuration		Success
Inventory		Success
Network		Success
Storage		Not Applicable
System Configuration		Warning

FIGURE 5-11 A Failover Cluster Validation Report

Once the hardware configuration of the cluster has been validated successfully, you can proceed to create the cluster, using the Create Cluster Wizard or the New-Cluster cmdlet. To do this, you specify the name of the servers that you want to add as nodes in the cluster. You also specify a name for the cluster, which is how it will be addressed on the network, as shown in the following example:

```
new-cluster -name cluster1 -node server1,server2
```

The cluster is a separate entity, with its own name and IP address. If there is a DHCP server available on the network, the cluster will obtain an IP address from there. If not, then you must assign the cluster a static address, as in the following example:

```
new-cluster -name cluster1 -node server1,server2 -staticaddress 10.0.0.3
```

The cluster also has its own computer object in Active Directory, called a cluster name object (CNO). Once the application is running on the cluster nodes, the clients will address their requests to the cluster itself, not to an individual server.

This section covers how to:

- Implement Workgroup, Single, and Multi Domain clusters
- Configure quorum
- Configure cluster networking
- Restore single node or cluster configuration
- Configure cluster storage
- Implement Cluster-Aware Updating
- Implement Cluster Operating System Rolling Upgrade
- Configure and optimize clustered shared volumes (CSVs)
- Configure clusters without network names
- Implement Scale-Out File Server (SoFS)
- Determine different scenarios for the use of SoFS vs. Clustered File Server
- Determine usage scenarios for implementing guest clustering
- Implement a Clustered Storage Spaces solution using Shared SAS storage enclosures
- Implement Storage Replica
- Implement Cloud Witness
- Implement VM resiliency
- Implement shared VHDX as a storage solution for guest clusters

Implement workgroup, single, and multi domain clusters

Prior to Windows Server 2016, all of the servers in a failover cluster had to be joined to the same AD DS domain. This is now called a *single domain cluster.* As mentioned earlier, the Create Cluster Wizard and the New-Cluster cmdlet create an AD DS object representing the cluster by default.

Starting in Windows Server 2016, however, it is possible to create a cluster using servers joined to different domains, which is called a *multi-domain cluster,* or servers not joined to any domain at all, which is called a *workgroup cluster.*

Failover Clustering uses Active Directory for a variety of services, not least of which is locating the cluster itself. Without Active Directory support, it is necessary for the cluster to use DNS to register an administrative access point, also known as the cluster network name.

There are also Active Directory issues with some applications that prevent them from running on an multi-domain or workgroup cluster. Microsoft SQL Server functions well without Active Directory because it has its own authentication mechanism. However, a file server cluster without Active Directory authentication would require you to create user accounts on every node in the cluster.

Before you can create a multi-domain or workgroup cluster, you must complete the following tasks.

Create a local account

In a single domain cluster, one domain user account can provide access to all the nodes. Without Active Directory, access to the nodes for cluster communications is an issue. Therefore, you must create a local user account on every node, with the same user name and the same password. Then, you must add the user to the local Administrators group.

You can use the built-in Administrator account for this purpose, which is already a member of the Administrators group, if you assign it the same password on every node. However, if you do not use the Administrator account, you must set a registry key called LocalAccountTokenFilterPolicy on every node, using the following command in a PowerShell session with administrative privileges:

```
new-itemproperty -path hklm:\software\microsoft\windows\currentversion\policies\system
-name localaccounttokenfilterpolicy -value 1
```

Add DNS suffixes

Without Active Directory, a cluster must use DNS to locate the cluster nodes and the cluster itself. You must therefore specify a primary DNS suffix when assigning a name to each node, as shown in Figure 5-12.

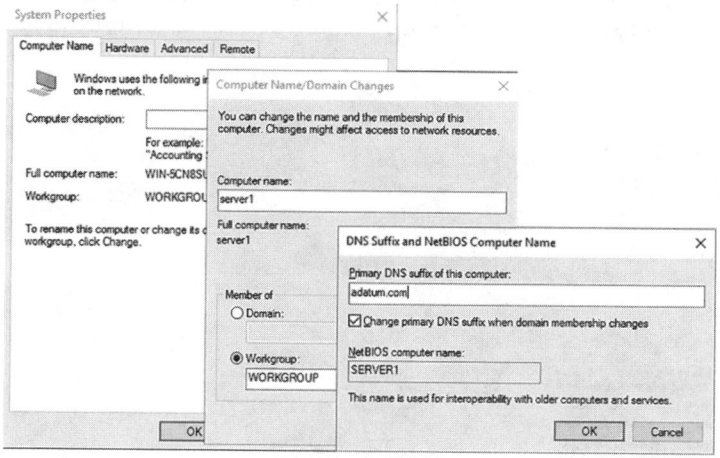

FIGURE 5-12 Assigning a primary DNS suffix

There is no direct way to configure the primary DNS suffix using PowerShell, but you can do so using Group Policy, by browsing to the Computer Configuration\Policies\Administrative Templates\Network\DNS Client folder and enabling the Primary DNS Suffix policy, as shown in Figure 5-13.

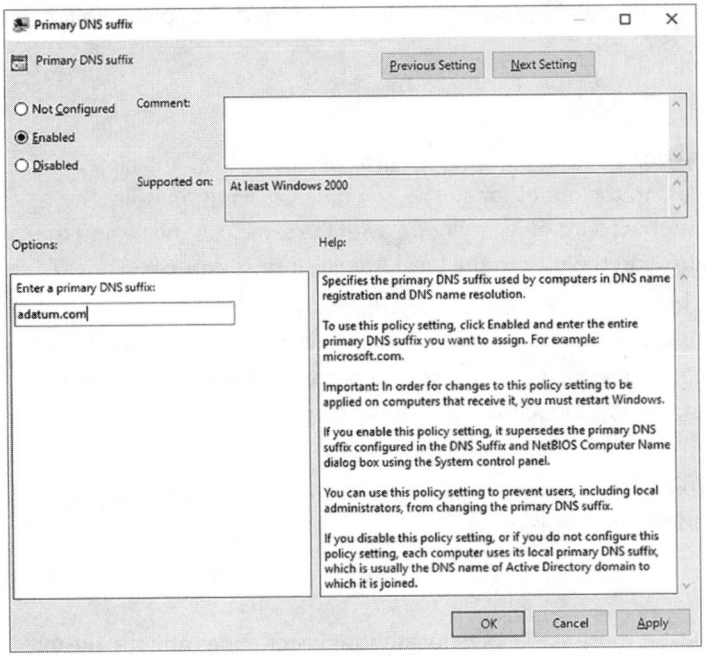

FIGURE 5-13 The Primary DNS Suffix policy dialog box

For a multi-domain cluster, you must also configure the Advanced TCP/IP Settings in every node with the DNS suffixes for all the domains represented in the cluster, as shown in Figure 5-14.

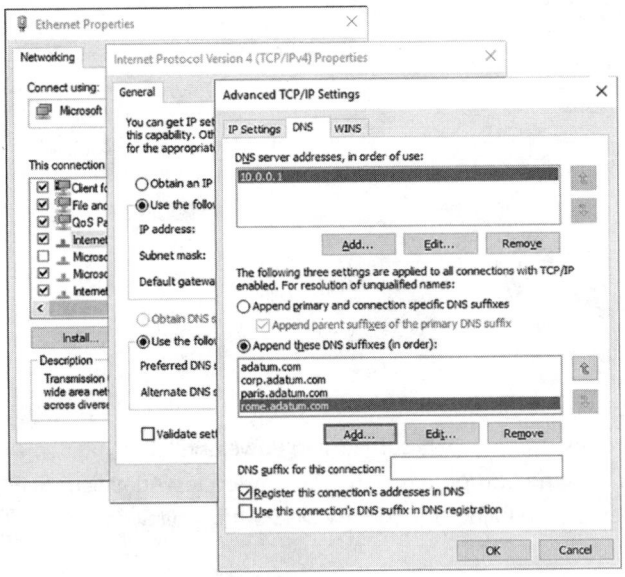

FIGURE 5-14 Specifying additional DNS suffixes

You can also do this using the Set-DnsClientGlobalSettings PowerShell cmdlet, as shown in the following example:

```
set-dnsclientglobalsettings -suffixsearchlist @("adatum.com", "corp.adatum.com", "paris.
adatum.com", "rome.adatum.com")
```

Creating a workgroup or multi-domain cluster

With these settings in place, you can proceed to create the cluster. When using PowerShell, you use the New-Cluster cmdlet, just as you would for a single domain cluster, but you must include the AdministrativeAccessPoint parameter with the DNS value, as shown in following example:

```
new-cluster -name cluster1 -node server1,server2,server3 -administrativeaccesspoint dns
```

The AdministrativeAccessPoint parameter causes the cmdlet to use a DNS name for the cluster and prevents it from creating a computer object in Active Directory. You can also use Failover Cluster Manager to create the cluster, if the computer you use is not joined to an AD DS domain.

Configure quorum

The function of *quorum* in failover clustering is to prevent a cluster from being split in two, with both halves continuing to run. This is called a *split-brain* situation. If, for example, a network failure causes a six-node cluster to be split into two three-node clusters, both could continue to function if it wasn't for quorum. If the cluster were running a database application, that would mean that there are two separate copies of the database being accessed and updated by different sets of clients at the same time. This could be disastrous for the integrity of the information in the database.

Quorum provides each node in the cluster with a vote, and in many cases, there is a witness disk adding another vote, to break potential ties. All of the nodes monitor the continual votes from the other nodes and the witness. If a node detects that the vote tally drops below 50 percent +1, it removes itself from the cluster. In the case of the six-node cluster split in half mentioned earlier, all the nodes would see the vote tally drop from 6 to 3. Because 3 is less than 50 percent +1, all the nodes would remove themselves, shutting down both halves of the cluster.

If there was a witness disk somewhere on this cluster, then the half that can contact the witness disk would have a vote tally of 4, which is 50 percent +1 of the original cluster. Therefore, the half with the witness disk would continue to function, while the nodes in the other half, with a tally of 3 votes, would remove themselves.

Quorum witnesses

When you create a failover cluster, the Create Cluster Wizard or the New-Cluster cmdlet creates a quorum configuration that, in most cases, is appropriate for the cluster, based on the number of nodes and the available storage resources. By default, each node gets one vote, and, if there is an even number of nodes, the wizard or cmdlet attempts to create a witness, to function as a tie-breaker. Like the nodes, the witness gets one vote.

A *witness* is a resource that, by its existence, casts a vote for the continued operation of the cluster. Failover clustering in Windows Server 2016 supports three types of witnesses, as follows:

- **Disk Witness** A dedicated disk in the cluster's shared storage that contains a copy of the cluster database. This is the typical option for a cluster located at a single site.
- **File Share Witness** An SMB file share on a Windows server with a Witness.log file containing information about the cluster. This is the typical option for clusters divided among multiple sites with replicated storage.
- **Cloud Witness** A blob stored in the cloud using standard Microsoft Azure services. This is a new option in Windows Server 2016, designed for stretched clusters split among multiple data centers at remote sites, which want to maintain a witness that is independent of all the data centers.

Dynamic quorum management

The default quorum configuration in Windows Server 2016 also includes *dynamic quorum management*, which is a feature that is designed to keep a cluster running in situations where it would be stopped in earlier versions of the Failover Clustering feature.

When a node leaves the cluster, dynamic quorum management automatically removes its vote, so that the functionality of the cluster is based on the quorum of the remaining votes. For example, in a five-node cluster without dynamic quorum management, if three nodes fail, the quorum vote drops to two out of five, and the remaining two nodes remove themselves, shutting down the cluster. In the same cluster with dynamic quorum management, the vote of each failing node is automatically removed from the tally, resulting in a quorum vote of two out of two, so the cluster continues to function. This feature, therefore, can enable a cluster to function, even when all but one of the nodes has failed.

Modifying the Quorum Configuration

Usually, the quorum configuration created by the Create Cluster Wizard or the New-Cluster cmdlet is suitable for the cluster and requires no adjustment. However, you can modify the quorum configuration, by running the Configure Cluster Quorum Wizard in Failover Cluster Manager, or by using the Set-ClusterQuorum cmdlet in Windows PowerShell. Using these tools, you can add or change a witness and specify which nodes should have votes in the quorum.

To run the Configure Cluster Quorum Wizard, you select the cluster in Failover Cluster Manager and, in the Actions pane, select More Actions | Configure Cluster Quorum Settings. On the Select Quorum Configuration Option page, shown in Figure 5-15, you have the following options.

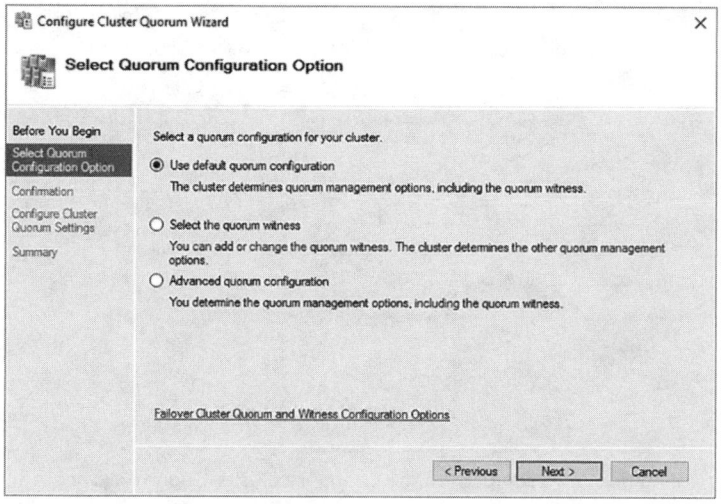

FIGURE 5-15 The Select Quorum Configuration Option page in the Configure Cluster Quorum Wizard

- **Use Default Quorum Configuration** Enables the wizard to configure an appropriate quorum configuration for the cluster without manual input.
- **Select The Quorum Witness** Enables you to add a witness, if none exists, remove an existing witness, and specify the type and location of the witness the quorum should use, as shown in Figure 5-16.

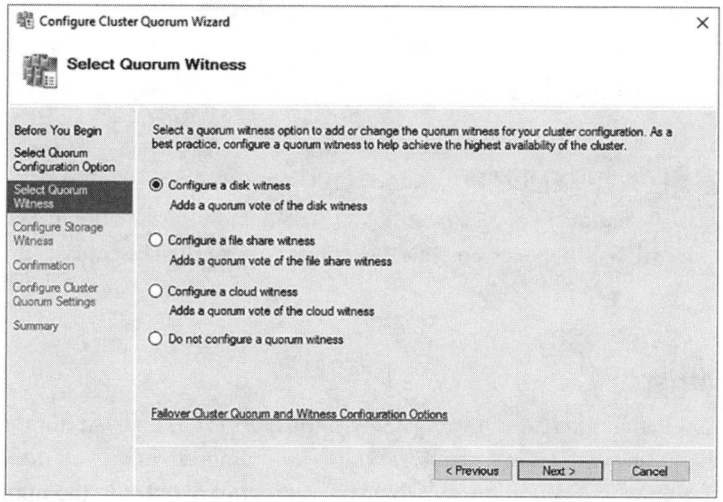

FIGURE 5-16 The Select Quorum Witness page in the Configure Cluster Quorum Wizard

- **Advanced Quorum Configuration** Enables you to specify which nodes should have votes in the quorum, as shown in Figure 5-17. It also configures the same witness settings as the Select the Quorum Witness option.

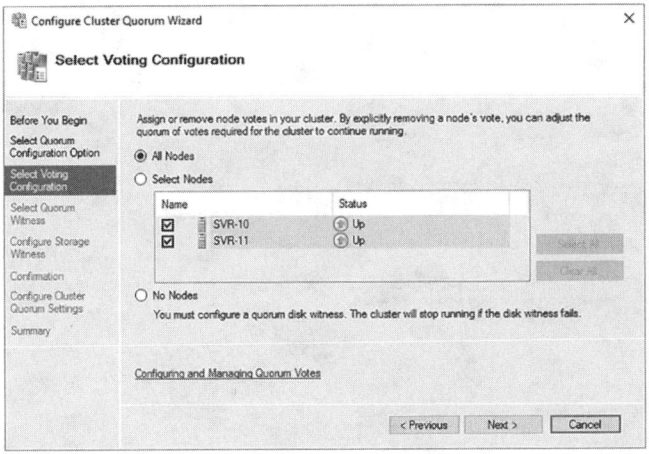

FIGURE 5-17 The Select Voting Configuration page in the Configure Cluster Quorum Wizard

To configure the quorum configuration with Windows PowerShell, you use commands like the following.

To configure the quorum to use a node majority, with no witness:

```
set-clusterquorum -cluster cluster1 -nodemajority
```

To configure the quorum with votes from each node and a disk witness:

```
set-clusterquorum -cluster cluster1 -nodeanddiskmajority "cluster disk 1"
```

To configure a cluster node to not have a quorum vote:

```
(get-clusternode clusternode1).nodeweight=0
```

> ***NOTE*** **RUNNING CLUSTERING CMDLETS**
>
> **Many of the PowerShell cmdlets in the FailoverClusters module do not function properly from a remote location. Whenever possible, you should try to run the cmdlets on a cluster node.**

Configuring a witness

In most cases, Failover Clustering creates a witness when the cluster has an even number of nodes. There can only be one witness in a cluster, and it is recommended that you do not create a witness in a situation where it would result in an even number of votes in the quorum.

When all the nodes in a cluster have access to the same shared storage, then a disk witness is the recommended configuration. The Configure Storage Witness page in the Configure Cluster Quorum Wizard, shown in Figure 5-18, enables you to select the disk that should function as the witness. The witness disk only must contain a small amount of data, so you should create a minimum-sized 512 MB NTFS disk for this purpose.

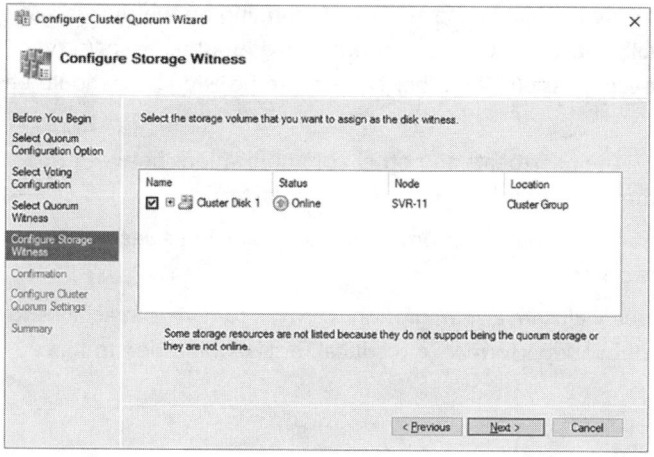

FIGURE 5-18 The Configure Storage Witness page in the Configure Cluster Quorum Wizard

The options to create a file share witness or a cloud witness are similar, enabling you to specify the location for the witness and, in the case of a cloud witness, the name and key for your Azure storage account.

Modifying quorum voting

In most cases, every node in the cluster should have a vote. It is possible to configure a cluster with no voting nodes and just a witness vote, and this might seem at first to be a viable option. If there is a node available that has access to storage, the cluster can run. However, in this configuration, the witness becomes a single point of failure. If the witness becomes inaccessible, the cluster goes down, even if all the nodes and the rest of the storage is functional.

There are situations in which you might want to revoke the votes of specific nodes in the cluster, however. For example, you might have cluster nodes at a remote site that are there strictly as a backup, for manual failover in the event of a disaster. You can revoke their votes so that they are not part of the quorum calculations.

> ***NOTE*** **NON-VOTING NODES**
>
> **Whether a node has a quorum vote has no bearing on its functionality in the cluster. Nodes that do not participate in the quorum are still fully active in the cluster.**

Configure cluster networking

The network connections are critical to maintaining the high availability of a failover cluster. Separating traffic into different networks and providing redundant connections at all point in the network path help to ensure the continued functionality of the cluster.

Depending on the role performed by the cluster, you might want to create separate networks for each of the following types of traffic:

- **Client Communications** Client access to the application running on the cluster is the highest priority. This is usually the default shared network used for other client/server communications, but whenever possible, the other types of traffic listed here should be kept off this network.
- **Cluster Communications** The heartbeats and other communications between cluster nodes are essential to the continued functionality of the cluster.
- **iSCSI** iSCSI and other storage area network communications should be separated from all other types of network traffic.
- **Live Migration** On a Hyper-V cluster, Live Migration is critical for virtual machines to continue functioning, and network performance is critical for Live Migration to function efficiently.

Selecting network hardware

For the network hardware, the object should be to provide as much redundancy as possible and to avoid single points of failure. Some of the hardware provisioning recommendations are as follows:

- Use separate network adapters, rather than adapters with multiple interfaces, to avoid the adapter card as a single point of failure.
- Use different makes of network adapter when possible, to avoid driver issues from affecting multiple adapters.
- Use separate physical switches, rather than configuring VLANs on a single large switch, to prevent the switch from being a single point of failure.
- Create redundant network connections whenever possible, especially for the client communication network.
- For networks without redundant connections, such as those for cluster communication and Live Migration, use NIC Teaming to provide failover capability in the event of a network adapter malfunction.

Modifying network defaults

When you create a cluster, the system evaluates each of the connected networks and assigns traffic roles to them, based on the following criteria:

- Any network carrying iSCSI traffic is disabled for any cluster communication.
- Networks without a default gateway address are configured for cluster communications only.
- Networks with a default gateway address are configured for both client and cluster communication.

The current states of the detected networks are displayed on the Networks page of Failover Cluster Manager, as shown in Figure 5-19, or by running the Get-ClusterNetwork cmdlet in PowerShell.

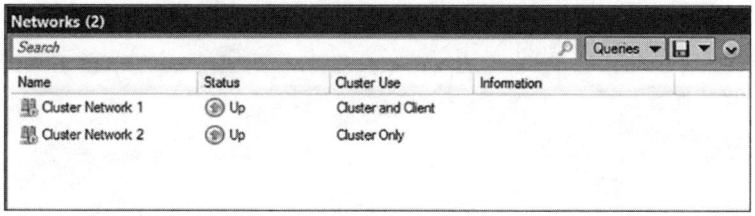

FIGURE 5-19 The Networks page of Failover Cluster Manager

It is possible to modify the default network settings created with the cluster, using Failover Cluster Manager or the Get-ClusterNetwork PowerShell cmdlet. To configure the network in Failover Cluster Manager, use the following procedure.

1. Open Failover Cluster Manager and browse to the Networks page.
2. Select a network and, in the Actions pane, click Properties.
3. On the Properties sheet shown in Figure 5-20, choose from the following options:
   - **Allow Cluster Communication On This Network** Enables the network to be used for cluster communication only.
   - **Allow Clients To Connect Through This Network** Enables the network to be used for client communication, as well as cluster communication.
   - **Do Not Allow Cluster Communication On This Network** Prevents the network from being used for any cluster communication.

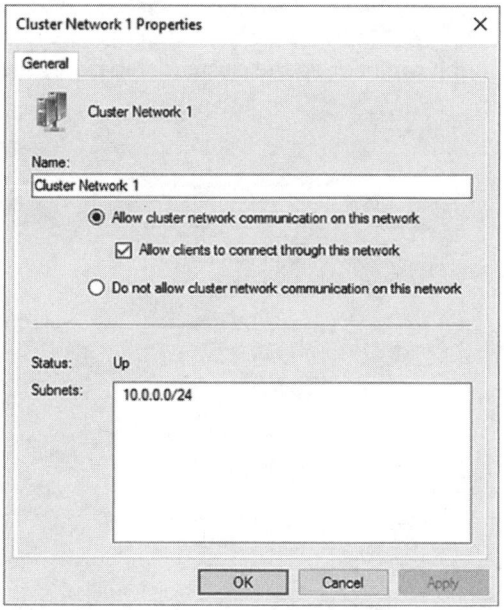

FIGURE 5-20 The Properties sheet for a network

4. Click OK.

To configure these settings in Windows PowerShell, you use the Get-ClusterNetwork cmdlet, as in the following example:

```
(get-clusternetwork "network1").role =1
```

The values for the Role property are as follows:

- 0 Disabled for cluster communication
- 1 Enabled for cluster communication only
- 3 Enabled for client and cluster communication

> ***NOTE*** **FAILOVER CLUSTER CMDLETS**
>
> **In many instances, the cmdlets in the FailoverClusters PowerShell module are less intuitive than those in other modules. Even experienced PowerShell users might find it more convenient to use Failover Cluster Manager many cluster configuration tasks.**

Restore single node or cluster configuration

Failover clusters might provide fault tolerance, but they do not absolve you from the need to back up your servers. Whatever shared storage solution you use for a failover cluster, you should have a backup strategy in place, even if it includes mirrors or parity-based data redundancy. However, the other issue regarding backups is the cluster configuration itself.

Windows Server Backup is limited in its ability to perform backups of Cluster Shared Volumes (CSVs) as part of the server backup, but it can back up the cluster database, as shown in Figure 5-21.

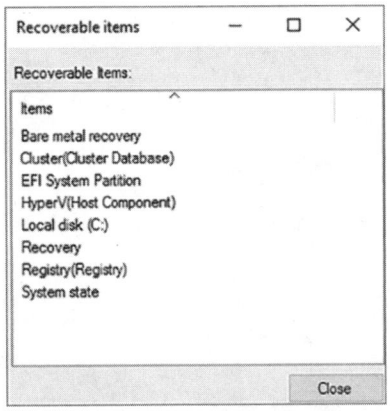

FIGURE 5-21 The Recoverable Items list for a Windows Server Backup job

The cluster database is stored on each node of a cluster, as well as on a disk witness, if one exists. The Cluster Service running on each node is responsible for seeing to it that the most recent version of the cluster database is replicated to each node. When you are performing a restore from backup on a cluster node, you must consider whether you want to perform an authoritative restore of the cluster database.

One of the more likely disaster situations for a failover cluster environment is the loss of a single node. If one node fails, and the rest of the cluster is running, you can probably just perform a full restore of that node from a backup. The version of the cluster database in the backup will be outdated, and the Cluster Service will overwrite it with the latest version as soon as the node comes up as part of the cluster. This is called a non-authoritative backup.

The other situation is when you want to perform an authoritative restore of the cluster database, that is, you want the cluster to use the version of the database from the backup, not the one that it is currently using. To do this with Windows Server Backup, you must perform the restore from the command prompt using the Wbadmin.exe program. You cannot use the GUI for this.

When you run the following Wbadmin command, it displays the backups that are available for restoration. The result is shown in Figure 5-22.

```
wbadmin get versions
```

```
PS C:\Users\administrator.ADATUM> wbadmin get versions
wbadmin 1.0 - Backup command-line tool
(C) Copyright 2013 Microsoft Corporation. All rights reserved.

Backup time: 11/13/2016 9:09 PM
Backup target: Fixed Disk labeled D:
Version identifier: 11/14/2016-05:09
Can recover: Volume(s), File(s), Application(s), Bare Metal Recovery, System State
Snapshot ID: {cfaee8b8-130c-4b2e-9a27-a2758e808a9e}
```

FIGURE 5-22 Results of the Wbadmin get versions command

Using the Version Identifier specified in the listing, you can now display the recoverable contents in the backup— including the cluster database— with a command like the following. The result is shown in Figure 5-23.

```
wbadmin get items -version: 11/14/2016:05:09
```

```
PS C:\Users\administrator.ADATUM> wbadmin get items -version:11/14/2016-05:09
wbadmin 1.0 - Backup command-line tool
(C) Copyright 2013 Microsoft Corporation. All rights reserved.

EFI System Partition
Volume ID = {3d9d7859-d63a-496c-aa59-fea6966f031e}
Volume '', mounted at C:
Volume size = 126.44 GB
Can recover = Full volume

Volume ID = {a84dd41a-1590-40f2-8f75-ece3e0a48112}
Volume 'Recovery', mounted at <not mounted> ('Recovery', mounted at <not mounted> at the time
the backup was created)
Volume size = 450.00 MB
Can recover = Full volume

Application = Cluster
Component = Cluster Database (\Cluster Database)

Application = Registry
Component = Registry (\Registry)

Application = HyperV
VM name: Host Component
VM caption: Host Component
VM identifier: Host Component
Total Size: <Not available>
```

FIGURE 5-23 Results of the Wbadmin get items command

To perform the authoritative restore, you use a command like the following.

```
wbadmin start recovery -itemtype:app -items:cluster -version:01/01/2008-00:00
```

The results, shown in Figure 5-24, indicate that the database has been restored successfully, and provide instructions for restarting the cluster.

```
PS C:\Users\administrator.ADATUM> wbadmin start recovery -itemtype:app -items:cluster -version:11/14/2016-05:09
wbadmin 1.0 - Backup command-line tool
(C) Copyright 2013 Microsoft Corporation. All rights reserved.

You have chosen to recover the application cluster.
The following components will be recovered:

Component = Cluster Database (\Cluster Database)

Warning:  This operation will perform an authoritative restore of your
cluster. After recovering the cluster database, the Cluster service will be
stopped and then started. This might take a few minutes.
Do you want to continue with an authoritative recovery of the cluster?
[Y] Yes [N] No Y

Preparing the component Cluster Database for recovery...
Recovering the files for the component Cluster Database, copied (100%).
Recovering the component Cluster Database.
The component Cluster Database was successfully recovered.
The recovery operation completed.
Log of files successfully recovered:
C:\Windows\Logs\WindowsServerBackup\ApplicationRestore-14-11-2016_06-20-23.log

Summary of the recovery operation:
----------------------

The component Cluster Database was successfully recovered.
Note:  To complete the restoration of the cluster associated with this node you
must do the following:
1.  Start the Cluster service on this node.
2.  Start the Cluster service on the nodes identified in the restored cluster
    database.
The Failover Clusters module for Windows PowerShell is installed with the
Failover Cluster feature. To see the list of nodes identified for the cluster
once the Cluster service is running, use the Windows PowerShell cmdlet
Get-ClusterNode.
```

FIGURE 5-24 Results of the Wbadmin start recovery command

You can start the Cluster Service on the other nodes remotely, by highlighting them in Failover Cluster Manager and selecting More Actions | Start Cluster Service in the Actions pane.

Configure cluster storage

For a failover cluster to host a highly available application, all the cluster nodes must have access to the application data. Therefore, the cluster must have some form of shared storage. Shared storage is a requirement of the Failover Clustering feature in Windows Server 2016. Before you can add storage to the cluster, you must make sure that all the servers that will become the cluster nodes have access to the storage that will hold the application data.

Windows Server 2016 supports several shared storage technologies, including the following:

- **Fibre Channel** One of the first storage area network (SAN) protocols, Fibre Channel, is a dedicated fiber optic network that, at the time of its introduction, ran at high speeds, but which required specialized equipment and expertise, both of which were extremely expensive. There is now a Fibre Channel variant that runs over standard Ethernet (Fibre Channel over Ethernet, or FCoE), which is more affordable, but is still the esoteric high end of SAN technologies.

- **Serial Attached SCSI (SAS)** Small Computer System Interface (SCSI) is a bus-based storage attachment protocol that, in its parallel form, was at one time the industry standard for high performance local storage. The SAS variant uses serial communications to increase the maximum length of the bus, while using smaller cables and connectors than the original, parallel devices.
- **Internet SCSI (iSCSI)** Another variant of the SCSI protocol that transmits the same SCSI command language over a standard IP network. As with SAS, iSCSI designates storage devices as targets and the servers and other devices that access the storage as initiators. A server running Windows Server 2016 can function as both an iSCSI target and initiator, making it possible to implement an iSCSI SAN wholly in software.

Each of these technologies is less expensive than the ones preceding it, with iSCSI SANs now realizable for little more than the cost of an unsophisticated disk array. While some high-end storage appliances include varying levels of intelligence, fault tolerance, and high availability, there are also storage arrays known as JBODs (Just a Bunch of Disks), which are low cost devices that are little more than standard hard disk drives in a cabinet with a common power supply.

EXAM TIP

Using Hyper-V and iSCSI, it is possible to implement a failover cluster on a single physical server, for evaluation, testing, and educational purposes. The performance level of the cluster is likely to be extremely limited, but an arrangement such as this will enable you to explore the Failover Clustering feature of Windows Server 2016.

Once you create the cluster, any disks that qualify should appear in Failover Cluster Manager when you select Add Disks on the Storage\Disks page, as shown in Figure 5-25. Once you add a disk, it is designated as Available Storage.

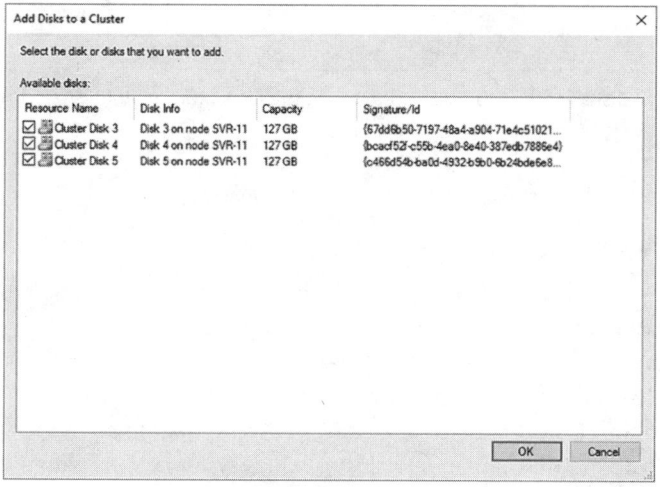

FIGURE 5-25 The Add Disks to a Cluster dialog box in Failover Cluster Manager

Alternatively, you can use the storage on the disks to create a clustered storage pool. The process is like that of creating a pool using Storage Spaces on a single Windows server, except that the storage is shared by all the nodes in the cluster.

A clustered storage pool requires a minimum of three disks of at least 4 GB capacity each, which must be connected to all the cluster nodes using SAS or iSCSI. To create a clustered storage pool, use the following procedure.

1. In Failover Cluster Manager, browse to the Storage\Pools page and click New Storage Pool in the Actions pane to launch the New Storage Pool Wizard.
2. On the Specify a Storage Pool Name and Subsystem page, type a name for the pool and select the primordial pool containing the disks you want to use.
3. On the Select Physical Disks for the Storage Pool page, select the disks you want to add to the pool and specify whether each one should be Automatic, Hot Spare, or Manual, as shown in Figure 5-26.

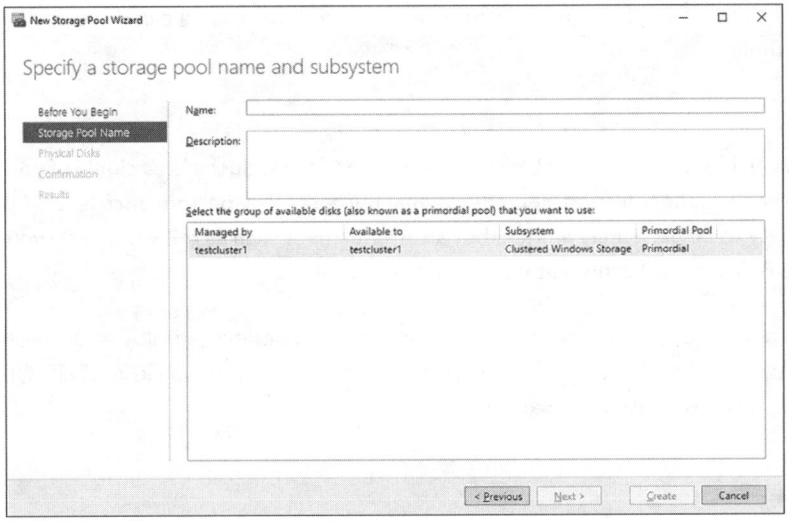

FIGURE 5-26 The Select Physical Disks for the Storage Pool page in the New Storage Pool Wizard

4. Click Create.

Implement cluster-aware updating

One of the important prerequisites for Failover Clustering in Windows Server 2016 is for all the potential cluster nodes to be running the same version of the operating system, with all of the same updates applied to them. The Validate Cluster Wizard issues warnings when it determines that the servers it is checking are not identically updated. What then do you do to keep your nodes updated once the cluster is operational? *Cluster-Aware Updating (CAU)* is a tool supplied with Failover Clustering that can update cluster nodes systematically with a minimum of down time.

CAU applies updates to a cluster in a round-robin fashion, called an Updating Run, using the following procedure:

1. Selects one node to update.
2. Moves any existing roles off the selected node to other nodes in the cluster, using Live Migration or other techniques that minimize client service interruptions.
3. Places the selected node into node maintenance mode.
4. Installs the required updates on the selected node and restarts it, if necessary.
5. Takes the selected node out of maintenance mode.
6. Moves on to the next node in the cluster and repeats the procedure.

This way, each node in turn is taken out of service temporarily and updated, until the entire cluster has had the same updates applied.

CAU requires a computer to function as the Update Coordinator, directing the updating activities for the cluster. The question of which computer performs this function is the primary distinction between the CAU's two operating modes:

- **Self-Updating Mode** In this mode, one of the cluster nodes has the CAU clustered role installed, enabling it to function as the Update Coordinator. The Update Coordinator node performs Updating Runs according to a schedule configured by an administrator, triggering updates on each of the other nodes in turn. When all of the other nodes have been updated, the CAU role on the Update Coordinator fails over to another node, enabling it to assume the Update Coordinator role. The original coordinator can then be updated itself. In this mode, the entire update process is performed automatically.
- **Remote Updating Mode** In this mode, a computer outside the cluster is configured to function as the Update Coordinator. From this computer, an administrator can manually trigger an Updating Run on the cluster. The Update Coordinator computer is not updated itself, and the process cannot be automated.

To use CAU in self-updating mode, each node in the cluster must have the Failover Clustering tools installed. The tools are installed by default when you add the Failover Clustering feature using Server Manager. However, if you install the feature using PowerShell, you must add the IncludeManagementTools parameter to the Install-WindowsFeature command.

For remote updating mode, the Update Coordinator must have the Failover Clustering tools installed, but the Failover Clustering feature is not required. The tools themselves are located under Remote Server Administration Tools in the Add Roles and Features Wizard. They are known as RSAT-Clustering in Windows PowerShell.

The CAU tools include a Cluster-Aware Updating console, as shown in Figure 5-27, and a ClusterAwareUpdating module for Windows PowerShell, which contains cmdlets for managing the service.

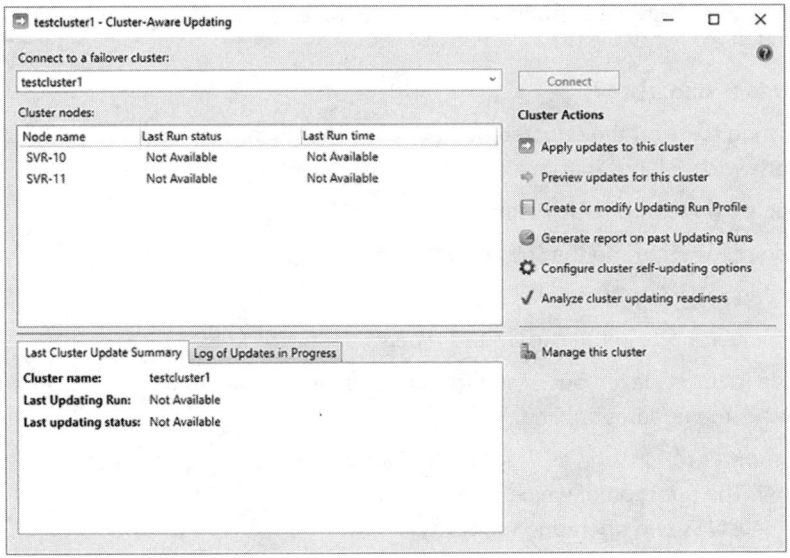

FIGURE 5-27 The Cluster-Aware Updating console

There are other prerequisites for using CAU, most of which are already satisfied in a properly installed Windows Server 2016 failover cluster. Clicking Analyze Cluster Updating Readiness in the console's Cluster Actions list or running the Test-CauSetup cmdlet in PowerShell on a cluster node performs a series of tests that assesses the readiness for the entire cluster, as shown in Figure 5-28.

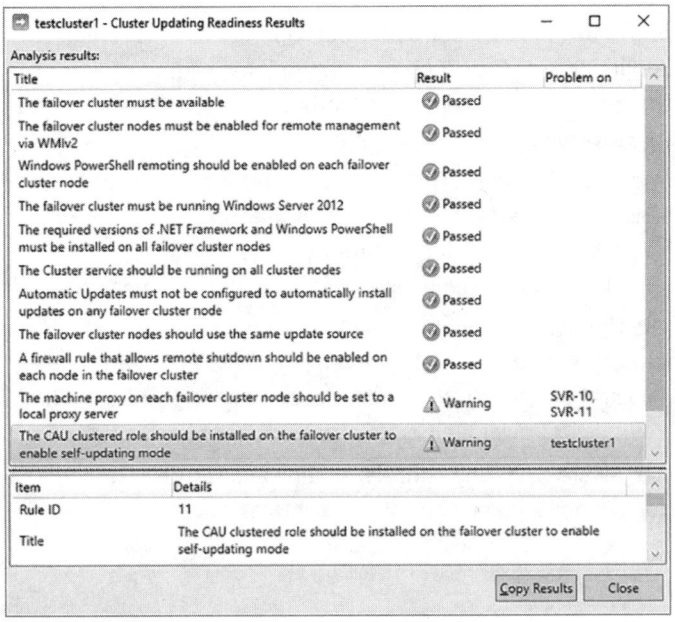

FIGURE 5-28 Cluster Updating Readiness Results

To use self-updating mode, once the cluster meets all the prerequisites, you install the CAU clustered role by clicking Configure Cluster Self-Updating Options in the console. This launches the Configure Self-Updating Options Wizard, which adds the clustered role and creates a schedule for the self-updates, as shown in Figure 5-29. You can also configure advanced updating options, such as the maximum number of retries allowed per node and the order in which nodes should be updated. You can also do these things with the Add-CauClusterRole cmdlet in PowerShell, as in the following example:

```
add-cauclusterrole -clustername "cluster1" -daysofweek sunday -weeksinterval 3
-maxretriespernode -nodeorder node2, node1, node3
```

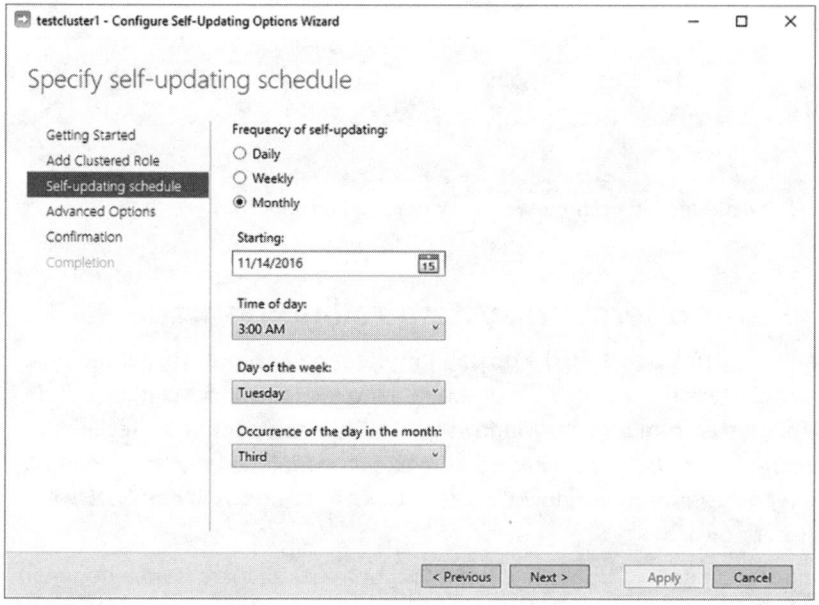

FIGURE 5-29 The Specify Self-Updating page of the Configure Self-Updating Options Wizard

Once the schedule is set, you can wait for it to run, or perform an Updating Run immediately, as shown in Figure 5-30, by clicking Apply Updates to this cluster or running the Invoke-CauRun cmdlet.

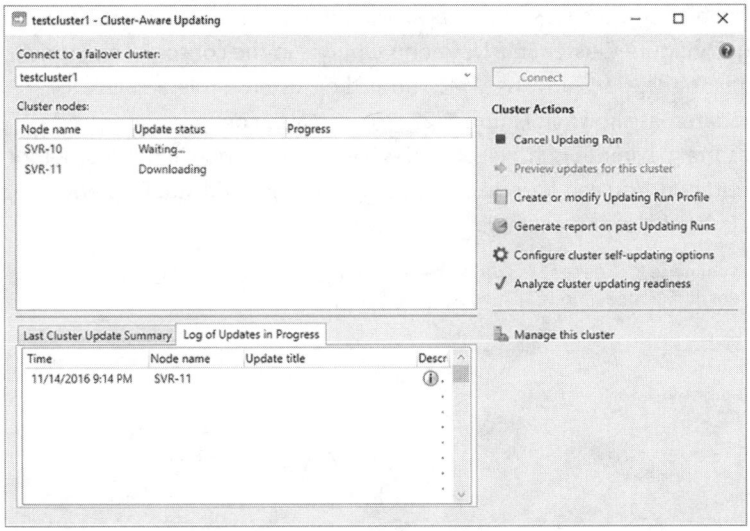

FIGURE 5-30 The Cluster-Aware Updating console with an Upgrading Run underway

Implement cluster operating system rolling upgrade

Prior to Windows Server 2016, upgrading the operating system on a failover cluster required you to take the entire cluster offline, install the new operating system on all the nodes, and essentially rebuild the cluster from scratch. Windows Server 2016 now supports a technique called *Cluster Operating System Rolling Upgrade* that makes it possible to upgrade a Hyper-V or Scale-Out File Server cluster from Windows Server 2012 R2 to Windows Server 2016 without bringing the cluster down.

Cluster Operating System Rolling Upgrade is not a tool or a wizard; there is no automated process for upgrading the cluster. It is rather a technique in which you bring each cluster node down in turn, perform a clean upgrade of the operating system, and add it back into the cluster. The feature that makes this possible is a new operational mode for Failover Clustering called *mixed-OS mode*. Unlike clusters in previous Windows versions, it is possible for a cluster to function, temporarily, with nodes running different operating system versions, specifically Windows Server 2012 R2 and Windows Server 2016.

The process for upgrading each Windows Server 2012 R2 node in the cluster is as follows:

1. Pause the node.
2. Drain the node of its workload by migrating it to other nodes.
3. Evict the node from the cluster.
4. Reformat the system drive and perform a clean installation of Windows Server 2016.
5. Configure network and storage connections.
6. Install the Failover Clustering feature.

- **SMB Direct** Uses Remote Direct Memory Access (RDMA) to perform direct memory-to-memory data transfers between remote systems, minimizing system processor utilization. Both the client and the server must be using SMB 3.0.
- **SMB Encryption** Provides end-to-end AES encryption between servers and clients using SMB 3.0.

When you create or modify a file server share in Failover Cluster Manager, the New Share Wizard presents a Configure Share Settings page, as shown in Figure 5-53. The Enable Continuous Availability checkbox, selected by default, activates the SMB Transparent Failover feature, and the Encrypt Data Access checkbox enables SMB Encryption.

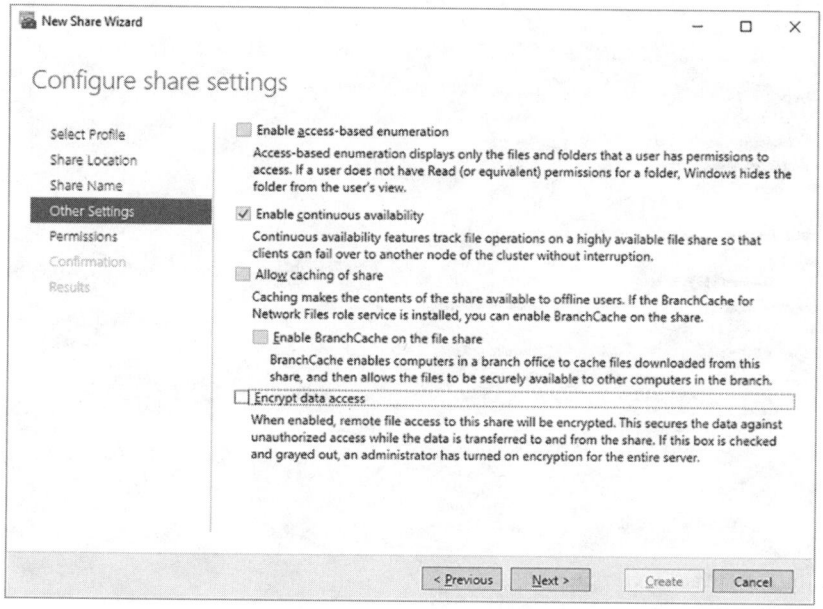

FIGURE 5-53 The Configure Share Settings page of the New Share Wizard

Configure VM monitoring

One of the advantages of running Hyper-V in a cluster is that the cluster is capable of monitoring specific services on the virtual machines, reporting when a problem occurs, and taking action that you can configure. This way, you can select the service associated with a critical application on the VM and configure the VM to restart it or failover to another node when a problem occurs.

To use VM Monitoring in Failover Clustering, the virtual machine must meet the following prerequisites:

- The VM must be in the same domain as the Hyper-V host.
- Windows Firewall on the VM must have the inbound rules in the Virtual Machine Monitoring group enabled.

- The Hyper-V cluster administrator must be a member of the local Administrators group on the VM.

To configure monitoring for a specific virtual machine, use the following procedure.

1. Open Failover Cluster Manager and click Roles to display the Roles page.
2. Select the Virtual Machine role you want to monitor and, on the Actions pane, select More Actions, Configure Monitoring.
3. On the Select Services dialog box appears, as shown in Figure 5-54, select the checkbox for the service you want to monitor and click OK.

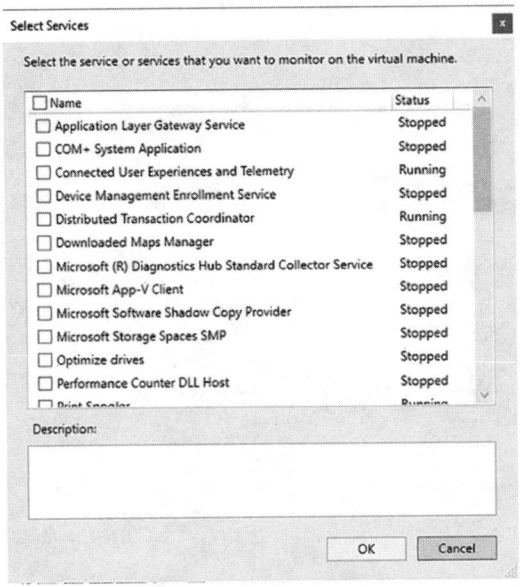

FIGURE 5-54 The Select Services dialog box

You can also configure monitoring using the Add-ClusterVMMonitoredItem cmdlet in a Windows PowerShell window, as in the following example:

```
add-clustervmmonitoreditem -virtualmachine clustervm3 -service spooler
```

When a service you've selected experiences problems, they are handled first by the Service Control Manager on the VM, which uses the properties of the individual service to control its actions, as shown in Figure 5-55. You can modify these properties to specify what actions the Service Control Manager should take, and how often.

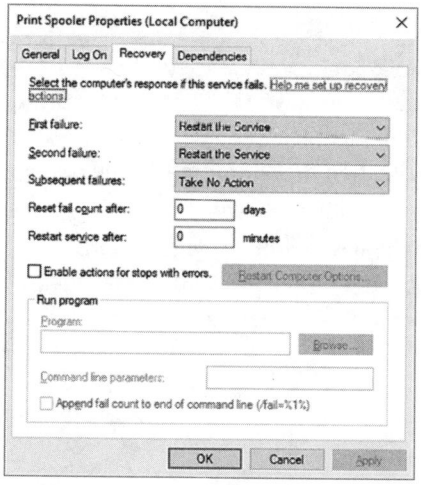

FIGURE 5-55 A service's Properties sheet

If the Service Control Manager's efforts fail, and the service is still malfunctioning, the cluster takes over and performs its own recovery actions, as follows:

- The cluster creates an entry in the host's System log with the Event ID 1250.
- The cluster changes the status of the Virtual Machine to Application in VM Critical.
- The cluster restarts the Virtual Machine on the same node. If the service continues to fail, the cluster fails the role over to another node.

You can modify these default restart activities by opening the Virtual Machine Cluster WMI Properties sheet, as shown in Figure 5-56. This is located on the cluster's main page, in the Cluster Core Resources box.

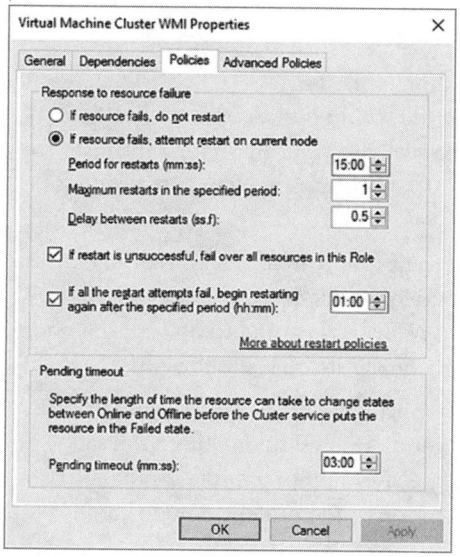

FIGURE 5-56 The Virtual Machine Cluster WMI Properties sheet

Configure failover and preference settings

A *failover* is when a role running on a cluster node can no longer continue to run, and the cluster moves it to another node. There are any number of reasons why a failover might occur: there could be a power failure, the software could malfunction, or an administrator might have to shut the node down for maintenance. A *failback* is when the cluster moves the role back to its original node, after the problem that caused the failover is fixed.

Administrators can control the behavior of the cluster with regard to node selections and failover behavior for a specific role by modifying its properties. In Failover Cluster Manager, on the Roles page, selecting a role and clicking Properties in the Actions pane displays the role's Properties sheet, as shown in Figure 5-57.

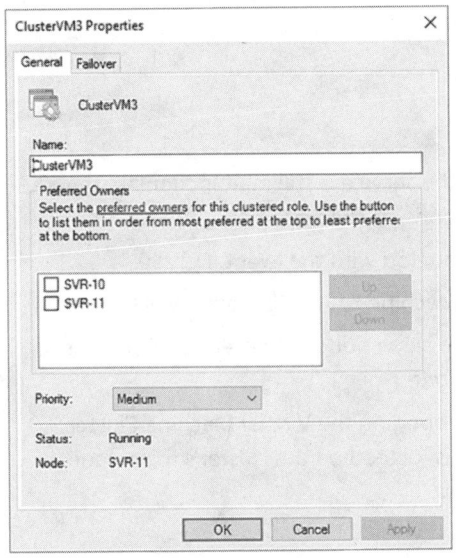

FIGURE 5-57 The General tab on a cluster role's Properties sheet

On the General tab, you can specify the node that you would prefer run the role. It shouldn't matter, since the nodes are functionally identical, but you can do it by selecting the checkbox for one of the nodes and using the Up and Down buttons to change the order of preference.

In the Priority drop-down list, you can specify the values High, Medium, or Low to indicate when the role should start, in relation to the other roles in the cluster. The values are relative only to those of the other roles, and there is also a No Auto Start setting to prevent the node from starting with the cluster. You must then start it manually, if you want it to run.

On the Failover tab, shown in Figure 5-58, you can specify the maximum number of times the cluster should attempt to restart a role or fail it over to another node during the time interval specified by the Period setting. You can also specify whether the role should fail back to the preferred node, and whether it should do so as soon as the preferred node comes back online, or wait an interval that you specify.

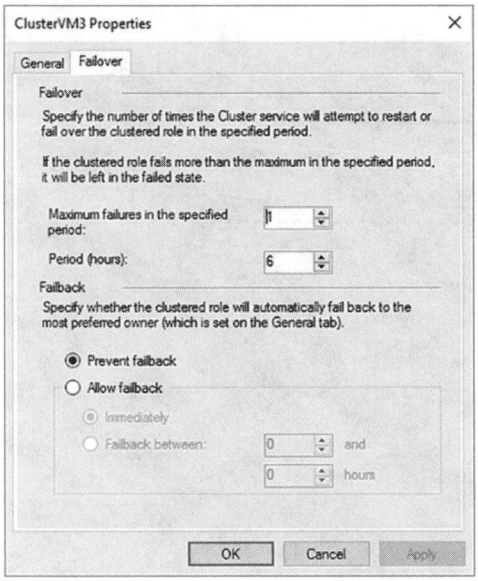

FIGURE 5-58 The Failover tab on a cluster role's Properties sheet

Implement stretch and site-aware failover clusters

Fault tolerance is about planning for any eventuality, and failover clusters are a means of anticipating hardware and software failures. However, sometimes failures occur on a larger scale, in which it's not hard drives and servers that are affected, but rather building and cities. For this reason, organizations that want to keep their applications running in any eventuality can create stretch (or stretched) clusters.

A *stretch cluster* is a cluster that has it nodes divided among different sites, often in different cities. This way, if a catastrophe occurs, such as a hurricane or earthquake, the cluster can failover its roles to nodes that are located far away from the problem. However, stretch clustering presents administrators with some difficult problems, such as how to ensure that cluster nodes in different cities are working with the same data and how to control failover behavior in a situation in which the nodes are not interchangeable.

Because it is usually not practical to create a shared storage solution that can connect all the nodes in a stretch cluster to the same disk drives, many stretch clusters use asymmetric storage, in which each site has its own shared storage solution. Administrators can then use the Storage Replica feature in Windows Server 2016 to synchronize the data between sites, as shown in Figure 5-59.

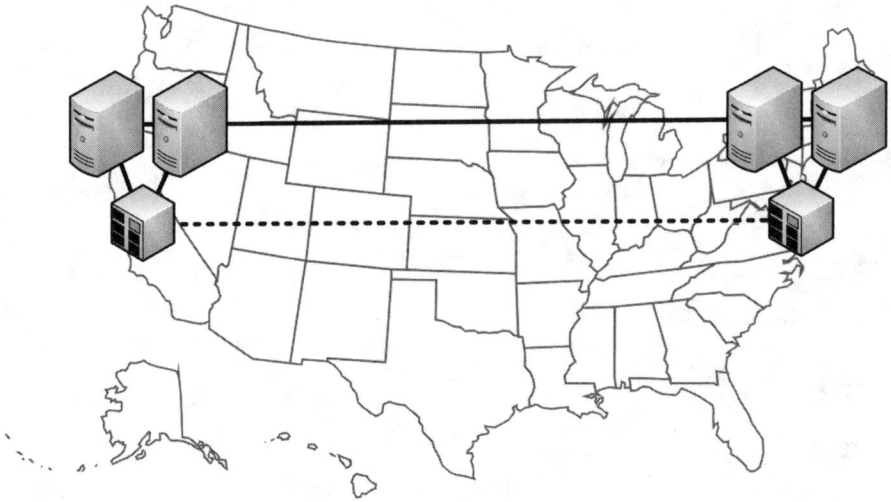

FIGURE 5-59 A stretched cluster with replicated storage

Even with the shared data problem resolved, however, there are other issues involved in stretch clustering. For example, in a failover situation, how is the cluster supposed to distinguish between the nodes located in New York and the nodes in San Francisco? Windows Server 2016 Failover Clustering addresses this issue by providing the ability to create site-aware failover clusters.

A *site-aware failover cluster* is a cluster that contains fault domains based on the values of a site property configured for each node. The cluster uses these fault domains to determine its behavior during failovers and other role transfers. To create a site-aware cluster, you first use the New-ClusterFaultDomain PowerShell cmdlet to define the sites. Then you use the Set-ClusterFaultDomain cmdlet to assign the cluster nodes to the sites you've created.

For example, to create sites for offices in New York and San Francisco, you could use commands like the following:

```
new-clusterfaultdomain -name ny -type site -description "primary" -location "new york
ny"

new-clusterfaultdomain -name sf -type site -description "secondary" -location "san
francisco ca"
```

Then, for a four-node cluster with two nodes at each site, you would assign the nodes to the sites using commands like the following:

```
set-clusterfaultdomain -name node1 -parent ny

set-clusterfaultdomain -name node2 -parent ny

set-clusterfaultdomain -name node3 -parent sf

set-clusterfaultdomain -name node4 -parent sf
```

Once these properties are configured, the cluster uses the site information to control activities involving resource transfers between nodes. When a node fails, for example, the cluster will attempt to fail it over to another node in the same site first. Only when all the nodes in that site are found to be unavailable will it fail over to a node at another site. This is known as *failover affinity*.

In the same way, when an administrator drains a node of its roles prior to bringing it down for maintenance, the cluster will move the roles to a node in the same site. Cluster Shared Volumes will also distribute connections among nodes in the same site, whenever possible.

It is also possible to configure the heartbeat settings that a cluster uses to determine that nodes are functional. In a stretch cluster, there are bound to be longer latency delays in communication between sites than between subnets, so you can modify the following settings to prevent nodes from being incorrectly designated as having failed:

- **CrossSiteDelay** Specifies the amount of time (in milliseconds) between heartbeats sent to nodes in different sites. The default setting is 1000.
- **CrossSiteThreshold** Specifies the number of missed heartbeats that must occur before a node at a different site is considered to have failed. The default setting is 20.

To configure these settings, you use PowerShell commands like the following:

```
(get-cluster).crosssitedelay = 2000

(get-cluster).crosssitethreshold = 30
```

You can also configure one of the sites you have created to be the preferred site for the cluster, using a command like the following:

```
(get-cluster).preferredsite = ny
```

When you do this, roles start at the preferred site during a cold start of the cluster, and the preferred site receives precedence during quorum negotiations, keeping the preferred site alive at the expense of the other sites, if necessary.

Enable and configure node fairness

Maintenance, failovers, and other activities can cause virtual machines on a Hyper-V cluster to be migrated in such a way that some nodes are overcommitted, while others are hardly being utilized. Windows Server 2016 includes a feature called *node fairness*, which attempts to balance the distribution among the nodes.

Node fairness works by evaluating the memory and CPU loads on each node over time, attempting to identify those that are overcommitted. When cluster detects an overloaded node, it balances the load by live migrating VMs to other nodes that are idle, while still observing fault domains and preferred owners.

Node fairness is enabled by default, but you can configure whether it runs and when load balancing occurs. You can also configure the aggressiveness of the load balancing that occurs. You do this in the cluster's Properties sheet, on the Balancer tab, as shown in Figure 5-60.

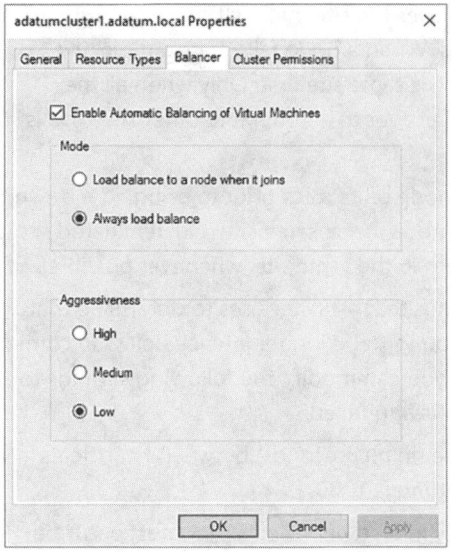

FIGURE 5-60 The Balancer tab of a cluster's Properties sheet

You can also configure these settings using Windows PowerShell, using the following commands:

- **(Get-Cluster).AutoBalancerMode** Specifies whether node fairness should run and how often it should balance the load, using the following values:
  - 0 Node fairness is disabled
  - 1 Load balancing occurs when a node joins the cluster
  - 2 Load balancing occurs when a node joins the cluster and every 30 minutes thereafter. This is the default.
- **(Get-Cluster).AutoBalancerLevel** Specifies the aggressiveness with which node fairness should evaluate the load on each node, using the following values:
  - 1 Low. Migrates VMs when the host is more than 80 percent loaded. This is the default.
  - 2 Medium. Migrates VMs when the host is more than 70 percent loaded.
  - 3 High. Migrates VMs when the host is more than 60 perecnt loaded.

Skill 5.5: Manage VM movement in clustered nodes

Once you have a cluster installed, configured, and operational, you will be likely to encounter situations in which it is necessary to change the distribution of virtual machines among the cluster nodes. Windows Server 2016 provides several methods for moving VMs and controlling their behavior when they are moved.

This section covers how to:

- Perform a live migration
- Perform a quick migration
- Perform a storage migration
- Import, export, and copy VMs
- Configure VM network health protection
- Configure drain on shutdown

Perform a live migration

When you create a Virtual Machine role on a cluster, you create the VM itself and then configure it for high availability. This latter action, which you perform with the High Availability Wizard or the Add-ClusterVirtualMachineRole cmdlet in PowerShell, enables Live Migration for the role. There is no need to manually configure the Hyper-V server to enable Live Migration or select an authentication protocol.

Once the virtual machine is created in the cluster, performing a live migration is simply a matter of right-clicking the VM on the Roles page and, on the context menu, selecting Move | Live Migration. You can let the cluster choose the best node or select any of the nodes in the cluster as the target, as shown in Figure 5-61.

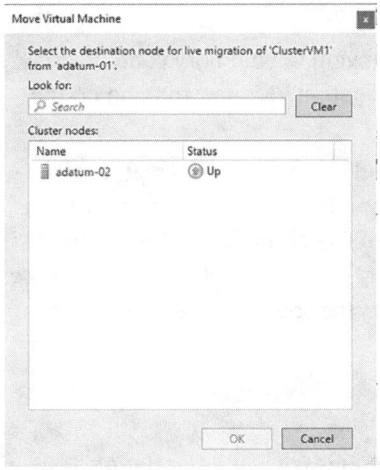

FIGURE 5-61 The Move Virtual Machine dialog box

To initiate a live migration in PowerShell, you use the Move-ClusterVirtualMachineRole cmdlet, as in the following example:

```
move-clustervirtualmachinerole -name clustervm1 -node server2
```

Perform a quick migration

Quick Migration is the predecessor to Live Migration, and was the original tool for moving a virtual machine from one cluster node to another. Largely replaced by Live Migration on Windows Server 2012, Quick Migration is still included in Windows Server 2016, because there are situations in which it is still useful.

Compared to Live Migration, in which the handover of a VM from one node to the other is, in most cases, nearly instantaneous, Quick Migration involves what is usually a brief pause. As with a live migration, the data files do not move during a quick migration. However, you can perform a quick migration on VMs that are either running or stopped. For a live migration, the VMs must be running. In practice, administrators typically use Quick Migration only when they can't perform a Live Migration.

A typical quick migration of a running virtual machine role proceeds as follows:

1. The cluster pauses the virtual machine role, suspending the I/O and CPU functions of the VM.
2. The cluster saves the source VM's memory contents and system state to shared storage and places the VM into the Saved state.
3. The cluster copies the symbolic link specifying the location of the source VM's files to the destination node and transfers ownership of the source VM's files to the destination VM.
4. The cluster removes the symbolic link from the source VM.
5. The cluster resumes the role from the Saved state, copying the memory contents and the system state from shared storage to the destination VM, now running on the destination node.

The fundamental difference between Quick Migration and Live Migration is that a quick migration copies the VM's memory first to disk and then from disk to the destination, while a live migration copies the memory directly from the source to the destination. The length of the pause in a quick migration depends on the size of the VM's memory and the performance of the storage subsystem. The only data copied directly from the source to the destination VM is the tiny symbolic link.

NOTE **QUICK MIGRATION IN STOPPED VMS**

When the virtual machine is stopped, a quick migration requires only the transfer of the symbolic link from the source to the destination. In this case, the process is nearly instantaneous.

The effect of the pause on the clustered role depends on the applications running on the VM. Some applications can recover easily from a pause of a few seconds, while others might not. However, the situation was important enough to the Windows Server 2012 developers that the creation of a nearly instantaneous migration tool, Live Migration, was a top priority for them.

The process of performing a quick migration is nearly identical to that of a live migration. You right-click the VM on the Roles page and, on the context menu, selecting Move | Quick Migration, and choose the desired destination node. As the migration proceeds, you can see the role enter the Saved state and then the Starting state as the role is resumed.

Perform a storage migration

Live Migration and Quick Migration are designed to move the memory contents and the system state from one virtual machine to another. They do not move the virtual hard disk files that the VM uses to store its operating system, application files, and data. In a failover cluster, these files are expected to be located on shared storage, so the destination VM already has access to them.

Storage Migration has the opposite effect: it moves a VM's virtual hard disk files, but not its memory and system state. There are relatively few limitations on Storage Migration. The virtual machine does not have to be part of a cluster, so you see it implemented in Hyper-V as well as Failover Clustering.

On a standalone Hyper-V server, you can move the files to any destination you have permission to access, including a different location on the same computer. This is helpful, because it updates the VM with the new locations of the files as it migrates them.

In Hyper-V, you use the Move Wizard to perform storage migrations, but there is a different tool in Failover Cluster Manager. When you select a virtual machine cluster role and click Move | Virtual Machine Storage, the Move Virtual Machine Storage dialog box appears, as shown in Figure 5-62.

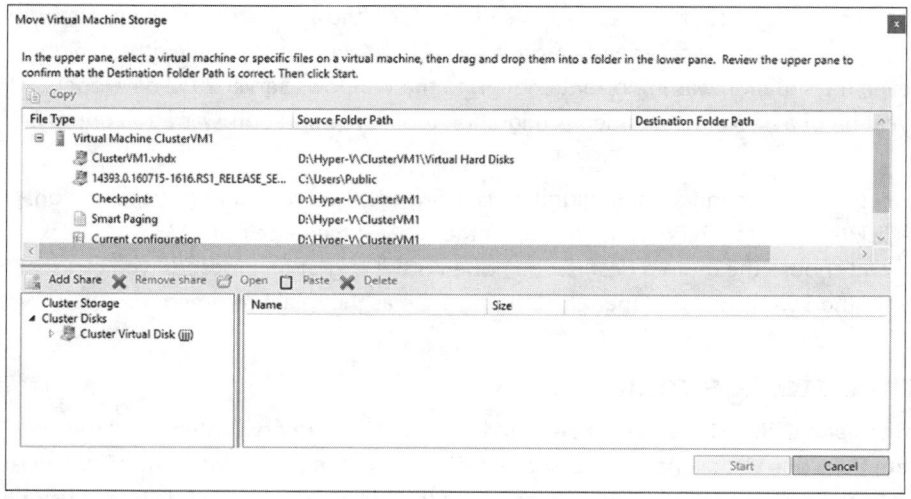

FIGURE 5-62 The Move Virtual Machine Storage dialog box

EXAM TIP

When preparing for the 70-740 exam, keep in mind that Storage Migration and Live Migration are separate processes. In Hyper-V Manager, the Move Wizard integrates Live Migration and Storage Migration capabilities into one interface, which can be confusing. Using this wizard, you can move a virtual machine to a different Hyper-V host; you can move a VM's storage, while leaving the VM in place; or you can move both the VM and its storage to a different host, effectively combining Live Migration and Storage Migration. Remember, however, that these are two separate tools and two separate procedures, although the wizard makes it seem as though it is one process.

In this dialog box, you can select any of the virtual machine's stored resources, including individual VHD and VHDX files, checkpoints, and Smart Paging files, and drag and drop them to a location anywhere in cluster storage. A new Destination Folder Path value appears, specifying to where the tool will move the file. When you have selected destinations for all of the files you want to move, you can click the Start button to close the dialog box and begin the storage migration process.

Import, export, and copy VMs

In Hyper-V, the ability to export and import VMs has several useful purposes. It is a simple, although tedious, way to move a VM from one host to another, complete with all its virtual hard disk, checkpoint, and Smart Paging files, without the prerequisites needed for Live Migration or Quick Migration. It is also a way to copy—or clone— a virtual machine, with all its updates, configuration settings, and applications intact.

Hyper-V Manager provides access to an Export Virtual Machine dialog box and an Import Virtual Machine Wizard, as described in Chapter 3, but there is no such interface accessible in Failover Cluster Manager. You can, however, use the Export-VM and Import-VM cmdlets in Windows PowerShell to effectively clone a clustered virtual machine.

To export a virtual machine, running or stopped, you use a command like the following:

```
export-vm -name clustervm1 -path d:\vm
```

You can run the command from any node in the cluster, but if you specify a local, unshared disk for the Path parameter, the VM will be exported to the specified path on the node where it is running. Specifying shared storage for the Path value is therefore preferable.

To import the virtual machine into the Hyper-V host, copy the files to the host's default folders and generating a new security identifier (SID) for the VM. , To prevent conflicts, use a command like the following:

```
import-vm -path "d:\vm\virtual machines\5ae40946-3a98-428e-8c83-081a3c68d18c.xml" -copy
-generatenewid
```

Once the process is complete, you will have a new virtual machine on that host. If the Hyper-V host is configured to store VM files on shared storage by default, you can then use Failover Cluster Manager to add that VM as a Virtual Machine role, configuring it for high availability.

Configure VM network health protection

Network health protection is a feature that detects whether a VM on a cluster node has a functional connection to a designated network. If it does not, the cluster automatically live migrates the VM role to another node that does have a connection to that network.

Without this feature, clustered virtual machines can lose contact with the network they are supposed to be servicing, and will continue to run as though nothing is wrong. If the problem is a simple one, such as an unplugged cable, other nodes in the cluster might still have access to that network, and migrating the VM to one of those nodes can keep it operational until the network fault is repaired.

Network health protection is enabled by default, but there are situations in which an administrator might not want a live migration to occur automatically. For example, if the cluster nodes are equipped with connections to redundant networks, you might not want live migrations to occur in response to one network's failure, when the node has access to others already.

To control whether network health protection is applied, open the Settings dialog box for the VM, either in Failover Cluster Manager or Hyper-V Manager, expand the network adapter providing the connection to the network in question, and display the Advanced Features page, as shown in Figure 5-63. When you clear the Protected Network checkbox, you prevent live migrations from occurring due to faults detected on that particular network.

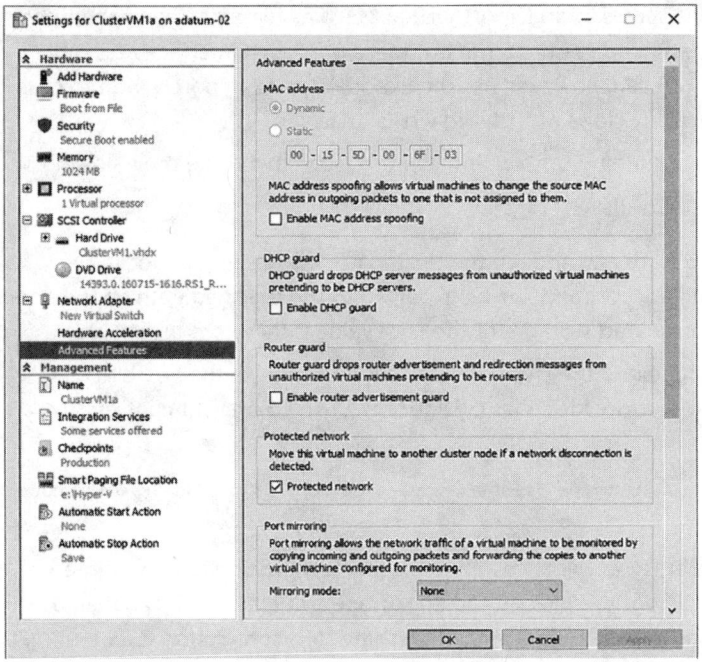

FIGURE 5-63 The Advanced Settings page for a network adapter in a VM's Setting's dialog box

Configure drain on shutdown

When you want to shut down a cluster node containing VMs, for maintenance or any other reason, the proper procedure is to drain the roles off the node (that is, live migrate them to other nodes) before you shut down the machine. In Failover Cluster Manager, you do this by selecting a node and clicking Pause | Drain Roles in the Actions pane. If you click the Roles tab at the bottom of the page, you should see each one live migrated to another node in the cluster.

In PowerShell, you can drain a node using the Suspend-ClusterNode cmdlet, as in the following example:

```
suspend-clusternode
```

At one time, if you failed to drain the node and just shut it down with the roles running, the roles would be placed into a Saved state, causing a service outage until the VMs could be moved to another node and resumed. Now, Windows Server 2016 Failover Clustering includes a feature called drain on shutdown, which automatically live migrates all the roles on a node before shutting down the system. It is worth noting, however, that Microsoft still recommends pausing a node and draining it before initiating a shutdown.

Drain on shutdown is enabled by default, as you can tell by running the (Get-Cluster). DrainOnShutdown command, as shown in Figure 5-64. A value of 1 indicates that the feature is enabled, and 0 is disabled.

```
PS C:\Users\administrator.ADATUM> (get-cluster).DrainOnShutdown
1

PS C:\Users\administrator.ADATUM> |
```

FIGURE 5-64 Output of the (Get-Cluster).DrainOnShutdown command

To disable drain on shutdown, you would therefore use the following command:

```
(get-cluster).drainonshutdown = 0
```

Skill 5.6: Implement Network Load Balancing (NLB)

The basic philosophy of a failover cluster is one of fault tolerance, in which one computer performs a service while others remain idle, waiting to serve as replacements in the event of a failure. *Network load balancing*, by contrast, is based on the idea that many computers are all providing the same service simultaneously. This arrangement provides fault tolerance also, but the primary objective is to distribute the traffic load among many computers, enabling the cluster to service more clients at once than a single computer ever could.

This section covers how to:

- Configure NLB prerequisites
- Install NLB nodes
- Configure affinity
- Configure port rules
- Configure cluster operation mode
- Upgrade an NLB cluster

Configure NLB prerequisites

A Network Load Balancing (NLB) cluster can consist of 2 to 32 servers—called hosts— each of which runs a separate copy of the desired application. NLB then uses TCP/IP addressing to send incoming client requests to the different hosts, balancing the load among them. NLB is best suited for stateless applications, such as web servers, with variable client loads. As traffic increases, it is possible to add hosts to the cluster, increasing its capacity. You can easily remove hosts as well, when the client load is diminished.

EXAM TIP

Failover Clustering clusters consist of *nodes*, while Network Load Balancing clusters consist of *hosts*. Remember this distinction for the 70-740 exam.

The NLB hosts in a cluster exchange messages called *heartbeats* once a second. These messages enable them to track the continued functionality of the other hosts. When the heartbeats from a single host stop for a given length of time, the other hosts remove it from the cluster. Whenever a host is added or removed, the NLB cluster performs a process known as *convergence*, during which it evaluates the current cluster membership and determines how client requests should be distributed among the hosts.

As with Failover Clustering, an NLB cluster has its own virtual identity on the network, with a name and IP address that clients use to connect to the application. For example, when you connect to any large web site on the Internet, you are connecting to a cluster address with some mechanism like NLB that forwards your request to one of the computers in a server farm. You have no idea which server you are accessing, and it doesn't matter, because they all provide the same service.

Because the application runs on all the hosts in the cluster, many of the complicated negotiations required for failover clustering are not needed. There is no quorum, and there are no questions of which the server is performing a specific role. They are all active. Thus, NLB is much simpler to set up and administer than Failover Clustering, and has fewer prerequisites.

Hardware prerequisites

NLB clusters can support up to 32 hosts. In general, there is no shared storage or other specialized hardware required for NLB. Unlike a failover cluster, the computers you use to create NLB hosts must not be identical. However, they should be similar in their capabilities, so that some hosts do not perform substantially worse than others.

All the hosts in an NLB cluster must be connected to the same subnet, and network latency must be minimized to allow the convergence process to proceed normally. The hosts don't need to be in the same server closet or data center, but dispersing the computers over long distances could result in hosts being dropped from the cluster.

NOTE **SITE-BASED FAULT TOLERANCE FOR NLB**

To provide site-based fault tolerance, in the event of a large-scale disaster, the best practice is to create separate NLB clusters at different locations, and use another mechanism to distribute client requests between the two sites. For example, *DNS round robin* is a technique that enables the DNS servers resolving the cluster name to supply different IP addresses to successive requests. This would effective split the incoming traffic between the sites, and NLB would split it again among the hosts at each site.

The NLB hosts can have as many network interface adapters as needed for other purposes, but the network adapters used for NLB must all use either multicast or unicast transmissions. The cluster parameters—and specifically the Cluster Operation Mode—influence the hardware configuration of your network. Because this is selected when setting up the NLB cluster, you will have to consider this point at that time.

Software prerequisites

Network Load Balancing has some software configuration requirements that you must consider before creating an NLB cluster, including the following:

- **Operating System** Windows Server has supported Network Load Balancing through several versions, and the implementations since Windows Server 2008 are largely the same. However, the best practice is to have all the hosts in an NLB cluster run the same version and the same edition of Windows Server.
- **IP Addresses** All the hosts in an NLB cluster must have static IP addresses. NLB does not support the use of Dynamic Host Configuration Protocol (DHCP), and will disable the DHCP client on the computers you configure as hosts. Therefore, you must be aware of the IP addressing used on the subnet and have appropriate IP addresses that you can assign to the hosts and the cluster. If the subnet uses DHCP for its other computers, you must have addresses that fall outside of the DHCP scope.
- **Local User Accounts** All the hosts in an NLB cluster should have an identical user account, with membership in the local Administrators group, which the Network Load Balancing Manager will use to access them. Without identical accounts, you must supply authentication credentials for each host you access. While membership in an Active Directory Domain Services domain is not required for an NLB cluster, it makes management easier, because the AD DS Domain Admins group is a member of the local Administrators group on every joined computer.

Install NLB nodes

Network Load Balancing, like Failover Clustering, is a feature included in Windows Server 2016. You must install the feature on all servers that will function as NLB hosts, by using the Add Roles and Features Wizard in Server Manager. Or, you can install this feature using the Install-WindowsFeature cmdlet in Windows PowerShell, using the following command:

```
install-windowsfeature -name nlb -includemanagementtools
```

You can also install the NLB management tools without the NLB feature, to administer a cluster from a remote workstation, using the following command:

```
install-windowsfeature -name rsat-nlb
```

Once the feature is installed on all the servers, you can proceed to create an NLB cluster, using the following procedure.

1. Launch the Network Load Balancing Manager console, shown in Figure 5-65, from the Tools menu in Server Manager.

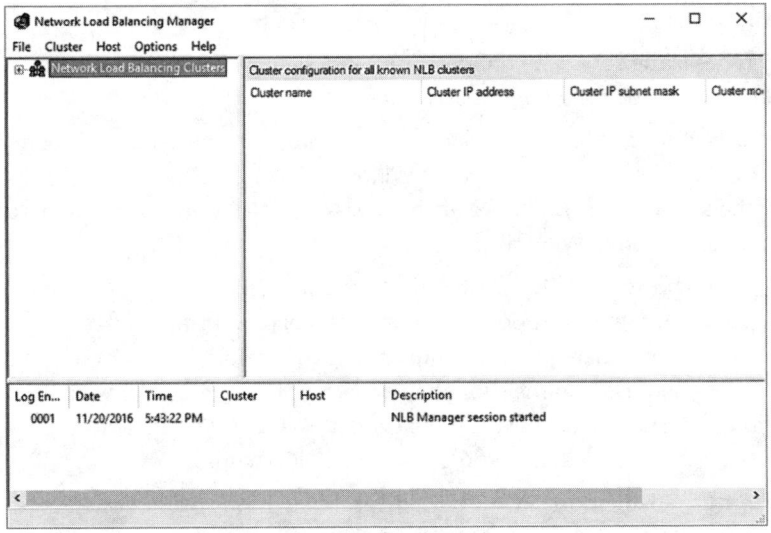

FIGURE 5-65 The Network Load Balancing Manager console

2. On the Cluster menu, click New.
3. On the New Cluster: Connect page, shown in Figure 5-66, in the Host text box, type the name of the first host you want to add to the cluster (even if it is the name of the local computer) and click Connect. The interface(s) and IP address(es) of the computer appear.

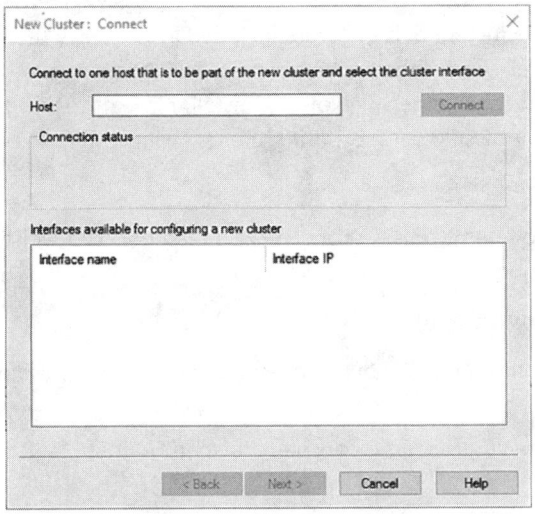

FIGURE 5-66 The New Cluster: Connect page

4. Select the interface the host will use for the cluster.
5. On the New Cluster: Host Parameters page, specify a Priority (Unique Host Identifier) value using the drop-down list. This value must be unique on each host you install. Any traffic that does not conform to the port rules configured for the cluster will be forwarded to the host with the lowest priority value.
6. On the New Cluster: Cluster IP Addresses page, click Add.
7. In the Add IP Address dialog box, shown in Figure 5-67, specify the IPv4 Address and Subnet Mask values that the cluster will use, and click OK. This creates the virtual identity for the cluster, which will be added to the network adapter configuration of every host in the cluster.

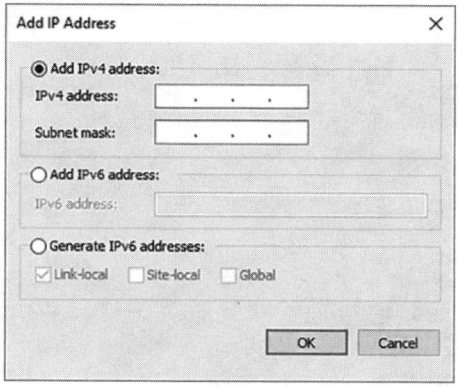

FIGURE 5-67 The Add IP Address dialog box

8. On the New Cluster: Cluster Parameters page, shown in Figure 5-68, specify the Full Internet Name value for the cluster. This is the name that clients will use to connect to the application running on the cluster. For a web server cluster, for example, this will be the server name in the web site's URL.

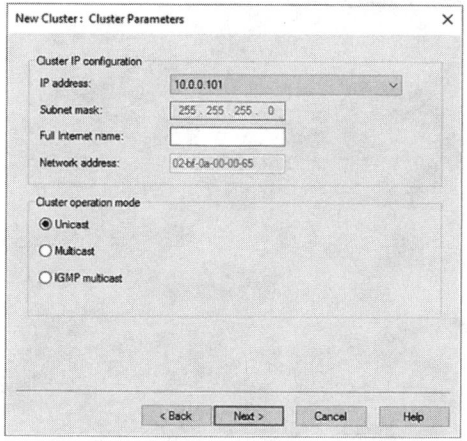

FIGURE 5-68 The New Cluster: Cluster Parameters page

9. In the Cluster Operation Mode box, select one of the following values:
   - **Unicast** Specifies that the cluster should use a unicast media access control (MAC) address for cluster communications.
   - **Multicast** Specifies that the cluster should use a multicast MAC address for cluster communications.
   - **IGMP Multicast** Specifies that the cluster should use a multicast MAC address for cluster communications, with Internet Group Messaging Protocol (IGMP), to prevent port flooding.
10. On the New Cluster: Port Rules page, shown in Figure 5-69, click Edit to modify the default port rule.

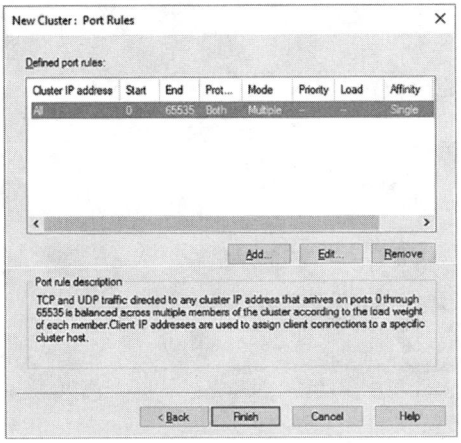

FIGURE 5-69 The New Cluster: Port Rules page

11. In the Add/Edit Port Rule dialog box, shown in Figure 5-70, modify the Port Range settings to specify the port(s) for the application the cluster will be running.

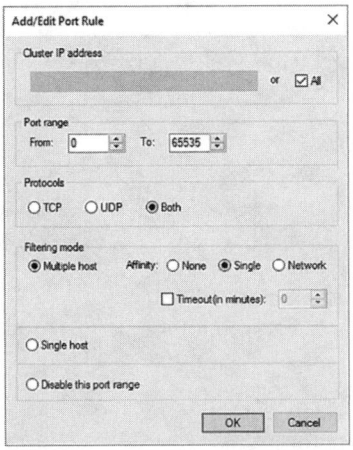

FIGURE 5-70 The Add/Edit Port Rule dialog box

12. In the Filtering Mode box, select one of the following options, and click OK to revise the settings in the port rule.
    - **Multiple Host** Enables incoming traffic conforming to the port rule to be handled by multiple cluster hosts. Select an Affinity setting to specify how repeat traffic from clients is distributed among hosts.
    - **Single Host** Enables incoming traffic conforming to the port rule to be handled by a single cluster host.
    - **Disable This Port Range** Causes the cluster to block all traffic confirming to the port rule.
13. Click Finish.

You have now created an NLB cluster and configured its first host. To add additional hosts to the cluster, select it in the console and click Cluster | Add Host. For each host you add, you must configure only the Connect, Host Parameters, and Port Rules pages. As you add each host, the cluster converges, until all the hosts have been recognized and incorporated into the cluster, as shown in Figure 5-71.

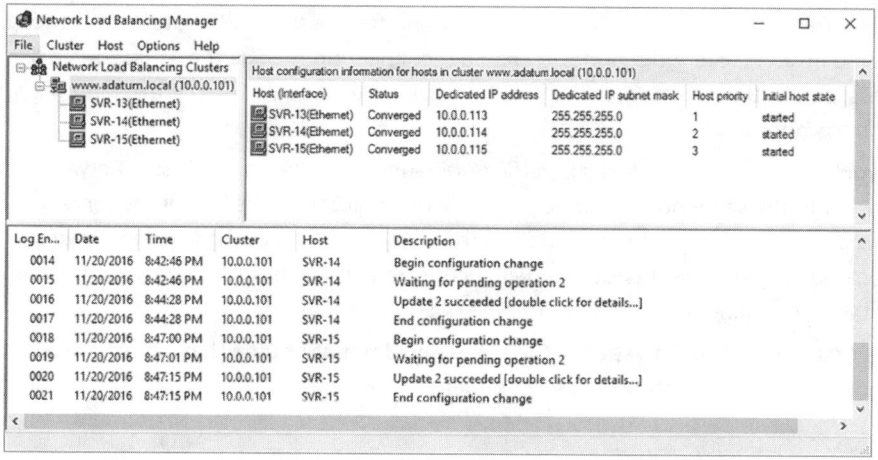

FIGURE 5-71 The Network Load Balancing Manager console, with a three-node cluster

Configure affinity

When you configure the Filtering Mode setting in a port rule, you specify how the cluster handles the traffic conforming to that port rule. If you select Single, you are essentially using NLB as a failover cluster for that rule, with fault tolerance, but no scalability. Only the host with the lowest Priority value will handle traffic for that rule. If that host should fail, then the next lowest priority host would take over.

Selecting Disable prevents the cluster from accepting any traffic conforming to the rule. You use this setting to creating a rule that blocks traffic using a specific IP address or port.

When you select the Multiple Host option, then the traffic conforming to that rule is distributed among all the hosts of the cluster. This provides both fault tolerance and scalability. The potential problem with this arrangement is that a client could conceivably disconnect and reconnect to the cluster, and be sent to a different host.

For some applications, this is not a problem. If, for example, you are running a web server that provides only static pages, then it doesn't matter if a client is shifted from one host to another. However, for an e-commerce web site, interrupting a session and moving the client to another host would interrupt the transaction. The Affinity settings for the Multiple Hosts option address this problem.

The Affinity setting you choose specifies how the cluster should react to repeated requests from the same client. The available settings are as follows:

- **None** With no client affinity, incoming requests from the same IP address can be handled by any host. You should avoid this setting for transaction based applications that require consistent connections to one host. You should also avoid this setting when the rule uses UDP or Both for the Protocols setting, so that IP fragments are not sent to different hosts.
- **Single** This setting ensures that all traffic coming from a single IP address is sent to the same host. If a client disconnects, then a reconnection will use the same source IP address, and NLB will recognize this and forward the traffic accordingly, allowing the session to continue.
- **Network** This setting enables all traffic originating from the same Class C network to be sent to the same host. In some cases, clients might use different proxy servers on the same network when connecting to the cluster. As long as those proxy servers are located on the same subnet, NLB will recognize that the traffic probably originates from the same client and send it to a single host.

Select the timeout checkbox to specify the maximum amount of time that can pass between connections before the affinity rule no longer applies.

Configure port rules

Port rules define what types of TCP/IP traffic the NLB cluster should handle and how it should handle each type. When you first create a cluster, the default port rule admits traffic using all IP address and all ports. You can modify this rule as needed, and create others to specify different settings for different types of traffic.

In addition to the Filter Mode and Affinity settings already described, the settings available in a port rule are as follows:

- **Cluster IP Address** A cluster can have multiple IP addresses, representing different services, such as different web sites hosted by Internet Information Services (IIS). By selecting a specific address, you can create a different rule for each service. Selecting the All checkbox creates a global rule for all the cluster's IP addresses.

- **Port Range** A cluster can also provide services that use different ports. For example, the well-known port for a web server is 80, but the well-known port for a secured web server is 443. If you are using NLB to balance traffic for a web server that runs multiple sites, you can create a rule for each site by specifying its IP address and/or its port number. A site that provides static web pages can use the Multiple Host filtering mode with no client affinity, but for a secure e-commerce site supported on only one host, you might use the Single filtering mode.
- **Protocols** Specifies whether the rule should apply to TCP, or UDP traffic, or both. TCP is typically used for longer transactions that require multiple packets, while UDP is often used for quick request/response transactions. Depending on the application you are running on the cluster, you might want to configure different affinity settings for each protocol.

When you access the port rules through the Properties sheet for one of the hosts, as shown in Figure 5-72, you cannot modify the rule settings listed earlier, but there are two host-specific settings that you can configure, as follows:

- **Load Weight** Accessible only in multiple host mode, specifies how much of the traffic conforming to the rule should be handled by the selected host. The default setting is to balance the traffic equally, but you can specify a relative value from 0 to 100.
- **Handling Priority** Accessible only in single host mode, specifies a priority for the host's handling of the traffic conforming to the rule. The host with the lowest value will handle all the traffic for the rule.

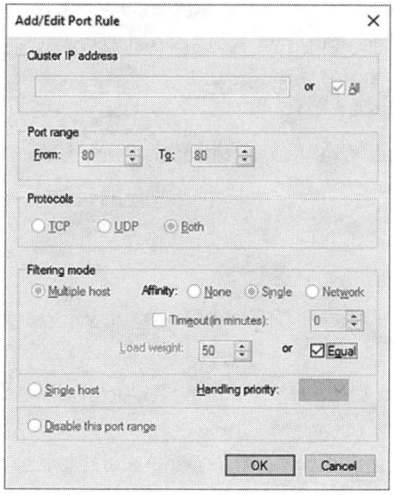

FIGURE 5-72 The Port Rules settings in a host's Properties sheet

Configure cluster operation mode

The Cluster Operation Mode setting specified what kind of TCP/IP traffic the cluster hosts should use. A unicast is a TCP/IP transmission that is addressed to a single destination. A multicast is a transmission sent to multiple destinations, using a special multicast IP address.

The MAC address is a unique six-byte value encoded into network interface adapters at the factory. When you select the unicast mode for a cluster, NLB replaces the hardware MAC address on the interface you select for each host with the cluster's virtual MAC address. This causes traffic addressed to the cluster to go to all its hosts. This practice also confuses your network switches, which are unable to determine which port the cluster MAC address belongs to, and therefore must forward the traffic out through all its ports, flooding the network in the process.

Unicast mode also prevents cluster hosts from communicating with each other using their designated cluster adapters. Because all the hosts use the same MAC address, outgoing traffic loops back and never reaches the network. You should therefore install a second network adapter in each host if you plan to use unicast mode and require normal communication between the hosts.

When you select the multicast option, NLB adds a second MAC address to the network interface on each host, which is a multicast MAC address that does not replace the original one. Because each host retains its unique MAC address, there is no need for a second network adapter. The multicast option also causes switch flooding, by default, but there are solutions for it. The IGMP multicast option uses the Internet Group Management Protocol to program the switches, so that traffic destined for the cluster's MAC address is only forwarded out through the switch ports connected to NLB hosts. Administrators can also create a virtual local area network (VLAN) in the switch that achieves the same results.

Multicast mode is the preferable option, except in cases when your network hardware does not support multicast transmissions or the use of multicasts seriously diminishes cluster performance.

Upgrade an NLB cluster

There are two ways to upgrade an existing Windows Server NLB cluster to the Windows Server 2016 version:

- **Simultaneous Upgrade** In this option, you bring the entire NLB cluster down, upgrade all the hosts, and then bring the cluster up again. Obviously, this entails a significant amount of downtime for the clustered application. This is only a viable option if you are comfortable with leaving your application unavailable for a time, or if you have a backup cluster available to take its place.
- **Rolling Upgrade** In this option, you remove the hosts from the cluster, one at a time, upgrade each one, and then add it back into the cluster. NLB is designed to accommodate the addition and removal of hosts, so the cluster will converge each time you remove or add one of the servers.

Chapter summary

- Hyper-V Replica is a feature that can duplicate virtual machine storage, either synchronously or asynchronously.
- Live Migration is the process by which the memory and system state of a virtual machine are transferred from one cluster node to another almost instantaneously.
- Storage Migration is a process by which a VM's virtual hard disk files are moved from one location to another, either on the same or a different Hyper-V host.
- Windows Server 2016 supports failover clusters containing nodes in a single domain, in multiple domains, and in workgroups.
- Quorum is the voting procedure that clusters use to determine whether it should continue to run or shut down during a failure.
- Failover Clusters require shared storage, so that the applications running on the cluster nodes can continue to function, despite a node failure.
- Cluster-aware Updating is a feature that ensures that all the nodes in a failover cluster receive the same updates in a timely manner.
- Cluster Operating System Rolling Upgrade is a new operational mode that enables cluster nodes with different operating systems to coexist temporarily.
- Cluster Shared Volumes are shared storage that is available on all a cluster's nodes simultaneously.
- Guest clustering is when you create a failover cluster using virtual machines on Hyper-V servers.
- A cloud witness is a voting quorum member that resides in Microsoft Azure, providing the decisive vote for multisite clusters.
- Storage Spaces Direct enables you to create cluster shared storage using the local disks in the nodes.
- Storage Spaces Direct can provide shared storage for a separate cluster or for roles running in the same cluster.
- VM monitoring enables you to specify a service running on a virtual machine, so that the cluster can take action if the service fails.
- A stretch cluster is one that is split between two or more sites. Site awareness is the ability to configure cluster nodes with their sites, to control their failover behavior.
- To perform Live Migrations and Storage Migrations, you can use Failover Cluster Manager or Windows PowerShell cmdlets.
- Quick Migration, the predecessor to Live Migration, copies memory contents to shared storage and then to the destination node.
- Network health protection automatically fails over a role to a different node when a network is inaccessible.

- Network Load Balancing is a Windows Server 2016 feature that enables you to create clusters in which all the servers are running the same application simultaneously.
- NLB clusters have their own identities, with names and IP addresses that clients use to access them.
- To create an NLB cluster, you use the Network Load Balancing Manager to add each host and configure the settings for the hosts and the cluster.
- Port rules enable you to identify the types of traffic that NLB cluster hosts can handle, by specifying IP addresses, protocols, and ports.

Thought experiment

In this thought experiment, demonstrate your skills and knowledge of the topics covered in this chapter. You can find answer to this thought experiment in the next section.

Alice is setting up a Network Load Balancing cluster consisting of five hosts running IIS to host an e-commerce web site. Each of the host servers has a single network adapter, and they are all connected to the same subnet. When creating the NLB cluster, Alice works at the first host server, adding the local machine, configuring the cluster to use Unicast transmissions, and modifying the default port rule to use the Multiple Host filtering mode with the Single affinity setting.

After adding the first host to the NLB cluster, Alice discovers that she cannot communicate with the four computers that are to be the other hosts in the cluster. She tries adding them to the cluster, and she is unable to connect. She tries pinging them, and the destination is unreachable. She even tries shutting down Windows Firewall, to no avail.

What is preventing the communication and what are two possible solutions Alice can use to remedy the situation?

Thought experiment answer

This section contains the solution to the thought experiment.

The unicast transmission setting has caused the MAC address on the host's network adapter to be replaced by the virtual MAC address of the cluster. Because that MAC address resolves to the cluster, Alice is, in effect, pinging herself when she tries to contact the other servers. To remedy the situation, she can either add a second network adapter to all of the host servers, or reconfigure the cluster to use multicast transmissions, which does not suppress the server's own MAC address.

CHAPTER 6

Maintain and monitor server environments

Once servers are installed and configured, there are still tasks for administrators to perform. Servers require maintenance, to ensure that they are updated and protected, and their performance must be monitored, to ensure their continued efficiency.

Skills in this chapter:

- Maintain server installations
- Monitor server installations

Skill 6.1: Maintain server installations

No matter what fault tolerance mechanisms you are using on your network, servers require regular maintenance to function efficiently. Administrators must apply updates to operating systems and applications, monitor antimalware software products, and perform regular backups to ensure data is protected against loss. Windows Server 2016 includes features that can perform these tasks, as described in the following sections.

This section covers how to:

- Implement Windows Server Update Services (WSUS) solutions
- Configure WSUS groups
- Manage patch management in mixed environments
- Implement an antimalware solution with Windows Defender
- Integrate Windows Defender with WSUS and Windows Update
- Perform backup and restore operations using Windows Server Backup
- Determine backup strategies for different Windows Server roles and workloads, including Hyper-V Host, Hyper-V Guests, Active Directory, File Servers, and Web Servers using Windows Server 2016 native tools and solutions

Quick check

Which of the following device types is Windows Server Backup unable to use for a backup drive?

1. **magnetic tape drives**
2. **internal disk drives**
3. **external hard disk drives**
4. **remote network shares**

Quick check answer

Windows Server Backup does not support magnetic tape drives (#1), but can back up to internal or external disk drives, as well as remote network shares.

Determine backup strategies for different Windows Server roles and workloads, including Hyper-V Host, Hyper-V Guests, Active Directory, File Servers, and Web Servers using Windows Server 2016 native tools and solutions

Some Windows Server 2016 components present special difficulties for a backup solution, and yet at the same time, those components are often the ones most worth protecting.

Backing Up Active Directory

The Active Directory database is a crucial resource on most Windows networks, one that backup administrators must not ignore. However, backing up and restoring Active Directory is an exceptional process in nearly every way. When you perform a scheduled backup of an Active Directory domain controller, or perform a single backup with the System State checkbox selected, Windows Server Backup includes the Active Directory database as part of the system state, among other things.

Active Directory domains should have at least two domain controllers, and if that is the case, and one of them fails or is lost, it should not be necessary to restore the Active Directory database from a backup. Instead, you can reinstall the Active Directory Domain Services role, promote the computer to a domain controller, and allow the replication process to rebuild the database on the new domain controller.

Performing a full server restoration includes the system state, and consequently the Active Directory database, but there might be occasions when you want to retrieve parts of Active Directory, such as objects you have inadvertently deleted.

NOTE BACKING UP THE SYSTEM STATE

You can only work with the system state as a single entity. You cannot back up or restore individual elements within the system state.

It is possible to restore just the system state from a backup, but you must use the Wbadmin.exe command line tool, as in the following example:

```
wbadmin start systemstaterecovery -version:11/27/2016-11:07
```

The date and time value following the version: parameter is the version identifier for the backup from which you want to restore the system state. To list the version identifiers of the available backups, use the following command, as shown in Figure 6-36:

```
wbadmin get versions
```

```
PS C:\Users\Administrator> wbadmin get versions
wbadmin 1.0 - Backup command-line tool
(C) Copyright 2013 Microsoft Corporation. All rights reserved.

Backup time: 11/27/2016 3:16 AM
Backup target: Fixed Disk labeled E:
Version identifier: 11/27/2016-11:16
Can recover: Volume(s), File(s), Application(s), System State
Snapshot ID: {5c44e1b1-fc26-4499-a95a-2bb144a1b7c6}

Backup time: 11/27/2016 8:31 PM
Backup target: Fixed Disk labeled E:
Version identifier: 11/28/2016-04:31
Can recover: Volume(s), File(s), Application(s), Bare Metal Recovery, System State
Snapshot ID: {e73de3af-c9d8-4187-b5b6-9ba094c7b737}

Backup time: 11/27/2016 11:18 PM
Backup target: Fixed Disk labeled E:
Version identifier: 11/28/2016-07:18
Can recover: Volume(s), File(s), Application(s), Bare Metal Recovery, System State
Snapshot ID: {53a990f6-99c7-4a7f-8de2-86b3c802d178}

PS C:\Users\Administrator> _
```

FIGURE 6-36 Output of the wbadmin get versions command

It is important for the administrator to understand that there are two types of system state restores: *authoritative* and *nonauthoritative*.

- **Nonauthoritative** When you open a Command Prompt window in a standard Windows session and restore the system state, you are performing a nonauthoritative restore. This means that the program will restore the Active Directory database to the exact state it was in at the time of the backup. However, the next time an Active Directory replication occurs, the other domain controllers will update the newly restored system with any changes that have occurred since the backup took place. This means that if you are trying to recover AD objects that you accidentally deleted, the replication process will cause the system to delete the newly restored objects.
- **Authoritative** To restore deleted objects, you must perform an authoritative restore, and to do this, you must restart the computer in Directory Services Repair Mode (DSRM) by pressing F8 during the boot process and selecting the appropriate entry from the Advanced Boot Options menu. After logging on using the Administrator account and the DSRM password specified during the Active Directory Domain Services installation, you can perform the system state restore using Wbadmin.exe. Once the restoration of the system state is complete, you can use the Ntdsutil.exe tool to specify the objects that you want restored authoritatively.

Backing up group policy objects

Group policy objects (GPOs) are a special case. You cannot use the authoritative restore procedure to restore GPOs that you have accidentally deleted. To back up and restore GPOs, you must use the Group Policy Management console. When you right-click a GPO in the console and select Back Up from the context menu, a Back Up Group Policy Object dialog box appears, as shown in Figure 6-37, in which you can specify the location for the backup.

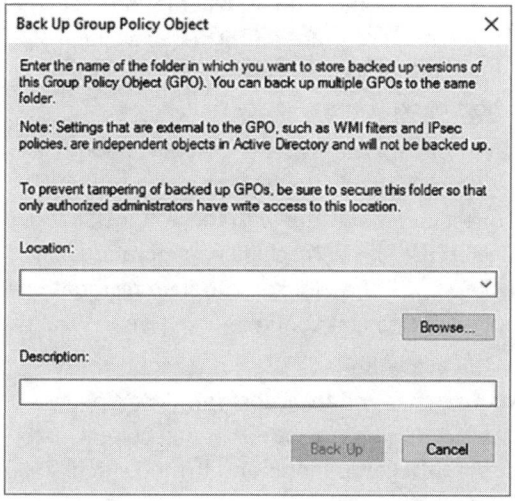

FIGURE 6-37 The Back Up Group Policy Object dialog box

To restore a GPO, right-click the Group Policy Objects container and, from the context menu, select Manage Backups. The Manage Backups dialog box appears, as shown in Figure 6-38, in which you can select the GPO you want to recover and click the Restore button.

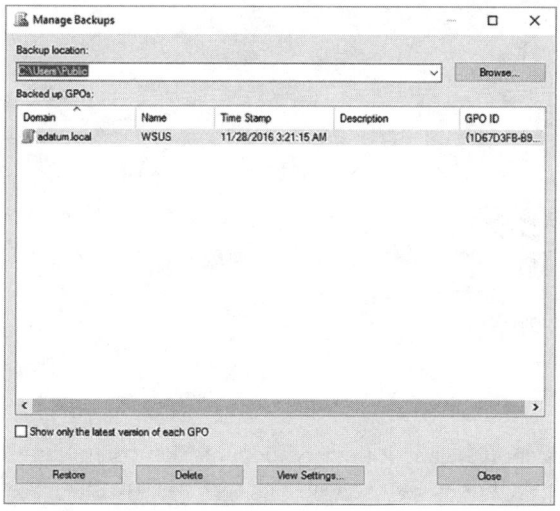

FIGURE 6-38 The Manage Backups dialog box

Backing Up Hyper-V

Hyper-V presents a problem for backup administrators. You can conceivably back up virtual machines as though they are separate systems, by running Windows Server Backup in the guest operating system. You can also back them up as part of the host server, by backing up the virtual machine files and the virtual hard disks.

Backing up from within the guest OS can provide access to resources that are not available through the host, such as pass-through disks, but it saves none of the virtual machine settings. If you must perform a restore of the guest, you must recreate the virtual machine first, with the appropriate settings, and then restore the guest OS. Microsoft recommends that administrators use this method in addition to a host backup, not in place of it.

Backing up virtual machines from the Hyper-V host uses the Hyper-V Volume Shadow Copy Requestor service in the guest operating system to enable the host to back up the VM while it is running. The requestor service in the guest communicates with the Volume Shadow Copy Service (VSS) in the host, enabling it to back up the virtual machine configuration files, the virtual hard disks, and any checkpoints associated with the VM. You can then restore the virtual machine from the host, if needed, without having to first configure it in Hyper-V.

Windows Server Backup includes support for the VSS writer and the guest requestor service, making it a simple matter to backup virtual machines and their host settings. When you create a backup of a Hyper-V host, the Select Items dialog box includes a Hyper-V item, as shown in Figure 6-39, that enables you to select the host components and the individual VMs running on the server.

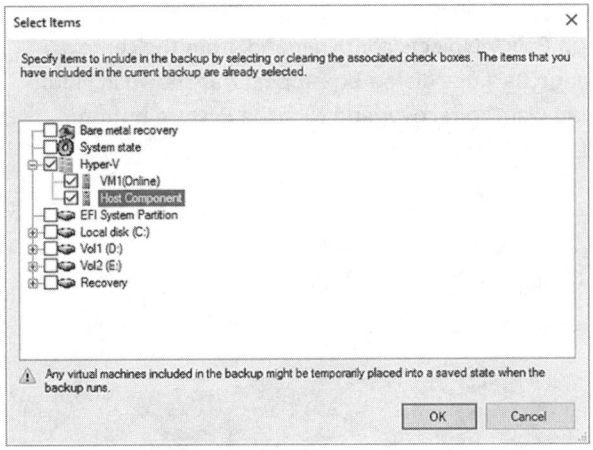

FIGURE 6-39 The Select Items dialog box on a Hyper-V host

Backing up IIS

Web sites running Internet Information Services (IIS) can include components that complicate the process of backing them up. The static files that make up a web site, such as HTML files, are not a problem, because they can be treated as files on a file server and backed up accordingly.

However, many web sites are connected to back-end databases, hosted by Microsoft SQL Server or other applications. The database can be located on the server running IIS or another server. To back these up, you must use a product that supports SQL Server backups. Windows Server Backup can perform VSS backups of SQL Server databases.

The third possible components of an IIS web site are the configuration files, including ApplicationHost.config, Administration.config, and Redirection.config. These are XML files, located in the Windows\System32\inetsrv folder, which contain the configuration settings for the IIS sites and applications.

Because these are XML files, they are not a problem to back up, but administrators must remember to select them for backup. It is also possible to back these configuration files up using an IIS utility called Appcmd.exe. To perform a backup of the IIS configuration files, you run a command like the following in the Windows\System32\inetsrv folder:

```
appcmd add backup configbackup1
```

To restore the configuration files from a previously performed backup, you use a command like the following:

```
appcmd restore backup configbackup1
```

Skill 6.2: Monitor server installations

Server performance can change over time for a variety of reasons. Workloads can change, and so can hardware components. Part of the server administrator's job is to track the ongoing performance of servers, to ensure that they continue to function efficiently. Windows Server 2016 includes tools that you can use for this performance tracking, such as the Performance Monitor console.

This section covers how to:

- Monitor workloads using Performance Monitor
- Configure Data Collector Sets
- Determine appropriate CPU, memory, disk, and networking counters for storage and compute workloads
- Configure alerts
- Monitor workloads using Resource Monitor

Monitor workloads using Performance Monitor

Performance Monitor is a tool that displays system performance statistics in real time. Using Performance Monitor, you can display hundreds of different statistics (called performance counters) and create customized graphs containing any information you choose.

When you open the Performance Monitor console from the Windows Administrative Tools group, you see an Overview page containing a system summary. Click the Performance Monitor icon and you see a line graph, updated in real time, showing the current level for the % Processor Time performance counter, as shown in Figure 6-40.

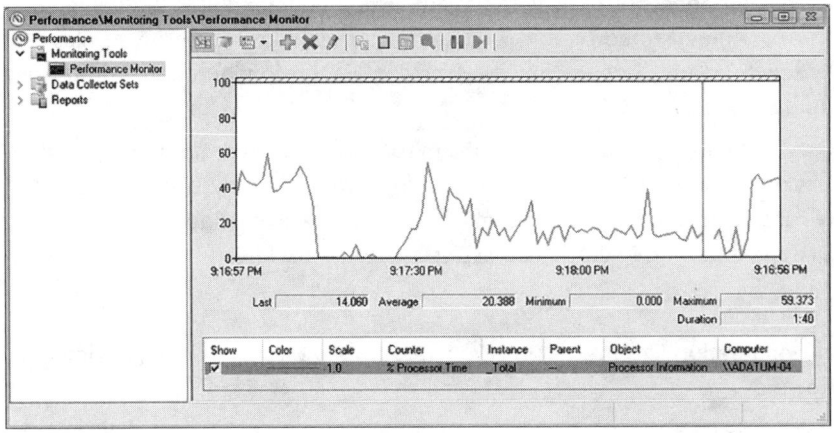

FIGURE 6-40 The default Performance Monitor display

A performance counter is a measure of the current activity in one aspect of a specific hardware or software component. The % Processor Time counter measures the percentage of the system processor's clock cycles that are being utilized by non-idle tasks. This is one of the basic measures of computer activity. A % Processor Time counter that is consistently pegged at 100 percent indicates that the processor is unable to keep up with the tasks it must perform.

There are counters available that measure processor performance in other ways, as well as counters for many other system components. You can add as many counters to the graph as you want, although adding too many can make the display difficult to interpret. By viewing the statistics generated by these counters and learning their significance, you can evaluate the performance of the computer in many ways.

Modifying the graph view

The legend beneath the Performance Monitor graph specifies the line color for each counter added to the display, the scale of values for each counter, and other identifying information. When you select a counter in the legend, its current values appear in numerical form at the bottom of the graph.

NOTE **HIGHLIGHTING COUNTERS**

When you have multiple counters in the Performance Monitor graph, clicking the Highlight button in the toolbar (or pressing Ctrl+H) changes the selected counter to a broad line that is easier to distinguish from the others.

If your computer is otherwise idle, you will probably notice that the line in the default graph is hovering near the bottom of the scale, making it difficult to see its exact value. You can address this problem by modifying the scale of the graph's Y (that is, vertical) axis. Click the Properties button in the toolbar (or press Ctrl+Q) to display the Performance Monitor Properties sheet and click the Graph tab, as shown in Figure 6-41. In the Vertical Scale box, you can reduce the maximum value for the Y axis, thereby using more of the graph to display the counter data.

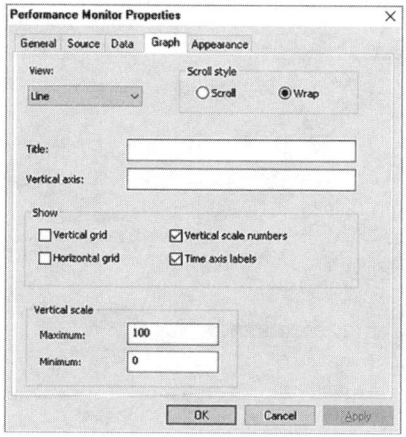

FIGURE 6-41 The Graph tab on the Performance Monitor Properties sheet

Depending on the nature of counters displayed in the graph, you might want to raise or lower the Maximum and Minimum values in the Vertical Scale box to create an ideal range for the Y axis. Different counters use different units of measurement for the data they present; they are not all percentages. Part of the skill in using Performance Monitor effectively is selecting counters with units of measurement and value ranges that work well together on the same graph.

On the General tab of the Performance Monitor Properties sheet, you can also modify the sample rate of the graph. By default, the graph updates the counter values every one second and displays 100 seconds worth of data at a time, but you can increase this value to display data for a longer period of time on a single page of the graph. This can make it easier to detect long-term trends in counter values.

NOTE **MODIFYING THE GRAPH APPEARANCE**

The Performance Monitor Properties sheet contains a few other controls that you can use to modify the appearance of the graph. For example, on the Graph tab, you can add axis titles and gridlines, and in the Appearance tab, you can control the graph's background and select a different font.

Other graph views

In addition to the line graph, Performance Monitor has two other views of the same data, a histogram bar graph and a report view. You can change the display to one of these views by clicking the Change Graph Type toolbar button. The histogram view is a bar graph with a separate vertical bar for each counter, as shown in Figure 6-42. In this view, it is easier to monitor large numbers of counters, because the lines do not overlap.

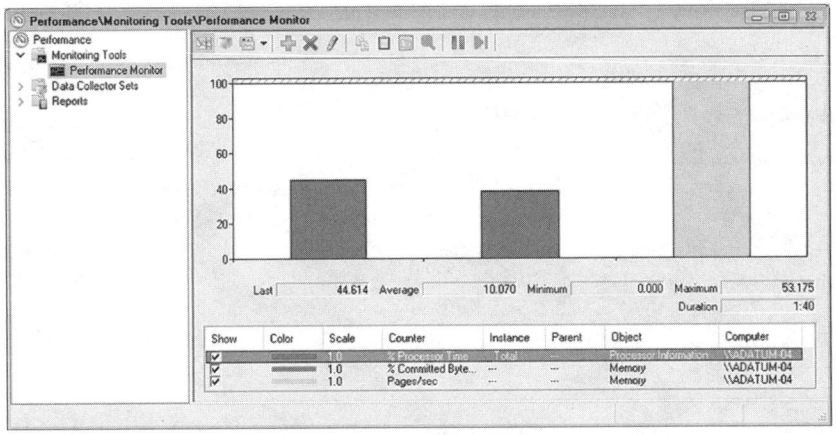

FIGURE 6-42 The Performance Monitor histogram view

The report view, shown in Figure 6-43, displays the numerical value for each of the performance counters.

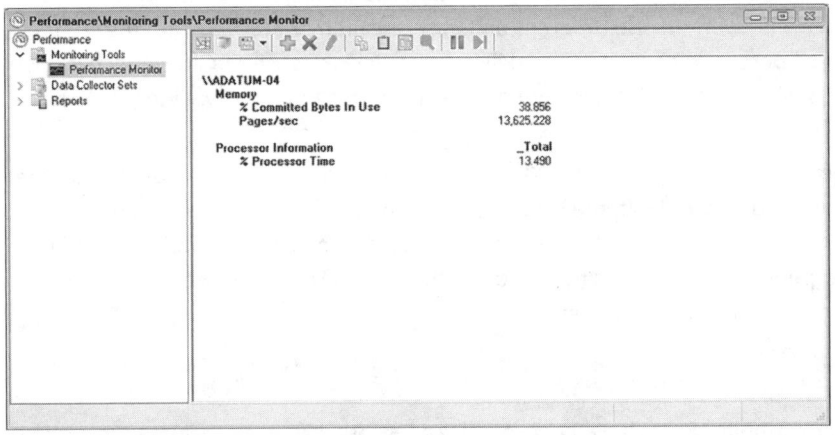

FIGURE 6-43 The Performance Monitor report view

As with the line graph, the histogram and report views both update their counter values at the interval specified on the General tab of the Performance Monitor Properties sheet. The main drawback of these two views, however, is that they do not display a history of the counter values, only the current value. Each new sampling overwrites the previous one in the display, unlike the line graph, which displays the previous values as well.

Adding performance counters

To add counters to the Performance Monitor display, click the Add button in the toolbar or press Ctrl+I, to display the Add Counters dialog box, as shown in Figure 6-44.

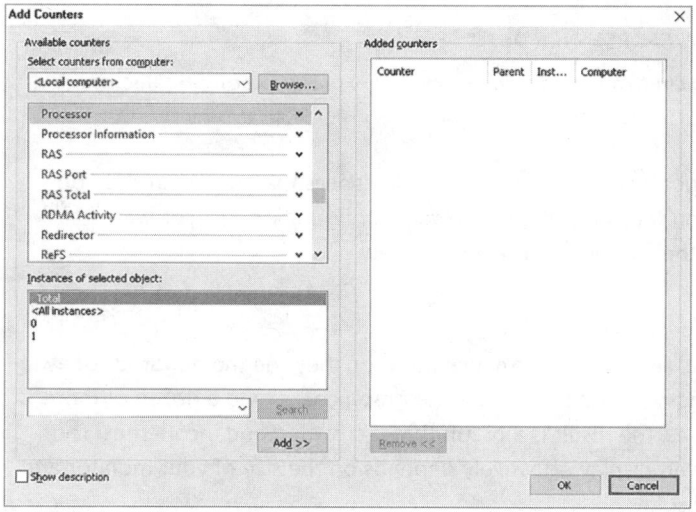

FIGURE 6-44 The Add Counters dialog box

In the Add Counters dialog box, you must specify the following four pieces of information to add a counter to the display:

- **Computer** Specifies the name of the computer you want to monitor with the selected counter. Unlike most MMC snap-ins, you cannot redirect the entire focus of Performance Monitor to another computer on the network. Instead, you specify a computer name for each counter you add to the display. This enables you to create a display showing counters for various computers on the network, such as a single graph of the processor activity for all your servers.
- **Performance Object** Specifies the hardware or software component in the computer you want to monitor. Click the down arrow on a performance object to display the performance counters related to that component.
- **Performance Counter** Identifies a statistic representing a specific aspect of the selected performance object's activities.
- **Instance** Identifies a specific occurrence of the selected performance counter. For example, on a computer with two network interface adapters, each counter in the Network Interface performance object has two instances, enabling you to track the performance of each adapter individually. Some counters also have instances such as

Total or Average, enabling you to track the performance of all instances combined or the median value of all instances.

Once you have selected a computer name, a performance object, a performance counter in that object, and an instance of that counter, click Add to add the counter to the Added Counters list. The dialog box remains open so that you can add more counters. Click OK when you are finished to update the graph with your selected counters.

***NOTE* UNDERSTANDING PERFORMANCE OBJECTS**

Select the Show Description checkbox to display a detailed explanation of the selected performance object or performance counter.

The performance objects, performance counters, and instances that appear in the Add Counters dialog box depend on the computer's hardware configuration, the software installed on the computer, and the computer's role on the network.

Controlling the display

In many cases, when users first discover Performance Monitor, they see the hundreds of available performance counters and proceed to create a line graph containing a dozen or more different statistics. In most cases, the result is a graph that is crowded and incoherent. The number of counters that you can display effectively depends on the size of your monitor and the resolution of your video display.

Consider the following tips when selecting counters:

- **Limit The Number Of Counters** Too many counters make the graph more difficult to understand. To display a large number of statistics, you can display multiple console windows (by right-clicking Performance Monitor and selecting New Window From Here) and select different counters in each one, or use the histogram or report view to display a large number of counters in a more compact form.
- **Modify The Counter Display Properties** Depending on the size and capabilities of your monitor, the default colors and line widths that Performance Monitor uses in its graph might make it difficult to distinguish counters from each other. On the Data tab in the Performance Monitor Properties sheet, you can modify the color, style, and width of each counter's line in the graph, to make it easier to distinguish.
- **Choose Counters With Comparable Values** Performance Monitor imposes no limitations on the combinations of counters you can select for a single graph, but some statistics are not practical to display together, because of their disparate values. When a graph contains a counter with a typical value that is under twenty and another counter with a value in the hundreds, it is difficult to arrange the display so that both counters are readable. Choose counters with values that are reasonably comparable, so that you can display them legibly. Here again, if you must display counters with different value ranges, you might prefer to use the report view instead of the graph view.

Configure data collector sets

Performance bottlenecks can develop on a server over a long period, and it can often be difficult to detect them by observing performance levels at one point in time. This is why it is a good idea to use tools like Performance Monitor to establish baseline levels for a server. A *baseline* is a set of readings, captured under normal operating conditions, which you can save and compare to readings taken later. By comparing the baseline readings to the server's current readings at regular intervals, you can discern trends that might eventually affect the computer's performance.

To capture counter statistics in Performance Monitor console for later review, you must create a *data collector set*, using the following procedure.

1. Open the Performance Monitor console and expand the Data Collector Sets folder.
2. Right-click the User Defined folder and, on the context menu, click New | Data Collector Set. The Create New Data Collector Set Wizard appears, displaying the How Would You Like To Create This New Data Collector Set page, as shown in Figure 6-45.

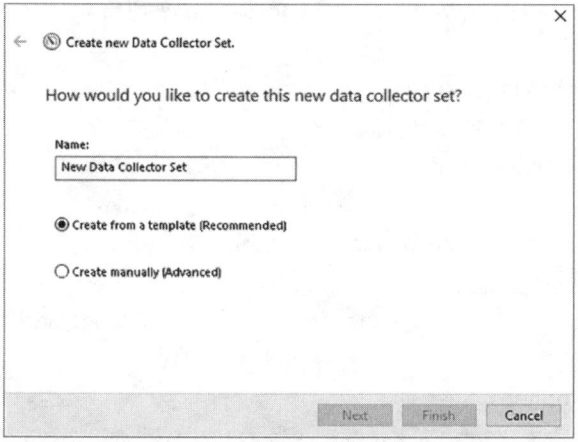

FIGURE 6-45 The How Would You Like To Create This New Data Collector Set page of the Create New Data Collector Set Wizard

3. In the Name text box, type a name for the data collector set. Then, select the Create Manually (Advanced) option.
4. On the What Type Of Data Do You Want To Include? page, shown in Figure 6-46, leave the Create Data Logs option selected and select the Performance Counter check box.

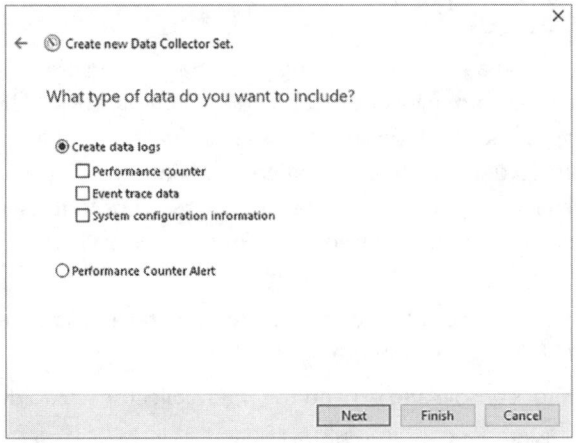

FIGURE 6-46 The What Type Of Data Do You Want To Include? page of the Create New Data Collector Set Wizard

5. On the Which Performance Counters Would You Like To Log page, click Add, to display the Add Counters dialog box.
6. Select the counters you want to log in the usual manner and click OK. The counters appear in the Performance Counters box.
7. Select the interval at which Performance Monitor should collect samples.
8. On the Where Would You Like The Data To Be Saved Page, type the name of or browse to the folder where you want to store the data collector set.
9. On the Create The Data Collector Set page, if the account you are currently using does not have the privileges needed to gather the log information, click Change to display a Performance Monitor dialog box in which you can supply alternative credentials.
10. Select one of the following options:
    - **Open Properties For This Data Collector Set** Saves the data collector set to the specified location and opens its Properties sheet for further modifications.
    - **Start This Data Collector Set Now** Saves the data collector set to the specified location and starts collecting data immediately.
    - **Save and Close** Saves the data collector set to the specified location and closes the wizard.
11. Click Finish. The new data collector set appears in the User Defined folder.
12. Right-click the new data collector set and, in the context menu, select Start. The console begins collecting data until you right-click and select Stop.

Once you have captured data using the collector set, you can display the data by double-clicking the Performance Monitor file in the folder you specified during its creation. This opens a Performance Monitor window containing a graph of the collected data, as shown in Figure 6-47, instead of real time activity.

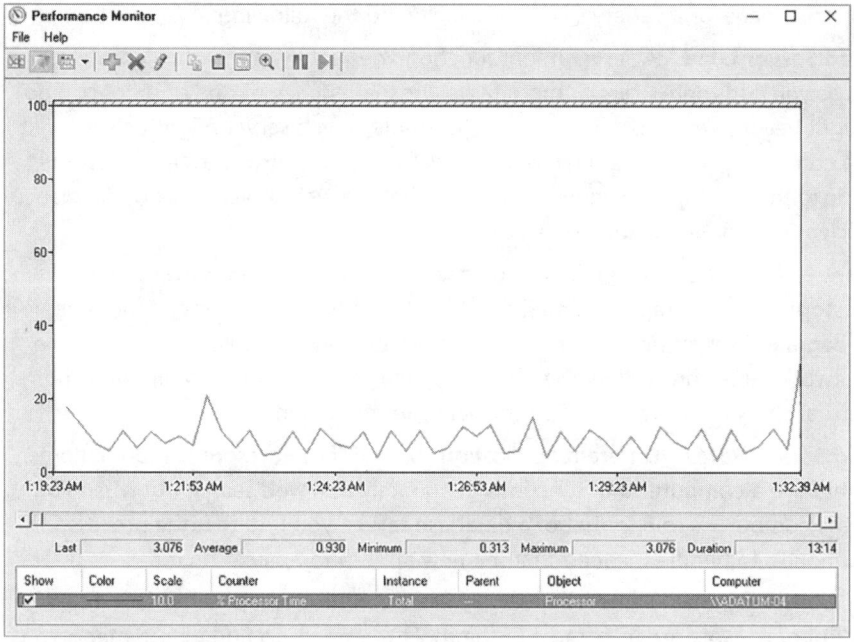

FIGURE 6-47 Performance Monitor information collected using a data collector set

By repeating this process later and comparing the information in the two data collector sets, you can often detect performance trends that indicate the presence of bottlenecks.

Determine appropriate CPU, memory, disk, and networking counters for storage and compute workloads

Once you learn how to operate the Performance Monitor console, the next step is to learn how to use it to monitor and troubleshoot a computer. Server administrators often encounter performance problems that are not attributable to an obvious cause, such as a hardware or service failure. Users might complain that a server's performance is slow at certain times of the day, or that performance has been declining gradually over the course of weeks or months. When this occurs, one of the most common causes is a performance bottleneck somewhere in the server.

A *bottleneck* is a component that is not providing an acceptable level of performance, compared with the other components in the system. For example, users might complain that their file server performance is slow, and you might spend a great deal of time and money upgrading your network, expecting to see a dramatic improvement. However, if the server is an older computer using an outdated processor, the improvement might be minimal because it is the processor, not the network, that is the bottleneck. All the other components might be running well, but the processor cannot keep up with the data capacity of the new, faster network.

Bottlenecks can appear for a variety of reasons, including the following:

- **Increased Server Load** A server might function adequately in a particular role at first, but as you add more users or more tasks, the inadequacy of one or more components might become more pronounced. For example, a web server might be sufficient to host a company's web site at first, but then the company introduces a new product and traffic to the site triples. Suddenly, you find that the web server's disk performance is insufficient to handle the additional traffic.
- **Hardware Failure** Hardware failures do not always manifest themselves as catastrophic stoppages. A component might malfunction intermittently for a long time, causing degraded server performance that is maddeningly inconsistent. For example, a faulty network cable connecting a server to a switch can cause occasional traffic interruptions that show up as degraded performance in the server.
- **Changed Server Roles** Different applications have different resource requirements. You might have a computer that functions adequately as a web server, but when you change the computer's role to that of a database server, you find that the processor is not fast enough to handle the load that the new application places on it.

Locating the bottleneck that is hindering performance can be a complicated task, but the Performance Monitor console provides most of the tools you need. To find a bottleneck, you usually examine the four main subsystems of a computer, which are covered in the following sections.

CPU counters

An inadequate or malfunctioning processor array can cause a server to queue incoming client requests, preventing the server from fulfilling them promptly. For general monitoring of the processor subsystem, consider using the following performance counters:

- **Processor: % Processor Time** Specifies the percentage of time that the processor is busy. This value should be as low as possible, with anything below 85 percent being acceptable. If this value is consistently too high, you should attempt to determine which processes are using too much processor time, upgrade the processor, or add another processor, if possible.
- **System: Processor Queue Length** Specifies the number of program threads waiting to be executed by the processor. This value should be as low as possible, with values less than 10 being acceptable. If the value is too high, upgrade the processor or add another processor.
- **Server Work Queues: Queue Length** Specifies the number of requests waiting to use a specific processor. This value should be as low as possible, with values less than four being acceptable. If the value is too high, upgrade the processor or add another processor.

- **Processor: Interrupts/Sec** Specifies the number of hardware interrupts the processor is servicing each second. The value of this counter can vary greatly and is significant only in relation to an established baseline. A hardware device that is generating too many interrupts can monopolize the processor, preventing it from performing other tasks. If the value increases precipitously, examine the various other hardware components in the system to determine which one is generating too many interrupts.

Memory counters

An inadequate amount of memory in a server can prevent the computer from caching frequently-used data aggressively enough, causing processes to rely on disk reads more than memory reads and slowing down the entire system. Memory is the single most important subsystem to monitor because memory problems can affect all the other subsystems. For example, when a memory condition causes excessive disk paging, the system might appear to have a problem in the storage subsystem, although memory is the culprit.

One of the most common conditions that can cause memory-related problems is a memory leak. A memory leak is the result of a program allocating memory for use but not freeing up that memory when it is finished using it. Over time, the computer's free memory can be totally consumed, degrading performance and ultimately halting the system. Memory leaks can be fast, causing an almost immediate degradation in overall server performance, but they can also be slow and difficult to detect, gradually degrading system performance over a period of days or weeks. In most cases, memory leaks are caused by third-party applications, but operating system leaks are not unprecedented.

To monitor basic memory performance, use the following counters:

- **Memory: Page Faults/Sec** Specifies the number of times per second that the code or data needed for processing is not found in memory. This value should be as low as possible, with values below 5 being acceptable. This counter includes both soft faults (in which the required page is found elsewhere in memory) and hard faults (in which the requested page must be accessed from a disk). Soft faults are generally not a major problem, but hard faults can cause significant delays because disk accesses are much slower than memory accesses. If this value is too high, you should determine whether the system is experiencing an inordinate number of hard faults by examining the Memory: Pages/Sec counter. If the number of hard page faults is excessive, you should either determine what process is causing the excessive paging or install more random access memory (RAM) in the system.
- **Memory: Pages/Sec** Specifies the number of times per second that required information was not in RAM and had to be accessed from disk or had to be written to disk to make room in RAM. This value should be as low as possible, with values from 0 to 20 being acceptable. If the value is too high, you should either determine what process is causing the excessive paging or install more RAM in the system.

- **Memory: Available MBytes** Specifies the amount of available physical memory in megabytes. This value should be as high as possible and should not fall below 5 percent of the system's total physical memory, as this might be an indication of a memory leak. If the value is too low, consider installing additional RAM in the system.
- **Memory: Committed Bytes** Specifies the amount of virtual memory that has space reserved on the disk paging files. This value should be as low as possible and should always be less than the amount of physical RAM in the computer. If the value is too high, this could be an indication of a memory leak or the need for additional RAM in the system.
- **Memory: Pool Non-Paged Bytes** Specifies the size of an area in memory used by the operating system for objects that cannot be written to disk. This value should be a stable number that does not grow without a corresponding growth in server activity. If the value increases over time, this could be an indication of a memory leak.

Disk counters

A storage subsystem that is overburdened with read and write commands can slow down the rate at which the system processes client requests. The server's hard disk drives carry a greater physical burden than the other three subsystems because, in satisfying the I/O requests of many clients, the drive heads must continually move to different locations on the drive platters. The drive head mechanism can move only so fast, however, and once the drive reaches its maximum read/write speed, additional requests can begin to pile up in the queue, waiting to be processed. For this reason, the storage subsystem is a prime location for a bottleneck.

To monitor the storage subsystem in Performance Monitor, you can use the following counters:

- **PhysicalDisk: Disk Bytes/Sec** Specifies the average number of bytes transferred to or from the disk each second. This value should be equivalent to the levels established in the original baseline readings or higher. A decrease in this value could indicate a malfunctioning disk that could eventually fail. If this is the case, consider upgrading the storage subsystem.
- **PhysicalDisk: Avg. Disk Bytes/Transfer** Specifies the average number of bytes transferred during read and write operations. This value should be equivalent to the levels established in the original baseline readings or higher. A decrease in this value indicate a malfunctioning disk that could eventually fail. If this is the case, consider upgrading the storage subsystem.
- **PhysicalDisk: Current Disk Queue Length** Specifies the number of pending disk read or write requests. This value should be as low as possible, with values less than 2 being acceptable per disk spindle. High values for this counter can indicate that the drive is malfunctioning or that it is incapable of keeping up with the activities demanded of it. If this is the case, consider upgrading the storage subsystem.

- **PhysicalDisk: % Disk Time** Specifies the percentage of time that the disk drive is busy. This value should be as low as possible, with values less than 80 percent being acceptable. High values for this counter can indicate that the drive is malfunctioning, that it is incapable of keeping up with the activities demanded of it, or that a memory problem is causing excess disk paging. Check for memory leaks or related problems and, if none are found, consider upgrading the storage subsystem.
- **LogicalDisk: % Free Space** Specifies the percentage of free space on the disk. This value should be as high as possible, with values greater than 20 percent being acceptable. If the value is too low, consider adding more disk space.

Most storage subsystem problems, when not caused by malfunctioning hardware, are resolvable by upgrading the storage system. These upgrades can include any of the following measures:

- Install faster hard disk drives, such as solid state drives (SSDs).
- Install additional hard disk drives and split your data among them, reducing the I/O burden on each drive.
- Replace standalone drives with a RAID (Redundant Array of Independent Disks) array.
- Add more disk drives to an existing RAID array.

Network counters

Monitoring network performance is more complicated than monitoring the other three subsystems because many factors outside the computer can affect network performance. You can use the following counters to try to determine if a network problem exists, but if you suspect one, you should begin looking for causes external to the computer:

- **Network Interface: Bytes Total/Sec** Specifies the number of bytes sent and received per second by the selected network interface adapter. This value should be equivalent to the levels established in the original baseline readings or higher. A decrease in this value could indicate malfunctioning network hardware or other network problems.
- **Network Interface: Output Queue Length** Specifies the number of packets waiting to be transmitted by the network interface adapter. This value should be as low as possible, and preferably zero, although values of two or less are acceptable. If the value is too high, the network interface adapter could be malfunctioning or another network problem might exist.
- **Server: Bytes Total/Sec** Specifies the total number of bytes sent and received by the server over all its network interfaces. This value should be no more than 50 percent of the total bandwidth capacity of the network interfaces in the server. If the value is too high, consider migrating some applications to other servers or upgrading to a faster network.

The bandwidth of the network connections limits the amount of traffic reaching the server through its network interfaces. If these counter values indicate that the network itself is the bottleneck, there are two ways to upgrade the network, and neither one is a simple fix:

- **Increase The Speed Of The Network** This means replacing the network interface adapters in all the computers, as well as the switches, routers, and other devices on the network, and possibly replacing the cabling as well.
- **Install Additional Network Adapters In The Server And Redistribute The Network** If traffic frequently saturates the network interfaces already in the server, the only way to increase the network throughput without increasing the network's speed is to install more network interfaces. However, connecting more interfaces to the same network will not permit any more traffic to reach the server. Instead, you must create additional subnets on the network and redistribute the computers among them, so that there is less traffic on each subnet.

Configure alerts

Performance Monitor is a useful tool, but few administrators have the time to sit around watching line graphs track server performance counters. This is why you can also use the Create New Data Collector Set wizard to create *performance counter alerts*, which monitor the values of specific counters and perform a task, such as sending an email to an administrator, when the counters reach a specific value.

To create an alert, you use a procedure like that of creating a data collector set, as follows.

1. Open the Performance Monitor console and expand the Data Collector Sets folder.
2. Right-click the User Defined folder and, on the context menu, click New, Data Collector Set.
3. On the How Would You Like To Create This New Data Collector Set? page, type a name for the data collector set and select the Create Manually (Advanced) option.
4. On the What Type Of Data Do You Want To Include? page, select the Performance Counter Alert option.
5. On the Which Performance Counters Would You Like To Log? page, click Add and select the counter you want to monitor.
6. In the Alert When drop-down list and the Limit text box, specify the value at which Performance Monitor should trigger an alert. The values you use for these fields depend on the nature of counter you select. For example, when monitoring the % Processor Time counter, you might want to trigger an alert when the value goes above 95 percent. Counters that do not measure percentages might use values based on other factors, however.
7. On the Create The Data Collector Set? page, if the account you are currently using does not have the privileges needed to gather the log information, click Change to display a Performance Monitor dialog box in which you can supply alternative credentials.

8. Select one of the following options:
   - **Open Properties For This Data Collector Set** Saves the data collector set to the specified location and opens its Properties sheet for further modifications
   - **Start This Data Collector Set Now** Saves the data collector set to the specified location and starts collecting data immediately
   - **Save And Close** Saves the data collector set to the specified location and closes the wizard
9. Click Finish. The new data collector set appears in the User Defined folder.
10. Select the new data collector set under the User Defined folder.
11. Right-click the alert and select Properties.
12. In the Properties sheet for the alert, select the Alert Task tab, as shown in Figure 6-48.

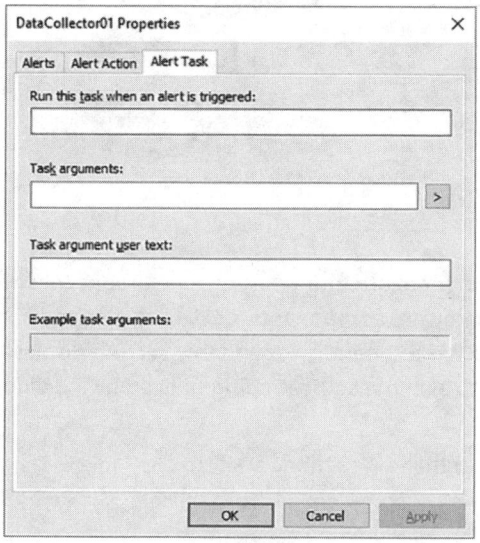

FIGURE 6-48 The Alert Task tab of a Properties sheet for a performance counter alert

13. In the fields provided, specify a Windows Management Instrumentation task or a script to run when the alert is triggered.
14. Click OK.

When you start the alert, it will monitor the selected counter and execute the task when it reaches the specified value. In the same Properties sheet, on the Alert tab, you can also configure the sample interval for the alert, so that it does not interfere with server performance or trigger unwanted alerts too often.

Monitor workloads using Resource Monitor

When you launch the Performance Monitor console, you can right-click the Monitoring Tools folder and, from the context menu, select Resource Monitor, to display the Resource Monitor window, as shown in Figure 6-49.

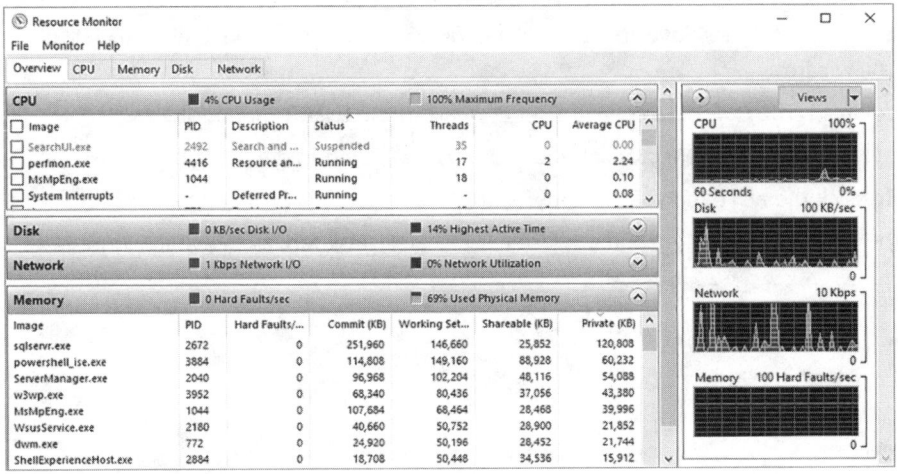

FIGURE 6-49 The Resource Monitor console

On the Resource Monitor's Overview tab, there are four real-time line graphs that display information about the server's four main hardware components: CPU, Disk, Network, and Memory. Each of the four components also has a separate, expandable section displaying more detailed information in text form, such as the resources being utilized by individual applications and processes.

The statistics displayed by the graphs and the text sections are listed in Table 6-1.

TABLE 6-1 Resource Monitor Line Graphs and Text Statistics

Component	Line graph statistics	Text statistics
CPU	■ Overall CPU Utilization (%)	■ **Image** The application using CPU resources ■ **PID** The Process ID of the application ■ **Status** Specifies whether the application is currently running or suspended ■ **Threads** The number of active threads generated by the application ■ **CPU** The number of CPU cycles currently being used by the application ■ **Average CPU** The percentage of the total CPU capacity being used by the application
Disk	■ Total Current Disk I/O Rate (In KB/Sec)	■ **Image** The application using disk resources ■ **PID** The Process ID of the application ■ **File** The file currently being read or written by the application ■ **Read** The speed of the current read operation (in bytes/sec) ■ **Write** The speed of the current write operation (in bytes/sec) ■ **Total** The speed of the current combined read/write operations (in bytes/sec) ■ **I/O Priority** The priority of the I/O task currently being performed by the application ■ **Response Time** The interval between the issuance of a command to the disk and its response (in milliseconds)
Network	■ Current Total Network Traffic (In Kb/Sec)	■ **Image** The application using network resources ■ **PID** The Process ID of the application ■ **Address** The network address or computer name of the system with which the computer is communicating ■ **Send** The speed of the current network send operation (in bytes/sec) ■ **Receive** The speed of the current network receive operation (in bytes/sec) ■ **Total** The combined bandwidth of the current network send and receive processes (in bytes/sec)
Memory	■ Current Hard Faults Per Second ■ Percentage Of Physical Memory Currently In Use (%)	■ **Image** The application using memory resources ■ **PID** The Process ID of the application ■ **Hard Faults/Sec** The number of hard faults currently being generated by the application ■ **Commit** The amount of memory (in KB) committed by the application ■ **Working Set** The amount of physical memory (in KB) currently being used by the application ■ **Shareable** The amount of memory (in KB) being used by the application that it can share with other applications ■ **Private** The amount of memory (in KB) being used by the application that it cannot share with other applications

Examining the resources utilized by specific applications and processes over time can help you to determine ways to improve the performance of a computer. For example, if all the system's physical memory is frequently being utilized, then the system is probably being slowed by large amounts of disk paging. Increasing the amount of physical memory or reducing the application load will probably improve the overall performance level of the computer.

Chapter summary

- Windows Server Update Services (WSUS) is a feature included in Windows Server 2016 that enables a local server on your network to function as the back end for the Windows Update client, just as the Microsoft Update servers do on the Internet.
- When you use multiple WSUS servers on your enterprise network, you create an architecture by specifying the upstream server from which each server should obtain its updates.
- In a replica WSUS server configuration, one central WSUS server downloads updates from the Microsoft Update site on the Internet, and the WSUS servers at other sites obtain the approved updates from that first server.
- Autonomous WSUS servers download all available updates from the central server, and administrators at each site are responsible for evaluating and approving updates for their own users.
- The process by which a WSUS downloads updates from an upstream server is called synchronization.
- To exercise control over which Windows Update clients on the network receive specific updates, WSUS uses a system of groups.
- Windows Defender is an antimalware solution that is automatically installed an enabled on all servers running Windows Server 2016.
- For Windows Defender to remain effective, it must have regular updates to its antispyware and antivirus definitions.
- In Windows Server Backup, single backup jobs provide more flexibility than scheduled ones, with the obvious disadvantage that someone must be there to create and start the job.
- When you create a scheduled backup job, the options are somewhat different from a single, interactive job.
- When you perform a scheduled backup of an Active Directory domain controller, or perform a single backup with the System State checkbox selected, Windows Server Backup includes the Active Directory database as part of the job.
- Windows Server Backup can back up Hyper-V hosts and the guest virtual machines as well.

- Performance Monitor is a tool that displays system performance statistics in real time. Performance Monitor can display hundreds of different statistics (called performance counters); you can create a customized graph containing any statistics you choose.
- A bottleneck is a component that is not providing an acceptable level of performance compared with the other components in the system.
- The Resource Monitor console contains four real-time line graphs that display information about four of the server's main hardware components.

Thought experiment

In this thought experiment, demonstrate your skills and knowledge of the topics covered in this chapter. You can find answer to this thought experiment in the next section.

Norton, an administrator at Adatum, Ltd., has been assigned the task of deploying new servers throughout the enterprise. The servers will be running Windows Server 2016, and Norton is in the process of creating a long-term plan to replace the servers at each of the company's five offices. He wants to install Windows Server Update Services on one of the servers at each office, so that clients can download updates from a local source, but is running into some administrative problems in the process.

The one Canadian office, in Winnipeg, operates under another name and has its own IT staff. However, their Internet connection is considerably more expensive than those of the US offices and is priced based on the bandwidth they use. The Minneapolis and Detroit offices have high-speed connections to the company headquarters in Chicago, but they do not maintain their own IT administrators. The newly-created branch office in St. Louis is tiny, with only two sales associates. They have a high-speed Internet connection, but use a VPN connection to connect to the headquarters network.

How should Norton configure the WSUS architecture for the home office and the four branches?

Thought experiment answer

This section contains the solution to the thought experiment.

The WSUS server at the headquarters in Chicago should be configured as the central server and should obtain its updates from the Microsoft Update servers on the Internet. The server at the Winnipeg office should download updates from the Chicago server, but the administrators there should evaluate and approve updates for themselves. The WSUS servers in the Minneapolis and Detroit offices should be replicas of the Chicago server. The server in the St. Louis office should have the Chicago server as its upstream server, but the Do Not Store Update Files Locally; Computers Install From Microsoft Update option on the Update Files and Languages dialog box should be selected, so that the server downloads the approval list from Chicago and the actual updates from the Microsoft Update servers on the Internet.

Index

A

access control entries (ACEs) 112, 115
access control lists (ACLs) 112
ACEs. *See* Access Control Entries (ACEs); *See* access control entries (ACEs)
ACLL. *See* Attempt Copy Last Logs
ACLs. *See* access control lists (ACLs)
activation models 35–42
  Active-Directory based 39–41
  Automatic Virtual Machine Activation 41–42
  Key Management Service 36–39
  multiple activation keys 35–36
activation threshold 37
activation validity interval 37
Active Directory
  backing up 421–422
Active Directory-based activation 39–41
Active Directory-detached clusters 337
Active Directory Domain Services (AD DS) 337
Add-ClusterSharedVolume cmdlet 153
Add-ClusterVirtualMachineRole cmdlet 304
Add-ClusterVMMonitoredItem cmdlet 362
Add-Computer cmdlet 20
Add-ContainerImageTag cmdlet 272
Add Roles And Features Wizard 11–15
Add-VMNetworkAdapter cmdlet 237
administrative access points 337
Administrators groups 269
advanced permissions 114–115, 120–121
allocation unit size 82–84
antimalware solution 405–410
asynchronous replication 148
Attach-Container cmdlet 280
authentication protocols
  for Live Migration 308–309
authorization 113
Automatic Virtual Machine Activation (AVMA) 41–42
AVMA. *See* Automatic Virtual Machine Activation
AVMAkey variable 42
Azure
  managing container images using 293
Azure Access Panel. *See* Access Panel

B

backups
  Active Directory 421–422
  before upgrading 30
  data deduplication and 162
  failover clusters and 324–326
  group policy objects 423
  Hyper-V 424–425
  IIS 424–425
  incremental 417–418
  mirrored 416
  restores from 418–421
  scheduled 415–417
  single job creation 412–415
  strategies for 421–425
  Windows Server Backup 411–421
balloon driver 188
bandwidth management 254–256
Basic Input/Output System (BIOS) 86
basic permissions 114, 117–120
BIOS settings 7
blob files 45, 46–47
Block-SmbShareAccess cmdlet 109
boot
  Secure Boot 205–208
  traditional 205
bottlenecks 433–434

C

cabinet (CAB) files 48, 74
checkpoints
  applying 229–230
  creating 228–229
  managing 228–230
  production 230–231
  standard 230
child partitions 167
Chkdsk.exe 94
chunks 159
chunk store 158
churn 158, 161
Close-SmbOpenFile cmdlet 108
Close-SmbSession cmdlet 107
cloud-based services 43
cloud deployment 4
cloud witnesses 345–348
Cluster-Aware Updating (CAU) 328–332
Clustered Storage Spaces 342–345
cluster name object (CNO) 313, 337
Cluster Operating System Rolling Upgrade 332–333
cluster shared volume (CSV) 153
cluster shared volumes (CSVs) 333–336, 341
cluster-to-cluster configurations 149, 151–155
CNA. *See* converged network adapter (CNA)
collector technologies 65
Compare-VM cmdlet 212
connectors. *See also* receive connectors; *See also* send connectors
containers. *See* Linux containers; *See* Windows containers
converged network adapter (CNA) 143
converged networks 143
convergence 376
ConvertTo-ContainerImage cmdlet 280
Convert-VHD cmdlet 228
Copy-Item cmdlet 180
CPU counters 434–435
CPU cycles 288–289
Create New Data Collector Set wizard 438–439
Credential Security Support Provider (CredSSP) 308–309
CSV. *See* cluster shared volume (CSV)

D

DAC. *See* Datacenter Activation Coordination
daemon.json 269–270
DAGs. *See* Database Availability Groups
DAS. *See* Direct-Attached Storage
databases. *See* mailbox databases
datacenter bridging (DCB) 142–145
Datacenter edition 4, 5, 41
data collector sets 431–433
data deduplication 155–162
  backup and restore solution with 162
  configuration of 155–158
  monitoring 160–161
  optimization rates 159
  usage scenarios for 158–160
  workload evaluation 159–160
Data Deduplication Savings Evaluation Tool 160
Data Protection Manager (DPM) 162
data replication 148–155
data storage. *See also* storage architectures; *See also* storage requirements
data volumes 286–287
DCB. *See* datacenter bridging (DCB)
DCBX Willing bit 143
DDA. *See* Discrete Device Assignment (DDA)
Ddpeval.exe 160
deduplication. *See* data deduplication
Deployment Image Servicing and Management (DISM.exe) 172
  adding drivers to image files using 72–74
  /disable-feature command 76
  /enable-feature command 76–77
  installing roles and features in offline images with 75–77
  umounting image with 74
  updating images with 70–72
  Windows PowerShell equivalents for 77–79
Desired State Configuration (DSC) 26–28
  creating configuration scripts 26
  deploying configurations 27–28
Desktop Experience 2
devices
  detecting 147
Device Specific Module (DSM) 145
  policies 148
DFS. *See* Distributed File Share

differencing disks 222–223
/disable-feature command 76
Discrete Device Assignment (DDA) 212–213
discretionary access control lists (DACLs) 93
disk counters 436–437
disk fragmentation 83
Disk Management console 84, 139–140
  creating VHD or VHDX files using 88–90
  mounting VHD and VHDX files with 91–92
disk partitions 9–10
disks
  adding to CSVs 336
  differencing 222–223
  GUID partition table 84–88
  initializing new 84–85
  MBR 84–85
  partition style selection 87
  pass-through 212, 225–226
  physical 125, 225–226
  storage layout options 125–131
  virtual. *See* virtual disks
disk sectors
  size configuration 82–84
disk volume
  allocation unit size 82–84
DISM.exe. *See* Deployment Image Servicing and Management
Dismount-VHD cmdlet 92
Distributed Component Object Model (DCOM) 25
Distributed File System (DFS) Replication 150
Djoin.exe tool 46
DNS round robin 376
DNS server addresses 270
Docker
  Attach command 279
  Build command 290
  Commit command 279
  Images command 273
  installation
    on Nano Server 267–268
    on Windows Server 266
  managing containers with 277–279
  Network Create command 285
  PowerShell and 270–271
  Pull command 271
  Push command 292
  RM command 279
  Run command 274–276, 285, 287, 288
  Start command 278
  start-up options 269–270
  Stop command 278
Dockerd.exe 266, 269
Docker.exe 266
dockerfile 289–290
DockerHub 271, 291–293
Domain Name System (DNS) 39
domains
  joining, with Nano Server 45–47
drive arrays 134
drivers
  adding to image files 72–74
DSC. *See* Desired State Configuration (DSC)
Dynamic Host Configuration Protocol (DHCP) 51
Dynamic Host Configuration Protocol (DHCP) server 11
dynamic least queue depth 148
dynamic memory
  allocations 188
  configuration 186–188
  limitations 187
  settings 186–188
dynamic quorum management 318

E

Edit-NanoServerImage cmdlet 49, 51, 77
EFS. *See* Encrypting File System
emulated adapters 248–249
Enable-DedupVolume cmdlet 157–158
/enable-feature command 76–77
Encrypting File System (EFS) 94
enhanced session mode 199–201
Enter-ContainerSession cmdlet 280
Enter-PsSession cmdlet 22, 56
ESRA. *See* EdgeSync replication account (ESRA)
Essentials edition 5, 6
Ethernet 142–143
Exit-PsSession cmdlet 22, 57
Exit-PSSession cmdlet 177
explicit remoting 176
Export-SmigServerSetting cmdlet 33
Export-VM cmdlet 210
Extended Page Tables (EPT) 263
Extensible Firmware Interface (EFI)-based boot partition 87
external network switches 239, 241

F

failback policy 148
failbacks 364
failover affinity 367
failover clusters 153, 220–221, 304, 311–351
  cloud witnesses 345–348
  Cluster-Aware Updating 328–332
  cluster configuration 324–326
  Clustered Storage Spaces 342–345
  cluster networking 321–324
  Cluster Operating System Rolling Upgrade 332–333
  cluster shared volumes 333–336, 341
  configurating without network names 337
  guest clustering 341–342, 349–351
  managing 359–368
  monitoring VMs in 361–363
  node fairness 367–368
  quorum 317–321
  role-specific settings 359–361
  Scale-out File Server 337–341
  shared VHDX files 349–351
  site-aware 365–367
  storage configuration 326–328
  stretch 365–367
  VM resiliency and 348–349
  workgroup, single, and multi-domain 314–317
failover policy 148
failovers 150
failover settings 364–365
fault tolerance 128–131
features
  implemention on Nano Server 48–50
  installation of 13–15
    in offline images 75–77
  offline installation 225
Fiber Channel over Ethernet (FCoE) 142
Fibre Channel 133, 326
  adapter 231–233
file compression 94
file ownership 122
file permissions 112–122
File Server cluster role 360
File Server Resource Manager (FSRM) 103
File Server role service 96
File Sharing dialog box 95
file systems
  NTFS 93–95
  ReFS 93–95
folder ownership 122
folder permissions 112–122
folder shares. *See* shares
Format-List cmdlet 161
FreeBSD
  virtual machines 201–203
FreeBSD deployments 61
FreeBSD Integration Services (BIS) 61
FreeBSD Integration Services (FIS) 204, 205
FSW. *See* File Share Witness

G

garbage collection 158
Generation 1 VMs 197, 214
Generation 2 VMs 197–199, 205, 215
generic volume licensing keys (GVLKs) 39
Get-Command cmdlet 21
Get-ComputerInfo cmdlet 274
Get-Container cmdlet 280
Get-DedupStatus cmdlet 161
Get-help cmdlet 21
Get-NetAdapter cmdlet 19
Get-NetAdapterVmqQueue cmdlet 252–253
Get-SmbClientConfiguration cmdlet 111–112
Get-SmbOpenFile cmdlet 108
Get-SmbServerConfiguration cmdlet 109–110
Get-SmbSession cmdlet 107
Get-SmbShareAccess cmdlet 108
Get-SmigServerFeature cmdlet 33
Get-SRGroup cmdlet 154
Get-VM cmdlet 177
Get-VMHostSupportedVersion cmdlet 209
Get-VM PowerShell cmdlet 208
Get-WindowsFeature cmdlet 15
globally-unique identifier (GUID) 86
GPT. *See* GUID partition table (GPT) disks
Grant-SmbShareAccess cmdlet 109
Grant-SRAccess cmdlet 153
Group policy objects (GPOs) 401–403, 409
  backing up 423
GRUB boot loader 202
GUID partition table (GPT) disks
  advantages of 86
  booting from 87–88
  compared with MBR 87
  configuration of 84–88

H

hard disk drives (HDDs) 131
hard disks. *See* disks
hardware address 244–246
hardware requirements 3–4
high availability 297–386
  failover clustering 311–351, 359–368
  in Hyper-V 297–310
  Live Migration 303–309, 369–370
  network load balancing 375–384
  Storage Migration 309–311
  Storage Spaces Direct (S2D) 352–358
  VM movement in clustered nodes 369–375
host bus adapter (HBA) 134
hotfixes 74–75
hot spares 130–131
hygiene. *See* message hygiene
hyperthreading 4
Hyper-V 165–258
  backing up 424–425
  checkpoints 228–231
  containers 261–264, 275–277
  converting from previous versions 208–209
  Discrete Device Assignment 212–213
  enhanced session mode 199–201
  export and import functions 209–212
  Fibre Channel adapter 231–233
  guest operating systems 203–208
  guests 165, 166
  hardware limitations 167–169
  high availability in 297–310
  hosts 165, 174–179
  installation 165–173
    hardware and compatibility requirements 166–170
    management tools 172–173
    using PowerShell 171
    using Server Manager 170–171
  Integration Services 195–196, 204
  Nano Server and 43
  nested virtualization 181
  networking 235–256
    bandwidth management 254–256
    MAC address configuration 244–246
    network isolation 246–247
    NIC teaming 249–251
    performance optimization 243–244
    Switch Embedded Teaming 253–254
    synthetic network adapters 247–249
    virtual machine queue 251–253
    virtual network interface cards 236–237
    virtual switches 238–242, 244, 247
  New Virtual Hard Disk Wizard 88
  permissions 174
  PowerShell Direct 180
  remote management 174–179
  resource metering 193–195
  smart paging 192–193
  storage 213–235
    differencing disks 222–223
    quality of service 233–235
    shared VHDX files 220–222
    VHDs 214–220, 223–225
    VHDX files 214–220
  supported guest VMs 61
  upgrading from existing versions of 173
  virtual machine configuration 182–213
hypervisor 166–167
Hyper-V Manager 172–173
  conflict handling 212
  container host installation in 262–263
  creating VHDs and VHDX files using 214–220
  creating virtual hard disks in 216–218
  importing VMs using 210–211
  remote management using 174–176
  virtual machine creation in 183–184
Hyper-V Replica 298–303
Hyper-V Server 168
Hyper-V Server edition 5

I

image files
  adding drivers to 72–74
  adding updates to 74–75
  committing 74
  container 261, 291–293
  for deployment 58–79
  installing roles and features in offline 75–77
  managing, using Windows PowerShell 76–78
  mounting 71–72
  removing 273–274
  umounting 74
  updating 70–75
implicit remoting 177, 178–179
Import-SmigServerSetting cmdlet 33
Import-VM cmdlet 211–212
inheritance
  permission 115–116

initiators
iSCSI 133–140
in-place upgrades 28–32
installation
MAP Toolkit 63
Nano Server 44–48
Server Core 17–19
upgrades 28–32
Windows Server 2016 1–18
activation models 35
clean installation 6–9
features and roles 11–17
mass deployment 11
partitions 9–10
requirements 2–4
Windows Server Migration Tools 33–34
Install-WindowsFeature cmdlet 15, 171, 377
Install-WindowsFeature PowerShell cmdlet 225
Institute of Electrical and Electronics Engineers (IEEE) 143
Integration Services 195–196, 204
integrity scrubbing 158–159
internal network switches 241
Internet Information Services (IIS)
backing up 424–425
Internet SCSI (iSCSI) 327
Internet Small Computer System Interface (iSCSI) 133–140
creating targets 134–138
initiators and targets 133–134
using initiators 138–140
Internet Storage Name Service (iSNS) 140–142
Inventory And Assessment Wizard 65–67
Invoke-Command cmdlet 180
IP addresses
configuration
Nano Server 51–53
iSNS Protocol (iSNSP) 141

J

just-a-bunch-of-disks (JBOD) arrays 123

K

Kerberos 308–309
Key Management Service (KMS) 36–39
client configuration 39
host installation 37–39
limitations 36–37
KMS. *See* Key Management Service

L

legacy network adapters 248–249
Lightweight Directory Access Protocol (LDAP) 66
Linux
Secure Boot and 206–208
virtual machines 201–203
Linux containers
managing
using Docker daemon 277–279
using PowerShell 279–281
Linux deployments 61
Linux Integration Services (LIS) 61, 204–205
Live Migration
CredSSP or Kerberos authentication protocol for 308–309
implementing 303–308
in cluster 304
of VM 369–370
Shared Nothing 307–308
without a cluster 305–307
local area network (LAN) 142
Local Configuration Manager (LCM) 26
local Hyper-V Administrators 174
local memory 189
log files. *See* transaction log files
logical unit number (LUN) 134
Lync Online. *See* Skype for Business

M

MAK Volume Licensing agreements 35–36
Management Object Format (MOF) files 27
MapSetup.exe 63–64
MAP Toolkit. *See* Microsoft Assessment and Planning (MAP) Toolkit
master boot record (MBR) 84–85, 87
maximum hardware configurations 4
MBR. *See* master boot record (MBR)
Measure-VM cmdlet 194, 234–235
Media Access Control (MAC) address
configuration of 244–246
memory
adding or removing, in VM 185–186
containers 288

dynamic 186–188
local 189
Non-Uniform Memory Access 189–192
remote 189
virtual 259
memory counters 435–436
Merge-VHD cmdlet 228
message transport. *See* transport
Microsoft Assessment and Planning (MAP) Toolkit 61–69
collection of inventory information 64–68
discovery methods 66
evaluation of results 68–69
functions of 62
installation 63–64
Microsoft Azure. *See* Azure
Microsoft Azure Active Directory. *See* Azure Active Directory (Azure AD)
Microsoft Management Console (MMC) snap-ins
using remotely 25–26
migrations. *See also* Live Migration
migration guides 34–35
P2V 60
Quick Migration 370–371
roles 32–33
servers 32–35
Storage Migration 309–311, 371–372
virtual machines 369–372
mirror storage layout 128
MOF files. *See* Management Object Format (MOF) files
Mount-DiskImage cmdlet 92
mounting
virtual hard disks 91–93, 224–225
mounting images
images 71–72
Mount-VHD cmdlet 92
MSU files 74
multi-domain clusters 314–317
Multipath I/O (MPIO) 145–148
multiple activation keys (MAKs) 35–36
Multipoint edition 5

N

namespace isolation 260
Nano Server 2, 4, 42–57
as container host 264–265
authentication screen 50
configuration 50–55
firewall rules 54–55
IP address 51–53
Docker installation on 267–268
features of 42, 43
image creation 44–45
installation 44–48
joining a domain 45–47
managing, using Windows PowerShell 76–78
remote management 265
remote management of 55–57
roles and features implementation on 48–50
shortcomings of 44
usage scenarios and requirements for 43–44
virtual machine creation 47–48
Nano Server Recovery Console 50–54
NAS. *See* network attached storage (NAS)
NAT. *See* network address translation (NAT)
nested virtualization 181
Netdom.exe tool 21
network adapters 246–247
enabling RMDA on 253–254
legacy 248–249
NIC teaming 249–251
synthetic 247–249
virtual 251, 283
network address translation (NAT) 269, 284
network attached storage (NAS) 123
network counters 437–438
Network File System (NFS) shares 96
creation of 101–103
network hardware 322
network health protection 373–374
networking
cluster 321–324
container 281–285
Hyper-V 235–256
bandwidth management 254–256
MAC address configuration 244–246
network isolation 246–247
NIC teaming 249–251
performance optimization 243–244
Switch Embedded Teaming 253–254
synthetic network adapters 247–249
virtual machine queue 251–253
virtual network interface cards 236–237
virtual switches 238–242, 244, 247
S2D 353–354
transparent networks 285
network load balancing (NLB) 375–384
affinity configuration 381–382

cluster operation mode configuration 384
cluster upgrades 384
node installation 377–381
port rules 382–383
prerequisites 375–377
New-Cluster cmdlet 337
New-Container cmdlet 275, 280
New-NanoServerImage cmdlet 44–49, 51, 52, 264
New-NetIpAddress cmdlet 19, 20
New-NetQosPolicy cmdlet 144
New-NetQosTrafficClass cmdlet 144
New-PsSession cmdlet 21–22, 55
New-PSSession cmdlet 177, 180
New-SmbShare cmdlet 106–107, 340
New-SRPartnership cmdlet 151
New-VHD cmdlet 90, 219, 223
New Virtual Hard Disk Wizard 88
New-VM cmdlet 47, 184
New-VM PowerShell cmdlet 197
NICs. *See* network interface cards (NICs)
NIC teaming 249–251
NLB. *See* network load balancing (NLB)
node fairness 367–368
nodes 311, 375
Non-Uniform Memory Access (NUMA) 189–192
nodes 189
node spanning 189–190
ratio 189
topology 190–192
N_Port ID Virtualization (NPIV) 232
NTFS file system 93–95
NTFS permissions 112–114, 117–122

O

Office Telemetry. *See* telemetry
operating system environments (OSEs) 5
Optimize-VHD cmdlet 228
organizationally unique identifier (OUI) 244

P

P2V migration 60
packages
Nano Server 48–49
parent partitions 167
parity storage layout 129
partitions 9–10, 167
pass-through disks 212, 225–226
patches 74–75
performance counter alerts 438–439
Performance Metrics Wizard 68
Performance Monitor
bottlenecks and 433–434
CPU counters 434–435
data collector sets 431–433
disk counters 436–437
memory counters 435–436
monitoring workloads using 425–430
network counters 437–438
permissions
advanced 114–115, 120–121
allowing 115, 116
assigning 117–121
basic 114, 117–120
configuration 112–122
denying 115, 116
Hyper-V 174
inheritance 115–116
NTFS 112–114, 117–122
resource ownership and 122
share 96, 104–106, 108–109, 112–113
understanding effective access 116–117
physical disks 225–226
adding 125
physical servers
migration to virtual 60
platform-as-a-service. *See* PaaS
Plug and Play (PnP) 147
port mapping 284
power-on self-test (POST) 205
PowerShell. *See* Windows PowerShell
PowerShell Core 57
Preboot Execution Environment (PXE) 198, 249
Preboot Execution Environment (PXE) feature 11
Priority-based Flow Control (PFC) 145
private networks 244
private network switches 241
production checkpoints 230–231
Pull Server 27–28

Q

quality of service (QoS) policies 144, 233–235
Quick Migration 370–371

quorum 317–321
  dynamic quorum management 318
  modifying configuration of 318–320
  voting 321
  witnesses 317–318, 320–321
quotas 94

R

Receive-SmigServerData cmdlet 33
redundancy 128, 145
ReFS (Resilient File System) 93–95
Remote Direct Memory Access (RDMA) 253–254
remote management
  configuration of 55
  Hyper-V 174–179
  Nano Server 265
  of Nano Server 55–57
  using MMC snap-ins 25–26
  using PowerShell 21–22
  using Server Manager 22–24
remote memory 189
Remote Server Administration Tools 174
Remove-Container cmdlet 281
Remove-ContainerImage cmdlet 273
Remove-SmbShare cmdlet 108
reparse point 158
replica servers 299–301
replication
  asynchronous 148
  DFS 150
  Hyper-V Replica 298–303
  Storage Replica 148–155
  synchronous 148
Reset-VMResourceMetering cmdlet 195
Resize-VHD cmdlet 228
resource governance 260–261
resource metering 193–195
Resource Monitor 440–442
resource ownership 122
restores
  data deduplication and 162
  from backups 418–421
Revoke-SmbShareAccess cmdlet 109
roles
  implemention on Nano Server 48–50
  installation 11–17
    in offline images 75–77
  migration of 32–33
  offline installation 225
round robin policy 148

S

SAN. *See* storage area network (SAN)
saved-state (.vsv) files 182
Scale-out File Server (SoFS) 337–341
SCCM. *See* System Center Configuration Manager
SCSI (Small Computer Systems Interface) controllers 214–215
sector sizes 82–84
Secure Boot 205–208
security identifiers (SIDs) 113
security principal 112
self-service deployment. *See* user-driven client deployments
Send-SmigServerData cmdlet 33
Serial Attached SCSI (SAS) 327
Server Core 2, 4, 42
  configuration 19–20
  Hyper-V Server and 168
  installation 17–19
  management of 21–25
    using Windows PowerShell 76–78
  Windows containers and 264
server folders
  sharing 95–109
Server for NFS role service 97
server installations
  maintaining 387–425
    backup strategies 421–425
    patch management 401–405
    Windows Defender 405–410
    Windows Server Backup 411–421
    Windows Server Update Services 388–405
  monitoring 425–442
    performance counter alerts 438–439
    using Performance Monitor 425–430, 431–438
    using Resource Monitor 440–442
Server Manager
  deduplication configuration using 155–157
  Hyper-V installation using 170–171
  installing roles using 11–15
  managing Server Core using 22–24
  share configuration using 95–106

If you're interested in reaching your potential as a writer, you need to pay attention to your own writing process. However you like to work, it's your writing, reading, rewriting, rereading, rewriting process that will take your rough path through new territory and transform it into a wonderful journey for other readers as well.

ASSUMPTIONS

This text is based on the following assumptions:

1. Writing is a repeated writing/reading process.
2. Students learn best from discovery and experimentation.
3. Students must be able to transfer their writing skills to other areas of their professional and private lives.
4. Students profit from studying models of both professional and student writing.
5. Students profit from individual and collaborative learning.

HOW THIS BOOK WORKS

This book begins with a general introduction to the writing process. The eight chapters that follow are each divided into three carefully integrated sections:

The Writing Process

Focus on Essays

Focus on Paragraphs

The Afterword, "You and Your Writing Process," summarizes the main points of the text.

Chapters Two to Nine focus on one of the eight primary purposes for writing: recalling (2), observing (3), explaining (4), investigating (5), researching (6), analyzing (7), persuading (8), and problem solving (9). The purpose is explained and then featured in a professional essay as well as a student essay before the readers are asked to compose an essay of their own.

Learning from Published Writers focuses on a provocative professional essay to introduce students to a specific purpose for writing. Each essay was chosen for its interest and readability and serves as a springboard in form and content for the rest of the chapter.

Learning from Your Peers walks students through the writing process using an actual student essay. Students witness the development of a peer essay that moves through the general reading/writing tasks of generating ideas, planning, developing, organizing, drafting, revising, editing. The revised draft is printed in each chapter with the student changes highlighted.

Writing Your Own Essay asks students to compose their own essays focusing on the purpose they have just studied. Following a brief review of the highlights of the chapter and the composing process, students are given at least four writing topics to choose from. After they draft, revise, and edit their essays, students are then asked some specific questions that require them to pause and reflect on their writing process before they start another chapter.

Focus on Paragraphs and Focus on Essays. The second and third sections of each chapter, Focus on Paragraphs and Focus on Essays, can be taught by themselves or in conjunction with the first section. The Focus on Paragraphs sections briefly review grammar and usage and develop understanding and ability with paragraphs. The Focus on Essays sections focus on the larger issues of essay organization and development; they progress from fairly simple to more complex revision strategies. Each of the Focus sections includes instruction and exercises that are drawn from the professional and student essays featured in the chapter. They begin with a checklist summarizing the tasks to be covered and end with collaborative work for individual, small group, or entire class projects.

UNIQUE FEATURES

Several unique and exciting features separate this book from other basic writing texts:

1. It moves students systematically through the personal and academic writing process.
2. It gives student writing more attention than professional writing.
3. It sees learning to write as a repeated reading/writing process.
4. It illustrates all aspects of the writing process.
5. It teaches revising and editing through the student essays in each chapter.
6. It focuses on individual aspects of both the sentence and the paragraph.
7. It features culturally diverse reading selections that are of interest to students.
8. It provides an appendix for sentence-level concerns of the editing process.

ACKNOWLEDGMENTS

We would like to acknowledge the support of the people at Pearson Education, Mount Royal College, our students, and especially our families.

CHAPTER **ONE**

The Writing Process

Without writing, I'm lost. Writing is the process of building a map, a map with an arrow that points to a specific place and says "you are here."

—**MAY MCLAREN**

GETTING STARTED

Good essays begin with good ideas. But, a good idea is sometimes the biggest problem in writing an essay. How do you come up with good ideas? Perhaps an instructor has assigned an essay topic. How do you find good ideas for an assigned topic? There are a number of techniques writers use to generate ideas for essays. Many writers use one or more activities to generate ideas, settle on a specific topic, and clarify the topic in their own minds. These activities are meant to help you think through your topic so they're an excellent help to you whenever you feel stuck for things to say.

Generating Ideas

One of the most difficult things for some writers is coming up with something to write. The problem of coming up with ideas is very old, and techniques for inventing topics have been around for a few thousand years. These techniques will help you originate and explore your ideas. Return to this list at any time during the writing process if you feel stuck, or you need more to write about.

Journal: Many times, ideas don't happen when you're ready to begin an essay. Ideas often come during the day, while you're doing other things. That's why many writers keep a notebook with them at all times, and others spend some time each day writing down their ideas, conversations, dreams, or things they've seen. Use paper or feed your ideas to your computer. Use whatever is comfortable and easy. Use your journal to record your ideas for your essays while you're in this class.

Reading: One great way to generate ideas is to read. A good essay will take you down paths you haven't taken before. When you read, take notes in your journal, or write notes in the margin of your book. It's also a good idea to reread some things over and over again. Often writers have favourite pieces that they like to read just to get them in the right frame of mind for writing.

List: Another technique to get your ideas on paper or on screen is a simple list. Write down every idea you can possibly think of, even if it doesn't seem all that great at the time. Seeing your ideas on paper often generates more thought, which leads to more ideas.

Freewrite: To freewrite, you can either begin with a topic or with nothing at all. Put your pen at the top of a blank page or open a new document on your computer. If you're writing on a computer, try shutting the monitor off. Then, glance at the closest clock, and make note of the time. Begin writing, and don't allow yourself to stop until you've written for five, seven, or ten minutes straight. If it's your first freewrite, try writing for five minutes. Don't worry about grammar and punctuation. Each time you freewrite, increase the length of time. Soon you will be able to comfortably write for greater lengths.

Brainstorming: You can brainstorm alone, with a friend, or, best of all, with a group. Brainstorming just means writing down all your ideas, in any way: pictures, words, diagrams. It doesn't matter how you do it, just write down *all* your ideas.

Clustering: Map your ideas as they come into your mind. To cluster, take a sheet of blank paper and write a key word, phrase, sentence, or draw a picture in the centre of the page, and draw a circle around it. Next, write down and circle any more ideas you have, and connect them with lines to the thoughts they came from.

Questioning: Journalists and many other writers ask questions to generate ideas on a topic. Question techniques can help you avoid omitting important details. Most often, the questions used to generate ideas and details on a topic are the five w's and one h: *Who, What, Why, When, Where,* and *How.*

Planning

Once you have an idea or several paragraphs of writing, you'll need to make some decisions to limit your topic and provide a focus for your essay. Jot down short answers to each of the following questions.

Who is your **audience**?

Who's going to read your essay? The person or people who will read it are your audience. The more you know about these people, the more likely you will successfully get your ideas across. Imagine yourself talking to this audience. How would you speak? What words would you choose? Would you be serious or funny, casual or formal? If you know who you're writing to, you'll make good decisions about how to write your essay.

What is your **purpose**?

Imagine your audience. What do you want your essay to do? How do you want your audience to feel, think, or act? How likely is it that your audience will respond the way you hope they will?

What **size** will your essay be?

Knowing the size of your essay ahead of time will help you to determine the scope of your topic and the amount of material it is necessary to generate. Your idea has to fit the essay's length. If your topic is how trains contributed to the Industrial Revolution, it's too big for a 750-word essay. It would make a great book, though. For a 750-word essay, you might be able to talk about how trains helped develop Montreal.

What **content** (person, event, object, etc.) do you want to focus on?

Each of your essays should *focus* on a few specific ideas. If you're good at coming up with ideas, this probably means you need to choose the best and most closely related ideas. Although this focus will become clearer to you as you write, make some general, preliminary decisions about your content before you begin to draft an essay.

What **perspective** will you take toward your topic? Perspective is *how you feel about your particular topic.* It is the stance that you take. For example, are you for or against jail sentences for young offenders? Or, how do you feel about a certain issue affecting your community? Or you personally? Once you choose a stance toward your topic, keep it for the entire essay.

Developing

Now that you know your audience, purpose, essay size, general content, and perspective, you are ready to expand some specific topics that will make up the bulk of your essay. If you have already developed paragraphs or a fair amount of text, from, say, a freewrite, you can begin to shape the material with your planning in mind. If you're expanding some seed ideas, add three or four more related details. If necessary, return to the questions of the generating and planning phases. Use these to help you flesh out your ideas and rethink your more focused topic.

Organizing

Once you have something down on paper, a few ideas or a few paragraphs, you need to consider the best way to present your ideas. Decide how you want to begin your essay. Think about each idea and where it should go in your essay. It's like putting together a puzzle—piece your writing together to make it the best it can be.

Organize your material in a way that will be most interesting to your audience. What's the most striking detail or fact about your topic? You might want to start with that. What meaning or significance does the topic have for you? You might want to end with that. Remember that those aspects of your topic that interest you are what you are most likely to write about effectively.

Outlining

An outline is a map. It tracks the order of your ideas in your essay. Outlines let you see the ideas you already have and how they connect. Many writers use an outline to set up the essays they write. Some writers don't use any outline at all. Sometimes an outline can tell you where you need further development or support. If you want to use an outline, you may want to update and revise your outline as you go.

Sometimes writers don't outline until after they've drafted the essay once or twice. Once they've got something down on paper, they want to see the order of their ideas. By examining your main point in each paragraph and setting it up as an outline, you can determine whether your organizational pattern works as you had intended. This type of outlining is called **organizational analysis**.

Drafting

Drafting, as you may have guessed, means writing out a first draft. At this point, you have been working both by yourself and in class, generating, planning, developing, and organizing your ideas on your essay topic. You may want to spread out your journal, clusters, lists, etc., to help you as you write.

Before you begin drafting, you might try writing your main idea at the top of the page or write it on a small piece of paper and tape it to the top of your computer screen. A **working title** is usually the topic of your essay combined with your purpose for writing combined into a single phrase. This working title can remind you of why you are writing and help you stay focused.

Now you're ready to begin writing what the business writer Peter F. Drucker likes to call the **zero draft**. In the first draft, you won't worry about spelling and punctuation: you'll fix that up later. For this zero draft, as you write, try to keep a steady flow of words going. Put as much as you can on paper.

Revising

Writing is a conversation between the writer and his or her words. Once you have something on paper, begin to look for what you don't like in your words and fix it. If you don't like the way something is worded, or you want to move your ideas around, this is called revising.

Revising means "seeing again" and that is exactly what you try to do. You try to look at your essay again with fresh eyes. One of the most effective ways to revise your essay is to put your draft aside for at least a day before you begin working on it again. You'll spot problems and see things you hadn't seen before.

The Focus on Paragraphs and Focus on Essays sections in each chapter of this book will help you revise your writing.

Editing

Editing means taking care of grammar, spelling, and punctuation—making sure it's all in the right place. Although writers keep an eye out for grammar, spelling, and punctuation errors while they draft, writers also check their writing with a final edit before they send it to its audience. Though most readers will be able to understand you even with errors, errors send a definite message: the writer doesn't know what he or she is doing. Writers want to be credible, so they avoid errors to save themselves embarrassment.

The Focus on Sentences section in the appendix of this book will help you edit your work and look for specific problems. Get someone to read your essay out loud to you. You'll hear awkward phrases and grammatical problems as you reader reads to you. Once you've caught most of the little errors, try a technique used by many professional editors: read your draft, sentence by sentence, from back to front. Reading in reverse will help you spot errors you hadn't seen as you read front to back.

HOW TO USE THIS BOOK

Each of the following chapters provides a look at one of eight main purposes for essay writing: recalling (2), observing (3), explaining (4), investigating (5), researching (6), analyzing (7), persuading (8), and problem solving (9). Each takes you through a professional essay and the writing process of a student before offering strategies for writing your own essay. At the end of each chapter are instructions and exercises to help you revise your essay and paragraphs and edit your sentences. The text ends with a summary chapter asking you to reflect on your own writing process.

CHAPTER **TWO**

Recalling

Reading and Writing to Remember

The world at large is the raw material of the writer. That world reaches the writer through the conduit of his sense, modified by perception and experience.

—"FACT INTO FICTION" TIM WYNNE-JONES

LEARNING OUTCOMES

This chapter will help you:

- Understand and write an essay about a past event;
- Recognize and shape an essay with its introduction, body paragraphs, and conclusion;
- Recognize and shape body paragraphs.

Recalling is the act of writing about something we remember: something we did, something that happened to us, a person or object that is important to us, or an exciting period in our lives. People who write their autobiographies reminisce about their entire lives. Recalling a shorter period or just one incident, however, is usually a far more manageable and satisfying task. In *The Art and Craft of Memoir* William Zinsser explains that writing about a particular time or incident enables the writer to achieve "a focus that isn't possible in autobiography." Recalling is a "window into life."

Recalling, however, is not simply writing down exactly what happened during a given time; that would be tedious and boring. Recalling means first determining why the event, person, or incident has **significance** for you. Did it teach you a lesson? Did it make you think about people or a person differently? Did it make you think you should change something about yourself or your lifestyle? An event can also be significant if it can help your readers recognize or remember something similar that happened to them. Recalling helps writers and readers alike discover that, despite the fact that people differ in many ways, as human beings we share many common experiences.

Robert MacNeil, the author of the memoir *Wordstruck*, recalls his childhood experiences of reading. The events are significant because they set up his love for words and his desire to become a writer.

> There wasn't a fire every night. Some fireplaces burned wood and some coal. The coal fire might have been a few years later. All of those things happened often, but I cannot remember whether they happened all at one time. It might have been spring with the liquid warble of an evening bird, echoing in the damp green air outside, like sounds intimate in a fog; or a long evening in summer with bees buzzing against screens and a chickadee plaintive in the distance. Often I was in bed when read to, pleading for a few more pages before going to sleep, or sick and listening lethargically. But in memory it feels like a winter night. What I remember precisely is the reading; both what was read and what I felt about it.

By recalling this incident, the writer shares with his readers the significant moments that have made a huge impact on his life. His recollection makes us recall our own memories of our early literary experiences.

LEARNING FROM PUBLISHED WRITERS

So that you can better understand how to write about something that occurred in your own life, you may find it helpful to read the following recollection by a published writer. Written by Bill Bunn, it describes an event that occurred when the author's first child was very young. It is significant in that Bunn expresses the difficulty of separation that parents often feel when they must trust their child to a caregiver. The final paragraph expresses the significance that the incident has given to his view of living.

Before You Read

Focus Your Attention

Before you read this recollection, take a few moments to respond to the following questions in your journal:

1. In the essay you are about to read, the writer describes the anxiety of a parent who must necessarily leave his child in someone else's care. Can you recall a time in your life when you felt the anxiety of separation from someone that you loved? Write down as many specific details as you can recall.
2. Bunn says that "death and goodbye are the same thing." Have you ever felt this connection? Write about it.

Expand Your Vocabulary

Read the following words in the sentences in which they appear. Jot down in your notebook what they mean in the context of the essay.

Siren (paragraph 3)

Claustrophobic (paragraph 3)

Existentially (paragraph 4)

Resurrection (paragraph 5)

Shroud (paragraph 5)

Bill Bunn

The Big, Short Party*

I actually wished he had started to kick and scream: it makes it so much easier when they kick and scream. But, he's a dedicated little boy, so he tries to take well most of what we throw at him. I watched him trying to manage his emotions as he contemplated me leaving him alone there. His chin trembled, and he blinked hard as I sat him down to take off his backwards boots, ones that he had proudly put on himself a few moments earlier. I watched his shoulders sag as the moment approached. 1

His body went limp as I removed his hat and coat. As soon as he was ready, he gave me a big hug and kiss, then went to the window as I prepared to leave him there. I stepped outside, toward the car, and turned to him, to that place in the window where his face usually was. He smiled weakly as I gave him my grin-and-bear-it smile—it's really facial advice. Then he started blowing kisses, as the tears rolled down his cheeks. I couldn't handle the sight any more, so I turned and ran back to my car, afraid that if I turned to look once more, I'd quit my job to stay home and play with him forever. 2

As I drove away, my eyes averting my siren son, I noticed an angular pain in my soul, one I'd not felt very often. After a short session of emotional arithmetic, I could only locate one other occasion I felt this particular kind of painful longing: my grandfather's death. He passed away when I was a teenager, and I remember struggling to understand what death meant in my lived experience. I couldn't understand the afterlife. How can you understand "forever"? I felt claustrophobic thinking about what it might be like to be sleeping inside a coffin under the ground. Instead, I learned to believe that death was simply absence: he was "gone." That parting of ways, and 3

*Published in *The Globe and Mail*, June 1, 2000

lingering absence conjured this odd, and particularly sharp sort of pain. Because I've learned to understand death as an absence, what my son and I suffered as we waved goodbye was nothing more than a small dying, a death, an on-the-spot, makeshift funeral.

4 You could accuse me of being overly dramatic. I've accused myself of the same thing. I've taken my feelings to task, insisting that I get over this inappropriate emotion immediately. But I can't. And, now, I don't believe I'm being overly dramatic. Death and goodbye are the same thing, existentially speaking: my son was absent from my day, just as my grandfather is. My emotions, no matter how much I tried to jimmy them into seeing things another way, will not budge. They have marked this kind of occasion for me as a death. So, death I must live with as I work through my professional day.

5 But, then, when the locks on my briefcase snap closed, I hop in the car to return to that day home. What a miracle moment it is: The dead are brought back to life. I witness the resurrection once we make eye contact. The morning's shroud buried itself in our reunion, and death's permanent marks are wiped away for a moment. These milliseconds of joy have become some of my favourite moments.

6 Our reuniting is one moment of pure life, for in that moment death is completely erased. My time with my son has not yet become tinged with the weight of future goodbyes, nor the sly death of taking one another for granted: it is my complete, momentary appreciation of my son, without the thought of what may lie ahead. A complete celebration of life. A huge party, lasting two heartbeats.

7 As I have come to understand goodbye and hello and their profound significance in my life, I don't let those moments go unlived. I've given up resenting them and embraced these daily deaths and resurrections. These are some of the mundane miracles that hold me close to the root of what living is about.

Questions For Critical Thinking

Thinking Critically About Content

1. What do you think Bunn means when he says "an on-the-spot, makeshift funeral"?
2. Does the author convince you that "death and goodbye are the same thing"? Is it a valid comparison? Why?

Thinking Critically About Purpose

3. What do you think Bunn's purpose is with this essay? Explain your answer.
4. How does the author garner his readers' sympathy?

Thinking Critically About Audience

5. What type of audience do you think would most understand and appreciate this recollection?
6. Does the writer succeed in making the audience feel the pain of a father having to leave a child?

Thinking Critically about Perspective

7. Would this essay have as much impact if it were written from a mother's perspective? How would it be different?
8. What other kinds of separation and loss does this essay make you think about?

LEARNING FROM YOUR PEERS

Recalling is an activity we all do every day in both speaking and writing. We learn from recalling, especially when we write, because it helps us understand our past and make better decisions in the future. It helps us understand ourselves and learn from our experiences. Although recalling comes to all of us naturally, writing about it goes through a recursive writing process. To better understand this process, we are going to follow a student named Tommy Poulos in response to the following writing assignment.

Tommy's Writing Assignment: Recalling

This is the topic Tommy's instructor assigned:

You have probably had many experiences that had predictable outcomes: getting a driver's licence, going to the mountains, landing a first job. Most of us, though, have had events in our lives that were not so predictable: an automobile accident while taking a driving test, a sudden storm coming up when we were hiking, sleeping in on the day of a job interview. Often we learn about ourselves by reflecting on these experiences. Write a recalling essay about an experience that did not turn out the way you thought it would.

The following outlines Tommy's individual writing process: generating ideas, planning, developing, organizing, drafting, revising, and editing.

Generating Ideas

After thinking about his assignment, Tommy starts **listing** all the places that were important in his childhood: his school, his church, the neighbourhood stores, the family restaurant, the playground, his favourite shortcuts through the neighbours' yards, and the treehouse his brothers built. In his mind, he recreates all the places he was most familiar with.

Then Tommy expands on his list by **clustering** some events that happened at those places. He takes a separate sheet of paper and writes down each of the places, leaving a large space between them. Then, he begins with all the "firsts" in his life. He thinks of his first day of school, but he cannot remember any details. He remembers his first communion, but he cannot think of anything unusual about it. He recalls going to the shops in his neighbourhood to buy new clothes for school. He remembers his first haircut at the barber just down from his family's restaurant. He realizes that many hours of his childhood were spent in the restaurant because his parents, grandparents, aunts, uncles, and cousins were all connected with it in some way.

Next Tommy begins another cluster, this time for the events he associates with the restaurant. What he sees from the points that he has written is that all the adults spent every day cooking, cleaning, and setting up the booths for business. When he was old enough, he learned to fold napkins and sort silverware. Tommy begins to realize his happiest memories were from his preschool days when he had no responsibilities. As long as he did not get into trouble, he was free to explore anything and everything in the restaurant. Suddenly, Tommy remembers the time when he was accidentally locked in the restaurant's walk-in freezer. He smiles to himself as he thinks about how funny that incident was and still is. It has become a story that is repeatedly told at family gatherings and has been embellished over the years.

Planning

Tommy begins to jot down the main points of the story:

> I thought I was a world class explorer. There was no place I could not go—upstairs, downstairs, inside, outside. That made me feel I could climb mountains and walk on the moon. But I had done it all, and I was getting bored. So one day I looked for a new challenge. There it was—the walk-in freezer. The rest of the story was inevitable.
>
> I got stuck inside. Everything got stuck. My feet got stuck—they were bare. I thought I was going to freeze to death. No one could hear me because the doors were too thick. I thought I would never get out.

Tommy takes his short summary to class the next day, and his peer response group tells him that it sounds like it can be developed into a good essay. They ask him the following questions:

- How old were you?
- How long were you trapped in the freezer?
- How did you get out?
- Were you punished?
- Did you get frostbite?
- Did you ever go into the freezer again?

Developing

The next day Tommy gets out his journal and looks at the questions from his group. He starts writing about his experience again, this time adding answers to the group's questions as he goes:

- How old were you? I was five years old, and I thought I was a real adventurer, on a par with astronauts and mountain climbers.
- How long were you trapped in the freezer? I was trapped in the freezer long enough to get very scared and very cold. I definitely thought I was going to die. I was very tired because I had worked my little body so hard trying to get the door open. And for what? Vegetables. That was the worst part. All that effort to get in, and only frozen vegetables as a reward. I had flopped my body in every direction, trying to get that door open.
- How did you get out? I got out when my grandfather came to the rescue. Everyone had been looking for me, but he found me and gave me some ouzo and wrapped me in a blanket.
- Were you punished? I didn't get punished because everyone was so happy to find me alive. Just before they found me, they were about to call the police.
- Did you get frostbite? I did practically get frostbite on my feet because I went in there with bare feet.
- Did you ever go into the freezer again? It took me a long time to even think of going in the freezer again. I must have been at least 12 before I would go in alone.

Organizing

During the next class, Tommy's peer group tells him that he is ready to start organizing his essay. Tommy goes to the library with his journal and looks over his notes. He starts a rough outline of the points he wants to include in his essay:

1. I was no ordinary kid—I was a true adventurer. The restaurant was my private domain. I could go anywhere and be anything. My only limit was my imagination. One morning, the walk-in freezer's unexplored mysteries compelled me to enter this forbidden territory.
2. I forced my way into the freezer with all my might, swinging my body from the enormous handle.
3. Once I was inside, there were only vegetables.
4. Worse, my feet stuck to the floor. (The restaurant floors had just been mopped and my bare feet were wet when I went into the freezer.)

5. I started to feel frozen—my eyes, my lungs, my nose, my feet. It felt like needles were poking into my body from all directions.
6. Suddenly praying became more important than exploring.
7. Finally, grandfather came to the rescue.

These points help Tommy decide how to organize his essay. He thinks that readers need to know something about his personality to make his story understandable. He decides to emphasize his adventurous spirit at the beginning of the essay. Then he will develop the essay in chronological order, ending with his rescue.

As he writes, he continues to add details and comparisons that emphasize the dramatic nature of the event.

Drafting

Tommy has spent time thinking, planning, developing, and organizing. He is now ready to begin writing the first version of his essay. We call this drafting. He spreads out his notes from his peer group, his journal, his clusters, and his rough outline. Then he writes his ideas from beginning to end.

Tommy's Essay: First Draft

Main Idea: Once my desire for adventure got me into more trouble than I was prepared for.

Tentative Title: The ice box

One day, I was at my family's restaurant. I considered myself to be a world-class adventurer and was always searching for undiscovered and uncharted territory. This morning, I was in a mood to find even larger booty. My adventurous soul was burning with curiosity. I had an urgent need to go "where no man had gone before."

Streaking through the kitchen in my bare feet, I tried to keep from slipping on the newly mopped floor. Suddenly, my destination loomed in front of me: the huge silver walk-in freezer, the only spot in the restaurant my father has strictly forbidden me to enter. I wondered what lay beyond that heavy door. I was determined to conquer the freezer's unexplored mysteries. Gathering all of my courage, I stretched to reach the huge latch that separated me from the hidden treasures within. Whatever stood in my way would be conquered. I climbed up on some boxes stacked nearby and leaped onto the handle like a frog attacking some forlorn fly. Nothing happened. But I was not going to be defeated. I changed strategies and started flapping my body back and forth like a trout on a line. My pride would not let me give up. Suddenly I felt a cool breeze, and the massive door creaked and opened just wide enough for my scrawny body to slip through the crack. Success! Tommy the Conqueror had landed! If I'd had a flag, I would have planted it on that hard, cold, metallic floor.

I looked around me, searching for the promised bounty within this forbidden metal chamber. Hurriedly trying to absorb all that was around me was tough. I scanned the boxes and bags stacked around the walls, looking for my private gold mine, but all I could see were vegetables. Drat! I hated vegetables. All that work, and what was my reward? Broccoli, cauliflower, and spinach. I didn't even like Popeye. Now what was I going to do? My big adventure had been ruined, so I turned toward the door just as it slammed shut. I tried to pick up my feet and run toward the door, but I could not move. My bare feet had frozen to the freezer floor. I forced them up, only to see chunks of my skin permanently attached to the freezer floor. Letting out a helpless whimper, I unashamedly called for my mommy. I felt helpless. But crying for my mom wasn't the answer. I made my way to the door and pushed with all my might. I threw myself against the door latch, but it didn't budge. I started kicking and screaming, but nothing happened. There was only silence and surrounding cold. I decided to sit down on a box of frozen spinach to await my doom. I started to realize that I would become cold and stiff as the multitude of vegetables that stared back at me. I realized there was nothing I could do except wait.

Suddenly, the cooling unit for the freezer kicked on. The air became even colder and drier. I felt pain everywhere. My stupid curiosity had done me in.

I started to pray. Surely I was too young to die. I was too innocent to have been given so harsh a punishment by God. I questioned how God could kill such a young, well-meaning child. While my mind was becoming unfocused, my body was starting to seem like a distant memory. I tried to cuddle my numb legs with my stiff arms. I hoped for the best, but expected the worst. Once I shut my eyes, I awaited my untimely death.

Suddenly, there was a *swoosh* as the gigantic door swung open. My grandfather's eyes met mine. His stern look vanished as he swept me into his arms and rescued me from the frozen tomb. He wrapped me in towels from the kitchen and took me to his office where he quickly poured a hot cup of ouzo, a Greek liqueur. After he touched it to my frozen lips, I swallowed it reflexively, feeling the warmth of its vapours spreading through my mouth and down to my stomach. The air in the heated office burned the frozen skin on my arms and legs and face. I didn't care because I was so relieved that the numbness was starting to leave my body and I had been brought back to life. My grandfather held me on his lap and kissed my forehead. Then he carried me around and let everyone know that the adventurer had returned. My whole family had a good laugh at my expense, and I had new respect for my father's warnings. I wouldn't say that this adventure was my last, but it was certainly my most memorable.

Revising

Once Tommy has finished his first draft, he knows that the task of revising lies ahead. At this point, his instructor wants the class to focus on various aspects of the essay, explaining that studying the separate parts will make the whole essay stronger and more effective. There are two parts to the revising process. The first is to look at the essay as a whole, and then to focus on the individual paragraphs.

Tommy first reviews the Checklist for Recognizing and Developing an Essay at the beginning of the Focus on Essays section of this chapter. His instructor explains to the class that revising means focusing on content, not grammar—concentrating on making the components of the essay work well together. Tommy reads the Focus on Essays section and completes the assigned exercises. When he is sure that he understands this overview of the essay structure, he moves on to pay closer attention to paragraphs.

The revising tasks in this chapter involve identifying the basic parts of an essay, analyzing the structure of certain paragraphs, and sometimes writing alternative paragraphs for specific essays. After reading the Checklist for Recognizing and Developing Paragraphs, and working through the Focus on Paragraphs section, Tommy learns that he can change the emphasis in a paragraph and even in an essay by including different information and organizing it in a variety of ways.

Returning to his draft, Tommy makes sure that each paragraph is fully developed and correctly placed in his essay. He finds that his meaning is hindered in some cases by paragraphs with missing parts, and in other cases by paragraphs that are out of place. He tries to remedy both problems in his revision.

Collaborative Work

Peer Group Activity

After you read the portions of Focus on Essays and Focus on Paragraphs that your instructor assigns, turn to Tommy's first draft (pp. 13–15), and complete the following tasks in small groups:

A. Underline the thesis statement. Does it appear in the introduction?

B. Underline the topic sentence in each body paragraph. Put an X at the start of each sentence that does not relate to the topic sentence of that paragraph.

C. Put brackets around the statements that show the significance of the recalling experience.

Compare your marks with those that your instructor will show you. Where do your marks differ from your instructor's? What do you need to review before writing your own essay?

Class Activity

As an entire class, look at the underlined portions of Tommy's revised draft (pp. 17–20) to see how he changed each sentence.

1. Did you identify the revision problems that Tommy corrected?
2. Discuss his changes. Do you think his changes are good ones?

Editing

Now that Tommy has made sure that his essay has all the parts it needs, he knows that he must do some final editing and proofreading before handing it in. His instructor tells the students that the Focus on Sentences sections in the appendix of the book give students a working knowledge of basic grammatical terms and usages. So Tommy shifts his focus from the content of his essay to specific points of grammar. He refers to the Focus on Sentences Appendix, and learns to recognize complete sentences and to identify the principal parts of the sentence. Then he uses the Checklist for Recognizing and Developing Sentences, and revises his draft according to these guidelines.

Collaborative Work

Peer Group Activity

After you read Focus on Sentences in the appendix of this book, turn again to Tommy's first draft and complete the following tasks in small groups.

1. Circle each subject and place each predicate in brackets.
2. Underline any sentence fragments.
3. Highlight any sentences that are missing end punctuation or a capital letter.

Compare your group's work with your instructor's. Where do your marks differ from your instructor's? What do you need to understand before you write your own essay?

Tommy's Revised Essay

The ~~ice box~~Ice Chamber

~~One day, I was at my family's~~It was an early Saturday morning at my home away from home, my family's restaurant. I was five years old, and I had been to every nook and cranny of our house and restaurant. I considered myself to be a world-class adventurer and was always searching for undiscovered and uncharted territory. I felt it was my mission to search attics, closets, basements, and dark hallways that held abandoned treasures. It was not unusual to find pennies, nickels, dimes, and even quarters under the restaurant booths. To adults, this was spare change. To me, it was comic book money, and I searched for it every morning without fail. This particular morning, though, I was in a mood to find even larger booty. My adventurous soul was burning with curiosity. I had an urgent need to go "where no man had gone before." Before my adventure was over, I would discover more than stray coins; I would learn the meaning of caution.

~~Streaking~~I made a quick tour of the restaurant. Streaking through the kitchen in my bare feet, I tried to keep from slipping on the newly mopped tile floor. I scampered through the storerooms like a running back through the defence. I whizzed past the silvery blur of kitchen equipment as fast as my short, stocky legs would carry me. Suddenly, my destination loomed in front of me: the huge silver walk-in freezer, the only spot in the restaurant my father ~~has~~had strictly forbidden me to enter. I wondered what lay beyond that heavy door. I was determined to conquer the freezer's unexplored mysteries. Gathering all of my courage, I stretched to reach the huge latch that separated me from the hidden treasures within. I grasped that latch as if it were my lifeline. I jumped and swayed feverishly, willing that door to open and let me in. I twisted and jerked, I leaped and turned, all to no avail. Since I was ready to give up, I sat down on the moist floor, panting and feeling my sore muscles. After a short rest, I steeled myself for another try. I was not going to fail. Whatever stood in my way would be conquered. I climbed up on some boxes stacked nearby and leaped onto the handle like a frog attacking some forlorn fly. Nothing happened. But I was not going to be defeated. I changed strategies and started flapping my body back and forth like a trout on a line. My pride would not let me give up. Suddenly I felt a cool breeze, and the massive door creaked and opened just wide enough for my scrawny body to slip through the crack. Success! Tommy the Conqueror had landed! If I'd had a flag, I would have planted it on that hard, cold, metallic floor.

I looked around me, searching for the promised bounty within this forbidden metal chamber. Hurriedly trying to absorb all that was around me was tough. I scanned the boxes and bags stacked around the walls, looking for my private gold mine, but all I could see were vegetables. Drat! I hated vegetables. All that work, and what was my reward? Broccoli, cauliflower, and spinach. I didn't even like Popeye. Now what was I~~going~~ to do? My big adventure had been ruined, so I turned toward the door just as it slammed shut. I tried to pick up my feet and run toward the door, but I could not move. My bare feet had frozen to the~~freezer~~ floor. I forced them up, only to see chunks of my skin permanently attached to the freezer floor. Letting out a helpless whimper, I unashamedly called for my mommy. I felt helpless. But crying for my mom wasn't the answer. I made my way to the door and pushed with all my might. I threw myself against the door latch, but it didn't budge. I started kicking and screaming, but still nothing happened. There was only silence and the surrounding cold. I decided to sit down on a box of frozen spinach to await my doom. I started to realize that I would ~~become cold and stiff~~soon become as still and cold as the multitude of vegetables that stared back at me. I realized there was nothing I could do except wait.

~~Suddenly,~~Suddenly the cooling unit for the freezer kicked on with a loud roar. The air became even colder and drier. ~~I felt pain everywhere.~~My lungs felt like there were hundreds of needles poking at them in all directions. I could feel my nostrils sticking together. My eyes hurt. I moved to the other corner of the freezer, hoping it would be slightly warmer than near the cooling unit, but there was no improvement. My stupid curiosity had done me in.

I started to pray. Surely I was too young to die. I was too innocent to have been given so harsh a punishment by God. I questioned how God could kill such a young, well-meaning child. While my mind was becoming unfocused, my body was starting to seem like a distant memory. I tried to cuddle my numb legs with my stiff arms. I hoped for the best, but expected the worst. Once I shut my eyes, I awaited my untimely death.

Suddenly, there was a *swoosh* as the gigantic door swung open. My grandfather's eyes met mine. His stern look vanished as he swept me into his arms and rescued me from the frozen tomb. He wrapped me in towels from the kitchen and took me to his office where he quickly poured a shot of ouzo, a Greek liqueur. After he touched it to my frozen lips, I swallowed it reflexively, feeling the warmth of its vapours spreading through my mouth and down to my stomach. The air in the heated office burned the frozen skin on my arms and legs and face. I didn't care because I was so relieved that the numbness was starting to leave my body and I had been brought back to life. My grandfather held me on his lap and kissed my forehead. Then he carried me around and let everyone know that the adventurer had returned.

My whole family had a good laugh at my expense, and I had learned a valuable lesson. The minutes that had seemed like hours in the freezer taught me a new respect for my father's warnings. I wouldn't say that this adventure was my last, but it was certainly my most memorable.

Collaborative Work

Practise Outlining

Spend time as a class generating ideas, planning, developing, and organizing a potential recalling essay.

1. Spend about 10 minutes sharing a few memories.
2. Once three or four have been suggested, choose one or two for the subject of a potential essay. What makes one idea better than another idea? What are we looking for?
3. Decide on the audience and the purpose.
4. Brainstorm this memory's possible significance to the audience. Have someone write ideas on the overhead or blackboard.

5. Develop the ideas to give a sense of what a person could write if he/she were to write this essay.
6. Organize the ideas so they appear in the best order for the best effect.

Could you write this essay? How long would it take you to finish this essay?

WRITING YOUR OWN RECALLING ESSAY

So far you have seen an essay from a professional writer and from a fellow student. You have also worked as a class to build most of an essay. As you've spent time in this chapter you've followed the writing process of another student from first to final draft, you have absorbed ideas and ways of explaining those ideas in words. All of these activities have prepared you to write your own essay focusing on one of your own meaningful memories.

What Have You Discovered?

Before you begin your own writing, let's review what you have learned in this chapter so far:

- Recalling is the act of writing about something you remember.
- The event, person, or incident in a recollection should have significance for you.
- Ordinary events can be as powerful as dramatic ones. Don't pressure yourself to choose a spectacular event for your essay topic. Bill Bunn's essay demonstrates the power of an ordinary memory.
- Include enough detail to help your memory come to life for your readers. Tommy's essay develops several key details for his readers.
- Organize (reorganize) your ideas to be sure they are in the most effective order.
- After you revise your essay, edit the grammar, usage, and sentence structure.

Your Writing Topic

Choose one of the following topics for your recalling essay:

1. Reflect on your own childhood and recall an incident or event that has significance for you. It doesn't have to be a major memory. It can be an ordinary one: feeling a sense of loss, learning from an experience, remembering a person, place, or thing of particular significance to you. Write an essay to explain this memory to someone who was not with you.

2. Your old high school has asked you to submit an essay to the newsletter recalling a significant learning experience. It can be about very early or later years. It can involve being taught directly or perhaps the editor has asked you to submit an essay recalling a job or volunteer experience that you enjoyed. The editor wants to show current high school students some options for volunteer and paid work.
3. The members of your English class are putting together a collection of essays paying tribute to people who encouraged them to go to college. You decide to submit an essay. Who gave you the courage and determination to pursue your education—a teacher, a relative, a supervisor at work? Was there a memorable event or conversation that helped you decide to continue your schooling? Record that memory and why it was important to you.
4. Create your own recalling topic (with the assistance of your instructor), and write an essay about it.

When you select one of these topics, begin to work through the writing process in the way that Tommy did. You may find his experience helpful in giving you ideas. If parts of the process seem to appear out of order, that adjustment is probably part of your own writing ritual. Follow your instincts, but make sure you work through all parts of the writing process. As you write, keep track of what you do to finish a final draft that you're proud to hand in.

Reflect On Your Writing Process

After you hand in your essay, take some time to reflect on what you did to complete it. You'll want to become familiar with what you need and like to do to write well. In a single page, write a short version of what you did to write your essay. Include how and where you got your ideas, right up to the finished essay you handed in.

Once you've documented your writing process, ask yourself if you would like to change anything about it for your next essay. Write a short paragraph explaining parts of the writing process that you'd like to change.

Drafting

Here is Sitara's essay.

Sitara's Essay: First Draft

I can spend an entire day looking at how people are dressed and watching the way they interact with each other. Outdoor concerts and street fairs are some of the best places to watch people without fear of being discovered. Another place that almost anyone can go to watch people is the local mall.

I think I can always pick out the ones on a first date because they do not seem comfortable with each other. One may be dressed in a business suit; the other may be wearing jeans and an old T-shirt. Others have lived and shopped together so long that they look like they belong together. At one outdoor concert that I attended recently, a man and woman who had obviously been taking dancing lessons were all dressed up, and as soon as the music started, they showed off their steps. Their obvious enjoyment of their skills was appreciated by dozens of people. The crowd applauded them like they did the musicians. There was another couple who fell into the first-date category. She was dressed for a concert in a cocktail dress and high heels. Her hair was styled, and her makeup was perfect. She even carried a sequined bag. He was dressed for the outdoor concert they were attending: running shoes, T-shirt, and baggy shorts. You could call him casual. It would be interesting to know if they ever had a second date.

The beer drinkers often bring their own coolers. Then they secretly drink one beer after another. However, no matter how secretive they are, their drinking begins to show because they begin to lose their coordination and look a little drunk after a while. The people who come for the food make a great ceremony of getting a sandwich or a good dessert. They can be quite obsessive, so they always stand out in a crowd. I was close enough recently to eavesdrop on a man and woman who were obviously on a first date. The woman asked the man some questions about his interests and hobbies, but the man didn't respond. He was unable to answer because his attention was completely focused on the amount of ice cream, whipped cream, and strawberries that was rapidly being transferred from his dish to his mouth. He kept saying, "You should really try some of this." He was a glutton. What do you think she did? She kept refusing and changing the subject while her fork fiddled with the small pile of granola and fruit chunks on her own plate. I suspect that that was their first and last date, but you never know.

Running around and climbing and jumping and chasing each other, some of them just give me fits. Others really listen to the music and dance. At the mall some of them are amazed at the seasonal decorations. Meanwhile, others ask for all the latest offerings in consumer land. Some of their parents are tolerant, but others try so hard to control their children that they make themselves and everyone around them miserable.

Sometimes while I was sitting drinking cappuccino, I saw groups of junior high and senior high students. I call them prowlers, and they deserve this name. You might expect to see variations in appearances, but they usually travel in same-sex groups that dress alike. There is almost always a group of teenage girls who have gone to great lengths to appear casual, coincidentally wearing the same makeup and hairstyles. There is a group of teenage boys who act nonchalant and uninterested around girls. The two groups often check each other out before they can get together. Sometimes the boys and girls make contact; however, usually it's a standoff with no one making a move.

They probably see me as a loner, but I plan to write a novel about my hometown one of these days. Perhaps I will include that child with personality or that sulky-looking young woman with her arm in a cast. As you can see, I never get tired of watching people and trying to imagine what their lives are like.

Revising

Sitara, essay in hand, went to class the next day. The instructor asked the students to work on their introductions. He emphasized how important it is for writers to catch their readers' attention. Since Sitara didn't write with an outline, and may have strayed away from her main idea, she realized she needed to go back and make sure her introduction introduced her essay.

First, Sitara reviewed the Checklist for Writing Thesis Statements and Introductions at the beginning of the Focus on Essays section in this chapter. Then she read the Focus on Paragraphs section and did the assigned exercises. Sitara learned that most introductions can be made clearer and more interesting. In her own essay, for example, she thought she could do a better job of introducing and narrowing her topic. Sitara approached her revision determined to develop her introduction as effectively as possible.

Collaborative Work

Peer Group Activity

After you read the Focus on Paragraphs and Focus on Essays sections, turn to Sitara's first draft and complete the following tasks in small groups:

A. Put a caret (^) at points in the essay where you think Sitara needs more detail. What kinds of detail should she include?

B. Use an asterisk (*) to indicate the points at which Sitara could use stronger controlling ideas for her paragraphs.

C. Look at Sitara's introduction. Does she have a thesis statement? Underline it.

D. Does her introduction narrow the topic well? Why or why not?

E. Rewrite her introduction in different words, making sure to include a thesis statement. Make sure your introduction narrows the topic to what's covered in the rest of her essay.

Compare your group's marks and rewrites with those your instructor shows you. Where do they differ? What do you need to review before writing your own essay?

Class Activity

As an entire class, look at the underlined portions of Sitara's essay to see the changes she makes.

1. Did you identify the **revision** problems that she corrects?
2. Do you think the changes are good ones? Discuss them.

Editing

Once Sitara rewrote her introduction, she needed to do some final editing and proofreading before handing in her essay. In class, the instructor explained that a working knowledge of basic sentence structure is a necessity for effective writing. Sitara read the relevant section of the Focus on Sentences Appendix to learn about pronouns and modifiers. Then, she set out to apply this information to her own writing.

Collaborative Work

Peer Group Activity

After you have read the Focus on Sentences section, turn to Sitara's first draft and complete the following tasks in small groups:

A. Circle all of the modifiers in the first couple of paragraphs. Draw arrows to the words that they modify.

B. Draw a box around the pronouns. With arrows, connect the pronouns to the nouns they replace.

Compare your answers with those from another group. Where do your answers differ from theirs? What do you need to review before writing your own essay?

Sitara's Revised Essay

Crowds

My favourite activity is watching people in crowds. I can spend an entire day looking at how people are dressed and watching the way they interact with each other. Outdoor concerts, and street fairs, and malls are some of the best places to watch people without fear of being discovered. Another place that almost anyone can go to watch people is the local ~~mall~~. mall. People-watching is a bit like searching for treasures in a secondhand store. One day a small child (about six years old) caught my eye, and I ended up following him and his mother through the entire mall. The stores they stopped in and the purchases they made gave me a lot of information about their personalities. I spend as much free time as possible people-watching, always looking for the most conspicuous characters, observing how they look and act, and wondering what happens after I've noticed them. Some of my best people-watching discoveries have been couples, concert-goers, children, and teenagers on the prowl.

Couples of all ages are always fun to watch. I think I can always pick out the ones on a first date because they do not seem comfortable with each other. One may be dressed in a business suit; the other may be wearing jeans and an old T-shirt. Others have lived and shopped together so long that they look like ~~they belong together~~.bookends out for a stroll. At one outdoor concert that I attended recently, a man and woman who had obviously been taking dancing lessons were all dressed up, and as soon as the music started, they showed off their steps. Their obvious enjoyment of their new skills was appreciated by dozens of people. The crowd applauded them ~~like~~as heartily as they did the musicians. There was another couple who fell into the first-date category. She was dressed for a symphony concert in a black cocktail dress and high heels. Her hair was freshly styled, and her make-up was perfect. She even carried a sequined bag. He was dressed for the outdoor concert they were attending: running shoes, T-shirt, and baggy shorts. You could call him casual. It would be interesting to know if they ever had a second date.

At the concerts some people come for the beer, and some come for the food. The beer drinkers often bring their own coolers. Then they secretly drink one beer after another. However, no matter how secretive they are, their drinking begins to show because they begin to lose their coordination and look a little ~~drunk~~bleary-eyed after a while. The people who come for the food make a great ceremony of getting ~~a~~the perfect sandwich or ~~a good~~the most delectable dessert. They can be quite obsessive, so they always stand out in a crowd. I was close enough recently to eavesdrop on a man and woman who were obviously on a first date. The woman asked the man some questions about his interests and hobbies, but the man didn't respond. He was unable to answer because his attention was completely focused on the ~~amount~~sublime mountain of ice cream, whipped cream, and strawberries that was rapidly being transferred from his dish to his mouth. He kept saying, "You should really try some of this." He was a glutton. What do you think she did? She kept refusing and changing the subject while her fork fiddled with the small pile of granola and fruit chunks on her own plate. I suspect that that was their first and last date, but you never know.

I also like to watch children at these events. Running around and climbing and jumping and chasing each other, some of them just give me fits. Others really listen to the music and ~~dance.~~cannot resist swaying and dancing to the rhythms. At the mall some of them are amazed and wide-eyed with wonder at the seasonal decorations. Meanwhile, others ~~ask~~whine and beg for all the latest offerings in consumer land. Some of their parents are tolerant, but others try so hard to control their children that they make themselves and everyone around them miserable.

~~Sometimes while I was sitting drinking cappuccino, I saw groups of junior high and senior high students.~~Another common sight in these places is gangs of teenagers. I call them prowlers, and they deserve this name. You might expect to see variations in appearances, but they usually travel in same-sex groups that dress alike. There is almost always a group of teenage girls who have gone to great lengths to appear casual, coincidentally wearing the same make-up and hairstyles. There is a group of teenage boys who ~~act~~betray their interest in the girls by acting nonchalant and ~~uninterested around~~

~~girls.~~uninterested, their combs peeking out of the back pockets of their jeans. The two groups often ~~check each other out before they can get together.~~circle the crowd in opposite directions so they can look for subtle signs of acceptance before anyone makes a move on the other group. Sometimes the boys and girls make contact; however, usually it's a standoff with no one making a move.

If I am feeling very brazen in these settings, I will take out a small notebook and a pen and write down my impressions of these people. They probably see me as an eccentric loner, but I plan to write a novel about my hometown one of these days. Perhaps I will include that adorable child with ~~personality~~the red curly hair and the denim cap with the sunflower on it or that sulky-looking young woman with her arm in a cast. Perhaps she fell while she was having a fight with her boyfriend. Maybe she was trying to rescue the neighbour's cat from a tree, or maybe she has an incurable disease of the bone marrow. As you can see, I never get tired of watching people and trying to imagine what their lives are~~ like~~.like. If they ever close the mall in my hometown, I will just have to drive until I find another one.

Practise Outlining

As a class, spend time generating ideas, planning, developing, and organizing a potential observing essay.

1. Spend five minutes brainstorming a few memories of strong observations.
2. Choose five for the subject of a potential essay. Discuss what makes one idea better than another. Choose the best one.
3. Decide on the audience and the purpose.
4. Draw a cluster of this memory's possible significance to the audience.
5. Develop the ideas to give a sense of what a person might potentially write.
6. Organize the ideas so they appear in the best order for the best effect.

What would be the main topics for each paragraph? Could you write this essay? How long would it take you to complete a first draft?

WRITING YOUR OWN OBSERVING ESSAY

So far, you have seen a professional writer and a fellow student at work trying to communicate an observation or experience that was significant to them. As you read the published essay and followed the writing process of another student from first to final draft, you absorbed ideas and ways of giving those ideas a form of their own. These reading and writing activities have prepared you to write your own essay focusing on an observation that is meaningful to you.

What Have You Discovered?

Before you begin your own writing task, let's review what you have learned in this chapter so far:

- Good observers use all their senses: seeing, hearing, touching, smelling, and tasting.
- When you write an observation, you cannot simply tell your reader what you saw; you must show your reader.
- Your ultimate goal in writing an observing essay is to use your words to recreate your experience for your readers.
- You should have a dominant impression you want to communicate.
- You must choose details that best express your dominant impression.
- To present your observations effectively, you need to organize your ideas.
- To help you shape your essay, you should learn as much as possible about your readers.
- Before you write a draft, you need to decide on a point of view toward your subject.
- After you write a draft, revise your essay for meaning and organization.
- After you revise your essay, edit its grammar, usage, and sentence structure.

Your Writing Topic

Choose one of the following topics for your observing essay:

1. Choose a person you know or remember well and write an essay that provides a detailed explanation of the way that person looked, the place where that person lived, and the things that person did each day.

2. Many places seem to have particular atmospheres, such as hospitals, churches, graveyards, and greenhouses. Choose one that evokes a particularly strong memory for you. Describe that experience. Use as many sensory details as are necessary to provide a dominant impression.
3. A national travel magazine is asking for honest descriptions (positive or negative) of places people have visited. They are offering $100 to the writers of the essays chosen for publication. You may decide to write about a place with a marvellous beach or about a dreadful place where you were forced to live because of circumstances beyond your control. The mood of the essay will help determine its form, so find ways to reveal your feelings about the place you choose.
4. Create your own observing topic (with the assistance of your instructor), and write an essay in response to it.

Write your essay and keep track of how you like to work. Although how you specifically write may differ from other writers, you need to go through all parts of the writing process. Compare the process you go through to the one Sitara took to complete her essay. Include a small description of your writing process with your essay when you hand in your assignment.

Writing Thesis Statements and Introductions

Checklist for Writing Thesis Statements and Introductions

- ✓ Does the introduction catch the readers' attention with a description, story, statistic, fact, definition, or comparison?
- ✓ Does the thesis state the controlling idea for the entire essay?
- ✓ Does the thesis statement give the essay focus and direction?
- ✓ Is the thesis statement as complete as it can be?
- ✓ Does the thesis appear as the first or last sentence in the first paragraph of the essay?

Imagine yourself at a party. A person walks up to you and begins to tell you a detailed description of his life. As you listen, you wonder if this information has a point–a focus. Without a focus, you'd tend to believe that this person was wasting your time, and after he finished relating all the information, you would have trouble remembering what he said.

One of the ways you can help your readers as you write an essay is to let them know your essay has a focus. That's one of the main functions of an essay's thesis statement. The thesis statement is a summary of your entire essay in a single sentence. In some ways, the thesis statement is a bit like a promise you make to your readers. It tells the readers where you're going to take them, and good writers always take readers where they say they're going to go. They keep their promise.

Most often, the thesis statement ends up in the introduction. If you put your thesis statement in the introduction, it generally makes the essay clearer. Sometimes it finds its way into the conclusion. If you want to create a sense of mystery, and keep your reader wondering where you're taking them, then put your thesis statement in the conclusion.

In addition to presenting your thesis, the introduction has to hook your readers' attention. You want your readers to be excited and interested about where you're going to take them, so you need to use a few different writing techniques to make sure your introduction is a strong one.

Finding Your Focus

Finding your focus is sometimes quite difficult. Your assignments throughout college are most often broad topics, and you're often given very few pages to communicate what you have to say. So your thesis can't be too large—it can't promise to cover the entire subject in three or four pages. And it can't be too small, or you'll run out of things to say before you reach your word limit. Since your thesis statement is your controlling idea for the entire essay, one good way to begin your first draft is to write your thesis statement at the beginning of your paper. Your thesis statement may change several times before your essay is finished. Still, making this statement is very good for your essay. Some writers, after writing a tentative thesis statement, turn their thesis into a question, a question their essay will answer.

In the title of his essay at the beginning of Chapter 5, "Illiterate Like Me," Dan Zollmann suggests that he is going to talk about illiteracy. This is a broad topic with little to distinguish it. But Zollmann uses his introduction to narrow his topic and settle on a focus in his thesis statement (boldfaced here):

> Most Canadians believe that something should be done to help the illiterate. Yet other social issues often take precedence when it comes to distributing tax dollars. If illiteracy were simply an inconvenience suffered by a handful of Canadians, then the low priority we accord to dealing with it would be justified because time and money are finite, and we must allocate these scarce resources on the basis of importance. However, illiteracy is not merely an inconvenience, nor does it afflict only a few Canadians. Instead, it is nothing less than the political, economic, and social alienation of a large number of individuals from their society. **As such, illiteracy is as urgent as any other social problems we face.**

In reviewing her essay, Sitara decided that the topic "Crowds" would be too big to handle in six to eight paragraphs. Since Sitara couldn't possibly cover everything she's ever observed in crowds in 500 to 700 words, she needed to find a more specific focus for her essay. She started reworking her first paragraph:

First Draft: I can spend an entire day looking at how people are dressed and watching the way they interact with each other. Outdoor concerts and street fairs are some of the best places to watch people without fear of being discovered. Another place that almost anyone can go to watch people is the local mall.

As she looked at her introduction again, she realized that she did not include a clear thesis that focuses her subject: she wasn't sure she had a thesis at all. So she read her whole essay over and wrote a thesis statement based on what she had already written:

Thesis: I spend as much free time as possible people-watching, always looking for the most conspicuous characters, imagining what they are thinking and what their lives are like.

As Sitara studied her draft, she decided that even though her revised statement revealed her purpose, it didn't serve the other major function of a thesis statement, which is to limit her topic. As she looked back over her essay, Sitara realized that she wasn't really imagining what people are thinking or what their lives are like—she observed people and wondered how they'd end up. Plus, she noticed she hadn't mentioned the four groups she wanted to talk about. Instead of putting those groups into her thesis statement, she put them in another sentence, following her thesis statement:

Revised Thesis: I spend as much free time as possible people-watching, always looking for the most conspicuous characters, observing how they look and act, and wondering what happens after I've noticed them. Some of my best people-watching discoveries have been couples, concert-goers, children, and teenagers on the prowl.

After she placed her thesis statement at the end of her introduction, her essay was clear. She'd made a promise to her readers that she knew she could keep.

Exercise E3-1

Write an alternative thesis statement for Zollmann's Essay "Illiterate Like Me."

Exercise E3-2

Write an alternative thesis statement for Sitara's first draft (pp. 43–45).

Exercise E3-3

Read the following sentences and decide which ones would make good thesis statements for the topic provided. Write a new thesis statement for any that you think are too broad.

1. Pets: For many reasons, cats make better pets for apartment dwellers than dogs do.
2. Education: Everyone needs a good education.
3. Gun control: Carefully observed gun control laws that require licensing for weapon owners will prevent many tragic deaths caused by young people who do not observe safety rules or cannot control their tempers and find guns easy to obtain.
4. Television: Parents are finding it harder and harder to limit the violence and smut that comes into their homes via their TV sets; therefore, the new V chip that allows them to block unsuitable programs is a valuable tool for them.
5. Television: A strictly observed rating system for TV shows like the one used for movies will make the V chip unnecessary.

Exercise E3-4

Read the following introductory paragraph and compose a thesis statement for it.

As our society changes, more and more students must have part-time or full-time jobs. These students often find their stress levels rising as a result of too much to do and too little time in which to do it. Tragically, many of them give up on furthering their education when some careful thinking and scheduling could have prevented their dropping out.

Introducing Your Topic

Experienced writers know the importance of catching their audience's attention at the beginning of an essay. For example, in Chapter 2's essay, Bunn begins with a detailed description of his son's reaction to his leaving:

> I actually wished he had started to kick and scream: it makes it so much easier when they kick and scream. But, he's a dedicated little boy, so he tries to take well most of what we throw at him. I watched him trying to manage his emotions as he contemplated me leaving him alone there. His chin trembled, and he blinked hard as I sat him down to take off his backwards boots, ones that he had proudly put on himself a few moments earlier. I watched his shoulders sag as the moment approached.

Another strategy that writers sometimes use to begin their essays is a brief story. In Chapter 9 of this book, Kelly Kaur begins her problem-solving essay by recounting her situation:

> I did not want to be a 10-year-old girl who was bound by patriarchal ideals and restrictions in a very strict and suffocating East Indian upbringing that constantly reminded me that my future would be one determined for me: I had to learn how to cook, clean and eventually be married to a man chosen for me by my family. I lived a childhood feeling the shackles of tradition on my imagination.

Kaur catches her audience's attention by giving background information that leads naturally to her purpose for writing.

Still another strategy that works well for introducing certain topics is offering various interesting facts, statistics, or definitions to catch the readers' attention:

> Nationwide, women have a median income that is 52% of the median income of men. Some observers believe this huge income gap is not a cause for concern. They point out that a major reason for this discrepancy is child-rearing activities. Women are much more unlikely to be steady participants in the work force and thus, not surprisingly, they have a much lower median income.

As Sitara looked back over her first draft and the Checklist for Writing Introductions, she decided that she could use a combination of these methods. The thesis statement she added is indicated by boldface type in her revision.

First Draft: I can spend an entire day looking at how people are dressed and watching the way they interact with each other. Outdoor concerts and street fairs are some of the best places to watch people without fear of being discovered. Another place that almost anyone can go to watch people is the local mall.

Revision: My favourite activity is watching people in crowds. I can spend an entire day looking at how people are dressed and watching the way they interact with each other. Outdoor concerts, and street fairs, and malls are some of the best places to watch people without fear of being discovered. Another place that almost anyone can go to watch people is the local mall. People-watching is a bit like searching for treasures in a secondhand store. One day a small child (about six years old) caught my eye, and I ended up following him and his mother through the entire mall. The stores they stopped in and the purchases they made gave me a lot of information about their personalities. **I spend as much free time as possible people-watching, always looking for the most conspicuous characters, observing how they look and act, and wondering what happens after I've noticed them. Some of my best people-watching discoveries have been couples, concert-goers, children, and teenagers on the prowl.**

Sitara's revision is informative and very interesting. In her introduction of her topic (people-watching), she gives the readers some background information, compares people-watching to searching for treasures, and tells a brief story about one of her people-watching expeditions.

Exercise E3-5

In your opinion, what is most effective about Amy Tan's introductory paragraph? Explain your answer.

Exercise E3-6

Rewrite Sitara's introductory paragraph using at least one of the methods explained in this chapter.

Exercise E3-7

Using chapters from your textbooks for other classes, find examples of four different methods of introducing a topic. Photocopy and label them.

Exercise E3-8

Using a recent newspaper or magazine, find examples of four different methods of introducing topics and share them with your classmates.

Collaborative Work

After writing a draft of your own observing essay, exchange papers with a classmate. Having read the essay, do you think its purpose and focus are clearly stated in the thesis? If not, suggest revisions. Complete the following tasks:

A. Make sure the thesis statement is either the first or last sentence in the introductory paragraph.

B. Decide whether the introduction to the essay effectively catches your attention. If it doesn't, suggest revisions.

C. Does the introduction leave any questions in your mind? If so, note them in the margin. Then return the paper to its writer, and use the information in this section to revise your draft.

Composing Topic Sentences

Checklist for Composing Topic Sentences

✓ Are your topic sentences clear?
✓ Are they focused?
✓ Are they specific?

Newspaper headlines are always an easy-to-read summary of the entire news story. The headlines say what the entire news story says. When we write paragraphs, they should include one sentence that summarizes the entire paragraph, the same way a newspaper headline summarizes an entire news story. Without that topic sentence, a paragraph will seem like a loose collection of ideas, without much of a point. Read the following paragraph:

> Running around and climbing and jumping and chasing each other, some of them just give me fits. Others really listen to the music and cannot resist swaying and dancing to the rhythms. At the mall some of them are amazed and wide-eyed with wonder at the seasonal decorations. Meanwhile, others whine and beg for all the latest offerings in consumer land. Some of their parents are tolerant, but others try so hard to control their children that they make themselves and everyone around them miserable.

Now, take the following sentence, a topic sentence, and read it before you reread the previous paragraph: **I also like to watch children at these events**. Clear, strong topic sentences are key to building a strong essay.

Clear Topic Sentences

A **topic sentence** should clearly summarize the information in the entire paragraph in a single, complete sentence. Look at Sitara's essay. Each paragraph in her essay contains one sentence that summarizes the entire paragraph. The topic sentence, or controlling idea, tells the reader what is being developed in that particular paragraph.

Look at the following paragraph. We know the paragraph is going to be about "gangs of teenagers" because the topic sentence lets us know all about it. The topic sentence makes a statement about the contents of the paragraph. The rest of the paragraph describes the setting of the experience:

> **Another common sight in these places are gangs of teenagers.** I call them prowlers, and they deserve this name. You might expect to see variations in appearances, but they usually travel in same-sex groups that dress alike. There is almost always a group of teenage girls who have gone to

great lengths to appear casual, coincidentally wearing the same makeup and hairstyles. There is a group of teenage boys who betray their interest in the girls by acting nonchalant and uninterested, their combs peeking out of the back pockets of their jeans. The two groups often circle the crowd in opposite directions so they can look for subtle signs of acceptance before anyone makes a move on the other group. Sometimes the boys and girls make contact; however, usually it's a standoff with no one making a move.

Notice the topic sentence is the first one in the paragraph. Topic sentences are usually the first or last sentence in the paragraph. Topic sentences at the end of the paragraph tend to create a sense of mystery or anticipation. A topic sentence at the beginning of the paragraph promotes clear writing.

As Sitara revised her observing essay, she decided that her topic sentence for another paragraph was awkward, and it did not clearly summarize the paragraph:

First Draft: Sometimes while I was sitting drinking cappuccino, I saw groups of junior high and senior high students.

Revision: Another common sight in these places is gangs of teenagers.

She realized as she looked at this topic sentence that she didn't talk about herself at all in the paragraph. She had just included her observations of these teenage groups. So she decided to cut herself out of the topic sentence and simplify it by referring to one group of students instead of two.

Exercise P3-1

Highlight the controlling idea for each paragraph of Sitara's essay. Develop one paragraph by adding details she might have included.

Exercise P3-2

Reread Sitara's first draft. Divide it into paragraphs and provide each paragraph with a clear topic sentence. Add details where needed.

Exercise P3-3

Underline any of the following topic sentences that could be developed in one paragraph.

1. Children who watch television every day are exposed to the highest-pressure advertising in mass media.
2. I have tried several relaxing hobbies.
3. The University of Windsor in Ontario was the best choice for me.
4. Universities often have different areas of strength and weakness.
5. I learned one easy way to make friends.
6. Cats make better pets than dogs.

7. There are several ways to avoid being disappointed in love.
8. Lasting relationships are built on a foundation of mutual interests and mutual respect.
9. I will never forget the day I got my driver's licence.
10. Riding Mountain National Park is a great place for a holiday.

Exercise P3-4

Compose a topic sentence for the following paragraph.

For example, we spent a great deal of time generating ideas about something or someone we had observed closely. Then, we chose the idea that we felt we could develop with a great many relevant details. After settling on a controlling idea for the essay, we planned the body of the paper.

Focused Topic Sentences

Topic sentences have to be focused. If they don't fit the paragraph well, they make your writing blurry and unclear. Topic sentences have to summarize the paragraph, and just the paragraph.

As Sitara began revising paragraph 4 of her observing essay, she realized that the new small paragraph lacked focus. What it needed was a topic sentence to help the reader understand what the paragraph was about. She also realized that the pronoun "them" in the first sentence didn't clearly refer to anything previously. So she wanted to fix that problem, too:

First Draft: Running around and climbing and jumping and chasing each other, some of them just give me fits. Others really listen to the music and dance. At the mall some of them are amazed and at the seasonal decorations. Meanwhile, others ask for all the latest offerings in consumer land. Some of their parents are tolerant, but others try so hard to control their children that they make themselves and everyone around them miserable.

Revision: **I also like to watch children at these events.** Running around and climbing and jumping and chasing each other, some of them just give me fits. Others really listen to the music and cannot resist swaying and dancing to the rhythms. At the mall some of them are amazed and wide-eyed with wonder at the seasonal decorations. Meanwhile, others whine and beg for all the latest offerings in consumer land. Some of their parents are tolerant, but others try so hard to control their children that they make themselves and everyone around them miserable.

The topic sentence clarifies the paragraph and provides a strong focus for the reader.

Exercise P3-5

Review Sitara's first draft. Which of the paragraphs could still use a topic sentence? Write topic sentences for those paragraphs.

Exercise P3-6

Write a topic sentence that would give shape and direction to a paragraph developing each of the subjects listed below.

1. The best feature of my college.
2. The ideal spot to study.
3. The most entertaining sport.
4. The sport that is the best to participate in.
5. The most misleading advertising claim.
6. The cleverest ad on television.
7. Choosing an outfit.
8. My favourite musicians.
9. My least favourite foods.
10. A good book.

Exercise P3-7

Write a topic sentence for the following paragraph to make the controlling idea as clear as possible.

At Olds College, classes are small enough for your instructors to know you personally, yet the college has enough students to offer a wide variety of courses. Because Olds is in a rural setting, peace and quiet surround you; however, Calgary, a major city housing several colleges and a university, is only an hour's drive away. Olds' students are motivated to achieve without feeling pressure to compete.

Collaborative Work

After writing a draft of your own observing essay, exchange papers with a classmate, and do the following tasks:

A. Underline each topic sentence.

B. Put brackets around any topic sentences that do not make the controlling idea clear.

C. In the margin, suggest changes to make the topic sentences clearer and more meaningful.

Then return the paper to its writer, and use the comments you received and the information in this section to revise your draft.

CHAPTER **FOUR**

Explaining

Think of prospective paragraphs as *files;* the task...is to sort the ideas and the evidence into appropriate files, and to be sure that nothing is misfiled or left out in the cold.

—**CONSTANCE ROOKE,** ***THE CLEAR PATH***

LEARNING OUTCOMES

This chapter will help you:

- Understand and write an essay that explains a topic to the audience;
- Recognize and apply methods of reasoning used in an essay;
- Write focused and unified paragraphs.

It would likely be impossible for us to function if we didn't have a chance to explain ourselves: what we meant when we said something; why we were late for work or school; why we didn't get an assignment done; how we feel about social issues, politics, religion. Whether we are speaking or writing, we continually engage in explanations. **Explaining** is an essential part of all forms of communication. The ability to explain through writing may be one of the most important skills we possess as human beings. Through explaining, we communicate and share ideals and values—we help each other know, understand, and respect our ideas or feelings.

Explaining essays fall into two categories: (1) offering reasons for why things are the way they are (justifying); (2) explaining something we know to someone else (procedures and process descriptions).

If you're writing a *justifying* essay, you explain why something has happened, or why you acted in a certain way: why you didn't pay the rent on time, why you chose to go to school, or why fossil fuels endanger the ozone. You explain yourself to your readers to help them understand what you know about a topic, how you feel about it, and why you feel the way you do. Your readers may not agree with what you're saying, but at least they will understand why you are saying it.

In an essay called "For They Know Not What They Do," which was published in *The Globe and Mail*, in an effort to understand her son's suicide, Edna Weber tries to justify her reactions to her son's announcement that he was homosexual. The essay outlines the family's misunderstandings that have resulted from an intolerant society. The following paragraph from Weber's essay is a good example of the author explaining through justification:

> Still at sea over this astonishing occurrence, I did what Christians do when they don't know what to do: I fell back on the Bible. I read to my son from Leviticus 20:13: "If a man also lie with mankind, as he lieth with a woman, both of them have committed an abomination; they shall surely be put to death...." Then I went on to suggest that maybe his teacher had been right and that his abnormal schedule had resulted in arrested social development; maybe he needed psychiatric help. I offered to pray with him for guidance. But none of this was what my son wanted to hear, and he shook his head sadly and walked out.

In offering this justification, Weber helps us to recognize and understand her reactions and her feelings of being at a loss in a society which is intolerant of difference.

When you're writing a justifying essay, there is no set pattern of organization. These kinds of essays can be ordered in a number of different ways. You'll have to rely on your sense of how your ideas can be most effectively organized.

In the other kind of explaining essay, you might explain how something should be done, or how something works: changing a tire, planting a tree, or making paper. This other kind of explaining essay can be divided into two types: process description and procedure. A **process description** gives readers a general sense of how something happens, but the readers don't have to complete the process themselves. If you were to read an essay called "How a Mosquito is Born" you would soon realize that you are supposed to understand the process a mosquito goes through in order to be born. You aren't supposed to do the steps yourself. Here are some other examples: "How a Car Engine Works;" "How the Canadian Justice System Works;" and "How Tires are Recycled in Alberta." This kind of writing explains something in a general way. Here's a small sample of a process description:

> Quality coffee is roasted, not in big batches, but small 30 to 70 pound batches by a professional master roaster. The beans drop into the roaster for a gentle 12- to 18-minute roast to coax out their character. After the beans roast, they need to cool down quickly to halt the roasting process and protect them from absorbing other flavours and aromas. The beans drop into an air-cooling tray to allow them to return to room temperature.

This is a process description because it explains how something is done, but readers are not expected to carry out any task.

Other times, you'll want to explain how to do something in specific detail so readers understand how something happens and they'll know how to do it themselves. We call this a **procedure**. When you explain a procedure, you want readers to carry out your instructions. You might explain how to drive a standard-shift car, or make a pizza. Other examples of explaining a process come in the form of instruction manuals, maps, menus, and directions for assembling products. Here is a typical example from a recipe book:

> You'll need a mixing bowl, a mixing spoon, measuring utensils, and a 9-inch square pan. In the mixing bowl, mix the following ingredients in the order given, mixing after adding every ingredient:
>
> 1 egg
>
> 1 cup of sugar
>
> 1 teaspoon of soda
>
> 1 teaspoon of vanilla
>
> 1½ cups of flour
>
> 2 cups of fruit cocktail and syrup
>
> ½ cup of chopped nuts
>
> Stir the batter until most of the lumps have disappeared. Then, pour it into a 9-inch square pan. Sprinkle a ¼ cup of brown sugar on the top. Bake at 350 degrees Fahrenheit for 45 minutes.

You can tell that these instructions are supposed to be carried out. Readers are expected to use this writing to complete a task.

Process descriptions and procedures follow a typical pattern. Both begin, most often, by introducing the process or task. In the introduction, the writer helps the reader understand what the situation is like before the process or task begins. Next, process descriptions and procedures show stage by stage or step by step how the process or task moves to completion. Finally, both end by explaining what the situation is like once everything has been completed. You need to make sure you explain yourself carefully enough that you answer any and all of your readers' questions before they arise.

LEARNING FROM PUBLISHED WRITERS

The essay you are about to read, written by Candace Savage, is a fascinating account of different people's understandings of the aurora. It can be classified as process description because it explains the aurora phenomenon. What is different about this process description is that the explanations are based on mythological rather than scientific data.

Before You Read

Focus Your Attention

Before you read this explanation, take a few moments to respond to the following questions in your journal.

1. In the essay you are about to read, Candace Savage sets out various people's explanations for the aurora. What are your experiences of the aurora?
2. Think of a natural phenomenon that you have witnessed that also has mythological explanations. Why do you think those beliefs came about?

Expand Your Vocabulary

Here are some words that are important to your understanding of Savage's essay. Find each word in the essay, and write down a definition of what that word means in the context of the sentence in which it appears.

Benevolence (paragraph 3)

Celestial (paragraph 3)

Decorous (paragraph 4)

Deity (paragraph 5)

Intimations (paragraph 16)

Lurid (paragraph 16)

Circumpolar (paragraph 17)

Macabre (paragraph 17)

Pestilence (paragraph 19)

Portent (paragraphs 19 and 23)

Presage (paragraphs 19 and 23)

Calamitous (paragraph 19)

Conflagrations (paragraph 20)

Penance (paragraph 21)

Placated (paragraph 26)

Candace Savage

Aurora: Myth and Mystery*

"They're scary," my daughter said. Yes. 1

The aurora is both wondrous and alien. In its presence, we may feel delight or dread or some uneasy mixture of conflicting emotions. These responses give us a living connection to the powers that are at work in the heavens. At the same time, our feelings offer us an important connection to other members of the human tribe. Through countless millennia, people have stood and wondered under the polar lights. In different places and times, our ancestors created radically different interpretations of what was going on. But their contradictory emotional responses seem always to have been much the same as our own. 2

On the one hand, the lights appeal to people with their loveliness. Under their spell, the universe may come to life with gaiety and benevolence. Thus, the Eskimos of the lower Yukon River in Alaska described auroras as the dancing souls of their favorite animals: deer, seals, salmon and beluga whales. The Finns were put in mind of magical "fire foxes" that lit up the sky with sparks that flew from their glistening fur. In a similarly joyful mood, the people of the Hebrides thought they could make out a tribe of shining fairies known as the "nimble men." To the Scots the lights were "merry dancers" and to the Swedes a polka, or folk dance. Old-timers in French Canada knew them as "marionettes." A tale from Estonia imagines them as the glow from a celestial wedding, in which horses and sleds of the guests all shine with mysterious radiance. 3

In Scandinavia tradition has it that the lights are the final resting place for the spirits of unmarried women who busy themselves above the mountain Konnunsuo by making fires, cooking fish, dancing and waving their white-gloved hands. "The women of the North are hovering in the air," the Finns used to say, or "Sibylle is burning her woolen blanket." In a less decorous spirit, the Samis of Sweden sometimes addressed the aurora as "Girls running around the fireplace dragging their pants." 4

And if there are half-naked women up there, perhaps there will be childbirth. The Chuvash people of central Asia identified the lights as the god (or goddess) Suratan-tura (Birth-giving Heaven); it was said that the sky gave birth to a son when the lights rolled and writhed. Fittingly, this deity could be called upon to ease women through the pains of labour. There was also a suspicion in some cultures that the lights were connected to the life-giving mysteries of conception. The Lakota Sioux thought the aurora might be the spirits of future generations waiting to be born, and there is an old Chinese record of "the mother of the Yellow Emperor" who, in 2600 B.C., 5

*From *Aurora*. Copyright © 1994 by Candace Savage. Published in Canada by Greystone Books, a division of Douglas and McIntyre. Reprinted by permission of the publisher.

"saw a big lightning circulating around the Su star of Bel Don [in the Big Dipper] with the light shining all over the field" and "then became pregnant." To this day, dozens of Japanese honeymooners visit northern Canada each year, persuaded that children conceived in the spell of the lights will be fortunate.

The aurora has also been thought to enhance the fruitfulness of the earth. A Swedish tradition has it that "when the northern light is burning, the seed will be abundant." Some Nunamiut Eskimos believe that if the sky is divided in half by auroral displays, animals will be plentiful in the area the next day. Dene elder Alexis Arrowmaker says the lights are there to show hunters where they can find the most game. Similarly, Scandinavian fishing people used to interpret the lights as sunshine glinting off schools of herring in the northern sea and, hence, as a welcome omen of rich catches in the offing. **6**

The power of the lights could also be invoked to cure disease. When Knud Rasmussen visited the Inuit of the central Canadian Arctic in the 1920s, he found the aurora to be "in great demand as a helping spirit for the best shamans." It was a basic responsibility of all Inuit healers to make "spirit journeys" into the lights, to obtain advice about treatments and to rescue souls from death. As recently as the 1950s, a healer on Kodiak Island, Alaska, relied on the lights to cure heart ailments. A boy who experienced this procedure remembered that "his mother sent for a woman who held him up to the northern lights and then pulled something out of his chest." Unfortunately, we are not told if he was healed by this treatment. **7**

But we do know of an instance in which the aurora provided religious guidance and spiritual healing to an entire community. It happened among the Lakota Sioux in 1805, when the people wished to revive an important ceremony that had been abandoned several years earlier. Performing the ritual correctly was a matter of life and death, and the leaders were not sure exactly what to do. So, as John Blunt Horn recalled in the early years of this century, the elders and shamans "said they would counsel and make medicine and talk with the spirits and find out about this thing": **8**

> They went into the council lodge and stayed there two days and two nights. . . . And many persons saw ghosts the first night. The second night the ghosts danced so that it was light like the moon (the Aurora Borealis). While the ghosts were dancing, the old men and the wise men and the medicine men came out of the council lodge and danced in a circle around it. Many saw ghosts dancing with them. So all were afraid and went into their tipis. **9**
>
> In the morning one of the old men called aloud to the people to come out of the tipis and look on the sun when it was rising. And all the people came out and stood looking at the sun, and while it was rising, the old man cried in a loud voice that the spirits were pleased, [and] that they had told them how to perform the ceremony ... **10**

And, indeed, after that, the ceremony was revived in a new form, following the auroral spirits' instructions. **11**

Even Christians could sometimes benefit from the aurora's spiritual help. **12** In 1397 a Russian monk named Kirill heard a voice urging him to establish a monastery. When he went to the window, he saw a great aurora radiating over the northern sky and pointing with its fingers towards the chosen location. Guided by this instruction, Kirill established the Kirill-Beloszerskij monastery at White Lake, near Novgorod, a strategic location in which he and his community enjoyed both influence and wealth.

So it seems, in large ways and small, that the aurora can reflect the favour **13** of heaven to humans watching below. The Ottawas of Manitoulin Island in Lake Huron expressed this thought in the form of a myth. According to a tradition recorded in the 1850s by Francis Assikinack, the lights are a message from the creator-hero Nanahboozho, who restored the earth after the Flood and then went to live in the North. Before he left, he told his people that he would always take a deep interest in their well-being. As a sign of his good will, he promised to light large fires that would glow against the sky and appear to the people as the northern lights. Thus, like the rainbow in the Old Testament, the aurora stands as a sign of harmony and trust between humans and their creator.

The Dogrib people have a similar belief—but with a crucial twist. Ac- **14** cording to their mythology, the hero Ithenhiela first laid out the landscape of northwestern Canada and then journeyed to his rest in the Sky Country. He is up there still and sometimes beckons to his people with long, gauzy fingers of lights, calling them to the home he has found for them in the land beyond the sky. But it is a decidedly double-edged message, since to join him you first have to die.

That's the rub, in life and in auroral traditions. *You have to die*, and people **15** have long harboured a suspicion that the lights are somehow implicated in this tragedy. Indeed, the whole of the North has often been mythically linked with death and dying. As mythologist Uno Holmberg points out, since the night is the time when spirits move about, it follows "that the underground world of the dead lies towards the sunset, or towards the dark north." In old Scadinavian texts, the road to Hel always leads "downward and northward," and the way is barred by a "trembling road" and a "flaming whirlpool"—both possible references to the aurora at the boundary between the worlds. "I seemed to be lost between the worlds, while around me burned the fires," laments the shaken narrator of the Hervarar Saga. And while the cold flames of the aurora flickered in the North, cold flames of the same ghastly fire flickered above the graves of the old Norse ancestors.

The Iroquois people were troubled by similar intimations. They imagined **16** the aurora as the entry point into the Land of Souls, where the sky rose and fell to let spirits into the world beyond. For many other northern aboriginal peoples, the lights were seen as the actual spirits of dead ancestors. Sometimes their progress across the sky was interpreted as a torchlight procession or a joyful dance (perhaps inspired by the "cheerful" thought of relatives who would soon die and join them), but more often their erratic movements conjured up alarming images, especially when the lights were tinged a lurid red.

According to a circumpolar tradition shared by Eskimos in Alaska, Inuit of Canada and Greenland, Samis in Scandinavia and Russia, and various Siberian peoples, the northern lights are the souls of those who have died through loss of blood, whether in childbirth, by suicide or through murder. Elevated to the frozen snowfields of the sky, these spirits dash to and fro playing a macabre game of soccer. Sometimes the ball they kick is a human skull; sometimes it is a walrus head. In certain traditions, the head is alive and can be heard chattering its jaws in pleasure or roaring viciously as it slashes at the players with its tusks. According to the Chukchi people of Siberia, spirits who have hanged themselves are honoured spectators at the auroral game. On the rare occasions when they join in the sport, they play awkwardly because of the ropes that still dangle from their necks. The souls of dead infants can be seen up there, too, trailing their long, gory ribbons of afterbirth. **17**

But to many observers, the violent play of the lights did not resemble a game of ball, however bizarre. To them it looked like war. Sometimes the heavenly battle was bloodless and abstract, as in the Finnish belief that the Archangel Michael stood arrayed in light to fight Beelzebub. In that case the aurora was understood to be a fiery warning to resist one's own sinfulness. But usually the conflict was pictured as a literal combat among the souls of those who had died through violence, especially warriors who continued fighting after death. The Samis sometimes referred to the lights as *runtisjammij* ("some who are killed by the use of iron") and described them as quarrelsome spirits that lived together in a large hall. When a brawl broke out among them, they stabbed each other to death, and the floor of their quarters was stained blood red. If blood from an auroral battle rained down over the Hebrides, it might congeal into the coloured pebbles that are known as blood stones or fairy blood. As recently as 1871, an auroral observer in London declared that he had heard the distant clash of weapons when the lights raged overhead. **18**

Bad enough that the very heavens should be aflame with battle; worse yet to know that this sign foretold calamity on earth—death, pestilence, assassination, political upheaval and armed combat. Not surprisingly, this portent was most troubling for people who lived outside the auroral zone where strange lights in the night sky were a rare and terrible occurrence. (As it happens, the great auroras that appear at low latitudes are also more likely to be red, which gives them an even more threatening appearance.) Thus the Roman author Pliny the Elder declared in 112 B.C. "there is no presage of woe more calamitous to the human race" than "a flame in the sky," or a display of the northern lights. **19**

Who could doubt it then or since? In 507 A.D. the citizens of Rome awoke to the sight of glowing armies in the sky and sounds of ghostly trumpets, just as their empire crumbled under an attack by the Longobards. Several hundred years later, Henry of Huntingdon saw the skies of Northumberland, England, aflame with light and sparks and took it as a sign of terrible bloodshed and conflagrations to follow—predictions that were tragically confirmed during an ill-fated rebellion in 1138. **20**

By the late Middle Ages, a brilliant display of aurora caused total, pathetic panic among Europeans. People fainted and went mad at the sight. Even in the sixteenth century, country people were so alarmed by these signs of divine displeasure that they poured out of their villages to make penance at many cathedrals. Thus, as auroral scholar Alfred Angot reports, **21**

> In the month of September 1583 eight or nine hundred persons of all ages and both sexes, with their lords, came to Paris in procession, dressed like penitents or pilgrims ... "to say their prayers and make their offerings in the great church at Paris; and they said that they were moved to this penitential journey because of signs seen in heaven and fires in the air, even towards the quarter of the Ardennes, whence had come the first such penitents, to the number of ten or twelve thousand, to Our Lady of Rheims and to Liesse." The chronicler adds that this pilgrimage was followed a few days afterwards by five others, and for the same cause. **22**

More than three centuries later, on 13 October 1917, Our Lady of the Rosary, Mother of God, appeared miraculously to three children in Fatima, Portugal, and warned of "a night illuminated by an unknown light" when a "terrible war will begin." And, just as prophesied, on 25 January 1938, the heavens over western Europe "filled with a strange and terrible crimson fire" that, to some, presaged the Nazi invasion of Austria three months afterward. Four years later, violent displays of the aurora flared over the United States for three nights straight, as far south as Cleveland, Ohio—an awful portent, it was later said, of the Japanese assault on Pearl Harbor. **23**

By treating the lights with holy dread, people have traditionally attempted to keep their evil influences at a distance. The auroral spirits can be spiteful and easily irritated. A folktale from Norway tells of a boy who dared to chant at them– **24**

> The northern light is running lip, lip, lip **25**
> with fat in its mouth lip. Lip, lip
> with a hammer in its skull lip, lip, lip
> with an axe on its back lip, lip, lip –

whereupon the lights zoomed down and burned him to a crisp.

Although some traditions suggest the aurora can be placated by singing, most northern peoples agree that whistling and singing at the lights are highly risky. The lights get aroused when they hear these sounds and think they are being teased. At the very least, they run faster and writhe into new forms; at worst, they take offense and come plunging down. People are said to have been blinded, paralyzed and decapitated by these assaults; others have been abducted into the lights' cold brilliance. In French Canada, a fiddler who charmed the lights with his music was seized by the rays and bewitched. **26**

"When the Aurora Borealis falls," warns a Gwich'in text, "when it runs close to man, the human brain goes mad and man is seized by the Heart and **27** killed. That is why we are frightened of it and why we reject it utterly and have done for a long time."

To people who live in the spirit-filled world or traditional cultures, one fact was clear. The forces that dance in the polar dark are awe-inspiring—alien, uncontrollable and immensely vigorous. With that conclusion, at least, modern science would have no argument. **28**

QUESTIONS FOR CRITICAL THINKING

THINKING CRITICALLY ABOUT CONTENT

1. Why do you think Candace Savage provides us with only brief glimpses of these particular mythologies? Why does she include so many myths?
2. Why do you think Savage chooses to provide more detail about a few specific myths such as the Lakota Sioux myth (paragraphs 8-11) and the Norwegian folktale (paragraph 25)?

THINKING CRITICALLY ABOUT PURPOSE

3. In your view, what is Candace Savage's purpose in this essay? Explain your answer.
4. Why does she include her first line, the words of her daughter who does not appear in the rest of the essay?

THINKING CRITICALLY ABOUT AUDIENCE

5. What group of readers would be most interested in this essay? Why?
6. Why does Savage end with the final line that she does? To whom, specifically, is it addressed?

THINKING CRITICALLY ABOUT PERSPECTIVE

7. Describe in a complete sentence the writer's perspective. How do you know this? Choose specific examples from her essay to support your answer.

LEARNING FROM YOUR PEERS

Explaining through speaking is often easier than it is in writing. When you have conversations, you know from the expressions of those with whom you are conversing that they understand or that you have provided them with too much or too little information. When you write, however, you must anticipate how much information is needed by your particular audience. If you don't explain yourself fully, clearly, and convincingly, your readers will be confused and frustrated. If you provide them with too much information they may lose interest in your topic. To see how one person learned to compose an explanation, we will follow the writing process of a student named Eden Bailey.

Eden's Writing Assignment: Explaining

This is the topic Eden's instructor assigned:

All of us possess an amazing variety of skills that we take for granted: tuning up a car, shopping for the best bargains in fashion, planning and cooking a formal dinner, even pursuing childhood hobbies such as collecting stamps or baseball cards. Explain to an audience of your peers a complicated process that you have learned. Be as specific and clear as possible.

Eden goes through the process as outlined in Chapter 1: generating ideas, planning, developing, organizing, drafting, revising, and editing.

Generating Ideas

Eden is a "senior citizen" in her writing class. She married during her first year of college, raised a family, and is back in school to finish her degree; she hopes to graduate at the same time as her oldest child. Eden's first reaction to this assignment is that she does not know how to do anything special. She approaches the assignment by freewriting.

> Well, this is bound to be interesting. I sure don't know how to tune up a car. I've never collected stamps. I can cook, but a really elaborate meal at our house these days means sprinkling some almonds on the salad from the Healthy Sprouts Deli.
>
> Sometimes I long for the good old days I thought I was tied to the house when the kids were tiny. They seemed to need food or sleep all the time, and it was just easiest to stay until they could walk around on their own. I used to sit and sew while they napped. That sounds good about now. No cares in the world. Just the creative process unfolding before me. I made quilts for every baby and all the relatives. Not to mention wall hangings and potholders. I've still managed to get to some quilt shows and keep up my membership in my quilt guild. Perhaps I could write about making quilts. I guess most people wouldn't know about that.

Planning

Eden meets with her peer editing group once a week. At the next meeting, she asks them what they think about her topic. They all tell her that they know nothing about quilting, not even what questions to ask, so in the library after class Eden starts listing everything she knows about quilts.

What I know about quilts:

- Different types: pieced, appliquéd, whole-cloth.
- Different sizes: wall hangings, baby bed quilts, regular bed quilts.
- Colour combinations—wild, contemporary to traditional, subdued.
- How to make one: start with the top; add the stuffing; add the backing.
- Stitch through the sandwich.
- Take small stitches; don't create any toe catchers.
- Quilter's idea of a dream vacation: go to big quilt shows, go to lots of quilt and fabric shops, take seminars with famous quilters. (Why does my family always want to go to the ocean, where there is no quilt shop for miles around?)
- Even cowboys quilt. It's not just for old ladies!

Developing

Eden's list gives her peer editing group a basis for asking her questions when she meets with them again. This is what they ask:

1. What is the difference between pieced, appliquéd, and whole-cloth quilts?
2. How did you learn to quilt? Did you always know how to sew?
3. Were there any other quilters in your family?
4. What is the most common size for a quilt?
5. Do most people use quilts just to sleep under?
6. What kinds of quilts do cowboys make?

Eden then answers these questions in her journal, letting her mind run freely over the details of her quilting experiences and the memories they trigger. Here are her journal entries:

1. Pieced quilts are made up of small pieces of fabric—often remnants of cloth or cut-up clothing, old pillow cases and sheets—that are laid out and sewn together in geometric designs of several colours. Whole-cloth and appliquéd quilts start with large pieces of new material. Their design comes from what is added to their base fabric; an appliquéd quilt has pieces shaped in specific designs (flowers, stars, eagles) sewn to its base, and a whole-cloth quilt's design comes from the pattern of its quilting stitches.
2. When I was very young, I stayed with my grandmother during the day. To keep me busy, she taught me how to sew. Grandmother would give me scraps of materials that I would cut, baste, and sew into clothes for my dolls. As I began to sew

more complicated things, I started making dolls. Eventually, I checked out books from the library about quilting. I found one about doll quilts. Grandmother and I would rummage through her scrap box and piece together pretty quilts for each of my favourite dolls.

3. I am the first quilter in my family; however, my grandmother Marian was a seamstress. She would make me pretty frilly dresses, drapes for my bedroom, and satin pillowcases for my bed, and she sewed all of her dresses for church. From my grandmother I learned how to make lasting stitches and small neat stitches, to choose fabrics for my sewing projects, and to design and lay out my quilts tops.
4. The most common quilt size is the double. A double quilt will fit on a double bed or a queen-sized bed. A dust ruffle is often used with a double quilt on a queen-sized bed.
5. Yes, most people sleep under quilts; however, quilts are also used in decorating. We often see quilts hanging from walls in country-style homes, quilted throw pillows and wall hangings, and quilted Christmas tree ornaments and table runners.
6. Cowboys made tied quilts. These were made from scraps of material cut from their own clothes, blankets, and bedding. The pieces were stitched together to form a top. This top would be attached to an old blanket and stuffed with batting. Then the cowboy would take yarn and tie the top, batting, and base together in sections. The edges would be sewn together as well. The tied quilts were not the prettiest quilts made during that time, but they were functional—they kept the cowboys warm.

Organizing

Eden does her best writing in the library, away from the telephone and the distractions of home. She usually goes to the library at least three evenings a week to read, write, or do research. She has a favourite table that is hidden in a corner, and she likes the solitude there for writing. She looks at her list of questions and her "What I know" list and starts making notes so she can organize her essay. Then she underlines key words that identify the topic or main idea in each entry:

What I like best about quilting—the unique creations, completely my own.

I cannot remember when I started to sew. I think I always had a needle and thread in my hand. I made dolls and doll quilts when I was a child. Later, I did some for my kids. In between, I learned how to do pillows and wall hangings and table runners, all the usual stuff.

You make a quilt the same way you make a sandwich. Start with the top and bottom and put a batting layer in between.

Your top can be appliquéd, pieces, or whole-cloth. This depends on the effect you want and how good you are at any of the skills. They all demand different talents. Patience, of course, is something you need no matter what.

All quilters love to find out what is new in their craft. They like to go to quilting shops and read quilting magazines and get new equipment.

Quilting as my profession.

Eden looks at her notes and decides that, since she knows her subject so well, she is ready to start writing.

Drafting

Eden's Essay: First Draft

Main Idea: People make quilts for different reasons, but I use quilting to express myself.

My hobby is making quilts. I liked nothing better than spending hours in my sewing room with a huge stack of books and little pieces of fabric. Sketching ideas and trying them out, creating something that no one else will ever duplicate. I give my hobby a great deal of creative energy. Using quilting as a way to express myself.

I cannot remember when I started sewing, but I must have been very young. Some of my first library books. These were about making dolls. I used to try to duplicate the ones that I saw in the pictures. But I never had the right materials, so they never turned out very well. One of my favourite books. Had instructions to make some simple doll quilts. My efforts at the doll quilts were more successful than my doll-making ventures. Which frustrated me to no end. Even though my doll quilts would not have won any prizes. I was persistent. I kept trying until I developed some colour sense, and I learned as much as possible about my hobby. No one in my family had ever made quilts, so I had to work on my own. To learn everything from books.

After the doll quilts, I made several small projects like potholders and placemats and tote bags. After a few years, I started developing more confidence in my design abilities, and I started making more complicated projects. I experimented with colour combinations and block patterns. Learning how to sew projects very rapidly on the sewing machine. Traditional quilting was done by hand, but that is one tradition that I am willing to break. A hundred years ago, quilters probably worked by candlelight, but that did not make their quilts any better. It just ruined their eyesight at an early age.

To make a quilt, you start out with the top layer, which is where the designs appear. There are three basic methods of construction for quilts. The ones we see most often are pieced quilts. Appliquéd quilts are made by using a base fabric and sewing smaller pieces onto it. The last category of quilts is the whole-cloth quilt.

Once the quilt top is made, another piece of fabric is cut to match it, this will form the backing. Then a piece of batting or stuffing (or wadding, as the British call it) is cut to form the filling of the sandwich. This makes the quilt squeezable. The sandwich is temporarily fastened together with safety pins or long, loose stitches called basting stitches then the work of quilting begins. Quilting stitches go through all three layers and follow many different kinds of designs. Some of the pieced quilts are outlined with quilting. Appliquéd quilts are interesting and intricate. Often have quilting stitches around the designs and large areas where quilting stitches form the only design. Whole-cloth quilts follow the planned design very carefully, because there is nothing to distract the viewer's eye from the patterns formed by the stitches. Quilting stitches were traditionally done by hand, and the skill of the person doing the stitches was very obvious. The most desirable stitches are tiny puckers. In the fabric. Some expert quilters can make 20 stitches to the inch. Large, loose stitches are called toe-catchers because if people were to sleep under a quilt with loopy stitches, they might catch their toes in the loops. Machine stitching has made it possible to disguise a person's lack of talent with hand stitching, but it requires a completely different set of skills, and some people prefer to keep tradition.

Most quilters I have met would rather quilt than do anything else in their spare time. Many of them belong to one or more quilting guilds. Organizations whose members challenge each other to develop their skills and encourage and praise each other when they finish a project or try something different. For vacations, they go to national or international quilt shows. Shopping trips are not complete unless they include a stop at the fabric store. To see what is new. The best days of the month for them are the days they find new issues of the quilting magazines in their mailboxes at least an hour is required to look at each new magazine and fantasize about making a multitude of new projects. If it has been too long since a magazine arrived. A trip to a bookstore or quilt shop to check out the latest shipment of books is the next-best solution.

Most people know that women used every scrap of fabric they could find. Recycling these bits into works of functional art for everyone in their families to enjoy. I saw one once at an art show and it had little faces woven into it. Men too. Some quilts were even made by cowboys on the range. They salvaged the good parts of the garments and tied them together to make "tied quilts" that served as rugged bedrolls and saddle blankets. When their work clothing was worn out.

Although quilting is my hobby, I hope someday to make it my profession. In the meantime, I am not going to quit my day job. I am going to study graphic design and accounting to make sure that I will always be able to make a living and afford to buy all the quilt books and fabric that my heart desires.

Revising

Eden feels that her first draft says what she wants it to say. Writing about this hobby that has been a part of her life since she was a child was satisfying in many ways. But she knows she still has to revise her work. Eden's instructor has asked the class to focus on different methods of developing their ideas. If the student writers can develop their ideas fully at this point in the course, they can build on this ability for the rest of the term as their writing gets more complex.

Eden reviews the Checklist for Developing an Essay at the beginning of the Focus on Essays section of this chapter. Right now, the instructor wants the students to work with whole essays, not just with isolated parts, and to concentrate on the relationship of ideas to one another. The instructor explains that these methods of development are really ways of thinking and processing information. These skills will help them, insists the instructor, in all of their classes. That's all Eden needs to hear to take these guidelines seriously; she has learned that developing her ideas is a part of everything she does.

Eden reads the Focus on Essays section and does all the assigned exercises. She learns that an idea can be developed in one of seven ways (definition, description, example, classification, cause-effect, comparison-contrast, and analysis) and that the method of development must be suited to the idea. So Eden takes her essay apart paragraph by paragraph, checking to see whether her ideas are developed as fully as possible and in the most appropriate way for what she is trying to say. She finds problems in her essay and sets out to improve each paragraph so that her essay as a whole will be more effective.

Then, she turns her attention to the Focus on Paragraphs section to learn about paragraph focus and unity. She does the assigned exercises, and once again looks over her essay draft.

Collaborative Work

Peer Group Activity

After you read the portions of the Focus on Essays and Focus on Paragraphs sections that your instructor assigns, turn to Eden's first draft (pp. 75–77) and complete the following tasks in small groups:

A. Underline the topic sentence in each of Eden's body paragraphs.

B. Put brackets around any sections of the essay that are not fully developed.

C. In the margin, suggest a method for expanding the undeveloped sections you identified: definition, description, examples, classification, cause-effect, comparison-contrast, and analysis. (For definitions, see pp. 85–90.)

D. Use a wavy line to identify sentences that your group thinks do not logically fit in their current paragraphs.

E. Put a slash between sentences that are not related to each other.

Compare the brackets and underlining your group recorded with those your instructor will show you. Where do your marks differ from your instructor's? What do you need to review before writing your own essay?

Class Activity

As an entire class, look at the underlined portions of Eden's revised draft (pp. 79–82) to see how she changed each sentence.

A. Did you identify the revision problems that Eden corrected?

B. Do you think her changes are good ones? Discuss her changes.

Editing

Now that Eden's paragraphs are fully developed, she needs to do some final proofreading and editing before handing in her essay. The instructor helps the students see the importance of choosing correct forms and tenses for verbs in each sentence. So Eden shifts her focus from the content of the essay to the finer matters of individual sentences. She reads the relevant Focus on Sentences section in the appendix and reviews how to recognize a verb, and then learns some tips about strengthening this core part of the sentence.

Collaborative Work

Peer Group Activity

After you read Focus on Sentences in the appendix, turn again to Eden's first draft and complete the following tasks in small groups.

A. Look at each sentence. Does each sentence contain a verb? Circle each verb.

B. Put an asterisk (*) by each verb that is not in the correct tense.

C. Put a number sign (#) by each verb that is not in the right form.

Compare the marks your group recorded with those your instructor will show you. Where do your marks differ from your instructor's? What do you need to review before writing your own essay?

Eden's Revised Essay

~~Main Idea: People make quilts for different reasons, but I use quilting to express myself.~~

Quilts

My hobby is making quilts. ~~I liked~~Quilts began as an economy measure; women used scraps from outgrown clothing or other sewing projects to provide warm covers for their families. Quilts basically consist of a top layer of pieces of fabric and a bottom layer of whole cloth with stuffing between the layers. Today, many people consider quilts an art form. I like nothing better than spending hours in my sewing room with a huge stack of books and little pieces of ~~fabric. Sketching~~fabric, sketching ideas and trying them out, creating something that no one else will ever duplicate. At times like these, I feel like an artist who creates a great mural like the one on the ceiling of the Sistine Chapel. I give my hobby a great deal of creative ~~energy. Using~~energy, using quilting as a way to express myself.

I cannot remember when I started sewing, but I must have been very young. Some of my first library books~~. These~~ were about making dolls. I used to try to duplicate the ones that I saw in the pictures. But I never had the right materials, so they never turned out very well. One of my ~~favourite books. Had~~favourite books had instructions to make some simple doll quilts. My efforts at the doll quilts were more successful than my doll-making ~~ventures. Which~~ventures, which frustrated me to no end. Even though my doll quilts would not have won any ~~prizes.~~prizes, I was persistent. I kept trying until I developed some colour sense, and I learned as much as possible about my hobby. No one in my family had ever made quilts, so I had to work on my ~~own. To~~own to learn everything from books.

After the doll quilts, I made several small projects like potholders and placemats and tote bags. Once I quilted a set of placemats in flower designs for a Mother's Day gift. My mom particularly loves the one that looks like a bouquet of bright red poppies and another that looks like a huge sunflower. After a few years, I started developing more confidence in my design abilities, and I started making more complicated projects: lap quilts, pillows, wall hangings, and a few bed quilts. I experimented with colour combinations and block patterns. Learning how to sew projects very rapidly on the sewing machine gave me confidence. Traditional quilting was done by hand, but that is one tradition that I am willing to break. A hundred years ago, quilters probably worked by candlelight, but that did not make their quilts any better. It just ruined their eyesight at an early age.

To make a quilt, you start out with the top layer, which is where the designs appear. There are three basic methods of construction for quilts. The ones we see most often are pieced quilts made of small pieces of fabric sewn together, forming geometric designs of many colours. Appliquéd quilts are made by using a base fabric and sewing smaller pieces onto it, forming flowers ~~it.~~or animals or other more complicated designs. The last category of quilts is the whole-cloth ~~quilt.~~ quilt made by taking one large piece of fabric and stitching an elaborate design that will cover the whole surface with quilting stitches.

Once the quilt top is made, another piece of fabric is cut to match ~~it, this~~it. This will form the backing. Then a piece of batting or stuffing (or wadding, as the British call it) is cut to form the filling of the sandwich. This makes the quilt squeezable. The sandwich is temporarily fastened together with safety pins or long, loose stitches called basting ~~stitches then~~stitches. Then the work of quilting begins. Quilting stitches go through all three layers and follow many different kinds of designs. Some of the pieced quilts are outlined with quilting. Appliqued quilts are interesting and ~~intricate. Often have~~intricate, often having quilting stitches around the designs and large areas where quilting stitches form the only design. Whole-cloth quilts follow the planned design very carefully, because there is nothing to distract the viewer's eye from the patterns formed by the stitches. They are like beautiful tapestries we often see in museums. Quilting stitches were traditionally done by hand, and the skill of the person doing the stitches was very obvious. The most desirable stitches are tiny ~~puckers. In~~puckers in the fabric. Some expert quilters can make 20 stitches to the inch. Large, loose stitches are called toe-catchers because if people were to sleep under a quilt with loopy stitches, they might catch their toes in the loops. Machine stitching has made it possible to disguise a person's lack of talent with hand stitching, but it requires a completely different set of skills, and some people prefer to keep tradition.

Most quilters I have met would rather quilt than do anything else in their spare time. Many of them belong to one or more quilting ~~guilds.~~

~~Organizations~~guilds, organizations whose members challenge each other to develop their skills and encourage and praise each other when they finish a project or try something different. For vacations, they go to national or international quilt shows. Shopping trips are not complete unless they include a stop at the fabric ~~store. To~~store to see what is new. The best days of the month for them are the days they find new issues of the quilting magazines in their ~~mailboxes a~~tmailboxes. At least an hour is required to look at each new magazine and fantasize about making a multitude of new projects. If it has been too long since a magazine ~~arrived. A~~arrived, a trip to a bookstore or quilt shop to check out the latest shipment of books is the next-best solution.

Every time I see a quilt, I am reminded of the sewing skills of our frugal, hardworking ancestors. Most people know that women used every scrap of ~~fabric they could find. Recycling~~fabric, material usually left over from sewing projects and pieces of worn clothing. They worked hard to recycle these bits into works of functional art for everyone in their families to enjoy. You may be surprised, however, to ~~I saw one once at an art show and it had little faces woven into it. Men too. Some~~find out that some quilts were even made by cowboys on the range. When their work clothing was worn ~~They~~out, they salvaged the good parts of the garments and tied them together to make "tied quilts" that served as rugged bedrolls and saddle ~~blankets. When their work clothing was worn out.~~ blankets.

Although quilting is my hobby, I hope someday to make it my profession. In the meantime, I am not going to quit my day job, and I am planning my college career so that it will both benefit my job now and help me convert my hobby into a business later. I am going to study graphic design and accounting to make sure that I will always be able to make a living and afford to buy all the quilt books and fabric that my heart desires. In addition, the effect of taking these courses is to make me a better quilter who can run her own business when the time comes.

Collaborative Work

Practise Outlining

Spend time as a class generating ideas, planning, developing, and organizing a potential explaining essay.

1. Spend about five minutes brainstorming potential topics for an explaining essay.
2. Discuss what makes one topic better than another.
3. Choose one to work with and decide on the audience and purpose.
4. List the main points that the writer might include if he or she were to write this essay.
5. Organize the details in the best order for the best effect.
   Could you write this essay? What changes would you make?

WRITING YOUR OWN EXPLAINING ESSAY

So far, you have seen a professional writer and a fellow student at work trying to explain an experience or process they felt was worth talking about. As you read the published essay and followed the writing process of another student from first to final draft, you absorbed ideas and ways of giving those ideas a form of their own. These reading and writing activities have prepared you to write your own essay explaining an experience or process that is meaningful to you.

What Have You Discovered?

Before you begin your own writing task, let's review what you have learned in this chapter so far:

- Explaining is an essential part of all forms of communication.
- Explaining in writing is more difficult than explaining in speech because you cannot get immediate feedback from readers about the clarity of your message.
- Explaining falls into two categories: (1) justifying and (2) procedures and process description.
- Organize your ideas to explain effectively.
- To help you shape your essay, learn as much as possible about your readers.
- Before you write a draft, decide on a perspective toward your subject.
- After you write a draft, revise your essay for meaning and organization.
- After you revise, edit for grammar, usage, and sentence structure.

Your Writing Topic

Choose one of the following topics for your explaining essay:

1. In the professional essay that you read at the beginning of this chapter, "Aurora: Myth and Mystery," Candace Savage explains the significance of the aurora for various peoples. Rather than providing a scientific explanation, she provides a series of mythologies. Write an essay in which you explain the mythological significance of another natural phenomenon that is of interest to you.
2. Create an explaining "myth" for a particular phenomenon that is often shrouded in mystery. Make certain that the myth clearly explains the phenomenon and its significance to a particular group of people.
3. Explain an incident that made you appreciate your own life and circumstances more deeply. This event may have been something that happened to you personally, an event in the news, or segments of a novel or film that changed your perspective. Explain the incident and your response to it so that your classmates can understand its impact on your life.
4. Have you ever taken on a project or a job that required organization and specific skills? You may have decorated a room, planted a garden, or constructed a model ship or airplane. You may have worked on a job that required you to learn a special method of doing things. Write an essay in which you explain the methods and skills you learned in completing your project. (Some examples of what *not* to do might help make your point with your readers.)
5. Create your own explaining topic (with the assistance of your instructor), and write a response to it.

When you have selected one of these topics, you may begin your writing process in the same way Eden did. (You may find her experience helpful in giving you ideas.) This time your purpose is to write your own explaining essay. If some tasks occur out of order, that adjustment is probably part of your personal writing ritual. Follow your instincts, but make sure you've worked through all the parts of the writing process to your final draft.

Then, turn in your revised draft to your instructor.

Reflect on Your Writing Process

When you have completed your own essay, answer these four questions in your journal:

1. What was most difficult about this assignment?
2. What was easiest?
3. What did I learn about explaining by completing this assignment?
4. What did I learn about my own writing process: how I prepared to write, how I wrote the first draft, how I revised, and how I edited?

Developing an Essay

Checklist for Developing an Essay

- ✓ Are the writer's ideas developed fully and completely in each paragraph?
- ✓ Are the methods of reasoning used in the essay best for what is being said at different points in the essay: definition, description, examples, classification, cause-effect, comparison-contrast, and analysis?

A gardener begins with a controlling idea—a design for a beautiful outdoor garden. Then he or she spends days, months, even years developing that garden. The gardener may plant a hedge of roses to define the space, select one beautiful and rare plant to stand alone as a focal point, build a pool and install a fountain, or follow various other plans to develop the garden to fit the original idea.

Developing paragraphs in essays can be like developing a garden, though the task shouldn't take years the way gardens often do. Just as a garden would be bland and boring if all the beds contained the same kinds of plants, or blooms of only one colour, so, too, would an essay if only one type of development method were used. Most writers, like most gardeners, mix a number of methods for developing an essay and its paragraphs so that the whole essay is colourful and meaningful. They usually choose from the following methods: defining, describing, giving examples, classifying, assigning cause-effect, comparing-contrasting, and analyzing.

Definition

When you explain the meaning of a term, you are **defining** it so that your audience understands specifically what you mean. For example, in the professional essay in this chapter, Candace Savage might have defined the term aurora if she felt that her audience would be unfamiliar with the phenomenon. She might have provided a scientific definition, something about the electrically charged particles in the atmosphere, or a brief dictionary definition that describes the coloured bands of light in the night sky, but because she wants her readers to be immersed in the mythological explanations for the aurora, she deliberately avoids defining the term. Because the essay itself provides a mythological explanation and definition, a definition is not necessary.

As Eden Bailey began to revise her essay, she decided that paragraph one in her first draft about her quilting hobby would be better developed if she included a definition of quilting:

First Draft: My hobby is making quilts. I liked nothing better than spending hours in my sewing room with a huge stack of books and little pieces of fabric. Sketching ideas and trying them out, creating something that no one else will ever duplicate. I give my hobby a great deal of creative energy. Using quilting as a way to express myself.

Revision: My hobby is making quilts. **Quilts began as an economy measure; women used scraps from outgrown clothing or other sewing projects to provide warm covers for their families. Quilts basically consist of a top layer of pieces of fabric and a bottom layer of whole cloth with stuffing between the layers. Today, many people consider quilts an art form.** I like nothing better than spending hours in my sewing room with a huge stack of books and little pieces of fabric, sketching ideas and trying them out, creating something that no one else will ever duplicate. **At times like these, I feel like an artist who creates a great mural like the one on the ceiling of the Sistine Chapel.** I give my hobby a great deal of creative energy, using quilting as a way to express myself.

Eden defines not only quilting, a term that might be unfamiliar to her audience, but also her role as a quilter, comparing it to an artist. Now her audience is sure to understand her paragraph.

Description

A **description** uses words to draw a picture of a place, an object, a person, group, or a situation. It gives a fine level of detail that can make a subject come alive for the reader. For example, in paragraph four of his essay in Chapter 2, Tommy Poulos paints a vivid picture of the young boy locked in the freezer:

> Suddenly the cooling unit for the freezer kicked on with a loud roar. The air became even colder and drier. My lungs felt like there were hundreds of needles poking at them in all directions. I could feel my nostrils sticking together. My eyes hurt. I moved to the other corner of the freezer, hoping it would be slightly warmer than near the cooling unit, but there was no improvement. My stupid curiosity had done me in.

Eden decided that she could develop her fourth paragraph by describing the three construction methods for quilts:

First Draft: To make a quilt, you start out with the top layer, which is where the designs appear. There are three basic methods of construction for quilts. The ones we see most often are pieced quilts. Appliquéd quilts are made by using a base fabric and sewing smaller pieces onto it. The last category of quilts is the whole-cloth quilt.

Revision: To make a quilt, you start out with the top layer, which is where the designs appear. There are three basic methods of construction for quilts. The ones we see most often are pieced quilts **made of small pieces of fabric sewn together, forming geometric designs of many colours.** Appliquéd quilts are made by using a base fabric and sewing smaller pieces onto it**, forming flowers or animals or other more complicated designs**. The last category of quilts is the whole-cloth quilt **made by taking one large piece of fabric and stitching an elaborate design that will cover the whole surface with quilting stitches.**

Now Eden's readers know exactly what the three kinds of quilts are and how they are made because she has described them.

Examples

If a picture is worth a thousand words, then writing an **example** is priceless. Giving an example of something you are writing about is a technique that shows your readers what you mean. Candace Savage's essay in this chapter explains primarily through examples. Paragraph three provides seven examples of how "the universe may come to life with gaiety and benevolence" under the influence of the aurora:

> On the one hand, the lights appeal to people with their loveliness. Under their spell, the universe may come to life with gaiety and benevolence. Thus, the Eskimos of the lower Yukon River in Alaska described auroras as the dancing souls of their favorite animals: deer, seals, salmon and beluga whales. The Finns were put in mind of magical "fire foxes" that lit up the sky with sparks that flew from their glistening fur. In a similarly joyful mood, the people of the Hebrides thought they could make out a tribe of shining fairies known as the "nimble men." To the Scots the lights were "merry dancers" and to the Swedes a polka, or folk dance. Old-timers in French Canada knew them as "marionettes." A tale from Estonia imagines them as the glow from a celestial wedding, in which horses and sleds of the guests all shine with mysterious radiance.

Studying her essay, Eden decided to give an example of one of her early projects so that she could show rather than tell her readers about this stage of her quilting abilities. As Eden revised paragraph three, she included some details about a gift that especially pleased her mother.

First Draft: After the doll quilts, I made several small projects like potholders and placemats and tote bags.

Revision: After the doll quilts, I made several small projects like potholders and placemats and tote bags. **Once I quilted a set of placemats in flower designs for a Mother's Day gift. My mom particularly loves the one that looks like a bouquet of bright red poppies and another that looks like a huge sunflower.**

This addition makes Eden's paragraph much more lively and interesting to read.

Classification

Another way to develop an idea is by **classification**, grouping similar items in a paragraph. People might be classified by occupation, hobbies, regions where they live, political beliefs, and so on. For example, in a paragraph in an essay called "Words," essayist William Zinsser groups the many synonyms for the word villain that can be found in *Roget's Thesaurus*:

> Look up "villain," for instance, and you'll be awash in such rascality as only a lexicographer could conjure back from centuries of iniquity, obliquity, depravity, knavery, profligacy, frailty, flagrancy, infamy, immorality, corruption, wickedness, wrongdoing, backsliding, and sin.

Eden decided she could improve her essay by classifying. In paragraph 3, she added more examples of complicated projects:

First Draft: After a few years, I started developing more confidence in my design abilities, and I started making more complicated projects.

Revision: After a few years, I started developing more confidence in my design abilities, and I started making more complicated projects: **lap quilts, pillows, wall hangings, and a few bed quilts.**

These categories help her readers more fully understand the types of quilts she made.

Cause-Effect

Explaining causes that lead to a particular effect or the effect that results from a particular cause is an important tool for writers. The papers that you will need to write for your other courses in college—history and science, for example—often draw on making **cause-effect** connections. Candace Savage uses cause-effect reasoning in paragraph 27 of "Aurora: Myth and Mystery" to explain why some people are afraid of the Northern Lights:

> "When the Aurora Borealis falls," warns a Gwich'in text, "when it runs close to man, the human brain goes mad and man is seized by the Heart and killed. That is why we are frightened of it and why we reject it utterly and have done for a long time."

Eden found a place in paragraph eight of her draft that could be improved with the use of cause-effect reasoning:

First Draft: Although quilting is my hobby, I hope someday to make it my profession. In the meantime, I am not going to quit my day job. I am going to study graphic design and accounting to make sure that I will always be able to make a living and afford to buy all the quilt books and fabric that my heart desires.

Revision: Although quilting is my hobby, I hope someday to make it my profession. In the meantime, I am not going to quit my day job**, and I am planning my college career so that it will both benefit my job now and help me convert my hobby into a business later.** I am going to study graphic design and accounting to make sure that I will always be able to make a living and afford to buy all the quilt books and fabric that my heart desires. **In addition, the effect of taking these courses is to make me a better quilter who can run her own business when the time comes.**

With these additions, Eden clarifies the relationship between taking certain college courses and her career goals.

Comparison-Contrast

When you point out similarities, you are using **comparison** to develop your ideas. When you emphasize differences, you are using **contrast**. To make your ideas clear about things in the same category, the **comparison-contrast** technique is useful. It is another skill that will prove helpful in other courses such as literature or political science. In the professional essay, Savage compares various stories about the lights' reaction to people whistling and singing:

> Although some traditions suggest the aurora can be placated by singing, most northern peoples agree that whistling and singing at the lights are highly risky. The lights get aroused when they hear these sounds and think they are being teased. At the very least, they run faster and writhe into new forms; at worst, they take offense and come plunging down. People are said to have been blinded, paralyzed and decapitated by these assaults; others have been abducted into the lights' cold brilliance. In

> French Canada, a fiddler who charmed the lights with his music was seized by the rays and bewitched.

Eden decided to use comparison-contrast to make paragraph 5 of her essay more informative:

First Draft: Whole-cloth quilts follow the planned design very carefully, because there is nothing to distract the viewer's eye from the patterns formed by the stitches.

Revision: Whole-cloth quilts follow the planned design very carefully, because there is nothing to distract the viewer's eye from the patterns formed by the stitches. **They are like beautiful tapestries we often see in museums.**

With this addition, Eden helps her audience make a connection between her description of whole-cloth quilts and tapestries in museums.

Analysis

To **analyze** an idea, you must first break it into its basic parts. Then you need to explain the relationship between those parts. Analysis is a major component of essays on many serious topics. You might find this skill especially useful in writing for sociology, science, and psychology classes.

In paragraph two of the professional essay in this chapter, Savage begins to analyze people's reactions to the aurora:

> The aurora is both wondrous and alien. In its presence, we may feel delight or dread or some uneasy mixture of conflicting emotions. These responses give us a living connection to the powers that are at work in the heavens. At the same time, our feelings offer us an important connection to other members of the human tribe. Through countless millennia, people have stood and wondered under the polar lights. In different places and times, our ancestors created radically different interpretations of what was going on. But their contradictory emotional responses seem always to have been much the same as our own.

Eden found a weak example of analysis in paragraph four of her essay, so she strengthened the paragraph with more detailed information:

First Draft: To make a quilt, you start out with the top layer, which is where the designs appear. There are three basic methods of construction for quilts. The ones we see most often are pieced quilts. Appliquéd quilts are made by using a base fabric and sewing smaller pieces onto it. The last category of quilts is the whole-cloth quilt.

Revision: To make a quilt, you start out with the top layer, which is where the designs appear. There are three basic methods of construction for quilts. The ones we see most often are pieced quilts **made of small pieces of fabric sewn together, forming geometric designs of many colours.** Appliquéd quilts are made by using a base fabric and sewing smaller pieces onto it**, forming flowers or animals or other more complicated designs.** The last category of quilts is the whole-cloth quilt **made by taking one large piece of fabric and stitching an elaborate design that will cover the whole surface with quilting stitches.**

The entire paragraph is now clearer and more interesting to read.

Exercise E4-1

In Candace Savage's essay "Aurora: Myth and Mystery" (pp. 66–71), find one example (other than the ones used in this section) of each of the methods of development you have just studied.

Exercise E4-2

Mark places in Eden's first draft (pp. 75–77) that could be developed further using at least three of the methods you have studied in this chapter. Write down the method you suggest.

Exercise E4-3

Complete the following paragraphs using a combination of the strategies described in this chapter: defining, describing, giving examples, classifying, assigning cause-effect, comparing-contrasting, and analyzing.

1. Washing my car can be a rewarding and frustrating experience. Depending on the weather, my schedule, and my energy level, my car's outward appearance may or may not be shiny and clean.
2. Budgeting time in today's hectic world is a worthwhile task. Even with a job, classes to attend, family obligations, and social activities, an organized person can certainly achieve all of his or her goals and manage to have time for recreation and other fun activities.
3. Many people today are concerned about the ecology of the world we live in. Efforts to prevent pollution, recycle, and use safer, nontoxic materials have benefited human beings.

Collaborative Work

After writing a draft of your own explaining essay, exchange papers with a classmate and complete the following tasks:

A. Put brackets around any sections of the essay that could be developed more fully.

B. Considering all the techniques of paragraph development that you have just studied, suggest ways to develop each paragraph further.

Then return the paper to its writer and use the information in this section to revise your draft.

Writing Focused Paragraphs

Checklist for Writing Focused Paragraphs

- ✓ Do all paragraphs **focus** on a single controlling idea?
- ✓ Should any paragraphs be **divided** into additional paragraphs?
- ✓ Are the sentences in each paragraph related to the topic sentence to form a **unified** whole?
- ✓ Are the sentences in each paragraph related to one another, following a **logical** train of thought?

Have you ever tried to find a single document in a filing cabinet drawer so packed that you couldn't move the file folders? To restore order to a filing cabinet, you need to sort all the papers into piles by category, throw out the useless or outdated items, then sort the piles into logical groups. Sometimes the paragraphs in your essays can resemble an overloaded filing cabinet. Just as organizing a filing cabinet makes important papers easier to find, clearing your paragraphs of unrelated ideas, organizing essential ideas logically, and connecting ideas with supporting details will help an audience understand the important contents of your essay.

Focus

To organize a filing cabinet, you might begin by sorting the contents into three piles: papers to put back in the cabinet, papers to store elsewhere, and papers to discard. Writers often use a similar method to **focus** their body paragraphs (the paragraphs that fall between the introduction and conclusion of an essay) on a single controlling idea. For many writers, the first step in revising is making sure the controlling idea for each paragraph is clear to their audience. Usually, they state this idea in a topic sentence at the beginning of the paragraph. Then they sort the sentences in that paragraph into (1) those that contribute to the controlling idea, (2) those that support another idea and need a separate paragraph, and (3) those that need to be thrown out entirely.

Look at paragraph six of Candace Savage's "Aurora: Myth and Mystery":

> The aurora has also been thought to **enhance the fruitfulness** of the earth. A Swedish tradition has it that "when the northern light is burning, the seed will be abundant." Some Nunamiut Eskimos believe that if the sky is divided in half by auroral displays, animals will be plentiful in the area the next day. Dene elder Alexis Arrowmaker says the lights are there to show hunters where they can find the most game. Similarly, Scandinavian fishing people used to interpret the lights as sunshine glinting off schools of herring in the northern sea and, hence, as a welcome omen of rich catches in the offing.

Savage focuses this entire paragraph on the controlling idea stated in the first sentence, that the aurora was influential in providing plenty from the natural world. Each of her examples developed this idea. Note that she connects this paragraph to the previous one with the transitional phrase "the aurora has **also** been thought to enhance..."

Unity

To be **unified**, a paragraph not only focuses on one point, but develops that point. Each paragraph should form a unified whole, with all of its topic sentences relating directly back to the thesis of the essay. A good way to check for unity at this point is to make a scratch outline. To do this, read each paragraph and jot down its controlling idea. Do each of the topic sentences relate back to the main idea of the essay. If a paragraph isn't focused on one idea, consider your options for achieving unity. Should some ideas be moved to other paragraphs? Do you need to divide the material into two paragraphs? Do some of the ideas need to be deleted altogether?

After rereading the first draft of her explaining essay, Eden realized she had to rework her second paragraph to focus more clearly on a single controlling idea.

First Draft: Most people know that women used every scrap of fabric they could find. Recycling these bits into works of functional art for everyone in their families to enjoy. I saw one once at an art show and it had little faces woven into it. Men too. Some quilts were even made by cowboys on the range. They salvaged the good parts of the garments and tied them together to make "tied quilts" that served as rugged bedrolls and saddle blankets. When their work clothing was worn out.

Revision: **Every time I see a quilt, I am reminded of the sewing skills of our frugal, hardworking ancestors.** Most people know that women used every scrap of fabric they could find, **material usually left over from sewing projects and pieces of worn clothing. They worked hard to** recycle these bits into works of functional art for everyone in their families to enjoy. ~~I saw one once at an art show and it had little faces woven into it. Men too.~~ **You may be surprised, however, to find out that some** quilts were even made by cowboys on the range. When their work clothing was worn out, they salvaged the good parts of the garments and tied them together to make "tied quilts" that served as rugged bedrolls and saddle blankets.

Eden adds a topic sentence to introduce a historical aspect to making quilts. As she rewrites her paragraph she realizes that although all her ideas are focused on the controlling idea, the historical aspects of quilts, there are some that go off on a tangent. Because of this tangent, the paragraph is not unified. It has a focus on its clear topic sentence, but to give this paragraph unity, Eden has to delete all the irrelevant details that don't directly relate to the paragraph's topic sentence. In the revision, Eden has made her paragraph unified as well as focused, strengthening the main ideas and making the paragraph more effective. Her revision also reflects some of the other corrections that she makes while editing.

Exercise P4-1

Underline the controlling idea that focuses each paragraph of Candace Savage's "Aurora: Myth and Mystery" (pp. 66–71).

Exercise P4-2

Find the sentence that states the controlling idea for each paragraph in Eden's first draft (pp. 75–77) and move or delete any that do not explain that idea.

Exercise P4-3

Rewrite the following paragraph, deleting all irrelevant material so that the paragraph focuses on one controlling idea.

Astronomy is the oldest of all the sciences. It began several thousand years ago, when people first wondered about the stars at night. Life was simple then. I sometimes enjoy using a telescope to look at the stars. Most of the people who used to wonder about the stars were hunters and shepherds, although I'll bet people from other professions also wondered about the stars. Shepherds and hunters could not write then, perhaps because they did not have a school system like we have today, and we do not know much about their thoughts. Yet they used the stars as guides on their journeys. Those days must have been interesting.

Exercise P4-4

Read the following sentences and group them into two unified paragraphs. Drop sentences that don't fit into either paragraph.

1. The first day of classes is always a confusing time at my campus.
2. Today, we know a great deal more about the ways in which diseases can be transmitted than was known in the nineteenth century.
3. Finding new buildings and locating classrooms takes a lot of time.
4. The bookstore is inevitably a crowd scene, with long lines going out the door and around the corner.
5. We know that mosquitoes, not noxious fumes in the air, carry malaria.
6. It's fun seeing old friends in classes again, though.
7. We know that typhoid comes from an unclean water or food supply.
8. For instance, we would never casually drink water from an old well.

9. Old wells can be dangerous if children play near them and fall in.
10. Long ago people had some funny ideas.

Collaborative Work

After writing a draft of your own explaining essay, exchange papers with a classmate, and do the following tasks:

A. Put brackets around each sentence that seems unrelated to its paragraph's controlling idea.

B. Draw an arrow to another paragraph if any sentences you found in task A seem to belong somewhere else, or put a question mark beside sentences you think should be deleted.

C. Place a paragraph symbol where a division should be made in a paragraph to form two paragraphs.

Then return the paper to its writer and use the information in this section to revise your draft.

CHAPTER **FIVE**

Investigating

What else is writing but investigation?

—**LINDA EDMUND**

LEARNING OUTCOMES

This chapter will help you:

- Investigate and report a topic in an essay format;
- Learn to develop several specific paragraph patterns;
- Learn to organize essays in specific patterns.

A good investigative journalist is someone who finds out all the facts and gets answers to as many questions as possible. Investigation happens to be an important part of education as well. Students often write investigating essays, particularly in college. In fact, most college research and term papers are based on the basic principles of investigative journalism—answering the questions who, what, where, and when, helping the writer address the bigger questions of why and how.

Investigating means gathering as much information about a person, place, event, or topic as possible. You can gather information for an investigative essay from several sources: interviews, lectures, TV shows, videos, the Internet, archives (places where books, letters, personal papers, maps, legal documents, and other records are kept), books, newspapers, magazines, journals, or CDs. Or, you can go to experience something for yourself. No matter how you gather your information, you must be certain to answer the who, what, where, and when questions. If you do a thorough and careful job of this part of the investigation, you will usually find the answers to the why and how questions.

Once the research ends, the writing of your essay becomes your primary concern. The investigating essay lays out information in a clear and convincing way. And your research inspires confidence in your knowledge, helps your reader become an expert in the subject as he or she reads, and helps win your readers to your point of view.

In an essay titled "A Woman's Work," published in *Harper's* magazine in 1993, Louise Erdrich, who had just given birth to a baby girl, wondered why so little was written about being a mother of a new infant and why, although writing is her occupation, she had no time to write. After thinking carefully about the situation, she wrote the following analysis:

> One reason there is not a great deal written about what it is like to be the mother of a new infant is that there is rarely a moment to think of anything else besides the infant's needs. Endless time with a small baby is spent asking, What do you want? I do what she "tells" me to do—feed, burp, change, amuse, distract, hold, look at, help to sleep, reassure—without consciously choosing to do it. I take her instructions without translating her meaning into words but simply bypassing straight to action. Until I've satisfied her need, my brain is a white blur. I lose track of what I've been doing, where I've been, who I am.

This process of analysis helped Louise Erdrich understand why she could not write about the birth of her new baby—or do much of anything else, for that matter.

LEARNING FROM PUBLISHED WRITERS

The following investigation by a writer examines what it means to be illiterate. Dan Zollmann built his investigation from his personal experience after moving to Quebec to study French. He examines illiteracy and some of its practical effects on the attitudes and experiences he had in a particular community.

Before You Read

Focus Your Attention

Before you read this investigation, take a few moments to respond to the following questions in your notebook.

1. Think of a time when you have found yourself in a situation that was very unfamiliar to you. Why were you there? What was it about that situation that made you feel uncomfortable?
2. How do you feel about illiterate Canadians? Do you think illiteracy is a big problem? How do you think an illiterate person might feel?

Expand Your Vocabulary

Here are some words that are important to your understanding of the essay. Read the words in context and write a definition for each.

Illiterate (paragraph 1)

Alienation (paragraph 1)

Paraplegic (paragraph 2)

Disastrous (paragraph 3)

Oligarchy (paragraph 8)

Dan Zollmann

Illiterate Like Me*

Most Canadians believe that something should be done to help the illiterate. Yet other social issues often take precedence when it comes to distributing tax dollars. If illiteracy were simply an inconvenience suffered by a handful of Canadians, then the low priority we accord to dealing with it would be justified because time and money are finite, and we must allocate these scarce resources on the basis of importance. However, illiteracy is not merely an inconvenience, nor does it afflict only a few Canadians. Instead, it is nothing less than the political, economic, and social alienation of a large number of individuals from their society. As such, illiteracy is as urgent as any other social problems we face. 1

What is it really like to be illiterate? I do not know, nor will I ever be capable of knowing, any more than I could know what it would be like to be blind, or to be a paraplegic. Four years ago, however, I moved to Quebec City to study French at Laval University, an experience that provided me with some insight into the reality of illiteracy. As someone who had learned to speak French by ear, I knew the alphabet, could recognize a few words, but had almost no practical experience reading and writing French. In other words, at age 20 I joined the ranks of the illiterate. 2

How does an illiterate survive in a situation requiring a higher level of literacy than most jobs in Canada require, namely, as a university student? With great difficulty. Although in high school I had participated a great deal in class discussions, in university I stopped offering my opinions because I had no confidence in my understanding of the texts under discussion. Always a good writer in high school, I now found myself incapable of finishing 3

*Dan Zollmann. "Illiterate Like Me." *Contest: Essays by Canadian Students*, Third Edition. Ed. Murray McArthur, pp. 205-208. Copyright © 1998 by Harcourt Brace & Company, Canada, Ltd. All rights reserved. Reprinted by permission of Harcourt Canada, Ltd.

an essay exam question within the time limit, never mind producing logical, concise answers. Even the basics of dealing with the university's administration became a struggle: calendars, course changes, registration forms, regulations, all were a complete mystery to me. Sometimes the results were disastrous: for example, I accidentally signed a form that forced me to spend hours in the following year trying to get readmitted to the university. Moreover, I had no idea how services such as guidance, tutoring, or the ombudsman could help me deal with these problems since I was incapable of fully comprehending my student handbook.

Not only was attending university difficult, but many problems that literate people daily overcome suddenly became insurmountable. I opened a bank account without even attempting to understand the form I had to sign. My furnace broke down several times in the winter, yet I had no idea to whom I should complain. Moreover, I was incapable of writing a letter of complaint even if I had known where to send it. Although I had some idea of the basics of written French, using it every day was extraordinarily difficult because I knew that when I wrote in French I made mistakes in grammar that most people stopped making after Grade 3. This embarrassed me to the point that I was afraid to put up an advertisement on the bulletin board to sell last term's textbooks, or to fill out a job application, or to leave a note for someone on my apartment door, or even to write down a phone message for a roommate. I became paralyzed with fear when faced with the most trivial of daily tasks. **4**

My inability to read or write also had a profound effect on the way I related to my community. I constantly saw things around me that aroused my anger, yet I was powerless to change them. For example, I wanted to write a letter of complaint to the owners of the pulp mill that filled my lungs with sulfur dioxide gas every time I passed by on the way to the university, yet I knew that any letter I wrote would first be laughed at, and then ignored. Since we tend to judge a person's intelligence by his or her ability to write, how could I expect the owners of the pulp mill, or the editors of a newspaper, to take seriously the complaint of someone who appeared to be too ignorant to write beyond the primary school level? **5**

Gradually, I became divorced from the world in which I lived. I voted in the provincial elections, but I did not understand the brochures delivered to my apartment by the candidates. I occasionally bought *Le Devoir* with the intention of reading it cover to cover, yet found myself incapable of following any article longer than a few paragraphs. Unable to read newspapers, I had to accept the second-hand reports of literate people around me. Unable to understand political debate, I judged on the basis of appearance, rather than issues. Incapable of communicating with my own community, I renounced all personal responsibility, hoping that others would write the letters, circulate the petitions, and lobby the local officials. In short, I gave up, resigning myself to the frustrated yet passive existence of the alienated. **6**

The comparison between my experiences in Quebec City and those of someone who is truly illiterate, however, can only go so far. After all, I was **7** already literate in one language and was in Quebec by choice, not necessity. In contrast, the millions of Canadians who can neither read nor write either official language cannot simply pack their bags and return to their home province when they grow tired of their alienation. Moreover, it is quite possible that most of these people are not even aware of the extent to which they are isolated from society because they know no other existence, no other way of living. This, in turn, highlights the ultimate tragedy of illiteracy, namely that those who suffer from it are powerless to exert the political pressure necessary to change their situation.

Illiteracy is, therefore, more than merely a minor inconvenience. In Canada, and in all other Western societies, an inability to read and write means alienation from one's community and from one's country. At a political level, illiteracy makes a mockery of the democratic process by creating an oligarchy composed of an educated elite. At a personal level, illiteracy means subjection to economic and political marginalization; in short, the exploitation of one of the most vulnerable groups in society. **8**

Questions For Critical Thinking

Thinking Critically About Content

1. How does Zollmann investigate illiteracy? Do you think his investigation was a good one? Why or why not?
2. What does Zollmann's investigation allow us to see that a government study of illiteracy wouldn't show us?

Thinking Critically About Purpose

3. What do you think Zollmann's purpose is in this essay?
4. What effect did the essay have on you?

Thinking Critically About Audience

5. Who is the main audience for this essay? How can you tell?
6. Can this audience do anything about illiteracy? Why did he aim his essay at this audience?

Thinking Critically About Perspective

7. How would this essay be different if Zollmann had followed an illiterate person around and recorded what he or she did?
8. Do you think Zollmann might have felt as disconnected from the community if he had temporarily lost his sight or hearing?

LEARNING FROM YOUR PEERS

The first thing most people think of when they hear the word investigating is detective work. Actually, satisfying your curiosity about any unfamiliar subject often requires some investigation. You may go to the library or the telephone directory in search of the answers to a particular question. When you ask friends and neighbours how to find a good used car or what restaurants have the best meals, you are investigating. From this basic sense of investigating, your goal is to construct an essay that is informative and interesting to readers. To this end, we are going to follow the writing process of a student named Anto Celotto in response to an investigating essay assignment.

Anto's Writing Assignment: Investigating

This is the topic Anto's instructor assigned:

When we meet people who have unusual occupations, we often wonder what led them to pursue that line of work. Maybe you know someone who appraises real estate or installs computer systems. This writing assignment will give you an opportunity to find out about people who work in fields that you find interesting, whether or not they are related to your future profession. For this assignment, you should interview someone about his or her decision to work in a specific career and then write an essay summarizing your findings.

Anto went through his own writing process similar to the one outlined in Chapter 1: generating ideas, planning, developing, organizing, drafting, revising, and editing.

Generating Ideas

Anto tried to think of people he knew who had unusual careers. He made a list of his relatives, neighbours, and acquaintances from church, but he couldn't think of anyone he found interesting. He called his girlfriend, Tonja, and asked her how her day was going. She told him that her cousin was visiting and she wanted them to meet each other. Anto jumped in his car and drove to Tonja's house. "I don't feel like studying, anyway," he told himself.

When he arrived at Tonja's house, Travis greeted him at the door. Anto tried to conceal his surprise: Tonja never mentioned that Travis was in a wheelchair. After a few minutes of small talk, Travis began chatting about his life.

When Anto discovered that Travis was a drug and alcohol counsellor, Anto asked him if he would mind talking about the reasons for his career choice. Travis agreed, so Anto ran back to his car to get a notebook from his knapsack. Several hours later, Anto was pleasantly surprised to discover that he had done some class preparation in spite of himself. He asked Travis for permission to call him back and ask him more questions if he needed to. Travis smiled. "I am always happy to share my experience," he said.

Planning

Anto looked over his notes the next day. He found he had most of what he needed to write an essay about Travis and his situation. These are his notes:

> Travis started drinking heavily in high school and became a paraplegic after he dove into an empty swimming pool at a party. He didn't quit drinking, though. In fact, he started doing drugs and wasting his life because of this tragedy. Tried to escape reality. For 10 years.
>
> But his life just kept getting worse. Finally, his mama told him to get sober or get out. His whole family was sick of him stealing and wasting his life. He was sick and tired of being sick and tired himself. Finally he went into counselling. He found a clinic that would let him stay for a month. He thought it would cool things down at home.
>
> He was surprised that he really wanted to change. Being with other people who wanted to change was real helpful.
>
> When he got out of the clinic, he studied with a tutor. Then he applied to the community college. He was admitted and liked to study. His friends ragged on him, but he was determined to change his life.
>
> He was offered a job at the clinic as soon as he finished his associate's degree.

Developing

The next time Anto looked at his notes, he noticed something was missing. He asked Tonja to look over his notes. She agreed with him. Anto took Travis's interesting life and as he wrote about it, made him sound like a world-class bore.

Anto called Travis trying to get some quotable information to make the person in his essay sound more like the "real" Travis. Anto took detailed notes as he spoke with Travis, making sure he captured some of Travis's actual words:

- "You might say that I 'dove' right into my career."
- "I was never happy with myself when I was a young teenager, so I used to drink when I was hanging out with the older boys in my neighbourhood. Back in those days, I thought it made us more attractive to the ladies. Now I know better."
- "I had some help making my decision. My mama said, 'Travis, get sober or get out of my house.' Since I had no idea how I could function without all the care my mama gave me, I decided to sober up quickly."
- "I had never heard of any paraplegic bank robbers."
- "The problem with drinking is that it is like a roller-coaster ride. You can only go so high, and then you come crashing down. After being through so many highs and lows, I was ready for some level ground."

- "There were many people who called me an inspiration. I think that's quite a reputation to live up to, and I take that as an obligation."
- "My life today, along with my future, holds rewarding, challenging, and interesting opportunities. There is no way I can make my family and friends forget what a low-life scoundrel I was, but I can assure them I will never sink that low again."

Organizing

Now all that Anto had to do was take his notes and add Travis's quotes. After he read the essay over again, he decided to add some more material. He tried to remember what Travis looked like and he wove the descriptions through his text and explained Travis's family situation in more detail. Here is the order Anto decided on for the information he had:

1. Travis's immediate background
2. Hitting rock bottom
3. Self-evaluation and rehab
4. Education
5. Career and life goals

Anto began his essay with one of Travis's remarks because Travis spoke so well for himself.

Drafting

Here is Anto's essay.

Anto's Essay: First Draft

Main idea: Alcohol abuse was part of what made Travis a paraplegic; then he turned his life around and became a drug and alcohol counsellor.

"You might say that I dove right into my career," said Travis Lawrence. He is a drug and alcohol counsellor at a local rehabilitation clinic. He started drinking at the age of 15 and soon found himself a paraplegic after jumping off a diving board into the deep end of an empty swimming pool. "That ended one night of drinking," he said, "but it led to many more nights and days trying to escape reality by using and abusing drugs and alcohol."

"I was never happy with myself when I was a young teenager, so I used to drink when I was hanging out with the older boys in my neighbourhood," Travis explained. "Back in those days, my buddies and I were trying to make ourselves more attractive to the ladies. Now I know better."

Travis Lawrence, with help from his friends and supporters, has been sober for five years now. But he had a 10-year drinking career before he came to the decision that alcohol and drugs were making him more miserable than he already was. He had never fully adjusted to life in a wheelchair, and he realized that drinking his life away was not going to solve that problem. "Actually," he said, "I had some help making my decision. My mama said, 'Travis, get sober or get out of my house.' Don't you think this got my attention? Since I had no idea how I could function without all the care my mama gives me, I decided to sober up quickly." When someone sinks as low as he did, you have to take action.

Travis had been fighting with his sister about some missing money, and he became enraged and pushed her down the stairs. He knew that he had given up hope of having a normal life, so he gave himself excuses for treating others in what he now sees as inexcusable ways. For example, he kept borrowing money from family members and never paid any of it back. When they stopped loaning him money, he started stealing from them. He said he was unable to go anywhere else and steal to support his habits because his getaway vehicle was too easy to identify. He said he had never heard of any paraplegic bank robbers. His mother told him that she did not want another crippled child, so he had to learn to resolve his differences with his sister without resorting to violence.

He looked at himself honestly for the first time. Everybody had been trying to get him to wise up. He saw that he was not going anywhere. He understood how important his family was and how badly he had treated them. Travis realized that his anger at his paralysis was being misdirected, and he decided to get some counselling. One of the most important things he learned was that he was responsible for his own moods and that "getting high" was almost inevitably followed by "getting low." He told me, "The problem with drinking is it is like a roller-coaster ride. You can only go so high, and then you come crashing down. After being through so many highs and lows, I was ready for some level ground." He along with his mom were able to find a clinic that let him stay for a month and learn all about the disease of alcoholism and how to overcome it. Most of the month's stay was an eye-opening experience.

Alcohol addiction isn't an easy habit to kick. Addiction, the dictionary says, is the state of being addicted. And to be addicted means that you cannot say "no" to whatever you're addicted too. At that point, you need help. After a month in the clinic, Travis decided to get his high school equivalency diploma, so he studied with a tutor until he was ready to take the test. About three-fourths of the test were easy, simple enough for Travis to pass with no problem. The day he got his certificate, he went to the local community college and applied for admission. He said that when his friends in the neighbourhood found out that he was going to college, they teased him all the time and called him "school boy." They were not supportive. Everyone took their digs at him. He told me that was better than many of the things they had called him in the past, so he kept going to school and kept going to support group meetings.

When Travis finished his associate's degree, the clinic where he first started recovering from his addictions hired him to help counsel newcomers. Not only his supervisor, Nancy Jeffries, but also his co-workers was impressed with his sense of humour and his ability to get along with others. "Imagine that," he said to me. "There were many people who called me an inspiration. I think that's quite a reputation to live up to, and I take that as an obligation." He knows that for him, he cannot drink and have a happy life. People who don't know him probably looks at him and feel sorry for him because of his mode of transportation. But they can't even guess how far down he was and how far back he's come since he started using the chair. Travis says, "My life today, along with my future, holds rewarding, challenging, and interesting opportunities." He works with a group of people who cares about him and wants him to succeed at his career. His family and friends have forgiven him for the bad deeds he has done. The majority of the money he stole have been paid back. He makes sure he's generous with his family and friends at holidays and birthdays. He feels everyone have been supportive. "There is no way I can make my family and friends forget what a low-life scoundrel I was, but I can assure them I will never sink that low again," says Travis. Everybody still has their opinion of him. But he hopes it's changed for the better.

Like Travis's co-workers, my friends and I was truly impressed with Travis's wit and wisdom. I am sure that the clinic supervisor made an excellent decision when they decided to hire him to help others recover from their addictions.

Revising

Anto was genuinely moved by Travis's energy and enthusiasm for his newfound career. Anto marvelled at how easy and painless it was to write an essay he hadn't wanted to write in the first place. The words just came tumbling out after his interview with Travis. Anto knew that revising this essay would likely take more time than the first draft because he didn't pay much attention to the way he was making his statements; he just wanted to get his first draft on paper. His philosophy was "Write now, revise later."

Then came the revisions. The instructor's revision guidelines for this assignment involved focusing on methods for organizing paragraphs and essays. Anto turned to the Checklist for Organizing Paragraphs and Essays (p. 115) and completed the exercises his instructor assigned. From the readings, he learned that he had several options for organizing the ideas in each paragraph and for arranging the paragraphs in the essay.

Anto returned to his essay, revising cautiously because he knew he had a lot of work to do. As he reread his draft, Anto found several problems with ideas that weren't logically arranged, and he began marking changes he wanted to make.

Collaborative Work

Peer Group Activity

After you read the portions of the Focus on Paragraphs and Focus on Essays sections your instructor assigns, turn to Anto's first draft (pp. 104–107), and complete the following tasks in small groups:

A. Put brackets around any sentences, paragraphs, or ideas that are not arranged as effectively as they could be.

B. In the margin, suggest a better way of organizing any material you put in brackets: general to particular, particular to general, time order, space order, or movement between extremes. (For explanations, see pp. 115–123.)

Compare the marks your group recorded with those your instructor will show you. Where do your marks differ from your instructor's? What do you need to review before writing your own essay?

Class Activity

As an entire class, look at the underlined portions of Anto's revised draft (pp. 109–112) to see how he changed each sentence.

A. Did you identify the revision problems that Anto corrected?

B. Do you think his changes are good ones? Discuss his changes.

Editing

Now that Anto has reorganized portions of his essay, he needs to do some final proofreading and editing before handing it in. He refers to the section in the Focus on Sentences Appendix to learn about recognizing and developing clauses, interjections, and phrases and begins correcting problems one by one to strengthen his essay.

Collaborative Work

Peer Group Activity

After you read the portions of the Focus on Sentences section in the appendix that your instructor assigns, turn to Anto's first draft (pp. 104–107) and complete the following task in small groups:

> Circle any pronouns (for a definition see p. 267) and the nouns the pronoun is replacing. Make sure the pronoun clearly refers to a previous noun, and that the pronoun doesn't shift (see page 290 – 293).

Compare the marks your group recorded with those your instructor will show you. Where do your marks differ from your instructor's? What do you need to review before writing your own essay?

Anto's Revised Essay

An Accidental Career

"You might say that I dove right into my career," said Travis Lawrence. He is a drug and alcohol counsellor at a local rehabilitation clinic. He started drinking at the age of 15 and soon found himself a paraplegic after jumping off a diving board into the deep end of an empty swimming pool. "That ended one night of drinking," he said, "but it led to many more nights and days trying to escape reality by using and abusing drugs and alcohol." Finally, a combination of his mother's tough love and an honest look at his own behaviour convinced Travis that he had to change his life.

Travis then told me about some mistaken ideas that had influenced him to drink. "I was never happy with myself when I was a young teenager, so I used to drink when I was hanging out with the older boys in my neighbourhood," Travis explained. "Back in those days, my buddies and I ~~was~~were trying to make ourselves more attractive to the ladies. Now I know better." Now, Travis knows about the realities of drinking, and he can help others avoid his mistakes.

Travis Lawrence, with help from his friends and supporters, has been sober for five years now. But he had a 10-year drinking career before he came to the decision that alcohol and drugs were making him more miserable than he already was. He had never fully adjusted to life in a wheelchair, and he realized that drinking his life away was not going to solve that problem. "Actually," he said, "I had some help making my decision. My mama said, 'Travis, get sober or get out of my house.' Don't you think this got my attention? Since I had no idea how I could function without all the care my mama gives me, I decided to sober up quickly." When someone sinks as low as he did, ~~you have~~he or she has to take action.

~~Travis had been fighting with his sister about some missing money, and he became enraged and pushed her down the stairs.~~ He knew that he had given up hope of having a normal life, so he gave himself excuses for treating others in what he now sees as inexcusable ways. For example, he kept borrowing money from family members and never paid any of it back. When they stopped loaning him money, he started stealing from them. With ~~He~~a twisted smile, he said he was unable to go anywhere else and steal to support his habits because it would have been difficult to avoid police when his getaway vehicle was ~~too~~so easy to identify. ~~He said~~ "Besides," he said, "I had never heard of any successful paraplegic bank ~~robbers.~~ robbers." It all came to a head ~~His~~one day when Travis had been fighting with his sister about some missing money, and he became enraged and pushed her down the stairs. Then, his mother told him that she did not want another crippled child, so he had to learn to resolve his differences with his sister without resorting to violence.

~~He~~That very night, he looked at himself honestly for the first time. ~~Everybody~~For years, everybody had been trying to get him to wise up. ~~He~~Finally, he, too, saw that he was not going anywhere. ~~He~~

~~understood~~After thinking for a while, he realized how important his family was and how badly he had treated them.

Travis realized that his anger at his paralysis was being misdirected, and he decided to get some counselling. ~~One of the most important things he learned was that he was responsible for his own moods and that "getting high" was almost inevitably followed by "getting low." He told me, "The problem with drinking is it is like a roller coaster ride. You can only go so high, and then you come crashing down. After being through so many highs and lows, I was ready for some level ground."~~

He along with his mom ~~were~~was able to find a clinic that let him stay for a month and learn all about the disease of alcoholism and how to overcome it. Most of the month's stay ~~were~~was an eye-opening ~~experience.~~ experience.

One of the most important things he learned was that he was responsible for his own moods and that "getting high" was almost inevitably followed by "getting low." He told me, "The problem with drinking is it is like a roller-coaster ride. You can only go so high, and then you come crashing down. After being through so many highs and lows, I was ready for some level ground."

~~Alcohol addiction isn't an easy habit to kick. Addiction, the dictionary says, is the state of being addicted. And to be addicted means that you cannot say 'no' to whatever you're addicted too. At that point, you need help.~~ After a month in the clinic, Travis decided to get his high school equivalency diploma, so he studied with a tutor until he was ready to take the test. About three-fourths of the test ~~were~~was easy, simple enough for Travis to pass with no problem. The day he got his certificate, he went to the local community college and applied for admission. He said that when his friends in the neighbourhood found out that he was going to college, they teased him

> see her regularly. I suppose I wanted to live in one of those spotless homes on a fancy street lined with trees, and have supper waiting on the table when I got home from playing basketball with my friends. But mom doesn't like to cook much, and she's often gone at meal times. Now that I'm older, I realize how hard she works and that she really loves us. What I treasure are the special times, like pizza Fridays when we are all together, and the only thing we have to worry about is which movie to watch and to make sure the frozen pizza doesn't burn in the oven. I guess that this doesn't really say what motherhood is all about, but I do know that there is more to it than meets the eye.

Alexa now needs to sort out how to incorporate the quote from "MotherHOOD" into her own paragraph. She turns her attention to the Focus on Paragraphs section of this chapter, and then uses that information to revise her paragraph:

> In her essay, Beth Everest says that "the problem isn't that mothers are celebrated or honoured, but that the ideal [of motherhood] is honoured, and mothers are expected to conform to that ideal" (134). I know that raising my sister and me wasn't always easy, and it was pretty tough for my mom. We didn't have a lot of money, so we never had the clothes and things that my friends seemed to have. Our house was always a mess, and being a nurse, mom often worked shifts so we didn't see her regularly. I suppose I wanted to live in one of those spotless homes on a fancy street lined with trees, and have supper waiting on the table when I got home from playing basketball with my friends. But mom doesn't like to cook much, and she's often gone at meal times. Now that I'm older, I realize how hard she works and that she really loves us. What I treasure are the special times, like pizza Fridays when we are all together, and the only thing we have to worry about is which movie to watch and to make sure the frozen pizza doesn't burn in the oven. I guess that this doesn't really say what motherhood is all about, but I do know that there is more to it than meets the eye.

Alexa's new paragraph is long, but it is coherent and each detail relates back to her topic sentence, the quote from Everest's essay. She has incorporated the quote by introducing the author, and followed it with a citation. She knows that because she has used the author's surname in the introduction that it is not necessary to include it in the citation. The citation, then, includes only the page number. The rest of the citation material will be included in a Works Cited page. Note, too, that she clarifies *the ideal* by adding *of motherhood* in brackets.

Paraphrasing

Next, Alexa's instructor wants to make certain that her students know how to paraphrase, or reword someone else's words. After explaining how to paraphrase, this is what she has asked her students to do:

Read the section on paraphrasing in Focus on Paragraphs in this chapter. When you are confident that you know what to do, choose a paragraph from "MotherHOOD," and do a line by line paraphrase for the entire paragraph. Make sure you introduce the paraphrase and end it with a citation.

Alexa chooses paragraph four for her paraphrase. This is what she writes:

> There is a problem with worshipping motherhood because it is seen as an ideal. Nowadays we expect moms to be "supermoms" who work all day long and still do everything for their kids by participating on every committee and team that their kids are associated with. And we expect them at least once a week to bake fresh goodies for the kids' snacks, do all the chores without complaining one little bit and happily cook all the meals. Even though it seems that everyone wants this to happen, and many try to do it, it is not something that can really happen.

Then, she rereads the Focus on Paragraphs section that tells her how she is meant to introduce the paraphrase and to show that it has ended. This is how she revises her paragraph:

> The essay "MotherHOOD" in this chapter talks about the problem with worshipping motherhood as an ideal. In one of the paragraphs, the author says that what happens nowadays is that we expect moms to be "supermoms" who work all day long and still do everything for their kids by participating on every committee and team that their kids are associated with. And we expect them at least once a week to bake fresh goodies for the kids' snacks, do all the chores without complaining one little bit and happily cook all the meals. Even though it seems that everyone wants this to happen, and many try to do it, it is not something that can really happen (Everest 134).

Alexa introduces the paraphrase by noting the title of the essay and the main idea. She ends the paraphrase with a citation which includes the author's surname and the page number of the paragraph as it appears in the textbook. She knows that the rest of the citation material will be included on a Works Cited page.

Summarizing

The final task that Alexa's instructor wants her students to do before tackling their own research essays is to try writing a summary—to summarize means to condense someone else's words. After explaining to them how to do summaries, she asks them to do the following:

Read the section on doing summaries in the Focus on Paragraphs section of this chapter. Then, summarize in a single paragraph the essay "MotherHOOD."

Alexa sets out to do this. She looks at each paragraph and tries to come up with a main point for each. This is what she writes:

1. New mothers often are afraid to talk about what they really feel about being a mother because they are trying to live up to others' expectations.
2. Pregnant and new mothers have created a big market for business.
3. Myth and religion also have worshipped the mother.
4. The supermom is the way that we now worship the mother as an ideal.
5. Some women try to be the ideal and because they say how wonderful it is they make it harder for others who can't be like them.
6. Mother's Day is a celebration that has ancient roots, but we still have and it adds to the problem.
7. The definition of motherhood is size and power.
8. Mother also means good, but hood is a cover that prevents someone seeing what is really underneath.
9. A hood is a criminal, and mother has some negative meanings like scum.
10. The definitions contrast and this creates a problem.
11. Mothers need to speak about what they really feel or they will always be stuck having to live up to the ideal.

After Alexa lists the main ideas in each paragraph of the essay, she formulates them into a paragraph. Here is her paragraph:

> New mothers often are afraid of what they really feel about being a mother because find that they can't live up to others' expectations. It is expectations that cause problems. First, there is a big market for business which poses a particular image of what mothers need to have. Myth and religion also have worshipped the mother and tell what the ideal mother is like. Mother's Day is a celebration that has ancient roots, but we still have it and it adds to the problem. The supermom is the way that we now worship the mother. Some women try to be the ideal and because they say how wonderful it is they make it harder for others who can't be like them. The dictionary shows motherhood as size and power. Mother also means good, but hood is a cover that prevents someone seeing what is really underneath. A hood is also a criminal, and mother has some negative meanings like scum. The definitions mean so many different things, and this creates a problem. What is under the hood? Mothers need to speak about what they really feel or they will always be stuck having to live up to the ideal.

Alexa tries to keep her ideas in the order in which they appeared in the essay, and except for the detail about Mother's Day, which seemed better placed a bit earlier, she manages to do this. She tinkers with the sentences and then works on introducing and concluding the summary. This is her revision:

> Beth Everest's essay on "MotherHOOD" looks at how our society worships mothers and motherhood. She says that new mothers often are afraid of

> failure because they find that they can't live up to others' expectations of what it means to be a mother. It is expectations that cause problems. First, there is a big market for business and business poses a particular image of what mothers need to have. Then, myth and religion worship the mother and tell what the ideal mother is like, and these go back a long time. Mother's Day is a celebration that has ancient roots, but we still have it and it adds to the problem. These things set up an ideal of the mother. The supermom is how we now worship the mother. Some women try to be the ideal and because they say how wonderful it is they make it harder for others who can't be like them. The dictionary has so many definitions of motherhood that mean different things: size, power, and good. But mother has some negative meanings like scum, and a hood is a criminal or a cover that prevents someone seeing what is really underneath. All of the conflicting meanings cause problems. What is under the hood? Mothers need to speak about what they really feel or they will always be stuck having to live up to the ideal (Everest 134).

Alexa's summary is quite long, and she might decide later on to shorten the more repetitive ideas. She has, however, included most of the main ideas and, except for the ones that make better sense in other places, she has tried to keep them in the order in which they appear in the essay. She is now ready to begin generating ideas about her own research essay.

WRITING YOUR OWN RESEARCH ESSAY

Choose one of the following topics for your own research essay.

1. Listen to the news and scan the newspapers to find a current news story. Think about any issues that are involved: i.e., a local murder case in which a teen kills a person. Should the killer be tried in adult court? What are the legalities? What are the ramifications? How do the members of the community feel? Research various aspects of this issue and bring them together in a research paper. Use all sorts of sources from newspapers and magazines to books and the Internet. You may also want to do a personal interview. Your instructor might want you to hand in a copy of all articles that you use.
2. Research an issue that affects you directly or your community. What are the issues involved and who will it affect? Think about both sides: i.e., perhaps the government is trying to push a particular bill through parliament. What is the bill? What will it change? What are the benefits? To whom? What are the negative aspects? For whom? Why? Use all sorts of sources from newspapers and magazines to books and the Internet. You may also want to do a personal interview. Your instructor might want you to hand in a copy of all articles that you use.
3. Create your own research topic (with the assistance of your instructor). Use a variety of sources from newspapers and magazines to books and the Internet. You may also want to do a personal interview. Your instructor might want you to hand in a copy of all articles that you use.

Writing Coherent Essays

Checklist for Writing Coherent Essays

✓ Are **transition words**, **phrases**, and **clauses** used effectively?
✓ Are **key words** repeated wisely?
✓ Is **parallelism** used appropriately?

When computer engineers set up a new system, they must first plan a logical configuration. A big part of their planning involves finding a way to connect all the components in the system so that they work together. For your readers to follow your thoughts in an essay, you need to make logical connections between your paragraphs and between the sentences within your paragraphs in much the same way a computer engineer connects the parts in a new computer system.

Coherence in writing means achieving a consistent relationship among parts. **Cohesive devices** show the logical relationships between the various parts of an essay as well as between sentences and paragraphs. Cohesive devices include transitional words and expressions, repetition, and parallelism. These techniques are similar to ones used to unify paragraphs (see Chapter 7, Focus on Paragraphs).

Transitions

Words, phrases, and clauses that guide readers through ideas are often called **transitions**. Specific transition words, phrases, and clauses establish time, space or distance, contrasts, examples, additions, order, and conclusions. Here are some examples of these transitions that will be useful in your writing:

Time:	now, then, meanwhile, before, afterward
Space:	nearby, farther, on the other side, above, below, down
Cause-effect:	because, due to, whereas, since, thus, therefore
Contrast:	although, despite this, however, on the other hand
Example:	in fact, for example, for instance
Addition:	also, besides, furthermore, in addition, plus
Conclusion:	finally, lastly, since, thus, therefore

Transitions help your reader fit the pieces of your essay together in the way you intended because they establish logical relationships between your ideas. For example, in "MotherHOOD," Beth Everest links paragraphs 4, 5, and 6 by using transitional words and phrases. Paragraph 4 begins with a question about the problems with worshipping the ideal, provides an example of the epitome of the ideal, and then ends the paragraph with another question.

> Is there anything wrong with worshipping the ideal? *Yes* is the simple answer. Even in contemporary times we worship the mother through deeply entrenched cultural idols of the supermom . . . . In fact, this epitomizes the ideal of motherhood. Who can realistically match it?

Then, paragraph 5 opens by partially answering the question and providing research that shows women trying to live up to the ideal. Note the use of the word *obviously* which provides the transition from question to answer.

> **Obviously**, some women try. In a Mother's Day article featuring interviews with several mothers, Rita Zak speaks about her experiences with motherhood . . . Although what Zak advocates is admirable, evidently, even members of the motherhood promote a type of silence. The ideal is upheld, and social strictures make it impossible for most of us to do anything but fail.

She reminds her reader at the end of the paragraph that meeting the ideal is impossible, and then links her next idea, which she develops in paragraph 6, by using an addition type transition.

> **Moreover**, the ideal is exacerbated by institutions such as Mother's Day. Although this celebration has its roots in pagan festivities honoring Rhea, The Mother of the Gods, and later by English Christians celebrating Mothering Sunday (Kanner 38), in contemporary times Mother's Day has become a marketing phenomenon . . . . The problem isn't that mothers are celebrated or honored, but that the ideal is honored, and mothers are expected to conform to the ideal.

Note that each of Everest's paragraphs neatly flows from one to the next.

Repetition

The **repetition** of key words is another strategy that holds paragraphs together and contributes to the coherence of an entire essay. This device not only lends coherence to your writing but also emphasizes important ideas. Look at this example from paragraphs one and two of "MotherHOOD" (The repeated words are in bold type):

> For those already initiated, it is easy to identify the new ***mother***, and it isn't because of the rosy glow on her cheeks. Those sweet cheeks are blotched purple with the strain of a difficult labour. . . . She fears failure, almost as much as she fears talking about her initiation into this new **culture** called ***motherhood***, a **culture** that necessitates the wearing of a hood.

> We live in a **culture** that promotes the idea of the ***mother***, especially the ***mother***-to-be and the new ***mother***. . . . We can buy fashionable maternity clothes, bedding including pillows with large central cavities, baby albums, cradles, memorabilia, knickknacks—everything the baby and or expectant ***mother*** could ever wish for, if she had money enough. Our **society** tells us how to play the role of the ***mother***, and there is a big market for it.

These boldfaced words bind the various ideas in these paragraphs together. If repetition is used in moderation, as in this example, it emphasizes main ideas and stresses important details. But if it is overused, it loses its effect and becomes confusing.

Parallelism

Writers often put certain words and phrases in **parallel** form to show their relationship to one another. These words and phrases are parallel when they fall into the same grammatical pattern. In "MotherHOOD," Everest uses a parallel structure by opening paragraphs with questions and the paragraph develops an answer. Paragraph 4 opens and closes with a question, and paragraphs 10, 11, and 12 all begin with a question. Each question further develops the central theme of her essay.

> **Paragraph 4:** Is there anything wrong with worshipping the ideal? *Yes* is the simple answer . . . . In fact, this epitomizes the ideal of motherhood. Who can realistically match it?
>
> **Paragraphs 10, 11 and 12:** Why can mothers not talk about their experiences of motherhood? What prevents them from speaking? Is it because of the way they are defined by a culture that imposes an ideal? Are they hooded, concealed from speaking the truth?
>
> A hood is also a gangster. Is this too a part of the mothering culture? What crime has been committed and against whom? Who is it that is concealing the being of a mother, she who is hooded? At this point, it is interesting to note another denotation of mother, one that has to do with the process of fermentation. The mother, in this case, refers to the dregs, the scum. How does this impact on society's view of what is a mother?
>
> What is the impact of all of these conflicting definitions of motherhood? Rarely does the mythology surrounding childbirth speak of the new mother as a self, a being bodily, mentally and soulfully experiencing becoming a mother, a reconciliation with who she is in relation to all of the defining . . . How can we as mothers talk about the problems associated with giving birth and raising a child or children when we have to work against our defining.

This pattern of question-answer not only lays out the content but also establishes an interesting rhythm in the prose that builds up the readers' expectations for what the mother is.

Exercise E6-1

In the essay "MotherHOOD" underline and label other examples of the pronouns, transitions, repetitions, and parallel structures that connect and emphasize ideas.

Collaborative Work

After writing a draft of your own researching essay, exchange papers with a classmate and complete the following tasks:

A. Mark with a caret (^) places where you feel cohesive devices are needed, either within a sentence or paragraph or between sentences and paragraphs.

B. In the margin beside each mark you made, suggest a method or specific words, phrases, or clauses that the writer might use to make the sentence or paragraph more coherent.

Then return the paper to its writer and use the information in this section to revise your draft.

Including Other People's Words and Ideas in Your Essay

Checklist for Including Other People's Words

- ✓ Are you quoting, paraphrasing, or summarizing your sources?
- ✓ If you're quoting, have you quoted the words exactly as they appear in the original?
- ✓ Have you used quotation marks around all quoted material?
- ✓ Have you adequately introduced the quote?
- ✓ Have you offset quotes that are longer than four lines?
- ✓ Did you edit the quote—add or remove words and properly use ellipses or brackets— to make the quote say what it needs to say clearly?
- ✓ Did you introduce your paraphrased sources properly?
- ✓ Did you introduce your fragment quotes?
- ✓ Have you correctly cited all of your sources?
- ✓ Have you included a Works Cited page for all of your cited materials? (see Chapter 8 to learn how to set up a Works Cited page)

There is an art to including other people's words in your essays. This section will provide you with techniques that can help you get started. There are three ways to include a person's words in your essay: you can reword the person's words in your own words (paraphrase); you can condense some of the person's own words (summary); or, you can use the person's words exactly as they appear in the original text (quote). Each technique has its own effect. You need to choose the technique for a good reason. In each case there are some specific techniques you can use to make sure the other person's words are well integrated into your essay. Make absolutely certain, however, that whenever you use another person's words or ideas that you include citations so that your reader knows exactly where the words or ideas have come from. This is not only a matter of courtesy, but a matter of law.

Using a Quotation

How to Quote Other People's Words

When you take the exact words someone has written or spoken and use them in your essay, you are quoting their words. You'll want to use a direct quote if the quote is well worded, it makes your point better than your own words, or if you need to have someone else deliver the point.

Whenever you include someone else's words in your essay, you need to use your own words to introduce the quote—to guide your reader into the other person's words. There are two main techniques you can use. If your quote begins with a partial sentence—a sentence fragment—then you'll use the first technique. If your quote begins with a whole sentence, or is a single whole sentence, you'll want to use the second technique.

Quoting a Sentence Fragment

If the words you wanted to quote aren't a complete sentence, then introduce the quote with a phrase that completes the quoted sentence fragment. Let's say that you want to use a quote from paragraph 11 of Beth Everest's essay. Here is the paragraph:

> A hood is also a gangster. Is this too a part of the mothering culture? What crime has been committed and against whom? Who is it that is concealing the being of a mother, she who is hooded? At this point, it is interesting to note another denotation of mother, one that has to do with the process of fermentation. The mother, in this case, refers to the dregs, the scum. How does this impact on society's view of what is a mother?

Let's say you want to include this sentence of the paragraph in your essay:

> At this point, it is interesting to note another denotation of mother, one that has to do with the process of fermentation.

You won't want to use the first part of the sentence because it is likely irrelevant to your essay. And, you might not be talking about *another* denotation. Perhaps you simply want to quote a fragment of the sentence.

All quotes need an introduction, and this quote is no exception. Introduce the quote using one of three techniques. Introduce the quote by summarizing what the quote is about, announcing who the words belong to, or announcing who the words belong to and where they came from. Make your introduction flow right into the quoted words. Here's the same quote introduced three different ways:

Summarizing what the quote is about:

> The word mother has some negative associations too, such as its meaning that "has to do with the process of fermentation" (Everest 135).

Stating who the words belong to:

> As Beth Everest has noted, one of the denotations of mother "has to do with the process of fermentation" (135).

Stating who the words belong to and where they came from:

> In her essay called "MotherHOOD," Beth Everest has noted that a denotation of mother "has to do with the process of fermentation" (135).

Make sure the introduction and the quote taken together form a complete sentence, and that you use quotation marks around all the quoted words. Just a little advice about introducing quotes: make sure to vary the introductions to your quotes. If you introduce all your quotes with one technique, you're likely to bore your reader.

The other thing to note is the use of the citation. After each quote, summary, or paraphrase, we want to make it clear for our reader where the words or ideas have come from. We call this citing our sources. In the discipline of English, we use MLA (Modern Languages Association) format. MLA format requires that we include the author's last name and the page on which we found the words in parentheses immediately following the quote, summary, or paraphrase. The end punctuation, in this case a period, comes after the closing parenthesis of the citation. Note that if the author's name appears in the introduction to the quote, it is not necessary to repeat it in the citation.

It is important to note here, too, that whenever we include other people's words or ideas in our essays we also include a Works Cited page as the final page of our essay. This is a list of all of the sources that we have used in our essay. Each entry contains full bibliographic information on each source. See Chapter 8 for details.

What to Do If the Quote is Longer Than Four Lines in Your Essay

If the quote you're using takes up more than four lines of your essay, then you need to make the quote into its own paragraph and indent the paragraph on both sides. You still introduce the quote using the same technique as you used to introduce a shorter quote. The only difference between the quote of four lines and the quote under four lines, is that in the longer version of the quote, because you indent the quote, you can remove the quotation marks from the beginning and end of the quote. Here's an example of a longer version of our original quote:

As Beth Everest has noted, the word motherhood also has some negative implications, ones that end up

> concealing the being of a mother, she who is hooded[.] At this point, it is interesting to note another denotation of mother, one that has to do with the process of fermentation. The mother, in this case, refers to the dregs, the scum. How does this impact on society's view of what is a mother? (135)

Notice that the introduction still flows right into the quote, forming a complete sentence. There is no punctuation between the introduction and the quote because the introduction and the first phrase of the quote form a complete sentence. Notice, too, that there are no quotation marks around the quote. When the words are indented and separated from the main paragraph, your reader will realize that you are quoting someone else's words, so the quotation marks aren't necessary. Remember that any of the three introduction techniques could introduce this quote. The format for citations remains the same, except that the end punctuation comes after the quote rather than after the citation.

Quoting Whole Sentences

If the quote isn't a sentence fragment, then we're quoting a whole sentence. To introduce a whole-sentence quote, we must use a complete sentence. Let's say we want to include this sentence in our essay:

> The mother, in this case, refers to the dregs, the scum.

The quote is a whole sentence, and it needs an introduction. We must introduce the quote using one of the three introduction techniques described in Quoting a Sentence Fragment. We can introduce the quote by summarizing what the quote is about, announcing who the words belong to, or announcing who the words belong to and where they came from. Our quote comes from Beth Everest's essay titled "MotherHOOD." However, this time, instead of making the introduction and the quote form a complete sentence, the introduction must be a sentence by itself. Here is the same quote introduced three different ways:

Summarizing what the quote is about:

> There are some negative meanings to the word mother: "the mother, in this case, refers to the dregs, the scum" (Everest 135).

Stating who the words belong to:

> Beth Everest suggests another negative meaning: "the mother, in this case, refers to the dregs, the scum" (135).

Stating who the words belong to and where they came from:

> In her essay called "MotherHOOD," Beth Everest suggests another negative meaning: "the mother, in this case, refers to the dregs, the scum" (135).

Notice that the introduction for each example is a full sentence. Notice that the first word of the quote, even though it was capitalized in the source, is now lower case. Change the first letter of the full-sentence quote to lower case. Notice, too, that the introduction is followed by a colon. Use a colon whenever you use a full sentence to introduce your quote. The format for doing citations remains the same as it does for sentence fragment quotes.

How to Remove Words from a Quote

Sometimes, you might want to cut some words from the middle of a quote. You need to use some special punctuation to show that you removed some. The special punctuation is called an **ellipsis**. Let's use paragraph two from "MotherHOOD" as our example:

> We live in a culture that promotes the idea of the mother, especially the mother-to-be and the new mother. We mark this as a rite-of-passage with baby showers and quilting bees, and clever marketing strategies that convince us that we need books about developing fetus and body changes, diet, herbs, medication and prenatal tests, delivery procedures, choosing doctors/midwives, choosing names, and so forth. And we can take classes to make sure we exercise, eat, and birth correctly. We can buy fashionable maternity clothes, bedding including pillows with large central cavities, baby albums, cradles, memorabilia, knickknacks—everything the baby and expectant mother could ever wish for, if she had money enough. Our society tells us how to play the role of the mother, and there is a big market for it.

Suppose we want to remove some of the words in a couple of places in this quote. First, remove the unwanted words. Make sure that the quote still makes sense after you've removed the words. Then, where you removed the words, place three periods in a row (this is called an ellipsis). We use four periods if we either omit words up to the end of a sentence or omit words at the beginning of the next sentence. The ellipsis tells your reader that you removed some words from the quote. Here's how it works:

> We live in a culture that promotes the idea of the mother, especially the mother-to-be and the new mother. We mark this as a rite-of-passage . . . . And we can take classes to make sure we exercise, eat, and birth correctly. We can buy . . . everything the baby and expectant mother could ever wish for, if she had money enough. Our society tells us how to play the role of the mother, and there is a big market for it.

The first ellipsis indicates that we have omitted all of the words from the ellipsis to the end of the sentence (four periods in a row). A four period ellipsis could also indicate that you have omitted a full sentence or more from that space in a paragraph. The second ellipsis of our example shows that we have left out words in the middle of a sentence (three periods). We've shortened the quote considerably, yet it still makes sense. As long as it clearly supports what we're saying in our essay, then removing words helps.

How to Add Words to a Quote (After Removing Some)

Occasionally a quote might use a word that could confuse your readers, or the words used in the quote don't fit with the terminology of your paper. In this kind of situation you'll want to add words to your quote to help the quote support your essay in a stronger way. For example, if you wanted to quote the following sentence from paragraph one of "MotherHOOD," you might want to replace the pronoun:

> No one appears to blame **her** for getting the stroller caught in the revolving door, or for leaving the baby seat (baby buckled tightly inside) on the

> roof of the car as she drives away; they simply watch from the sidelines, aghast at her failings.

First, you'll want to remove the confusing words and replace them with an ellipsis, like this:

> No one appears to blame . . . for getting the stroller caught in the revolving door, or for leaving the baby seat (baby buckled tightly inside) on the roof of the car as she drives away; they simply watch from the sidelines, aghast at her failings.

Then, add the terms you want to use in square brackets within the quote, like this:

> No one appears to blame . . . [the new mother] for getting the stroller caught in the revolving door, or for leaving the baby seat (baby buckled tightly inside) on the roof of the car as she drives away; they simply watch from the sidelines, aghast at her failings.

When your readers encounter words in square brackets, they will realize that these are words you added to the original quote. You won't want to add too many words, however, or your reader will suspect that you're trying to force your source to say something it doesn't say.

Paraphrase

A **paraphrase** is a sentence by sentence restatement of the original source. When you paraphrase a source, you rewrite in your own words what is being said. A paraphrase does not need quotation marks, but readers know that you paraphrased your information when they see that you have included a citation for your source. This technique interrupts your own writing the least because you don't have to try and fit someone else's words into your essay. You rewrite their words with your own. The other reason this technique might make a good choice is if the person who authored the words and the way the quote is worded aren't important to your essay.

How to Paraphrase Other People's Words

Paraphrasing means that you put the other person's ideas in your own words. It isn't enough to simply substitute a few words with synonyms for those words. You will also want to change the sentence structure. While it isn't necessary in your restatement to mention where the idea came from, it is critical that you include a citation using correct citation format. Examine the following paragraph from Everest's original source, Kanner's article in the *Calgary Herald*:

> Mother's Day is now the third largest card-sending occasion in America behind Christmas and Valentine's Day, according to Hallmark cards, with 144 million expected to be dispatched this year (Kanner 38).

Here is the paraphrase as it appears in "MotherHOOD":

> Hallmark reports that it ranks right after Christmas and Valentine's as the celebration in which the greatest number of cards is commonly sent. The greeting card company estimated a huge number of sales in the year 2000: 144 million Mother's Day cards (Kanner 38).

Because Everest wants to really emphasize the fact that Mother's Day has become a marketing phenomenon, she uses a paraphrase of Kanner's ideas. The words "Hallmark reports..." indicates where the paraphrase begins, and the citation to the source indicates where the paraphrase ends. Note that the words in the paraphrase are different, and the sentence structure is completely different, but the ideas are the same. The length, too, remains approximately the same. The paraphrase fits better with what Everest wants to say, and especially how she wants to say it.

It is absolutely essential that the sources for paraphrases, like quotes, are properly cited. If a person forgets to document the source, there is nothing in the writing to indicate the ideas are someone else's. Either failing to cite a source, or incorrectly citing a source, is considered plagiarizing. Plagiarizing is using someone's words or ideas without giving credit. It is a serious offence. Be careful to quote, paraphrase, and summarize carefully and to cite your sources correctly!

Summarizing

A **summary** is a condensed version of the original. You use it to support whatever it is that you are trying to get across to your reader. When you write a summary, you reduce the original source to the most important ideas without the unnecessary details that flesh them out. Summarizing is an important skill in doing research, because it first demands that you read carefully for the author's purpose and perspective, and then write concisely and directly the author's central message. You might reduce a single paragraph or even a group of paragraphs to a single sentence. A whole essay or chapter might become a single paragraph in your essay. Summarize the ideas in the order that they appear in the original, and make certain that you don't follow the original wording too closely or you might inadvertently plagiarize. Don't forget to indicate where your summary begins, and use a citation to indicate the end of the summary and the source.

How to Summarize Other People's Words

A summary is a brief reporting of someone else's words or ideas. When you summarize, you want to give a general idea of what has been said and give the author credit at the same time. Often you will want to use the word "that" to indicate you are beginning a summary. Reread paragraph four of "MotherHOOD":

> Is there anything wrong with worshipping the ideal? *Yes* is the simple answer. Even in contemporary times we worship the mother through deeply entrenched cultural idols of the supermom, the professional who comes home from full time work to do full time work and still manages to be on parent advisory, to coach little league, to organize the phone committee, and to supervise the yearbook. And every Friday the kids come home to freshly baked chocolate chip cookies. Plus, the house is always spotless, and she never yells at anyone to put their dirty clothes in the laundry or to stop bickering or to help with the dinner preparations. In fact, this epitomizes the ideal of motherhood. Who can realistically match it?

If we were to summarize this paragraph, we would likely want to introduce the summary by including where the ideas have come from. The author's name is Beth Everest, so we might like to begin with a statement attributing the ideas to her. This shows our reader not only whose ideas we are referring to, but also that we are beginning a summary. Here is a possible summary:

> Beth Everest suggests that worshipping the mother is a problem because it plays itself out in our society with ideals such as the supermom, ideals that can not realistically be met (134).

Notice that the details of what Everest says in the original quote are omitted from the summary. The summary simply condenses the material to the main ideas. It is important that what you write in your summary is true to what the original source says. Note also that we include the citation at the end to attribute the source and to show that this is where this particular summary ends.

Exercise P6-1

Spend some time to complete the following exercise. Make sure you understand each technique:

1. Go to the library and find one six- to ten-sentence quote that you might use for your research essay.
2. Return to the class and spend time introducing a quote fragment, and/or a whole sentence.
3. Try working with the four lines quoting technique.
4. Try rewording and paraphrasing your quote.

Collaborative Work

After you revise your essay, exchange papers with a classmate and complete the following tasks:

A. Find any quotes, paraphrases, and rewordings used in the essay.

B. Check every quote to make sure it's been introduced and the introduction connects properly to the quote.

C. Does the essay vary the introductory techniques?

D. Should any of the quotes be turned into a paraphrase or summary? Should any of the paraphrases or summaries be quoted instead?

Then return the paper to your classmate. When you receive your essay, use the information in this section to edit your draft.

CHAPTER **SEVEN**

Analyzing

Meaning comes only through the act of taking things apart and putting them back together again.

—**Richard A. Orr**

LEARNING OUTCOMES

This chapter will help you:

- Understand and write an essay about a topic you have analyzed;
- Check the structure of your essay by examining your essay's varying levels of generality;
- Link paragraphs with unifying devices.

Detectives cordon off the crime scene and begin the tedious task of collecting hair fragments, blood samples, bits of paper, and anything else they think is related to the crime. From those fragments of evidence, they hope to accuse the person responsible, and send that person to prison. When you watch a basketball game, you evaluate the players' movements so that you can better understand their strategy. You do the same thing when you listen to a speech or read an article. You break down the parts of the article, speech, or basketball game, attempting to show your audience what is really being said or what is really happening in the game. In other words, you break a topic into parts and look at them from all angles so that you can understand the topic as fully as possible.

Analyzing is an important ability we use every day, and we use it in one of two ways. Sometimes when we analyze we're looking at a lot of little pieces and suggesting what those details mean and what might happen in the future. This kind of movement from details into general conclusions is called **induction**. Here's an example:

> Red sky at night, sailor's delight: red sky in the morning, sailor's warning.

This short saying makes sense of details that anyone might observe during the day–a red sky–and tells that person what that red sky means. The second kind of analysis we can use looks at the big picture and then moves to suggest some of the details that must be true in light of the big picture:

> We lost the game because our best players were out with injuries.

This kind of movement–from the general to the specific–is sometimes called **deduction**. Most analysis essays tend to move inductively, from the details and work towards a whole, or deductively from the whole to the details.

LEARNING FROM PUBLISHED WRITERS

In the following essay, titled "An Essay for My Father," poet Richard Harrison works through some of the detail of his father's life, analyzes it, and moves to some general conclusions about who his father was and why he loved poetry. It's an exploration of a bond of words between a son and his father.

Before You Read

Focus Your Attention

In the essay you are about to read, the writer analyzes his father's love of poetry, what those poems meant to his father, and how his father shared those poems with his son. Before you read this analysis essay, take a few moments to respond to the following questions. Jot down the answers in your notebook.

Think about a habit one of your parents nurtured. What was that habit? How did it affect you? How do you feel about that habit now? Does it have any special meaning to you?

Expand Your Vocabulary

Find each of the listed words in the following essay. Read them in context, and jot down a definition of each. Compare your definitions with those that you find in a dictionary.

Horrific (paragraph 1)

Romantic (paragraph 2)

Falcon/Falconer (paragraph 3)

Second Coming (paragraph 3)

Apocalyptic (paragraph 4)

Richard Harrison

An Essay for My Father*

I've spent a large part of my life trying to dream up what my father never told me about his war. The things he did and saw done. The things comic books and movies tell me are both horrific and things to be proud of. They were terrible things and of them he has never spoken. I've often thought of him as one of the young men who, as Enrich Remarque wrote in his preface to *All Quiet on the Western Front*, "escaped its shells," but "were destroyed by the war." 1

It's a Romantic image in its way: the man as living ghost. He lived. And maybe if I look at what he is rather than what he is not, I can find out something more important about him than what I don't know because he didn't tell me. Maybe I can find out what I should know because he did. 2

After all that death, my father came out of the war loving poetry. Before I was born he had memorized Robert Browning and Dylan Thomas, William Butler Yeats and Shakespeare. I remember him uttering marvelous words around me over and over not because he was teaching me, but because he was offering me the best language that he could. I remember the thrill of learning how to complete the sentence, "O pardon me thou bleeding piece of earth..." from Marc Antony's speech over the body of murdered Caesar. Or knowing that after the "falcon cannot hear the falconer" it was then that "things fall apart" to set in motion "The Second Coming." It was the thrill of speaking together with the man who had come through the war and decided to make a new life in spite of it. 3

Looking back on it now, I can see that the poems he remembered were mostly apocalyptic, poems about the ends of things—kings, towns, worlds. And in that sense I'm sure his choice of what words to say was influenced by their ability to talk about things in words he could not. But these words, committed to memory, were the things that he held on to. I've read about love like that: soldiers in Leningrad fighting the Nazis from shelled-out apartment buildings in the middle of Russian winter putting down their rifles for the night and scribbling out their poems in frozen rooms. Maybe they would die the next day, but even so, the words just might outlive them and they wouldn't have died without leaving their voices behind. 4

To love words is to love the best of them whether you wrote them or not. My father loved language that way. And he gave me that love, I now believe, because for him language became life and I was his son. And when we spoke a poem together, he wasn't teaching me about poetry, he was showing me how he survived. And how life goes on. As it must. 5

---

*Richard Harrison's "An Essay for My Father" first appeared in *Matrix* magazine No. 55 (Autumn, 1999).

Questions For Critical Thinking

Thinking Critically About Content

1. What is Harrison analyzing: what is he taking apart and examining? Does his essay move inductively or deductively?
2. Harrison says "maybe if I look at what he is rather than what he is not, I can find out something more important about him than what I don't know because he didn't tell me." In the light of his essay, what does this mean?

Thinking Critically About Purpose

3. What is Harrison's purpose in writing this essay?
4. What makes this an essay of analysis rather than a recalling essay?

Thinking Critically About Audience

5. What group of readers would find this essay most interesting? Why?
6. Harrison is writing about his own father. What makes his experience relevant to the reader?

Thinking Critically About Perspective

7. How does the author feel about his father's love of words? How do you know?
8. What specific incidents suggest that Harrison romanticizes the old ways?

LEARNING FROM YOUR PEERS

Analyzing helps us to understand why something happened and what the effects of the event are on our lives. When you write an analysis, you should make these connections very clear, both for yourself and for your readers. Learning to write analytically is a skill that will be useful to you in many areas of life. In other college classes, you may be asked to analyze a scientific process, a political or historical event, or a piece of literature. The skills you use to write essays of this type are basically the same: take the event apart, and put it together again in a way that makes sense to you. Watching another writer's analysis take shape can be an informative experience. To help you learn how to approach writing assignments requiring analysis, we are going to follow the writing process of a student named Chris Desiatnyk.

Chris's Writing Assignment: Analyzing

This is the topic Chris's instructor assigned:

Look for something in your everyday life that you feel strongly about. Then, spend some time and take that person, place, thing, or idea apart and try to discover what it is that makes you feel so strongly.

Chris went through the process as outlined in Chapter 1: generating ideas, planning, developing, organizing, drafting, revising, and editing.

Generating Ideas

Chris didn't know how to begin, and he had no idea what to write about. He sat at the desk in his room, frustrated for a good half-hour. He never had any ideas—that was his biggest problem. The instructor had asked the class not to think about a writing topic so much as something they felt strongly about, so Chris tried to put his paper out of his mind and concentrate on something he felt strongly about. Unfortunately, he still couldn't think of anything. Finally, after another 40 minutes, he tried putting his pen on a blank piece of paper. As he sat at his desk, his feet got quite cold, so he left his writing to find his slippers. When he returned to his desk, he sat looking out the window as snow fell, and found himself thinking about winter and cold. Finally, he wrote the word "cold" down in the middle of his paper. It didn't seem like much, but it was the only idea he'd had in an hour of work. He circled the word cold, and wrote the word "slippers." As he tapped his pen on his page, he realized he was sick with a cold, too. He began to wonder what the definition of "cold" was. He rummaged through his desk drawers looking for his dictionary.

Planning

He briefly read the dictionary's rendition of the word "cold" and made a few notes. He wrote down these words in a list:

Temperature

Sickness

Personality stuff

He wasn't sure what order he wanted to deal with each topic, but it was enough to get going.

Developing

Chris spent some time brainstorming each idea and adding thoughts and questions to the page. He did a separate freewrite and cluster session for each of his points. Then, he took his ideas and turned them into sentences around each of his points.

Organizing

Once he had developed his collection of thoughts around each idea, he had to sort through his ideas and reorder them in each paragraph. He spent a good deal of time cutting irrelevant material, paring it all down to one coherent paragraph on each topic. He wrote a topic sentence for each paragraph and made sure they were clear. Then, he started to shuffle the paragraphs around to see which paragraph worked best toward the beginning, and which worked best at the end. He was working on his computer, so tinkering with the essay's structure was simple.

Drafting

Once he settled on an order, he worked on the transitions between paragraphs to make sure one paragraph flowed nicely into the subsequent one. Then he wrote an introduction and conclusion. Here's what he wrote:

Chris's Essay: First Draft

What is cold? Who is cold? Where is cold? Or even how is cold? Sure people can be cold, but at the same time they can be cold. I know that I've been cold, and I'm certain that people around me have been cold. I've also had a cold. Was having a cold the result of being cold? The cold could have been given to me by people who had a cold, even though they may not have been cold at the time. How do you get a cold: from the weather, another person, a virus, or another person with a virus? I've learned you shouldn't be cold to people with colds, even if they are being cold to you, but if they are cold it might be nice to cook them some chicken soup or give them a blanket. The thing about cold is that even though it is a four-letter word, its definition depends on who and why someone says it. The most basic and common ways of using the word cold would be when describing the temperature of something, describing the mood of a person, or a health or medical condition.

Something can feel cold, or someone can feel cold. It is considered cold when the temperature is low. Usually things become cold because of the temperature of the things around them or that come in contact with them. For example, a drink will get colder if it is put in the fridge or if someone puts ice into it. The same rules apply to people as well. People are going to get cold if they are sitting in a cold room or outside in the winter. They may also get cold from drinking or eating something of a very low temperature. Really, though, what is feeling something cold, more than feeling something that is soft or hard, what is that feeling in us but the mere sensation of how our body tells us to react to that feeling. Is it not just a triggered impulse from the brain? How many time has another person in the same room, even sitting next to you, felt the opposite of you, cold when you're hot or hot when you're cold. Of course it has to be more than a mental reaction, or people would not suffer things like frostbite or hypothermia. Perhaps people's individual response to different levels of cold vary and are a mental response.

Cold is frequently used when describing the mood people are in. People are often overheard using such lines as "cold shoulder" or "cold look" or simply complain of being treated coldly. The word is used in order to describe a mood or demeanour, in short is usually used in order to describe someone unfriendly. The use of cold in such a way stems from the way the touch of cold makes you feel. Cold usually has a very sharp and unpleasant feel to it. It is that sharp, painful type look or feeling that people give that is referred to as cold.

The third most common use of cold is when describing a certain type of sickness. Having a cold is being stuffed up, having a sore throat, runny nose, and feeling tired and low in energy. People can also get cold sores in their mouths. The funny thing about having a cold, or a cold sore, is that it is not the result of being cold. It is curious to me that it is called a cold, because even though people may have a cold, they may be warm. The name has very little to do with describing the condition they may be in.

Bob Bartlett, who teaches a freshman sexuality class in a Richfield, Minn., high school, shares the following story of regret on the part of one of his students (we'll call her Sandy): **13**

> Sandy, a bright and pretty girl, asked to see Mr. Bartlett during her lunch period. She explained that she had never had a boyfriend, so she was excited when a senior asked her out. **14**
>
> After they dated for several weeks, the boy asked her to have sex with him. She was reluctant; he was persistent. She was afraid of appearing immature and losing him, so she consented. **15**
>
> "Did it work?" Mr. Bartlett asked gently. "Did you keep him?" **16**
>
> Sandy replied: "For another week. We had sex again, and then he dropped me. He said I wasn't good enough. There was no spark. **17**
>
> "I know what you're going to say. I take your class. I know now that he didn't love me. I feel so stupid, so cheap. (Bartlett 36) **18**

Sandy hoped, naively, that sex would keep the guy. Here is another high school girl writing to an advice column about a different kind of regret. She wishes she *could* lose the guy she's involved with, but she feels trapped by their sexual relationship. **19**

> I am 16, a junior in high school, and like nearly all the other girls here, I have already lost my virginity. Although most people consider this subject very personal, I feel the need to share this part of my life with girls who are trying to decide whether to have sex for the first time. **20**
>
> Sex does not live up to the glowing reports and hype you see in the movies. It's no big deal. In fact, it's pretty disappointing. **21**
>
> I truly regret that my first time was with a guy that I didn't care that much about. I am still going out with him, which is getting to be a problem. I'd like to end this relationship and date others, but after being so intimate, it's awfully tough. **22**
>
> Since that first night, he expects sex on every date, like we are married or something. When I don't feel like it, we end up in an argument. It's like I owe it to him. I don't think this guy is in love with me, at least he's never said so. I know deep down that I am not in love with him either, and this makes me feel sort of cheap. **23**
>
> I realize now that this is a very big step in a girl's life. After you've done it, things are never the same. It changes everything. **24**
>
> My advice is, don't be in such a rush. It's a headache and a worry. (Could I be pregnant?) Sex is not for entertainment. It should be a commitment. Be smart and save yourself for someone you wouldn't mind spending the rest of your life with. **25**
>
> —Sorry I Didn't And Wish I Could Take It Back (Landers, "A Not-So-Sweet. . . 20) **26**

Regret over uncommitted sexual relationships can last for years. I recently received a letter from a 33-year-old woman, now a psychiatrist, who is very much concerned about the sexual pressures and temptations facing young people today. She wanted to share the lessons she had learned about sex the hard way. After high school, she says, she spent a year abroad as an exchange student: **27**

> I was a virgin when I left, but I felt I was protected. I had gotten an IUD so I could make my own decisions if any when I wanted. I had steeled myself against commitment. I was never going to marry or have children; I was going to have a career. During that year abroad, from 17½ to 18½, I was very promiscuous. **28**
>
> But the fact is, it cost me to be separated from myself. The longest-standing and deepest wound I gave myself was heartfelt. That sick, used feeling of having given a precious part of myself—my soul—to so many and for nothing, still aches. I never imagined I'd pay so dearly and for so long. **29**

This woman is happily married now, she says, and has a good sexual relationship with her husband. But she still carries the emotional scar of those early sexual experiences. She wants young people to know that "sex without commitment is very risky for the heart." **30**

3. Guilt

Guilt is a special form of regret—a strong sense of having done something morally wrong. Guilt is a normal and healthy moral response, a sign that one's conscience is working. **31**

In his book for teenagers, *Love, Dating, and Sex*, George Eager tells the story of a well-known speaker who was addressing a high school assembly. The speaker was asked, "What do you most regret about your high school days?" **32**

He answers, "The thing I most regret about high school is the time I single-handedly destroyed a girl." **33**

Eager offers this advice to young men: "When the breakup comes, it's usually a lot tougher on the girls than it is on the guys. It's not something you want on your conscience—that you caused a girl to have deep emotional problems." **34**

One 16-year-old boy says he stopped having sex with girls when he saw and felt guilty about the pain he was causing: "You see them crying and confused. They say they love you, but you don't love them." **35**

Even in an age of sexual liberation, a lot of people who are having sex nevertheless have a guilty conscience about it. The guilt may come, as in the case of the young man just quoted, from seeing the hurt you've caused other people. **36**

The guilt may come from knowing that your parents would be upset if they knew you were having sex. Or it may stem from your religious convictions. **37**

Christianity, Judaism, and Islam, for example, all teach that sex is a gift from God reserved for marriage and that sexual relations outside marriage are morally wrong.

Sometimes guilt about their sexual past ends up crippling people when they become parents by keeping them from advising their own children not to become sexually involved. According to counselor Dr. Carson Daly: "Because these parents can't bear to be considered hypocrites, or to consider themselves hypocrites, they don't give their children the sexual guidance they very much need." (Personal communication.) 38

4. Loss of Self-Respect and Self-Esteem

Many people suffer a loss of self-esteem when they find out they have a sexually transmitted disease. For example, according to the Austin, Texas-based Medical Institute for Sexual Health, more than 80 percent of people with herpes say they feel "less confident" and "less desirable sexually" (*Safe Sex. . .*). 39

But even if a person is fortunate enough to escape sexually transmitted disease, temporary sexual relationships can lower the self-respect of both the user and the used. 40

Sometimes casual sex lowers self-esteem, leading a person into further casual sex, which leads to further loss of self-esteem in an oppressive cycle from which it may be hard to break free. This pattern is described by a college senior, a young woman who works as a residence hall director: 41

> There are girls in our dorm who have had multiple pregnancies and multiple abortions. They tend to be filled with self-loathing. But because they have so little self-esteem, they will settle for any kind of attention from guys. So they keep going back to the same kind of destructive situations and relationships that got them into trouble in the first place. 42

On both sides of dehumanized sex, there is a loss of dignity and self-worth. One 20-year-old college male confides: "You feel pretty crummy when you get drunk at a party and have sex with some girl, and then the next morning you can't even remember who she was." 43

Another college student describes the loss of self-respect that followed his first sexual "conquest": 44

> I finally got a girl into bed—actually it was a car—when I was 17. I thought it was the hottest thing there was, but then she started saying she loved me and getting clingy. 45
>
> I figured out that there had probably been a dozen guys before me who thought they had "conquered" her, but who were really just objects of her need for security. That realization took all the wind out of my sails. I couldn't respect someone who gave in as easily as she did. 46
>
> I was amazed to find that after four weeks of having sex as often as I wanted, I was tired of her. I didn't see any point in continuing the 47

relationship. I finally dumped her, which made me feel even worse, because I could see that she was hurting. I felt pretty low. (McDowell and Day)

People aren't things. When we treat them as if they were, we not only hurt them; we lose respect for ourselves. 48

5. The Corruption of Character and the Debasement of Sex

When people treat others as sexual objects and exploit them for their own pleasure, they not only lose self-respect; they corrupt their characters and debase their sexuality in the process. 49

Good character consists of virtues such as respect, responsibility, honesty, fairness, caring, and self-control. With regard to sex, the character trait of self-control is particularly crucial. The breakdown of sexual self-control is a big factor in many of the sex-related problems that plague our society: rape, promiscuity, pornography, addiction to sex, sexual harassment, the sexual abuse of children, sexual infidelity in marriage, and the serious damage to families many of these problems cause. It was Freud who said—and it is now obvious how right he was—that sexual self-control is essential for civilization. 50

Sex frequently corrupts character by leading people to tell lies in order to get sex. The Medical Institute for Sexual Health reports: "Almost all studies show that many sexually active people will lie if they think it will help them have sex." Common lies: "I love you" and "I've never had a sexually transmitted disease." 51

Because sex is powerful, once a sexual restraint is set aside, it easily takes over individuals and relationships. Consider the highly sexualized atmosphere that now characterizes many high schools. A high school teacher in Indiana says, "The air is thick with sex talk. Kids in the halls will say—boy to girl, girl to boy—'I want to f— you'." 60

In a 1993 study by the American Association of University Women, four of five high school students—85 percent of girls and 75 percent of boys—said they have experienced "unwelcome sexual behavior that interferes with my life" in school (American Association . . .). An example: A boy backs a 14-year-old girl up against her locker, day after day. Says Nan Stein, a Wellesley College researcher: "There's a Tailhook happening in every school. Egregious behavior is going on." 61

Another recently reported example of this corruption of character is the Spur Posse club at Lakewood High School in suburban Los Angeles. Members of this club competed to see how many girls they could sleep with; one claimed he had slept with 63. Sadly, elementary school-age children are beginning to mimick such behavior. In a suburb of Pittsburgh, an assistant superintendent reports that sixth-grade boys were found playing a sexual contact game; the object of the game was to earn points by touching girls in private parts, the most points being awarded for "going all the way." 62

In this sex-out-of-control environment, even rape is judged permissible by many young people. In a 1998 survey of students in grades six through nine, the Rhode Island Rape Crisis Center found that two of three boys and 49 percent of the girls said it was "acceptable for a man to force sex on a woman if they have been dating for six months or more (Kikuchi). In view of attitudes like these, it's easy to understand why date rape has become such a widespread problem. 63

In short, sex that isn't tied to love and commitment undermines character by subverting self-control, respect, and responsibility. Unchecked, sexual desires and impulses easily run amok and lead to habits of hedonism and using others for one's personal pleasure. In the process, sexual intercourse loses its meaning, beauty, and specialness; instead of being a loving, uniquely intimate expression of two people's commitment to each other, sex is trivialized and degraded. 64

6. Shaken Trust and Fear of Commitment

Young people who feel used or betrayed after the break-up of a sexual relationship may experience difficulty in future relationships. 65

Some sexually exploited people, as we've seen, develop such low self-esteem that they seek any kind of attention, even if it's another short-lived and demeaning sexual relationship. But other people, once burned, withdraw. They have trouble trusting; they don't want to get burned again. 66

Usually this happens to the girl. She begins to see guys as interested in just one thing: Sex. Says one young woman: "Besides feeling cheap [after several sexual relationships], I began to wonder if there would ever be anyone who would love and accept me without demanding that I do something with my body to earn that love" (McDowell and Day). 67

However, boys can also experience loss of trust and fear of commitment as a result of a broken relationship that involved sex. Brian, a college senior, tells how this happened to him: 68

> I first had intercourse with my girlfriend when we were 15. I'd been going with her for almost a year, and I loved her very much. She was friendly, outgoing, charismatic. We'd done everything but have intercourse, and then one night she asked if we could go all the way. 69
>
> A few days later, we broke up. It was the most painful time of my life. I had opened myself up to her more than I had to anybody, even my parents. 70
>
> I was depressed, moody, nervous. My friends dropped me because I was so bummed out. I felt like a failure. I dropped out of sports. My grades weren't terrific. 71
>
> I didn't go out again until I got to college. I've had mostly one-night stands in the last couple of years. 72
>
> I'm afraid of falling in love." (*Choose the Best . . .*) 73

7. Rage Over Betrayal

Sometimes the emotional reaction to being "dumped" isn't just a lack of trust or fear of commitment. It's rage. 74

Every so often, the media carry a story about a person who had this rage reaction and then committed an act of violence against the former boyfriend or girlfriend. Read these accounts, and you'll find that sex was almost always a part of the broken relationship. 75

Of course, people often feel angry when somebody breaks up with them, even if sex has not been involved. But the sense of betrayal is usually much greater if sex has been part of the relationship. Sex can be emotional dynamite. It can lead a person to think that the relationship is really serious, that both people really love each other. It can create a very strong emotional bond that hurts terribly when it's ruptured—especially if it seems that the other person never had the same commitment. And the resulting sense of betrayal can give rise to rage, even violence. 76

8. Depression and Suicide

In *Sex and the Teenager*, Kieran Sawyer writes: "The more the relationship seems like real love, the more the young person is likely to invest, and the deeper the pain and hurt if the relationship breaks up." Sometimes the emotional turmoil caused by the rupture of a sexual relationship leads to deep depression. The depression, in turn, may lead some people to take their own lives. 77

In the past 25 years, teen suicide has tripled. In a 1988 survey by the U.S. Department of Health and Human Services, one in five adolescent girls said they have tried to kill themselves (the figure for boys was one in 10). 78

This is the same period during which the rate of teenage sexual activity has sharply increased, especially for girls. No doubt, the rise in youth suicide has multiple causes, but given what we know about the emotional aftermath of broken sexual relationships, it is reasonable to suspect that the pain from such break-ups is a factor in the suicide deaths of some young people. 79

9. Ruined Relationships

Sex can have another kind of emotional consequence: It can turn a good relationship bad. Other dimensions of the relationship stop developing. Pretty soon, negative emotions enter the picture. Eventually, they poison the relationship, and what had been a caring relationship comes to a bitter end. 80

One young woman shares her story, which illustrates the process: 81

> With each date, my boyfriend's requests for sex became more convincing. After all, we did love each other. Within two months, I gave in, because I had justified the whole thing. Over the next six months, sex became the center of our relationship. . . . 82
>
> At the same time, some new things entered our relationship—things like anger, impatience, jealousy, and selfishness. We just couldn't talk 83

anymore. We grew very bored with each other. I desperately wanted a change. (McDowell and Day)

A young man who identified himself as a 22-year-old virgin echoes this 84
warning about the damage premature sex can do to a relationship:

> I've seen too many of my friends break up after their relationships 85
> turned physical. The emotional wreckage is horrendous because they have already shared something so powerful. When you use sex too early, it will block other means of communicating love and can stunt the balanced growth of a relationship. (Landers, "Despite Urgin'")

10. Stunting Personal Development

Premature sexual involvement not only can stunt the development of a re- 86
lationship; it also can stunt one's development as a person.

Just as some young people handle anxieties by turning to drugs and alco- 87
hol, others handle them by turning to sex. Sex becomes an escape. They aren't learning how to cope with life's pressures.

Teenagers who are absorbed in an intense sexual relationship are turning 88
inward on one thing at the very time in their lives when they should be reaching out—forming new friendships, joining clubs and teams, developing their interests and skills, taking on bigger social responsibilities.

All of these are important nutrients for a teenager's development as a per- 89
son. And this period of life is special because young people have both the time and the opportunities to develop their talents and interests. The growing they do during these years will affect them all their lives. If young people don't put these years to good use, they may never develop their full potential.

The risk appears to be greater for girls who get sexually involved and in 90
so doing close the door on other interests and relationships. Says New York psychiatrist Samuel Kaufman:

> A girl who enters into a serious relationship with a boy very early in 91
> life may find out later that her individuality was thwarted. She became part of him and failed to develop her own interests, her sense of independent identity. (qtd. in Lewis)

Reflecting on her long experience in counseling college students and 92
others about sexual matters, Dr. Carson Daly comments:

> I don't think I ever met a student who was sorry he or she had post- 93
> poned sexual activity, but I certainly met many who deeply regretted their sexual involvements. Time and time again, I have seen the long-term emotional and spiritual desolation that results from casual sex and promiscuity.
>
> No one tells students that it sometimes takes years to recover from 94
> the effects of these sexual involvements—if one every fully recovers. (Personal communication)

Sex certainly can be a source of great pleasure and joy. But as should be amply clear—and youngsters need our help and guidance in understanding this—sex also can be the source of deep wounds and suffering. What makes the difference is the relationship within which it occurs. Sex is most joyful and fulfilling—most emotionally safe as well as physically safe—when it occurs within a loving, total, and binding commitment. Historically, we have called that marriage. Sexual union is then part of something bigger—the union of two persons' lives. **96**

Works Cited

American Association of University Women. *Report on Sexual Harrassment*, June 1993.

Bartlett, Bob. "Going All the Way." *Momentum* April/May 1993: 124.

Bennett, William. "Sex and the Education of Our Children." *America* 14 Feb. 1987: 36.

Choosing the Best: A Values-Based Sex Education Curriculum [abridged]. Atlanta, GA, 1993.

"Condoms Ineffective Against Human Papilloma Virus." *Sexual Health Update*. Austin, TX: Medical Institute for Sexual Health. Apr. 1994.

Daly, Carson. Personal communication.

Eager, George. *Love, Dating, and Sex*. Valdosta, GA: Mailbox Club Books.

Kikuchi, J. "Rhode Island Develops Successful Intervention Program for Adolescents." *National Coalition Against Sexual Assault Newsletter* Fall. 1988.

Landers, Ann. "A Not-So-Sweet Sexteen Story" [abridged]. *Daily News*. 23 Sept. 1991: 20.

Landers, Ann. "Despite Urgin', He's a Virgin." *Daily News*. 15 Jan. 1994.

Lewis, Howard and Martha. *The Parent's Guide to Teenage Sex and Pregnancy*. New York: St. Martin's, 1980.

McDowell, Josh and Dick Day. *Why Wait: What You Need to Know About the Teen Sexuality Crisis*. San Bernardino, CA: Here's Life, 1987.

Medical Institute for Sexual Health. Austin, TX.

Noller, Kenneth. *OB/GYN Clinical Alert-t*. Sept. 1992.

Safe Sex: A Slide Program. Medical Institute for Sexual Health. Austin, TX: 1992.

Sawyer, Karen. *Sex and the Teenager*. Notre Dame, IN: Ave Maria, 1990.

"Some Teens Taking Vows of Virginity." *Washington Post*. 21 Nov. 1993.

Weller, Susan. "A Meta-Analysis of Condom Effectiveness in Reducing Sexually Transmitted HIV." *Social Science and Medicine*. June 1993: 12.

Questions For Critical Thinking

Thinking Critically About Content

1. Why do you think the writer presents the negative consequences of premature sexual involvement by numbering them 1 through 10 and giving each consequence a heading instead of presenting them in paragraph form? What effect does this strategy have on the essay?
2. Why do you think the writer includes so many quotes from teenagers about their sexual experiences?

Thinking Critically About Purpose

3. What do you think Thomas Lickona's purpose is in this essay?
4. Do you think the author is trying to persuade young couples not to have sexual relations before marriage? If not, what is he recommending?

Thinking Critically About Audience

5. Although this essay was published in a magazine for teachers, do you think other groups of people could benefit from reading it? Explain your answer.
6. What effect do you think this essay will have on teenagers who have already had sexual relationships?

Thinking Critically About Perspective

7. Describe in a complete sentence the writer's point of view.
8. This essay was written for teachers. If you were writing an essay about the same topic for students, how would it be different? How would it be the same? Rewrite the introduction and conclusion of this essay for a student audience.

LEARNING FROM YOUR PEERS

Because we live in a society that allows us to voice our opinions freely, many of us strive to learn how to express our disagreement in a polite and reasoned way. As a student, your life may be affected by unreasonable school policies; you may be asked to participate in debates or class discussions; or you may be assigned a particular point of view when writing about an important social or historical issue. At home, you may want to write a letter to a public official or an employer to explain your views on a certain topic, or you may want to write to a store or a manufacturer to ask for your money back on a recent purchase. In short, life in North America is filled with opportunities to try to persuade others of your point of view. Learning how to persuade others effectively and respectfully is a valuable skill that will always be useful. To see how to excel at this skill, we are going to follow the writing process of a student named Melinda Jackson.

Melinda's Writing Assignment: Persuading

This is the topic Melinda's instructor assigned:

No one is born with the skill to persuade another person to change his or her way of thinking; it is a skill we develop. Some combination of emotional and logical arguments is probably the most effective formula when trying to convince another person to see a situation from your point of view. For this assignment, choose a controversial topic that you are familiar with. Then take one side, and try to convince your readers that your stand on the issue is the correct one.

Melinda goes through the process as outlined in Chapter 1: generating ideas, planning, developing, organizing, drafting, revising, and editing.

Generating Ideas

After receiving this assignment, Melinda explains to her writing group that she doesn't feel like thinking of a topic today. She is upset because her brother, who is still in high school, was beaten up by one of his best friends at a school event yesterday. The friend had come to school after several hours of drinking, and his behaviour was alarming to his friends. Melinda's brother confronted his friend and tried to get him to leave the school grounds so the school officials wouldn't notice he was drunk. The friend responded by hitting Melinda's brother repeatedly in the face, knocking him to the ground, and almost choking him before help arrived. The school officials called the drunk boy's parents, but there were no consequences for his bad behaviour. Her brother, the innocent victim, had to go to the hospital for stitches and other necessary medical attention. Her writing group tells her how sorry they feel for her brother, and they encourage her to think about her topic later.

The next day Melinda is still upset about her brother's situation. He is home from the hospital but still in pain. She decides to write about her anger. At least she will have a journal entry for class. This is what she writes:

> I am really mad about what happened to Scott. It is not fair. He is a good kid, and he was just trying to keep his friend out of trouble. Well, he sure succeeded at that. That kid probably didn't even remember what he did while he was drunk. The school didn't do anything to him. Who knows what his parents did. Knowing them, the worst thing they can think of is to take his car away for a week. Of course, they will let him drive to school. He just won't be able to drive at night.
>
> And poor Scott. He might have permanent damage to his eyes. He wouldn't press charges because he said his friend was out of his mind and

> didn't know who Scott was or what he was doing to him. What is it with these people? They all seem to be helping the drunk. Who is helping Scott?

Melinda meets with her group the next day. They suggest that she write about the alcohol policy at her brother's high school. Maybe she can write a letter to someone in authority there and suggest a change in the policy or in the enforcement of the policy.

Planning

That evening, Melinda asks her brother for his school handbook. There she finds the current policy on drug and alcohol abuse. She sees that the policy is designed to be enforced only if the school authorities think it needs to be enforced. The policy has no "teeth" in it; there is no guaranteed punishment for offenders.

Melinda starts writing about possible policy changes at the school. This is what she writes:

> Innocent people are being hurt. Guilty people suffer no consequences. Everyone knows that drug and alcohol abuse is rampant, but no one does anything about it.
>
> There is no penalty for breaking the rules at that school. I think students could get away with murder as long as the parents would agree to pick them up and get them off the school grounds.
>
> The policy says that kids could get expelled from school. Not likely. Not in my experience. Maybe the school will suggest that Susie or William should go to a rehab program.
>
> Kids come to school events wasted all the time. They think they can't have any fun without some chemical high.
>
> So do mandatory drug tests. That might get rid of the problem for a while. A drastic solution, maybe. But what's the alternative?

Developing

Melinda knows she needs to do a little more research so that she can develop a few of her ideas more thoroughly before writing her first draft. First of all, she wants to make sure she quotes the actual school policy on drug and alcohol use: "School policy prohibits the unlawful use, manufacture, possession, distribution, or dispensing of controlled substances and alcohol on school grounds or at school-sponsored events." The wording of the penalty for breaking this rule ("may result in expulsion from school") is vague and tentative, and Melinda believes this is part of the problem.

In fact, there are several different aspects of this problem that Melinda feels the school isn't dealing with, so she records some more of these:

1. Students using drugs and alcohol at school.
2. Students coming to school or school events under the influence of drugs or alcohol.
3. Students not being punished at school or at home for substance abuse.

Melinda believes there are several reasons for substance abuse among high school students. She thinks these might be important additions to her essay:

1. Students are reckless and experimental at this age.
2. Peer pressure.
3. Some students don't feel they can have fun without drugs or alcohol.

Finally, Melinda has some ideas for punishments that might control substance abuse in high school:

1. Required drug tests for all students with results sent to parents.
2. Random sobriety tests by security officers on campus.
3. Random drug tests at school events.

Melinda also believes that once evidence of drug and alcohol use is found, students should be punished further. She feels, however, that students should not be expelled or suspended because they will fall too far behind in their studies. Here are some alternative forms of punishment Melinda has come up with:

1. Students should be barred from extracurricular activities for one month for their first offence.
2. Students should be barred from extracurricular activities for the rest of the school year—including all the big events, like the prom and football games—for their second offence.

Organizing

At the next class meeting, Melinda shows her notes to her writing group. They tell her that she has a good topic and some good ideas to support her point of view. They tell her to list the arguments that would be most convincing to the school board and to write her thoughts in a letter addressed specifically to that group. Once her audience and purpose are clear to her, she can decide on the tone that would be most effective.

Melinda goes home and talks to her parents, who are just as upset about Scott as Melinda is. They tell her that she has some good ideas and that she should address her letter to the school board.

Melinda goes over her notes and lists the most important points she wants to make. This is what her list looks like:

1. This school needs a stronger policy about drug and alcohol abuse.
2. Existing rules need to be enforced more strictly.
3. If students do not have drugs or alcohol on them, there is no problem. I think if drugs or alcohol are in them, the problem should not be ignored. Students have seen over and over again that being intoxicated is no problem. They can just claim they are silly teenagers, and their behaviour will be overlooked.
4. Parents should be willing to give permission for their children to be tested for drugs or alcohol. If they care about their kids, they will want to know if there is a problem. Ignoring it will not make it go away.
5. There should be punishments for being drunk, but students should still be able to go to school. Knowing they will miss an important game if they are caught drunk may stop them from taking that drink before coming to school.
6. If the school board decided to change the policy, there should be lots of hoopla. Television, news conferences. The works. Everyone should know about it and stand behind it.
7. Maybe there are other solutions. I don't know. I just know too many people are being hurt. Innocent people.

Melinda decides that she is ready to write her draft. She knows that she is still angry and that she will need to concentrate on being reasonable in her essay. Too much emotion could get in the way of her good ideas and encourage her audience to respond emotionally instead of listen to her logic.

Drafting

Here is Melinda's draft.

Melinda's Essay: First Draft

Main idea: We need to enforce the drug and alcohol policy at the high school.

Dear School Board Members:

I am a recent graduate of Sunnydale High School, and my experiences there tell me that you need to have a more stringent policy in regard to the drug and alcohol abuse that runs rampant throughout the student body. For too long, the attitude that reigns at our school has been one of tolerance and denial. It is high time to enforce existing rules more strictly and perhaps to add more drastic penalties to the Student Code of Conduct. We have been beating around the bush too long.

The current code states, "School policy prohibits the unlawful use, manufacture, possession, distribution, or dispensing of controlled substances and alcohol on school grounds or at school-sponsored events." Due to the fact that there is no specific penalty stated in the Code, it is my opinion that problems could arise. Although it falls in a category of behaviours that "may result in expulsion from school," who decides the penalties and if they will be given out fairly? The policy also has a vague statement which says the school has a responsibility to take all appropriate actions against violators, including referral to drug use/alcohol abuse assistance or rehabilitation programs. The problem with this rule, as I see it, is that students drink or use drugs before school or before coming to school-sponsored activities. By coming to school already under the influence of the substances, students do not risk being expelled. To remedy or correct this problem, it is my opinion that the school should allow drug and alcohol testing in cases where students are suspected of being intoxicated.

Some people may argue that drug testing is a drastic measure that violates their individual rights. However, it seems to me that a large amount of parents are concerned about the welfare of their children and would sign release forms allowing their children to be tested. Reports of all kinds of tests should then be sent to the student's parents and teachers. This would have several affects. Students would know that their behaviour at school and school-sponsored events is being watched, and they cannot claim that they are just being silly. If they are suspected of using drugs or alcohol, the test can be made as soon as a teacher or administrator suspects a problem. Students who feel pressured by their friends to use substances such as alcohol and drugs can use the threat of drug testing as a way to avoid drinking or drugging in the first place. Other students who stand by helplessly and see their friends become intoxicated everyday can hope that adults will use their authority to force the drinkers and druggers to abstain from their habits.

When evidence of drug or alcohol use is found, I believe that students should be excused from extracurricular activities for a period of one month. If the big dance or football game is coming up in the future, I myself believe students will not be so tempted to start celebrating with chemicals in advance of the event. If there is a second offence, I believe the student should be banned from all extracurricular activities for the remainder of the school year, including events such as the senior prom and graduation. Under no circumstances should the school board give those students a break.

I do not believe that students should be expelled from classes for these offences. Based on my experiences, students I know who were expelled from classes at school ended up getting behind in schoolwork and abusing substances even more than ever. If students are to be responsible adults, they need to learn to meet their obligations when they are students.

I think that these new policies should be implemented with a lot of fanfare. There oughta be a school-wide assembly with films or speakers from organizations like SADD (Students Against Drunk Driving) or AA (Alcoholics Anonymous) or the Council on Alcoholism. Students should be made aware that the policy will be strictly enforced if there is any sign that students is intoxicated.

I am sure that there are many solutions to the substance abuse problem at our school that I have not mentioned in this letter. Perhaps security officers at school events should be given permission to give students a sobriety test. Perhaps there should be random tests allowed. I do not know what the perfect solution is. I just know that the School Board needs to step on it. I just know that the four years I spent at Sunnydale High School were marred by many incidences at parties and football games that could have been avoided if students had not been drinking or drugging. Fights, fender benders, and verbal abuse may seem like normal parts of high school events, but many of those I observed were because of alcohol and drug abuse.

It is sometimes the responsibility of the school board to create policies that protect students from theirselves. It is clear as a bell that high school students are naturally reckless and take many unnecessary risks. By setting a firm and realistic policy that strongly discourages students from using drugs and alcohol, the school board will help these students succeed in school and in life. What is more important?

Revising

Melinda feels that she has made a worthwhile plea in her essay. Instead of just going through the motions to complete this assignment, she has spent her time writing about something she really believes in. Now her instructor wants each student to look closely at the effectiveness of his or her whole essay—paying special attention to the focus of the essay, its unity, its organization, and its support for the essay's main ideas.

Melinda is excited about revising this essay because she might actually send her letter to the school board. She reviews the Checklist for Writing Effective Essays at the beginning of the Focus on Essays section of this chapter. Melinda quickly sees how these guidelines are all related to one another, and she begins to restructure parts of her essay. As she rewrites her thesis statement and reorganizes several of her paragraphs, she realizes that her essay needs a lot more work than she originally thought, but the checklist gives her a focus for her revision. She reads the Focus on Essays section and does the exercises her instructor assigns.

Now Melinda goes back over each paragraph, thinking of each as an integral part of the whole essay. After she checks to see that each paragraph is fully developed, she reads her essay again to ensure that its paragraphs fit together smoothly and logically.

Collaborative Work

Peer Group Activity

After you read the portions of the Focus on Essays your instructor assigns, turn to Melinda's first draft (p. 197–199), and complete the following tasks in small groups:

A. Underline the thesis statement (for a definition, see p. 25) of the essay.

B. Put brackets around any of Melinda's paragraphs that your group believes are not directly related to the thesis statement.

C. Write the number 2 beside any paragraph that contains more than one main idea.

D. Put a question mark next to any paragraph that seems out of place; then draw an arrow to a better location for the paragraph.

Compare the marks your group made to those your instructor will show you. Where do your marks differ from your instructor's? What do you need to review before writing your own essay?

Class Activity

As an entire class, look at the underlined portions of Melinda's revised draft (p. 202) to see how she changed each sentence.

A. Did you identify the revision problems that Melinda corrected?

B. Do you think her changes are good ones? Discuss her changes.

Editing

Now that the essay says what Melinda wants it to say, she needs to do some final proofreading and editing before handing it in. The instructor emphasizes that all the students in the class need to have a working knowledge of diction and spelling. So Melinda shifts her focus from the organization and development of her essay to specific points of grammar. She reads the Focus on Sentences Appendix to learn about creating dramatic sentences. Then, she returns to her draft to apply what she has learned.

Collaborative Work

Peer Group Activity

After you read the portions of the Focus on Sentences that your instructor assigns, turn to Melinda's first draft (pp. 197–199), and complete the following tasks in small groups:

A. Highlight any dramatic sentences (see pp. 290–293).

Could Melinda use more or fewer dramatic sentences in her essay?

B. Underline Melinda's topic sentences. Are her dramatic sentences located in effective places?

C. Suggest any dramatic sentences you would add and show where you would insert them.

Compare your marks with those your instructor will show you. Where do your marks differ from your instructor's? What do you need to review before writing your own essay?

Melinda's Revised Essay

~~Main Idea: We need to enforce the drug and alcohol policy at the high school.~~

Dear School Board Members:

I am a recent graduate of Sunnydale High School, and my experiences there tell me that you need to have a more stringent policy in regard to the drug and alcohol abuse that ~~runs rampant throughout~~is rampant through the student body. For too long, the attitude that reigns at our school has been one of tolerance and denial. It is high time to ~~enforce existing rules more strictly and perhaps to add~~clarify and then enforce existing rules more strictly and perhaps to add more ~~more drastic penalties to the Student Code of Conduct. We have been beating around the bush too long.~~

~~The current code states, "School policy prohibits the unlawful use, manufacture, possession, distribution, or dispensing of controlled substances and alcohol on school grounds or at school sponsored events." Due to the fact that there is no specific penalty stated in the Code, it is my opinion that problems could arise. Although it falls in a category of behaviors that "may result in expulsion from school," who decides the penalties and if they will be given out fairly? The policy also has a vague statement which says the school has a responsibility to take all appropriate actions against violators, including referral to drug use/alcohol abuse assistance or rehabilitation programs. The problem with this rule, as I see it, is that students drink or use drugs before school or before coming to school sponsored activities. By coming to school already under the influence of the substances, students do not risk being expelled. To remedy or correct this problem, it is my opinion that the school should allow drug and alcohol testing in cases where students are suspected of being intoxicated.~~

~~Some people may argue that drug testing is a drastic measure that violates their individual rights. However, it seems to me that a~~

~~large amount of parents are concerned about the welfare of their children and would sign release forms allowing their children to be tested. Reports of all kinds of tests should then be sent to the student's parents and teachers. This would have several affects. Students would know that their behavior at school and school sponsored events is being watched, and they cannot claim that they are just being silly. If they are suspected of using drugs or alcohol, the test can be made as soon as a teacher or administrator suspects a problem. Students who feel pressured by their friends to use substances such as alcohol and drugs can use the threat of drug testing as a way to avoid drinking or drugging in the first place. Other students who stand by helplessly and see their friends become intoxicated everyday can hope that adults will use their authority to force the drinkers and druggers to abstain from their habits.~~drastic penalties to the Student Code of Conduct. But in order to make these changes, we must have a sure way to find out who the offenders are. To remedy and correct this problem, it is my opinion that the school should allow drug or alcohol testing in cases where students are suspected of being intoxicated. We need to take action now.

Some students and others may argue that drug testing is a drastic measure that violates their individual rights. However, it seems to me that a large number of parents are concerned about the welfare of their children and would sign release forms allowing their children to be tested. All test reports should then be sent to the students' parents and teachers. Knowing that parents and teachers would receive reports of drug tests would encourage many students to give up alcohol and drugs.

The reports would have several effects. Since students would know that their behaviour at school and school-sponsored events is being watched by a teacher or administrator for signs of intoxication and those exhibiting this behaviour are being tested, they cannot, as some have done in the past, claim that they are just being silly when they are actually high or intoxicated. Also, students who feel pressured by their friends to use substances such as alcohol and drugs can use the threat of drug testing as a way to avoid such behaviour in the first place. Other students who stand by helplessly and see their friends become intoxicated every day can hope that adults will use their authority to force the drinkers and drug users to abstain from their habits.

The current code has two flaws that make it ineffective in controlling alcohol and drug abuse: It is ambiguous about punishment, and it does not take into account drug use away from the school. The code states, "School policy prohibits the unlawful use, manufacture, possession, distribution, or dispensing of controlled substances and alcohol on school grounds or at school-sponsored events." Because there is no specific penalty stated in the code, I think problems could arise. Although drug and alcohol use falls in a category of behaviours that "may result in expulsion from school," who decides the penalties and if they will be given out fairly? The second problem with this rule, as I see it, is that students drink or use drugs before school or before coming to school-sponsored activities, but this problem could be avoided with drug testing.

When evidence of drug or alcohol use is found, I believe that students should be banned from extracurricular activities for a period of one month. If the big dance or football game is coming

~~When evidence of drug or alcohol use is found, I believe that students should be excused from extracurricular activities for a period of one month. If the big dance or football game is coming up in the future, I myself believe students will not be so tempted to start celebrating with chemicals in advance of the event.~~up, I believe students will not be so tempted to start celebrating with chemicals in advance. If there is a second offence, I believe the student should be banned from all extracurricular activities for the remainder of the school year, including events such as the senior prom and graduation. Under no circumstances should the school board give those students a break.

I do not believe that students should be expelled from classes for these offences. ~~Based on my experiences, students~~Students I know who were expelled from classes at school ended up getting behind in their schoolwork and abusing substances even more than ever. For example, a friend of mine was expelled for other reasons, and she fell so far behind in her schoolwork that she ended up dropping out of school completely. As a result of her school problems, she is now on welfare and making very little money working for a janitorial service. If students ~~are to be responsible~~like my friend are to be responsible, self-supporting adults, they need to learn to meet their obligations when they are students.

I think that these new policies should be implemented with ~~a lot of~~great fanfare. There ~~oughta~~should be a school-wide assembly with films or speakers from organizations like SADD (Students Against Drunk Driving) or AA (Alcoholics Anonymous) or the Council on Alcoholism. Students should be made aware that the policy will be strictly enforced if there is any sign that students ~~is~~are intoxicated.

I am sure that there are many solutions to the substance abuse problem at our school that I have not mentioned~~ in this letter~~. Perhaps security officers at school events should be given permission to give students~~a~~ sobriety tests. Perhaps there should be random tests allowed. I do not know what the perfect solution is. I just know that the ~~School Board needs to step on it. I just~~school board needs to take action now. I also know that the four years I spent at Sunnydale High School were marred by many ~~incidences~~incidents at parties and football games that could have been avoided if students had not been drinking or ~~drugging.~~using drugs. Fights, fender benders, and verbal abuse may seem like normal parts of high school events, but many of ~~those~~the incidents I observed ~~were~~occurred because of alcohol and drug abuse.

It is sometimes the responsibility of the school board to create policies that protect students from ~~theirselves. It is clear as a bell that~~themselves. Clearly high school students are naturally reckless and take many unnecessary risks. By setting a firm and realistic policy that strongly discourages students from using drugs and alcohol, the school board will help these students succeed in school and in life.~~What is more important?~~

WRITING YOUR OWN PERSUADING ESSAY

So far, you have seen a professional writer and a fellow student at work trying to persuade you to take some action or adopt a position on an issue. As you read the published essay and followed the writing process of another student from first to final draft, you absorbed ideas and ways of giving those ideas a form of their own. These reading and writing activities have prepared you to write your own persuading essay on a topic that is meaningful to you.

What Have You Discovered?

Before you begin your own writing task, let's review what you have learned in this chapter so far:

- In a persuading essay, you should choose a topic that is important to you, gather as much information as possible, and use this information to convince your readers to agree with you.
- Evidence is probably the most important factor in writing a persuasive essay.
- To present your persuading essay effectively, you need to organize your ideas.
- To help you shape your essay, you should learn as much as possible about your readers.
- Before you write a draft, you need to decide on a point of view toward your subject.

- After you write a draft, you should revise your essay for meaning and organization.
- After you revise your essay, you should edit its grammar, usage, and sentence structure.

Your Writing Topic

Choose one of the following topics for your persuading essay:

1. Choose an unjust practice, rule, activity, or policy that exists in your family, your school, your community, or society, and write an essay to persuade whoever is responsible to change or abolish the practice, rule, activity, or policy.
2. Write a letter trying to persuade an administrator at your college that a course requirement should be changed.
3. Write an essay trying to persuade your classmates to devote some of their time to doing volunteer work in your community.
4. Create your own persuading essay topic (with the assistance of your instructor), and write a response to it.

When you have selected one of these topics, you may begin your writing process in the same way Melinda did. (You may find her experience helpful in giving you ideas.) This time your purpose is to write your own persuading essay. If some tasks occur out of order, that adjustment is probably part of your personal writing ritual. Follow your instincts, and let them mold your own writing process. But make sure you've worked through all the stages to your final draft.

Turn in your revised draft to your instructor.

Some Final Thoughts

When you have completed your own essay, answer these four questions in your journal:

1. What was most difficult about this assignment?
2. What was easiest?
3. What did I learn about persuading by completing this assignment?
4. What did I learn about my own writing process from this assignment: how I prepared to write, how I wrote the first draft, how I revised, and how I edited?

Writing Effective Essays

Checklist for Writing Effective Essays

✓ Does the essay have a single controlling idea expressed in a thesis statement?
✓ Are all topic sentences in the essay related to the essay's thesis statement?
✓ Does each body paragraph develop only one main idea?
✓ Are body paragraphs arranged in the most logical order?

When medical researchers are working on large projects that require them to repeat the same experiment many times, they develop a set procedure or "protocol" for laboratory assistants to follow so that the experiments remain focused on the same goal and the results remain reliable and valid. This protocol leads the assistant step by step through the experiment to ensure that each repetition is conducted in exactly the same manner. If you follow a revising plan similar to a protocol, it will lead you to produce essays that are effective because they are focused, unified, logically organized, and well supported.

In no other type of essay are these qualities—focus, unity, organization, and support—as important as they are in a persuading essay. By establishing the focus or purpose of your persuading essay, clearing the essay and individual paragraphs of unrelated ideas, making sure the essay's organization is logical, and including sufficient support for your ideas, you may be able to convince an audience to consider and perhaps adopt your position on a particular issue.

Focus

Especially in a persuasive essay, writers need to make sure their essays are focused on a single controlling idea or purpose. In other words, you should determine whether the essay contains a **thesis statement** (or sentence about the essay's general topic). Having a clear focus is crucial in a persuasive essay because you are trying to convince your audience that your position on a particular issue is valid and worthy of consideration.

In "The Neglected Heart," Thomas Lickona provides a thesis statement in the middle of his first paragraph that guides us through the rest of his essay: "the destructive psychological consequences of temporary sexual relationships are very real." The rest of Lickona's essay addresses these concerns as thoroughly as he can.

When Melinda Jackson began to revise the letter she had written to the school board suggesting ways to better control alcohol and drug use in her brother's school and at extracurricular activities, she first needed to determine whether the focus of her essay—to persuade the school board to initiate drug and alcohol testing for students and then to enforce stricter punishments—was clear. Melinda read her first draft again and realized that she didn't really state her thesis until paragraph two, and even then the statement was too broad. Here is her original introductory paragraph:

First Draft: I am a recent graduate of Sunnydale High School, and my experiences there tell me that you need to have a more stringent policy in regard to the drug and alcohol abuse that runs rampant throughout the student body. For too long, the attitude that reigns at our school has been one of tolerance and denial. It is high time to enforce existing rules more strictly and perhaps to add more drastic penalties to the Student Code of Conduct. We have been beating around the bush too long.

As Melinda reread what she had written, she realized she needed to focus on her major suggestions for the school board: instituting drug testing at Sunnydale, clarifying and enforcing school rules related to drug and alcohol use, and adding more drastic penalties. Here is her revised paragraph:

Revision: I am a recent graduate of Sunnydale High School, and my experiences there tell me that you need to have a more stringent policy in regard to the drug and alcohol abuse that is rampant through the student body. For too long, the attitude that reigns at our school has been one of tolerance and denial. It is high time to **clarify and then** enforce existing rules more strictly and perhaps to add more drastic penalties to the Student Code of Conduct. **But in order to make these changes, we must have a sure way to find out who the offenders are. To remedy and correct this problem, it is my opinion that the school should allow drug or alcohol testing in cases where students are suspected of being intoxicated.** ~~We have been beating around the bush too long~~. **We need to take action now.**

Now Melinda's essay is clearly focused on her plan to reduce alcohol and drug abuse at her school, and she has established the best way to proceed with her essay. First, she will try to persuade her audience that drug testing is necessary to the process of reducing drug and alcohol abuse on campus. Then she needs to focus on the idea of enforcing the existing school rules after offenders are identified. Next she will argue for more drastic punishments and conclude her letter with a word about acting immediately.

Exercise E8-1

Draft a thesis statement for Melinda's essay (pp. 197–199) that suggests ways other than drug testing to control the abuse of drugs and alcohol by high school students.

Exercise E8-2

Draft a thesis statement that takes a position or makes a statement about each of the following broad topics.

1. Making divorces harder or easier to obtain
2. Raising or lowering the speed limit on interstate highways
3. Requiring all Canadian students to become fluent in both French and English
4. Requiring computer instruction for all Canadian students
5. Limiting the amount of time children can watch television

Exercise E8-3

Read the following introductory paragraph and write a thesis statement for it.

Many cars today are equipped with safety devices such as seat belts, child protective seats, and air bags. However, too many people don't use this equipment correctly or at all. Many highway patrol officers witness the senseless injuries and deaths of people in auto accidents that could have been prevented.

Unity

In a **unified** essay, each body paragraph is focused on one controlling idea that contributes to the essay's purpose and relates directly to the thesis statement. Usually this idea is stated in a topic sentence at the beginning of the paragraph. Only details that contribute to that topic sentence should be included in that paragraph.

In the following paragraph from "The Neglected Heart," Thomas Lickona is careful to relate each body paragraph to his general thesis statement. The author's subheadings help keep the essay unified, and each paragraph is related to the essay's main controlling idea (the psychological consequences of premature sexual involvement). Take paragraph 50 as an example. It considers some of the consequences of premature sexual relationships in a section titled "The Corruption of Character and the Debasement of Sex."

> Good character consists of virtues such as respect, responsibility, honesty, fairness, caring, and self-control. With regard to sex, the character trait of self-control is particularly crucial. The breakdown of sexual self-control is a big factor in many of the sex-related problems that plague our society: rape, promiscuity, pornography, addiction to sex, sexual harassment, the sexual abuse of children, sexual infidelity in marriage, and the serious damage to families many of these problems cause. It was Freud who said—and it is now obvious how right he was—that sexual self-control is essential for civilization.

This paragraph outlines some of the sexual problems associated with not exercising self-control, a basic virtue necessary for developing a good character. The corruption of character is part of Lickona's larger argument that attempts to convince people to avoid premature sexual involvement.

Another problem that threatens the unity of an essay is a body paragraph with more than one main idea. In the first draft of her essay, Melinda discovered that paragraph three dealt with two related but separate ideas: (1) the objections to drug testing and (2) the beneficial effects that she believed should outweigh the objections to drug testing.

First Draft: Some people may argue that drug testing is a drastic measure that violates their individual rights. However, it seems to me that a large amount of parents are concerned about the welfare of their children and would sign release forms allowing their children to be tested. Reports of all kinds of tests should then be sent to the student's parents and teachers. This would have several affects. Students would know that their behaviour at school and school-sponsored events is being watched, and they cannot claim that they are just being silly. If they are suspected of using drugs or alcohol, the test can be made as soon as a teacher or administrator suspects a problem. Students who feel pressured by their friends to use substances such as alcohol and drugs can use the threat of drug testing as a way to avoid drinking or drugging in the first place. Other students who stand by helplessly and see their friends become intoxicated everyday can hope that adults will use their authority to force the drinkers and druggers to abstain from their habits.

After studying this paragraph, Melinda divided it into two separate paragraphs, one focused on why she thinks many parents would support drug testing and another that explained the benefits that she thought would come about from drug testing:

Revision: Some ~~people~~ **students and others** may argue that drug testing is a drastic measure that violates their individual rights. However, it seems to me that a large number of parents are concerned about the welfare of their children and would sign release forms allowing their children to be tested~~. Reports of all kinds of tests~~ **All test reports** should then be sent to the students' parents and teachers. **Knowing that parents and teachers would receive reports of drug tests would encourage many students to give up alcohol and drugs.**

~~This~~ **The reports** would have several effects. Since s~~S~~tudents would know that their behaviour at school and school-sponsored events is being watched **by a teacher or administrator for signs of intoxication and those exhibiting this behaviour are being tested,** ~~and~~ they cannot, **as some have done in the past**, claim that they are just being **silly when they are actually high or intoxicated.** ~~If they are suspected of using drugs or alcohol, the test can be made as soon as a teacher or administrator suspects a problem.~~ **Also,** s~~S~~tudents who feel pressured by their friends to use substances such as alcohol and drugs can use the threat of drug testing as a way to avoid ~~drinking or drugging~~ **such behaviour** in the first place. Other students who stand by helplessly and see their friends become intoxicated every day can hope that adults will use their authority to force the drinkers and ~~druggers~~ **drug users** to abstain from their habits.

Now each of these paragraphs develops a single topic that is directly related to the essay's thesis statement.

Exercise E8-4

Identify the two ideas in paragraph two of Melinda's first draft (p. 198). Rewrite the paragraph by dividing it into two separate paragraphs with their own topic sentences.

Exercise E8-5

Read the following group of sentences and decide which ones contribute to the following thesis statement: "Most students are not particularly aware of political issues that affect their lives, such as proposed cuts in financial aid."

1. In my political science class, not a single student is aware of current proposed legislation that will severely limit the amount of student aid available.
2. Many students need to have outside jobs to stay in college.
3. The bill before Parliament would affect 90% of the students who receive financial aid.
4. Nobody is proposing cuts in provincial aid programs.
5. We all need more education in the Information Age.

Exercise E8-6

Read the following paragraph and revise it, deleting all irrelevant material so that the paragraph focuses on one main idea.

Small children need good role models in television programs that are produced for a very young audience. I really liked Kukla, Fran, and Ollie when I was growing up. For instance, cartoon programs that feature violence should be eliminated. Also, programs that contain dangerous actions that the children might try to imitate should not be allowed. I had to read for 30 minutes before bedtime every night when I was in elementary school. In their television programs, children need to observe characters who are solving problems in nonviolent ways and practising safety measures.

Logical Organization

Logical essays present information to their audiences in the most reasonable way possible. This means that logical essays follow a plan marked by the fact that one idea develops out of the previous idea.

In his essay "The Neglected Heart," Thomas Lickona proceeds step by step to build his case to counsel people that should make the decision to avoid premature sexual involvement. First he sets out the "physical dangers of uncommitted sex," and then moves on to the emotional and psychological consequences. It is the emotional and psychological consequences that he focuses on for most of his essay. These he neatly organizes into 10 categories and chooses to use a subheading to introduce each one. In other words, Lickona has given a step-by-step presentation of the material that allows his audience to proceed to each new phase of his persuasive essay.

As Melinda worked on her revision, she observed that paragraph two of her essay, which dealt with the school's policy on alcohol and drug abuse, was out of place, especially since she had moved her call for drug testing into her introduction. Her audience would need the information on drug testing first. Here is the order of her main ideas in her first draft:

- Explanation of problem/introduction
- School policy on drug and alcohol use
- Drug testing
- Punishment for offenders
- Expulsion
- Implementation of new policies
- Other solutions
- Summary/conclusion

Her revised plan for the essay places her arguments for drug testing earlier in the essay, puts the topic of the effects of testing (originally in the drug-testing paragraph) in a paragraph of its own, and places the paragraph on the school policy after drug testing and its effects, as paragraph four:

- Explanation of problem/introduction
- Drug testing
- Effects of drug testing

- School policy on drug and alcohol use
- Punishment for offenders
- Expulsion
- Implementation of new policies
- Other solutions
- Summary/Conclusion

After she reorganizes these paragraphs, Melinda's essay becomes more logical and easier to follow.

Then Melinda makes several internal revisions in the paragraph on school policy connected to drug and alcohol use so that it fits more logically into its new location as paragraph four. So Melinda not only moves the paragraph but develops its main idea more fully in the new location.

Exercise E8-7

Outline the main ideas and details of Melinda's revised essay (pp. 202–206), and discuss the logic of her order.

Exercise E8-8

Arrange the following topic sentences in the most logical order. Then explain the reasoning for your arrangement.

1. Tendons, ligaments, and bones may not always hold up under the stress of professional sports, but an education lasts forever.
2. More and more college athletes are entering the professional sports drafts before they have completed their college eligibility because that is where the big bucks are.
3. Many athletes who have played only one or two years in college are a big disappointment to the professional teams that draft them.
4. The national governing bodies need to take action to protect college athletics, athletes, and professional teams.
5. Colleges need to be realistic about their athletes' needs.

Exercise E8-9

Read the following thesis statement and plan the most logical way to develop it. Then make a list of main ideas that might support it if you were to develop it into an essay.

The images of extremely thin young women that are so prominent in magazines, films, and television productions contribute to the proliferation of eating disorders, low self-esteem, and the failure to mature.

Collaborative Work

After writing a draft of your own persuading essay, exchange papers with a classmate, and do the following tasks:

A. Underline the essay's thesis statement.

B. Put brackets around any topic sentences that are not directly related to the essay's thesis statement.

C. Mark each body paragraph that contains more than one idea with a paragraph symbol in front of the sentence where the paragraph should be divided.

D. List the main idea of each paragraph, and make sure the paragraphs are in the most logical order for what the writer is trying to accomplish.

Then return the paper to its writer and use the information in this section to revise your draft.

Documenting Your Sources

Checklist for Documenting Other People's Words

✓ Do you use an "in-text" citation every time you quote, paraphrase, or summarize a source?
✓ Is every source you use listed on the "Works Cited" page?
✓ Have you removed any sources that you didn't "cite" in your paper from your "Works Cited" list?

When you document your sources, you have to document the sources in two places. First, you have to include a documentation reference right after you use the other person's words or ideas in your essay. Second, you have to build a list of all the sources you included in your essay. The list is called "Works Cited," and you include it as the last page of your research essay. First we'll learn how to document a source right after you use it. Then, we'll learn how to make a Works Cited page.

How to Document a Source within Your Essay

If you use anyone's ideas or words, you need to tell your reader who and where you borrowed from. When you tell your reader where you borrowed words from, it's called **documenting your sources**. There are at least 20 different documentation styles. The most common one in English Departments is a documenting system called the Modern Languages Association (MLA) documentation style. It's the documentation style used by people who write essays for composition classes, and for most other classes in the humanities.

Documenting your sources is essential for a couple of reasons. First, if a person writes an essay and uses someone else's words but doesn't tell the reader that those words weren't his/her own, that person is guilty of a criminal offence called plagiarism. **Plagiarism** is when you use someone else's words or ideas in your essay but you don't tell the reader that you borrowed them: it's stealing someone else's words, images, or ideas.

Second, documenting your sources is important for convincing your reader and demonstrating you understand the field. The documentation system you use tells your reader you understand the field and work within it. Glitches in the documentation of sources demonstrate that the writer doesn't know what he/she is doing.

To document your sources properly with the MLA system, you include some short references to books right in your essay. We call these references **in-text citations**. Then, at the end of your essay, you include all the details of your sources in a list called the "Works Cited" list.

The bottom line is this: documenting your sources has to be done and done right to be an effective part of your essay. Below you'll find the details of the MLA documentation style for each of the following sources.

How to Do an "In-text" Citation

After you've paraphrased, summarized, or quoted from a source you need to include an "in-text" citation with enough information that the reader can identify which source you used from your "Works Cited" list. All the information needed to identify the source is put in parentheses right after you use the source.

The kind of in-text citation you use depends on the sources you're including in your essay. If you're using several sources, and none of the sources has the same title or author, you can use the standard in-text citation. If you're using two or more sources with the same author, you'll want to use the alternate in-text citation format.

Standard In-text Citations

If you only use one book by an author, then usually the author's name and the page number are enough for the reader to locate the source. This is the **standard in-text citation** format. When you use the author's name you only need to include the author's last name, dropping the first name.

If the Author is Named in the Introduction to the Source then Include the Page Number After You Use the Source

In Chapter 6 we learned different techniques to introduce quotes. One of those techniques uses the author's name to introduce the source. If you do introduce the source with the author's name, then just put the page number in brackets after you finish the paraphrase, summary, or quote. Here's an example:

> Thomas Lickona concludes that "The destructive psychological consequences of temporary sexual relationships are very real" (183).

Notice that the word "page" or the letters "p" or "pp" **don't** go in front of the page number. That's because the reader expects it to be the page number.

If the Author is Not Named in the Quote's Introduction then Include the Author's Name First Followed by the Page Number

If you don't name the author when you introduce your source, then you need to add the author's name to the information in the parentheses after you use the source. Put the author's name before the page number. Here's an example:

> It is evident that "The destructive psychological consequences of temporary sexual relationships are very real" (Lickona 183).

Note that there is no punctuation separating the author's surname from the page number.

Variations on the Standard In-text Citation

If Your Book Has Two or Three Authors

If you're using a source with two or three authors, you must either include the author's last names in the introduction or put them in parentheses at the end.

> Swift and Mooney state that they "arrived at a co-operative selection of poets and poems, striking what stands as an enriching balance of perspectives" (14).

> The editors state that they "arrived at a co-operative selection of poets and poems, striking what stands as an enriching balance of perspectives" (Swift and Mooney 14).

If Your Book Has Four or More Authors

If your source, like this text, has more than four authors, use the first author's name and the words "et al." Et al. is a Latin phrase that means "and others." Do not italicize or underline the Latin phrase. Here are some examples:

> In a landmark study of girls in schools, Shiffer et al. explore the problems that girls have with body image (235).

> A landmark study of girls in schools explores the problems that girls have with body image (Shiffer et al. 235).

> A landmark study of girls in schools explores the problems that girls have with body image (Shiffer, Zodel, Smith and Heaney 235).

If You Have a Corporate Author

Many sources don't mention an author's name as the originator of the material. If an institution or an agency claims the source, then use the name of the agency or corporation as you would treat the author's name.

> The Foothills Historical Society claims that its policies on collections are "as innovative as any invented" (127).

> The policies on collections are "as innovative as any invented" (Foothills Historical Society 127).

If the Author of a Source is Part of a Bigger Source, Written or Edited by a Different Author

Some books include articles that are written by people other than those who wrote or edited the book. Newspapers, magazines, Web sites, and edited pieces can do the same thing. This book, for instance, uses essays that were written by people other than those who wrote the book. In this instance, use the specific article's author as the author of the source. For instance, if you wanted to quote from the professional essay in this chapter, you would use the author of the essay, not the authors of this textbook, as the author of the work:

> As Lickona notes, "girls, especially, need to know in advance the sharp regret that so many young women feel after becoming sexually involved." (184).

> A big consequence is regret: "girls, especially, need to know in advance the sharp regret that so many young women feel after becoming sexually involved." (Lickona 184).

Alternative In-text Citations

If you use several sources in your essay and two or more of the sources share the same author, you'll need to use an **alternative in-text citation** format. The point of the in-text citation is to help the reader identify the source in your Works Cited list. If the author wrote two or more of the sources you're using, then the reader can't identify the quote if the citation only uses the author's name. Instead of using the author's name to identify the source, the title of the source will work.

Referring to the Title and Author in the Introduction

If you're using two or more sources by the same author, then include the book titles in your in-text citation. If you use the title of the book to introduce the quote, then just include the page number in parentheses:

> In *No More Teachers, No More Books*, Heather-Jane Robertson concludes that technologies "have their own politics" (235).

If the source's introduction doesn't use the name of the source or the author, then include a slightly abbreviated name of the source with the page number in parentheses after using the source. You can shorten the name of the source to save space, but it must be unique enough that the reader can find it in the "Works Cited" list. Here's a sample:

> Even something as banal as a tomato harvester carried social consequences: "the development of the mechanical tomato-harvester was not a political statement, but its introduction dramatically shifted power relations nonetheless" (*No More Teachers* 235).

Quoting Someone Who Quotes Someone Else

If you quote a source and that source is quoting another source, you're using an **indirect quote**. Use the original author's name, but attribute the quote properly to the source you found it in. Notice the addition to the information in parentheses: "qtd. in." It means "quoted in." Here are some samples:

> The health coordinator, Russell Henke, explains the problem that he sees at his school: I see kids going to the nurses in schools, crying a day after their first sexual experience, and wanting to be tested for AIDS" (qtd. in Lickona 184).

> The health coordinator explains the problem that he sees at his school: I see kids going to the nurses in schools, crying a day after their first sexual experience, and wanting to be tested for AIDS" (Henke qtd. in Lickona 184).

How to Build a "Works Cited" Page

Once your in-text citations are in place, you can put together your Works Cited page. The **works cited** page provides your readers with all the detail they need to locate the sources you've used. All of the sources are listed in alphabetical order, according to the author's surname (see page 192 of this chapter for a sample works cited page).

Works cited is different than a bibliography. In a bibliography, you include books you looked at but didn't use in your essay, but the works cited page includes only the sources you use in your essay. If you don't use an in-text citation to refer to the work, you can't include it in your works cited list.

There are specific techniques to help you document every possible situation and source you might come across. The following is a selection of the most common techniques and sources:

Documenting Books

If you're documenting books, most of the information you'll need to include them in your list of works cited is on the title page, inside the front cover. Here, you'll often find the complete title of the book and the publisher. On the back of the title page you'll find the details of the publication: the date, the place of publication, the edition, etc.

Most citations include the following bits of information: the name of the author(s), last name first; the name of the work; the name of the publisher; the city and province or city and state the book was published in; and the date of publication.

Books with One Author

List publication information in the order shown in the example. Remember to put the last name of the author first, followed by his/her first name.

Pura, Murray. Mizzly Fitch. Simon & Pierre: Toronto, Ont. 1988.

Books with Two or Three Authors

If you have a book with two or three authors, include each author's name in the citation listing. Remember to put the last name of each author first.

Downing, L., Carter, J.C., and McManus, T. Students In Our Midst. Toronto, Ont.: Doubleday, 1995.

More Than Three Authors

If your book has three authors or more, then you can abbreviate the list of authors. Write down the name of the first author, last name first, and afterward include the abbreviation "et al.," a Latin phrase meaning "and others," or you can include all of the authors.

Bunn, William et al. Stitching Lines. Toronto, Ont.: North Beach Press, 2000.

Bunn, William, Bert Shelby, Mary Stewart, and Josh Unger. Sewing for the Millennium. Edmonton, Alta.: Quilting Press, 2000.

Books with an Editor

If, instead of an author, your book has an editor, include the editor's name the way you would an author's; after the author's name include the abbreviation "ed." for "editor."

McArthur, Murray, ed. Contest: Essays by Canadian Students, Third Edition. Harcourt Brace: Toronto, Ont. 1998.

Books with Corporate Authors

Sometimes books and other publications produced by institutions and corporations don't have a person's name associated with the text. In cases like this, use the name of the corporation or institution as the name of the author.

City of Calgary. Our Future Through Diversity. Calgary, Alberta: City of Calgary. 1996.

Documenting Articles within Books

Edited books often include writing by other authors. When you list these kinds of books in your list of citations, you need to recognize the author of the piece and the editor of the book.

Signed Article/Edited Book

If the article is signed, include the author and name of the article first, and the book title and editor(s) afterward:

> Plato. "Phaedrus." Readings in Classical Rhetoric. Ed. Thomas Benson and Michael Prosser. Hermagoras Press: Davis, California. 1988.

Unsigned Article in a Dictionary, Almanac, or Encyclopedia

Though many of these books don't have a named author or editor, they're not the same as an institutional author. These books differ from books with corporate authors in that they aren't representing an institution or agency. Instead, they are products intended to supply information to readers.

Sometimes, dictionaries and some other reference-type books often don't have an author. Just include the name of the entry (the entry's title) in quotation marks, or if it's an entry in an encyclopedia or dictionary, include the name of the listing as the article title:

> "Grace." Webster's Third New International Dictionary of the English Language, Unabridged. G. & C. Merriam Company: Springfield, Massachusetts. 1976.

Multivolume Work

Encyclopedias and other kinds of books come in sets of multiple books called volumes. If you use one book from a set, you need to let your readers know that the book comes from a set. Include the volume number in the title of the source. Here's an example:

> "Peterson, Oscar" The Guinness Encyclopedia of Popular Music, Vol. 4. Middlesex, England: Guinness Publishing. 1995.

Documenting Magazines, Journals, or Newspapers

Newspaper Article with a Byline

Citing a newspaper is much the same as a book with different authors writing in it. The author of the specific article goes first with the name of the article afterward, in quotes. The name of the newspaper is underlined as the title of a book would be, followed by the date of publication and the section/page number:

> Nicholson, Blake. "Wind Power Works for Benedictines." The Chronicle-Herald. August 21, 1999: A16.

Newspaper Article with No Author

Some articles in newspapers have no named author. The listing is much the same as listings with an author, except the name of the author isn't included. Begin with the name of the article in quotes, then the name of the paper, underlined, followed by the date of publication and the section/page number:

> "Refugee Status Based on Specific Criteria." The Vancouver Sun. September 7, 1999: A6.

Documenting Internet Pages or CD-ROMs

A listing of a CD-ROM includes the name of the CD in quotes. After the name, the name of the medium, in this case a CD-ROM, is listed. Finish the listing with the name of the company or organization releasing the CD-ROM and the date of release:

> "Ban Landmines! The Ottawa Process and the International Movement to Ban Landmines." CD-ROM. Department of Foreign Affairs and International Trade. 1998.

Documenting Lectures or Conversations

If you want to use words from a lecture, put the name of the lecturer or speaker first, as you would the name of the author, then the name of the lecture, or if there isn't a name for the lecture, then include the topic of the lecture as the title. The name of the class is underlined. End the listing with the place and date of the lecture or speech:

> Everest, Beth. "Signs, Symbols and Myth." Introduction to Creative Writing. Mount Royal College, December 3, 1999.

If you want to quote from a personal conversation you've had with someone, put the name of the person you're quoting first, followed by the words "Personal Interview," followed by the date of the conversation.

> Patterson, Diana. Personal interview. October 31, 1999.

Documenting TV and Radio Programs

To quote from radio or TV shows, begin with the name of the episode or specific show first. If the show spotlights individuals, include their names after the show title. Underline the name of the series followed by the producers' information, and the date of the airing.

"My Healing Journey: Seven Years with Cancer." With Joe Viszmeg. Witness. CBC. National Film Board. Dec. 3, 1999.

Documenting Films, Videos, or Musical Recordings

To list a movie, begin with the director's name, followed by the abbreviation "dir.", meaning "director." Underline the title of the film and include the names of the principal actors. Include the name of the company that released the video and the date of release.

Duvall, Robert, dir. The Apostle. With Robert Duvall, Farah Fawcett, and Miranda Richardson. Universal, 1997.

If you're watching a video, the listing needs to inform the reader that it came from a video. The listing is similar to citing a film: it begins with the director's name and the abbreviation "dir." The title of the video is underlined. After the title, include the name of the medium, in this case "videotape." The listing ends with the name of the company releasing the video, the place and date of release, and the length of the video:

Jhally, Sut, dir. Peter Elbow on Writing: A Conversation With America's Top Writing Teacher. Videotape. Media Education Foundation: Northampton, MA. 1995. 43 min.

For a musical recording, the name of the group or musician performing the music goes first. The name of the recording goes next, followed by the names of the companies that released it. Almost every musical recording has a unique number assigned to it. Include the recording's number and end the listing with the year of release.

Jars of Clay. Much Afraid. Essential/Silvertone, 01241-41612-2, 1997.

Collaborative Work

Peer Group Activity

After you read the portions of the Focus on Paragraphs your instructor assigns, your instructor will put you into groups and send you to the library. When you get there:

A. Locate at least one source from each category of citation listing.

B. Document each source.

C. Compile a "Works Cited" page.

Return to class and exchange your "Works Cited" page with another group. Check their listings to make sure they're done properly.

CHAPTER **NINE**

Problem Solving

If writing won't help the living, it isn't much good.

—**Elise Victory**

LEARNING OUTCOMES

This chapter will help you:

- Understand and write an essay which offers a solution to a problem;
- Write an introductory paragraph that leads to your thesis; and,
- Write strong conclusions to your essay.

No matter how we try, we all find ourselves stuck with problems from time to time. Some of our problems are personal ones: we don't have enough money for tuition; we can't afford groceries; we're struggling with a relationship. No matter what our personal problems are, almost all of our own problems are problems that others share, too: poverty, hunger, divorce.

One reason we write about problems is to organize our thoughts and experiences so we can understand our situation better. In fact, problem solving is an especially satisfying form of essay writing because it helps us identify and fix what is wrong in our own lives, and because most problems are common ones, when we write about how we solve our own problems, we can help others in our communities, in our country, or in our world.

Charlotte Johansen, writing on the subject of pollution, documents some exemplary solutions to this difficult problem:

> Toronto has already set up a special committee on environment and has even passed laws that prohibit the manufacture and sale of those products that are harmful and contain chloroflurocarbons and halons. In addition to this, they have also set up local environment protection agencies to deal with hazardous waste and toxic chemicals by providing storage. This has been a cooperative effort by citizens and all levels of

government as well. Recycling centres have been built and a secretariat position was added to the province for coordinating local initiates and inter-city programs.

LEARNING FROM PUBLISHED WRITERS

In the following essay, Kelly Kaur relates elements of her own upbringing that she found difficult to face. Then, she read a book that gave her the strength to free herself from her tradition and move to build a life for herself.

Before You Read

Focus Your Attention

Before you read this problem-solving essay, take a few moments to respond to the following questions. Jot down your thoughts in your notebook.

1. Think about a problem that you recently solved. How did you go about solving the problem? Did you have to change your lifestyle or behaviour in some way, or did you have to convince other people to behave and think differently? Were you happy with the solution, or was it not as satisfying as you expected it to be?
2. In the essay you are about to read, the writer describes her experience of breaking free from tradition. Think about a time that you felt trapped. Did you try to break free? How? And did you find you were happier once you were free?

Expand Your Vocabulary

Find each of the listed words in the following essay. Without looking up dictionary definitions, jot down a definition for each. Compare your definitions with those in a dictionary. When you feel confident that you know the meanings of the words, write an original sentence for each that uses the words in context.

Patriarchal (paragraph 1)

Shackles (paragraph 1)

Savoured (paragraph 2)

Pixie (paragraph 3)

Emancipated (paragraph 4)

Kelly Kaur

My Friend George*

I did not want to be a 10-year-old girl who was bound by patriarchal ideals and restrictions in a very strict and suffocating East Indian upbringing that constantly reminded me that my future would be one determined for me: I had to learn how to cook, clean and eventually be married to a man chosen for me by my family. I lived a childhood feeling the shackles of tradition on my imagination. 1

Then I discovered George–George from Enid Blyton's *Five on Treasure Island.* My goodness—she was my key to the shackles. How she subverted patriarchy and rebelled against notions of what it was to be a "good girl." Oh no, not Georgina, who would only be called George. I savoured her tantrums and her stubbornness. No pretty dresses or girly-like behavior from my new best friend. She aimed to please no one. George, to me, attempted to carve her own identity and a new path for herself. Her adventures and beyond normal life adventures excited and thrilled me. 2

At 10, I formed the Famous Five club at school. I, of course, was George. There were not many mysteries to solve, but I joined the brass band, was a male pixie in a dance recital and wore only jeans and T-shirts–no dresses, thanks to George. 3

Five on Treasure Island was my first introduction to the world of the Famous Five, and I became a librarian so that I could borrow seven Famous Five books a week. To this day, I remember the classic torch-light-under-the-blanket trick as I was transported to a world where 10-year-olds could begin to be emancipated. 4

George would be terribly proud of me. My grandmother had an arranged marriage at 14, my mother at 16 and my sister, at 21. But I, bless George, learned to say "No!" and lived a life filled with adventure of my own making. 5

---

*Reprinted by permission of the author.

Questions For Critical Thinking

Thinking Critically About Content

1. Why do you think the author needed a book to help her break free?
2. How does playing in a brass band and dancing as a "male pixie" free the author? What is the author breaking free from?

Thinking Critically About Purpose

3. What is Kaur's purpose in writing this essay?
4. Do you think this essay would work to convince strict parents that they should let their children make their own decisions?

Thinking Critically About Audience

5. Who would benefit from reading this essay? Why?
6. How would this essay be different if she was trying to convince strict parents to loosen up?

Thinking Critically About Point of View

7. The author doesn't tell us how her choices affected her family. How do you think they reacted? If she included their reactions, how would it have changed the essay for her readers?
8. What parts of this essay would change if someone else wrote the essay–her mother or her married sister?

LEARNING FROM YOUR PEERS

In our lives, we face problems every day. Some problems have obvious solutions (finding things we need), and we handle them quickly. Others are more complicated (deciding where to go to college), and we may not be able to find a solution unless someone helps us. Sometimes we find that we are experiencing the same problem with minor variations over and over. Maybe we always seem to choose unreliable friends or loan money to the wrong people. Maybe we procrastinate whenever we are faced with a lot of work to do. Maybe we would rather rent a video than go to the library. Learning to analyze and solve problems is a valuable skill that we can develop throughout life if we are open to possibilities. In response to a problem-solving assignment, we are going to follow the writing process of a student named Azure Chen.

Azure's Writing Assignment: Problem Solving

This is the topic Azure's writing instructor assigned:

Most of us will never find the solutions to overwhelming social problems or the cures for devastating diseases, but we do manage to solve the smaller problems in life every day. Sometimes we can learn from people around us who have faced the same problems in their lives. Think of a problem you are trying to solve. Then talk to at least three people who have successfully solved a similar problem. Write an essay explaining how the people you talked to identified their problems and carried out their solutions.

Generating Ideas

Azure sat in the campus student centre staring blankly at the newspaper in front of her. She realized that she had been sitting there for 20 minutes. She knew that she should go to the library and start her homework, but she could not seem to force herself to get up and walk across the street. Just as she prepared to leave, her friend Marsie walked over to Azure's table, plunked down her book bag, and started talking.

Azure explained that she had to start working on her next essay, but she didn't know what to write about. "I've been wasting more time worrying about it than doing it," she complained. Marsie told her that she should stop worrying and just do her work. As Azure got up from the table, she said, "Easier said than done."

Marsie offered to talk about how she manages her time. Azure sat back down and listened as Marsie talked about scheduling classes, work, and family responsibilities.

Finally Azure said, "You've been very helpful, but now I feel more guilty than ever. I'd better be getting to the library."

Planning

At the library, Azure wrote in her notebook:

> I need to write about solutions to problems. Sometimes I think I have problems that have no solutions. Everyone else is so busy studying that I hate to ask them anything. And I don't even know for sure what I want to write about. Logically, I guess I could write about time management since that seems to be one of my biggest problems. I don't have to have solved the problem personally. I just have to talk to some people who think they are in control of their schedules. How long can that list be? I know exactly one person who claims to be on top of this: Marsie. And she says that the answer is to read all assignments before going to class. She reads everything when she gets up at four in the morning. I can just see that. My alarm clock would go off, and the next thing I would know the sun would be shining and the birds would be singing. I know I can't do that. Marsie just has more self-discipline than I do. I know that coming to the library is a good idea. Theoretically, at least. As long as I use my time productively. But sometimes I just sit and stare into space, just like I do in the cafeteria, so I might as well sit in the library.
>
> Perhaps there is something to be said for being in a certain place. Maybe that helps. But four hours of reading at one sitting! I don't think so.
>
> Well, I certainly didn't solve that problem.

Azure put her notebook in her book bag and reached for a reading assignment for her history class. Just then, her friend Mike came by and asked her how she was doing. She told him about the essay she was trying to develop. Mike told her that he was fairly disorganized when he first started college, but since then he had developed habits that work for him.

Azure stood up and said, "Great. Let's go to the cafeteria, and I'll buy you a cup of coffee while you tell me all about your great time-management skills. Then I can ignore my terrible ones and not feel guilty about them."

Developing

During the next week, Azure had several conversations with friends and friends of friends who gave her tips for organizing her time. She found that she had several pages of notes when she went to her next writing class.

Friends in her writing group asked about her topic. She told them that now she had so many ideas that she didn't know where to start. Her classmates encouraged her to keep asking people questions until she felt she understood exactly how time management worked. "Ask your friends how they manage to do everything else in their lives," the group said.

Azure returned to the cafeteria with a new list of questions, ready to ask anyone who would answer them. This is her list:

- When do you do your laundry?
- Do you buy groceries? If so, when?
- Do you go to the bank during daytime hours? If not, do you use teller machines?
- What habits have you developed that save you time and help you do other things you need to do, like studying?
- Do you have a clean house or apartment? How do you keep the Health Department away from your door?

Azure was surprised that so many of her friends took her questions seriously and were willing to take the time to answer them.

Organizing

Azure took her notes and attempted to find some patterns. She noticed that a few ideas surfaced over and over. She made a list of the most repeated bits of advice:

- Go to class, every class.
- Read your assignments before going to class.
- Block out four or five hours at a time to study. You can't study for 10 minutes or half an hour unless you're just trying to memorize a list of definitions or words or something like that.
- Find a place that is comfortable for you, and make an appointment with yourself on your calendar. For example: Saturday, 10-12, second floor of library. Reading.

Then Azure took out another piece of paper and labelled it "List 2: How much time do Real Students spend studying?":

- Most everyone says they study at least 20 hours a week, and they schedule their study time. They don't leave it to luck. (Plan for success, yes?)
- A few people spend 10-12 hours every Saturday and Sunday hitting the books–the pre-med contingent, no doubt.

Azure retrieved another piece of paper and labelled it "List 3: The School-Is-My-Career Syndrome:"

- 8:00 to 5:00; two 10-minute coffee breaks and a half hour for lunch. My friend Terry.
- Let's not talk about people who get up and read at 4 a.m.
- If you have a goal, you have to work at it every day.

Azure then got out another sheet of paper and titled it "List 4: The Get-a-Job (It Makes You More Efficient) School of Thought:"

- Some people think the more you work, the more you should study.
- If they work during the week, they study on weekends, and vice versa.
- Then again, some study all day and work all night.

Azure looked over her lists and concluded that she actually did have enough information to start writing her essay. The four lists have helped her see the main ideas that have emerged from her numerous interviews. As she began her draft, she decided to choose certain people to represent the groups she had created.

Drafting

This is Azure's draft.

Azure's Essay: First Draft

Main idea: After talking with some successful students at my college, I have some good ideas for managing my time as a student.

When I started college, managing my time effectively was very important to me, but I did not have any idea how to do it. Since I was constantly behind in my reading, every test and paper produced fear and trembling. During my first semester, I observed successful students and ask them what they did to keep up with all of their assignments and other obligations. all of the students I talked to called themselves extremely busy people, but everyone had made graduating from college their first priority. The one universal recommendation was to attend absolutely all classes and labs. In high school I never went to all of them. Nevertheless, since I have completed my interviews and collected students' experiences, I can confidently offer their advice to you.

Almost every person suggested reading through all assignments prior to attending class. In a study guide I bought at the bookstore, it said that keeping up with assigned reading is critical if you want to succeed. By reading the assignments ahead of time, students claimed that they have to take fewer notes and are able to ask more intelligent questions. You can really develop more confidence. They also calim that they spend less time reviewing for their classes and studying for tests. One student said that he spends the first week of classes skimming his textbooks to get an overview of each course. Then, if a class seems boring or too difficult, he can change to another class before it is too late.

Some students said every day that they study and make sure they spend a certain amount of time reading, writing, or doing research. Most of the students who do this blocked out four or five hours to study. Some prefer to study for no more than an hour or two at a time. Some people like to spend the entire time in the library while others like to study in a place where there are no distractions, like an empty classroom. Then they can do quick research, if necessary. Some students like to spend more time studying during the week and less time on weekends. However, I was surprised that several have jobs in the afternoons and evenings during the week and spend 10-12 hours every Saturday and Sunday reading and studying. All the students I talked to spend at least 20 hours a week in scheduled study sessions. They emphasize that they do not allow themselves to do anything else during that time. One woman said that she considers her time at school to be her most important job and that she does not waste time during the day. That way, she says, she can study and attend classes from 8 a.m. to 5 p.m. and spend her evenings earning money as a waitress. This schedule works out well for her, and she does any extra studying she needs to do during the weekend.

Other students schedule their classes in blocks of time that allow them to do their studying and research in large blocks of time. For instance, one student spends almost all day on Tuesdays and Thursdays in class. Reading all his assignments for the week on Mondays, some weeks this takes 12-15 hours. On Wednesdays, he spends the day in the library or in a study room at the Student Center. To keep on track, Friday is for writing. This schedule works for him because he takes several classes that require library research and lengthy papers. On the weekends, he works at the mall and earns enough money so he does not have to work during the week.

I talked to one student who is a pre-med student in the library and spends many hours a week in laboratory classes. He said every morning that he reads for four hours before he comes to campus. Then, between classes and labs he works on lab reports and homework is completed. These tasks do not require as much concentration as reading does for him. Working on Friday and Saturday nights at a restaurant, the job is about as much social life as his schedule will allow him right now.

One woman that I interviewed is married and has two small children. She does not take a full load of classes. She and a friend who works part time take care of each other's children. She worked in a bank for several years. She says that she does all her reading and homework before leaving campus. She wants to give all her attention to her family and her home when she is at home. She and her husband split all the usual chores like grocery shopping and laundry and cooking. She says that she would rather take a few more years to finish college than neglect them. If her children are ill, she might miss a class to take them to the doctor. She makes it a practice not to miss classes unless it is an emergency.

All of these students told me that they plan their study time and that they do not wait until they are given assignments or homework. They try to learn as much as possible from every class and to read supplementary material as often as possible. One political science major told me that she reads the newspaper every morning and clips articles that are interesting to her, making a note of the date and jotting down the page numbers. Then, when she needs to do library research, she already has files full of them. She still goes to the library and reads other sources, but her basic footwork is done. She says that she enjoys reading the newspaper, and it helps you feel less guilty if you can say that you're doing research at the same time.

Talking to these students has made me appreciate their self-discipline and dedication to their studies and has inspired me to commit to a specific schedule. I now know how to manage my time effectively by listening to the trials and tribulations of other students with complicated lives.

Revising

Now that she had a draft done, she knew she had to revise. Her instructor wants the class to look at the conclusions of their essays, paying special attention to how their conclusions relate to their thesis statements and to the main ideas in their essays. At this point in the course, the students know that every part of an essay has its own place and should be related to other parts of the essay.

Azure reviewed the Checklist for Comparing Introductions and Conclusions at the beginning of the Focus on Essays section of this chapter. Her instructor explained that at this stage, the revising process for students involves rethinking their conclusions and introductions, and making sure their final paragraphs are as effective as possible.

Azure reread her introduction and wrote her thesis statement on a separate piece of paper. Then she checked to see that her conclusion mirrored her introduction and summarized her essay. She found several parts of her conclusion that she wanted to change. After rewriting her conclusion, she looked at her essay a second time feeling that it fulfilled the revision guidelines and was a stronger essay.

Collaborative Work

Peer Group Activity

After you read the portions of the Focus on Essays and Focus on Paragraphs sections that your instructor assigns, turn to Azure's first draft (pp. 231–234), and complete the following tasks in small groups:

A. Highlight the main ideas in the introductory paragraph with a coloured marker. Formulate them into a thesis statement.

B. Underline the topic sentence of each body paragraph.

C. Put an X by any paragraph that lacks a topic sentence or has a topic sentence that is not directly related to her main ideas (thesis).

D. Put in brackets any details that do not support their topic sentences.

E. Make sure each paragraph is developed with vivid, interesting details. Put a check mark in the left margin next to paragraphs that would benefit from a few more details.

F. In the margin, make suggestions for improving the introductory and concluding paragraphs.

G. Highlight the essay's thesis statement and each topic sentence with coloured markers.

H. Circle any main ideas that are not represented in the conclusion. Suggest other ways she might end her essay.

Compare the marks your group came up with to those your instructor will show you. Where do your marks differ from your instructor's? What do you need to review before writing your own essay?

Class Activity

As an entire class, look at the underlined portions of Azure's revised draft (pp. 236–239) to see how she changed each sentence.

A. Did you identify the revision problems that Azure corrected?

B. Do you think her changes are good ones? Discuss her changes.

Editing

Now that the essay says what Azure wants it to say, she needs to do some final proofreading and editing before handing it in. The instructor explained that all the students in the class should have a similar understanding of sentence structure and variety. Azure refers to the Focus on Sentences Appendix before editing her draft.

Collaborative Work

Peer Group Activity

After you read the portions of the Focus on Sentences that your instructor assigns, turn to Azure's first draft and complete the following tasks in small groups:

A. Put an X through any pronouns that are remote, unclear, or broad.

B. Use an arrow to show where a modifier should be moved in a sentence so that the word(s) it modifies are clear to the reader.

C. Mark with a wavy line any part of a series that is not parallel in structure to the other items in the series.

D. Circle any words that are not consistent in tense, person, or number.

E. Put brackets around any sentences that are monotonous in their structure or type and should be varied.

Compare your marks to those your instructor will show you. Where do your marks differ from your instructor's? What do you need to review before writing your own essay?

Azure's Revised Essay

Time Management for College Students

I knew I had a serious problem. I knew I might not survive. I knew I needed to change. But, I couldn't. When I started college, managing my time effectively was very important to me, but I did not have any idea how to do it. Since I was constantly behind in my reading, every test and paper produced fear and trembling. During my first semester, I observed successful students and asked them what they did to keep up with all of their assignments and other obligations. All of the students I talked to called themselves extremely busy people, but everyone had made graduating from college their first priority. The one universal recommendation was to attend absolutely all classes and labs. In high school I never went to all of them. Nevertheless, since I have completed my interviews and collected students' experiences, I can confidently offer their advice to you. With it, I gave up ~~you can give up~~ surviving and learned to succeed.

Almost every person suggested reading through all assignments prior to attending class. In a study guide I bought at the bookstore, it said that keeping up with assigned reading is critical if you students want to succeed. By reading the assignments ahead of time, students claimed that they have had to take fewer notes and ~~are~~were able to ask more intelligent questions. ~~You~~Students can really develop more confidence. They also ~~calim~~claim that they spend less time reviewing for their classes and studying for tests. One student said that he spends the first week of classes skimming his textbooks to get an overview of each course. Then, if a class seems boring or too difficult, he can change to another class before it is too late.

Some students said ~~every day~~ that they study every day and make sure they spend a certain amount of time reading, writing, or doing research. Most of the students who do this blocked out four or five hours to study. Some prefer to study for no more than an hour or two at a time. Some people like to spend the entire time in the library so~~Then they can do quick research, if~~ they can do quick research, if necessary, while others like to study in a place where there are no distractions, like an empty classroom~~. necessary~~. Some students like to spend more time studying during the week and less time on weekends. However, I was surprised that several have jobs in the afternoons and evenings during the week and spend 10-12 hours every Saturday and Sunday reading and studying. All the students I talked to spend at least 20 hours a week in scheduled study sessions. They emphasize that they do not allow themselves to do anything else during that time. One woman said that she considers her time at school to be her most important job and that she does not waste time during the day. That way, she says, she can study and attend classes from 8 a.m. to 5 p.m. and spend her evenings earning money as a waitress. This schedule works out well for her, and she does any extra studying she needs to do during the weekend.

Other students schedule their classes in blocks of time so that ~~allow them to~~ they can do their studying and research in large blocks of time. For instance, one student spends almost all day on Tuesdays and Thursdays in class.~~,~~ r~~R~~eading all his assignments for the week on Mondays.~~,~~ S~~s~~ome weeks this takes 12-15 hours ~~some weeks~~. On Wednesdays, he spends the day in the library or in a study room at the Student Center. To keep on track, he sets aside Friday ~~is~~ for writing. This schedule works for him because he takes several classes that require library research and lengthy papers. On the weekends, he works at the mall and earns enough money so he does not have to work during the week.

I talked to ~~one student who is~~ a pre-med student ~~in the library and~~ who spends many hours a week in laboratory classes. He said ~~every morning that~~ he reads every morning for four hours before he comes to campus. Then, between classes and labs, he works on lab reports and completes his homework ~~is completed~~. These tasks do not require as much concentration as reading does for him. Working on Friday and Saturday nights at a restaurant, ~~the~~he says that his job is about as much ~~his only~~ social life as his schedule will allow him right now. He knows that he will be a student for several years to come, and he thinks that should be his first priority for now.

One woman that I interviewed is married and has two small children. She does not take a full load of classes. She and a friend who works part time take care of each other's ~~children. She~~children, so she is able to go to class. Even though she worked in a bank for several years, going to college is much harder for her because of the homework. She says that she does all her reading and homework before leaving campus. ~~She~~When she is at home, she wants to give all her attention to her ~~family and her home when she is at home~~. She and her husband split all the usual chores like grocery shopping and laundry and ~~cooking. She~~cooking, but she says that she would rather take a few more years to finish college than neglect ~~them~~her family. If her children are ill, she might miss a class to take them to the doctor, but ~~doctor. She~~she makes it a practice not to miss classes unless it is an emergency.

All of these students told me that they plan their study time and that they do not wait until they are given assignments or homework. They try to learn as much as possible from every class and to read supplementary material as often as possible. One political science major told me that she reads the newspaper every morning and clips articles that are interesting to her, making a note of the date and jotting down the page numbers. Then, when she needs to do library research, she already has files full of ~~them~~ material. She still goes to the library and reads other sources, but her basic footwork is done. She says that she enjoys reading the newspaper, and it helps ~~you~~her feel less guilty if ~~you~~ she can say that ~~you're~~ she's doing research at the same time.

Talking to these students has made me appreciate their self-discipline and dedication to their studies and has inspired me to ~~commit to a specific schedule. I now know how to manage my time effectively by listening to the trials and tribulations of other students with complicated lives.~~ change. And the change has helped me succeed. Just two simple pieces of advice can turn your academic life around: one, read all your assigned readings; two, schedule your study time. I met and talked with many different kinds of successful students and they used this same advice no matter how complicated their lives were. It worked for me. It can work for you. You can move from survival to success. Who wouldn't want to do that?

Practise Outlining

As a class, spend some time generating ideas, planning, developing, and organizing a potential problem-solving essay.

1. Spend five minutes writing a list of problems that might make a good essay topic. Choose your best three to write on the chalkboard.
2. When each member of the class has added theirs to those on the chalkboard, choose the best two to practise outlining.
3. Divide the class in half. Choose which of the two topics to outline.
4. Choose a group leader to monitor discussion, and another person to record your ideas. Spend five minutes talking about the problem and possible solutions.
5. Write a possible thesis statement for the proposed essay.
6. Write five possible topic sentences that relate directly to the thesis.
7. Arrange the topic sentences in the order that would best bring across the topic.
8. Suggest some ideas for a concluding paragraph.

WRITING YOUR OWN PROBLEM-SOLVING ESSAY

So far, you have seen a professional writer and a fellow student at work trying to solve a problem worth resolving. As you read the professional essay and followed the writing process of another student from first to final draft, you absorbed ideas to work with and ways of giving those ideas a form of their own. These reading and writing activities have prepared you to write your own problem-solving essay on a topic that is meaningful to you.

What Have You Discovered?

Before you begin writing, review what is necessary to write a problem-solving essay:

- Problem-solving essays identify a problem and present a possible solution if one can be determined.
- Ask yourself the following questions as a guide for your essay:
  - Does the problem have a solution?
  - Will the solution work, or is it so complicated, expensive, or farfetched that it is not practical?
  - Will the solution create more problems beyond the original problem?
- To present your problem-solving essay effectively, organize your ideas.

- To help you shape your essay, learn as much as possible about your readers.
- Before you write a draft, decide on a point of view toward your subject.
- After you write a draft, revise your essay for meaning and organization.
- After you revise your essay, do a final edit for grammar, usage, and sentence structure.

Your Writing Topic

Choose one of the following topics for your problem-solving essay:

1. Have you ever run into problems with feeling like you aren't allowed to be who you are? Write an essay in which you describe the problem as Kelly Kaur does, and suggest a possible solution.
2. Consider a possible problem that one or more people might have: It could be caused by a physical or mental disability; by discrimination, poverty, illness, or injustice; or by lack of caring and concern. Write an essay in which you describe the problem and the way it could be solved.
3. Imagine your college newspaper is running a special edition on proposed solutions to important campus problems. Write an essay for your school paper that identifies an important problem on your campus (such as a problem in the cafeteria or with parking), and suggest how this problem might be successfully solved.
4. Write a letter explaining a problem that you had with a business or organization to the CEO of that business or organization; then, offer your suggestions to this person for solving the problem.
5. Create your own problem-solving topic (with the assistance of your instructor), and write a response to it.

When you have selected one of these topics, you may begin your writing process in the same way that Azure did if it suits you. By now, though, you have probably found your own personal style to begin an essay. If some tasks occur out of order, trust that adjustment as part of your own way of thinking. Follow your instincts. But make sure that you have worked through all of the parts of the process.

Comparing Introductory and Concluding Paragraphs

Checklist for Comparing Introductions and Conclusions

- ✓ Does your introductory paragraph contain a strong thesis statement that captures your essay's major points?
- ✓ Do each of your topic sentences relate directly back to and develop your thesis?
- ✓ Does your conclusion reiterate the thesis?
- ✓ Do you repeat important words and phrases from your introduction in your conclusion?

Essays, in many ways, are circles. They start by presenting a thesis in the introduction, then present the body or supporting paragraphs to develop the thesis, and then finally they often circle around to where they began, and remind the reader of how the essay began and the significance of the word-journey they've just been on. Elegant essays often return to the topics and thoughts that began these essays as a way of concluding things. This section is designed to help you check to see if your essay's introduction and conclusion share some of the same information.

Does Your Introductory Paragraph Contain a Strong Thesis Statement that Captures Your Essay's Major Points?

As we discussed in Chapter Three, your essay needs a strong thesis that summarizes its main points. The thesis statement is the backbone of your essay and sets the expectations for the entire essay. Check your introduction to make sure all the pieces are in place.

As Azure reads over her first draft and compares it against the checklist for introductions in Chapter Three (page 52), she realizes that her introductory paragraph is weak. She needs to catch her audience's attention and state her thesis clearly:

First Draft: When I started college, managing my time effectively was very important to me, but I did not have any idea how to do it. Constantly behind in my reading, every test and paper produced fear and trembling. During my first semester, I observed successful students and ask them what they did to keep up with all of their assignments and other obligations. All of the students I talked to called themselves extremely busy people, but everyone had made graduating from college their first priority. The one universal recommendation was to attend absolutely all classes and labs. In high school I never went to all of them. Nevertheless, since I have completed my interviews and collected students' experiences, I can confidently offer their advice to you.

Revision: **I knew I had a serious problem. I knew I might not survive. I needed to change. But, I couldn't.** When I started college, managing my time effectively was very important to me, but I did not have any idea how to do it. Constantly behind in my reading, every test and paper produced fear and trembling. During my first semester, I observed successful students and asked them what they did to keep up with all of their assignments and other obligations. All of the students I talked to called themselves extremely busy people, but everyone had made graduating from college their first priority. The one universal recommendation was to attend absolutely all classes and labs. In high school I never went to all of them. Nevertheless, since I have completed my interviews and collected students' experiences, I can confidently offer their advice to you. **With it, I gave up surviving and learned to succeed.**

With the addition of an opening attention grabber, and a new final statement, Azure's introductory paragraph now introduces the problem and its causes and clearly states her thesis.

Does Each of Your Topic Sentences Relate Directly Back to and Develop Your Thesis?

Strong essays focus the reader's attention on the thesis statement even when relating information in a body paragraph. Topic sentences are part of the bones of your essay. Make sure each paragraph has one, and that each of them contributes to your thesis. You may want to return to Chapters Two and Three to remind yourself of what makes good topic sentences.

For example, in Dan Zollmann's essay in Chapter Five (page 99–101), his three main ideas are summarized, together, in his thesis statement:

> Instead, it [illiteracy] is nothing less than the political, economic, and social alienation of a large number of individuals from their society.

In his essay, Zollmann discusses the political, economic, and social effects of illiteracy, just as his thesis promises. Each of the effects is introduced with a clear topic sentence.

Political: Gradually, I became divorced from the world I lived. I voted in the provincial elections, but I did not understand the brochures delivered to my apartment by the candidates.

Economic: I opened a bank account without even attempting to understand the form I had to sign.

Social: My inability to read or write also had a profound effect on the way I related to my community.

Azure checked her paragraphs' topic sentences and made sure they all helped her thesis. She was happy with her topic sentences–they supported her thesis.

Does Your Conclusion Reiterate the Thesis? Does it Use the Same Words or Is the Thesis Restated in Different Words?

The conclusion is quite dependent on your introduction and thesis statement. Your conclusion usually returns to the thesis and restates it in different words. Good essays will restate the essay's thesis often in different words, and sometimes by repeating the thesis using the identical sentence or phrase.

As Azure studied the conclusion of her first draft, comparing it with the Checklist for Writing Conclusions in this chapter (page 248), she decided it needed strengthening in two ways.

First Draft: Talking to these students has made me appreciate their self-discipline and dedication to their studies and has inspired me to commit to a specific schedule. I now know how to manage my time effectively by listening to the trials and tribulations of other students with complicated lives.

Revision: Talking to these students has made me appreciate their self-discipline and dedication to their studies and has inspired me to change. And the change has helped me succeed. **Just two simple pieces of advice can turn your academic life around: one, read all your assigned readings; two, schedule your study time.** I met and talked with many different kinds of successful students and they used this same advice no matter how complicated their lives were. **It worked for me. It can work for you. You can move from survival to success. Who wouldn't want to do that?**

Azure's revised conclusion summarizes the main points in her essay and ends with a question. She tightened up some of the wording, too, to accommodate her other changes. The content takes the reader back to the beginning by repeating some of the actual words, and then goes one step further. The final sentence, in particular, could have taken the final thoughts in a number of different directions. Azure's choice challenges the reader to follow the advice and brings closure to the essay as well.

Do You Repeat Important Words and Phrases from Your Introduction in Your Conclusion?

One of the ways essays seem to cohere or have a unity to them is that important words or phrases are repeated from paragraph to paragraph. Nowhere is that more important than in your introduction and conclusion. Your conclusion should use similar terms, ideas, and themes as your introduction does. An excellent example of this is Beth Everest's essay, "MotherHOOD," from Chapter Six:

Introduction: For those already initiated, it is easy to identify the new mother, and it isn't because of the rosy glow on her cheeks, those sweet cheeks are blotched and purple with the strain of a difficult labour. Her eyes, half-mast, are ringed in red. No one appears to blame her for getting the stroller caught in the revolving door, or for leaving the baby seat (baby buckled tightly inside) on the roof of the car as she drives away; they simply watch from the sidelines, aghast at her failings. She fears failure, almost as much as she fears talking about her initiation into this new culture called **motherhood**, a culture that necessitates the wearing of a **hood**.

Conclusion: Mother is the source or origin of something ("Mother"); therefore, she is the one who will bear the next generation. While she is **hooded** from who she is as a mother, she cannot escape the tensions placed on her by her defining or the clucking tongues of others in the **hood**. It is necessary for her to escape: "from the Latin ex, meaning out, and cappa, meaning headcovering, cloak...we are slipping out from under our head-coverings or cloaks (ex-caping). Until then, there will be the tensions of knowing that somewhere under the **hood** of the idol is the real mother.

Everest's introduction introduces the word "hood" and Everest repeats the word in the conclusion, using it several different ways: her essay goes full circle.

Azure checked her introduction and conclusion to see if she repeated any important words or phrases in both:

Introduction: I knew I had a serious problem. I knew I might not **survive**. I knew I needed to change. But, I couldn't. When I started college, managing my time effectively was very important to me, but I did not have any idea how to do it. Since I was constantly behind in my reading, every test and paper produced fear and trembling. During my first semester, I observed successful students and asked them what they did to keep up with all of their assignments and other obligations. All of the students I talked to called themselves extremely busy people, but everyone had made graduating from college their first priority. The one universal recommendation was to attend absolutely all classes and labs. In high school I never went to all of them. Nevertheless, since I have completed my interviews and collected students' experiences, I can confidently offer their advice to you. With it, I gave up **surviving** and learned to **succeed**.

Conclusion: Talking to these students has made me appreciate their self-discipline and dedication to their studies and has inspired me to change. And the change has helped me **succeed**. Just two simple pieces of advice can turn your academic life around: one, read all your assigned readings; two, schedule your study time. I met and talked with many different kinds of **successful** students and they used this same advice no matter how complicated their lives were. It worked for me. It can work for you. You can move **from survival to success**. Who wouldn't want to do that?

Azure was happy with the repetition in the introduction and conclusion in her revised essay. Her essay's conclusion and introduction now looked like they came from the same essay.

Exercise E9-1

Rewrite the first paragraph from Azure's first draft (p. 231). Compare your introduction against her revised conclusion. What would you have to change in your introduction to make the introduction and conclusion share an effective structure?

Exercise E9-2

Revise the following paragraph to be an effective introduction. Then, write a conclusion that might mirror the introduction and bring the essay full circle.

I am a second year student in the School of Engineering. There are only a few of us girls in my class. We really have a lot of problems because of this. There should be ways to help this situation.

Exercise E9-3

Write an alternative conclusion for one of the essays that you have written during this school term. Hand your essay in with your revised conclusion.

COLLABORATIVE WORK

After writing a draft of your own problem-solving essay, exchange papers with a classmate and complete the following tasks:

A. Evaluate the introductory paragraph. Is it well structured? Suggest changes to make the introduction stronger.

B. Read the thesis. Is it strong, clear, and does it lead into the essay's main points? If not, suggest an alternative.

C. Put a line through any topic sentences that are not directly related to the essay's thesis.

D. Decide whether the conclusion is effective. If not, suggest revisions.

E. Compare the introduction and conclusion. What changes would you suggest?

Return the paper to its writer and use the information in this section to revise your draft.

Writing Conclusions

Checklist for Writing Conclusions

✓ Does the conclusion mirror the introduction?
✓ Does the conclusion summarize the main ideas of the essay, not adding any new material?
✓ Does the conclusion actually bring the essay to a close?

The writer of a mystery concludes a novel by tying up all the loose ends of the plot in some realistic and logical manner. At the close, the readers should have all their questions answered and feel satisfied that the plot is complete. An essay is like a mystery novel in that it presents several main ideas that need to be tied up at the end. So conclusions are just as important to essays as they are to novels.

Concluding paragraphs can be structured in several different ways, but the most effective ones follow some basic requirements that provide a clear, stimulating summary of the essay's main points. Beyond certain necessary features, writers can add a variety of options to their concluding paragraphs, each of which produces a different effect.

Basic Requirements

A summary of the main points of your essay is one of the basic ingredients of any conclusion. Not only should a summary highlight the main points of an essay, but it should also remind the readers of the thesis statement from the introduction and the topic sentences from each body paragraph in the paper. The summary, at its most basic level, can summarize each of the points that the body of the piece mentions. Another kind of summary rewords the thesis without restating each point that the essay develops.

In the last paragraph of "My Friend George" (p. 227), Kelly Kaur touches on her thesis, without referencing each of her primary points:

> George would be terribly proud of me. My grandmother had an arranged marriage at 14, my mother at 16 and my sister, at 21. But I, bless George, learned to say "No!" and lived a life filled with adventure of my own making.

Because Kaur's body points are smaller illustrations of her thesis, it isn't really necessary for her to recount each of her main points. If the essay is communicating information that isn't covered by restating the thesis, then the conclusion should recount each of the important points, like Dan Zollmann does in his essay entitled "Illiterate Like Me" (Chapter 5):

> Illiteracy is, therefore, more than merely a minor inconvenience. In Canada, and in all other Western society, an inability to read and write means alienation from one's community and from one's country. At a political level, illiteracy makes a mockery of the democratic process by creating an oligarchy composed of an educated elite. At a personal level, illiteracy means subjection to economic and political marginalization; in short, the exploitation of one of the most vulnerable groups in society.

Adding a Memorable Finish

Conclusions should also leave your reader with a lingering thought or idea that stays with him or her after they've put your essay away. Since the first job of the conclusion is to tie up loose ends, the conclusion begins with some kind of summary element. Then, from the summary element, the conclusion should try to impress its point on the reader in some lasting way.

One way to conclude an essay effectively after your summary is to leave your audience with a final question to mull over. This approach at the end of an essay leaves the readers with something to think about beyond the confines of the essay. It is especially effective for a complex topic that invites many perspectives. Here's an example of this kind of conclusion:

> It is sometimes the responsibility of the school board to create policies that protect students from themselves. Clearly high school students are naturally reckless and take many unnecessary risks. By setting a firm and realistic policy that strongly discourages students from using drugs and alcohol, the school board will help these students succeed in school and in life. What is more important?

The question at the end of this essay makes the readers think about the importance of succeeding in school and in life. This strategy can be very effective.

Another option for ending your essays effectively is to add a prediction to your summary. Such a conclusion might be just what your readers need to capture their long-term interest in your topic. In his essay titled "Definition: Cold" in Chapter 7, Chris Desiatnyk points toward the future:

> It is interesting to see how many different meanings can be attached to a simple four-letter word. Cold has three very distinct and well-known definitions, but there are probably more. Throughout history, and I'm sure in the future, words tend to evolve and change from generation to generation. It will be interesting to see what becomes of words such as cold through the next few decades.

In other essays, suggesting a solution is a good way to conclude, especially for a problem-solving essay. Such an approach leaves the readers with a positive suggestion to consider after you lay out a problem or conflict. Azure Chen ends her essay on study habits with a solution she discovered for her own difficulties:

> Talking to these students has made me appreciate their self-discipline and dedication to their studies and has inspired me to commit to a specific schedule. I now know how to manage my time effectively by listening to the trials and tribulations of other students with complicated lives.

Her last sentence adds a specific suggestion to the summary that brings the essay to an exciting close.

A frequent device used to conclude both problem-solving and persuasive essays is a call to action. Such an approach makes one last attempt to stir up the emotions and energy of the readers as the essay comes to a close. In this example from "Condom Use Will Not Help Prevent AIDS," the call to action is actually directed to Magic Johnson:

> This is Magic Johnson's unprecedented opportunity. He can use his heart-breaking ordeal to persuade society to change behavior or become just another public advocate for condoms.

With this plea, the author makes his readers aware of the seriousness of the issues connected with the AIDS epidemic and indirectly calls us all to action.

Sometimes a combination of these techniques will effectively conclude an essay. As Azure studied her first draft, she decided her conclusion needed strengthening in two ways. She needed a clearer summary of her main points and a concrete proposal for solving her time-management problems as a student. To accomplish this, she realized she needed to add a few sentences to her existing conclusion:

First Draft: Talking to these students has made me appreciate their self-discipline and dedication to their studies and has inspired me to commit to a specific schedule. I now know how to manage my time effectively by listening to the trials and tribulations of other students with complicated lives.

Revision: Talking to these students has made me appreciate their self-discipline and dedication to their studies and has inspired me to change. And the change has helped me succeed. Just two simple pieces of advice can turn your academic life around: one, read all your assigned readings; two, schedule your study time. I met and talked with many different kinds of successful students and they used this same advice no matter how complicated their lives were. It worked for me. It can work for you. You can move from survival to success. Who wouldn't want to do that?

Azure's conclusion now offers a more concrete solution to her time-management problems, and in the last sentence, she calls her classmates to action. Her revised conclusion gives her readers additional information, and it is much more engaging. Now Azure's essay is complete with both a summary and a proposed plan for solving her time-management problems.

Exercise P9-1

Look again at Kaur's concluding paragraph in "My Friend George" (p. 227). Write an alternative conclusion, using another method of bringing her essay to a close.

Exercise P9-2

Can you think of other ways Azure could have concluded her essay? Write a new conclusion using another method or a combination of the methods discussed in this section.

Exercise P9-3

Go back to the professional and student essays in Chapter 8 (p. 183 and p. 202). Write an alternative conclusion for each essay, using a different strategy in each case.

Collaborative Work

After writing a draft of your own problem-solving essay, exchange papers with a classmate and do the following tasks:

A. Decide whether the essay's conclusion is effective; if it is not, suggest revisions.

B. Survey the class and list all the different strategies your classmates used to conclude their problem-solving essays.

Then return the paper to its writer and use the information in this section to revise your draft.

Afterword

You and Your Writing Process

Now this house, mine, the old house. I want to put something down. The paint brush. I come down the ladder, go to my study, get a writing pad, begin to write, back against a wall, knees up for writing. The ache of that other house, the cottage on the lake, in my bones, but the words flow easily.

—Phyllis Webb, "Notes on the Creative Process"

The opening words come from an essay by Phyllis Webb. In the essay, she compares writing to fixing up an old house. Each part of the writing process is like adding another coat of paint or tackling another room. For her, the last corner is like the final draft. What she is doing, she says in the essay, is transforming "tacky darkness into light." We can see the first draft as the darkness, what we have to work with. As we move through the repetitive tasks of cleaning, scraping away old paint, adding new, we build the essay. Suddenly the whole room, house even, is transformed into something we might not even have imagined. It is brighter and cleaner than before. We can look at it with a sense of completion and satisfaction.

UNDERSTANDING THE WRITING PROCESS

Many student writers admit that some of their biggest barriers to writing came from what they thought the writing process was supposed to be, and how they thought essays were supposed to be written. When these writers discovered that they couldn't write the way they thought they were supposed to, they came to believe they were not writers. Nothing could be further from the truth. In this book we have asked you to look at what it is you do when you write. As you've written over the past few weeks and months, we hope you've discovered for yourself how the writing process works and what works for you.

Dispelling the Myths

Here is one of the great myths of the writing process: first you come up with a thesis statement; then you come up with an outline that clearly supports your thesis statement and includes an introductory paragraph, three body paragraphs, and a concluding paragraph; finally, you write out a draft of your essay and fill in your outline. To be fair, some writers do write this way, but most don't. Most writers can't come up with the thesis statement or the outline of the essay until they've written something. Often the act of writing itself teaches writers what it is that they want to say about a topic. As the student essays in this book demonstrate, there is no one right way to write an essay. In fact, there are many different ways, and they all depend on how each writer likes to write.

Many writers struggle with writing because of some mistaken beliefs about the writing process itself. For instance, many students believe that essays must always follow a set structure. Here's the classic structure: introductory paragraph, three body paragraphs, and a conclusion. Most of the professional essays in this book do NOT follow this particular structure. And many people struggle with their essay writing because they cannot work with this format. Good essays do not often follow the classic format. And, likely, your essay won't nicely fit this particular structure either.

Writing is Recursive

Many writers have a sense that good writers are people who can write something well the very first time they set pen to paper. Instead, we've tried to show you that to write well you don't have to get everything right the first time. The writing process is recursive, not linear. It is not a series of steps that must be taken in a specific order. Writing is revising, fixing your essay after you've written a draft or two. It's about getting words onto the paper and rewriting them until you're happy.

Most writers don't get it right the first time. They revise. They play with words because words are the key component. The following essay is by a professional writer writing about finding the right words.

William Zinsser

Words*

There's a kind of writing that might be called journalese, and it's the death of freshness in anybody's style. It's the common currency of newspaper and of magazines like *People*—a mixture of cheap words, made-up words and clichés that have become so pervasive that a writer can hardly help using them automatically. You must fight these phrases, or you'll sound like every hack who sits down to write. You'll never

*William Zinsser, *On Writing Well*, 4th ed. (pp. 35-40). New York: Harper Collins, 1990.

make your mark as a writer unless you develop a respect for words and a curiosity about their shades of meaning that is almost obsessive. The English language is rich in strong and supple words. Take the time to root around and find the ones you want.

What is "journalese?" It's a quilt of instant words patched together out of other parts of speech. Adjectives are used as nouns ("greats," "notables"). Nouns are extended into adjectives ("insightful"). Nouns are used as verbs ("to host"), or they are chopped off to form verbs ("enthuse," "emote"), or they are padded to form verbs ("beef up," "put teeth into"). This is a world where eminent people are "famed" and their associates are "staffers," where the future is always "upcoming" and someone is forever "firing off" a note. Nobody in America has merely sent a note or a memo or a telegram in years. Famed diplomat Henry Kissinger, who hosted foreign notables to beef up the morale of top State Department staffers, sat down and fired off a lot of notes. Notes that are fired off are always fired in anger and from a sitting position. What the weapon is I've never found out.

Here, for example, is an article from a famed newsmagazine that's hard to match for fatigue:

> Last February, Plainclothes Patrolman Frank Serpico knocked at the door of a suspected Brooklyn heroin pusher. When the door opened a crack, Serpico shouldered his way in only to be met by a .22-cal. pistol slug crashing into his face. Somehow he survived, although there are still buzzing fragments in his head, causing dizziness and permanent deafness in his left ear. Almost as painful is the suspicion that he may well have been set up for the shooting by other policemen. For Serpico, 35, has been waging a lonely, four-year war against the routine and endemic corruption that he and others claim is rife in the New York City police department. His efforts are now sending shock waves through the ranks of New York's finest. . . . Though the impact of the commission's upcoming report has yet to be felt, Serpico has little hope that...

The impact of the upcoming report has yet to be felt because it is still upcoming, and, as for the "permanent deafness," it's a little early to tell. And what makes those buzzing fragments buzz? I would have thought that by now only Serpico's head would be buzzing. But apart from these lazinesses of logic, what makes the story so infinitely tired is the failure of the writer to reach for anything but the nearest cliché. "Shouldered his way," "only to be met," "crashing into his face," "waging a lonely war," "corruption that is rife," "sending shock waves," "New York's finest"—these dreary phrases constitute writing at its most banal. We know just what to expect. No surprise awaits us in the form of an unusual word, an oblique look. We are in the hands of a hack, and we know it right away. We stop reading.

Don't let yourself get in this position. The only way to fight it is to care deeply about words. If you find yourself writing that someone recently enjoyed a spell of illness or that a business has been enjoying a slump, stop and think how much they enjoyed it. Notice the decisions that other writers make in their choice of words and be finicky about the ones that you select from the vast supply. The race in writing is not to the swift but to the original.

Make a habit of reading what is being written today and what has been written before. Writing is learned by imitation. If anyone asked me how I learned to write, I'd say I learned by reading the men and women who were doing the kind of writing I wanted to do and trying to figure out how they did it. But cultivate the best models. Don't assume that because an article is in a newspaper or a magazine it must be good. Sloppy editing is common in American newspapers, and writers who use clichés by reflex are likely to work for editors who have seen so many clichés that they no longer even recognize them as they go limping by.

Also get in the habit of using dictionaries. My favorite for handy use is Webster's New World Dictionary, Second College Edition, though, like all word freaks, I own bigger dictionaries that will reward me in their own fashion when I'm on some more specialized search. (Careful writers cling to their copy of any Webster dictionary based on the superb Second Edition, because the Third Edition is quite permissive.) If you have any doubt of what a word means, look it up. Learn its etymology and notice what curious branches its original root has put forth. See if it has any meanings you didn't know it had. Master the small gradations between words that seem to be synonyms. What's the difference between "cajole," "wheedle," "blandish," and "coax"? Get yourself a dictionary of synonyms.

And don't scorn that bulging grab bag Roget's Thesaurus. It's easy to regard the book as hilarious. Look up "villain," for instance, and you'll be awash in such rascality as only a lexicographer could conjure back from centuries of iniquity, obliquity, depravity, knavery, profligacy, frailty, flagrancy, infamy, immorality, corruption, wickedness, wrongdoing, backsliding, and sin. You'll find rogues and wretches, ruffians and riffraff, miscreant and malefactors, reprobates and rapscallions, hooligans and hoodlums, scamps and scapegraces, scoundrels and scalawags, jezebels and jades. You'll find adjectives to fit them all (foul and fiendish, devilish, and diabolical), and adverbs, and verbs to describe how the wrongdoers do their wrong, and cross-references leading to still other thickets of venality and vice. Still, there's no better friend to have around to nudge the memory than Roget. It saves you the time of rummaging in your own memory—that network of overloaded grooves—to find the word that's right on the tip of your tongue, where it doesn't do you any good. The thesaurus is to the writer what a rhyming dictionary is to the songwriter—a reminder of all the choices—and you should use it with gratitude. If, having found the scalawag and the scapegrace, you want to know how they differ, then go to the dictionary.

Also bear in mind, when you are choosing words and stringing them together, how they sound. This may seem absurd: readers read with their eyes. But in fact they hear what they are reading—in their inner ear—far more than you realize. Therefore, such matters as rhythm and alliteration are vital to every sentence. A typical example—maybe not the best, but undeniably the nearest—is the preceding paragraph. Obviously I enjoyed making a certain arrangement of my ruffians and riffraff, my hooligans and hoodlums, and the reader enjoyed it too—far more than if I had provided a mere list. He enjoyed not only the arrangement but the effort to entertain him. He wasn't enjoying it, however, with eyes. He was enjoying it in his ear.

E. B. White makes the case cogently in *The Elements of Style* (a book that every writer should read at least once a year) when he suggests trying to rearrange any phrase that has survived for a century or two, such as Thomas Paine's "These are the times that try men's souls":

Times like these try men's souls.

How trying it is to live in these times!

These are trying times for men's souls.

Soulwise, these are trying times.

Paine's phrase is like poetry, and the other four are like oatmeal, which is the divine mystery of the creative process. The good writer of prose must be part poet, always listening to what he writes. E. B. White continues to be my favorite stylist because I'm conscious of being with a man who cares about the cadences and sonorities of the language. I relish (in my ear) the pattern that his words make as they fall into a sentence. I try to surmise how in rewriting the sentence he reassembled it to end with a phrase that will momentarily linger or how he chose one word over another because he was after a certain emotional weight. It's the difference between, say, "serene" and "tranquil"—one so soft, the other strangely disturbing because of the unusual "n" and "q."

Such considerations of sound and rhythm should be woven through everything you write. If all your sentences move at the same plodding gait, which even you recognize as deadly but don't know how to cure, read them aloud. (I write entirely by ear and read everything aloud before letting it go out into the world.) You'll begin to hear where the trouble lies. See if you can gain variety by reversing the order of a sentence, or by substituting a word that has freshness or oddity, or by altering the length of your sentences so they don't all sound as if they came out of the same mold. An occasional short sentence can carry a tremendous punch. It stays in the reader's ear. Remember, then, that words are the only tools you've got. Learn to use them with originality and care. Value them for their strength and their precision. And remember: somebody out there is listening.

The Last Word

In this course you've likely written several essays. The process of writing them has taught you not only what it takes to create interesting essays, but what you need to do to write your best. It is this that you can take from this course and apply to other writing situations in other times and places. You may have even learned a few habits to feed your writing skills and keep them well tuned. And, perhaps, through writing the essays, you have learned a bit more about what you think and why you think in that way. These insights are what we hoped to help you find, for this is how great writers are born.

Appendix
Focus on Sentences

Recognizing and Developing Sentences

Checklist for Recognizing and Developing Sentences

✓ Does every sentence end with a period?
✓ Does every sentence begin with a capital letter?
✓ Does each sentence contain a subject and a predicate?

Writing an essay is a little like assembling a building. You think about what you want to do before you pick up the hammer. You start with the smallest bits of construction material and nail the pieces together carefully. You want to build something that's not going to fall apart and will suit your purpose. You might be able to build a little shack with four bare walls to house your dog, but you wouldn't want to live in it yourself. You'd probably prefer something with more to it, something with heat, water, and electricity.

Instead of lumber and nails, essays work with basic building blocks: sentences. Not only do your sentences need to be grammatically complete, they need to develop your ideas, to make your meaning strong and clear. You'll certainly want your essay to hold together. The strength of every sentence depends on how you treat the most important parts of the sentence: the subject and the verb. How you build and arrange your sentences depends on who you're writing to and what you want to do.

In the next sections you will learn to recognize a sentence, a subject, a predicate, and a verb. And, you'll learn when to use a period.

Recognizing Sentences

If the basic building block of our essays is the sentence, then it makes a good deal of sense to find out what a sentence is and get some idea of how to recognize one. It sounds easy, but it might be more difficult than you first think.

Complete sentences always contain two elements: a **subject** and a **predicate**. The subject tells you what the sentence is about, and the predicate makes a comment about the subject.

Subject	Predicate
Susan	Ran to the store for ice cream

In this example you can see that the sentence's topic is *Susan* and that the predicate gives us a comment on the subject telling us that *she ran to the store for ice cream*.

To make the sentence clear to our readers we give them some clues that what we have just written is a sentence. To show our readers that we are beginning a sentence we capitalize the first letter of the first word in the sentence. To show our readers that we are ending a sentence we put a period, a question mark, or an exclamation mark at the end.

We will confuse our readers if we don't have a complete sentence, but we begin it with a capital and end it with a period.

Ran to the store for ice cream.

This example looks like a sentence, but it isn't. If we look for a subject and a predicate, we discover that the subject is missing. We can confuse our readers if we don't show them where sentences start and end.

Susan ran to the store for ice cream the store was closed.

If you look at the sentence carefully you'll discover that there is a subject and a predicate followed by another subject and predicate. There are, in fact, two sentences, but these two sentences only have one capital letter and one period. Because of these signals, the reader will try to treat these two sentences as one sentence, and then the meaning will not be clear.

How to Find a Subject

A subject names the topic of the sentence. It has to be a person, place, or thing–the name of something. To find the subject, ask yourself this question: what or who is this sentence about? The subject usually appears at the beginning of the sentence.

Susan ran to the store for ice cream.

What is at the beginning of this sentence? The word *Susan* is first. *Susan*, then, is the subject of the sentence. This sentence is about "Susan." Let's try this with another sentence:

Nervous excitement runs through my body.

What or who is this sentence about? *Nervous excitement* comes first in the sentence and it is the subject of the sentence.

Finding a subject is usually simple, but there are a few tricky bits. There are four kinds of subjects a sentence can have. A subject can name a person, place, or thing; the name of a group of persons, places, or things; a feature of a person, place, or thing; an idea; or, an activity. Here are some examples of each kind of subject.

Sentences can name a person, place, or thing

Person

John likes to feed his hamster.

Place

Canada is a country with multiple personalities.

Thing

Super glue won't solve every problem.

A group of people, places, or things

People

The audience gasped as the actor fell from the stage.

Places

Tropical countries are great places to live.

Things

That flock of sheep is the wrong colour.

Televisions are difficult to fix.

A feature of a person, place, or thing

John's ugliness is something of a wonder.

Susan's anger flares up when she drives.

An idea

Communism never understood love.

Frank's view of a good time frightens me.

An activity

Writing isn't easy.

Snowboarding makes me tired.

Sentences can replace subjects with words designed to act like subjects and nouns (nouns indicate persons, places, or things). These words are called pronouns. In some sentences you encounter, you may find a pronoun acting as the subject of the sentence. Here are some examples.

Noun as subject: *Steve and Ruth* think that is stupid.

Pronoun as subject: *They* think that is stupid.

They is a pronoun and it replaces *Steve and Ruth* from the previous sentence. These are some of the most common pronouns:

I, my, mine, me, we, our, ours, us, you, your, yours, he, his, him, they, their, theirs, them, she, her, hers, it, its.

Most subjects are easy to find, but there are some special cases. Sometimes subjects may be taken out of the sentence, or words that seem like a subject might not actually be the subject. Sometimes the sentence has a subject but the subject isn't written down. If you were to ask what or who these sentences are about, you would see that the answer isn't written down.

Recycle!

Pay attention!

These sentences do have a subject–the subject is *you*. They're commands and the reader understands the subject automatically. We could rewrite these sentences to include the subject:

You recycle!

You pay attention!

With commands, like in those examples above, the subject *you* is implied or understood by the reader.

Sometimes, sentences are addressed to a specific person, place, or thing. Whoever or whatever the sentence is addressed to is not the subject of the sentence.

Person

John, *the car* has been blown to bits.

Place

Oh Canada, *we* stand on guard for thee.

Thing

Computer, *I* need some information.

In the first sentence, *John* is not the subject, *the car* is. In the second example *Canada* is not the subject of the sentence, *we* is. In the third sentence *Computer* is not the subject of the sentence, *I* is.

Keep an eye out for sentences that have more than one subject. A sentence can have two or more subjects. Look at these examples:

Susan and Patsy moved to Sudbury yesterday.

Canada and the U.S. signed the accord.

Hard bread and molasses make a good combination.

And there is one last tricky subject you need to understand. Subjects most often appear at the beginning of a sentence. But, there are times when they can be moved to other places within a sentence. Here's an example:

To the arena prepared to do battle, I head.

In this case the end of the sentence has been moved to the front. The subject is still *I*, but it has moved in the sentence. Even though the subject is now in a different position within the sentence, the question will still help you determine what the subject is.

Who or what is the sentence about? Is it about *to the arena prepared to do battle*? That doesn't make too much sense. Is it about *head*? That doesn't make much sense either. The sentence, then, is still about *I*. If you encounter a sentence that doesn't begin with the subject, you can usually take the information at the beginning of the sentence and move it to the end of the sentence like this:

To the arena prepared to do battle, **I head**.

I head to the arena prepared to do battle.

When you move the extra information to the end of the sentence, it's much easier to see what the subject is.

How to Find a Predicate

Every complete sentence has a predicate to explain what the subject is or does. The predicate often sounds like a comment about the subject. It finishes the thought the subject introduces.

One way to find the predicate is to find the subject first. If you find the subject of the sentence the rest of the words form the predicate. Here are some samples.

I head to the arena prepared to do battle.

Nervous excitement runs through my body.

The arena is now within my sight.

All the strategies and plays I have learned throughout the many previous practices flash through my mind.

I is the subject of the first sentence, so the words *head to the arena prepared to do battle* must be the predicate. *Nervous excitement* is the subject of the second sentence, so *runs through my body* is the predicate. *The arena* is the subject of the third sentence, so underline the predicate. The fourth sentence is a little more difficult: *All the strategies and plays I have learned throughout the many previous practices* is the subject. Whatever is not the subject is the predicate.

Understanding Sentence Fragments

If a group of words is missing a subject or a predicate, we call it a **sentence fragment.** We use the word fragment to describe sentences that aren't complete—they're pieces of a whole sentence. Most of the time, sentence fragments are easy to detect. The easiest way to figure out if you have a sentence fragment is to read the sentence out loud. You can hear that it's missing something. Then, when you examine the sentence in detail, you will notice that the subject or the predicate is missing.

Understanding the Sentence

Punctuation marks are the road signs of writing. Punctuation tells the reader when to slow down, when to turn, and when to stop. Punctuation helps the reader move through your words so they can arrive at the destination you want to take them to: your main point. Without punctuation, your readers are less likely to understand what you are saying because they don't know how you want them to read things. Read the following lines out loud:

What does Joe do he is a garbage collector his job is full time and he walks to work he lives near the dump there he goes now

How easy are these lines to read? You probably read the lines several times because you didn't know where the sentences started and stopped. Try reading these sentences:

What does Joe do? He is a garbage collector. His job is full time, and he walks to work. He lives near the dump. There he goes now!

This collection of sentences is much easier to read: you know when to start and stop. The punctuation helps you understand what is being said.

End Punctuation

There are three punctuation marks you can use to end a sentence: the **period** (.), the **question mark** (?), and the **exclamation mark** (!). The period is the most frequently used punctuation mark. A period is like a stop sign. It asks the reader to pause–to stop reading for a moment. The pause, when a person is speaking out loud, tells the listener that one thought has ended and another one is going to begin. When you see a period it means that what is before the period is one complete sentence on one topic.

What is a complete sentence? The smallest complete sentence must have a subject and a predicate. You can add extra subjects and predicates to a sentence or expand the subject and predicate, but every sentence must have at least one of each. We can also call a subject and predicate a sentence or an **independent clause.**

Identifying and Using Modifiers and Pronouns

Checklist for Identifying and Using Modifiers and Pronouns

✓ Is each pronoun in its correct form for its position and function in the sentence?
✓ Is each modifier positioned to emphasize the noun or verb to which it refers?
✓ Does each pronoun clearly refer back to the noun that it replaces?

If you're having some friends over for dinner and you're cooking, you'll probably use some spices to flavour your food. Without spice, the food we eat is certainly less interesting, sometimes bland. No spice makes for less than interesting eating. On the other hand, too much spice means the food won't be enjoyed either. Food needs just the right amount of spice.

Modifiers are a lot like spice. They flavour words and make for some tasty sentences, but they can be overused. Here's a little information about putting spice, using modifiers, in your sentences.

Modifiers

Modifiers are words that add flavour to the meaning of another word or group of words. There are two main groups of modifiers: one group of modifiers, adjectives, flavour the meaning of nouns; the other group, adverbs, flavour verbs.

Adjectives

Adjectives are words that describe or modify nouns or pronouns. Adjectives normally come before the nouns or pronouns they modify, adding specific information that makes the sentence more colourful and interesting:

> It was a **hot, muggy** day, the day that my grandma brought me to a very old and shoddy looking building.

Adjectives can also appear after the noun they modify. Note the changes in the following sentences:

> It was a day, **hot and muggy**, that my grandmother brought me to a very old and shoddy looking building.

> It was a hot, muggy day, the day that my grandmother brought me to a building, **very old and shoddy looking**.

Comparative Adjectives

Adjectives can be used to compare two things and express the difference between them. Look at the following examples:

Mount Athabasca is high.

(Mount Athabasca is not being compared to any particular mountain.)

Mount Alberta is higher.

(Mount Alberta is being compared to one other mountain.)

Mount Robson is the highest.

(Mount Robson is being compared to more than two other mountains.)

Most short adjectives, one or two syllables, add *-er* and *-est* at the end to form their comparative adjective. Longer adjectives, three syllables or more, add the words *more* and *most* (or *less* and *least*) before them to form their comparative adjective.

Examples: Charlene is **more** agreeable

Andrea is the **most** agreeable

Katelyn is **less** patient

Ian is the **least** patient

Some adjectives can form their comparatives either way, like *lovely* (*lovelier* or *more lovely*; *loveliest* or *most lovely*). Other adjectives cannot be compared at all. For example, if something is *dead*, how can it be *deader* or *deadest*? The following adjectives have no degrees of comparison:

Complete	Favourite	Pregnant	Vertical
Empty	Eternal	Finite	Impossible
Round	Unique	Parallel	Unanimous
Endless	Equal	Horizontal	Square

Be Careful with the Spice

Be careful with adjectives: don't use both an adjective with an *-er* or *-est* ending and *more*, *most*, or *less* and *least* together.

Irregular Adjectives

Adding the endings *-er* and *-est* and the words *more*, *most*, *less*, or *least* are ways to form comparisons for regular adjectives. Some adjectives, however, are irregular, meaning they change spelling to form their comparative forms. Here are the most common irregular adjectives:

Bad	Worse	Worst
Good	Better	Best
Many, much	More	Most
Little	Less	Least

Adverbs

Adverbs are words used to flavour verbs. Occasionally, they modify adjectives, other adverbs, and, in some cases, entire sentences. Here are some examples:

She **repeatedly** called his name.

(Repeatedly modifies the verb called.)

The sun was **brightly** shining.

(Brightly modifies the verb phrase was shining, and appears between parts of the verb.)

She mumbled **almost inaudibly**.

(Almost tells us to what degree she was inaudible, and inaudibly tells us in what manner she mumbled.)

Now she spoke with a weird deep voice.

(Now tells us when she spoke.)

Pronouns

A **pronoun** is a word used in place of a noun. We use different pronouns to replace the same noun depending on where the pronoun appears in the sentence and how it functions—as a subject or an object, or to show possession—and whether it replaces a singular or plural pronoun.

Subjective pronouns appear in the place of the subject or follow linking verbs.

Singular: **She** is the priest at our church.

Plural: **They** attend our church.

Objective Pronouns serve as objects of the sentence; that is, they receive the action of the sentence.

Singular: Grandmother sent **us** boxes of bagels and cookies.

Plural: By way of Canada Post, Grandma sent **them** to us.

Possessive Pronouns indicate ownership.

Singular: These are **her** gloves; she forgot them at **your** house.

Plural: **Their** house is being built next to **yours**.

The following chart shows all of the forms that personal pronouns can take:

	Subjective	Objective	Possessive
Singular	I	Me	My
	You	You	Your, yours
	She, he, it	Her, him, it	Her, hers, his, its

Understanding and Identifying Verbs

Checklist for Understanding and Identifying Verbs

- ✓ Are verbs in their correct forms?
- ✓ Are verbs in their correct tenses, changing to show differences in time?
- ✓ Are nouns used correctly according to case?
- ✓ Are adjectives close to the words they modify?
- ✓ Are comparative adjective forms used correctly?
- ✓ Are adverbs located near the words they modify?
- ✓ Are comparative adverb forms used correctly?

What Verbs Do

Verbs are important for several reasons. First, every complete sentence must have a verb. Second, verbs communicate the action of the sentence. Third, verbs tell time. They tell the reader when something happened. The verb tells the reader that something happened in the past, something is happening at the moment, or something is going to happen.

Frank baked the beans. (Past)

Frank is baking the beans. (Present)

Frank will bake the beans. (Future)

Types of Verbs

Every sentence has at least one verb. There are two basic types:

1. Action: communicating something happening

   Linking: showing existence, condition, or appearance.
   With these kinds of verbs we communicate a "state of being."

Action Verbs	The player raced down the court. The government filed the documents.
Linking—existence	I am. (A verb can tell us that something or someone exists.)
Linking—condition	I feel happy. (The verb tells us the condition of a person or thing.)
Linking—appearance	I look happy. (A verb can report on the appearance of a person or thing.)

Action Verbs

Action verbs are like the verb in the first sentence of the previous examples: raced is an action verb. Action verbs express what something or someone does, has done, or will do. Writers often strive to use action verbs because these words help their writing become lively and descriptive.

Linking Verbs

Verbs like *is*, *feel*, and *looks* are **linking** verbs. These verbs don't express action. Instead they express states of being–information about a person or thing's existence, condition, or appearance—describing or renaming the verb's subject. Linking verbs also serve as connectors, joining words that come before and after them.

The scenery was gorgeous and green.

Her name is Amy.

The verb in the first example, *was*, serves as a bridge between the subject *scenery* and *gorgeous*. The verb helps the sentence report on the "state of being" of the scenery. In the second example, the linking verb *is* connects the subject *name* with the word *Amy*, a word that restates the subject.

Most linking verbs are forms of the verb *be*: be, being, been, am, is, are, was, and were. Other verbs like *appear, become, feel, grow, look, seem, smell, sound,* and *taste* can also function as linking verbs.

Here's a partial list of some of the most common linking (helping) verbs:

Be	Do	Have	Can	Shall
Am	Does	Has	Could	Should
Is	Did	Had	May	Will
Are			Might	Would
Was			Must	
Were				

How to Identify Verbs

The first step in understanding verbs is being able to identify them.

Locate the Action

There are two questions you can use to help you find the verb. First, find the subject of the sentence and ask yourself this question: what is the subject doing? If you can point to the word or words that answer this question, you're probably pointing to the verb (remember, too, that the verb is a part of the predicate.

Change the Verb Tense

The verb is the only part of the sentence that controls when the action happened. We call the verb's ability to indicate time "tense": past, present, future. Since the verbs are the only words that use a tense, you can change the tense of the sentence by changing the verb. Look at the following sentences:

Azmina honked her horn at the man.

The president said she could not attend Wednesday's meeting because she was sick.

Honked and *said* are the main verbs of the sentences. Both verbs tell you the action and also communicate when the action occurred. To make sure, we'll rewrite the first sentence and change the event from the past to the present.

Yesterday, Azmina honked her horn at the man.

Today, Azmina **honks** her horn at the man.

Honked is the word we had to change to change the tense. Therefore, *honked* is the verb.

Linking verbs are harder to spot. The first question won't work. Use this second question (technique) to help you locate the verb. The second question, though, will help you identify the verb because a linking verb, though not a strong action, always helps to tell you when the event occurred.

Jurgen's voice is soothing and mellow.

Vince is taking a course at the college.

Is and *is taking* are the verbs in these sentences. To be sure, let's try rewriting these sentences and see which words we have to change.

Today, Jurgen's voice **is** soothing and mellow.

Yesterday, Jurgen's voice **was** soothing and mellow.

Today, Vince **is taking** a course at the college.

Tomorrow, Vince **is going to take** a course at the college.

In both sentences we end up having to change some words to change when the event occurred. The words we have to change in the original sentence are the verb.

Words that Look Like Verbs, but Aren't

Often, you'll find words that look like verbs, but aren't. They seem to be the action of the sentence, but they're not.

I hope to swim today.

Carol likes drinking coffee inside on rainy days.

In these sentences, *swim* and *drinking coffee* are not verbs. You can tell they're not because they don't answer the first question properly. What is the subject of the sentence doing? In the first sentence the subject is *I* and *I* is hoping. So, the verb is *hope*. In the second sentence, the subject is Carol and Carol *is liking*. *Likes*, then, is the verb (*likes* is a linking verb, so it doesn't look as much like an action).

The second question can help you, too. Verbs give you a sense of when the action occurred. Nouns, when they name an activity, can sound like verbs except they won't clarify when the action is occurring: they won't communicate a sense of time. If you rewrite the sentences to change the time of the sentence, you can see the verb:

I **hope** to swim today.

I **hoped** to swim today.

Carol **likes** drinking coffee inside on rainy days.

Carol **liked** drinking coffee inside on rainy days.

See if you can spot the difference between nouns and verbs in these sentences:

Stating an action (a verb)	Naming an activity (a noun)
Dave jogs every day.	Dave thinks jogging is fun.
Statistics Canada reports on crime, now.	Statistics Canada believes reporting is important.

How to Identify Verb Phrases

Often verbs work together in groups of words called "verb phrases." Verb phrases may consist of as few as two words or as many as four. One of the words is called the main verb while the other words are called auxiliary or helping verbs. The helping verbs always come first in the phrase. Look at this example:

We **were excited** about the weekend.

The verb in this example is two words: were and excited. These two words form the verb of the sentence–a verb phrase.

Check the list of helping/linking verbs on page 270. Note that the verbs in the first three columns—other than the word *be*—can function by themselves as main verbs; they do not necessarily require helpers.

Words that Aren't Part of the Verb Phrase

Negatives Aren't a Part of the Verb

Words like *not* and *never* are called negatives, and they are not part of the verb or verb phrase, even though they appear right in the middle of the verb phrase:

I **am *not* going** to the Stampede without my boots.

The word *not* in the previous sentence is not part of the verb. One easy way to tell is to rewrite the sentence changing its tense.

I **did *not* go** to the Stampede without my boots.

When the verb phrase changes to the past tense, the word "not" doesn't change with it. That means "not" is not a verb or a part of the verb.

Adverbs Aren't a Part of the Verb

Words that end in -ly are words we call adverbs. Like negatives, adverbs sometimes appear in the middle of a verb phrase, but they're not a part of the verb:

Robert **could *hardly*** catch his breath after running the marathon.

The word *hardly* in this sentence is an adverb, so it is not a part of the verb. Again, if we rewrite the sentence and change the tense, the adverb doesn't change, so it isn't a part of the verb:

Robert **will *hardly*** catch his breath after running the marathon.

Questions Sometimes Interrupt the Verb

Sometimes questions interrupt the verb phrase with other words. To identify the verb phrase, rewrite the question in sentence form. Here's an example:

Will *Robert and Brian* be going fishing?

Robert and Brian will be going fishing.

The question has been rewritten as a statement, so the verb will be easier to locate.

How to Identify Verb Forms

Verbs change their forms to show tense or time. Understanding the principal forms and tenses of verbs will help you communicate more successfully and your writing will become more confident overall.

The Four Verb Forms

Every verb in the English language can appear in four different forms: present, present participle, past, and past participle.

Present	I run.
Present Participle	I am running.
Past	I ran.
Past Participle	I had run.

The Present or Base Form

The present or base form expresses action that occurs now, in the present: I run. We run. You run. They run. He, she, or it runs.

Here is a verb in its present form:

> Dr. Smith firmly believes that television programs misinform young children about people with dark skin or heavy accents.

The Present Participle Form

The present participle expresses action that continues in both the past and present. To make a past participle verb, simply add -ing to the present verb form.

> Verb (in present form) + *-ing* = Past Participle
> Run + ing = running

The present participle form cannot function alone in a sentence. A present participle must be paired with one or more linking or helping verbs to make the main verb in the sentence: I am running. We were running. You are running. They have been running. He, she, or it is running. The following sentence uses a present participle and a helping or linking verb:

> Dr. Phyllis A. Smith, director of the Institute for Research on Social Problems in Ottawa, Ontario, **has been studying** children and their perceptions about people.

The Past Tense Form

The past tense and past participle forms both express action that has happened in the past. Regular verbs form the past tense and past participle forms by adding -d or -ed: lived, died, learned, moaned. However, irregular verbs form the past and past participles by changing their spellings entirely: run, ran; know, known; see, saw. Of course, past forms of verbs can function as main verbs, as this sentence shows:

> She **found** that children begin to notice differences in skin colour as early as six months old.

The Past Participle Form

Like present participles, past participles require helping verbs, forms of be and have, before they can function as the main verbs of sentences: I have run. We had run. You were known. They were seen. He, she, or it is known. The following sentence depends on a past participle and a helper as its main verb:

One white girl had decided by the time she was four years old that blacks were "bad."

You can't rely on a rule to help you with irregular verbs: these verbs vary widely between the past and past participle forms. You either have to know each irregular verb, and you probably know several, or you need to keep a reference chart handy so you can look each one up.

Time and Tense

Verbs relate a sense of time to the reader. The general sense of when an action or a state of being occurs we call the verb's "tense." Writers write a verb in one of six tenses.

The Simple Tenses—Present, Past, and Future

The first three tenses, called the **simple** tenses, denote an action or state of being that occurs in the present, past, or future.

Present: Inez *works* on her writing assignment every night.

Past: Inez *worked* on her writing assignment last night.

Future: Inez *will work* on her writing assignment tomorrow night.

The present tense refers to action that happens now or immediately, while the past tense denotes action that has already occurred. Finally, the future tense expresses action that has not yet been completed.

The Perfect Tenses: Present Perfect, Past Perfect, and Future Perfect

The other tenses are called the **perfect** tenses. They denote action completed by a certain time. The past participle form of the verb—plus certain helping verbs—goes into each of the perfect tenses, as these sentences illustrate:

Present Perfect: Inez *has worked* on her essay all week.

Past Perfect: Inez *had worked* on her essay for a week before she turned it in.

Future Perfect: Tomorrow Inez *will have worked* on her essay for a week.

The present perfect tense refers to action that began in the past but continues or is completed in the present. The past perfect tense indicates action that both began and ended in the past. The future perfect tense expresses action that will be completed at some specific time in the future.

Recognizing and Developing Clauses, Interjections, and Phrases

Checklist for Recognizing and Developing Clauses, Interjections, and Phrases

- ✓ Does each clause contain a subject and a verb?
- ✓ Does each sentence contain at least one independent clause?
- ✓ Is each independent clause joined to a dependent clause with an appropriate conjunction?
- ✓ Are sentences containing multiple clauses punctuated correctly?
- ✓ Do your interjections simply provide an emotional pause in the sentence?
- ✓ Are all sentences containing interjections punctuated correctly?
- ✓ Does each phrase work as a single unit as part of a larger sentence? Remember that phrases do not stand alone, because they do not contain a subject and verb.
- ✓ Does each phrase modify something else in the sentence?

Clauses

A group of words that contains these two essential elements, both a subject and a predicate, is called a **clause**. There are two main types of clauses: independent and dependent clauses.

Independent Clauses

An **independent** clause can stand alone as a sentence because it contains a subject and a verb and expresses a complete idea. When an independent clause stands alone as a sentence, it is called a simple sentence.

Dependent Clauses

Like an independent clause, a **dependent clause** contains a subject and a predicate. However, the words that introduce a dependent clause make its meaning dependent on an independent clause. A dependent clause is not a complete thought and, therefore, cannot be a sentence on its own.

My father wasn't happy until everyone was eating.

This example contains two subjects and two verbs: there are two clauses in each sentence. One clause is independent, the other is dependent. The dependent clause begins with a subordinating conjunction, which, when added to the subject and verb, turns that clause from an independent clause into a dependent one.

Some dependent clauses are a bit tricky to identify:

My father is one who believes **that this works**.

That is a subordinating conjunction introducing the dependent clause that this works. My father is one is the independent clause.

You can turn independent clauses into dependent clauses with a few different kinds of pronouns, too. We'll look at subordination in greater detail on p. 286.

Interjections

Interjections express strong feeling or sudden emotion. The word interjection comes from Latin words meaning to throw between. Unlike other parts of speech, interjections have no grammatical relation to other parts of the sentence. They are simply thrown between, acting as an emotional pause for the reader. An interjection can be almost any word added that breaks up the flow of the sentence.

Some common interjections include the following: ah, aha, alas, eh, goodness, gracious, hallelujah, help, hey, mmm, oh, ouch, shucks, well, whew, wow, yeah, yippee. Curse words also fall into this category:

Whew! It's hot!

Mmmm! These are marvellous muffins.

The degree of emotion expressed is indicated by punctuation. Interjections expressing mild feeling are set off by commas; interjections indicating strong emotion are followed by an exclamation mark. Note how to punctuate an interjection.

Phrases

After reviewing how interjections can function as parts of speech, you will find that forming, using, and understanding phrases is much the same. A phrase is a group of words that does not include a subject and a verb:

After dinner, I saw the cookbook with the red cover.

After dinner and with the red cover are phrases that tell us when the cookbook was seen, and what the colour of the book's cover was.

Phrases are groups of words that tell us more about something in the sentence. The words in a phrase work together within a sentence and function as a single unit. They are added like interjections, but work as modifiers. Notice how the phrases in the following sentence make the content more interesting:

Outside it was dark with only a fraction of light from a single star high above the horizon.

The independent clause in the first example is it was dark. All of the other bits of the sentence tell us more about this darkness. We can say that they modify the independent clause, it was dark, telling us more about some aspects of this darkness:

where it was dark (inside)

how dark it was (with only a fraction of light)

where was the light (from a single star)

where was the window (high above the horizon)

There are various types of phrases, and each of them is classified by the part of speech that it modifies. Like interjections, they can appear in almost any part of the sentence. The best position for them, however, is close to the word or words they modify.

Prepositional Phrases

The simplest phrases to identify are **prepositional phrases**. Prepositional phrases begin with **prepositions**. Prepositions, like conjunctions, are connecting words. Prepositions join phrases to the parts of the sentence that they modify. A preposition always connects a noun, a pronoun, or a word group working as a noun to another word in the sentence. The preposition plus the connected noun, pronoun, or word group is the prepositional phrase. Here are some common prepositions:

Common Prepositions				
about	before	except for	next to	through
above	behind	for	of	throughout
according to	below	from	off	to
across	beneath	in	on	toward
after	beside	in addition to	onto	under
against	besides	in back of	on top of	underneath
along	between	in case of	out	unlike
along with	beyond	in front of	out of	until
among	by	in place of	outside	up
apart from	by means of	inside	over	upon
around	concerning	in spite of	past	up to
as	despite	instead of	prior to	with
as for	down	into	regarding	within
at	during	like	since	without
because of	except	near		

Prepositional phrases are modifiers, and they usually function as adjectives or as adverbs.

Adjective: My son is the boy in the green overalls.

Adverb: Our dog, Pepper, hides his toys under the carpet.

Building Compound Sentences

Checklist for Building Compound Sentences

- ✓ Are both clauses in the compound sentence complete?
- ✓ Have the sentences been joined correctly using one of the three techniques to build a compound sentence?
- ✓ Does the combined sentence (the compound sentence) communicate meaning precisely?

What is a Compound Sentence?

Those who have read many essays tend to think that a varied sentence structure makes for more elegant and sophisticated writing. There are three kinds of sentences that will help you achieve this goal: compound sentences, complex sentences, and compound-complex sentences.

The compound sentence combines two or more independent clauses (simple sentences). There are three simple techniques to help you understand how to build compound sentences: the FANBOYS technique, the semicolon technique, and the colon technique.

Joining two independent sentences is easy enough to do, but the most important thing to remember is that when you join sentences, you can alter the meaning of both sentences by the way you join them. Aim to combine sentences to better communicate your meaning.

Notice how the meaning changes when we use different words to join two sentences. Here are our two sentences:

Sentence 1: They're not trying to save the machine.

Sentence 2: They are enjoying watching it burn.

Let's put these two sentences together in a few different ways:

Combination 1: They're not trying to save the machine, so they are enjoying watching it burn.

This sentence suggests that the people watching the machine burn are enjoying the fire because they don't have to try to put it out. The sentence changes meaning, however, if we change the word we use to join the two sentences:

Combination 2: They're not trying to save the machine, for they are enjoying watching it burn.

This sentence suggests that people around the burning machine aren't putting out the fire because they're enjoying it. Here's another change:

Combination 3: They're not trying to save the machine, yet they are enjoying watching it burn.

In this sentence, the people watching the fire are enjoying the blaze even though they're not helping to put it out.

The meaning changes every time we change the way we join the sentences. Which of these three combinations is right? All three combinations are combined correctly, so they're right in the grammatical sense. The important question, then, is which combination says what you're trying to say most accurately?

The FANBOYS Technique

One way to combine sentences is to use a coordinating conjunction. There are seven of them, and you'll remember all seven of them if you remember the word "FANBOYS." Here's what each letter stands for:

F = for
A = and
N = nor
B = but
O = or
Y = yet
S = so

These are all of the coordinating conjunctions.

When you have two sentences, or independent clauses, you can join them together with one of the FANBOYS using this formula:

Independent clause , F A N B O Y S Independent clause .

Let's say you have two independent clauses and you want to combine them using a conjunction:

Sentence 1: I like my computer.

Sentence 2: It helps me write.

According to our formula, we can join them this way:

Combination 1: I like my computer, and it helps me write .

Here you can use any one of the FANBOYS. Try each one on the above sentences and note the change in meaning.

A Variation on the FANBOYS Technique

Instead of using one of the FANBOYS by itself, try using a FANBOY with an extra word or two at the beginning of the first independent clause. Here is an example of this technique:

Either the cow can talk, or Bob has lost his mind.

You'll recognize "or" as one of the FANBOYS. The extra word is the word "either." A few of the FANBOYS can take an extra word or words in this kind of pattern. Besides the famous either/or combination from the previous example, you can add "neither" to "nor" and "not only" to "but." Here's the formula:

Either Neither Not only	Independent clause ,	or nor but (also)	Independent clause .

Here are two sentences we can join with this technique:

Sentence 1: I like my computer.

Sentence 2: It helps me write.

And, when we join them, here's what we get:

Either I like my computer, or it helps me write.

The sentence doesn't make much sense, but it is correct. You can see it's not too difficult.

The Semicolon Technique

The second way to join two independent clauses is with a semicolon. A semicolon is different than a period. It is a weak version of the period. It's too weak to end a sentence the way a period does. It always has to be followed by a sentence ending in a period.

Punctuation means something just as words do. The semicolon means the same as the word *and*. It's an elegant piece of punctuation, but be careful not to overuse it. One semicolon every paragraph is enough in most situations.

Here is the formula for how to use it:

Independent clause ; Independent clause .

Here is an example:

Sentence 1: I like my computer.

Sentence 2: It helps me write.

If we combined them, they would look like this:

I like my computer ; it helps me write .

A Variation on the Semicolon Technique

We can add one complication to the technique we just learned. We can use a semicolon and an extra word to change the relationship of the independent clauses. The words we use with the semicolon are logical and sound quite formal. We call them conjunctive adverbs. Here are several of them:

Accordingly	However	Otherwise
Consequently	Likewise	Then
Furthermore	Moreover	Therefore
Hence	Nevertheless	Thus

Here is the formula for using conjunctive adverbs with a semicolon:

[Independent clause] ; [conjunctive adverb] , [independent clause] .

Let's combine these two sentences:

Sentence 1: I like my computer.

Sentence 2: It helps me write.

The two sentences form one compound sentence that should look something like this:

I like my computer ; therefore, it helps me write .

As with some of the other techniques, you don't want to use this one too often—aim for variety in your sentences.

The Colon Technique

The third technique for joining two independent clauses is the colon technique. Using the colon isn't much different than using a semicolon, except the colon has a different meaning. The colon is roughly equivalent to the mathematical equal sign. When you use it, it means that the sentence before the colon is equal in meaning to the sentence after the colon.

The house was falling apart: there were no doors or windows left in place.

The first sentence is equal to the second part of the sentence—both sentences are saying the same thing in different words. Most of the time, the first sentence will make a general observation and the second sentence gives some specific detail. The important thing to remember is that the meaning of the sentences has to be equal. If the meaning is not equal, then the colon has been used incorrectly.

Coffee has been blamed for many ailments: the trees are in full bloom.

This example uses the colon properly in the grammatical sense. But the relationship between the two sentences is not equal, so the colon isn't being used properly. Here's the formula for using the colon:

[Independent clause] : [Independent clause] .

Here are our two demonstration sentences:

Sentence 1: I like my computer.

Sentence 2: It helps me write.

Let's join our two sentences to see how this works:

I like my computer : it helps me write .

Note, you do not need to capitalize the first letter of the second sentence. Colons can easily be overused the way semicolons can. One colon per paragraph is plenty in most situations.

Other Uses for the Colon

As we've seen, the colon can be used to join two independent clauses. But the colon has other uses, too: use it to help introduce a list, introduce a quote, or emphasize a few words.

Introducing a List

Colons are often used to introduce a list. Here's an example:

> Here are the things I need to buy at the grocery store: tape, gum, salad dressing, Kleenex, and bleach.

This is a fairly obvious list, where the sentence before the colon introduces the list in quite an obvious way. Here's another list where the introduction is a little less obvious:

> Most of the pets I've owned have died on me: the hamster, the dog, the salamander, the flounder, and the pigeon.

In some ways, the colon in the list has the same meaning as it did when it brings two sentences together. The colon is like an equal sign, and the first sentence gives a general summary of the items in the list. So the colon still means the same as it did when it joined two sentences. Here's the formula for introducing lists with a colon:

[Independent clause] : [list item] , [list item] , and [list item] .

Let's use it to try and bring this sentence and this list together.

Sentence: I use my computer for many different tasks.

List: Writing, budgeting, surfing, and faxing.

Here's what it could look like:

I use my computer for many different tasks : writing , budgeting ,

surfing , and faxing .

Introducing a Quote

Writers often use the colon to introduce a quote. The colon's meaning hasn't changed for this technique either: it still means that what goes before the colon and what comes after are equal in their meaning. In this case, put an independent clause before the colon, an independent clause that introduces the quotation in a general way. Here's an example:

Frank's words criticize the Canadian people: "the government is not responsible for everyone's life."

Make sure you put an independent clause before the colon. The quote should be an independent clause, too. Here's the formula:

Independent clause : " Quote (independent clause) . "

Here's our introductory sentence and sentence quote:

Sentence: We can summarize Jill's attitude toward computers with her own words.

Quote: "I can't live without my computer."

Let's combine them:

We can summarize Jill's attitude toward computers with her own words: "I can't live without my computer."

Emphasizing a Few Words

You can also use a colon to emphasize a few words. Here's an example:

I changed to please one person: my aunt.

In this example, "one person" is emphasized. The words after the colon repeat part of what is expressed in the sentence before the colon and often add a little to the idea. "One person" was mentioned in the first sentence, and that person was identified in the words after the colon: "my aunt."

The colon still means the same thing as it did in all the other techniques. It's like an equal sign. What comes before the colon should equal what comes afterward.

This technique also works well if you introduce something without mentioning it in the first sentence, then use the words after the colon to identify it. Usually, it's best to pick the last main noun mentioned in the first sentence as the one to expand on after the colon. Here's an example:

Simon likes to run a marathon every year: the Boston Marathon.

What comes after the colon is not a complete sentence: it's a piece of a sentence, a sentence fragment. Sentence fragments are only allowed in a few specific places. This is one of them. Here is the formula:

Independent clause : noun or noun phrase .

Let's try it on this test sentence:

Sentence: Jasmine started her own company.

Detail: a cosmetics firm

Here's what we get:

Jasmine started her own company: a cosmetics firm.

We have now emphasized and added detail to the words "a cosmetics firm."

Other Uses of the Semicolon

Semicolons are not as versatile as the colon, but you can do one other thing with a semicolon: punctuate a list. The semicolon is used to separate items in a list if the list items use other punctuation or each list item is a sentence. The list is introduced by a full sentence and ends with a colon as we learned in the previous section. Here's an example:

Here's what everyone wants for Christmas: Dave needs a ski suit; Lynn needs some new clothes; Judith wants a comfy chair; and, I want a new guitar.

Here's an example with punctuation in each list item:

Here are the people on our new committee: Dave, president of the company; Susan, one of the shareholders; Frank, the founder of the group; and, Lola, the head engineer.

It's fairly easy to use. Here's the formula:

Independent clause : List item ; list item ; list item .

Here's a sentence and a list:

Sentence: Each Western province has its own flower.

List: British Columbia, the dogwood.

Alberta, the wild rose.

Saskatchewan, the Western red lily.

We notice that there is punctuation in each list item, so we cannot use commas to separate these list items. This is a job for the semicolon. Here's the combined sentence:

Each Western province has its own flower: British Columbia, the dogwood; Alberta, the wild rose; and Saskatchewan, the Western red lily.

Building Complex Sentences

Checklist for Building Complex Sentences

✓ Is at least one of the clauses independent?
✓ Have you made into a dependent clause those details that are subordinate to the main idea?
✓ Have the dependent clauses been joined correctly using subordinating conjunctions?
✓ Do the combined clauses communicate precisely what you mean?

What is a Complex Sentence?

The complex sentence combines an independent clause with one or more dependent clauses. The dependent clauses begin as independent clauses, but become dependent clauses when they take an extra word or phrase. The extra word or phrase subordinates that independent clause, making it less important than an independent clause. When we use dependent clauses, we begin to build sentences with a more complex structure; we call these sentences complex sentences.

Subordination

Subordination helps our readers distinguish between the most important ideas in the sentence and the details that simply tell us more about the main ideas. The main ideas are expressed in the independent clause, and the details that tell us more about the main ideas are expressed as a dependent clause or in a series of dependent clauses.

Example: Loya ate jellybeans because she could.

In this example, *because she could* is the dependent clause. It depends on the independent clause, *Loya ate jellybeans*, for its meaning. The main idea of the sentence is expressed in the independent clause. The dependent clause tells us more about the main information, so it is not the most important idea in the sentence. It has a subordinate meaning. This is why it is sometimes called a subordinate clause.

There are two ways to make a complex sentence. You can use **subordinating conjunctions** or **relative pronouns**.

Subordinating Conjunctions

The subordinating conjunction joins two complete thoughts by making one thought dependent upon the other.

Example: I am hungry.

I hear the ice cream truck.

To make the second idea dependent on the first, we add a subordinating conjunction to the beginning of the clause that we wish to subordinate.

I am hungry **because** I hear the ice cream truck.

We could also begin this sentence with the dependent clause and the sentence would still make sense.

Because I hear the ice cream truck, I am hungry.

If you do begin the sentence with the dependent clause, remember to put a comma after the dependent clause. Don't use a comma if the independent clause comes first.

Here's a list of many of the common subordinating conjunctions:

Common Subordinating Conjunctions		
after	even though	though
although	how	unless
as	if	until
as if	in order that	when
as long as	since	whenever
as soon as	so	where
as though	so that	wherever
because	than	whether
before	that	while
even if		

Implied Conjunctions

Sometimes the conjunction joining the clauses does not seem to be present. In these cases, the subordination is implied, or understood. The sentence contains the conjunction, but for the sake of brevity in speech, it has been dropped. This most often happens with the subordinating conjunction *that*.

We all know school starts tomorrow.

In order for this sentence to be correct, the two clauses *we all know* and *school starts tomorrow* must be joined by a conjunction. We can almost hear the *that*. *We all know* ***that*** *school starts tomorrow*.

Subordinating Using Different Kinds of Pronouns

In Chapter 3 we talked about personal pronouns, words used in the place of a noun to avoid repetition. We can create dependent clauses—complex sentences—using relative, interrogative, and demonstrative pronouns.

Relative Pronouns

Another kind of pronoun, called a relative pronoun, is also used to avoid repetition, but it is used to avoid repetition among clauses. There are only five of them:

Who is used when the antecedent (what the pronoun refers to) is a person; unlike whom, it is used for a subject.

That is used to refer to either persons or things.

Which is used to refer to anything except persons.

Whom refers to a person and is used for an object; it is a form of who.

Whose refers to either persons or things and is also a form of who.

Relative pronouns always introduce a subordinate clause and they tell us more about some aspect of the information in the independent clause:

Sometimes gambling promotes addiction, which can cripple a person's ability to operate normally.

The thing to note is that the relative pronoun relates directly back to a noun in a previous clause. If that, which, who, whose, whom do not appear to be introducing a subordinate clause, then they are likely performing some other pronoun function in the sentence, either as an interrogative pronoun or as a demonstrative pronoun.

Sometimes when we use relative pronouns in a sentence it is easy enough to figure out the subordinate clause that it introduces, but the independent clause is much trickier to identify. This is because the subordinate clause might appear in the middle of the independent clause, or because it appears to be sharing some words with the independent clause.

My boss, who is generally punctual, was an hour late for work.

In this example, the subordinate clause appears in the middle of the independent clause.

Example: What we can expect is a mystery to me.

Here, the sentence begins with the subordinate clause introduced by the relative pronoun what. The whole subordinate clause can be considered as the subject of the independent clause.

Interrogative Pronouns

Interrogative pronouns, *who? which? what? whose?*, are used to ask questions:

Who brought in the snake?

In this example, *who* is an interrogative pronoun. *Who* serves as the subject of the sentence.

Which of the films was the most interesting?

Here, *which* is the interrogative pronoun and it introduces the phrase *which of the films*. This phrase appears in the place of the subject of the sentence.

Demonstrative Pronouns

Demonstrative pronouns, *this, that, these, those*, are used to point out some particular person or object.

That was an X-rated movie.

That is a demonstrative pronoun: it refers to a particular movie. It also serves as the subject of the sentence.

Martyn should not have brought those books.

Here, *those* is a demonstrative pronoun. *Those books* serves as the object of the verb.

Building Dramatic Sentences

Checklist for Dramatic Sentences

- ✓ Are your dramatic sentences in the right place?
- ✓ Did you use the dramatic technique correctly?
- ✓ Did you use too many (too few) of these techniques in your essay?
- ✓ Do the dramatic techniques improve your essay or ad clutter?

Most people have far too much to read and become impatient with things that don't present ideas well. So, we have to work hard to make our writing interesting to our audience. One of the ways to hold your reader's interest is to add variety and excitement to your sentences. It's just a matter of learning a few different techniques and then using them to polish the draft of your essay.

These techniques don't guarantee you'll have a wonderful essay. But, if you have a good essay already, these techniques add finishing touches to your writing. Like any good thing, these techniques can be used too often. One technique per paragraph is the maximum for most situations. Remember, when you use one, use it in the right place.

Are Your Dramatic Sentences in the Right Place?

What is a good place to use a dramatic sentence? These sentences attract a lot of your reader's attention. So make sure you ask your reader to focus on the right material in your essay. You should use these kinds of techniques to emphasize your main points or material in your essay. Often, your paragraph's topic sentence is a good candidate for one of these techniques because the topic sentences should be your main points. You can also try one of these techniques on support sentences in your paragraph, if you think that attracting extra attention to that sentence helps you make your point. Finally, these techniques are often used to open or end an essay. Introductions and conclusions are places where you want to help focus the reader's attention on what you're trying to say.

A Few Types of Dramatic Sentences

The following techniques are only a few of the many techniques a writer can use. These ones were included because these are some of the most popular techniques used for essay writing.

Include a Piece of Conversation

For some reason, people are more interested in reading words that someone has actually spoken than words committed directly to paper. So, you can help your reader keep his/her attention focused on your essay and add a little variety if you use bit of conversation to help you make your point.

I said, "it couldn't be possible!" But it was.

If you're going to use a conversational chunk be sure you use the quotation marks and commas properly.

Staccato Sentences

A staccato is a musical term for a short, sharp sound. When you write, put three short sentences together in a row for a fast action, punchy effect:

He jumped. The shot exploded. It was over.

Compare Your Idea to Something Else the Reader Understands

Sometimes people may have a hard time understanding something you wrote. If you compare what you're trying to explain to something else, you can make your point more clearly for your reader.

That man treated me the way couriers treat a parcel.

Choose Words that Begin with the Same Letter

Try to begin as many words as you can in a particular sentence with the same letter or sound.

Foul, cried the fair-faced fellow.

Open Two or Three Sentences with the Same Words or Phrase

Several of the sentence techniques in this section have been around since writing was invented. Just use the words you use to open a sentence to open the next one or two sentences.

I didn't like what I saw. I didn't like what I ate. I didn't like what I paid.

End Two or Three Shorter Sentences with the Same Word

To create this type of sentence, repeat a word at the end of several clauses or short sentences:

He did nothing but eat healthy, dream healthy, and live healthy.

Begin a Sentence with the Words that Ended the Previous Sentence

This technique is quite subtle, so some of your readers won't notice it. This technique starts a sentence with the last word of the previous sentence for three or four sentences:

> He struggled to pound the spike into the ground. The ground crumbled as he pounded the spike with his hammer. His hammer had all it could take, and as he raised it, the handle broke. The handle broke at the worst possible time.

Use the Same Word to Start and End a Sentence

This technique requires that you use the same word to start and end a sentence:

> Blood begets blood. Power calls to power.

Reverse the Order of the Words in the First Half of the Sentence to Finish the Sentence

With this technique, you reverse the phrase you used to start the sentence to end the sentence:

> One should eat to live, not live to eat.

Use More Conjunctions than Normal with a List

Try using more conjunctions than normal in a sentence. Most often, this technique is used with a list. Look for a list and try it. It draws attention to the sentence:

> There were donuts and ice cream and bagels and cheese.

End Two Sentences or Clauses with a Rhyme

This kind of sentence uses rhyming words at the end of two clauses or sentences:

> He stopped on a dime, though he wasn't on time.

Use a Rhetorical Question

A rhetorical question is a question your readers should be able to answer without you having to answer it for them.

> Aren't politicians always honest?

Using Strong Verbs

Verbs are the muscle of the sentence. If you choose weak verbs, your writing might become boring or sound rather flat. For example, if we write "Kiona walked down the street" we don't tell as much to our readers as if we were to write "Kiona sauntered down the street." The second verb gives us a sense of Kiona's mood and identifies her actions with greater accuracy. When you are trying to improve verbs, look for two things: first, look for weak verbs that you can strengthen; second, look for linking verbs that you can replace with action verbs.

Replace Weak Verbs with Stronger Ones

If you replace weak and vague verbs with strong, precise verbs, your writing gains a lot of power and your readers will be more interested in what you have to say. Here are some examples:

Instead of	You could write
Jeremy cut the orange.	Jeremy slashed the orange.
I cried when I remembered her.	I wept when I remembered her.
Everything smelled like fish.	Everything reeked of fish.
Frank is going to succeed in life.	Frank plans to succeed in life.

Use Action Verbs, Not Linking Verbs, As Often As Possible

If you replace linking verbs with action verbs when you can, your sentences become more lively. Sometimes, you can just take out the linking verb and you can improve the sentence. Take a look at these sentences:

Instead of	You could write
Violet was in the middle of the road.	Violet froze in the middle of the road.
The car was hanging over the edge.	The car teetered over the edge.
City Hall was changed forever.	City Hall changed forever.

Writing Successful Sentences

Checklist for Writing Successful Sentences

✓ Do **modifiers** describe or refer to the **correct word**?
✓ Do **modifiers** clearly refer to only **one word**?
✓ Are sentences grammatically **parallel**?
✓ Are sentences **consistent** in tense, person, and number?
✓ Do sentences **vary** in structure and type?

At one time or another, you have probably been a member of a team. You may have actively participated in sports at school or in your community recreation leagues. Perhaps your part-time job at a fast-food restaurant depends upon your interaction with other people. Or maybe you have taken part in classroom discussion groups or special projects that required your interaction and cooperation with your peers. Whatever the situation, teamwork is important in many everyday situations. To be a good team member, you must perform your individual duties and work with others.

Sentences also require good teamwork. Each individual sentence must function independently, possessing all the necessary elements to form a complete thought. But expressing ideas is not enough. To be truly successful, sentences must connect with each other and express similar ideas, working toward the common goal of communicating their meaning.

In this section, you will learn to compose successful sentences that work in harmony. You will learn to isolate and correct the errors that keep sentences from fulfilling their communication goals: you will encounter problems with pronoun reference, modifiers, and parallelism, as well as unnecessary shifts in tense, person, and number. You will also learn more about sentence variety. Incorporating specific sentence-building strategies will help your writing become more engaging and cohesive as you achieve your goals of clarity and unity.

Parallelism

When you think of parallelism, you probably remember geometry class and a discussion of lines running side by side that never intersect. Parallelism in writing has a similar meaning: ideas of equal weight should appear in equivalent forms. Simply put, in a series or comparison, words should be used with words, phrases with phrases, and clauses with clauses. Moreover, the words, phrases, and clauses in parallel structures should follow the same grammatical form:

Words: We always said, "Yuck, what is that?" when we saw the latest concoction of cranberries, whipped cream, and walnuts.

Phrases: One year there was so much stuff that smelled like cinnamon in our house that I would have dreams about cooking in a bakery or working in a spice warehouse.

Clauses: During another year, she would decide that everything should smell like evergreens, that our house would look like a pine forest.

Sometimes words, phrases, and clauses in a series or in comparisons are not in a similar form within sentences. When this happens, we call the error faulty parallelism. To correct faulty parallelism, simply replace the word, phrase, or clause in question so that all constructions are equal in structure and form, as in the following examples:

Faulty: During our trip to New York City, we have many things to do, people to visit, and sights that should be seen.

Revision: During our trip to New York City, we have many things to do, people to visit, and sights to see.

Each item in a series in the revisions begins with the same part of speech, and each item is equivalent to the other items. Parallelism helps make the message clear and straightforward.

Unnecessary Shifts

Unless they are reading a mystery or suspenseful story, most readers dislike surprises. They prefer to follow a smooth path, anticipating what comes next in the sentence. Sometimes sudden changes within sentences throw readers off course, making the sentences misleading and confusing. We call these stumbling blocks unnecessary shifts, changes that usually occur in tense, person, and number.

Shifts in Tense

Verbs in sentences usually keep the same tense unless expressing action that occurs at different times is logically necessary.

Future **Present**

The college **will send** your transcript after you **complete** a request form.

Sometimes writers shift tenses unnecessarily, producing sentences that are misleading and illogical. Usually the shift occurs from present to past or from past to present. Correcting unnecessary shifts in tense is easy: simply make the verbs match up.

Shift in Tense: Azure **tends** to get upset when she **got** writer's block.

Revision: Azure **tends** to get upset when she **gets** writer's block.

Shifts in Person

English makes use of three persons: first person (*I*), the person speaking; second person (*you*), the person spoken to; and third person (*he, she, it*), the person spoken about. The most common shift occurs when a sentence starts out in the first person (*I*) and changes to the second person (*you*). When this shift occurs, the writer is usually trying to make a generalization by referring to a large group of people, whether specifically identified or unidentified. The simple rule to follow is to keep your person references consistent, as in the following sentences:

Shift in Person: I took a driving course where you learned how to parallel park and how to change lanes correctly.

Revision: I took a driving course where I learned how to parallel park and how to change lanes correctly.

Shifts in Number

Number means whether a noun or pronoun is singular or plural. Shifts in number are probably the most difficult to correct. We hear these mistakes so often that they readily find their way into our writing.

Shifts in number usually occur when indefinite pronouns (all, everyone, somebody, etc.) appear in a sentence. Learn which indefinite pronouns are singular, which are plural, and which can be either singular or plural. Then read the sentence closely, making sure that singular nouns are paired with singular pronouns and that plural nouns agree with plural pronouns.

Shift in Number: Someone left their keys in the copy room.

Revision: Someone left his or her keys in the copy room.

Sentence Variety

A good writer always strives for sentences that flow smoothly, allowing the readers to follow the ideas easily. But when readers cease anticipating and begin predicting repetitious writing patterns, the writer is in trouble. Prose that is boring and monotonous causes sentences, paragraphs, and entire essays to lose their impact.

One of the best ways to keep readers interested in your writing is to vary sentence structures. Often, writers rely too heavily on the standard subject-verb pattern, as in the following paragraph:

> We decided last weekend to take a spur-of-the-moment trip. We didn't want to go very far. We wanted to save some of our money for a concert next month. We went to a nearby forest preserve. It was only 45 miles away. It had a creek for tubing and many hiking trails. We took our camping supplies and spent one night. It was too hot. We went home the next day.

Notice that every sentence begins with a subject followed by a verb. You probably began to be bored or irritated with the "choppy" effect of the repeated pattern after just a few sentences. With just a little effort, we can add sentence variety to produce a much more interesting paragraph:

> Last weekend we decided to take a spur-of-the-moment trip. We didn't want to go very far because we wanted to save some of our money for a concert next month. So we went to a forest preserve that was only 45 miles away. It had a creek for tubing and many hiking trails. We also took our camping supplies, but we spent only one night because it was too hot. The next day we went home.

The main subjects and verbs appear not just at the beginning but at different points in the sentences.

On the following pages, you will learn how to add words, phrases, and clauses to sentences and how to shift sentence elements to improve sentence variety. You will also learn how to combine sentences to make more complex structures that will keep your readers anticipating, but not predicting, what comes next.

Varied Structure

Good writing displays a variety of sentence structures that keep thoughts flowing smoothly. Look closely at this paragraph and how it employs a variety of sentence structures rather than any one structure:

> (1) Laura and I knew that Mom wanted our holidays to be perfect, but she didn't have to keep buying all those decorations and strange foods. (2) A couple of magazine articles even said that people should not overdo things at holidays and feel pressure to spend money just because everyone else is. (3) We told her so, and she acted really surprised. (4) Of course, we also told her that we didn't believe in Santa Claus any more and that we really did not care for persimmons and pomegranates. (5) We wanted to help her make the holidays fun, but not crazy. (6) After talking things out, we agreed to buy some convenience foods that we really liked, things that are some of our timeless favourites. (7) Also, we each offered to make some cookies, quick breads, and other simple foods, so we could save more time and money that we could spend on gifts. (8) To help matters even more, we would buy a turkey breast and roast it so that we

would not have all those leftovers. (9) One of us had to tell her side of the story. (10) Think about it. (11) Doesn't our compromise solution sound much better?

When you write, try to allow sufficient time to work with your sentences to ensure that you don't overuse any one structure. Sometimes you may rely on the same structure several times in succession, but try to use different sentence beginnings to vary the basic pattern. Just remember that a good mix of sentence structures will refine your writing as you communicate with confidence.

Varied Types

There are four sentence types: declarative sentences, questions, commands, and exclamations.

A sentence in question form seeks an answer and ends with a question mark:

When did Azure finish her paper?

A command, sometimes called an imperative sentence, asks someone or something to perform an action:

Turn off the stereo. Call home before it gets too late.

An exclamation is a statement that expresses strong feeling: anger, surprise, fear, disappointment, disgust. An exclamatory sentence always ends with an exclamation point:

I won!

Azure, look out for the bee!

Usually, you'll use declarative sentences. However, for variety's sake, try to use questions, commands, and exclamations every now and then.

Index

A

action verbs, 269, 270, 293
addition
  as transition, 143, 176
  words to quotation, 151–152
adjectives
  comparative, 266
  defined, 265
  irregular, 266–267
adverbs, 267
alliteration, 291
alternative in-text citations, 219–220
American Educator, 181
analysis
  deduction, 157
  essay development, 90–91
  explaining essays, 90–91
  general to particular, 157
  induction, 156–157
  organizational, 4
  paragraph development, 128
  particular to general, 156–157
  purpose of, 159
analyzing essays
  development, 160
  drafting, 161–162
  editing, 164
  ideas, 160
  organization, 161
  outline, 166
  planning, 160
  published writers, learning from, 157–158
  revising, 163
  student sample, 161–162, 164–166
The Art and Craft of Memoir (Zinsser), 6
audience, 2–3
"Aurora: Myth and Mystery" (Savage), 66–71, 88–89, 93

B

base form of verb, 274
"The Big Short Party" (Bunn), 8–9, 24, 25–26
body paragraphs, 23, 27, 31, 93, 170–171
brainstorming, 2
Bunn, Bill, 7, 8–9, 24, 25–26, 31, 55

C

cause-effect connections
  essay development, 88–89
  paragraph development, 127
  as transition, 143
checklists
  citations, 216
  clauses, 276
  coherent essays, 143
  complex sentences, 286
  compound sentences, 279
  conclusions, 242, 248
  documenting other people's words, 216
  dramatic sentences, 290
  effective essays, 208
  essay development, 23, 85
  focused paragraphs, 93
  generality, varying levels of, 168
  interjections, 276
  introductions, 52, 242
  modifiers, 265
  organization of paragraphs and essays, 115
  paragraph development, 30, 124
  phrases, 276
  pronouns, 265
  quotations, 147
  successful sentences, 294
  thesis statements, 52
  topic sentences, 58
  unified paragraphs, 175
  verbs, 269
chronological order, 118–119
citations, 149
  alternative in-text, 219–220
  author and title in introduction, 219
  author not named in quote's introduction, 217–218
  author's name in quote's introduction, 217
  checklist for, 216
  corporate author, 218
  importance of, 216
  in-text, 216, 217–220
  MLA format, 149, 216
  part of bigger source, 219
  plagiarism, 216
  quotation within quotation, 220
  standard in-text, 217–218
  two or three authors of book, 218
  Works Cited page. *See* Works Cited page
clarity, topic sentences, 58–59
classification
  essay development, 88
  paragraph development, 126
clauses
  checklist for, 276
  defined, 276
  dependent, 276–277
  independent, 264, 276
  subordinating conjunctions, 276–277
  types of, 276

clustering, 2, 11
coherence
checklist for, 143
parallelism, 145
repetition, 144–145
transitions, 143–144
colon
emphasis on words, 284–285
list, introduction of, 283–284
quotation, introduction of, 284
technique for compound sentences, 282–283
commands, 298
comparative adjectives, 266
comparison
defined, 89
and dramatic sentences, 291
as transition, 176
comparison-contrast technique
essay development, 89–90
paragraph development, 127
complex sentences
checklist for, 286
defined, 286
demonstrative pronouns, 289
implied conjunctions, 287
interrogative pronouns, 288–289
relative pronouns, 288
subordinating conjunctions, 286–287
subordination, 286–289
compound sentences
checklist for, 279
colon technique, 282–283
defined, 279
FANBOYS technique, 280–281
semicolon technique, 281–282
techniques for building, 279
concluding paragraph, 27–28, 30, 244–246
conclusions, 23, 27–28
basic requirements, 248–249
checking, 172–173
checklists, 242, 248
memorable finish, 249–251
repetition of words from introduction, 245–246
and thesis, restatement of, 244–245
as transition, 143, 176
conjunctions, 278
and dramatic sentences, 292
implied, 287
subordinating, 276–277, 286–287
content, 3, 23
contrast, 89, 143, 176
controlling idea, 31
conversation, 290–291

D

declarative sentences, 298
deduction, 157
definition
essay development, 85–86
paragraph development, 126
definition-styled paragraphs, 125, 126
demonstrative pronouns, 289
dependent clauses, 276–277
description
essay development, 86–87
paragraph development, 126
development, 3
analyzing essays, 160
essays. *See* essay development
explaining essays, 73–74
investigating essays, 103–104
observing essays, 42
persuading essays, 195–196
problem-solving essays, 230
recalling essays, 12
documenting your sources. *See* citations
dominant impression, 35
drafting, 4
analyzing essays, 161–162
explaining essays, 75–77
investigating essays, 104–107
observing essays, 43–45
persuading essays, 197–200
problem-solving essays, 231–234
recalling essays, 13–15
dramatic sentences
action verbs, 293
alliteration, 291
checklist for, 290
and comparison, 291
conjunctions, use of, 292
conversation, 290–291
linking verbs, 293
placement of, 290
repetition, 291
reverse order of words, 292
rhetorical question, 292
rhyme, end with, 292
staccato sentences, 291
start and end with same word, 292
strong verbs, 293
types of, 290–292
weak verbs, replacement of, 293
words beginning with same letter, 291
words ending previous sentence, 292
Drucker, Peter F., 4

E

editing, 5
analyzing essays, 164
explaining essays, 79
investigating essays, 108
observing essays, 46
persuading essays, 201
problem-solving essays, 235
recalling essays, 16–17
effective essay-writing
checklist for, 208
focus, 208–209
logical organization, 213–214
thesis statements, 208
unity, 210–212
ellipsis, 150–151
emphasis on words, 284–285
Erdrich, Louise, 98
essay development
analysis, 90–91
basic features, 23
body paragraphs, 23, 27
cause-effect connections, 88–89
checklist for, 23, 85
classification, 88
comparison-contrast technique, 89–90
conclusions, 23, 27–28
content, 23
defining terms, 85–86
description, 86–87
examples, 87–88
introduction, 23, 25–26
organization, 115–122
subtitles, 23
thesis, 25–26
title, 23, 24
"An Essay for My Father" (Harrison), 118–119, 157, 158, 168–169, 171
Everest, Beth, 133–136, 149, 245
evidence, 180
examples
explaining essays, 87–88
persuading essays, 181
as supporting detail, 128–129

as transition, 143, 176
exclamation mark, 264
exclamations, 298
experts, 132
explaining essays
analysis, 90–91
cause-effect connections, 88–89
classification, 88
comparison-contrast technique, 89–90
description, 86–87
development, 73–74
drafting, 75–77
editing, 79
examples, 87–88
explaining, defined, 62
ideas, generation of, 72
justifying essay, 62
organization, 74–75
outline, 83
planning, 72–73
procedure, 63–64
process description, 63
published writers, learning from, 64–71
revising, 77–78
student sample, 75–77, 79–82
terms, defining, 85–86
extremes, movement between, 120–122

F
facts, 129, 180–181
FANBOYS technique, 280–281
focus
effective essays, 208–209
introduction, 52–54
paragraphs, 93–96
thesis statements, 52–54
topic sentences, 60
and unity, 94–95
focused paragraphs, 93–96
"For They Know Not What They Do" (Weber), 62–63
freewrite, 2
future perfect tense, 275
future tense, 275

G
general statements
conclusions, checking, 172–173
paragraphs, checking, 171–172
thesis, 170–171
topics, 168–170
general to particular, 115–117, 157
general topics, 168–170

H
Harrison, Richard, 118–119, 157, 158, 168–169

I
ideas
analyzing essays, 160
brainstorming, 2
clustering, 2, 11
controlling, 31
explaining essays, 72
freewrite, 2
generating, 1–2
investigating essays, 102
journal, 1
list, 2, 10
observing essays, 40–41
persuading essays, 194–195
problem-solving essays, 229
questioning, 2
and reading, 2
recalling essays, 10–11
"Illiterate Like Me" (Zollmann), 53, 99–101, 116, 117, 120–121, 248–249
implied conjunctions, 287
in-text citations, 216, 217–220
independent clause, 264, 276
induction, 156–157
interjections, 276, 277
interrogative pronouns, 288–289
introduction, 23, 25–26
checklist for, 52, 242
conclusion, repetition in, 245–246
focus, 52–54
topic, introduction of, 55–56
introductory paragraphs, 25, 30, 242–243
investigating, defined, 97
investigating essays
development, 103–104
drafting, 104–107
editing, 108
ideas, 102
organization, 104
outline, 113
planning, 103
published writers, learning from, 98–101
student sample, 104–107, 109–112
irregular adjectives, 266–267

J
Johansen, Charlotte, 225–226
journal, 1
"journalese," 253–254
Joy Luck Club (Tan), 36–39
justifying essay, 62

K
Kaur, Kelly, 55, 226, 227, 248

L
Lickona, Thomas, 181, 183–192, 208, 210, 213
linking verbs, 269, 270, 293
list, 2, 10, 283–284, 292

M
MacNeil, Robert, 7
"Magpies" (Tan), 36–39
memorable finish, 249–251
MLA format, 149, 216
Modern Languages Association (MLA) documentation style. *See* MLA format
modifiers
adjectives, 265
adverbs, 267
checklist for, 265
comparative adjectives, 266
defined, 265
irregular adjectives, 266–267
prepositional phrases, 278
Moore, Robert B., 181
"MotherHOOD" (Everest), 133–136, 245
movement between extremes, 120–122
multiple (four or more) authors of book, 218
"My Friend George" (Kaur), 227, 248
myths, dispelling, 253

N
narrative paragraphs, 125, 127–128
"The Neglected Heart" (Lickona), 181, 183–192, 208, 210, 213
non-fiction, 23
numbers, 129, 296

O
objective details, 35

objective pronouns, 267
observing essays
development, 42
dominant impression, 35
drafting, 43–45
editing, 46
ideas, generation of, 40–41
objective details, 35
organization, 42
outline, 49
planning, 41
published writers, learning from, 35–39
revising, 45
student sample, 43–45, 46–49
subjective details, 35
organization, 4
analyzing essays, 161
checklist for paragraphs and essays, 115
chronological order, 118–119
essays, 115–122
explaining essays, 74–75
general to particular, 115–117
investigating essays, 104
logical, 213–214
movement between extremes, 120–122
observing essays, 42
paragraphs, 115–122
particular to general, 117–118
persuading essays, 196–197
problem-solving essays, 230–231
recalling essays, 12–13
space order, 119–120
time order, 118–119
organizational analysis, 4
outline, 4
analyzing essays, 166
explaining essays, 83
investigating essays, 113
observing essays, 49
problem-solving essays, 240
recalling essays, 20–21

P

paragraph development
analysis, 128
basic features, 30
cause-effect connections, 127
checklist for, 30, 124
classification, 126
comparison-contrast technique, 127
controlling idea, 31
definition of terms, 126
description, 126
kinds of paragraphs, 124–125
supporting detail, 128–129
supporting sentences, 32–33
topic sentences, 31–32
types of paragraphs, 30–31
paragraphs
body. *See* body paragraphs
checking, 171–172
concluding, 27–28, 30, 244–246
defined, 30
definition-styled, 125, 126
development of. *See* paragraph development
focused, 93–96
introductory, 25, 30, 242–243
narrative, 125, 127–128
organization, 115–122
unified. *See* unified paragraphs
unity, 94–95
parallelism
coherence, 145
and successful sentences, 294–295
unified paragraphs, 177
paraphrase
quotations, 152–153
in research essays, 139–140
particular to general, 117–118, 156–157
past events, essay about. *See* recalling essays
past form of verb, 273, 274
past participle form of verb, 273, 274–275
past perfect tense, 275
past tense, 275
perfect tense, 275
period, 264
person, shifts in, 296
perspective, 3
persuading essays
development, 195–196
drafting, 197–200
editing, 201
evidence, 180
examples, 181
facts, 180–181
ideas, 194–195
organization, 196–197
planning, 195
quotations, 181
revising, 200
student sample, 197–200, 202–206
phrases
checklist for, 276
defined, 277
prepositional, 278
purpose of, 277
types of, 278
plagiarism, 216
planning, 2–3
analyzing essays, 160
explaining essays, 72–73
investigating essays, 103
observing essays, 41
persuading essays, 195
problem-solving essays, 229–230
recalling essays, 11
possessive pronouns, 268
predicate, 259–260, 263
prepositional phrases, 278
prepositions, 278
present form of verb, 273, 274
present participle form of verb, 273, 274
present perfect tense, 275
present tense, 275
problem-solving essays
development, 230
drafting, 231–234
editing, 235
ideas, 229
organization, 230–231
outline, 240
planning, 229–230
published writers, learning from, 226–227
purpose of, 225
revising, 234
student sample, 231–234, 236–239
procedure, 63–64
process description, 63
pronoun reference, 176
pronouns
checklist for, 265
defined, 267
demonstrative, 289
interrogative, 288–289
objective, 267
possessive, 268
relative, 286, 288
subjective, 267
and subordination, 287–289

published writers, learning from
analyzing essay, 157–158
explaining essay, 64–71
investigating essay, 98–101
observing essay, 35–39
persuading essay, 181–192
problem-solving essay, 226–227
recalling essay, 7–9
research essay, 132–136
punctuation, 264
purpose, 3

Q

question mark, 264
questioning, 2
questions
and ideas, 2
rhetorical, 292
sentences, 298
and verb phrases, 273
quotations
addition of words to, 151–152
checklist for, 147
colons and, 284
direct, 137–139
documenting sources. *See* citations
ellipsis, 150–151
longer than four lines, 149
paraphrasing, 152
persuading essays, 181
within quotation, 220
removing words from, 150–151
sentence fragment, 148–149
summarizing, 153–154
whole sentences, 150

R

"Racist Stereotyping in the English Language" (Moore), 181
reading
before, 7
and ideas, 2
recalling essays
defined, 6
developing, 12
drafting, 13–15
editing, 16–17
idea, generating, 10–11
organization, 12–13
outline, 20–21
planning, 11
published writers, learning from, 7–9
revising, 15–16
and significance, 6
student sample, 13–15, 17–20
recognizing
essays. *See* essay development
paragraphs. *See* paragraph development
sentences. *See* sentences
recursive writing, 253–256
relative pronouns, 286, 288
repetition
coherence, 144–145
dramatic sentences, 291
unified paragraphs, 177–178
research, 131–132
research essays
paraphrasing, 139–140
published writers, learning from, 132–136
quotation. *See* quotations
summarizing, 140–142
Works Cited page. *See* Works Cited page
result, as transition, 176
revising, 5
analyzing essays, 163
explaining essays, 77–78
observing essays, 45
persuading essays, 200
problem-solving essays, 234
recalling essays, 15–16
recursive writing, 253
rhetorical question, 292
Roget's Thesaurus, 88
Rooke, Carrie, 34–35

S

sample essays. *See* student sample essays
Savage, Candace, 64, 66–71, 88–89, 89–90, 93–94
semicolon
other uses for, 285
technique for compound sentences, 281–282
sentence fragment, 148–149, 264
sentences
checklist for successful, 294
commands, 298
complex. *See* complex sentences
compound. *See* compound sentences
declarative, 298
dramatic. *See* dramatic sentences
exclamations, 298
independent clause, 264
numbers, shifts in, 296
person, shifts in, 296
predicate, 259–260, 263
punctuation, 264
questions, 298
recognizing, 259–260
staccato, 291
structure, varied, 297–298
subject, 259–263
successful, 294–298
supporting, 32–33
tenses, shifts in, 295
topic. *See* topic sentences
types, varied, 298
understanding, 264
unnecessary shifts, 295–296
variety, 296–297
whole, quotation of, 150
shifts in person, 296
shifts in tense, 295
simple tenses, 275
size of essay, 3
sources, documenting your. *See* citations
space
order, 119–120
as transition, 143, 176
staccato sentences, 291
standard in-text citations, 217–218
student sample essays
analyzing essay, 161–162
analyzing essays, 164–166
explaining essay, 75–77, 79–82
investigating essay, 104–107, 109–112
observing essay, 43–45, 46–49
persuading essays, 197–200, 202–206
problem-solving essay, 231–234
problem-solving essays, 236–239
recalling essay, 13–15, 17–20
subject
defined, 259–260
finding the, 260–262
tricky, 262–263
subjective details, 35
subjective pronouns, 267
subordinating conjunctions, 276–277, 286–287
subordination, 286–289

subtitles, 23
summarizing
  quotations, 153–154
  in research essay, 140–142
summary, 153
supporting detail, 128–129
supporting sentences, 32–33
synonyms, 177

T
Tan, Amy, 36–39
tenses
  shifts in, 295
  of verbs, 271, 275
thesis statements, 25–26
  checklist for, 52
  effective essays, 208
  focus, 52–54
  introductory paragraph, 242–243
  support for, 170–171
  topic, introduction of, 55–56
time
  order, 118–119
  as transition, 143, 176
  verbs and, 275
title, 4, 23, 24
topic sentences, 31–32
  checklist for, 58
  and clarity, 58–59
  focused, 60
  introducing your topic, 55–56
  thesis, relation to, 243–244
topics
  general, 168–170
  introduction of, 55–56
transitions
  coherence, 143–144
  unified paragraphs, 176–177
tricky subjects, 262–263

U
unified essay, 210–212
unified paragraphs
  checklist for, 175
  parallelism, 177
  pronoun reference, 176
  repetition, 177–178
  synonyms, 177
  transitions, 176–177
  unifying devices, 175
unifying devices, 175
unity, 94–95, 210–212
unnecessary shifts, 295–296

V
verb phrases
  identifying, 272
  negatives and, 272–273
  and questions, 273
verb tense, 271, 275
verbs
  action, 269, 270, 293
  base form, 274
  checklist for, 269
  forms, 273–275
  future perfect tense, 275
  future tense, 275
  identifying, 270–271
  linking, 269, 270, 293
  locate the action, 270
  past form, 273, 274
  past participle form, 273, 274–275
  past perfect tense, 275
  past tense, 275
  perfect tenses, 275
  present form, 273, 274
  present participle form, 273, 274
  present perfect tense, 275
  present tenses, 275
  purpose of, 269
  simple tenses, 275
  strong, 293
  and tense, 275
  and time, 275
  types of, 269–270
  verb phrases, 272–273
  verb tense, change the, 271
  weak, 293
  words that look like, 271–272
vocabulary expansion, 8, 36, 65, 99, 132–133, 157, 182–183, 226

W
Webb, Phyllis, 252
Weber, Edna, 62–63
"A Woman's Work" (Erdrich), 98
"Words" (Zinsser), 88, 253–256
Wordstruck (MacNeil), 7
working title, 4
Works Cited page, 149, 216, 220–224
  articles within books, 221–222
  books, documenting, 220–221
  CD-ROMs, 223
  conversations, 223
  corporate author (book), 221
  editor (book), 221
  films, 224
  Internet pages, 223
  journals, articles in, 222–223
  lectures, 223
  magazines, articles in, 222–223
  multiple (more than three) authors (book), 221
  multivolume works, 222
  musical recordings, 224
  newspaper article with byline, 222
  newspaper article with no author, 223
  radio programs, 223–224
  signed article, 222
  single author (book), 220–221
  TV programs, 223–224
  two or three authors (book), 221
  unsigned article, 222
  videos, 224
writing process
  myths, dispelling, 253
  recursive writing, 253–256
  understanding the, 252–256

Z
zero draft, 4
Zinsser, William, 6, 88, 253–256
Zollmann, Dan, 53, 98, 99–101, 116, 243, 248–249